# A HISTORY OF
# PRIVATE LIFE

Philippe Ariès and Georges Duby
General Editors

## I · From Pagan Rome
## to Byzantium

# A HISTORY OF PRIVATE LIFE

## I · From Pagan Rome to Byzantium

Paul Veyne, Editor

Arthur Goldhammer, Translator

The Belknap Press of
Harvard University Press
CAMBRIDGE, MASSACHUSETTS
AND LONDON, ENGLAND
1987

Originally published as Histoire de la vie Privée, vol. 1,
*De l'Empire romain à l'an mil*, © Editions du Seuil, 1985.

This book is printed on acid-free paper, and its binding
materials have been chosen for strength and durability.

*Library of Congress Cataloging-in-Publication Data*

Histoire de la vie privée. English.
   A history of private life.

   Translation of: Histoire de la vie privée.
   Bibliography: p.
   Includes index.
   Contents: v. 1. From pagan Rome to Byzantium /
Paul Veyne, editor.
   1. Manners and customs—Collected works. 2. Family
—History—Collected works. 3. Civilization—History—
Collected works. 4. Europe—Social conditions—
Collected works. I. Ariès, Philippe, II. Duby,
Georges. III. Title.
GT2400.H5713 1987   390'.009   86-18286
ISBN 0-674-39975-7 (v. 1: alk. paper)

# Contents

# Foreword to
# A History of Private Life

*Georges Duby*

THE IDEA of preparing a history of private life for a broad audience came originally from Michel Winock. Philippe Ariès took it up, and it was he who initiated this undertaking. The work that we have done, with him for a number of years and then, sadly mourning his premature death, without him, is dedicated to the memory of this generous historian, who pursued his fresh and penetrating insights wherever they carried him. The boldness of his work is well-known: he was the first to illuminate what had seemed impenetrable reaches of modern history, opening new pathways for research and inviting other pioneers to follow him in the investigation of childhood, family life, and death, in seventeenth- and eighteenth-century Europe. That we have been able to finish this work at all we owe to Ariès's enthusiasm— and to his boldness, wonderfully unfettered by academic routine. Without these qualities of his we might have lost heart, but guided by his judicious counsel, freely offered at planning meetings, at our medievalists' colloquium at Sénanque in September 1981, and at the final stop on his scientific itinerary, a colloquium that he himself chaired in Berlin, we were able to carry on.

Our project was fraught with peril. The ground we hoped to explore was untouched. No one had sifted through or even identified useful source materials, which at first glance seemed abundant but scattered. We had to clear away the brush, stake our claim, and, like archaeologists approaching a site known to contain riches too great to be systematically explored, settle for excavating a few preliminary trenches. We took our bearings without deluding ourselves into thinking that the time was ripe for a synthetic overview. Obliged to feel our way as we went, we decided from the outset that we would present our readers with a program of research rather than a finished summary. The five parts of this book ask many more questions than they answer. We hope that they will arouse curiosity and encourage other researchers to continue our work, to explore new ground, and to dig deep where we have only scratched the surface.

We faced another, less obvious but more troublesome problem. We had decided that our research should cover all of Western history and that it should emphasize the *longue durée*. To a period of more than two millennia and to all of Europe, with its diversity of regional ways and customs, we would therefore be applying a concept—that of personal life—that had come into common use in certain parts of Europe only quite recently, in the nineteenth century. How should we go about writing the prehistory of such a concept? How should we define the realities that it subsumed over the ages? We needed to circumscribe the topic precisely in order to avoid wandering off into yet another investigation of "daily life." When it came to discussing the history of residential dwellings, for example, we hoped to avoid using bedrooms and beds as a springboard for speculation about the history of individualism, or worse, of intimacy.

We started from the obvious fact that at all times and in all places a clear, commonsensical distinction has been made between the public—that which is open to the community and subject to the authority of its magistrates—and the private. In other words, a clearly defined realm is set aside for that part of existence for which every language has a word equivalent to "private," a zone of immunity to which we may fall back or retreat, a place where we may set aside arms and armor needed in the public place, relax, take our ease, and lie about unshielded by the ostentatious carapace worn for protection in the outside world. This is the place where the family thrives, the realm of domesticity; it is also a realm of secrecy. The private realm contains our most precious possessions, which belong only to ourselves, which concern nobody else, and which may not be divulged or shown because they are so at odds with those appearances that honor demands be kept up in public.

An indoor business, a matter of events that take place behind closed doors and under lock and key, private life might seem to be walled off from prying eyes. But, on either side of that "wall," whose integrity the bourgeois of the nineteenth century so vigorously defended, battles constantly rage. Private individuals must use what power they have to fend off the encroachment of the public authorities on their domain. And inside that domain the desire for independence must be contained within bounds, for every private dwelling shelters a group, a complex social organism, within which inequalities and contradictions present in the larger society are brought to a head. Here the clash between male and female power is fiercer than it is outside, the old and the young are locked in struggle, and overbearing masters must cope with impudent servants.

Since the Middle Ages, the tendency of our cultural development has been to sharpen this conflict. As the state grew stronger, its intrusions became more aggressive and invasive, while the launching of new economic initiatives, the declining importance of collective rituals, and the internalization of religious attitudes tended to promote and liberate the individual and increase the importance of other social centers outside the family and the home, making private life more diverse. Starting in cities and towns, the private realm came more and more to be divided into three distinct parts: the home, to which feminine existence remained confined; private places of business, such as the workshop, the commercial shop, the office, and the factory; and places for private gathering and relaxation, such as the café or club.

The aim of the volumes in this series is to make visible the changes, some rapid, others quite slow, that affected the nature and the idea of private life. For the very quality of private life was subject to constant transformation. At each stage, "some of its features originated in the very distant past," as Philippe Ariès noted in one of the working documents he left us. Other features, "of more recent origin, are destined to evolve, either by undergoing further development or by having their evolution cut short or by changing to the point of becoming unrecognizable." Once made aware of the inextricable connections between continuity and innovation, the reader may feel less disoriented by ongoing changes, whose accelerating pace may at times seem troubling. Space for private sociability outside the home and the workplace, for example, may be disappearing. And the distinction between masculine and feminine, which history shows to have been strongly rooted in the distinction between the outside and the inside, the public and the private, is rapidly becoming a thing of the past. There is, I think, an urgent need to protect the essence of individuality from headlong technological progress. For unless we are careful, individual men and women may soon be reduced to little more than numbers in some immense and terrifying data bank.

London

Atlantic Ocean

Rhine River

Paris    Trier    Mainz

Orléans    Lügenfeld

Saint Gall

Danube River

Bordeaux

Po River

Douro River

Marseilles

Ravenna

Florence

Tagus River

Tiber River

Rome

Córdoba

Ostia

Pompeii

Palermo

Sicily

Morocco    Hippona

Carthage

Tunisia

Mediterranean Sea

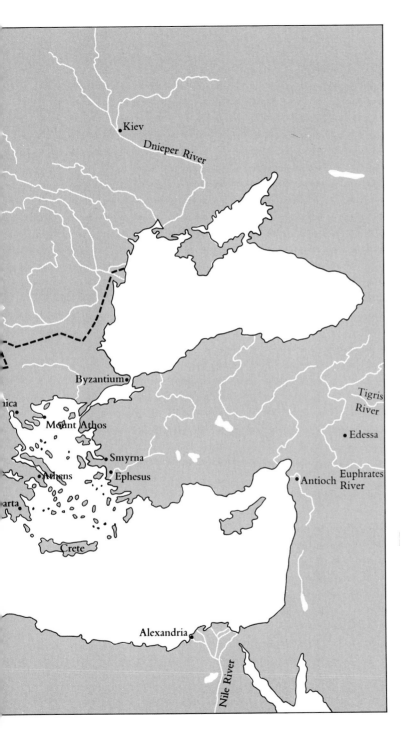

For the reader's convenience, the poetry of ancient place names has been sacrificed; only modern names are given. To understand the true scale of the map, remember that journeys by land could cover at most twenty to forty miles a day, official messengers somewhat more. By sea, depending on the wind, it took at least two weeks to travel from Rome to Syria, and sometimes much longer. If possible, people avoided sea travel between November and March. Nevertheless, they traveled a great deal, and they organized their lives to accommodate their travels. The most important cities, after Rome, were Carthage, Alexandria, Antioch in Syria, and Ephesus. The most prosperous regions were Tunisia, Syria, and Turkey.

The Empire was unique in being bilingual. In its western half, the language of government, business, and culture was Latin; in its eastern half, Greek. The total population was 50,000,000, perhaps as high as 100,000,000. The largest cities had populations of 100,000 to 200,000; Rome's was between 500,000 and 1,000,000. The standard of living varied from province to province, ranging from that of a poorer to that of a richer Middle Eastern country today.

# A HISTORY OF
# PRIVATE LIFE

## From Pagan Rome
## to Byzantium

# Introduction

*Paul Veyne*

FROM Caesar and Augustus to Charlemagne and even the accession of the Comnenus dynasty in Constantinople, this book spans eight and a half centuries of private life. There are, however, major gaps in what is covered—deliberate gaps. An exhaustive inventory would have held little appeal for the cultivated reader. Too many centuries are known to us from sources so impoverished as to be lifeless. The fabric of this millennium is full of holes. It is an oversized and tattered greatcoat, which we felt would prove more serviceable if we cut it up into pieces of sensible size with some life still left in them.

One piece covers the Roman Empire in pagan times. The story is told in sufficient detail to bring out the dramatic contrast with Christianization. We are grateful to that fine historian Peter Brown for having kindly consented to pour the acid that is Christianity on our Roman reagent. What emerges is a diptych that tells a dramatic story: that of the transition from "civic man" to "inward man."

Another segment deals with the physical setting of private life. We look at housing in both pagan and Christian antiquity in great detail, not so much at its material aspects as at its functions, its art, and its life. We feel that this part of our work breaks new ground and hope that readers will agree that the considerable amount of space we have devoted to it is justified. We also felt the need to satisfy the public's widespread interest in archaeology. It is common nowadays to see large numbers of tourists, guidebooks in hand, flocking every summer to the sites of excavations. But guidebooks do not tell all: they cannot teach us how to see, how to interpret scant remains, how to rebuild in our minds the walls, floors, and roofs of a crumbled dwelling, or how to imagine the people who once lived there, to think about what they did and how they lived, whether in isolation or intimacy.

The last two sections cover the early Middle Ages in the West and in the Byzantine East. In the fifth century A.D., the Roman Empire lost its western provinces, from which various barbarian peoples carved their kingdoms. Reduced to its eastern half, the Roman Empire endured. Byzantine civilization perpetuated Roman civilization, which was gradually transformed by the passage of time. Two portraits, in the style of the "new history," depict the contrast between life in the

Merovingian and Carolingian West and life in the Byzantine Empire under the Macedonian dynasty.

Given our avowed aims, the reader has every right to ask two questions: Why begin with the Romans? Why not the Greeks?

Why the Romans? Because their civilization is supposed to be the basis of our own? I am not convinced of that: Christianity, technology, and the rights of man are far more important than anything the Romans have left us. Nor am I quite sure what purpose the notion of a "basis of civilization" might serve, except to justify certain opinions about politics or pedagogy. In any case, historians have better things to do than to perpetuate the genealogical fantasies of *parvenus*. History is a journey into otherness. Surely it has as much right to help us overcome our limitations as to make us feel at home with them. The Romans were very different from us—no less exotic than the Indians of North America or the Japanese. That is one reason for beginning with them: to bring out the contrast, not to sketch the future of Western Europe in embryo. The Roman "family," to take just one example, has little in common with its legendary image or with what we would call a family.

Well, then, why not the Greeks? Because the Greeks are in Rome, are the essence of Rome. The Roman Empire is Hellenistic civilization brutally manhandled by a state apparatus of Italian origin. The civilization, culture, literature, art, and even religion of Rome came almost entirely from the Greeks, over a half-millennium of acculturation. From its inception, Rome, a powerful Etruscan city, was no less Hellenized than the other cities of Etruria. If the upper reaches of the state apparatus, the Emperor and the Senate, remained largely untouched by Hellenism (such was the Roman will to power), the second institutional level, that of municipal life, was entirely Greek. (The Roman Empire was like a body whose cells were thousands of autonomous cities.) Life in a city in the Latin West in the second century B.C. was identical to life in a city in the eastern half of the Empire. And for the most part it was in this municipal setting, completely Hellenized, that private life unfolded.

At the time our story begins, a universal civilization (universal for that time, at any rate) spanned the territory from Gibraltar to the Indus: Hellenistic civilization. The Romans, a marginal people managed to conquer this territory and complete their own Hellenization. Their purpose was to share in a civilization that they experienced not as alien or Greek but as civilization itself, the Greeks being merely the first to possess it. The Romans were determined not to leave a monopoly of that civilization to the Greeks. Rome adopted as its own the culture of another nation, Greece. The will to power of the Roman rulers was so great that they had no fear of "losing their national identity." Thus, this volume begins by describing private life in the Empire that is called Roman but might just as well be called Hellenic. Such is the basis of our history: an old, abolished empire.

Bacchus, half-life-size bronze. This beardless, long-haired adolescent bends his head, slightly turned, to look out over the edge of his pedestal. His lips, eyes, and somewhat disquieting charm reveal his divine nature. (Paris, Petit Palais, Dutuit Collection.)

# 1

# The Roman Empire

Paul Veyne

# ✌ Introduction

WITH them the mirror is soon broken: to know them we have only to look them in the eyes. They look back at us in the same way. It is not every age whose portrait art embodies such a direct exchange of gazes.

This man and this woman are not objects, for they look at us. But they do nothing to challenge or seduce or persuade us, nothing to show us a glimpse of inner life, which we would not presume to judge. They do not so much bare themselves to us as offer themselves tranquilly to the world's eyes. Our presence is taken for granted, and they take themselves for granted. They are what they are and stare at us as equals, sharing common values.

This Greco-Roman humanity was long regarded as classic. It seemed natural, neither dated nor constricted. Man and wife do not pose, nor do they mimic. Their clothing betrays no signs of social rank, no political symbolism. Clothes do not make the man. The background is empty. Against this neutral backdrop the individual is himself, and would be the same anywhere else. Truth, universality, humanity. The woman's elegance is in her hair; she wears no precious gems.

Today, however, we believe not in universality but in the arbitrariness of custom and the finiteness of history. To awaken ourselves from the humanist slumbers in which these Romans still sleep, a single argument, external though it is, will suffice: this man and this woman are wealthy enough to have had their portrait painted. Hence they are "individuals" only in appearance: this portrait, so like a snapshot, establishes their identity by depicting them, as if by chance, at a canonical age, when one is fully grown but has not yet begun to grow old. These are not flesh and blood people caught at some

Painting in the so-called Terentius Neo House, Pompeii: portrait of a couple, prior to 79 B.C. The "Fayoum portraits" of Roman Egypt were similar. (Naples, Archaeological Museum.)

arbitrary moment in their lives but individualized types belonging to a society that conceived of itself as both natural and ideal. The moment captured in the portrait coincides with a timeless truth, and the individual is an essence.

Husband and wife hold undeniable and personal attributes of their superior social status: not symbols of wealth or power such as a purse or a sword, but a book, writing tablets, and a stylus. This ideal of culture is taken for granted: the book and the stylus are obviously familiar tools and are not ostentatiously displayed. Oddly enough, given the reluctance of ancient artists to portray familiar gestures, the man is resting his chin expectantly on top of his book (actually a scroll), and the woman has brought the stylus meditatively to her lips. She is searching for a line, for poetry was an art practiced by women as well as men. Michelangelo would have relished these "unconscious" gestures (his Moses absentmindedly rubs his beard); for him, such gestures revealed the shadow of a doubt or dream. But here no one is dreaming; they meditate, sure of themselves. Their unconscious gestures prove that they are intimate with culture. They are not privileged people. If they hold books, it is because they are fond of reading. The subtlety and naturalness of a deceptive beauty create the grandeur of the Greco-Roman world. Are these people bourgeois, or are they nobles?

If friendship and grief have claims on us, let me dedicate the pages that follow to the memory of Michel Foucault, so towering a man that with him I felt the pleasure of living beside a mountain. One source of my energy is gone.

Detail from a sarcophagus, mid-2nd century. A woman seated in a high-backed armchair, a sign of privilege, nurses a baby. Holding a scroll, a mark of his class, the father leans nobly on a convenient pillar. (Paris, Louvre.)

# ❧ From Mother's Womb to Last Will and Testament

THE birth of a Roman was not merely a biological fact. Infants came into the world, or at any rate were received into society, only as the head of the family willed. Contraception, abortion, the exposure of freeborn infants, and infanticide of slaves' children were common and perfectly legal practices. They would not meet with disapproval or be declared illegal until a new morality had taken hold, a morality which for the sake of brevity I shall describe simply as Stoic. A citizen of Rome did not "have" a child; he "took" a child, "raised" him up (*tollere*). Immediately after the birth it was the father's prerogative to raise the child from the earth where the midwife had placed it, thus indicating that he recognized the infant as his own and declined to expose it. The mother had just given birth (in a seated position, in a special chair, away from male eyes). Had she died in labor, the child would have been cut out of her uterus. But birth alone did not signify that a scion had come into the world.

A child whose father did not raise it up was exposed outside the house or in some public place. Anyone who wished might claim it. An absent father might order his pregnant wife to expose her baby as soon as it was born. The Greeks and the Romans thought it peculiar that Egyptians, Germans, and Jews exposed none of their children but raised them all. In Greece it was more common to expose female infants than males. In 1 B.C. a Greek wrote his wife: "If (touch wood!) you have a child, let it live if it is a boy. If it is a girl, expose it." It is not at all clear, however, that the Romans shared this prejudice. They exposed or drowned malformed infants. This, said Seneca, was not wrath but reason: "What is good must be set apart from what is good for nothing." The Romans

Midwife's sign in terra-cotta. One midwife supports the woman about to deliver, who clutches the chair, while the other midwife prepares to deliver the child. (Ostia, Archaeological Museum.)

also exposed the children of their daughters who had "gone astray." More important, some Romans abandoned their legitimate children because they were poor, and others because they wished to bequeath a decent fortune to their surviving heirs. The poor abandoned the children they could not feed. Other "paupers" (in the ancient sense of the word, which we would translate as "middle class") exposed their children, "so as not to see them corrupted by a mediocre education that would leave them unfit for rank and quality," in the words of Plutarch. The middle class, the mere notables, preferred to concentrate their efforts and resources on a small number of offspring, for reasons of family ambition. In the eastern provinces, peasants agreed to divide their offspring. If a household with four children already had too many mouths to feed, the next three sons might be given to friends, who would welcome these future workers as "sons." Jurists never could decide whether children thus "taken in" (*threptoi*) were free or slaves of the family that raised them. Even the wealthiest Roman might have reasons not to keep an unwanted child, especially if the birth disrupted plans for division of his estate. A rule of law stated that "the birth of a son (or daughter) breaks a will" sealed previously, unless the father were willing to disinherit in advance any offspring that might be born after the will was sealed. Some fathers may have felt that it was better to do away with a child than to disinherit it.

What became of children who were exposed? Few survived, according to pseudo-Quintilian, who distinguishes, however, between the rich and the poor: when the rich exposed a child, they hoped never to see it again, while the poor, compelled by poverty alone, did all they could to ensure that the infant might someday be reclaimed. Sometimes exposure was faked: the child's mother would, without her husband's knowledge, entrust the newborn to neighbors or subordinates, who would raise it in secret. When the child grew up, it became the slave of its educators, who would eventually set it free. In extremely rare cases such a child might win recognition of its freeborn status. Vespasian's wife was one such.

A legitimate and deliberate act, the decision to expose a child was at times a statement of principle. A man who suspected his wife of infidelity would expose a child he believed to be the product of adultery. The little daughter of a princess was abandoned, "stark naked," at the gates of the imperial palace. Exposure could also be a political or religious statement: when the well-loved prince Germanicus died, the plebs indicated their displeasure with the gods' government by smashing their temples, and some parents apparently exposed their infants as a sign of protest. After the murder of Agrippina by her son Nero, an unknown person "exposed his child in the middle of the forum with a sign on which he had written: *I will not raise you, lest you cut your mother's throat.*" If exposure was a private decision, was there any reason why on occasion it should not be public? One day a false rumor circulated among the plebs: that the Senate, having learned from soothsayers that a king was to be born that year, would attempt to force the people to expose every newborn child. The Massacre of the Innocents inevitably comes to mind (this, I might add in passing, was probably an authentic occurrence and not a mere legend).

The "voice of blood" spoke very little in Rome. What mattered more than blood was the family name. Bastards took their mother's name, and legitimation or recognition of paternity did not exist. Forgotten by their fathers, bastards played almost no social or political role in the Roman aristocracy. This was not true of freed slaves, often quite wealthy and powerful individuals, some of whom pushed their children into the equestrian order and even the Senate. The ruling oligarchy replenished its ranks with its own legitimate children and with the sons of former slaves. Freed slaves adopted the

Fragment of vase with reliefs, 1st century. A servant hastens with a pail of water to a busy couple. A purifying bath after intercourse was ritualistic. (Lyons, Museum of Gallo-Roman Civilization.)

family name of the master who set them free. This custom accounts for the frequency of adoptions: the adopted child took the family name of its new father.

*Birth and Contraception*    Adoptions and the social advancement of freed slaves compensated for the low rate of natural reproduction, for the Romans made no fetish of natural kinship. Abortion and contraception were common practices, although historians have distorted the picture somewhat by overlooking the Roman use of the term "abortion" to describe not only surgical practices that we today would call abortion but also techniques that we would call contraceptive. Precisely when after conception a mother got rid of offspring she did not wish to bear mattered little to Romans. The most stringent moralists might argue that a woman had a duty to preserve the fruit of her womb, but even they never dreamed of according to the fetus a right to live. All classes of the population certainly made use of contraceptive techniques. Saint Augustine, who speaks of "embraces in which conception is avoided," gives no indication that these were rare; he condemns the practice, even between legitimate spouses. Augustine distinguishes between contraception, sterilization by means of drugs, and abortions, only to condemn them all. Alfred Sauvy (private communication) states his opinion that, "based on what we now know of the multiplicative powers of the human species, the population of the Roman Empire should have grown much more than it did and overflowed its borders."

What contraceptive procedures were used? Plautus, Cicero, and Ovid allude to the pagan custom of washing after sex, and a vase decorated with reliefs found in Lyons shows a man carrying a pitcher to a couple busily occupied in bed. Dressed up as a ritual of purification, the custom may have been contraceptive. The Christian polemicist Tertullian held that the sperm was already a child immediately after ejaculation (and hence that fellatio was in fact cannibalism). In the *Veil of the Virgins* he alludes, with obscene truculence that obscures his meaning, to false virgins who give birth to children who, oddly enough, exactly resemble their own fathers, only to kill them, apparently with a pessary. Saint Jerome, in his twenty-second epistle, speaks of young girls who "savor their sterility in advance and kill the human being even before its seed has been sown," an allusion to a spermicidal drug. As for the menstrual cycle, the physician Soranus taught the theory that women conceive either just before or just after their periods; fortunately, this doctrine remained esoteric. All these methods were the responsibility of the woman. No mention is made of *coitus interruptus*.

How many children did Romans have? The law accorded special privilege to mothers of three children, who were seen as having done their duty, and this number seems to have been canonical. The evidence of epitaphs is difficult to interpret with assurance, but the texts mention families of three children with particular frequency, almost proverbially. When a writer of epigrams wishes to castigate a woman who, out of greed, starves her offspring, he writes, "her three offspring." A Stoic preacher shouts: "Do you suppose you have done great things because by bringing two or three wretched brats into the world you have helped to perpetuate the human race?" These Malthusian attitudes served dynastic ends. As soon as a man has more than one child, Pliny writes to one of his correspondents, he must think of finding a wealthy son- or daughter-in-law for his younger offspring. No one liked to eat away at an inheritance. To be sure, the older morality eschewed calculation of this kind, and even in Pliny's time this was still the morality of certain old-fashioned heads of family, who "did not allow their fertile wives to lie fallow, even though in our time most people hold that an only son is already a heavy burden and that it is advantageous not to be

Ex-voto to the nurturing goddesses, 2nd or 3rd century. Mother and child offer a tray of fruit to the statue of the seated goddess, who is suckling an infant. The Nurses or Mothers or Matrones were protective deities of the Celts. (Marburg Museum.)

overburdened with posterity." Do things change as we move toward the end of the second century A.D. and Stoic and Christian morality begins to take hold? The orator Fronto, Marcus Aurelius' teacher, "lost five children" to childhood maladies. He must have had many more. Marcus Aurelius himself had nine sons and daughters. After three centuries Rome returned to that golden age in which the exemplary Cornelia, mother of the Gracchi, had given twelve children to the fatherland.

## Education

Shortly after birth the newborn boy or girl was handed over to a wet nurse. Breast-feeding by a child's natural mother was a thing of the past. But the "nurse" did much more than just offer the child her breast. She was responsible for education up to the age of puberty, in conjunction with a "pedagogue," also called a "nurse" (*nutritor, tropheus*). Marcus Aurelius' pedagogue taught him to take care of himself and not to become excited by the races at the Circus. Children lived and took meals with their nurses, but dined in the evening with their parents and guests at what was something of a ceremonial dinner. Nurse and pedagogue remained important figures even after a child was grown. Marcus Aurelius speaks with suitable piety of his natural father, his adoptive father, and his (male) "nurse," and the emperor Claudius would hate his pedagogue throughout his life because of the free use the latter had made of the whip. When a girl married, her mother and nurse together offered last-minute advice for her wedding night. Pedagogue, nurse, and foster child formed a kind of surrogate family and enjoyed all sorts of indulgences in later life; they were free to ignore the law. Nero, murdering his mother, Agrippina, was aided by his pedagogue. Later, when he was abandoned by everyone and facing death at the hands of his rebellious subjects, only his nurse stood by to console him. It was she who, with the help of his concubine Acte, wrapped him in a winding-sheet after his suicide. Yet Nero had been harsh toward his foster brother, to whom he should have shown respect. A Stoic philosopher once delivered a sermon on love of the family. Filial love, he explained, is in accordance with Nature, and Nature is the same thing as Reason; hence it is reasonable for a child to love its mother, its nurse, and its *pedagogus*.

In noble households the surrogate family lived in healthy rural surroundings, far from temptation, under the watchful

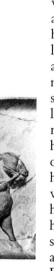

Sarcophagus. Boy at play, driving a cart hitched to a small animal. Axle shafts had not yet been invented. (Paris, Louvre.)

Paintings from underground tomb, 2nd century A.D. Left: ball game. Below: child learning to walk with a wheeled walker. (Rome, Museum of the Baths.)

eye of a strict older relative. "To its [the surrogate family's] tried and proven virtues all the progeny of the household were entrusted. It governed the children's studies and disciplines as well as their games and distractions." Caesar and Augustus were raised this way. The future emperor Vespasian was "raised under the direction of his paternal grandmother on his Cosa estates," even though his mother was still alive. A paternal grandmother's duty was to be strict, whereas the role of the maternal grandmother was one of total indulgence. Uncles differed in the same way: symbols of severity on the one side and of indulgence on the other.

The truth about education may be far from what self-satisfied educators imagine. One Roman teacher tells a very different story, though, to be sure, he is particularly severe, as his profession required. (In Rome, philosophers and some rhetors occupied a place apart in society, rather like priests today.) The child raised in its parents' home received, in this teacher's estimation, an education in indulgence. He dressed as sumptuously as his elders and, like them, was carried about by porters. His parents delighted in his most impudent words. At dinner he heard off-color jokes and bawdy songs. He saw concubines and pet young men about the house. In Rome, as we shall see, common sense held that the world was perverted and decadent. It was also believed that morality consists not in the love or habit of virtue but in having the strength to

Child's sarcophagus. Figure of boy playing with hoop (*trochus*). (Rome, Vatican Museums.)

Child's sarcophagus, 2nd century. Girls throw a ball at the wall, while boys slide a nut down an inclined plane to demolish a tower of nuts. (Paris, Louvre.)

resist vice. The cornerstone of every individual character, therefore, was the strength to resist. In theory, the purpose of education was to temper a person's character while there was still time, so that later, when he or she was fully grown, the germs of luxury and decadence, omnipresent in these vicious times, could be successfully warded off. The Roman attitude toward the teaching of virtue was rather like our own insistence that children participate in sports because we know full well that they will spend the rest of their lives seated behind desks. In practice, the antidote to self-indulgence was activity, *industria,* which, it was thought, strengthened the moral sinew that self-indulgence withered. Tacitus tells of one senator who was born into "a plebeian family, but a very old and distinguished one. He impressed more by his good nature than by his energy, although his father had raised him strictly."

Only severity, which terrifies appetites susceptible to temptation, can give strength of character. Accordingly, says Seneca, "parents subject the still malleable characters of their children to what will do them good. Let them cry and struggle as they will, we swaddle them tightly lest their still immature bodies become deformed rather than grow up straight and tall. Later we instill liberal culture by means of terror if they refuse to learn." Severity was part of the father's role; the mother pleaded for leniency. A well-brought-up child always addressed its father as "sir" (*domine*). Parvenus were quick to imitate this aristocratic custom. The distance between parents and children was dizzying. The professor of rhetoric just quoted lost a son of ten whom he adored and who preferred him, he writes, to his nurses and to the grandmother who raised him. This son had been destined for a splendid career in judicial eloquence (the most visible, "high-society," and busiest part of literary life—rather like the theater today). The child's exceptional gifts justified the father's public mourning. As is well known, the so-called maternal or paternal instinct

does not exist. In some cases love between parent and child develops from natural affinity (which is neither more nor less likely to occur between parent and child than between any two individuals brought together by chance). More often, no doubt, parental sentiments are "induced" by the prevailing morality. In Rome the prevailing morality taught that fathers should love their children as bearers of the family name and perpetuators of its grandeur. Tenderness was misplaced. But it was legitimate to mourn the ruin of a family's hopes.

---

Our teacher had yet another reason to mourn his beloved son: a great personage, a consul, had just adopted the boy, thus ensuring that he would enjoy a splendid public career. The frequency of adoption is yet another proof that nature played little part in the Roman conception of the family. Apparently one gave a child for adoption as one might give a daughter in marriage, particularly a "good" marriage. There were two ways to have children: to conceive them in legitimate wedlock or to adopt them. Adoption could prevent a family line from dying out. It was also a means of acquiring the quality of paterfamilias, which the law required of candidates for public honors and provincial governments. Everything that could be had through marriage could also be had through adoption. Just as a testator, in choosing an heir, also made him the continuator of the family name, a man who adopted a youth was careful to choose a successor worthy to bear his name. The future emperor Galba was a widower, and his two sons died. Having long since discerned the merits of a young noble by the name of Piso, he had a will drawn up naming Piso his heir and finally adopted him. A man could adopt a son even if his own sons were still alive, as Herodius Atticus did. The histories mention the practice of adoption by will, but no trace of such a thing survives in legal documents. The most striking instance of an inheritance linked to adoption involves a certain Octavius, who became the son and heir of Caesar and eventually the Emperor Octavius Augustus. In some cases adoption, like marriage, was a means of controlling the flow of wealth. A father-in-law impressed by his son-in-law's deference might adopt him as a son after the young man inherited his father's fortune, in order to gain control of the inheritance. In return he would see to it that his adopted son enjoyed a brilliant career in the Senate. Adoption could have great influence on a man's career.

*Adoption*

Children who were moved about like pawns on the chessboard of wealth and power were hardly cherished and coddled. Such matters were left to the servants. It was the nurse who taught the child to talk. Noble households employed Greek nurses so that the child might learn the language of culture in the cradle. The pedagogue was responsible for teaching the child how to read.

## School

Was literacy a privilege of the upper class? From Egyptian papyruses we can be sure of three things: there were illiterates who employed others to write for them; some people of the lower orders knew how to write; literary texts, classics, could be found in the smallest towns (here is the "culture" of which the ancient world was so proud). Books of the fashionable poets quickly found their way to the end of the world—meaning Lyons. Beyond this we have only hints. (Historians of literacy in early modern Europe are familiar with the problems involved.) In one fictional tale a former slave is proud of his ability to read capital letters. In other words, he did not know how to read the cursive script of books, private papers, and documents, but he could decipher shop and temple signs and posters publicizing elections, plays, houses to rent, and auction sales, to say nothing of epitaphs. Although only wealthy families could afford private teachers, Ulpianus tells

Funerary relief, 2nd century. Girls playing quoits. (Ostia, Archaeological Museum.)

Another detail of the sarcophagus shown at the start of this chapter. Grandly costumed, the son does his homework in rhetoric before his father (not his teacher). The boy's fingers are making a rhetorical gesture; these were codified and taught in school. The scroll in his left hand is not a genuine detail but a symbol of culture, hence of social rank. (Paris, Louvre.)

us that "in the cities and towns there were teachers who taught the rudiments of writing." School was a recognized institution. School vacations were determined by the religious calendar, and children attended school in the morning. We find large numbers of documents written by simple folk: artisans' accounts, naive letters, graffiti, magical tablets. To write for oneself was one thing, however; to write for people of higher station was something else entirely. One had to know the rudiments of high style and, to begin with, spelling (of which the graffiti writers were ignorant). So, when it came to drawing up a public document—a petition or even a simple contract— people who strictly speaking knew how to read and write felt that they were "illiterate" and turned to a public writer (*notarius*). Nevertheless, a fairly substantial number of young Romans attended school up to the age of twelve, girls as well as boys (as the physician Soranus confirms), together, in fact, in the same schools.

At age twelve the lives of boys and girls diverged, as did the lives of the rich and the poor. Only the boys continued their studies, and then only if they came from well-to-do families. Under the whip of a "grammarian," or teacher of literature, they studied classical authors and mythology (of which they believed not a word, but knowledge of mythology was the mark of a cultivated person). In rare instances fathers of young girls might hire a tutor to teach them classics. At age twelve a girl was considered nubile. Some were even married off at this tender age, and the marriages were consummated. By age fourteen a girl was considered an adult: "Men then call them 'madame' (*domina, kyria*), and seeing that there is nothing left for them but to share a man's bed, they dress themselves up and think of nothing else." The philosopher who penned these lines concluded: "It would be better to persuade them that nothing will make them more estimable than to appear modest and reserved." In good families girls of this age and older were confined in the wall-less prison known as "women's work," as visible proof that they were not misusing their time. If a woman learned to sing, dance, and play a musical instrument (singing, dancing, and music went together), people praised her and appreciated her talents, but hastened to add that she was nevertheless a decent woman. In the end, it was the husband who completed the education of a young woman of good family. A friend of Pliny had a wife whose epistolary talents earned her praise: either her husband was the real author of the letters attributed to her, we are told, or he had been clever enough to cultivate the talents of "this girl he married as a virgin" and hence deserved the credit for himself. Seneca's mother, on the other hand, was forbidden to study philosophy by her husband, who saw such study as the road to dissolution.

Meanwhile, young boys attended school. Why? In order to become good citizens? To learn a trade? To acquire the means to understand their world? No: to embellish their minds, to cultivate themselves through the study of *belles lettres*. It is a peculiar error to think that schools always perform the same function, that of shaping man or adapting him to society. Roman education was neither formative nor utilitarian. Rather, it conferred prestige, primarily through the study of such subjects as rhetoric. It is rare in history that the purpose of education is to prepare a child for life and equip him with an image of society. The history of education is generally a history of ideas about childhood; the social function of education does not explain why things change. In Rome the minds of little boys were decked out with rhetoric, much as in the last century the bodies of little boys were decked out with sailor suits or military uniforms. Childhood is an age that we disguise by embellishing, by using it to embody our ideals.

I have so far said nothing about education in the Greek

portions of the Empire, which differed from the foregoing description in several respects. Nilsson's views on this question are sound: Roman schooling was an imported product and, as such, separate from everyday life, from religious and political activity. Greek schooling, on the other hand, was a part of public life; it look place in the palestra and gymnasium. The gymnasium was like a second public square, a place where anyone could go and where activity was not limited to gymnastics. But gymnastics were an important part of schooling; in my opinion, the major difference between Greek education and Roman education was that sport took up half the time of the Greek student. Even literary subjects (Greek, Homer, rhetoric, a little philosophy, and a great deal of music, even under the Empire) were taught in a corner of the gymnasium or palestra. Schooling, which lasted until the child was about sixteen, was followed immediately by one or two years of ephebia, the program of which was identical.[1]

Apart from the public character of Greek education, its music and gymnastics, there was another difference between it and Roman education. No Roman of good birth could call himself cultivated unless a tutor had taught him Greek language and literature, whereas the most cultivated Greeks thumbed their noses at the thought of learning Latin and haughtily ignored Cicero and Virgil (with a few exceptions, such as the functionary Appian). Greek intellectuals who, like sixteenth-century Italians, went abroad and sold their talents naturally used Greek when practicing medicine or teaching philosophy, for Greek was the language of these sciences. In Rome they picked up a little broken Latin. Even in late antiquity Greeks would study Latin systematically only if they wished to make careers in the imperial bureaucracy.

---

*Adolescence*

At age twelve the young Roman of noble birth completed his elementary education. At age fourteen he shed his child's clothing and was allowed to do what every young man loves to do. At age sixteen or seventeen he might choose a public career or join the army—like Stendhal, who enlisted as a hussar at sixteen. There was no such thing as a legal age of majority. In Rome there were no minors, only prepubescents, who ceased to be so whenever their fathers or tutors judged they were ready to wear a man's garb and start trimming their mustaches. Take, for example, one senator's son. At sixteen he became an equestrian, and at seventeen assumed his first

Young prince, procession of the altar of the Peace of Augustus, 9 B.C. His great-uncle the emperor leads the procession. Beneath the gaze of the adults, the boy may as well not be there. This is unimportant, for the main thing is to belong to the imperial family, whose private life became public, as this image, as much a family as an official portrait, proves. The boy is characterized by his youth—not yet old enough to be officially himself. (Paris, Louvre.)

public office. He was put in charge of the Roman police, supervised executions, and governed the mint. From then on he rose steadily, becoming in turn general, judge, and senator. Where did he learn his craft? On the job. From his elders? More likely from his subordinates: he would have carried himself with enough aristocratic hauteur to seem to be making decisions that others in fact made for him. One noble was a colonel by age sixteen, as well as a state priest; he had already pleaded his first cases at the bar.

Civic and professional matters were learned on the job; culture was studied in school. (The lower orders *had* a culture but not the ambition to cultivate themselves.) School was the means by which one cultivated oneself, and this altered the nature of the culture acquired; certain writers came to be viewed as "classics." (Just as now, with the formation of a "canon" of tourism, there are sites that one "must" visit, monuments that one "must" see.) The schools taught subjects that brought prestige to anyone familiar with them but that actually interested only a few, even among those who admired from afar. And since any institution soon becomes an end in itself, the schools taught, and called "classic," what was easiest to teach. Ever since Athens' golden age rhetoricians had been developing a predigested doctrine, ready to teach. So, from age twelve to age eighteen or twenty, Romans learned to read their classics and then studied rhetoric. But what exactly was rhetoric?

It was most assuredly not utilitarian; it contributed nothing to "society." Eloquence at the podium and the bar played an important role in the Roman Republic, but its prestige derived from its brilliance as literature, not from its civic function. Cicero, who was not the son of an oligarch, enjoyed the rare honor of being admitted to the Senate, because his brilliance as an orator lent prestige to that institution. Under the Empire the public followed trials the way we follow literature; poets, for all their glory, were not wreathed with popularity to compare with the renown of talented orators.

Because of the popularity of eloquence, rhetorical art, or eloquence reduced to formulas, became the sole subject matter, apart from the classics, of Roman education. All Roman boys learned typical speeches suitable for use in politics and the courts, complete with model developments and catalogued effects (our "rhetorical figures"). Did they quickly learn to speak eloquently? No, because rhetoric as taught in the schools soon became an art unto itself, an art whose rules had to be learned. There was a gulf between true eloquence and rhetorical teaching, which the ancients never ceased to deplore even as they delighted in it. The subjects assigned to young Romans for their speeches had nothing to do with the real world. On the contrary, the more mystifying a subject was, the more it stimulated the imagination. Rhetoric became a society game. "Suppose that a law holds that a seduced woman may choose either to have her seducer condemned to death or to marry him, and, further, that in one night a man rapes two women, one of whom demands his death, while the other insists on marrying him." Such a theme gave free rein to virtuosity and to the Roman taste for melodrama and sex. It offered the pleasure of paradox and vicarious amusement. Amateurs long since done with school but highly trained in the rhetorical art continued to play such games at home, before an audience of connoisseurs. The genealogy of ancient education was as follows: from culture to the will to culture, from there to the school, and from the school to the scholastic exercise as an end in itself.

---

While the young Roman, under his teacher's watchful eye, "advised Sulla to abdicate the dictatorship" or weighed the choices open to the victim of rape, he also reached puberty. This marked the beginning of a period of indulgence. It was common knowledge that, as soon as a young man donned his adult garb, his first thought was to buy himself the favors of a servant or hasten to Suburra, Rome's quarter for mischief. Or perhaps a woman of good society might take it into her head to initiate the young man. (The ways of the Roman aristocracy were as free as those of the French aristocracy in the eighteenth century.) To physicians such as Celsus or Rufus of Ephesus, epilepsy was a disease that healed itself at puberty, that is, when girls have their first menses and boys their first sexual encounter. In other words, puberty and sexual initiation were synonymous for boys, while the virginity of young girls remained sacrosanct. For boys, the time between puberty and marriage was a time of parental indulgence. Such strict moralists as Cicero and Juvenal, as well as the Emperor Claudius in his capacity as censor, all admitted that allowances had to be made for the heat of youthful passions. For five or ten years young men chased prostitutes or lived with mistresses. Gangs of youths were known to break down the doors of a prostitute's house and rape her.

*Youth*

It was, moreover, a semiofficial practice for youths to form associations of their own. Organizations of young men were common in Greek sectors of the Empire and also existed (as *collegia juvenum*) in the Latin parts, although their precise role remains obscure, probably because they served many purposes and in any case tended to exceed the limits imposed on them (the blood of youth being hot). Young men participated in sports, duels, and hunting. They gathered in amphitheaters to grapple with wild animals, to the admiration of their compatriots. Unfortunately, they did not limit themselves to such laudable physical activities, derived from the physical education practiced by the Greeks. Taking advantage of their numbers and their official status, they created public disturbances. A privilege always accorded well-born youths in Rome was the freedom to wander the streets at night in gangs, beating passersby, manhandling women, and smashing shops. (The young Nero was no stranger to this custom; once he nearly suffered a thrashing at the hands of a senator attacked by his gang, who failed to recognize the Emperor among his attackers.) Groups of young men claimed this right as their due. "Come home from dinner as soon as possible," we read in one Latin tale, "for a gang of hotheaded youths from the best families is pillaging the city." These same youths cheered armies of gladiators and charioteers who clashed in pitched battle, for this, too, was considered sport by the Roman public. One jurist writes that "certain people, who usually call themselves The Young Men, have been seen to cheer the sides in certain public disturbances. If that is the extent of their crime, they should first be admonished by the governor, and, if they repeat the offense, they should be whipped and then released."

The privileges of youth were also the privileges of youths as a social group. Once a man married, the time for mistresses was over, and so was the time for handsome male lovers. That, at least, is what we are told by the poets who composed epithalamiums and who, in their nuptial songs, do not hesitate to describe the young bridegroom's past mischief, while assuring their audience that the bride is so pretty that none of these things will ever happen again.

Such was Rome's first moral code. But during the second century A.D. a new code gradually took hold, in theory supplanting the older morality. Backed by medical myths (and bear in mind that ancient medicine had about as much scientific validity as medicine in the time of Molière), the new morality

Tomb of the Haterii (detail), ca. A.D. 100. This child's face is a convention of Roman art, but a delightful one. (Rome, Lateran Museum; now at the Vatican.)

attempted to confine sexuality to marriage, even for young men, and encouraged parents to keep their sons virgins until their wedding day. To be sure, love was not a sin but a pleasure; the only trouble was that pleasure, like alcohol, is dangerous. For the sake of health, it was advisable to limit the amount consumed, and more prudent still to abstain altogether. This was not puritanism but hygiene. Conjugal pleasures were another thing entirely. They were part and parcel of the civic, and natural, institution of marriage and hence a duty. The Germans, whom Tacitus describes as noble savages, "know love only late in life, so that the strength of youth in them is not drained," as it was among the Romans. The philosophers, rationalizers by vocation, supported the movement. One wrote: "Regarding the pleasures of love, you must keep yourself pure until marriage, so far as it is possible to do so." Marcus Aurelius, philosopher as well as emperor, congratulated himself "for having preserved the flower of his youth, for not having performed the virile act too soon, and for waiting perhaps even longer than necessary." He was also proud of having touched neither his slave Theodotus nor his servant Benedicta, even though he felt the desire to do so. Physicians prescribed gymnastics and philosophical studies to cool the sexual energies of young men. Masturbation was to be avoided, not because it sapped a man's strength but because it ripened him too quickly and hence produced fruit imperfect because immature.

*Patricide*

The new morality was bolstered by arguments drawn from the old morality, with its civic and patrimonial concerns. Over the centuries these gave rise to an idea new to the Roman Empire, the notion of majority. Coming of age ceased to be a physical fact recognized in customary law and became instead a legal fiction: the prepubescent child was replaced by the legal notion of the "minor" child. A young man who abused his license to indulge in pleasure lost forever the opportunity to temper his character. The emperor Tiberius, a severe ruler and a Stoic as well, sent his young nephew Drusus to command a regiment, "because he showed too great a proclivity for the pleasures of the capital." Early marriage was proof that one's youth was not misspent. Jurists had always been more concerned with patrimony than with morality. A youth of fourteen who had not yet come into his inheritance might borrow at usurious rates of interest to pay for his

Funerary statue: sorrow for the dead or of death. This statue, whose face is a portrait, is a masterpiece of Greco-Roman sculpture, the existence of which is too often neglected by a public that has eyes only for Greek originals, for the supposedly all-Roman art of portraiture, and for the elements of Roman originality. (Rome, Museum of the Conservators.)

pleasures, as he was legally entitled to do, and thus squander his patrimony in advance of receiving it. Usurers (which in Rome meant everybody) "seek the notes of young men who have only recently donned the manly toga while continuing to live under the cruel authority of their fathers." Laws, renewed on several occasions, decreed that anyone who lent money to the scion of a noble house forfeited the right to collect the loan even after the youth's father had died. No one was allowed to borrow money before the age of twenty-five. There were other ways of dealing with the problem: a grandfather or paternal uncle might compel an adolescent orphan to obey a pedagogue who had shown that he was capable of asserting his authority. As a matter of principle, however, any fatherless adolescent was his own master. Quintilian tells, with no particular astonishment, the story of a young noble who just had time to bequeath his fortune to his mistress before dying in the flower of youth, aged eighteen.

This brings us to a point that seems important and may in fact be so. A peculiarity of Roman law that astonished the Greeks was that every male child, past puberty or not, married or not, remained under the authority of his father and did not become a Roman in the full sense of the word, a paterfamilias, until the father's death. More than that, the youth's father was his natural judge and could privately sentence him to death. A testator had almost unlimited discretion: fathers could disinherit their sons. Hence it was possible for an eighteen-year-old orphan to make his mistress his heir, yet a grown man could take no legal action on his own while his father was alive. "Where a son is involved," one jurist writes, "public officials have nothing to say; though he were consul, he would have no right to borrow money." Such, at any rate, was the theory. What was the practice? Morally it was even worse.

There were of course legal limits to paternal power. Not every father disinherited his children, and to do so one had to be sure not to die intestate. A son deprived of his inheritance could contest the will in the courts. In any case, only three-quarters of his patrimony could be taken away. As for a father sentencing his son to death, a notion that played a large role in the Roman imagination, the last instances date from the time of Augustus and outraged public opinion. Still, a child had no fortune of his own: whatever he earned or inherited belonged to his father. The father could, however, grant him a certain capital, the so-called *peculum,* to use as he saw fit. Or

Greek funerary relief from Thyrea (Laconia), 2nd or 1st century B.C. This wealthy young horseman and hunter had been taught to wage war with the breastplate and helmet exhibited by his slave. In the upper right is the vase that adorned his grave. The man sets an example by feeding a serpent, who is none other than the deceased, now a good spirit to be fed by his survivors. (Athens, National Archaeological Museum.)

the father could decide quite simply to emancipate the boy. Sons therefore had grounds for hope and means to act.

But the latter were mere expedients, and hopes were attended by risks. Psychologically, an adult male whose father was alive found himself in an intolerable situation. He could do nothing without his father's consent: he could not sign a contract, free a slave, or draw up his will. He possessed only his *peculum,* like a slave, and even that could be revoked. Apart from these humiliations there was the risk—quite real—of being disinherited. Leaf through Pliny's letters: "So-and-so has made his brother residuary legatee, cutting out his own daughter"; "So-and-so has disinherited her own son"; "So-and-so, whom his father disinherited." Public opinion, which, as we shall see, exerted a powerful influence over upper-class attitudes, did not censure automatically; it weighed the facts of each case. "Your mother," writes Pliny again, "had a legitimate reason for disinheriting you." We know, in any case, the demographic facts of life before Pasteur: society was filled with widows and widowers; many women died in childbirth; many others remarried after their husbands died. And since fathers were almost entirely free to draw their wills as they saw fit, the sons of a first marriage feared their stepmother.

Sons had one last yoke to bear: without their father's consent they could make no career. A youth, if of noble birth, could always have himself named a senator—or, if a mere notable, a member of his city's Council. But how could he meet the considerable expenses attached to such honors in an age when bread and circuses were the means by which public men got ahead? No youth would attempt to become a senator or councillor without his father's consent, for the necessary funds could be taken from his patrimony only if his father approved. On many public buildings in Roman Africa—buildings built by councillors to honor themselves—we find inscriptions stating that the father has borne the expense on behalf of the son. The father exercised sovereign authority in deciding the fate of his children. The number of places in the Senate and municipal councils was limited, and few families could claim more than one for their sons. The attendant expenses were considerable, so only the son chosen by the father could enjoy the costly honor of a career. Other sons were duly praised for their sacrifice. I should add that the eldest son enjoyed no legal privilege, though tradition encouraged younger sons to respect the priority of the eldest.

---

*Wills*

The father's death meant that, barring mishap, his children could enjoy their inheritance. It also signaled the end of a kind of slavery. The sons became adults, and the daughters, if they had not married or had divorced, became heiresses, free to marry whomever they wished. (Although the law required that a woman consent to her own marriage, it also assumed that she always did consent, so in practice girls had to obey their fathers.) Of course I am assuming that the new heiress did not become subject to another authority, that of her paternal uncle. A strict uncle might forbid his niece to take lovers and assign her to work with distaff and spindle. The poet Horace took tender pity on the fate of such unfortunate women.

In these circumstances the obsession with parricide—a relatively common crime—is not surprising. The reasons for committing such a horrible act are quite comprehensible and require no Freudian feats of explication. "During the civil wars and their attendant proscriptions," writes Velleius of a time when denunciations were common, "the loyalty of wives was greatest, that of freedmen less great, that of slaves not insignificant, and that of sons nil, so hard it is to bear the postponement of hope!"

The only Romans who were men in the full sense of the word were therefore free citizens, either orphans or legally emancipated sons, who, married or not, were "fathers of families" and who possessed a patrimony. The paterfamilias occupied a place apart in the prevailing moral system, as the following discussion, reported by Aulus Gellius, suggests: "Must one always obey one's father? Some say, 'Yes, always.' But what if your father orders you to betray your country? Others respond subtly that one never obeys one's father because it is morality that one obeys, to whose dictates he gives voice." Aulus Gellius replies intelligently that there is a third order of things that are neither good nor immoral, such as the decision to marry or remain celibate, to enter one profession rather than another, to leave home or to stay, to seek public office or not. It is over this third order of things that paternal authority is exercised.

The symbol, and weapon, of the father's familial authority and social dignity was the will. The will was a kind of

The opening of a will. Every will was required to be opened in a public place, a forum or "basilica," during the day and in the presence of witnesses. Here a noble has died, and the magistrate, with his official seat and lictors, has come in person for the opening. All are dressed in togas. (Rome, Palazzo Colonna.)

confession in which social man revealed himself fully and by which he would be judged. Had he chosen the worthiest heir? Had he made bequests to all his faithful clients? Did he speak of his wife in terms that would certify her as a good spouse? "What a long time we spend deliberating in our heart of hearts over whom we should name in our wills, and how much we should leave them! None of our decisions is more thoroughly examined." All kin, close or distant, were supposed to get something, along with all members of a man's household: deserving slaves were set free by their master's will, and loyal freedmen and clients were not forgotten.

The public reading of a will was an event of some significance. More was involved than just legacies and bequests; the will had the value of a manifesto. The custom of designating "substitute heirs," who received nothing unless the principal heir refused to accept his due, enabled the testator to name anyone he wished and to assign to each person he named a theoretical fraction of his estate, a measure of his esteem for that individual. A man could also insult, postmortem, anyone he had secretly despised, and praise anyone he had esteemed. The custom among nobles was to make a bequest to fashionable writers of the moment. Pliny, a famous orator in his day, went to every will-reading and remarked with satisfaction that he was always left the same amount as his friend Tacitus. (He did not lie, and epigraphists have found a will in which he is named.) Politics played a part. A senator who had always been taken seriously lost his reputation when his will was opened, because in it he flattered Nero (obviously to avoid having his will set aside and his estate confiscated by the Imperial Tax Collector). Others insulted the freedmen who served the sovereign as all-powerful ministers and even had rather unflattering things to say to the emperor himself, be he Nero or Antoninus Pius. A will was such a fine thing, of which people were so proud, that many a testator in his cups found it difficult to keep from reading his will so as to give his legatees a foretaste of their good fortune and win their respect.

In other societies the deathbed ritual and the dying man's last words were of great importance. In Rome what mattered was first of all the will, which expressed the social individual, and second, as we shall see, the epitaph, which manifested what can only be called the public individual.

Painting at Herculanum, 79 B.C. Unmarried life as it exists in painting. This couple, accustomed to it, are in no rush to take their pleasure. She is half nude, and he drinks wine from a raised vessel (with a hole in the bottom that one held closed with a finger; the vessel was usually emptied in a single swallow). (Naples, Archaeological Museum.)

# ✎ Marriage

ROMAN Italy, in the first century before or after Christ, was home to five or six million free citizens, male and female. They lived in hundreds of rural territories, at the center of which stood a cluster of monuments and private dwellings (the *domus*); these were called "cities." In addition, some one or two million slaves served as domestic servants and agricultural laborers. Little is known about how they lived, beyond the fact that marriage, at this time a private institution, was forbidden to them and would remain so until the third century. Slaves, it was believed, lived in sexual promiscuity, save for a handful of trusted servants who acted as stewards for their masters or, as slaves of the emperor himself, served the state as functionaries. These privileged slaves lived monogamously with a single concubine, sometimes given them by their masters.

*Criteria for Marriage*

Let us restrict our attention, then, to free men. Some of these were born free, the fruit of legitimate marriage between male and female citizens. Others were bastards, born to mothers who were citizens. Still others, born slaves, had been subsequently freed. All were nonetheless citizens, entitled to participate in the civic institution of marriage. To us this institution seems paradoxical: Roman marriage was a private act, which did not require the sanction of any public authority. Bride and groom did not have to appear before the equivalent of a priest or justice of the peace. No written document was necessary: there was no marriage contract, only a contract for the bride's dowry (assuming she had one), and the whole procedure was quite informal. Notwithstanding all that has been said on the subject, no symbolic act was required. In short, marriage was a private event, like engagement today. How, then, could a judge decide, in case of litigation over an inheritance, whether or not a man and a woman were legally married? In the absence of a formal act or contract, he based his decision on certain signs, much as courts do today in establishing matters of fact. What signs? Well, for instance, such unambiguous actions as the constitution of a dowry, or acts that proved a man's intention to be a husband, such as referring habitually to the woman with whom he lived as his wife. Or witnesses might testify that they had attended a small ceremony whose nuptial character was manifest. Ultimately, however, only husband and wife could be certain that in their own minds they were married.

It was, nevertheless, important to determine whether or not a man and a woman were legitimately married. For even though marriage was a private institution, with no written instrument or even formal ceremony to certify its existence, it was a fact with legal consequences. The children of a marriage were legitimate; they took their father's name and continued his line; upon his death they inherited his estate, assuming he had not disinherited them. Divorce, from a legal standpoint, was as easy for the wife as for the husband and as informal as marriage. It was enough for either party to leave home with the intention of divorcing his or her spouse. Certain cases gave jurists pause. Was there a true separation or a simple quarrel? Strictly speaking, it was not even necessary to notify an ex-spouse of the divorce, and cases are recorded in which husbands were divorced by their wives without their knowledge. Whether or not a woman took the initiative in divorce, she left her husband's household with her dowry, if any. On the other hand, children apparently always remained with their fathers. Divorce and remarriage were quite common, and nearly every family had children born of different mothers.

A marriage ceremony involved witnesses, useful in case the marriage was contested. The custom of marriage gifts existed. The wedding night took the form of a legal rape from which the woman emerged "offended with her husband" (who, accustomed to using his slave women as he pleased, found it difficult to distinguish between raping a woman and taking the initiative in sexual relations). It was customary for the groom to forgo deflowering his wife on the first night, out of concern for her timidity; but he made up for his for-

bearance by sodomizing her. Martial and Seneca the Elder state this as a proverb, and the *Casina* confirms it. The same custom existed in China. Women abstained from sexual activity during pregnancy. Elian and pseudo-Quintilian found such modesty natural, because they believed it was shared by animals. Since conjugal pleasures were legitimate, wedding guests had the right and even the duty to praise them bawdily. In one epithalamium the poet went so far as to promise the bridegroom an afternoon of love. Such boldness was pardonable on the day after a marriage, but in other circumstances making love during the daylight hours would have been considered shamelessly libertine.

Why did people marry? For money (obtaining a dowry was one honorable way to get rich) and for children who, as legitimate heirs, were entitled to inherit an estate; those children, moreover, perpetuated the state by replenishing the ranks of its citizenry. Politicians called upon families to do their duty as citizens and preserve the city. Pliny the Younger, a senator no more pompous than most, added appropriately that there was another way to make new citizens: by freeing deserving slaves.

Wedding night, reproduction of a Greek original. The veiled bride sits on the edge of the bed, as Persuasion encourages her. At the foot of the bed sits the god Hymen, bold and relaxed, awaiting his moment. Venus, or one of the Graces, leans on a pillar, ready to perfume the bride in preparation for her lawful violation, from which, thanks to the woman's charm, matrimonial harmony would grow. (Rome, Vatican Museums.)

*The Transformation of Marriage*

Stabies, portrait of a couple, prior to 79 B.C. Mediocre but cruelly accurate. Between the man and the woman is a small Bacchus. (Naples, Archaeological Museum.)

Whether in legitimate marriage or concubinage, monogamy was the rule. But monogamy was not synonymous with "couple." I shall consider here not what everyday married life was actually like, but what prevailing moral codes required husbands to think about their wives in different periods. Was the wife a person in her own right, her husband's equal, his queen as it were, and as such entitled to appear together with him in a "royal portrait" (even if she served him as handmaiden under a more respectable name)? Or was she a perpetual child, whose only importance was as personification of the institution of marriage? The answer is simple. In the first century B.C. a man was supposed to think of himself as a citizen who had fulfilled all his civic duties. A century later he was supposed to consider himself a good husband; as such he was officially required to respect his wife. At some point people began to internalize, as a moral code, what had been a civic and dotal institution: monogamous marriage. Why this change? Michel Foucault thinks that the role of men, of males, changed when the Empire supplanted the Republic and the independent cities of Greece. The members of the ruling class, formerly citizen-soldiers, became local notables and loyal subjects of the emperor. The Greco-Roman ideal of self-discipline and autonomy was associated with the desire to exert power in public life. (No one is worthy to govern who cannot govern himself.) Under the Empire, sovereignty over oneself ceased to be a civic virtue and became an end unto itself. Autonomy secured inner peace and made a man independent of Fortune and of the power of the emperor. This was preeminently the Stoic ideal, and Stoicism was the most widespread of those sects of wisdom, or "philosophy," that enjoyed as much influence with the Romans as religions or ideologies do with us. Much Stoic preaching concerned the new conjugal morality. Note, however, that everything I am about to say applies to only a tenth or a twentieth of the free population, to the class of the wealthy, who also considered themselves cultivated. Given the nature of our sources, this is the best we can do. In rural Italy free peasants, whether smallholders or sharecroppers on the lands of the rich, were married. That is all we know about them. The choice between the civic and Stoic ideals was not an option for them.

The code of civic morality, then the morality of the couple. When, over the course of a century or two, the transition was made from one to the other, what changed was not the way people behaved (let's not be overoptimistic), or even the rules they were supposed to follow, but something else, something more abstract and yet somehow more crucial: the very ground of morality, that which justified all the prescriptions, and hence the way in which moral agents were perceived—as soldiers with a civic duty to perform or as responsible moral individuals. Form determined content. The older moral code said: "To marry is one duty of the citizen." The newer said: "To be a good man, one must make love only in order to have children. Marriage is not a means to sexual pleasure." The older code did not question the reasons for the rules: the rule was that the only way to father a citizen was to take a wife, so citizens obeyed and married. Less militarist, the newer code sought to discover the grounds of social institutions. Marriage outlives the duty to produce children, it was argued, so there must be some other reason why it exists. Husband and wife, both reasonable beings, live together all their lives. Thus marriage, the Stoics deduced, must be a kind of friendship, a durable affection between two good people who make love only in order to perpetuate the human race. In short, the new morality sought to justify its prescriptions to reasonable people. But it was incapable of criticizing existing institutions. Rational grounds for marriage had to be found. This mixture of good intentions and conformity gave rise to the myth of the couple. In the old civic code, the wife was nothing but an accessory to the work of the citizen and paterfamilias. She produced children and added to the family patrimony. In the new code, the wife was a friend, a "life's companion." As a rational person it was her duty to recognize her natural inferiority and obey her husband. Her husband would respect her as a leader respects his devoted subordinates—friends but inferiors. In short, the couple came to the West when moralists began to wonder why a man and a woman should spend their lives together and ceased to regard marriage as a sort of natural phenomenon.

---

*Marriage as a Duty*

The new moral code said: "Here are the duties of the married man." By contrast, the old civic code had said: "Marriage is one of the duties of the citizen." Teachers of ethics accordingly had made a point of reminding their pupils of the existence of this duty. In 100 B.C. a censor could say to the assembly of citizens, "marriage, as we all know, is a source of trouble. Nevertheless, one must marry, out of civic duty."

Pompeii. Idealized figures conversing. A fabulous or theatrical model of elegance for the real world. Gynaeceum scene, perhaps a pastiche of Hellenistic painting. The figures are not placed at random; their respective positions establish the grandeur of the composition. (Naples, Archaeological Museum.)

Each citizen was called upon to ask himself whether or not he would fulfill this obligation. Marriage was not taken for granted but openly discussed as an issue. This created the illusion of a "marriage crisis," a spread of celibacy. (Such collective obsessions, as we know all too well, cannot be countered by mere statistical evidence.) The Romans suffered from this illusion before their historians took it up, and the emperor Augustus promulgated special laws to encourage citizens to marry.

Marriage was therefore perceived as a duty among other duties, an option to elect or reject. It was not a matter of "establishing a family" or setting the course of a life, but one of many dynastic decisions that a noble Roman had to make. Should he enter public life or seek to enhance his family's wealth in the private realm? Should he become a soldier or an orator? And so on. The nobleman's wife was not so much his life's companion as the object of a major decision. She was so much an object, in fact, that two noblemen could amicably pass her back and forth. Cato of Utica, that model of every virtue, lent his wife to a friend and later remarried her, picking up an enormous inheritance for his incovenience. A man by the name of Nero "affianced" his wife Livia to the future emperor Augustus ("affianced' was the word used).

Marriage was but one of a life's acts, and the wife was

but one of the elements of a household, which also included children, freedmen, clients, and slaves. "If your slave, your freedman, your woman, or your client dares to answer you back, you get angry," writes Seneca. Lords, heads of household, settled things among themselves, dealing with each other as sovereign to sovereign. If one of them had to make an important decision, he convoked a "council" of friends rather than discuss the matter with his wife.

Did husband and wife make a "couple"? Did the man of the house allow his wife to see visitors as we in the West do today, or did she quickly retire as in Islamic countries? When a man was invited out to dinner, was it proper to invite his wife as well? From the few indications in the sources, I have not been able to arrive at any firm answers to these questions. The one thing that is clear is that wives were allowed to visit women friends, albeit in the company of chaperones.

A woman was like a grown child; her husband was obliged to humor her because of her dowry and her noble father. Cicero and his correspondents gossip about the caprices of these lifelong adolescents, who, for example, might seize upon the absence of a husband sent to govern a remote province in order to divorce him and marry another. These women's antics nevertheless had real consequences for political relations among the nobility. Needless to say, it was impossible for a woman to make a fool of her lord and master. Cuckoldry (as we know it from Molière) was not a part of the Romans' conceptual universe. Had it been, Cato, Caesar, and Pompey would all have been illustrious cuckolds. A man was the master of his wife, just as he was the master of his daughters and servants. If his wife was unfaithful, the man did not thereby become a laughingstock. Infidelity was a misfortune, neither greater nor less than the misfortune of a daughter who became pregnant or a slave who failed of his duty. If a wife betrayed her husband, the husband was criticized for want of vigilance and for having, by his own weakness, allowed adultery to flourish in the city—much as we might criticize parents for overindulging or spoiling their children, allowing them to drift into delinquency and thus making the cities unsafe. The only way for a husband or father to avoid such an accusation was to be the first to publicly denounce any misconduct by members of his family. The emperor Augustus detailed the affairs of his daughter Julia in an edict; Nero did the same for the adultery of his wife, Octavia. The point was to prove that the man had no "patience," that is, connivance, with vice.

Painting of an underground tomb, 2nd century A.D. (Rome, Museum of the Baths.)

People wondered whether the stoic silence of other husbands deserved praise or blame.

Because deceived husbands were aggrieved rather than risible and divorced women took their dowries with them, divorce was common among the upper class (Caesar, Cicero, Ovid, and Claudius married three times), and perhaps also among the urban plebs. Juvenal tells of a woman of the people who consults an itinerant soothsayer about whether she should leave her tavernkeeper husband to marry a secondhand clothing merchant (a prosperous profession in a time when the lower orders bought their clothing used). Nothing was more alien to the Romans than the biblical notion of taking possession of the flesh. Roman men did not hesitate to marry divorced women. The emperor Domitian remarried a woman he had divorced, who had subsequently married another man. For a woman to have known only one man in her life was considered a merit, but only the Christians would undertake to make such fidelity a duty and attempt to prohibit widows from remarrying.

*The Harmonious Union*

Since marriage was a civic duty and a private boon, all that the old moral code required of spouses was to have children and run the household. There were two degrees of virtue: one for discharging strict marital duties, and another, higher level of virtue for achieving a harmonious union. It is here that the couple makes its first appearance in the West, but the appearance is deceiving. The household is the household, and husband and wife each have their respective duties to perform. If they happen to get on well together, so much the better; but mutual understanding is not essential. People were glad to hear that husband and wife got on well, as did Ulysses and Penelope in ancient times, or even that they adored each other, as did the Philemon and Baucis of legend. But not every couple was so fortunate. Marriage was one thing, happy couples were another.

Love in marriage was a stroke of good fortune; it was not the basis of the institution. Marital difficulties were commonplace, and people resigned themselves to this. Moralists said that by learning to put up with a wife's moods and the flaws in her character, a man prepared himself to face the trials and tribulations of the world. In many epitaphs a husband will speak of his "very dear wife"; in others, no less numerous, he will say rather, "my wife, who never gave me any reason to

Probably 2nd century A.D. This is not a fanciful image but a funerary portrait set in a shell— a common device. Evidently there were women painters; this one, with her pots of paint, is working with a nude model. Note the sophisticated hairdo (a similar hairdo can be seen in the portrait of a girl in the Museum of Thessalonica). (Rome, Villa Albani.)

complain" (*querella*). Historians compiled lists of couples who remained together until they died. Nevertheless, when the time came to pay one's respects to a new husband, people emulated Ovid and said: "May your wife equal her husband in exhaustible good nature! May quarrels rarely trouble your life together!" Ovid was too shrewd and courtly a poet to have committed a gaffe and embarrassed his audience.

Because treating one's wife well was not compulsory, it was all the more praiseworthy, all the more meritorious to be "a good neighbor, amiable host, kind to his wife, and lenient to his slave," to borrow Horace's words. Ever since Homer, tenderness toward one's wife had been held up as an ideal beyond the strict obligations of marriage. Bas-reliefs depict husband and wife holding hands, and this, whatever may have been said on the subject, was a symbol not of marriage but of this desirable additional concord. Ovid, exiled, left his wife in Rome, where she administered his property and attempted to win his pardon. Two things united them, he said: the "marital pact," but also "the love that makes us partners." It was possible for conflict to arise between duty and these extraneous tender feelings. What to do, for instance, if one's wife turned out to be sterile? "The first man who repudiated his wife on grounds of sterility had an acceptable motive but did not

Bronze mirror bracket: Jupiter, Juno, and Cupid, 1st century B.C.? In Italy, for five centuries, scenes from Greek mythology were de rigueur in elegant boudoir decoration. (Paris, Louvre.)

escape censure [*reprehensio*], because even the desire to have children should not have outweighed lasting devotion to his wife," according to the moralist Valerius Maximus.

*The New Illusion*

Had the couple arrived in the West? No. A merit is one thing, a duty another. Note the shade of difference: harmony was praised where it existed, not held up as a norm implicit in the institution of marriage, in which case disagreement between husband and wife would have been seen as shocking rather than only too predictable. And this was in fact the case under the new moral code, related to Stoicism, which imposed the couple as an ideal that husbands and wives should emulate. Hypocrisy was the result. To suspect disharmony in a marriage was now regarded as slander or defeatism. One symptom by which we can recognize the champions of the new morality of marriage is their edifying style. When Seneca and Pliny speak of their married lives, they do so in a sentimental style that exudes virtue and deliberately aims to be exemplary. One consequence was that the place of the wife ceased to be what it had been. Under the old moral code she had been classed among the servants, who were placed in her charge by delegation of her husband's authority. Under the new code she was raised to the same status as her husband's friends, and friends played an important role in the social life of the Greeks and Romans. For Seneca the marriage bond was comparable in every way to the pact of friendship. What were the practical consequences of this? I doubt that there were many. What changed was more than likely the manner in which husbands spoke of their wives in general conversation or addressed them in the presence of others.

What can be said about this moral transformation is approximately the same that can be said of any "event" in the history of ideas. After a century of cultural sociology, many historians frankly admit that they are incapable of explaining cultural mutations and, even more, that they haven't the slightest idea what form a causal explanation might take. Let it be noted simply that the cause was not Stoicism. The new morality had its champions among the enemies of the Stoics as well as among Stoics and neutral onlookers.

Plutarch, a Platonist philosopher, was at pains to mark his distance from Stoicism, the still triumphant rival of neo-Platonism, its challenger for philosophical supremacy. He nevertheless sets forth his theory of conjugal love, which he regarded as a higher form of friendship. A senator, Pliny belonged to no sect; he had chosen eloquence rather than wisdom. In his letters he paints himself as a good man, and he pronounces his opinion on every subject with dogmatic certainty typical of the Roman senator. He decides, for example, that remarriage is laudable even if the age of the parties rules out procreation as its purpose, for the true end of marriage is the aid and affection that the spouses bring each other. He claims that his relations with his own wife are noble and sentimental and that he shows her the greatest respect and bears toward her the profoundest feelings of friendship, marked by all the virtues. The modern reader must make an effort to recall that the woman in question was a child bride who came to Pliny in a marriage of convenience made for money and for the sake of his career. Another neutral senator, Tacitus, admitted that, contrary to republican tradition, a woman might accompany her husband on a mission to govern a province, even though this was practically a military function and the female sex was barred from all things military. The wife's presence would lend moral support to her husband, strengthening rather than weakening his soldierly resolve.

In these circumstances it is hardly surprising that the

This couple, 1st century B.C., has such an "old Roman" look that at first we do not notice that the sculptor has clothed them in the Greek manner. The Greeks sculpted Romans without their togas, retaining only the shoes of their usual costume. (Rome, Museum of the Conservators.)

Stoics, too, adopted the new morality, for it had emerged triumphant and would henceforth be taken for granted. But because there were so many Stoics, and their voices were so powerful, they appear, misleadingly, to have been the propagators rather than the dupes of the new moral outlook. I use the word "dupes" advisedly, for nothing in Stoic doctrine obliged them to preach submission to the reigning morality. Indeed, the contrary was true. Stoicism, in its original version, taught that mortals should strive to become the equals of the gods, self-sufficient and indifferent to Fortune's blows. They could achieve this end by applying critical reason to discover the natural route to self-sufficiency and then courageously sticking to this path. Individuals were obliged to accept their social roles only insofar as these were compatible with the end of achieving self-sufficiency and with the natural sympathy that each man feels for his fellow human beings. Such a philosophy could easily have led to a critique of the institutions of politics and the family, and originally Stoicism did lead to such a critique. But it became the victim of its success with a clique of rich and powerful men of letters and was reduced to little more than a sophisticated version of prevailing morality: a man's duties to himself and others were identified with institutions, which this bastard doctrine ingeniously sought to internalize as moral precepts. Marriage, for example, was conceived as a friendship—an unequal friendship—between a man and a woman. We are far from the time when Stoics speculated about desire for beauty and love for boys (which they considered typical of love in general).

Typical tomb of Byzantium and Mysia, 1st century B.C., showing a couple (but not their children) and a symbol of marital harmony. At the left is a servant; in the middle a slave standing with his legs crossed (ready to obey his master's orders). The omnipresent scroll indicates the husband's high social class. (Paris, Louvre.)

## Chaste Spouses

Apart from the deliberate conformity of the later Stoic philosophy, there was a more genuine affinity between Stoicism and the new conjugal morality. The new morality did more than just prescribe certain marital duties. It exhorted husband and wife to emulate a certain ideal of the couple, relying on feelings of friendship, constantly tested, to dictate their duties. Stoicism was a doctrine of moral autonomy, which held that the reasonable individual ought to guide himself, from within. But it was essential that he pay constant attention to every detail along life's path. This had two consequences: first, all the rigor of the matrimonial institution was incorporated into conformist Stoicism; and, second, the institution was made more rigorous than ever, by requiring husband and wife to control their every gesture and to dem-

Cameo. Octavia, sister of Augustus. Beautiful princesses, treated as stars, added luster to the new monarchy. (Paris, Bibliothèque Nationale, Cabinet des Médailles.)

onstrate, before giving in to any desire, that it conformed to the dictates of reason.

Perpetuation of the institution. One must marry, according to Antipater of Tarsus, in order to provide one's country with new citizens and because the divine plan of the universe requires propagation of the human race. The foundation of marriage, according to Musonius, is procreation and mutual support. Adultery is theft, according to Epictetus: to take one's neighbor's wife is as thoughtless as to snatch his serving of pork from his plate. "Similarly, for women, the portions have been distributed among men." Marriage, according to Seneca, is an exchange of obligations, possibly unequal or, rather, different, that of the woman being to obey. Marcus Aurelius, the Stoic emperor, congratulated himself on having found in his empress "so obedient a wife." Since husband and wife were both moral agents and contracts were mutual, adultery on the part of the husband was considered as grave an offense

Detail of sarcophagus, 3rd or 4th century. Muse with bare arms in melancholy daydream, leaning against frame of cultivated man's epitaph. (Paris, Louvre.)

as adultery on the part of the wife (in contrast to the old morality, which judged sins not according to a moral ideal but according to civic reality, recognizing male privilege as a fact).

It is clear that the requirements of marriage had become more stringent than ever. Because marriage was friendship, husband and wife could make love only in order to have children, and even then with care not to indulge in too many caresses. A man must not treat his wife as he would treat a mistress, Seneca admonishes, citing Saint Jerome approvingly. His nephew Lucan was of the same opinion. He wrote an epic, a sort of realistic historical novel, in which he describes in his own fashion the story of the civil war between Caesar and Pompey. He shows Cato, model of the Stoic, taking leave of his wife (the same wife he lent for a time to a friend) as he prepares to go off to war. Even on the eve of such a lengthy separation, they do not make love, as Lucan is at pains to point out, explaining as he does the doctrinal significance of the fact. Even that semigreat man Pompey, although no Stoic, does not sleep with his wife on the farewell night. Why the abstinence? Because a good man does not live for petty pleasures and is careful about every action. To give in to desire is immoral. There is only one reasonable ground for a couple to sleep together: procreation. It was a question not of asceticism but of rationalism. Reason asked: Why do this? By nature a planner, reason found it difficult to accept "Why not?" as an answer. Stoic *planism* bears a misleading resemblance to Christian asceticism. In any case, Christianity was not a monolithic religion. In its first few centuries it evolved far more than Stoicism did; and it was quite a varied religion to begin with. The Christian Clement of Alexandria was influenced by Stoicism to the point of copying out the conjugal precepts of the Stoic Musonius, without mentioning their true author. Saint Jerome would have found this doctrine far too sensual. As for Saint Augustine, one of the most prodigious inventors of ideas the world has ever known, it was easier for him to create his own doctrine of marriage than to copy someone else's.

Clearly we must not argue in terms of stereotypes and imagine a conflict between pagan and Christian morality. The real cleavage lay elsewhere: between a morality of matrimonial duties and an internalized morality of the couple. The latter, which originated somewhere in the heart of pagan culture, was commonplace by A.D. 100, shared by both pagans and Christians under Stoic influence. Stoics believed that this mo-

Venus. Roman replica of a Greek original from the 5th century B.C., cloaked in "wet drapery." (Rome, Museum of the Conservators.)

Portrait of an unknown woman, early Christian era. (Paris, Petit Palais, Dutuit Collection.)

Portrait of an unknown man, found in Annecy, 2nd century. (Paris, Petit Palais, Dutuit Collection.)

rality was morality par excellence, hence necessarily their own invention. To affirm, on abundant evidence, that late pagan morality was identical with almost all Christian morality is not to confound paganism and Christianity but to blur the outlines of both. There is no point arguing about those massive but flimsy inventions; rather, we must take them apart in order to study the more subtle mechanisms at work within them, mechanisms that do not correspond to traditional blueprints.

Besides, a moral code is more than just a collection of precepts. Even if some pagans and some Christians shared identical rules of marital behavior, questions would remain. At a certain point in history both pagans and Christians said: Do not make love except to have children. But the consequences of such a declaration differ, depending on whether it is made by a philosophy that offers advice to free individuals, who may take it or leave it as they find its arguments convincing or not, or by an all-powerful Church, which sees its mission as one of securing salvation in the hereafter through the regulation of consciences here below and seeks to lay down the law to all men without exception, whether convinced or not.

Rome, statuette of Venus or a Season. The hairdo would have been fashionable in the early Christian era. Did she once hold a mirror? This would account for the resigned gesture of the index figure beneath the chin. At the waist is the buckle of a girdle that lifted the woman's dress so that it would hang with more folds. (Paris, Petit Palais, Dutuit Collection.)

Fragment of sarcophagus, 2nd or 3rd century. Scenes like this occur infrequently on tombs. Either the man buried here was a wealthy landowner, or the plowing depicted had something to do with a myth, such as that of Triptolemus. Summer carries a full basket of fruit. The yoke is attached, not very efficiently, to the ox's withers. (Museum of Benevento.)

# ⚘ Slavery

At any moment, Seneca says, death may catch you unawares: you may fall victim to shipwreck or bandits, "and, leaving aside higher powers, the least of your slaves holds over you the power of life and death." A worried Pliny wrote to alert one of his correspondents that his friend Robustus had left on a journey accompanied by some of his slaves and had disappeared. No one had seen him since. "Had he been the victim of an attack by his servants?" In Mainz an epitaph immortalizes the tragic end of a thirty-year-old slaveowner murdered by his slave, who then committed suicide by jumping into the Main. The Romans lived in unspoken fear of their slaves. Though by nature an inferior being, the slave was a member of his master's family, one whom the master "loved" and punished paternally and from whom he expected obedience and "love" in return. The slave's relationship to his master was ambivalent, hence dangerous. Love could suddenly turn to hatred. The annals of modern criminology record any number of bloody crimes committed by maids who had previously given every appearance of being devoted servants. Ancient slavery is a subject for Jean Genet.

Opinions to the contrary notwithstanding, the slave was not a thing; he was considered a human being. Even "wicked masters," who treated their slaves inhumanely, set them the moral duty of being good slaves, of serving with loyalty and devotion. One does not impose moral obligations on animals or machines. Yet this human being was also a possession, the property of its owner. There were two kinds of property in the ancient world: men and things. My father, wrote Galen, always taught me not to look upon material losses as tragic. If an ox or a horse or a slave of mine dies, therefore, I do not

Tomb of the freedman Cornelius Atimetus, who manufactured and sold knives, 1st century A.D. In this scene knives are being sold. According to his epitaph, Atimetus owned several slaves. Shown on the right wearing a tunic, he displays his merchandise to a client wearing a toga. (Rome, Vatican Museums.)

carry on. Plato, Aristotle, and Cato shared these sentiments. Similarly, in our own day an officer may say, I lost a machine gun and twenty men.

Because a slave was owned property, he was an inferior being. And since this inferiority of one man made another man, his owner, a man of power, the master, confident of his majesty, consecrated that power by holding that the slave's inferiority was a fact of nature. A slave, it was said, is subhuman by fate and not by accident. Today's closest psychological analogy to ancient slavery is racism. Furthermore, the master's power over his human implement was not governed by rules; it was absolute. The personal relation between master and slave was therefore unlike the relation between employer and employee; the slave was a devoted servant who obeyed in his very soul. Though unequal, the master-slave relationship involved two human beings. The master "loved" his slave, for what master does not love his dog, what employer does not love his good workers, what colonist does not love his loyal natives? The officer who lost twenty men loved them and was loved by them. Ancient slavery was a peculiar legal relationship, which gave rise to common sentiments of dependence and personal authority; it was an emotional relationship between individuals, with little about it that was anonymous.

Slavery was not, or at any rate not simply, a relation of production. Though sharing a common inferiority, slaves played the most varied roles in the economy, society, and even politics and culture. A handful were richer and more powerful than most free men. Their ethnic origin was of no significance. The subjugation of vanquished peoples and slave trade at the borders of the empire supplied only a small fraction of the servile work force. Slaves reproduced themselves; their ranks were swelled by abandoned infants and free men sold into slavery. Children born to a slave mother belonged to her master, regardless of who the father was, just as the offspring of livestock belonged to their owner. It was the master's choice whether to raise his slave children or expose them—or even drown them as one might drown unwanted kittens. A Greek tale tells of the distress of a slave-mistress, who trembles at the thought that her master-lover might kill the child she is expecting by him. A collection of "jokes," the *Philogelos*, contains this good one: "The Absent-minded Fellow had a child by one of his slaves, and his father advised him to kill the child. But the Absent-minded Fellow responded, 'You tell me

Top: Relief, 1st or 2nd century. A family workshop (note the child at the left) in which metal vessels were manufactured. A vessel's price depended on its weight, which accounts for the scales. (Naples, Archaeological Museum.) Bottom left: Tomb of Cornelius Atimetus. Knives are being forged. Bottom right: Detail of a sarcophagus, 2nd or 3rd century. A cobbler and a ropemaker who lived together were buried together because they were friends. (Rome, Museum of the Baths.)

to begin by killing my children; next thing you'll be telling me to kill yours.'" As we have seen, the abandonment of children was common, and not only among the poor. Slave traders picked up babies exposed in temples or at public dumps. Last but not least, poverty drove the indigent to sell their newborn to slave traffickers (who took children scarcely out of the womb and still covered with blood, before their mothers had had a chance to see and develop affection for them). Many adults sold themselves in order not to die of hunger. Some ambitious men did the same in the hope of becoming the stewards of noblemen or imperial treasurers. This, in my view, was the story of the all-powerful and extremely wealthy Pallas, scion of a noble Arcadian family, who sold himself into slavery so that he might be taken on as steward by a woman of the imperial family and who wound up as minister of finance and *éminence grise* to the emperor Claudius.

---

*The True Nature of Slavery*

In the Roman Empire the emperor's slaves and freedmen played a role analogous to that played in French history by such illustrious royal ministers and advisers as Colbert or Fouquet. Most of those whom we would call functionaries or bureaucrats were also imperial slaves and freedmen: they handled the administrative chores of the prince, their master. At the opposite end of the spectrum were slaves who worked as agricultural laborers. To be sure, the age of "plantation slavery" and Spartacus' revolt belonged to the distant past, and it is not true that Roman society was based on slavery. The system of large estates cultivated by slave gangs was limited to certain regions such as southern Italy and Sicily. (The slave system was no more essential a feature of Roman antiquity than slavery in the southern United States prior to 1865 is an essential characteristic of the modern West.) Elsewhere, estates were worked by sharecroppers and hired laborers as well as slaves; in some provinces, such as Egypt, rural slavery was virtually unknown. Large landowners used slaves to cultivate portions of their estates not rented to sharecroppers. These slaves lived in dormitories under the authority of a slave overseer or steward, whose official concubine prepared meals for all the slaves. Philostratus tells the story of a modest vintner who resigned himself to tending his vineyard by himself because his few slaves cost too much to keep.

Most artisans seem to have been slaves. Slaves and freed-

men made up the entire staff of the pottery shops at Arezzo, where a host of small, independent businesses employed from one to sixty-five workers. In agriculture we find mainly small independent peasants and sharecroppers, who worked for large landowners. Additional labor was needed at times, however, and we find both hired day laborers, free but miserable, and "chained slaves," a phrase I interpret to mean slaves who had misbehaved and were punished by being sold on condition that the buyer keep them as prisoners in a kind of private prison. Slave labor supplemented the vast peasantry already on the land. For slavery to have become the primary relation of production, the Romans would have had to subjugate this free peasantry. At a rough estimate, slaves accounted for a quarter of the rural work force in Italy. Given that the peasants were the beasts of burden of the Roman Empire, the lot of the slave was harsh indeed.

A slave who did not work the land was most likely to be a domestic servant. An upper-class Roman employed dozens of servants in his household, and a middle-class Roman (who would have been wealthy enough to live without doing anything) had one, two, or three. According to Galen, "there was at Pergamum a grammarian who had two slaves. Every day the grammarian went to the baths with one of them [who dressed and undressed him] and left the second locked up at home to watch the house and prepare the meal." Domestics lived in a variety of situations, ranging from that of the slattern to that of the powerful overseer mentioned by Galen, who had charge of all of his master's affairs and who was seen by the greatest doctors when he fell ill. Relations between servants and their masters varied just as widely, and the slave who was the accomplice of his master and led him about by the nose was not just a figure of comedy (although the master could, in a fit of rage, send him off to a life of hard labor should their ambivalent relationship turn sour). Master and mistress could set trusted slaves to spy on their "friends" and clients or on preceptors, philosophers, and other freeborn servants. These slaves reported the scandals and absurdities of the household directly to the master. Certain types of work were normally performed by slaves, who obtained secure positions in the service of some great personage: grammarians, architects, singers, and actors might be slaves of the master who employed their talents. Intimacy with one of the great was less sordid than working for a daily pittance, and eventually the masters of these slaves would set them free.

Chariot race at the Circus. This relief telescopes two different phases of the race. The magistrate who presides over and pays for the games (identifiable from his scepter) prepares to throw down a handkerchief signaling the start, and one chariot pulls ahead of the others, indicating the finish. (Rome, Vatican Museums.)

Roman physicians were normally succeeded by slaves whom they trained and then manumitted (there being no medical schools at the time). The relation of employer to hired labor was not seen as a neutral one governed by rules; it was looked down on because it was not a personal bond. Personal ties were highly unequal, and it was this inequality that was common to all slaves, however different their conditions might be in other respects. This common condition—involvement in an unequal personal relation with a master—is what makes "slavery" a meaningful word. Whether powerful or wretched, all slaves were spoken to in the tone and terms used in speaking to children and inferior beings. Slavery was an extraeconomic relationship, and it was more than just a legal category. What is inconceivable and distasteful (to us) is that it was a social distinction not based on the "rational" criterion of wealth, which is why we compare it to racism. In the United States fifty years ago a black could be a famous singer or wealthy businessman and yet whites would speak to him in familiar terms and address him by his first name, as though speaking to a servant. As Jean-Claude Passeron has observed, there can be hierarchies, evident from visible signs of esteem, that have nothing to do with wealth or power. Slavery, racism, and nobility offer numerous examples.

Cover plate, 1st century. Prior to construction of the Coliseum, fights between gladiators and wild animals were held in the Circus. The seven boulders indicate that the chariots have completed seven laps. (Rome, Museum of the Baths.)

Slave collar in bronze, found around the neck of a skeleton in southern Rome: "If captured, return me to Apronianus, minister in the imperial palace, at the Golden Napkin on the Aventine, for I am a fugitive slave." (Paris, Petit Palais, Dutuit Collection.)

Bronze plaque, 3rd–4th century. "I am Asellus, slave of Prejectus attached to the ministry of markets, and I have escaped the walls of Rome. Capture me, for I am a fugitive slave, and return me to Barbers' Street, near the Temple of Flora." A slave who managed to escape had virtually no way to earn a living other than to sell himself to a slave dealer in the hope of being resold to a better master than the one from whom he had fled. (Paris, Petit Palais, Dutuit Collection.)

The slave was inferior by nature, whatever he was or did. This natural inferiority went hand in hand with legal inferiority. If the master decided to set the slave up in business in order to claim the profits for himself, he gave the slave a sum of money called a *peculum* and full financial autonomy, along with the right to sign contracts on his own initiative and even to plead in court, so long as his master's affairs were involved and the peculum was not revoked. Despite such useful sham freedoms, the slave remained a person who could be sold at any time. If the master, who had the right to punish a slave at will, decided that he deserved the ultimate punishment, he would hire the municipal executioner to do the job, paying only the cost of the pitch and sulfur needed to burn the unfortunate victim. In the public courts slaves could be subjected to torture to force them to confess crimes of their masters; free men were exempt from the threat of torture.

The barrier between humans and subhumans was supposedly impregnable. It was indecent to point out that such and such a slave had been born free and sold himself into slavery, indecent even to speculate about the possibility that a

*The Unquestioned Nature of Slavery*

Scene from a Greek comedy (or a Latin comedy with Greek costumes). Four masked actors: an angry master, ready to beat his slave, is restrained by an old friend. At right, the slave seeks the protection of a third party. Meanwhile, a woman plays a double "flute" (actually, a double clarinet). (Naples, Archaeological Museum.)

free man might sell himself that way. It was legitimate to buy futures—for example, a harvest "whenever it is ripe"—but it was not legitimate to offer a price for a man, "whenever he is forced to sell himself into slavery." This taboo was similar to one that existed in the Ancien Régime in France, where a respectful silence was maintained about the numerous offspring of poor nobles who lived obscurely as commoners. Since no ambiguity between freedom and servitude could be tolerated, Roman law had a rule of presumption "in favor of liberty," which held that when in doubt, a judge should decide in favor of liberty. If, for example, there was doubt as to the interpretation of a will that seemed to emancipate a late testator's slaves, the judge should choose the more positive interpretation, in favor of emancipation. Another rule was that once a slave had been freed, the decision could not be revoked, for "freedom is the common property" of all orders of free men, as the Senate reaffirmed in A.D. 56. To cast doubt upon the manumission of a single slave would be to threaten the liberty of all free men.

The principle of deciding in favor of the more humane alternative was humanitarian in appearance only. Suppose we had a rule that if a jury is divided equally between acquittal and execution, the verdict should be innocent; it does not follow from this that the execution of persons proven guilty will give anyone pause. The principle is established in the interest of the innocent, not in the interest of the guilty. The paradox in the Roman case is clear: judges should opt for freedom, but only in case of doubt. No one was concerned about those slaves whose servile status was unambiguous. To hate judicial errors is not to challenge the sanctity of justice but to uphold it.

Slavery was an undeniable reality. Humanitarians did not attempt to free slaves, merely to behave as good masters. So assured were the Romans of their own superiority, that they looked upon slaves as overgrown children. A slave was usually called "little one" or "boy" (*pais, puer*), even if he was an old man. Slaves addressed each other in the same way. Like children, slaves fell under the jurisdiction of that domestic court over which their master sat in sovereign judgment. If their crimes brought them before the public courts, they could be subjected to corporal punishment, from which free men were exempt. Lacking social importance, slaves had neither wives nor children. Their lovemaking and childbearing were like the breeding of livestock: the master rejoiced when his herds increased. Their proper names differed from those of free men (just as we call our dogs Fido and Rover). Slave names were of Greek origin, at least in appearance. (Greeks did not use these names, which were merely Roman pastiches of Greek names, made up for the purpose.) Slaves being children, slave rebellions were like parricide. When Virgil consigned to the lowest circle of his Hell all "those who have taken part in impious wars and renounced the faith due their masters," he had in mind Spartacus and his followers.

Romans looked with contempt on slaves' private lives, which they regarded as puerile. Yet slaves did have a life of their own. They participated in religion, for example, and not just the religion of the household, which was after all their own. Away from home a slave might well serve as the priest of some sect or even of the Christian Church—which never for one moment considered abolishing slavery. It is plausible that slaves should have been particularly attracted to things religious, whether pagan or Christian, for few other areas of life were open to them. They also took a passionate interest in public spectacles—theater, Circus, and arena—for on holidays they were given leave to stop work, as were the courts, the schools—and the beasts that toiled in the fields and on the roads.

Romans smiled or smirked about such matters. The feelings of slaves were not those of adults. A Roman would have found it as humorous to imagine a slave passionately in love as a Frenchman would to imagine a peasant of Molière's racked by Racinian passions and jealousies. And what if masters had been obliged to concern themselves with the sentimental caprices of their servants? "They fall in love now, do they, the slaves from around here?" asks the shocked hero of one of Plautus' fey comedies. A slave was supposed to live for his work, and that was all. Horace amused his readers with stories of the private life of his slave Davus, who went with cheap whores in the back streets and stared wide-eyed at paintings immortalizing the great matches of the gladiators. Judges were less amused: religious fanaticism, excessive lust, and immoderate passion for spectacles and paintings ("posters" may be closer to the mark) were all defects that slave traders were required to make known to prospective buyers. "Defects" in the sense of defective merchandise? No: slaves were men, and their defects were moral wrongs and psychological flaws.

It was commonly agreed that the psychology of servants was different from that of their masters. A slave's psychology came down to this: was he fit or unfit for his work, and did he have feelings of loyalty toward his master? Historians and moralists approvingly recount instances of slaves who carried devotion to the point of performing humble acts of heroism, who died to save their masters or who followed them to their deaths. But there were far too many "bad slaves." The adjective says it all. A bad slave was not a slave with certain flaws, as we might say, an "overweight plumber" or a "lazy lawyer." He was rather a slave unfit for his purpose, a "bad tool," a slave who was not a slave.

Like the psychology of a child, the psychology of a slave was the result of the influences he had absorbed and the examples he had been set; his soul had no autonomy. It was often said that imitating bad slaves could make any slave a

Small bronze of a grotesque character of fantasy, 1st century (?). A short, fat man should not take such long strides, especially when dressed in an improvised garment held together with one hand and ever so slightly too short. (Paris, Petit Palais, Dutuit Collection.)

gambler, a drunkard, or an idler, and that the example of a wicked master could make a slave lustful or lazy. The law permitted recourse against any person who corrupted one's slave. It was an offense to knowingly offer asylum to a fugitive slave or to encourage a slave to flee. Victims were all too often primarily responsible for their slaves' misdeeds. A master who wants to be respected by his servants should not joke with them, says Plato, and he must be the first to rise each morning. Many masters were weak and were censured for their weakness by public opinion. A Roman grammarian offers a curious detail: "In light comic sketches comic poets are allowed to show slaves wiser than their masters, something that would not be permissible in more formal comedies." In a short sketch it was possible to envision a maliciously inverted world; realistic comedy had to show the noble truth.

---

How did slaves endure such misery and humiliation? Did they feel smoldering rage or cunningly harbor thoughts of rebellion that occasionally erupted in slave uprisings or slave wars? Or did they resign themselves to their fate? Between utter passivity and active rebellion lies a middle term, which no doubt comes closer to describing everyday life: accommodation. Like a Pullman traveler in an uncomfortable berth, slaves adjusted their frame of mind so as to minimize their suffering: unable to burn the master, they loved him. In the slaves' argot the master was *ipsimus* or *ipsissimus* (roughly, "most himself"). "I was a slave for forty years," a freedman tells Petronius, "yet no one could tell whether I was a slave or a free man. I did all I could to gratify my master, who was an honorable and worthy man. And in the house I was dealing with people who would have liked nothing better than to trip me up. But in the end I came out on top, praise be to my master! Now, that is real merit, because to be born free isn't very hard at all." Thus, some saw slavery as a kind of career in which to outperform other slaves.

With nothing else to guide them, slaves shared the values of their master, admired him, and served him jealously. Like voyeurs they watched him live his life with a mixture of admiration and scorn. They took up his cause, defended his person, and jealously guarded his honor. In case of riot or even civil war they were the master's right hand, his soldiers. Let the master assert over a slave or his slave's concubine his *jus primae noctis*; the slave bore the blow with the aid of a

*Evidence of Slavery*

proverb: "There is no shame in doing what the master orders."
When a master came to visit his farm, his steward's wife
naturally slept with him. Obedience was the slave's cardinal
virtue, and slaves reproached other slaves for their refusal to
bend to discipline. "Your stupid masters don't know how to
make you obey," said one former slave to a "bad" slave.

It is not hard to imagine how such love, if frustrated or
offended, could turn to bloody rage against a master deemed
unworthy of affection. The slave uprisings led by Spartacus
and his emulators had a different cause, however. The down-
trodden did not think of fighting for a less unjust society from
which slavery would have been banished. To escape their
wretched condition, they embarked upon an adventure comparable to that of the Mamelukes or the buccaneers, attempting to carve a kingdom of their own out of Roman lands. A
generation before Spartacus, at the time of the great rebellion
of slaves in Sicily, the rebels established a capital, Enna, made
one of their number king, and even began striking coinage. It
is hard to believe that in this kingdom of former slaves slavery
would have been prohibited. Why should it have been?

No man has ever been able to look beyond the changing
backdrop of the historical dramas in which he is caught up
and peer deep into the wings of history's theater, for there are
no wings. No slave, no master, was ever able to imagine a
world in which the institution of slavery did not exist. What
slaves wanted—or what most of them wanted (for it was better
to serve than to be free and die of hunger)—was to escape
from servitude individually, to be set free. Masters themselves
regarded the manumission of slaves as a handsome deed. "My
friends," declaims Trimalchio in his cups, "the slaves, too, are
men and have sucked the same milk as us, even if fate has
struck them down. They shall nevertheless taste the water of
freedom before too long (but let us not tempt fate by speaking
of this, for I wish to remain alive!). In short, I set them all
free in my will." In speaking and acting this way a master
honored himself. Far from undermining the legitimacy of
slavery, he was in fact drawing the logical consequences of the
paternal authority he enjoyed over his slaves. A master who
loved his slaves would set them free, since freedom was what
they wanted most. By setting them free, he did not show that
he believed slavery to be an injustice rather than an accident
of fate; he proved only that he wished to be a good master.

To free slaves was a merit but not a duty: everything
hinges on that distinction. A king acts within his rights when

he condemns a criminal to death, and commands respect when he grants him pardon. But the pardon is a free act, and the king is not in the wrong if he refuses to grant it. The pleasure masters took in freeing their slaves confirmed the authority that allowed them not to free their slaves. The master commanded with love, and love knows no law. The subordinate could not claim clemency as his due. The father had a double image: he punished and he pardoned. Because granting the pardon was not a duty, it could not be solicited by the slave himself, but only by a third party, born free, like the master. The intermediary honored himself by persuading the father to substitute clemency for severity. At the same time he honored the authority of masters in general over slaves in general.

A free man solicits a master to pardon one of his slaves: this is a typical episode of Roman life, which writers and even the *Digest* delighted in portraying because they sensed vaguely that its paradoxical flavor somehow contained the key to the authority of the slave system. Ovid counseled the clever lover to cast the woman he desired in the role of kindly aunt, while the lover himself played the severe father: "When you might easily on your own do something that you must do in any case, always use your mistress as an intermediary. Have you promised freedom to one of your servants? See to it that he begs your mistress to intervene with you on his behalf. Do you exempt a slave from his punishment? Let it be your mistress who persuades you to do what you were going to do anyway." Roman law did not regard as a fugitive a slave who fled in order to ask a friend of his master to beg indulgence of the latter. A master could be severe in individual cases without damaging the reputation for kindness of the master class as a whole. For clemency could be requested and decided only between peers. A slave who asked for clemency would have been regarded as impudent for having taken it upon himself to prejudge which of the two paternal masks the master would choose to wear.

If the master's indulgence was not the homage that slaveholding paid to humanitarianism but merely the merit of an individual, cruelties and even atrocities committed by some masters were demerits that attached to individuals only, not to the master class. Cruelty to slaves was not unusual. This is clear from the advice that Ovid gives in his manual of seduction: a woman who scratches her hairdresser or stabs her with

*The Two Aspects of the Master*

Hydraulic organ, 4th-century tombstone. Water pressure caused the pipes to vibrate. The sonority of the organ contrasted with the usual high pitch of ancient music. (Rome, Museum of Saint Paul's Outside the Walls.)

a needle does not make herself attractive. One day the emperor Hadrian, refined though he was, stabbed one of his slave secretaries in the eye with his pen. He later called this slave in and asked him what gift he would like as compensation for the loss of his eye. The victim stood silent. The emperor repeated his question, adding that the slave could have whatever he wished. The answer was: "I want nothing but my eye." Shortly before Christianity's final triumph, the council of Elvira condemned Christian mistresses who, "out of jealous rage beat their servingwomen so severely that they die, provided that said death occurs within four days."

A cruel or wrathful master brought moral condemnation upon himself and could do himself material harm. Once their rage had passed, many repented of cruel acts. Consider this incident from the second century A.D. The physician Galen had left Rome bound for his home in Pergamum (near the Turkish coast), accompanied by a man from Crete. This fellow was not without virtues: simple, friendly, and honest, he was not too demanding when it came to the daily expenses of travel. But he was susceptible to fits of rage, during which he went so far as to beat his slaves personally, kicking them and beating them about the head with whip or cudgel. Upon reaching the Isthmus of Corinth, the travelers dispatched their baggage to Athens by sea from the port of Cenchreae. They hired a coach to carry themselves and their slaves to Athens by the coastal route via Mégara. They had passed Eleusis when Galen's companion noticed that his slaves had loaded on the ship some baggage that should have been kept for the road. He fell into a rage and, finding nothing at hand with which to beat his men, took his sheathed traveling dagger from his belt and proceeded to beat his slaves about the head. But the knife cut through the scabbard, and two slaves received head wounds, one quite serious. Thereupon the master, overwhelmed by what he had done, went from one extreme to the other: handing a whip to Galen and removing his clothes, he begged Galen to beat him, "as punishment for what he had done under the influence of this accursed anger." Galen laughed in his face, gave him a philosophical sermon on anger (he was a philosopher-physician), and drew from the incident the following moral for his readers: A master should never punish his slaves with his own hands, and he should always postpone the decision to punish until the following day.

This anecdote sheds light on one piece of conventional wisdom: the idea that slavery, under the influence of Stoicism, became progressively more humane during the three centuries of High Empire. This alleged humanization of slavery was in reality a moralization, resulting not from some "natural" tendency of civilized humanity but from a particular historical development, which we have already described in discussing the origins of the couple. This moralization of master as well as slave was in no sense humanitarian, nor did it cast doubt on the legitimacy of slavery, nor was it a ruse or ideological camouflage intended to preserve the institution from some sort of agitation by slaves. Once we refuse to allow our thinking to be confined by these rigid yet inept generalizations, it is easy to see that the moralization of slavery made it no less harsh than before. Nor was the moralization of slavery the consequence of imperial legislation. This legislation, alleged to have improved the slave's lot, comes down to a single edict, whose real significance was quite different. Under Antoninus, anyone who killed his own slave was subject to death or deportation unless he could prove to the satisfaction of a judge that he had good reason for what he did. What must be understood, however, is that for a master to kill his own slave was different from sentencing the slave to death before the domestic tribunal over which the master presided. Antoninus' edict merely revived the ancient distinction between legal murder and murder pure and simple. If an enraged master sentenced a slave to death with a minimum of formalities, no one could reproach him. But if, in his rage, he killed the slave with his dagger, he would have to trouble himself to explain to the judge that his rage had been legitimate (so legitimate that, had he been given the time to set himself up as domestic judge, he would surely have sentenced to death the slave he had just stabbed). As long as the formalities were respected, anyone could punish his slaves as he pleased without difficulty: Antoninus confirmed this. Similarly, Hadrian condemned a father who had killed his son during a hunt, claiming that the murder had been committed in the name of paternal authority.

---

Other measures aimed to moralize, if not improve, the condition of the slave. Imperial legislation became more and more prudish as time went by, and what we shall now consider is a minor chapter in the history of sexual morality. The new laws that afforded the slave moral protection could be enforced only by the master, through exercise of his paternal power. Slaves were commonly sold under restrictive conditions (for

*Morality*

example, a seller might stipulate that a bad slave be kept in chains). When females were sold, it was sometimes specified that they could not be used as prostitutes by their new owners. If an owner went ahead and made a prostitute of a woman sold under such a condition, the emperor declared that the slave must be set free and that the buyer should lose his property. A less well-known aspect of the moral order was the new custom of allowing slaves to marry (mentioned by Tertullian around A.D. 200). It had previously been unthinkable that these childlike creatures should have families. Later, however, when marriage came to be looked upon less as a sign of a power than as a token of morality, it was opened to slaves. More married slaves are mentioned in the *Digest* than one might think. Michel Foucault found the earliest reference to a married slave in Musonius. Remember, marriage was nothing more than a private decision marked by a private ceremony, so slave marriage was more a matter of evolving custom than of revolution in the law.

Moral evolution. Free men in republican Rome had been hard on themselves as well as on their slaves, because their sense of duty was based on civic status, without the illusory but comforting involvement of moral conscience. There were as many codes of ethics as there were statuses, and the morals of a slave were different from those of a citizen. "Tolerance of adultery," said one orator, "is infamous on the part of a free man. On the part of a freedman with regard to his master, it is the effect of a proper sense of gratitude. On the part of a slave, it is duty pure and simple." But now morality seemed to derive from the conscience of mankind in general. The slave remained a slave, but ethics became universalist.

Slave owners have, at different times, conceived of slavery in different ways, without making the institution any less tyrannical. In the southern United States masters had their blacks baptized because they believed that all God's creatures have souls. They were no less authoritarian as a result. In the Roman Empire the prevailing morality gradually shifted from a concept of "political man" to a concept of "inner man." Stoicism and Christianity would shape in their different ways this new conception of man, which also affected ideas about slaves. No longer was the slave always a human being whose inner life was limited simply to understanding his duty to submit to his masters. He became a human being with a moral conscience, who obeyed his master not so much out of loyalty to his private duties as out of a sense of moral duty in general.

To the slave were imputed duties to his wife, for he was now allowed to marry, and duties to his children, for he was now allowed to raise children, who became his morally even if they remained indisputably the property of his master. Legal and literary documents provide evidence of a growing tendency not to separate families of slaves, not to sell the husband without his wife and child. And Latin and Greek epitaphs show evidence of a growing tendency to bury slaves according to the proper formalities rather than simply disposing of their corpses or leaving it to other slaves to bury their own.

The institution of slavery thus changed from within, because everything around it was changing. We would be taking too sanguine a view if we ascribed these changes to humanitarian scruples, and it would be pedantic to try to explain them as safety valves. They are signs of an autonomous change in the prevailing moral climate. What is most striking of all is the inability of Roman society to question or even alleviate the harshness of the institution for a single moment. It was all well and good to remind the paterfamilias of his duties as a judge to respect the formalities and to allow slaves to marry, but the formalities altered none of slavery's cruel punishments, malnutrition, physical and moral misery, or tyranny.

This was all that the moralists, including the Stoics, were able to accomplish. What some scholars say about Seneca's attitude toward slavery is no more than projection of our own brand of moralism. For Seneca, slavery was not a product of "society" but an individual misfortune, a misfortune that might befall any one of us, for we are all men, subject to the same tricks of fate as these unfortunates. In wartime even the noblest of men could be reduced to slavery. It is Fortune that determines each man's fate. What, then, is the good man's duty? To do whatever he has to do wherever fate has placed him, be he king, citizen, or slave. If he is a master, he must be a good master. The Romans had more respect for good masters and good husbands than for bad ones. Philosophy took this merit of some individuals and imposed it as a duty on all who would be wise. Thus, Seneca taught his disciple to comport himself as a good master toward those "humble friends," his servants. Had he deigned to give lessons to the slaves themselves, he would have taught them to comport themselves as good slaves—as Saint Paul and Epictetus actually did.

# &#8258; The Household and Its Freed Slaves

A ROMAN household consisted of a number of domestic slaves or former slaves, a paterfamilias, his legitimate wife, and two or three sons and daughters, along with a few dozen free men known as "clients," who waited each morning in the antechamber of their protector or "patron" to pay him brief homage. A household was not a "natural" family. The affections it induced are as dated as our own nostalgic family emotions—though certainly more picturesque.

Nor was the Roman household a clan, an extended patriarchal family—the *gens* or some weakened or disintegrated form of that vast, archaic entity (despite the legend to the contrary, which Yan Thomas has attempted to debunk). It is not true that the father gradually ceased to reign over the family as a monarch. In fact he never did reign. Archaic Roman society did not consist of a number of clans, each ruled by an ancestral monarch. Archaic Rome was an Etruscan city, one of the largest. It does not hark back to some prehistoric stage of human development. Let us therefore set aside these political myths of origin and consider the facts: the father was a husband, a propertyowner, a slavemaster, and a patron to freedmen and clients. Over his sons and daughters he exercised judicial authority delegated to him, in a manner of speaking, by the city. This amalgam of heterogeneous powers did not derive from any primitive unity.

Once orphaned and emancipated, every son became the head of a family in his own right and felt no attachment to his brothers and uncles but that dictated by private feelings or family strategy. Whether or not a group of brothers would live together in the family mansion was simply a question of convenience and money. The family was a conjugal unit; every

An elegant dressing room. Was it permissible to paint a lady smaller than the slave who does her hair? Yes, provided the lady was very young. This woman (a child becomes a woman at the magic age of fifteen) is being dressed for her wedding. (Naples, Archaeological Museum.)

family head preferred to have a home of his own, and every son wished for the same thing. The sons of Cicero and of his friend Celius rented an apartment so they would no longer have to live at home with their fathers. If they damaged their neighbors' property, the law held that they themselves should be held responsible and that their fathers should bear none of the blame. These children led their own lives. The father was master primarily of the patrimony and the patrimonial rights. His children were bound to him by money and hopes of inheritance. But he did not insist that they remain at his side, and newlywed couples, if they had the means, preferred to live in homes of their own.

## The Mistress of the House

The paterfamilias was, in principle, head of the household. It was he who, every morning, gave the slaves their orders and assigned their duties, he who went over the accounts with the steward. And the mistress of the house? This was a point of friction: some husbands, but not all, put their wives in charge (*cura*) of the household and, if they deemed her worthy, gave her the keys to the strongbox. Cicero's sister-in-law made a scene one day when she was treated as a stranger in his house, because a servant had been put in charge of preparing lunch. Division of power over the household gave rise to frequent quarrels, if we are to believe the Church Fathers, enemies of marriage that they were. To marry was to submit to a woman's authority, they said, or at least to oblige oneself to suffer her recriminations. Physicians, for their part, recommended that wives be given charge of the house, because it was healthy for women to have some activity: "to supervise the slave baker, oversee the steward's purchases of supplies, and tour the house to make sure that everything is in order." These duties were not insignificant, for normally a wealthy woman had nothing to do but occupy herself with distaff and spindle, killing time in a traditional and honorable way.

Remember that these people had slaves constantly at their beck and call and were never alone. They were not allowed to dress themselves or put on their own shoes (although they could brush their teeth rather than have them brushed by a slave). On funerary steles in the museums of Piraeus and Larissa we see maids kneeling to remove their mistresses' shoes. The gospel phrase "I am not worthy to undo his sandals" means precisely that "I am not even worthy to serve him as a slave."

Woman's toilet kit, found at Cumae. (Naples, Archaeological Museum.)

The vast Roman houses we can visit at Pompeii, Vaison, and a hundred other places did not allow their owners to enjoy the pleasures of wide, open space; they were more densely occupied than today's low-rent apartment houses. Were husband and wife alone in the bedroom at least? Not always. A lover taken by surprise in one lady's bedroom claimed that he was there not for the lady of the house but for the servant girl who slept in the same room. The lady slept alone, but she had a slave, or several slaves, close to her bed. More commonly, slaves slept at the door to the master's bedchamber, over which they stood guard. "When Andromache mounted Hector," one satirist tells us, "their slaves stood with their ears glued to the door, masturbating." Slaves apparently slept all over the house. When the master or mistress wished to spend an evening alone, they had the slaves move their cots to some remote corner of the house.

The omnipresence of slaves was tantamount to constant surveillance. True, slaves did not count, and their presence could easily be overlooked. The poet Horace says: "I am accustomed to walking alone." Five lines later we learn that one of his three slaves is with him. Lovers never knew where to meet in secret—his place or hers? Their servants would know everything, and they gossiped. The only solution was to borrow the house of an indulgent friend (who risked being charged as an accomplice in adultery) or to rent the chamber of a sacristan, whose sacred office compelled him to maintain a loyal silence. Decency and concern for station required that ladies of rank never go out without maids, companions (*comites*), and a mounted servant known as a *custos*, often mentioned by erotic poets. This mobile prison, which followed a woman everywhere, was the Roman equivalent of the gynecaeum, or monogamous harem, in which a Greek woman concerned for her reputation insisted that her husband lock her up during the night. Even boys never went out without a *custos*, for there was as much concern for their virtue as for that of the fair sex. In any case, old-fashioned women proved their modesty by going out as little as possible and never showing themselves in public without a partial veil.

To be the mother of a family was an honorable prison, a rather constricted dignity to which a proud noblewoman could devote herself. But the daughters of the nobility inherited the pride of their fathers, who lent them as it were to their husbands. (An unhappy Roman wife who left her husband did not "go home to mother"; she went home to father.) Aristocratic pride was bolstered by wealth; wives often had fortunes

Statue of deceased woman, 1st–3rd century. The posture mimics that of draped statues in the Hellenizing manner; the artist's intentions are evident in the drapery of the left shoulder. This may be an early example of the ornamental, graphical style that supplanted the plastic naturalism of antiquity. We see here the decadence of the classical style. (Aquileia, Archaeological Museum.)

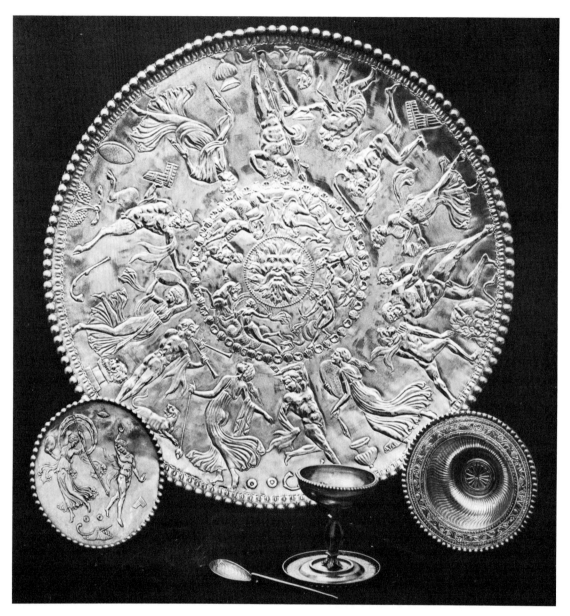

Silver from the 4th-century
crypt of Mildenhall, found not
far from a small villa. (London,
British Museum.)

of their own, which did not become the property of their husbands. Women were the equals of men insofar as the laws of inheritance were concerned, and they had the same right to make a will. Brides also had their dowries. Some women, nobler and wealthier than their husbands, refused to submit to their authority. Some played important political roles because, along with their patrimony, they inherited their lineage's hereditary clienteles. Others, not content merely to devote themselves to their husbands, showed the quality of their blood by following them into exile or even suicide. (Seneca, jealous of his wife's influence over his entourage, attempted to extort from her and from his disciple Lucilius promises of suicide.) Women were more than capable of defending their marital interests when their husbands were exiled or forced into hiding. They were also capable of an act that earned them far less praise and that is symptomatic of the impasse in which women found themselves: using a misfortune such as the loss of a son as a pretext, they deliberately renounced the world and cloistered themselves in perpetual mourning.

---

*Widows, Virgins, and Concubines*

What if our wealthy heiress was a widow, or, rather, a *vidua*, a woman without a man, widow or divorcée? Or a virgin, yet the "mother of a family" because her father was dead? Relatives would hasten to fortify her virtue by providing her with a custos. An imperial edict compared the loves of a vidua to adultery and rape, but it was never enforced. Imagine a woman or girl, mistress of her own house and her own patrimony: the wealthy widow was a period figure. She was not flirtatious but "imperious," because she no longer had any master over her. She was surrounded by suitors, who lusted after her inheritance. She might remarry or take a lover. Such liaisons, sometimes made respectable by promises of marriage, were often known and almost openly admitted. The affairs of young girls, by contrast, had to remain secret. They were always suspected of having lovers, and people liked to think that the guilty party was the girl's slave steward. For how could a woman possibly manage her life without a lord and master? The Church Fathers were horribly malicious about the morals of widows and orphans, though they uttered no slander. Had the state of affairs they described not been true, where would Ovid have found the bevy of wealthy and independent women to whom he taught the art of sin with his

Funerary stele, 1st century. A woman, half-faces the spectator; a freedwoman looks at her. (Arles, Lapidary Museum.)

*Lover's Handbook (Ars amatoria)*? These women enjoyed the best fate Rome had to offer the female sex. Their lovers had to take pains to please them in bed, to the dismay of Seneca and Martial.

What about the opposite situation—the widower father? He might sleep with his servants or remarry, or he might take a concubine. The word concubine had two different meanings: pejorative at first, "concubine" eventually acquired an honorable interpretation. Originally the word was applied to the woman or women with whom a man, married or not, habitually slept. Emperors, even when married, kept a harem of slave concubines in the palace, and Claudius was known to sleep with more than one at a time. But public opinion eventually came to tolerate relations with a concubine, so long as they were durable and exclusive, like marriage; and only the social inferiority of the woman prevented the man from converting the liaison into a legitimate marriage. The jurists followed suit. For them, concubinage was a de facto situation, but an honorable one, which did not degrade a woman to the level of those whom decent men were obliged to hold in contempt. It was necessary, however, that concubinage should resemble marriage in every respect. In the second—and only honorable—meaning of the word, a concubine had to be a free woman (slaves were not allowed to marry), and the union had to be monogamous. It was unthinkable for a married man to have a concubine or for any man to have two concubines at once. In short, concubinage was a substitute where marriage was impossible. The typical case was that of a man who had sexual relations with a freed female slave but who was reluctant to marry a woman of such inferior station. The emperor Vespasian, a widower, took as his concubine his secretary, a freed imperial slave, and "treated her almost like his wife." Some fifteen cases are known in which a man had an epitaph written for himself, his late wife, and the concubine who replaced her. Other epitaphs honor the memory of a man's two successive wives.

Unlike lawful marriage, concubinage had no legal consequences. The jurists, notwithstanding their indulgence toward concubinage as an institution, were uncompromising on this point. Children born of an honorable concubinage were free, since they were the children of a free mother; but since the woman was not married, they were bastards and bore their mother's name. They could inherit from their mother, but not from their natural father. Hence concubinage had nothing but its honorable status: it conferred upon the woman a dignity that would not have been possible had her relations with the man not been stable and monogamous. Finally, what about the case in which a patron overcame his initial hesitation and decided to marry his freed slave and concubine? The woman would have been proud to have been deemed worthy of donning the traditional robes of the true "mother"; however, aware of her definitive inferiority, she would always refer to her husband, in their epitaph, as "patron and husband," as if the first quality were indelible and even conjugal affection could never erase the taint of slavery. These, then, were the families of the left hand, composed of a man, his concubine, and his natural children. There were also more irregular combinations, with which jurists did not concern themselves: a man, his servingwomen, and his "pets." Before saying more on this subject, we must penetrate the secret recesses of the slave system and remind ourselves that the Roman Empire, like colonial Brazil, was an empire of miscegenation.

Bronze keys. Some keys turned in the lock, causing a bolt to advance or recede; others withdrew a pivoting bolt. (Paris, Louvre.)

*Unrecognized Bastards*

After Vespasian lost his cultivated concubine, he whiled away his hours in the company of one of his many servants. Anyone who owned slaves might have done the same: opportunity creates temptation. There was a word for husbands who gave in to that temptation: *ancillariolus*, maid-chaser. Their wives despaired of them. One cruel master drove his slaves so far that they murdered him, castrating him as well; they must have had their reasons. When the bloody news reached the house, "his concubines hurried in, screaming and sobbing." Slavery had its lyrical side. Horace delicately, even poetically, described the emotions of a master following the movements of a young female slave with his eyes. She is not far from the age when she might know a man, and the master savors the moment in advance. In short, the master might have good reason to believe that some of the infants born to his servants, who became his property, were his own children. Neither he nor anyone else was supposed to say so, however. It was essential that free status be above suspicion, unambiguously distinct from the condition of slavery; it was unthinkable that a master should scheme to recognize a slave as his own son. This was one of the tacit laws of the slave system. Yet everyone knew what the real story was: as one jurist put it, "It sometimes happens that a slave is the child of his master by a slave mother." Of course the master could always free

"The *fanciulla* (maiden) of Anzio"; found in one of Nero's villas at Anzio. This celebrated flat-chested "young woman" is, in my opinion, a young male. He carries various cult objects on a tray. This statue-portrait was probaby consecrated in a temple by the model (or by his parents, if he was a *pais amphithales*). This is either an original from the 4th or 3rd century B.C. or a Roman copy, as the somewhat sketchy indication of the folds in the drapery suggests. The lower portion was carved in different marble from that used for the head and bust, so it may be a Greek original whose lower part was restored in Roman times. Original or copy, this masterpiece is a landmark in the history of imperial art and taste. (Rome, Museum of the Baths.)

his child without saying why he chose to favor that particular slave, but he could not recognize or adopt the child, even after manumission: the law forbade it.

A curious custom permitted him to do more, however, while keeping up appearances. The Romans liked to have about the house a little boy or girl slave or foundling, whom they brought up (*alumnus, threptus*) because they were fond of the child (*deliciae, delicatus*) and found it cute. They kept the child with them at dinner, played with it, put up with its whims; sometimes they gave it a "liberal" education, in principle reserved for free men. This custom was useful because of its ambiguity: the pet child might be a plaything, but it might also be a sexual object. It might have been adopted in all innocence, or it might be the master's own child, enjoying his secret favor. I should also mention the corps of adolescent valets that, had they been well born, we might be tempted to call pages; but they, too, were slaves.

Keeping a boy for sexual purposes was a minor sin for gentlemen of quality, and their inferiors smiled respectfully. Brutus, Caesar's murderer, loved a boy so beautiful that reproductions of a sculpture of him could be seen everywhere. The lover of the terrible emperor Domitian and Antinous, Hadrian's celebrated lover, were praised by court poets (whose successors would praise Madame de Pompadour similarly). Jealous wives refused to allow their husbands to kiss a beloved boy in their presence. Did husbands go further still when out of sight? By convention no one in good society asked such questions. The pet usually served his master as a squire or cupbearer, pouring his drink as Ganymede, Jupiter's boy lover, had done for the god. The corps of "pages" (*paedagogium*) consisted of handsome boys who had no other responsibility but to serve at table, to grace the hall with their presence and add pomp to the ceremonial trappings. The first sign of a mustache resulted in a major change in the life of a page. The pretext of ambiguous sexuality having been eliminated, it would have been scandalous to treat the now adult male as a passive sex object. The pet lamented the loss of his position, but the master caused his long, girlish locks to be cut—to the great relief of the mistress of the house. Some stubborn masters kept their pets even after they had stopped growing (*exoletus*), but such behavior was considered reprehensible.

Masters sometimes had more innocent motives to delight in their pets. A boy might be a sort of plaything with which the master amused himself affectionately at table, as he might

Antinous, after 131. This Greek work from the Roman era bears the "signature" (or name, if it is a replica) of Antoninianos of Aphrodisias (Turkey), a celebrated artistic city. Hadrian's deceased lover is compared to the god Sylvanus, whose pruning knife he holds. This apotheosis may have been a poetic notion of the artist, implying no cult, or the work may have been commissioned by an individual or confraternity that championed the monarchy and worshiped Antinous as a "new Sylvanus." The first explanation is more in keeping with the pictorial nature of the work. (Rome, Museum of the Baths.)

do with a pet animal. In those days the most valued toys were living creatures—birds, dogs, and, for little girls, rabbits (cats were not yet domesticated in Rome). A master might even feel genuine affection for a slave child. Plutarch writes: "Sometimes people who are unalterably opposed to marriage and children are eaten away by regret and freely mourn the death of a servant's child or a concubine's infant." This was not always because a man believed the child to be his own. There were men with a vocation for fatherhood, who took under their wing children born to members of their households; the kisses lavished on these children were quite innocent. Though opposed at first, kissing on the lips as a sign of affection between men became fashionable; the adolescent Marcus Aurelius exchanged some very sentimental kisses with his mentor Fronto. The poet Statius has left some moving lines about the death of a child whom he loved so well that he freed him at birth: "No sooner was he born that he turned toward me, and his wailing enveloped me and penetrated to my heart. I taught him to use words, I comforted his hurts and sorrows when he was still crawling on the ground, and I bent down to take him in my arms and cover him with kisses. As long as he was alive, I desired no son." These are the poet's best verses. Was he the child's father? That is not certain: paternal sentiment could be lavished more easily on a child without social importance than on one's legitimate son, who, as the scion and secret enemy of the man who now possessed what would one day be his, had to be raised strictly. It is true that in other poems by Statius or by Martial, the pet boy or girl is certainly the father's unrecognized child. Such children were treated like free men: dressed like princes, covered with jewels, they never went out without an escort. All they lacked was the garb worn by free-born adolescents (*praetexta*). The poet is at pains to make this clear. These children are freed slaves and must remain so.

Epitaph of a young girl, 1st or 2nd century. This important historical document is one of the two earliest pieces of evidence for the domestication in Europe of the cat. (Bordeaux, Aquitaine Museum.)

The question remains: Whose freedman was the slave? Forgive this insistence on precision, but it will lead us into another circle of hell: unusual relations among freed slaves. Suppose a master had a child by a servant, whom he then freed. Too late. The infant, conceived in the womb of a slave mother, was born a slave of its own father. Suppose, further, that the father freed his newborn child; then the child would have its own natural father for its patron. But sometimes the

*The Tribulations of the Freed Slave*

Sign for shop of the fuller Verecundus, Abundance Street, Pompeii, shortly before 79. In the center four men in short pants wring out cloth around an oven. Three men kneeling at benches draw cloth. At right, the master shows off a clean piece of fabric. The inscription, which pertains to an election, should not have been affixed to this sign.

mother, a wealthy freedwoman, could afford to purchase the child from its master. Then her child became her slave or freedman or -woman. Nor was it unusual for a son, out of filial piety, to purchase his mother, who had remained a slave; she then became the slave or freedwoman of her son. Epitaphs and legal documents prove that such situations were not at all hypothetical but in fact quite common. From here anything was possible. A son who became the freedman of his mother might have his own father for a slave, or a man might be the freedman of his own brother. Family feeling may have counted for more than the provisions of law in such matters. Yet feelings, however powerful, had to contend with the authority that legally belonged to anyone who purchased his or her blood relative as a slave. Such purchases often involved heavy financial sacrifice. The laws of inheritance also played a part. The family life of former slaves must have been a veritable hell, filled with conflict, ambivalence, and resentment. A father might never forgive his son for his crushing generosity; a son might never forgive his father for behaving like a ingrate.

Freed slaves usually did not live in the home of their former master, although they continued to come there to pay him homage. Set up in business as artisans, shopkeepers, or merchants, they accounted for less than 5 percent of the total population; yet they formed a group that was highly visible socially and very important economically. Although not all shopkeepers were freed slaves, all freed slaves were shopkeepers and traders. Hence a certain image attached to the group, earning it the enmity of many. Freedmen were seen as avaricious exploiters, especially since many former slaves were wealthier, sometimes far wealthier, than the majority of the free population, which deemed itself dishonored by the prosperity of individuals not born to freedom. People found it hard to accept opulence in a freedman that they would have found legitimate and admirable in a noble. The status of freedmen was ambiguous, at once superior and inferior to that of most of their fellow citizens. Privately they suffered from this ambiguity and accordingly developed a culture of their own.

It seems that freedmen lived more often in concubinage than in marriage. This at least is the conclusion that emerges from comparison of the views of Plassard and Rawson. Clearly the reason for this was not the concubine's social inferiority. Many slaves during their years of servitude lived as couples, especially the luckier ones—stewards of large estates and imperial slaves, or state functionaries. A servingwoman who lived for a long period with a single man might be called a concubine. If the servingwoman and her companion were both freed, their union, which now became a union between a free man and a free woman, would have been considered honorable. The problem was that the couple, while

Funerary relief commemorating a well-known merchant. Rome, 1st century(?). Two customers are seated; five clerks are standing, including one woman, shown in profile (a slave). The architecture is remarkable, but it seems likely that the columns were of stucco rather than marble. Note the arrangement of round and flat roofing tiles ("Roman tiles"). The floor is not tiled. (Florence, Uffizi.)

Tomb of freedman and freedwoman with their son and his
pet pigeon. Note the faces and
the clumsy attempt to enliven
the composition by the tilt of
the man's neck. The man holds
a number of tablets rather than
a book; though not educated in
the liberal arts, he knows how
to read and write. The woman's hairstyle is typical of the
fourth decade of the first century or the second decade of
the second century. (Rome,
Museum of the Baths.)

still slaves, might have had children; legally speaking, those children would have been either bastards or slaves of their mother. Even if the two freed slaves married legitimately, the father was not permitted to acknowledge his natural son. Even if the freed couple redeemed their slave son from his master, they could not make him their son, only their freedman. In Ancona is the tomb of the freedman Titius Primus, who became so notable a figure in that city that he asked the stonecutter to represent him dressed in a toga, which had become a ceremonial costume. At his right hand he had the sculptor carve his "concubine" (this is the word used in the epitaph), a freewoman (no doubt a freed slave) by the name of Lucania Benigna, who holds in her arms a baby girl named Chloé. Since the child has only one name, she is a slave: she was born when her mother was still a mere servingwoman. The best her natural father could do was to take her for his pet (*delicium*), and in the epitaph she is given no other title. Nature and affection were powerless in the face of the law. On the right is another freedwoman (there is nothing surprising about this grouping: household tombs were commonplace). It is hard to think of any reason why this couple should have wished to "remarry" in a legitimate ceremony. Theirs was a second type of concubinage, which stemmed from indifference to marriage.

---

Everywhere we encounter signs of what tormented freed slaves: uncertainty as to their true place in society. The scale of social conditions did not coincide with the status hierarchy, and freed slaves fell in the gap between the two. They suffered from a lack of legitimacy. Their wealth enabled them to live luxuriously. In Rome many a costly tomb with sculpted portrait belonged not to a noble but to a freedman. With their dress, clients, slaves, and freedmen of their own, they imitated good society—but, as demi-citizens, without hope of entering it. With cruel lucidity their totally imitative existence is portrayed in Petronius' *Satyricon*. Their base origins were betrayed by their lack of cultivation; the children of slaves did not attend school. They were not parvenus, as some have said, but refugees who bore an indelible stain that kept them out of good society: the barriers between status groups were unbreachable. People of good society found the freedmen's imitation of good manners absurd; they saw only pretentiousness and vulgarity. Worse still, freedmen did not even constitute a social class

*Further Tribulations of the Freed Slave*

SEX·TITIVS·SEX·L·PRIMVS
VI·VIR
LVCANIAE·BENIGNAE
CONCVBINAE
TITIAE·CHRESTE
CHLOE·DELICIVM

Tomb of the freedman Titius
Primus. (Museum of Ancona.)

worthy of the name. They could not console themselves with class pride. There could be no "dynasties" of freedmen, for the status died out after a single generation. The son of a freedman was a full-fledged citizen. It would be a mistake to regard as a social class what was only a transitional group. What is more, the Roman upper class replenished its ranks largely by admitting the sons of wealthy freedmen and freed imperial slaves: many a senator was the grandson of a freed slave. All in all, the chance of rising socially was somewhat better for slaves than for men born free but poor, who had virtually no chance at all.

The possibility of upward mobility was available to freedmen because of wealth. This wealth they owed to their vocation for trade, and that vocation must in turn be understood as a result of the conditions under which they had been set free. As much as, or even more than, the relations of production, it is such minor details, the consequences of which are often unexpected, that explain social structure. Roman nobles preferred their freedmen to their impoverished fellow citizens because, as we shall see, freedmen remained loyal to their former masters, who knew them personally.

What factors moved masters to free slaves? At least three are worth mentioning. The impending death of a slave was one. Masters often felt compelled to give slaves the consolation of dying in freedom and being buried as freedmen. When a master died, he might free some or all of his slaves in his will, leaving them freedom as a legacy just as he distributed other bequests to all his loyal retainers. Since the will was a kind of manifesto, the master who freed his slaves upon his death proved that he was a good master by giving them what they most desired: freedom. Finally, manumission often involved a financial arrangement of some sort. A master might use his slave as an agent in a business venture in which he offered the slave a share of the profits; the two would agree beforehand on the price of the slave's freedom. Or the master might offer the slave his freedom as a reward, in return for which the latter would continue to act as the master's agent with the rank of freedman. Manumitted slaves were rarely turned out to face life without some resources. When a master freed worthy old servants at his death, he left them a small plot or a pension (*alimenta*), as, later, wealthy people used to do with their servants. A slave businessman's future was assured. Last but not least, I imagine that many freed slaves remained in the master's household and went right on doing what they always had done, but with greater dignity than before. Others were set up in business or a trade, the profits of which they would share with the master as the price of freedom. The number of conceivable arrangements is limitless. Usually slaves were freed only if they were capable of earning money. One type of slave was never freed, however: the slave who handled his master's finances, even if the master was the emperor himself and the slave the imperial treasurer. Freedom, to which imperial slaves looked forward as a promotion at a certain stage in their careers, was not accorded the treasurer. This would have precluded the possibility of torturing him, and it was thought useful to retain the threat of torture and private justice in case the slave should be tempted to dip into his master's funds.

Some freed slaves remained in the household of their former master, in his service; others were set up on their own elsewhere and became completely independent. In either case the freed slave maintained a symbolic tie with the household of his master, who now became his "patron." He was obliged to pay homage (*obsequium*) to his master, who set great store by this custom. This homage was due the master in gratitude for his good deed in freeing the slave. If a freed slave neglected this duty (which was difficult to enforce), he was stigmatized

Mosaic from Pompeii, of "three itinerant musicians wearing theatrical masks, with an urchin looking on." (Naples, Archaeological Museum.)

Mosaic from Carthage, 4th century. These buildings at the water's edge might seem to be figments of the artist's imagination. But when it comes to architectural landscapes, Roman reality was stranger than fiction. In the islet of Brioni (Istria), a bay was surrounded by an unbroken semicircle of buildings: a magnificent villa with hemicyclic portico, three temples, baths, docks, a covered promenade along the water, and so on. The entire bay was turned into a decorative scene. (Tunis, Bardo Museum.)

by all of society as an "ingrate." Ingratitude, said to be one of the major problems of the day, provoked the Romans to outrage. Freed slaves who left a family were supposed to surround it with an aureole of obsequiousness, thereby proving to the world how great the family was. The role of "clients" was identical.

Romans were torn between two concepts of society: one was civic, the other based on relations of loyalty between man and man. On the one hand, because freedom was supposed to be unquestionable, a master was not supposed to hinder that of a freed slave by hedging it about with obligations. On the other hand, the freedman owed a debt of gratitude to his master and was supposed to remain forever his loyal servant. If he did not, his patron had good grounds for punishing him by striking him from the list of legatees and banishing him from the household tomb—or, indeed, by beating him with a stick. In principle, no Roman was allowed to raise a hand against a free man. Yet it was "not to be tolerated that an individual who was only yesterday a slave should come to complain of his master, who has turned him out, beaten him a little, or inflicted some punishment on him." The club, after all, was a symbol! Still, the family and monetary interests of even a newly liberated slave were sacred. A patron could not require the freedman to do more work than had been agreed upon beforehand, and he could not subject manumission to restrictions so severe that the former slave would have been free in name only. In particular, he could not make the freedman promise to forgo marriage and children in order to secure the patron's own rights as master to the former slave's estate. He could not even (as a general rule, at any rate) forbid the slave to go into competition with him in his own line of work.

Materially free within the limits of the manumission agreement, the former slave remained symbolically under the authority of his patron, and the Romans, much given to vaguely paternalistic pronouncements, often repeated that a freedman had the duties of a son—duties of piety—toward his former master, whose family name had become his own. At one time freed slaves were required to appear twice a day at the home of their former master, to bid him good morning and good evening, but this duty fell into neglect. Piety required that freedmen pay their respects, however, and the *Cistellaria* shows how grim the scene was. The freedman was exasperated by the burden of a symbolic yoke that had outlived its real power to compel. The master knew that his power was gone and that his ex-slave, if he did not still fear him, hated him, so he played up his own importance all the more. These unduly prolonged relations were particularly burdensome when the slave had obtained his freedom by agreeing to perform certain specified work for his master after being set free (*operae libertorum*). It seems that freedmen, unlike clients, were not required to pay the patron a protocol visit (*salutatio*) every morning. But they were often invited to dinner, where they found the master on his couch surrounded by those same clients. Dinnertime brawls between the two groups of loyal but unequal retainers were common. Poor clients

*Clientage*

Silver found at Pompeii. (Naples, Archaeological Museum.)

resented having to compete with prosperous ex-slaves for the master's attention. The poets Juvenal and Martial, reduced to paying court to the great in order to live, hated wealthy ex-slaves as well as Greek clients, for these were their competitors.

With a "court composed of clients and toilsome, not ungrateful freedmen," as Fronto puts it, a household made a brilliant place for itself on the public stage—a necessary and sufficient condition to be deemed worthy of membership in the ruling class. "I had many clients," wrote one very wealthy former slave as proof of his success. What was a client? A free man who paid court to the paterfamilias and openly declared himself the client of his patron; he could be rich or poor, miserable or powerful—sometimes more powerful than the patron to whom he paid respects. There were at least four kinds of clients: those who wished to make a career in public life and counted on their patron for protection; men of affairs whose interests could be served by the patron's political influence, particularly when he stood to profit from their success; poor devils such as poets and philosophers, often Greek, many of whom had nothing to live on but what their patron gave them and who, not being commoners, would have found it dishonorable to work rather than live under the protection of a powerful man; and, finally, those clients who were powerful enough to move in the same circles as the patron himself and who might legitimately aspire to be remembered in the patron's will in gratitude for their homage. This last-named group would have included leading statesmen and imperial freedmen, all-powerful administrators. A wealthy old man without heirs would have had many clients of this kind.

Such was the mixed crowd that lined up in regulation order every morning in front of the patron's door at the hour when the cock crows and the Romans awoke. The clients numbered in the tens, sometimes even hundreds. Neighborhood notables were also besieged, but by smaller crowds. Far from Rome, in the cities of the Empire, the few powerful rural notables also had their clienteles. That a wealthy or influential man should have been surrounded by protégés and self-seeking friends is hardly surprising. But the Romans erected this unremarkable custom into an institution and a ritual. Unimportant people, Vitruvius wrote, are those who make visits but receive none. A man who was the client of another man proclaimed the fact loudly, boasting of his own importance and stressing the patron's influence. People re-

Small bronze pot, 8 inches in diameter, found at Doudeville. Probably used to carry to the bath or gymnasium the oil that the ancients used instead of soap. The scene depicts a goatherd leaning on his crook, with his goats. (Paris, Petit Palais, Dutuit Collection.)

ferred to themselves as "the client of So-and-so" or "a familiar of Such-and-such a household." Those who were not themselves commoners would pay for the erection of a statue of their patron in a public square or even in the patron's own home. The inscription on the base would list the patron's public duties and spell out the name of the client. When shrewd patrons protested that the word "friend" was more appropriate than "client," "friend" became a flattering synonym for client.

The morning salutation was a ritual; to fail to appear was to disavow one's bond of clientage. Clients lined up in ceremonial costume (*toga*), and each visitor received a symbolic gift (*sportula*), which enabled the poorest to eat that day; in fact this custom supplanted the earlier practice of simply distributing food. Clients were admitted into the antechamber according to an inflexible hierarchical order that duplicated the civic organization by ranks. At dinners, too, guests of different rank were served different dishes and wines of different quality, according to their respective dignities. Symbolism reinforced the sense of hierarchy. The paterfamilias did not simply receive individual greetings from certain of his friends; he admitted into his home a slice of Roman society, respecting public rank and inequalities. Over this group he exerted moral authority, and his knowledge of proper behavior always exceeded that of his clients: "A wealthy patron," writes Horace, "governs you as a good mother might do and requires of you more wisdom and virtue than he possesses himself."

---

*Moral Authority*

The economic power that the household exerted over its peasants, bound by sharecropping contracts, was coupled with a kind of moral authority. When the Christian Church was being persecuted, frightened Christian landowners who decided to sacrifice to the idols compelled their farmers and clients (*amici*) to emulate their apostasy. Other masters, with a stroke of a magic wand, converted all the residents of their estates by deciding one fine day that the rustic religion of their peasants should henceforth be supplanted by worship of the one true God; the pagan sanctuary was demolished and a church erected in its place. The aura of prestige that surrounded the household defined the limits of its authority. Three centuries earlier Catiline had involved his sharecroppers in his revolt against the Senate. And Cicero, on the eve of his exile, had the consolation of hearing his friends offer to place at his disposal "their bodies, their children, their friends, their clients, their freedmen, their slaves, and their property."

The household exerted both material and moral power over those who lived in and around it. In the public mind what qualified a family for membership in the governing class of its city, and indeed of the Empire as a whole, was its power over this small group of people. Even in Rome, Tacitus tells us, "the sound segment of the populace saw everything through the eyes of the great houses." Wealth and power (the two were one and the same) over a small circle qualified a man for political leadership. Obviously I do not mean to imply that the collective consciousness was somehow directly aware of the power that each household exerted over its circle of clients. Underlying this state of affairs was an implicit idea: that governing men is not a specialized activity but the exercise of a natural right, that the larger animals are entitled to rule over the smaller. Because social importance and political legitimation went together, the performance of public duties was not a specialized profession as it is, say, in the civil service today. Nobles and notables physically made up the membership of the Roman Senate and city councils. This was true even when the number of seats was so limited that not all could be accommodated.

On the subject of social and political power, a more general if less important point should also be made: any man who bore a great name was obliged to take part, to play an honorific role, in all activities of interest to his clients. This was one of the more harmless aspects of that multifaceted phenomenon, clientage. The Roman Empire, an indirect form of government, was a federation of autonomous cities. Every member of the nobility, whether senator or equestrian, sought to be named or to earn the title of patron of one of those cities or, if possible, of several. The title was in fact nothing more than an honorific. Some gift or service to the city by the patron was its cause or consequence. Patrons might donate money to the municipal treasury, build or repair an edifice of some kind, or defend the city in court in a dispute over boundaries. In exchange, the patron was allowed to display in his antechamber an official letter of honor sent him by the city. Deaths in his family became local events: duly informed of the death, the city would respond with a decree of consolation. If the patron visited the city, he was received officially and made a formal entry, in the manner of a king. The collecting of cities as clients was one of the careers open to those avid for symbolic tokens. Even the many associations (*collegia*) where common people met for the pleasure of one another's company had noble patrons. Because the main purpose of these "colleges" was putting on banquets, the patron had no real power other than deciding, perhaps, the menu of the feast paid for by his donation. Ambition for symbols was one of the leading passions in the Greco-Roman world. No celebrated person could go out without a train of admirers. Actors and charioteers had fans, as did even some physicians, who had become "stars" in their profession.

There were minor variations from region to region. Italy was the kingdom of clientage. In Greek areas, as everywhere else, the influence, economic power, and powerful contacts of the wealthy—natural allies of the Roman occupiers—were of great importance. Powerful men periodically tyrannized the cities whose patrons they were. But in these places the ceremonies and salutations associated with clientage were unknown. Freedmen did not play leading roles (in Athens they accounted for about half the demi-citizens whose epitaphs mention no deme), nor did they form entourages around former masters. The ruinous passion to accumulate symbols of patronage—recently dubbed "evergetism"—was particularly prevalent in Greece, however. The Italians picked up this vice from the Greeks.

Oil lamp, 6 inches long, in the shape of a foot, with a chain for hanging. (Paris, Petit Palais, Dutuit Collection.)

Statue portrait, early Christian era. A faceless noble (the head is a modern restoration) exhibits the busts of his ancestors; the busts capture likenesses but neglect small details. The dynastic purpose of Roman portraiture is here displayed with impressive naiveté. Roman portrait art was a byproduct of Hellenistic portrait art, and the Romans never matched the Greeks when it came to recreating reality. (Rome, Museum of the Conservators.)

# ✤ Where Public Life Was Private

WHAT did a Roman possess? What did he lose if sent into exile? His patrimony, his wife and children, his clients, and also his "honors." Cicero and Seneca tell us so. Honors were public offices that a man might hold, generally for a year's tenure, after which his having held the office served as a token of nobility. Roman nobles had a keen sense of the authority and majesty of their Empire, but nothing like our notion of public service. They made no clear distinction between public functions and private rank, or between public finances and personal wealth. The grandeur of Rome was the collective property of the governing class and the ruling group of senators. Similarly, the thousands of autonomous cities that formed the fabric of the Empire were controlled by local notables.

In these cities, as in Rome, legitimate power was in the hands of the governing elite, which stood out by its opulence. The elite had the exclusive right to judge whether or not a particular family was worthy of membership. Legal criteria such as election or wealth of some specified amount were fictions, necessary conditions perhaps, but not at all sufficient. If wealth had been the real criterion, thousands of landowners might have contended for every seat in the Senate. The real method of selection was cooptation. The Senate was a club, and club members decided whether or not a man had the social profile necessary for membership, whether or not he could add to the prestige of the group. Senators did not select new members directly, however; this chore was left to innumerable clientage networks. Public offices were treated as

*Cooptation*

Sacrifice, A.D. 2. The four priests wear ritual veils, as does the oboist. Telescoping time, two of the priests burn incense, while the other two appear to be pouring a libation. At the left is a lictor, because this sacrifice was part of a public cult. (Rome, Museum of the Conservators.)

Above right: Libation on a table of offerings, prior to immolation of an ox, 1st or 2nd century. At left, a man representing the crowd tweaks his ear, a gesture whose conventional meaning was: "Look meditative." (Milan, Archaeological Museum.)

though they were private dignities, access to which depended on private contacts.

Too many historians, forgetting that Rome was not a modern state, have mistaken these ancient principles for a perversion of modern ones. Some have protested that Rome was rife with corruption, bribery, and clientage; others have passed over these matters in silence, on the grounds that such "abuses" hold little more than anecdotal interest. To our modern way of thinking, a man ceases to be a true public servant if he lines his pockets with the spoils of office or if he places personal ambition above the common good. But the modern state is not the only effective form of rule: organized crime, for example, functions quite well under different rules. The Mafia that protects and exploits Italian immigrants in some American cities and immigrant workers in France performs a "public" function. It administers justice in an immigrant population and, relying on ethnic solidarity, protects it from a hostile society. It must serve its community well or risk losing credibility; by serving the interests of its clients, it rules paternally, and it is particularly assiduous in this because otherwise it could never extort money from the immigrants it is supposed to protect. Whoever protects controls, and whoever controls pillages. Like an old Roman, even the most insignificant Mafia *capo* will make edifying speeches about his devotion to the common cause and try to establish personal and confidential relations with each of his protégés. A Roman noble (or even a mere notable) has more in common with this "godfather" than with a modern technocrat. Getting rich through public service has never stood in the way of taking public service for one's ideal. If it had, it would be surprising.

The honest functionary is a peculiarity of modern Western nations. In Rome every superior stole from his subordinates. The same was true in the Turkish and Chinese empires, where baksheesh was the general rule. Yet all these empires proved capable of governing effectively for many centuries. Similarly, the Roman army was quite a capable fighting machine in spite of some rather curious customs. "Soldiers traditionally bribed their officers for exemption from service, and nearly a quarter of the personnel of every regiment could be found idling about the countryside or even lounging around the barracks, provided their officer had received his kickback . . . Soldiers got the money they needed from theft and banditry or by doing the chores of slaves. If a soldier happened to be a little richer than the rest, his officer beat him and heaped duties upon him until he paid up and received dispensation." It is hard to believe that these are the words of Tacitus. Every public function was a racket; those in charge "put the squeeze" on their subordi-

Arch of Lepcis (Libya), A.D. 203. According to Epictetus, people are always cursing either the gods or the emperor, on whom they blame all their woes. But the emperor was also the champion of Romanness: on a chariot, Severus and his two heirs apparent enter a city as conquerors. At the right, a child is carried away with enthusiasm. Figures are shown frontally in this naive work. The youth who holds the horses' bridles and who wears a portrait of the prince around his neck is probably a slave page (*paedagogium*).

nates, and all together exploited the populace. This was true during the period of Rome's greatness as well as during the period of its decline.

Even the least important public positions (*militia*), such as apparitor or clerk of the courts, were sold by their incumbents to aspiring candidates, because every position carried with it a guaranteed income in the form of bribes. A new officeholder was supposed to pay a substantial gratuity (*sportula*) to his superior. In the Late Empire even the highest dignitaries, appointed by the emperor, paid such a gratuity to the imperial treasury. From the very beginning of the Empire, every dignity bestowed by the emperor, from consul to mere captain, imposed upon the person honored the moral duty to make a bequest to his benefactor, the emperor. Failure to fulfill this duty meant running the risk of having one's will set aside for ingratitude and one's estate confiscated by the imperial treasury. And, since every nomination was made on the recommendation of "patrons" with court connections, these recommendations (*suffragia*) were sold or, in any case, paid for.

The heart of Rome. The open space shown in the middle of this photo originally was tiled (the agora at Athens was not). This was the center of Rome, the forum, from 600 B.C. to A.D. 700—or what was left of the forum after the construction of various monuments. In the foreground are three columns from the temple of the Greek demigods Castor and Pollux, founded in 494 B.C. In the background, on the left, is the arch of Severus (after 203) and, on the right, with a modern roof, the Senate, between which stood the republican electoral enclosure, destroyed during the Empire. To the top left of the photo, imagine the Capitoline Hill, the acropolis of Rome, on which stood the temple of Jupiter (founded in 509 B.C.), god of Rome. Agora and acropolis constituted the city.

If the patron did not keep his word, the victim did not hesitate to complain to the courts. Courtiers (*proxenetae*) specialized in buying and selling recommendations and clientage (*amicitiae*), though their profession was denounced as disreputable.

---

*The Empire of Baksheesh*

Public officials paid themselves. The troops that patrolled the countryside and were responsible for rural administration forced the towns and villages under their jurisdiction to vote them gratuities (*stephanos*). Every official had his palm greased before taking the slightest action. But, because it was important not to skin the animals one fleeced, an official schedule of bribes was eventually established and posted in every office. Suppliants were careful to bring gifts whenever they visited a functionary or high dignitary. The gift was a tangible symbol of the superiority of rulers over ruled.

In addition to bribery, high mandarins practiced extortion. After the Roman conquest of Great Britain, the military administration forced the conquered tribes to take the grain they paid as tax to remote public storehouses and then took bribes for granting permission to use storehouses located closer to home. Demanding payment of illegal taxes was big business among provincial governors, who bought the silence of imperial inspectors and split the profits with their department heads. The central government allowed these abuses to continue, content to receive its due. To pillage the provinces of which one was governor, Cicero said, was the "senatorial way to get rich." A good example was Verres, who ran his province, Sicily, with an iron fist and conducted a bloody reign of terror.

The notion that the government of a province was like a private economic enterprise persisted, albeit on a less spectacular scale, as long as the Empire. It was no secret. Erotic poets waited impatiently for the husbands of their beloved paramours to leave town for a year to make their fortunes in the provinces. The poets professed to live for love alone and to care nothing for career or wealth (the two being interchangeable). Officials enriched themselves in part at public expense. One governor was paid colossal sums for costs incurred in the course of his mission; he never rendered an accounting. Under the Republic, these costs accounted for the bulk of the state budget. Apart from extortion, moreover, the governor engaged in business. In the first century B.C. Italian traders took over the economy of the Greek Orient with the help of gov-

A high-ranking officer wearing a "muscled breastplate" (which reproduced the pectoral muscles in its relief) and a smaller centurion with a "swagger stick." (Museum of Syracuse.)

Rome, Trajan Column, ca.
A.D. 110, detail: civilization
conquers Romania. Trajan
(lower left) oversees the construction of a fortified bridge-
head. We see ramparts,
haystacks for the horses, and
crenellated walls of sun-dried
brick (instead of the indigenous
wooden construction). The column tells the story of an an-
nexation, and its 200 yards of
comic strip depict much building of this type, in contrast to
the battles and massacres of the
barbarians shown on the
Column of Marcus Aurelius.
Without composition or style,
this art was intended to be a
pastiche of the painted signs
used to explain military conquests to the populace.

ernors sent to the region, who profited from their complicity.
Roman governors backed Roman merchants because of corruption, not "economic imperialism."

Until the past century it was not considered improper to
enrich oneself through government service. In Stendhal's
*Charterhouse of Parma,* when Count Mosca resigns his ministry
he is able to give the grand duke incontrovertible proof of his
honesty: when he took office he had only 130,000 francs; on
leaving it he has only 500,000. Cicero, after a year as governor
of a province, was making the equivalent of a million dollars
a year and prided himself on his scrupulousness: the sum was
considered quite small. Ancient bureaucracy was nothing like
our bureaucracy. For millennia sovereigns relied on racketeers
to extort taxes and control their subjects.

The cardinal virtue of the official was tact, not honesty—
rather like the merchant who must not let his clients think
that he is in business for his own sake rather than theirs. Even
as governors served themselves in serving the emperor, oppressed people wanted to believe that their paternal masters
oppressed them for their own good. "Be obedient and the
governor will love thee," Saint Paul wrote. A good governor
knew how to fill his coffers without undermining such beliefs.
Just because officials get rich by governing does not prove
that government itself is not disinterested. Now and then an

example was made of some unfortunate governor, subjected to public trial and then executed or, if lucky, disgraced. One particularly clumsy governor displayed his cynicism in a letter to his mistress that unfortunately fell into the wrong hands: "Joy! Joy! I am coming to you free of debt after selling out half the people in my charge." (This is one of three or four extant examples of ancient love letters.) The emperor and his high officials proved their disinterest by disowning their subordinates. The emperor openly criticized the tax collector, who was merely the governor of the imperial estates. Occasionally he granted the request of peasants who came to him complaining of exactions made by his agents. And periodically he would issue an edict outlawing corruption: "An end must be put to the rapacity of all officials. I repeat: an end." Top officials established a regular schedule of bribes, an act tantamount to legalizing bribery.

Functionaries, soldiers, and governors did not think of themselves as members of a corps whose reputation had to be preserved but as an elite group with no specialized role—simply superior in every way. Within this elite, gradations of rank were created by the level of office that an individual held, whether in the state apparatus or, in the case of local notables, in the municipalities. Officials told themselves that by serving their emperor or their city for a year, they enhanced their own "dignity" as well as the dignity of their house; henceforth they could appear in the ancestral portrait gallery in official garb. "Dignity" was a great word. It connoted not a virtue, like respectability, but an aristocratic ideal of glory. To the great of the world, dignity was as much a matter of importance as honor to El Cid. Dignity was acquired and increased; it could also be lost. Cicero, exiled, fell into despair; his dignity was gone, he was reduced to nothing. Because public dignity was private property, it was acknowledged that holding public office was a matter of pride and that a man might defend his possession of office as legitimately as a king might defend his crown. If he acted on such grounds, he was absolved of guilt. No one could hold it against Caesar that he crossed the Rubicon, marched on his fatherland, and plunged it into civil war. The Senate had taken away some of his dignity, when Caesar had made it clear that dignity mattered to him more than anything else, including his life.

Certain outward signs indicated membership in the ruling

*Dignity*

Fragment of scene of sacrifice, 1st or 2nd century. It shows man with an axe, who will immolate the ox, and two lictors (rather than five or more), whose knouts have no blades for decapitation of the condemned. These were indications of rank that everyone could read: these two lictors serve a municipal magistrate, not a representative of the remote and awesome state apparatus. (Museum of Portogruaro.)

class. Manners, however, were not the most important sign in Roman society, which set little store by salons and the like. Not aesthetes to the same degree as the Greeks, Romans were suspicious of elegance and attached no social significance to it. Gravity of gesture and language was a better indicator of the man of authority. Every notable was supposed to have a good education (*pepaideumenos*), capped by literary culture and knowledge of mythology. In choosing senators and even department heads preference was given to men known for their culture, on the pretext that they would be able to draft official papers in fine prose. Schools of rhetoric became the training ground of future administrators because culture enhanced the image of the governing class in its own eyes. The first naturalized Greeks to become members of the Senate were aristocrats renowned for their culture. What effect this had on the lower orders is doubtful, but it certainly proved disastrous for the conduct of government affairs. By the first century, imperial edicts were couched in language so euphuistic and archaic as to be almost incomprehensible and all but unenforceable, for cultivated writers eschewed technical terms, even in decrees pertaining to matters of finance.

Broadly speaking, the governing class sought to recruit not capable rulers but individuals who would reflect the private qualities that it held in esteem: opulence, education, natural authority. It preferred to judge these qualities with its own eyes because they could not be pinned down in regulations. That is why cooptation tacitly continued to govern entry into the ruling class and promotions in rank. The choice of the elect was not made by the class as a whole. Each of its members had his own stable of protégés whom he would recommend to his colleagues, who in turn recommended their protégés. Even the emperor depended on these recommendations for nominations to the highest positions. This system guaranteed that every important personage could enjoy the pleasure of reigning over an army of aspirants—his clientele, if you will, but be careful of this vague and misleading term. There are two kinds of clientele: in one the client needs a patron; in the other the patron courts clients for the sake of his glory. In the former, the patron exercises real power. In the latter, patrons compete for clients; the clients are the real masters, for the patron needs them.

*The Two Forms of Clientage*

Alas, not every clientele system was of this sort! "In Istria," Tacitus wrote, "the house of Crassus always had clients, lands, and a name forever renowned." In rural areas there prevailed a form of patronage comparable to the South American caciquism. Large landowners tyrannized and protected the peasants who occupied the land surrounding their estates. Whole villages delivered themselves into the hands of one of these protectors in order to be safe from the others. At other times patronage was more a wager on the future than a consequence of the status quo. During a civil war, Tacitus reports, the city of Fréjus supported the winning party, which was led by a local boy who had grown up to become an important personage; it did so out of "zeal for one of its own and in the hope that he would one day be a powerful man."

Actually "clientage" and "patronage" were terms that the Romans used indiscriminately to describe a wide range of relations. A protected nation was called the "client" of a more powerful state. An accused person was defended in court by his patron—or perhaps he recognized as his patron the person who was willing to defend him. Nothing is more misleading than studies of vocabulary. Sometimes a man offered protection because he already enjoyed power; at other times a man was chosen as patron to provide protection. The latter case

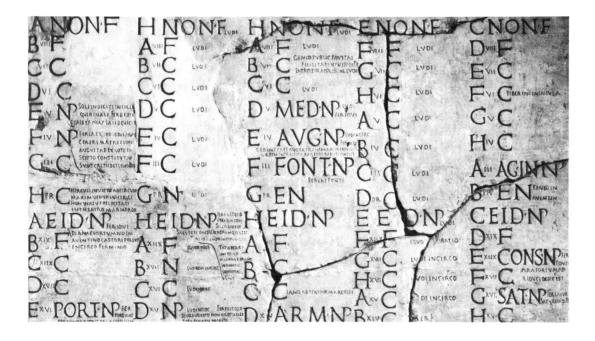

The pace of life: detail of a calendar ca. A.D. 25. Weeks did not exist; days of rest were religious feast days (a day of work was sacrificed to the gods), distributed throughout the year. On feast days magistrates, free men, students, slaves, and animals all ceased work. The word LVDI that appears in various places means "games" (such as chariot races) or theatrical spectacles. Gladiatorial combats were not religious and do not appear on the calendar. (Museum of the Aquila.)

was associated with the patronage of careers. An ambitious young man seeking promotion had little in common with the poor folk subject to a powerful neighbor and obliged to honor him, serve him, and rely on his support. The only problem the young man faced was which patron to choose. A compatriot? A well-placed old friend? A man who had supported him in the early stages of his career? Once selected, the protector would recommend the young man, possibly a stranger the day before, simply because the ambitious fellow had chosen him as protector, knowing that if he did not accept the proffered loyalty, it would be given to another. The Romans were in the habit of transforming generalized relations into personal ones, ritualizing them in the process. The younger generation divided itself into a thousand clienteles and went every morning to hail its patrons.

In return for his protection, the patron took pleasure in the knowledge that his peers' protégés did not outnumber his own. The circulation of political elites depended on personal connections. Oral promises, if not kept, resulted in charges of ingratitude. Patrons deluded themselves into thinking that they advanced the careers of young men out of pure friendship. They liked to give advice about careers. (Cicero adopts a condescending tone toward young Trebatius that he does not allow himself with other correspondents.) They wrote innumerable letters of recommendation, which, though usually quite devoid of content, became almost a distinctive literary genre. The essential thing was to inform one's peers of the name of some protégé. Each patron trusted his peers and used his influence in their behalf, as they used theirs in his. Some aspirants were no doubt omitted when recommendations were made. Only those likely to win the approval of the governing class could be recommended; otherwise the patron risked forfeiting his credibility. And credibility was everything. The man with many protégés and many places to distribute was hailed every morning by a small mob. By contrast, the man who turned his back on public life was abandoned: "He will have no more entourage, no escort for his sedan chair, no visitors in his antechamber." Neither in law nor in custom was there a clear dividing line between public life and private life. Certain philosophers urged such a division, but that was all. "Leave your clients, then, and come dine peacefully with me," said the wise Horace to a friend.

---

*Nobility of Office*

Given the vague distinction between public and private, in identifying a person it was customary to indicate his place in civic life, his political or municipal titles and dignities, if any. These became a part of a man's identity, much as an officer's rank or a noble's titles serve as identifying characteristics for us. When a historian or writer introduced a character, he specified whether he was a slave, a plebeian, a freedman, an equestrian, or a senator. If a senator, he could be either a praetorian or a consular senator, depending on whether the highest rank held in the course of his career was consul or merely praetor. If the man was a professional soldier, who chose to command a regiment in some province or on the borders of the Empire rather than return to Rome to take up one of these annual posts (a duty deferred until later in life), he was referred to as "young So-and-so" (*adulescens*), even if he carried forty years beneath his breastplate; his real career had yet to begin. So much for senatorial nobility. As for the notables in each Roman city, here is how Censorinus characterizes his protector (*amicus*), a man to whom he owes everything and dedicates his book: "Yours has been a distinguished municipal career. Of all the leading men of your city, you have been singled out for honor by being named priest of the emperors. And you even rise above your provincial rank, thanks to your dignity as Roman equestrian." Thus, municipal life, too, had its hierarchy. A man who was not a plebeian and who belonged to the local council (*curia*) was a true luminary. He became a leading man, a "principal," after he had held all available annual posts, including the highest (which were also the costliest).

"Engaging in political life," which meant simply "holding public office," was not a specialized activity. It was something that any man worthy of the name, and member of the governing class, was expected to do—an ideal of private behavior. To be deprived of access to public office and hence to the city's political life was to be less than a man, a person of no account. Erotic poets seeking to elicit smiles from their readers with an amusing paradox used to say that they felt nothing but scorn for a political career, that the only campaign that interested them was that of love (*militia amoris*). Philosophers, experts on the subject, usually held that, if absolutely essential, political life (*bios politikos*) could be sacrificed, but only to philosophical life, that is, to full devotion to the study of wisdom. In practice, municipal offices and, a fortiori, senatorial offices were accessible only to wealthy families. But this privilege was also an ideal, almost a duty. Conformists, the Stoics held that the political life was life lived in accordance with Reason. A man could be as rich as he liked, but he did not count among the "first men of the city" unless he cut a figure on the public stage. Of course a wealthy man might not be allowed to live by himself, undisturbed. Others of his class might exhort him to become involved, or the people of his city might wrest him from his estates by gentle coercion, thrusting him into the political limelight. For the exercise of any office, which lasted only a year but conferred a rank for life, involved lavish expenditure on public pleasures, to which the people were addicted.

The individual who held public office paid dearly for his lifetime of honor. The lack of distinction between public and private funds was not a one-way affair. The curious institution of public benefaction by government officials has been called "evergetism." Any man named praetor or consul was expected to spend billions from his own pocket to pay for public spectacles, plays, chariot races at the Circus, and even ruinous gladiatorial battles in the Colosseum, to amuse the people of Rome. Afterward the newly appointed official went to the provinces to replenish his coffers. Such was the lot of families included in the senatorial aristocracy—one family out of every

Consul about to throw a handkerchief onto the track to signal the start of a chariot race, 4th century. (Rome, Museum of the Conservators.)

ten or twenty thousand. The true nature of evergetism, however, can be seen most clearly among the municipal notables: perhaps one family in twenty. For them there was no compensation for the financial sacrifices that evergetism obliged them to make.

---

In the least of the Empire's cities, whether Latin was spoken or Greek or even Celtic or Syriac, perhaps the majority of public buildings now explored by archaeologists and visited by thousands of tourists every year were built by local notables who bore the expense out of their own pockets. These same men paid for the public spectacles staged each year to the delight of the populace. Anyone who acceded to municipal office was expected to pay into the city treasury a sum of money, which went to finance spectacles during his tenure or else to construct public buildings. If an officeholder found himself in straitened circumstances, he was expected to make a written promise that he or his heirs would some day pay the expected sum. More than that, apart from the holding of public office, notables made spontaneous gifts of buildings, gladiator fights, public banquets, and festivals to their fellow citizens. Such endowments were even more common in Rome than in the United States today, with the difference that in Rome the gifts of the wealthy were almost exclusively intended to embellish the city and add to the pleasure of its citizens. By far the majority of amphitheaters, those stony monuments to wealth, were freely given by patrons, who thereby left a definitive mark on their city.

Were these gifts a product of private generosity or public duty? Both. The proportion varied from donor to donor and every case was special. What began as a desire on the part of the rich to make ostentatious display of their wealth increasingly came to be seen as a duty imposed upon wealthy citizens by their cities. Cities obliged wealthy men of rank to make a habit of what they might have been inclined to do from time to time. By their generous gifts notables demonstrated membership in the governing class. Satirical poets mocked the pretensions of the nouveaux riches, who hastened to provide fellow citizens with the desired spectacles. Cities became accustomed to a level of public luxury that they began to consider their due. The nomination of annual officials provided the occasion. Every year, in every city, little dramas took place, as new sources of wealth were found and milked. Every

*Evergetism*

Chariot race (relief destroyed in 1944), 2nd or 3rd century. Statues of the gods are everywhere; the races were offerings to the gods, who took as much interest in the events as did men.

council member protested that he was poorer than his peers but that So-and-so was a fortunate and prosperous man and such a magnificent person that he would surely accept an office that required him, say, to pay for the cost of heating the water in the public baths. But the man designated might complain that he had already held this office. The more stubborn of the two would win the argument. In case of stalemate, the provincial governor might take a hand. Or the plebs of the city, fond of its hot water, might intervene peacefully by hailing the designated victim, extolling his spontaneous generosity, and electing him to office by unanimous acclamation. Or, again, an unexpected patron might come forward and spontaneously offer to help his city. The city would then show its gratitude by having the council name him to some high local office or by awarding a special title, such as "patron of the city," "father of the city," or "magnificent and spontaneous benefactor," a title that might be inscribed on the man's tombstone. Or the city might vote to erect a statue of its benefactor, the cost of which he would of course volunteer to bear.

These practices explain why local dignitaries gradually ceased to be elected by their fellow citizens and instead were designated by the council oligarchy, which chose officials from its own ranks. The problem was not too many candidates but too few. Since holding office was a matter more of disbursing funds than of governing, people were willing to allow the council to immolate one of its own members; the best candidate was the one who agreed to pay up. Notables enjoyed the dubious satisfaction of maintaining that the city belonged to them because they had paid for it. In return, this class had the privilege of assessing imperial taxes to its own advantage, shifting as much as possible of the tax burden onto the shoulders of the poor peasants. Every city was divided into two camps: the notables who gave and the plebs who received. A man was not a local luminary if he did not at least once in his life pay for a public building or banquet. This was the way the ruling oligarchy was formed. Was it also a hereditary oligarchy? The question is not easily answered. A father's dignities imposed a kind of moral obligation on his son, who was expected to make gifts simply because he was his father's heir. In seeking out victims cities always turned first to those whose fathers had held high office (*patrobouloi*), hoping that the sons would wish to emulate the generosity of their fathers. In case of a shortage of sons of officeholders, municipal councils resigned themselves to admitting into their ranks the scions of merchant families, say, to whom costly offices might then be assigned.

Fragment of sarcophagus, 4th century. An important man (he holds a scepter and is preceded by a lictor) travels by carriage; a secretary adds to his luster. An empty sedan chair follows. When the man reaches the city gates he will switch to the chair, being shrewd enough not to make an ostentatious entrance in his carriage. (Aquileia, Archaeological Museum.)

Notables put up with this system only because custom obliged them to. Protest was as common as silent submission. The central government also had doubts. Sometimes to ensure its own popularity it required notables to give the people pleasures that "will ward off unhappiness." Sometimes it sought the support of the notables by seeking to stem the tide of popular demands. Still other times it pursued its own interests and attempted to protect the rich from their penchant for ostentatious display: Did it not make more sense to provide a city with a new pier than to pay for a festival? The tendency was to give the populace whatever it found amusing, or to build buildings that flattered the vanity of the donor. It was only during times of famine that the plebs thought of asking its leaders to sell cheaply the grain held in their storehouses. The wealthy paid for the amusements of their fellow citizens out of civic spirit and for buildings out of ostentation. Civic spirit and ostentation—the twin roots of evergetism—again blurred the distinction between the public man and the private.

*Aristocratic Civism*

Ostentation meant spontaneity, civic spirit meant duty. The duty to give was paradoxical, in that it required the donor to give the city more than its due. The citizens of a modern state pay only the taxes they are required to pay, to the cent. But Greek cities, and the Roman cities patterned after them, held to a principle, or an ideal, that was far more exacting. When possible, they treated their citizens as a modern political party treats its militant activists: zeal is all or nothing and party members are expected to devote themselves fully to the cause. Ancient cities expected wealthy citizens to show similar devotion. It would take us too far afield to explain why this devotion went mainly to provide expensive amusements. (Briefly, officials found it most difficult to turn down requests to spend money on activities that were also acts of piety; when one of them honored the gods of the city by staging a festival or public spectacle, he always made a contribution to the public treasury.)

Besides civic duty, there was the ostentation of the nobility. The wealthy had always considered themselves public figures. They invited all fellow citizens to their daughters' weddings. If a rich man's father died, the entire city was invited to the funeral banquet or the gladiator fight in honor of the deceased. Such acts of generosity soon became obligatory. Throughout the Empire any notable whose adolescent son first donned adult garb or who took a new wife was expected to hold a public celebration or to donate money to the city. If he wished to avoid this obligation, he had to take refuge on one of his estates and celebrate the marriage there. But to do so was to forgo public life entirely and to moulder in oblivion. Nobles were proud men, who wanted their memories to endure, so rather than provide the citizens some fleeting amusement, they had buildings built with their names engraved on them. Or they established permanent foundations, another fashionable form of giving since every year on the founder's birthday the city celebrated his memory, paying for the celebration with the income from capital bequeathed for the purpose. Sometimes a festival named for a wealthy donor was celebrated in his honor.

All of these were ways in which wealthy men, living or dead, could confirm their status as local luminaries. A luminary is no longer a private person, however; stars are devoured by their fans. The relation between a benefactor and his city was a physical affair, a matter of face-to-face contact. In this it resembled the relation under the Roman Republic between ordinary citizens and political leaders, who made decisions from the rostrum before the eyes of the crowd, visible, like yesterday's generals, on the field of battle. Emperors, shut up in their palaces, wanted to continue this republican tradition by appearing personally in the amphitheater or circus, where the plebs could examine them and gauge their responsiveness to the wishes of the public, the one true judge.

The fate of municipal notables was similar. In a small town in Tunisia archaeologists have found a mosaic in which a powerful local figure named Magerius celebrated his own generosity. The mosaic, which had served as decoration in his antechamber, depicts a fight between four gladiators and four leopards; the name of each gladiator is recorded next to his portrait, as is the name of each animal. The mosaic is no mere decoration, but a truthful record of a spectacle which Magerius paid for out of his own pocket. It also records the acclamation of the public, which heaped praise upon its benefactor: "Magerius! Magerius! May your example serve to instruct those who come after you! May your predecessors also heed the lesson! When has anyone else done so much, and where? You offer a spectacle worthy of Rome, the capital! You pay from your own purse! Today is your great day! Magerius is the donor! That is true wealth! That is true power! The very thing! Now that it is over, give the gladiators something extra to

Rome, Villa Albani, between 177 and 180. The imperial government defended merchants against excessive customs duties. This decision was recorded in stone, because law enforcement was never automatic or assured.

CRISPINVS                    HILARINVS

The mosaic of Magerius
(overview with two details),
at Smirat (Tunisia).

send them on their way!" Magerius agreed to this last wish, and the mosaic shows the four bags of silver (each marked with an amount) that he sent to the gladiators in the arena.

The applause of the populace was normally followed by honorific titles and marks of honor awarded for life by the municipal council. Though obliged to bestow these honors, the city had the right to determine who deserved them. A notable could distinguish himself from his peers only by paying homage to his city. The honorific titles awarded to a benefactor, the public offices that he held, were no less important than, say, titles of nobility in prerevolutionary France, and they aroused just as much passion. The Roman Empire offers us the curious paradox of aristocratic civism. The hereditary presumption of the noble had to be confirmed by an ostentatious display of civic spirit, by a generous act that made the benefactor stand out but within a civic setting. Superior to the plebs of his town, the notable was an important man because he was worthy in the eyes of his fellow citizens, who benefited from his largesse. The city was both the beneficiary and the judge of its native son's devotion. The plebs was so keenly aware of this ambiguity that people often left the spectacle unsure whether they had been honored or humiliated by their benefactor. A phrase that Petronius imputes to one spectator captures this feeling well: "He gave me a spectacle, but I applauded it. We're even: one hand washes the other."

Thus, patriotic devotion cohabited with lust for personal glory (*ambitus*). Already, under the Roman Republic, members of the senatorial class sought popularity by staging public banquets and spectacles, more to please the plebs than to corrupt the electors. Even after election to high office had been eliminated, they carried on in the same tradition. Georges Ville said: "Behind self-interested ambition often lurked what one might call disinterested ambition, which sought the favor of the crowd for itself and was satisfied with that and nothing else."

---

Enough about the Roman "bourgeoisie." Like the clientele system, evergetism cannot be understood in terms of class interest. It was, rather, the consequence of an aristocratic mind-set, with its penchant for useless building and for erecting honorific statues to the glory of family dynasties. This heraldic art was fed by fantasies of nobility. To try to explain these in terms of Machiavellian strategy, redistribution of

*The Uniqueness of Evergetism*

This young Roman wears a toga, although he is not yet an adult (as is indicated by the *bulla* around his neck, which youths ceased to wear when they donned the toga of adulthood). Several copies of this statue have been found, which indicates that it was a widely reproduced official portrait. This young prince must be either the unfortunate Britannicus or the man who murdered him, Nero. But because effigies of Nero were destroyed after his death, and one of these statues was found in the Forum of Velleia, this is Britannicus. (Paris, Louvre.)

wealth, depoliticization, and a calculated effort to erect symbolic barriers between the classes is to oversimplify and rationalize a phenomenon whose cost and symbolic complexity went far beyond what was socially necessary. What confuses us is that this nobility, with its apparently civic symbolism, its "public" buildings and magistrate's titles, seems so different from the familiar European nobility of blood and landed titles. The Roman aristocracy was a unique historical entity, which, rather than extol the purity of its blood, sang its own praises in terms drawn from the vocabulary of the ancient city.

The group of curials did not coincide exactly with the class of the wealthy, if only because the number of seats available on the municipal council was generally limited to one hundred. The municipal council of a Roman city was an aristocratic club; not all the wealthy were admitted. Imperial laws insisted that, in case of financial need, wealthy merchants, however vulgar, should be admitted. But the wealthy nobles already in the club preferred to put pressure on one of their own, to force him to ruin himself for the sake of his city. Some nobles chose to flee the gentle violence of their peers. According to the last book of the *Digest,* they took refuge on their estates, with their farmers (*coloi praediorum*), for the power of the public authorities did not extend far outside the cities and into the countryside, where Christians like Saint Cyprian fled from their persecutors.

The official class was aristocratic in another sense: families that had attained prominent position tended to hold onto it for long periods. True, nouveau-riche dynasties were allowed to crash this exalted circle, but it is no less true that the leading families maintained their position for centuries, intermarrying and breeding among themselves. The marriage patterns of the few great families in one city have been studied by Philippe Moreau, who took Cicero's *Pro Cluentio* as his starting point. In Greece abundant epigraphic evidence has enabled scholars to trace the history of many a noble family over two or three centuries, in Sparta especially, as well as in Boeotia and elsewhere. Family trees fill entire folio-sized pages in our anthologies of Greek inscriptions of the imperial period. The time of the Empire was a time of stability for the aristocracy.

Evergetism was a point of honor among the aristocracy, whose caste pride was the driving force behind the various civic and liberal motives that historians have ably, but too exclusively, described: civic spirit, zeal in largesse, desire for distinction. But the historians are too subtle; the reality was far simpler. Noble pride was a fact, as was the existence of a patrimonial, indeed a hereditary, nobility. Every noble wanted to outdo his rivals so that he might claim to be the "first" or the "only" person ever to engage in some unheard-of act of generosity: previous officeholders may have distributed free bath oil to the populace, but along comes a new champion who prides himself on being the first to distribute perfumed bath oil.

"I want to make money," says one of Petronius' heroes, "and to have such a fine death that my funeral will become proverbial." No doubt he will order his heirs to stage a public banquet for the occasion. Bread and Circuses, or, rather, buildings and spectacles: authority was more often a matter of seizing the limelight than of obliging others to do one's bidding through the wielding of public or private power. It was monumentalization and theatricalization. Evergetism was not as virtuous as its most recent commentators believe. Nor was it as Machiavellian as some earlier commentators, imbued with vague Marxism, maintained. Nobility resided in a competition that was as irrational in a political and economic sense as ostentation was wasteful. Evergetism far exceeded what was needed to maintain one's rank or to mark class barriers, and there is no basis for reducing so fundamental a phenomenon as competition through waste to social terms, according to the modern taste in historical explanation. Nor does it make sense to rely on the explanations given by the ancients themselves: patriotism, festivals and banquets, generosity, and so forth. The phenomenon is as peculiar as the practice of potlatch that anthropologists have discovered among many "primitive" peoples. Among the Romans the passion to give was as all-consuming as the passions unleashed in "civilized" nations today by the desire for "political" power and "economic" wealth and nothing else, nothing more mysterious—or so we like to think.

View of the city of Alba Fucens (in the Abruzzi) ca. A.D. 50. It is difficult to interpret because it has been simplified. Instead of expansive, sumptuous villas or huge multistory apartment buildings, this may have been a city of tall, narrow houses. (Rome, Torlonia Collection.)

# ❧ "Work" and Leisure

SLAVERY was an important part of the Roman economy. Men could also be imprisoned for debt, sequestered by the creditor along with their wives and families and forced to work. And there was the state sector: condemned men, slaves of the innumerable imperial states, toiled under the whips of slavedrivers; many Christians suffered this fate. But for the most part Roman workers were legally free. Small independent farmers worked to pay taxes. As Peter Brown has written, the Roman Empire gave free sway to local oligarchies, to whom it delegated responsibility for administrative chores. Little was required of these local notables in the way of taxes, and imperial authorities refrained from exhibiting too much curiosity about the way in which taxes were extorted from the peasantry. (Unencumbering government of this kind has been the basis of much colonial rule in recent times.) Other peasants worked for these same notables as sharecroppers. Farm workers, laborers, and artisans hired to perform specific tasks reached agreements with their employers on the terms of employment, though this rarely took the form of written contracts (except when workers were accepted as apprentices). Just as the Napoleonic Code stipulated that the word of a master should be accepted in a dispute with a servant over wages, so did the Roman master mete out his own justice if robbed by an employee, as though the employee were a slave. Cities were essentially places where Roman notables (like the "urban nobility" of the Italian Renaissance) spent the money generated by land. The Roman Empire thus stands in sharp contrast to the France of the Middle Ages, where the nobility lived scattered about the countryside in fortified castles.

In the Roman city urban notables were surrounded by

Detail of mosaic from the Baths of Caracalla, 3rd or 4th century. In the 3rd century Rome rivaled Olympia as a center of athletic competitions in the Greek manner. This elderly gentleman trained professional athletes who came to Rome from all over the world to compete. (Rome, Lateran Museum.)

artisans and merchants who catered to the needs of the wealthy. Roman "cities" and modern cities have little in common but the name. A Roman city could be recognized by the presence of an idle class, made up of what I call "notables." Idleness was the cornerstone of "private life"; in fact, in the ancient world it was considered a virtue.

The urban nobility looked upon the countryside with disdain, and upon the cities, filled with workers, with suspicion. The imperial government did the same. In A.D. 215 an emperor decided to expel from Alexandria the Egyptian peasants who had gathered there in large numbers, because "their way of life proves that rural people are not suited to civic life." The Empire was really an empire only in its cities, where the notables in control of the municipal councils could regiment the working population. Romans were contemptuous of central Turkey whose cities were mere country towns inhabited by well-to-do farmers, wealthy enough to claim immortality by paying to have their epitaphs engraved.

Around 1820 an astrologer says to the young hero of Stendhal's *Charterhouse of Parma*: "In a century perhaps nobody will want idlers any more." He was right. It ill becomes anyone today to admit that he lives without working. Since Marx and Proudhon, labor has been universally accepted as a positive social value and a philosophical concept. As a result, the ancients' contempt for labor, their undisguised scorn for those who work with their hands, their exaltation of leisure as the sine qua non of a "liberal" life, the only life worthy of a man, shocks us deeply. Not only was the worker regarded as a social inferior; he was base, ignoble. It has often been held, therefore, that a society like the Roman, so mistaken about what we regard as proper values, must have been a deformed society, which inevitably paid the price of its deformity. The ancients' contempt for labor, the argument goes, explains their economic backwardness, their ignorance of technology. Or, according to another argument, the reason for one deformity must be sought in another: contempt for labor, we are told, had its roots in that other scandalous fact of Roman life, slavery.

And yet, if we are honest, we must admit that the key to this enigma lies within ourselves. True, we believe that work is respectable and would not dare to admit to idleness. Nevertheless, we are sensitive to class distinctions and, admit it or not, regard workers and shopkeepers as people of relatively little importance. We would not want ourselves or our children to sink to their station, even if we are a little ashamed of harboring such sentiments.

Therein lies the first of six keys to ancient attitudes toward labor: contempt for labor equals social contempt for laborers. This contempt persisted until about the time when the *Charterhouse of Parma* was written. Then, in order to maintain class hierarchy and discourage class conflict, it became necessary to recognize labor as a true value, shared by all. Social peace was bought at the price of hypocrisy. There is no mystery about the ancient contempt for labor; it is just that the social war had not yet reached the stage of a hypocritical and temporary armistice. A social class proud of its superiority sang hymns to its own glory (such is the nature of ideology).

*The Virtue of Wealth*

1. The first key to ancient attitudes toward labor is that the source and character of a social group's wealth determined its value. In classical Athens, when comic poets characterized men by occupations (Eucrates the scrap dealer or Lysicles the seller of sheep), they had no intention of doing them honor; to be fully a man, one had to live in leisure. According to Plato, a well-organized city is one in which citizens are fed by the rural toil of their slaves and the trades are filled with people of no importance. The "virtuous" life, the life lived by a man of quality, is supposed to be one of "idleness." (As we shall see, this meant the life of a landowner, who did no "work" but spent his time overseeing his estates.) Aristotle failed to see how slaves, peasants, and shopkeepers could be expected to lead "happy" lives, meaning lives at once prosperous and noble. Such lives were the exclusive province of men who could afford to live as they pleased, according to their ideals. Only such men of leisure conformed to the ideal of humanity. Only they were worthy of full citizenship: "The perfection of the citizen cannot be predicated of the man who is merely free, but only of the man who is free from such necessary tasks as are performed by serfs, artisans, and manual laborers; the latter will not be citizens if the constitution awards public charges to virtue and merit, since no one who leads the life of a worker or laborer can practice virtue." Aristotle is not saying that a poor man has scant means and little opportunity to exhibit certain virtues, but that poverty is a defect, a kind of vice. For Metternich, mankind began at the rank of baron; for the Greeks and Romans, it began with the landowner. Greek and Roman notables did not consider themselves to be supe-

Fragment of sarcophagus, 3rd century. A goatherd milks a goat in front of a reed hut. This sarcophagus was a popular model (the same shop produced a number of copies). The pastoral scene aestheticized death and dispelled sadness. (Rome, Museum of the Baths.)

rior to the average run of humanity. They believed purely and simply that they *were* humanity, hence that the poor were morally inferior. The poor did not live as men ought to live.

Wealth was virtue. Demosthenes, in a trial in which he stood as defendant and the Athenian mob as his judge, hurled the following insults in the teeth of his adversary: "I am worth more than Eschinus and I am better born than he; I do not wish to seem to insult poverty, but I am bound to say that it was my lot as a child to attend good schools and to have had sufficient wealth that I was not forced by need to engage in shameful labors. Whereas you, Eschinus, it was your lot as a child to sweep, as might a slave, the classroom in which your father served as teacher." Demosthenes won a decisive victory in this case.

Greek thinkers confirmed this natural conviction in the Romans. "The common arts, the sordid arts, are according to the philosopher Posidonius those practiced by manual laborers, who spend all their time earning their living. There is no beauty in such occupations, which bear little resemblance to the Good," writes Seneca. Cicero did not need to read the philosopher Panaetius, whose conformism he respected, to know that "wage labor is sordid and unworthy of a free man, for wages are the price of labor and not of some art; craft labor is sordid, as is the business of retailing [as opposed to large-scale wholesale trade]." No egalitarian, socialist, or Christian ideals existed to check this spontaneous contempt.

The ancients extolled the man who lived on unearned income as immoderately as the old French aristocracy accused commoners of beggary. A class of wealthy and more or less cultivated notables, determined to maintain exclusive control over the levers of power, exalted its idleness as the sine qua non of a liberal culture and a political career. Workers, Aristotle said, would not know how to govern; they cannot govern, he added, they should not govern, and, what is more, they scarcely even think of governing. In fact, according to Plato, all too many of the wealthy took no part in public affairs and concerned themselves solely with their pleasures and with increasing their wealth. The rich, wrote the mystic Plotinus, are all too often disappointing, but at least they have the merit of not having to work, hence "they constitute a species with some remembrance of virtue," whereas "the mass of manual laborers is a contemptible mob, whose purpose is to produce objects needed by men of virtue."

The rich of course had no need to work. The problem, according to Plato, was that many of them worked nevertheless, out of greed. Their love of wealth "leaves them no respite to concern themselves with anything other than their private property. The soul of the citizen today is entirely taken up with getting rich and with making sure that every day brings its share of profit. The citizen is ready to learn any technique, to engage in any kind of activity, so long as it is profitable. He thumbs his nose at the rest."

Rome, detail of butcher's tomb, 2nd century(?). The man cutting chops may have been a small shopkeeper or a major wholesaler. (Dresden Museum.)

Historians have too often studied the ancients' ideas about labor as though these were doctrines elaborated by jurists and philosophers. In fact, they were confused collective notions, as well as class ideologies. The ancients laid down no principles. They did not say, for example, that "labor" existed only if one worked for another man or for a wage. But their representations were broadly applicable to inferior social

*Class Struggle*

Tomb of mosaicist, 3rd or 4th century. Two seated workmen are cutting small cubes with large hammers. Two hod carriers bring colored stone or haul away the mosaic tiles. At top right, a figure invites spectators to admire the scene. (This sort of "deictic gesture" was to become very popular in medieval art.) (Ostia, Archaeological Museum.)

groups, whose members were reduced to earning their living by wage labor or by entering the service of others. The point was not to establish rules of conduct applicable to all, but to ascribe value to a social class in which some worked as servants, some as hired laborers. All were accused of "labor" so that the entire class might be held in contempt. Workers were reviled not because they worked, but because they belonged to this inferior class. Conversely, the class of notables, rich, cultivated, and powerful, was exalted because it possessed either the virtue of not having to work or that of ruling the city; it made no difference which. Thus, the "ancients' ideas about labor" were not so much ideas as evaluations, positive for the powerful, negative for the humble. Evaluation was the essential point; the details of their arguments are of no interest.

2. In making class evaluations, Romans used whatever argument came to hand. Xenophon explains that the manual trades feminized the men who worked in them, "because these men are forced to remain seated in the shade and sometimes even to spend entire days at fireside." Artisans, moreover,

"haven't time to be concerned with their friends and contribute to the safety of their city." By contrast, working in the fields accustoms a man to endure extremes of heat and cold and to get up early in the morning and encourages him to defend the land that feeds him.

If we are willing to concede that class interest plays a role in history, one historical mystery is easily solved: Why was commerce almost universally devalued until the industrial revolution? The key to the mystery lies in the fact that commercial wealth belonged to the newly rich, while old wealth was based on land. Inherited wealth defended itself against upstart merchants by imputing to them every conceivable vice: merchants are rootless, greedy, the source of all evil; they promote luxury and weakness; they distort nature by traveling to far-off lands, violating the natural barrier of the seas and bringing back what nature will not permit to grow at home. These ideas persisted from archaic Greece and India down to Benjamin Constant and Charles Maurras. In Rome citizens were divided, on the basis of wealth, into civic "orders" (simple citizens, decurions, equestrians, and senators). In establishing wealth, however, the census took account only of property in land. A wealthy trader could raise his status in civil society only by acquiring land. As Cicero wrote, if a merchant, tired of adding to his fortune, aspired to return to port and place his money in rural properties, he could shed his contemptible merchant's character and win high praise.

Sign for a shop that was undoubtedly called "Two Monkeys and a Snail," an allusion, I imagine, to the qualities of the clerks who sold fruit and game. The snail can be seen to the right of the women shown in profile.

The devaluing of nonlanded wealth amounted to a rejection of the parvenu. As long as cultivated land remained the principal form of wealth and agriculture the major source of income, to be wealthy meant to own land; it was the universal investment. Commerce was only a means to an end, a way to become rich. Landed property distinguished the heir from the parvenu. Commerce was a means of acquiring a desirable thing; land was the thing itself. This system of values had one peculiar consequence: a man who was already wealthy and who owned land was not disdained as a merchant if he decided to engage in trade. The important thing was not to begin in trade.

---

*A Definition of Labor*

Commerce is sordid, Cicero said, "if it is a small affair in which one buys only to resell immediately what one has bought. But if it is high trade, grand commerce, it no longer merits much scorn." He adds that, while all artisans' work is sordid, the liberal professions, such as architecture and medicine, are honorable. They might not suit persons of the highest rank, but anyone who did not belong to the cream of society could practice these professions without opprobrium.

3. But did practice of the liberal professions constitute "work"? What does the word mean? It has no exact equivalent in Latin or Greek. Was a writer a worker? A minister? A housewife? A slave did not "work": he obeyed, he did what his master ordered him to do. Similar questions may be asked in our own society. Is a soldier a "worker"? He follows orders. Plato, in *Laws*, establishes that a true citizen should not work; but two pages later he states that the same citizen should "spend several hours each night completing his political chores if he holds a public office or, if not, finishing off his business." By this Plato means the management of his estates, worked of course by his slaves. The physician and philosopher Galen mentions a teacher of his who was forced to give up the teaching of philosophy, "because his leisure was gone. His fellow citizens had induced him to take on various political tasks." This, however, was not work.

Consider the "philosophers, rhetors, musicians, and grammarians" mentioned by Lucian, "all those who feel they must accept a position in a household and receive a salary in return for giving lessons," because they are poor (that is, in the ancient meaning of the word, because their personal wealth is inadequate to their needs). Did they work? No. Some writ-

Coppersmith at work.
(Estonian Museum.)

Sign of a shop or dwelling called "The Four Sisters," three of whom were none other than the graces. (Berlin Museum.)

ers held that they practiced a profession truly worthy of a free man, a "liberal" dignity; others held that they were "friends" (the polite term) of the master who paid them. Still others held that these teachers were poor devils forced to earn their daily bread and to lead a life that was basically the life of a slave: their time was not their own; like household slaves, they heeded the bell that marked the beginning and end of the working day in all good houses. Strange "friendship, that speaks so much about labor and fatigue!" Tutors were not even allowed to become true freemen, because they were not allowed to acquire fortunes of their own. "Their wages, assuming they were paid, and paid in full, had to be spent down to the last cent. They could not put anything aside." Liberal profession, friendship, or wage labor? It is idle to ask how the Romans, or even their jurists, would have answered this question, for they had no answer. They held all three opinions at once, expressing astonishment at the paradox that an activity as "liberal" as scholarship (or "grammar") should fall to the lot of a poor devil with no money. Romans simultaneously felt respect and contempt for their domestic grammarian, their children's tutor. Friend or mercenary? In this society no one was a worker; all social relations were conceived in terms of friendship or authority.

Let us consider, finally, the activities that involved the holding of high office and personal dignity, namely, public functions. Here again we encounter an amalgam of prejudice

Gismondi model of Rome, near the Aracoeli, an apartment building from the 2nd century. This was a fairly large building of five stories divided into numerous apartments; the ground floor was occupied by shops.

A deceased merchant about to depart on a journey with his horse and slave; his son will be a worthy successor. One of Apuleius' heroes was such a merchant: he sold honey, cheese, and so forth to innkeepers and was always on the road, ready to go wherever he heard there was good cheese for sale at a reasonable price. (Aquileia, Archaeological Museum.)

and historical tradition. If a senator was sent to govern the province of Africa and received a fabulous salary for his work, there was no ambiguity. He held a glorious position, fully in keeping with the ideal that a noble should engage in political activity. Yet the man sent to govern the province of Egypt was not considered to hold high office. The difference was that Africa's governors were chosen from the ancient Senate, whereas Egypt's came from the corps of imperial "functionaries" created in the early days of the Empire.

Did these imperial functionaries serve the state and their prince? Their enemies charged that they were nothing more than slaves of their master, the emperor, who was supposed to use his servants to help him run the Empire much as he might use them to run his private estates. But one of these high functionaries, the writer Lucian, who served as high treasurer of Egypt, spoke for all when he said that there was no difference between an imperial functionary and a senator-governor. He was right, but collective judgments are not always based on reason. The physician Galen, who treated one imperial functionary, saw him as a kind of slave, since the man worked all day long for his master, the emperor, and "became himself once again, independent of his master, only at nightfall." The same ambiguity attached to another important role: steward for a great family. This post was generally entrusted to the scion of a ruined old family. Plutarch speaks of his steward in a tone of commiseration: he is an inferior brother.

---

4. What determined whether a governor of Egypt was a public man or a mere worker? Was it his position? No. Was it his "lifestyle," his lordly ways or submissive demeanor? No. What mattered was not what he was or did; judgment was imposed from outside. Ancient conceptions of labor contain quite an array of "outside judgments." Consider an analogy. How do we decide whether the powerful Medici family was a family of bankers or nobles? Were they bankers who lived like nobles or nobles who happened to be in the banking business? Is it their lifestyle that determines the answer, as Max Weber maintained? No. The judgment depends not on them, but on their contemporaries, who either agreed or did not agree to count the Medicis among the noble families of the day. And if they did agree to count them as noble, then their banking activities cease to be their profession and become a mere anecdotal detail. "Outside judgments" are a trap for unwary historians. Merely because the notables of the ancient world declared themselves to be men of leisure, it is wrong to conclude that they did not engage in banking and commerce.

In France today, a duke who runs a steel company remains a duke who happens to own some steel mills, while a steel

## Outside Judgments

Below left: An oculist. Detail of sarcophagus, 2nd or 3rd century. Some eye diseases were endemic and were treated with lotions, cupping, bleeding, and washing. On the right and left hang two oversized cupping glasses. (Ravenna, Church of San Vittore.)

Below right: Tomb of Athenian physician, 1st century B.C. Patients were examined nude, so women often preferred female doctors or midwives. In the lower right corner is an oversized cupping glass. (London, British Museum.)

Gismondi model of Rome. The Tiber and two of the eight bridges, the larger of the two circuses, two of the eleven aqueducts, the Coliseum, and the rectangular park of the Temple of Claudius Apotheosized.

executive who is not a duke derives his whole identity from his position. In the ancient world a notable was not identified as a shipper or an estate owner; he was himself, a man. To speak anachronistically for a moment, his business card contained nothing but his name. Everyone regarded managing one's estates as a prosaic necessity and nothing more, no more characteristic of a man than the need to get dressed in the morning. If we could travel back in time to a Roman city and ask the man in the street what he thought of, say, a dynasty of shipowners who lorded it over his city, he would answer: "They are important people, powerful, wealthy men. They take part in public affairs and with their donations they've done the city a lot of good and paid for some magnificent games." Later in the conversation we would no doubt learn that they had also fitted out a great many ships, though that fact alone would not reduce them to the level of mere ship-owners. One historian recently showed that the ancients scorned commercial profits as the fruit of greed, yet considered it a merit for a noble to accumulate wealth by every possible means, including commerce. They held professional merchants in contempt, but regarded nobles as statesmen and men of leisure. Was their thinking contradictory? Logically, yes. But the Romans themselves were not aware of the contradiction. A notable who engaged in trade was not classed as a trader but as a notable, one of the most powerful of men. To be sure, the law forbade Roman senators to engage in maritime commerce. But senators violated the law without scruple, because what mattered was that one should not be *in business*. Senators *did* business but were not *in* business; appearances were preserved.

No notable or noble was ever defined by what he did. A poor man, on the other hand, *was* a cobbler or a laborer. In order to be himself and nothing else, he had to possess a patrimony. When, in his epitaph, a notable proclaimed himself a "good farmer," he meant that he had the talent necessary to ensure that his lands were well cultivated, not that he was a cultivator by trade. What facts did the epitaphs of notables mention? In the first place, the political offices they had held, and possibly liberal activities in which they engaged by predilection or "profession," much as nobles of a later age would make profession of a monastic vocation. Notables and nobles honored themselves by studying philosophy, eloquence, law, poetry, or medicine, and, in Greek parts of the Empire, by athletic prowess. Cities honored them with statues commemorating these achievements: "professions" were publicly honored. People defined themselves in terms of their professions; for example, one said, "former consul and philosopher." Now we understand the meaning of the title that Marcus Aurelius has claimed in posterity: "emperor and philosopher." With these words he signified that he had capped his political dignity with his philosophical profession.

---

5. To scorn working people socially is one thing, but every member of the ruling class knows that labor is useful to the state. It secures social peace. Isocrates writes that "in the good old days the lower orders were encouraged to go into farming and commerce, because people knew that idleness gives rise to indigence and indigence to crime." Ancient phi-

*In Praise of Labor*

losophy did not hold that a state is a "society" organized in such a way that each man works for the benefit of all the others. It maintained instead that a "city" is an institution imposed upon natural human society in order to allow men to live more nobly. According to this view, the poor work not to contribute to society but to keep out of mischief: crime and sedition. But there was one ancient thinker who believed that work, or at least commerce, benefited all citizens by securing necessary goods. Given the esteem for other activities that contributed to the common good, he was surprised by the contempt in which merchants were generally held. This was none other than Plato, the same thinker who freely expressed his disdain for people of low social rank. Even here Plato does not say that society is sustained by the labor of all, including tillers, artisans, and merchants. He mentions only commerce. For him, every citizen is sustained by his patrimony (cultivated by his slaves), a resource as "natural" as the air we breathe. Man begins to render service to his fellow man only when it becomes necessary to obtain goods not "naturally" available. Commerce complements inherited wealth.

Detail of sarcophagus, 2nd century or later. Visible are two barrels (which had replaced amphoras). On the left is a customer, purse in hand; on the right, the late merchant, holding a cup and tap. Since uninherited wealth bestowed no rank, this major wine wholesaler indicates only the most concrete details of his business, giving no idea of its size; he could be mistaken for a mere tavernkeeper. (Museum of Ancona.)

Work was, moreover, the only resource of the masses. The emperor knew this and, as the "conservator" of Italian society, attempted to preserve the traditional resources of every group. Caesar ordered that one-third of all shepherds be free men (because slave labor was putting free shepherds out of work). Augustus sought to protect the interests of peasants as well as traders. Vespasian refused to use machines in constructing the Colosseum, for fear of reducing the lower orders of Rome to famine. Roman policy had two aspects. It sought, first, to defend the state apparatus and augment its power in the face of internal and external threats. And then there was the *cura*. The emperor treated much if not all of Roman society as though he were its "curator," or guardian. He worked to ensure that society as traditionally constituted should prosper, much as a guardian is charged with overseeing a ward's affairs without disrupting whatever prior arrangements have been made.

6. I have been examining the opinion of labor current among notables and politicians, who held their inferiors in contempt or manipulated them. The inferiors themselves had a different view of things.

In Petronius' *Satyricon* the wealthy freedman Trimalchio makes a fortune speculating on maritime commerce and then retires, living as a notable on the income from his estates and on interest from loans. He is neither a notable nor a man of the people, but a man proud of having made a fortune according to the values of his own subgroup, through zeal, talent, and willingness to take risks. He orders the sculptor working on his tomb to depict the banquet he staged for his fellow citizens. The whole town attended. Richer than his peers, Trimalchio wants to be "recognized," if not by the upper class then at least by the civic corps of his city. Even if the notables despise him, and others, poorer than he, disparage him in private, all show him the outward signs of respect by coming to eat and drink at his expense.

Even more numerous were those who subscribed unreservedly to the values of their own class and enjoyed their work, prosperity, and good professional reputation without seeking recognition from their betters or the transient satisfaction of a momentary public glory. Archaeologists have unearthed hundreds of tombstones on which the dead had themselves sculpted as they appeared in their shops or workshops. Like most of Roman culture, these tradesmen's tombstones are Greek-inspired, for in Athens as early as the fifth century artisans had a "class consciousness" of their own.

A more positive idea of labor, which we should have suspected all along, has been revealed by documents of popular origin. This coexisted with the ideal of leisure cum political activity that scholars have long held to be typical of ancient society. In Pompeii some fine houses, filled with paintings and marble statues, were owned by bakers, fullers, and ceramics-makers, who proudly displayed the insignia of their trades; some of these men belonged to the municipal senate. In Africa a wealthy farmer asked a poet to prepare a verse epitaph, in which he tells how work made him wealthy. Those merchants and artisans and farmers who had epitaphs drawn up for themselves were wealthy men (epitaphs were expensive), and all made a point of indicating their occupation. One states that a man "worked hard"; another that he was a "well-known money changer"; still another that he was a "noted dealer in pork and beef." It should be mentioned that at this time a potter or baker stood higher in the social hierarchy than a potter or baker today (an oven represented a fairly large investment). In Petronius' *Satyricon* a young man of letters is put in his place by a freedman trader, who professes faith in himself and others of his kind: "I am a man among men. I walk with my head held high. I don't owe a cent to anyone. I've never received a summons, and no one has ever said to me from the forum, 'Pay me what you owe.' I've been able to buy some land and save some money, and I support twenty people, to say nothing of my dog. Come with me to the forum and ask for a loan. You'll quickly discover whether I have credit, despite my mere freedman's iron ring." We can understand why the tombstones of shopkeepers detailed their shops' interiors, showing merchandise, fine counters, beautiful women being handed fabric cuttings, and the tools or machines of the trade. Merchandise and tools were valuable capital: signs of wealth rather than insignia of a trade. Such funerary sculpture does more than just indicate the profession of the deceased, like a death certificate. It celebrates his position as the owner of a shop. But no one is ever shown working with his hands.

Properly understood, these images express the opposite of plebeian humility: they illustrate the wealth of a middle class determined to distinguish itself from the plebs by means of a costly display of bas-reliefs. I say "middle class," even though this was not a large group; in terms of percentage of the population it numbered in the single digits. Its situation, however, was intermediate and ambiguous. These bakers, butchers, and wine, clothing, and shoe merchants were not municipal notables. They did not belong to the privileged civic "order"—at least not yet. But they were as rich as many notables. And, like Saint Paul (an eminent representative of the middle class and the son of the owner of a shop that manufactured tents and surely employed a number of slaves), they knew how to read and write. They probably attended school until they reached the age of twelve.

In antiquity bakers, butchers, and shoe merchants were not poor shopkeepers but wealthy men. A baker, for instance, was also a miller, who owned grain mills and the slaves or animals needed to operate them. A butcher had to be wealthy enough to buy a whole steer. A shoe merchant was not just a cobbler working in a stall, or *taberna*, but a man who owned a number of slaves who both produced and sold footwear. For the sake of clarity, we should distinguish between three levels of economic status. (1) A plebeian owned nothing, simply earning his daily bread day after day. As in Ricardo's day, wages were set at the subsistence level. (2) A poor shopkeeper (a cobbler, say, or tavernkeeper) disposed of so little ready cash that every morning he had to buy the merchandise he would sell during the day. If a demanding client asked for a good bottle of wine, the tavernkeeper would have to go out and buy that wine from a wealthy wine merchant in his neighborhood. Even today in Greece or the Middle East a merchant's cash reserves often amount to no more than a single day's business. (3) A wealthy merchant was one who could afford to keep on hand several barrels of wine or sacks of flour or sides of beef. He was not a wholesaler but a merchant who

Blacksmith's tomb, 1st or 2nd century. The epitaph states that this smith kept a number of slaves and freedmen (or freedwomen). Center: the smith works at anvil; left: the furnace and bellows. (Aquileia, Archaeological Museum.)

sold to private individuals as well as to lesser merchants. A small butcher, for example, might buy a few chops from his wealthy neighbor to sell to his customers during that same day. Wealthy butchers, bakers, and clothing merchants lived in houses with patios, just like notables. They invested all their profits in these sumptuous dwellings, which set them apart from poorer merchants. The latter had only their stalls and slept above their shops, in attics accessible only by ladder.

In Pompeii the sumptuous homes with their patios and celebrated murals stand out quite clearly from the poor shops. But there are more sumptuous homes than there are shops. Were the rich in Pompeii more numerous than the poor? One has to assume, I think, that the richer homes were often rented out to a number of poorer families, each of which occupied several rooms.

## Aesthetic Disdain

What about the four-fifths of the population who really worked? Theirs was a bitter struggle for survival, and no doubt they lived by the precept of Saint Paul: "He who does not work shall not eat." This was both a lesson to the industrious and a warning to the lazy, who might have hoped to share the meager pittance earned by others by the sweat of their brow.

Of this hard-working crowd of peasants, fishermen, and shepherds, some slaves, others free, we know very little. We know at least how the upper class viewed them: with the eye of the connoisseur. It was as a delightful exotic species that laborers were depicted in bucolic poetry (which has nothing but the name in common with modern pastoral) and Hellenistic genre sculpture.

Modern pastoral takes aristocrats and dresses them up as well-bred shepherds. But ancient bucolic was imbued with the ethics of the slave system, just as the blackface musicals attended by whites in the United States were imbued with racism. The bucolic poets took slaves, idealized them somewhat, polished them up, allowed them to speak their own language and tell their own jokes, but disguised them as lovers and poets. The point was to amuse "white" masters by making them imagine a naive and touching little world, so far beneath the real world that all is innocence: an idyll that survives no longer than a dream. The living is easy in this Garden of Eden—so, presumably, is the sex.

Genre sculpture, which decorated the homes and gardens

of the wealthy, depicted conventional types: the Old Fisherman, the Plowman, the Gardener, the Drunken Old Woman. These figures were represented with brutal, exaggerated naturalism. The veins and muscles of the Old Fisherman stand out with such relief that his desiccated body is reminiscent of an anatomical illustration; his face is so abstracted that for a long time this statue was thought to be of Seneca dying. This picturesque style is midway between expressionism and caricature. Old age and poverty are here nothing but a spectacle for the diversion of indifferent aesthetes; the onlooker does not penetrate beneath the surface, nor does he ever put aside his fundamental disdain. Physical deformity is an occasion for

Left: Old fisherman. The sculptor has realistically detailed the fish in the basket. (Rome, Museum of the Conservators.)

The so-called dying Seneca, a Roman copy of Hellenistic original. This is another elderly fisherman carrying his basket of fish. (Rome, Vatican Museums.)

smiles, like looking at midgets and giants at a carnival. Roman naturalism was full of condescension, without scruples. The philosopher Seneca was a scrupulous soul, who believed that harsh treatment of slaves was demeaning to a master. But this same Seneca one day happened to cast his eyes on the slave posted as a guard by his door and found him so unprepossessing that he turned to his majordomo, saying: "Where does this decrepit creature come from? You did well to post him at the door, for he seems on the verge of leaving this house for good and finding his final resting place! Where did you come up with this death's-head?" Whereupon the slave, hearing what Seneca had said, spoke up: "But Master, don't you recognize me? I am Felicio, with whom you used to play when you were little." Seneca then turned his gaze upon himself and wrote a meditation on the ravages that old age had wrought on his own person, from which he drew a lesson in wisdom and conclusions about the ontology of time.

To belong to the upper class, to the unmaimed, fully human part of humankind, it was necessary, first of all, to be wealthy enough to make a show of things that only money could buy, tokens of elite status. You also had to be master of your own time, at no one's beck and call, for only independent men were truly human. It was easier to meet these conditions by inheriting a fortune than by running a shop. With inherited wealth came standing, independence, and authority.

Rich and poor. What would seem striking to a modern observer transported back to the Roman Empire is the contrast between extremes of luxury and misery, not unlike what we might see in an underdeveloped country today. Ammianus Marcellinus wrote in substance that Aquitania was a prosperous province because the common people there did not go around in rags as they did elsewhere. When the poor get their clothing from the ragpicker (*centonarius*), luxury begins with new clothing.

The ancients did not scorn labor; they did scorn those who were compelled to work in order to live. It is wrong to imagine that ancient physicists neglected the technological applications of science because they disdained labor and idealized pure science. The error is threefold. First, it is hard to see what contemporary scientific discoveries would have lent themselves to technological application. Second, technology is in large part independent of science. (Ferrari, the automobile-maker, knew nothing about mathematics.) Finally, it is true that Greek engineers invented a kind of theodolith, which they used only for astronomical and never for geodesic purposes. This, however, was not because they were enamored of pure contemplation but because the vernier was not invented until the sixteenth century. Without a vernier a theodolith is precise only to within a half a degree (approximately the angle subtended by the moon in the sky), which is far too rough for surveying work. Greek mechanics invented amusing steam-operated automata but never developed the steam engine; the crankshaft and connecting rod were not invented until the Middle Ages, and without a crankshaft it is impossible to transform longitudinal into circular motion.

The ancients, nevertheless, did show great interest in practical and profitable activity. Disdain for the working poor has never prevented their being exploited.

Funerary relief, 2nd and 3rd century. A landowner checks his sharecroppers' accounts in a large account book or polyptych (consisting of five wooden tablets covered with wax). The so-called Saint Augustine's curtain is proof that the man was not easily accessible. (Trier, Landesmuseum.)

# ☙ Patrimony

ALL men, even slaves, are equal in humanity, but those with a patrimony are more equal than others. Patrimony played as central a role in the ancient economy as the firm or corporation plays in the modern economy. But in order to understand it correctly, we must first shed notions more applicable to early modern Europe than to the Roman Empire. In Rome, to engage in business was no derogation of nobility. Usury and commerce were not the exclusive province of a specialized class or order, whether "bourgeoisie," freedmen, or equestrians. Not all nobles and notables were absentee landlords or "lazy aristocrats." Autarchy, that philosophers' myth, was in no way the aim of their management, and they did not limit exploitation of their estates so as to produce just what they needed to maintain their rank. Landowners sought to increase their wealth, to make money in any way they could. The key word is not autarchy or laziness or derogation, but business—noble business, to be sure. In ancient Rome the employer, the business executive, was the paterfamilias, the head of an extended household and master of a patrimony. Patrimony was the basis of all business dealings.

The economy, accordingly, was part of private life, in contrast to today's economy, which is based on publicly owned corporations. Today's economic actors are moral persons: firms or corporations. These moneymaking machines channel wealth into the pockets of individuals. By contrast, in Roman society the economic actors were private individuals, heads of families. In our economy an import-export firm does not change identity simply because some shareholders sell their stock to other individuals. With the Romans, a patrimony did not change its identity simply because its master decided to abandon ocean commerce and invest in land in-

Mosaic of Saint-Roman-en-Gal, 2nd–3rd century. Mosaics illustrating feasts or labors of the months are not unusual. September is apple-picking time; December is for olive-pressing, using a press with a horizontal screw. (Saint-Germain-en-Laye, Museum of National Antiquities.)

stead. It is wrong to conclude that the Roman family head sought only to secure the future of his household rather than to maximize his profit. The difference between the modern economy and the ancient one lies elsewhere.

"Let us behave as heads of family should," Seneca wrote Lucilius, repeating a proverb. "Let us increase what we have inherited. Let the estate that I pass on to my heirs be larger than the one I received." To squander one's patrimony was to wipe out the family dynasty and fall into the realm of the subhuman. Ruined nobles were potential malcontents and conspirators, accomplices of would-be Catilines, while the son of a parvenu or wealthy freedman might enter the equestrian order and dream of seeing his own son a senator. Acquisitive virtues were noble virtues. An upper-class child who was not a ne'er-do-well should choose a career in public service, said Cicero, for then at least he could help to increase the family patrimony. A neglected aspect of Roman education concerns the way in which young Romans learned to manage patrimonial interests. In 221 B.C. the Roman people heard a funeral eulogy for a very great lord named Cecilius Metellus, one of whose merits was to have "amassed a great fortune by honest means." Of course there was no dishonor in being "poor," as most people obviously were; some, like Horace, even made poverty a sign of wisdom.

The trouble is that the word "poor" does not mean the

same thing in Latin and English. For us "poor" establishes an implicit comparison between the majority who are poor and the handful who are rich; the whole of society is included in this comparison. For the Romans, however, the majority did not count, and the word "poor" took its meaning as a relative term within the minority that we would consider rich. The poor were the rich who were not very rich. Horace, who made a virtue of poverty, said he was prepared to see his ambitions come to nought, for his poverty would serve as his life raft. This "life raft" consisted of two estates, one at Tivoli and the other in Sabine, where the master's house covered some 6,000 square feet. Poverty in the Christian and modern sense was inconceivable.

Did the business of amassing wealth, or at least of tending to one's patrimony and affairs, mean forgoing leisure? No. Business activities were not an essential part of a person's identity (T. S. Eliot, to take a modern example, was a poet rather than a bank clerk). Managing a patrimony in land meant supervising the planting of estates, watching over a steward or slave overseer, and selling what the estate produced at the best possible price. Money had to be lent out at interest and never allowed to lie idle. All of these activities were implicit in the rights of ownership; indeed they constituted the exercise of those rights. Other ways of "amassing a great fortune," some honest, some not, involved the exercise or abuse of civil rights and civic honors: one could marry a dowry, seek out legacies and bequests, extort money by abuse of office, and pillage the public treasury.

*An Unclassable Class*

Only common folk worked for a living. People of quality managed, that is, they engaged in the activity referred to as *cura* or *epimeleia*, which one might translate as "government," in the sense in which Olivier de Serres spoke of the "domestic government" of an estate. This was the only activity worthy of a free man, for it involved the exercise of authority. A family head's management of his patrimony, a public mission assigned to an individual, and even the government of the Empire were all instances of exercising authority, at least for those philosophers who liked to think of the emperor as a patriarchal sovereign. It hardly mattered that Scipio Africanus, in governing his estates, guided the plow with his own hand, like some latter-day Cincinnatus; he was nevertheless the master. As long as a man was master, it was a virtue to be "hard-

Bronze scale, checked by the authorities in A.D. 47. The pan that hung from the chains has disappeared. (Paris, Petit Palais, Dutuit Collection.)

working," energetic. The adjective referred to a moral quality, not an identity. When Virgil writes that with hard work one can accomplish anything, he is not stating Holy Writ but simply pointing out that with zealous application one can overcome any obstacle. Not to be lazy was a virtue, born of necessity. As Plutarch said, the man who never bestirred himself, who neglected his friends, his glory, and public affairs, lived like an oyster. A high official was an energetic man who from morning till night minutely examined the accounts of the treasury, line by line. "Don't gather rust" was a maxim of Cato, that truly great man.

It is clearly impossible to give a medieval or modern equivalent for the class that I have been calling, for want of a better term, the notables: nobles plus "middle class" or "gentry." These were men as proud as the nobles of prerevolutionary France, as universal in outlook and assiduous in business as the modern bourgeoisie, as dependent on the land for their income as the European aristocracy in general, and, though hard-working, convinced that they constituted a leisure class. And that is not all. In the Roman world we do not find the (to us) familiar connection between social class and economic activity. There was no Roman bourgeoisie, because the class that owned the land also engaged, without making a fuss about it, in more "bourgeois" activities. When we look for a class of traders, manufacturers, speculators, usurers, and tax farmers in Rome, we find it everywhere: freedmen, equestrians, municipal notables, and senators all took part in these activities. What determined whether Cato the Elder invested in maritime commerce, or whether a family of prominent municipal notables engaged in trade extending all the way to the Danube, was not social class but individual character and geographical location; there were considerable differences from person to person and region to region. As a matter of fact, Cato "invested his capital in solid and sure ventures. He bought lakes stocked with fish, thermal springs, land for fulling mills, starch factories, grazing land, and forests. He made maritime loans, the most reviled of all forms of usury. To that end he set up a company of fifty individuals and took a share of the capital through his freedman Quintio." Local traditions were also important. One city lived shut off from the outside world and was really no more than a peasant town of the kind that one sees today in southern Italy or Hungary. Not fifteen miles away, however, was the city of Aquileia, an ancient Venice or Genoa. Its notables were maritime traders who did business with the four corners of the world.

Left: Weighing balls of yarn with a similar type of scale. (Trier, Landesmuseum.)

Right: Shop interior, with wholesale trade indicated. In upper left corner is a scale, suspended at an oblique angle. (Rome, Museum of the Conservators.)

Rural scene, 3rd or 4th century. The hooded jacket was commonly worn. This is a simple and accurate image of rural labor. (Trier, Landesmuseum.)

Land ownership, individual investment, and family enterprises tell only part of the story. Keen for profit, Romans were quick to seize on business opportunities, particularly the wealthy, who were joined by some rather shady speculators. If a noble Roman learned from friends about a chance to make a killing, he was quick to act, even if he had no experience in that particular line of business and had to improvise as he went along. A piece of confidential information was too good a stroke of fortune to pass up; one could always put a freedman in charge of the business. The absence of an open market multiplied opportunities of this kind, as did the difficulty of obtaining information and the importance of political backing. The ruling and owning class connived with speculators who enjoyed access to information and influence over policy; these outweighed the laws of the market. The patrimonial economy was not exactly patriarchal, nor was it liberal.

The nature of Roman economic activity varied with the individual, the time, and the place. How do we know what a Roman fortune involved? Just because Juvenal speaks satirically of an ox driver and the young Virgil makes fun of mule drivers, it does not follow that the ox driver drove his own oxen or that the mule driver led his own mules. Reading on, we discover that the one headed a company that ran mule teams over the muddy roads of the Po Valley, while the other owned huge herds of livestock. Similarly, the Baron de Charlus [in Proust's *Remembrance of Things Past*] speaks contemptuously of Mrs. Singer [of the Singer Sewing Machine fortune] as though she were a woman who worked all day at a sewing machine. If the ox driver in question had owned only one or two oxen, the texts would never have mentioned him, at least not as an object of mockery.

## Entrepreneurs

Suppose we have a text that refers to a Roman by name without indicating the man's occupation. How might we determine the nature and origin of his wealth? Since the patrimonial economy was not fully professionalized, this wealth could have come from many sources. A paterfamilias received part of his income from the earnings of certain of his freedmen and slaves, to whom he granted a measure of financial autonomy and legal rights, allowing them to do business as free men but for the master's benefit. This business "staff" worked to increase the master's fortune. They were the real businessmen of the Roman Empire, along with the steward, another

Sarcophagus, 2nd–3rd century. A moneychanger. (Rome, Palazzo Salviati.)

hero worthy of Balzac. More often a slave than a free man, the steward ran his master's estate and sold its produce, in some cases managing all of the master's affairs. The Roman economy rested on its stewards.

Many stewards were born free but sold themselves into slavery in order to further their careers. Masters trusted them. Accounting was not yet what it has become in our day. Stewards did not open books for inspection regularly; masters let their accounts run for years. The steward was expected to keep an accurate record of income and expenditures and to be ready to give an accounting whenever necessary—when the master died, perhaps, or the slave retired, or the estate was sold, or simply when the master was angry. Woe unto the steward who could not then come up with a sum of cash representing the difference between the total income and the total expenditures! The steward whose books balanced (*pariari*) earned the appellation *pariator,* an honor he might mention in his epitaph. Landlords also allowed their farmers to maintain open accounts for years on end. If the landlord died or sold his property, the amount of rent due (*reliqua colonorum*) was then calculated. Farmers were not systematically held in debt; it was just that accounts were not settled periodically. Such methods surely encouraged the idea that debt established a bond as between patron and client and that the debtor who sought to pay what he owed was a disloyal client who wished to renounce his benefactor.

Notables were ubiquitous throughout the economy. Some headed rural and commercial enterprises (not hesitating to transform, if need be, their private residences into shops for displaying their wares). As landlords, they sometimes acted as silent partners in businesses run by their stewards. Notables took shares in commercial companies and tax farms. The humbler of them occasionally did work themselves. Among Galen's patients was a man who cared little about the finer things and ran about town constantly on business: "He bought, sold, and often got into disputes, so that he perspired more than he should."

---

*Noble Enterprise*

The social and institutional character of the Roman economy was so different from that of our own that it is tempting to call it archaic. It sustained, nevertheless, a high level of production and was as dynamic and ruthless as capitalism. For, if Roman aristocrats distinguished themselves by their culture and their interest in philosophy, they were still avid for profit. The greatest nobles talked business. Pliny, a senator, in letters intended to be specimens of the finest in the genre, held up his behavior as a wealthy landlord as an example for others to follow. When a noble wished to get rid of old furniture or building materials, he held a public auction. (Auctions were the normal way for private individuals to sell their used belongings; the emperors themselves auctioned off unwanted palace furniture.) Money was not supposed to lie idle. Even loans to friends and relatives earned interest (not charging interest on such loans was considered a mark of special virtue). A woman's father had to pay interest to her husband

Christian sarcophagus. Possibly a scribe writing on parchment (with a tanned skin suspended overhead). The arch is somewhat flattened by license of the sculptor; no such arch was built before the Middle Ages. (Milan, Palace of the Sforza.)

if transfer of her dowry was delayed. Usury was a part of daily life; modern anti-Semites might have made ancient Rome the object of their obsession instead of the Jews. In Rome commerce and money-lending were not left exclusively to professionals or to any one class of society. Any toil, no matter how pleasurable, merited payment. One picturesque aspect of amorous customs among the Romans was that the female partner in a high-society affair was paid for her trouble. A matron who deceived her husband received a large sum or, in some cases, an annual income from her lover. Some cads reclaimed these gifts when affairs were broken off, and on occasion the courts became involved. The practice of accepting gifts from lovers was considered not prostitution but work for hire. The woman did not give herself because she was paid, the jurists held; she was rewarded for giving herself of her own free will. She who loved best was most handsomely paid. Women sought the wages of adultery as eagerly as men sought dowries.

This universal busyness effaced not only the boundaries between social classes (or civic "orders") but also the distinctions between economic categories. Men engaged in occasional business ventures in addition to their regular activities; they were speculators as well as professionals (whether they called themselves that or not). Men amassed wealth by the old-fashioned means of gaining control of established fortunes as well as by the modern means of creating wealth through investment. They made money by producing and selling goods as well as by extraeconomic means, some legal, some not: inheritances, dowries, bribes, violence, legal chicanery. They counted on the law of supply and demand as well as on political influence and contacts with other "men of the world." Apart from their involvement in business, notables were the major landowners. Ancient society therefore consisted of an immense and impoverished peasantry and a wealthy urban class engaged in a variety of business activities. It is this variety that makes the ancient world shine so brilliantly for us. Since medicine was a costly business in those days, Galen's clients were all notables, and males to boot. They lived in the cities, supervised the work of their stewards, sweated in business, practiced a profession (like Galen himself), helped run their cities, and at home read or copied out the philosophical works of their favorite sect. In old age they retired to their estates.

Ostia, 2nd–3rd century. A ship enters Rome's primary port, sailing in front of the lighthouse, where a flame is visible. Statues of gods are everywhere. The large eye on the right, a good-luck charm having no relation to the picture, countered the evil eye of the envious, who would have liked to cast a spell on the hero of this relief. The naked figure holding a horn of plenty who seems to be offering a wreath to the ship is Bonus Eventus, god of happy endings. (Rome, Torlonia Collection.)

When they died, their estates were held to consist of three principal parts: cultivated land (with its farming equipment), buildings (with their furniture), and notes of credit (*nomina debitorum*). Bank accounts, known to have existed during the Republic and early Empire, are not attested in the late Empire.

The usurers of the time were not bankers but notables and senators. Every family head kept a strongbox, or *kalendarium,* which contained a calendar of due dates on loans along with notes of hand and cash awaiting borrowers. The Roman expression for "setting aside money for loans" was "put it in the *kalendarium*." Every man had his own strategy when it came to money-lending: some lent only a small fraction of their wealth, others a much larger proportion; some lent small sums to many borrowers, others large sums to a few borrowers. Notes passed easily from creditor to creditor, either by formal dation or, more simply, by outright sale. They served as a means of liquefying debt and as an object of speculation: an expandable supply of currency. A man could bequeath his *kalendarium* and, with it, claims on his debtors and capital intended for usury to one of his heirs.

---

Usury was considered a noble means of acquiring wealth, the same as farming, dowries, and legacies. Among the Romans it was as common to court a wealthy old man in the hope of being remembered in his will as it is to flatter the boss today. Although such behavior was universally derided, everyone did it. It was customary for a testator to honor his friends and reward faithful clients with a bequest. Because of this custom wealthy men were surrounded by attentive courtiers; these became the sign that a man was of some importance.

A man or woman gained, Tacitus said, by not having children, for then he or she met with even greater consideration from others. Demographic research tells us that in pre-revolutionary France an average family had four or five children, only two of whom lived to the age of twenty. The average Roman family had only three children. This suggests that not a few Romans outlived their children. Thus, quite a few inheritances must have been ripe for the taking, especially since under Roman law and custom testators enjoyed great freedom. With each new generation a considerable fraction of the national wealth was up for grabs. Who got what? Virtuosos when it came to chicanery, Romans knew what they were

*Other Ways of Acquiring Wealth*

about. One divorced woman named her son as heir but, knowing that her ex-husband was of dubious reputation, stipulated that the son could receive his inheritance only if, when her will was opened, he was no longer under his father's power (for in that case the estate would have passed to the father). In other words, the son would inherit only if his father were dead. As it happened, the father was still living when the will was opened, but he hit upon a stratagem: he emancipated his son, who then inherited from his mother. Was the father a better man than his reputation suggested? The story is not yet over. The man set about courting his own son with gifts of toys and pets. In other words, he went fortune-hunting with his own son's inheritance as quarry, and he got what he wanted: the spoiled child died and left his estate to his father.

Public opinion did not condemn fortune-hunting, but some ways of going about it were considered more praiseworthy than others. "So-and-so, a man who in life had been surrounded by fortune hunters, died and left everything to his daughter and grandsons. Judgments varied: some called him a hypocrite and ingrate who neglected his friends, while others were delighted that this old man had frustrated the hopes of the self-seekers." Spoken by a senator, these words have the ring of truth.

Gismondi model of 2nd-century houses in Ostia. Even in Rome, not all apartment buildings were four or five stories tall. In Ostia apartment buildings were two to four stories, with shops at the street level and a mezzanine.

There were more ruthless ways of acquiring wealth. The Roman Empire had no real police force. Some imperial soldiers (such as the centurion Cornelius mentioned in the Bible) put down riots and tracked thieves, but they showed little concern about routine insecurity, which posed less of a threat to the image of sovereign authority that the Roman authorities wished to maintain. Daily life in the Roman Empire resembled daily life in the wild and wooly American West: no police in the streets, no deputies in the countryside, no public prosecutor. Every man had to defend himself and mete out his own justice, and the only practical solution for the powerless and the not-so-powerful was to place themselves under the protection of a strong patron. But who would protect these clients from their patrons, and these patrons from one another? Sequestrations, usurpations, and private prisons for debtors were commonplace. Cities lived in fear of local and regional tyrants, sometimes well enough ensconced to defy even so powerful a personage as the provincial governor. A powerful man did not hesitate to seize the property of one of his poorer neighbors, or even, riding at the head of an army of henchmen and slaves, to attack the "ranch" of another potentate. What could be done against such depredations? The chance of obtaining justice depended on the good will of a busy provincial governor, who for reasons of state was obliged to go easy on powerful landlords and who in any case would have been tied to them by bonds of friendship and common interest. His justice, if he chose to mete it out, would have been an episode in interfamilial warfare, an attempt to shift the balance of power among rival clans.

In addition to ordinary violence there was judicial violence. The Romans are reputed to have been the inventors of law. True, they wrote many remarkable lawbooks and took glory and pleasure from knowing and using the arcana of civil law. Law was a matter of culture, a sport, and a subject of national pride. It does not follow, however, that law actually governed daily life in Rome. Legalism merely introduced into the chaos of Roman affairs an additional complication, not to say a weapon: chicanery. In Greek regions of the Empire judicial blackmail and paralegal extortion went by the ancient name, "sycophancy" (from the Greek for "false accuser").

Suppose that a noble covets the estates of another noble who happens to be out of favor with the imperial family. The first man might then accuse the second of lese majesty. As accuser, he stood to receive a portion of the accused's estate if

Villas at the water's edge. Painting from the house of Lucretius Fronto in Pompeii. Architecture in a virgin landscape, and close to reality.

the latter were put to death. Or suppose that, far from Rome, a notable who had placed his hopes in a rich man's will was disappointed. He might claim that the man had not died of natural causes but had committed suicide or that he had been poisoned and that his heirs had failed to prosecute the murderer and avenge the death of their benefactor. The will might then be set aside and the estate confiscated by the imperial treasury, with a bonus paid to the informer. The imperial treasury was not so much a tax collection authority as it was a repository for estates confiscated by the emperor for want of an heir or because of some irregularity. The treasury had its own court, in which it sat as both judge and party. By this means the emperor soon became the greatest landowner in the

Empire. The treasury was therefore quite ready to believe denunciations by informers who provided opportunities to seize still more estates. This was common knowledge, so some testators, bent on frustrating their heirs, named the emperor as colegatee. The treasury then saw to it that the emperor received the entire estate. In short, the law served as a weapon in the struggle over patrimonies. No one could feel secure in the peaceful possession and transmission of his property. One newly wed fellow was even robbed of his wife's dowry: jealous relatives accused him of using black magic to seduce the woman.

The more industrious ways of getting rich suggest that the Empire was a chaotic place where anything was possible. One could obtain a government concession to exploit some resource, usually with monopoly rights, or take advantage of a disorganized economy by establishing, say, a needed transport service that nobody had yet undertaken to provide, some for want of capital, others for want of initiative. More than one Third World economy offers a similar spectacle today. In these circumstances, it is not surprising that many a notable found himself in charge of a host of unrelated businesses and other activities with which he had become associated simply because the opportunity was too good to pass up. One man might easily be involved in real estate, fabrics, dyeing, shipping on the Rhine and the Aegean, and farming, in addition to teaching rhetoric for a fee and importing merchandise from Egypt and Athens. It would be a mistake to think of an august Roman personage as resembling a simple country squire, living tranquilly amid fields and meadows. He led a more colorful life, more like that of a modern South American dignitary. In a society in which the contrast between rich and poor was stark, he carried himself like a noble, with nothing of the tradesman in his bearing.

---

*Land*

All of this varied business activity derived from ownership of land. A man's property might be scattered over many provinces, an estate here, a farm in some remote corner of the world. Every parcel, however, was recorded in the accounts (*rationes, libellus*) of the head of the family, which reflected the organization of the patrimony. Were the baths part of his household or a separate business? We need only consult the accounts, where the rent for the baths is recorded in a separate account, distinct from the household accounts per se. Were

Painting from Ostia. The name of the ship is *Isis of Geminus;* its captain and pilot is Pharnaces. This is a single-masted commercial boat called a *corbita.* The picture is a simplified representation of an ocean vessel, not a realistic image of a river boat (*caudicaria*). The passengers on board prayed to the goddess Isis for a good crossing. (Rome, Vatican Library.)

taxes paid by the landlord or his sharecroppers? What was the "law" or "custom" established by the landlord? The account books contain the answers. They also tell us whether tenants were farmers who sold their produce themselves or sharecroppers who paid the landlord in kind, leaving him to sell the crop personally or assign the job to his steward.

Landed property meant more than just agricultural estates. Buildings could be rented out in their entirety or divided into apartments. The land supported businesses of every kind. Notables may have owned not only the cultivated land but also the second great source of wealth: urban dwellings. On their property they constructed port facilities, taverns, brothels, and storehouses (that is, docks that were rented out for the storage of cargo and of precious objects and documents to be protected against damage by fire). They schemed to obtain that "princely boon," the right to hold a market on their property and collect a tax on all transactions. They exploited mines and quarries in conjunction with farming and industrial activities, such as brickmaking and the manufacture of pottery, which were done on the estate either under the landlord's control or by a concessionaire. Agricultural laborers were shifted to these activities during the off season. A contract recently discovered in Egypt tells of a potter who agreed to work for a period of two years for a landlord who had ovens on his estates. The potter was supposed to produce 15,000 jars per year, but the landlord was to provide the clay (it was customary to provide masons and artisans with needed materials).

We must be careful lest this diversity mislead us. Agriculture was still the primary form of production on which all other business depended. Crop yields were too low to allow land to be what it has become today in the developed countries: a resource so abundant that only a fraction of the population is employed on it. Today overproduction is a greater danger than famine. In antiquity agriculture yielded too little to permit much development of industry. The vast majority of the population had to work the soil to ensure their own survival and sustain the few noncultivators. This fact, as we shall see, greatly influenced the private strategies of the wealthy.

Each man who cultivated the land with his own hands fed no more than two or three others: his own family and the notable who owned the land. Yields were too low to sustain masses of industrial workers, though high enough to enable the wealthy to transform the surplus into monumental splendor, typical of class societies prior to the industrial revolution. Yet this feat depended on the ability to sell what the soil produced, that is, on a lively commerce. Wheat had to be exchanged for columns and statues. If the Roman world had been, as some have imagined, an empire without trade in foodstuffs, tourists and archaeologists would have far fewer ruins to explore. Agriculture and commerce were not antithetical but identical.

Land was at once a repository of wealth, a means of survival, and a source of trade goods. One ploy of the wealthy was speculation in essential commodities. Storehouses were filled with grain awaiting a bad harvest and higher prices: "They refuse to sell the products of the soil at their just price," wrote the jurist Ulpianus, "and, since they wait for the famine years, they are driving up the price." Regional specialization was also practiced. Archaeologists are convinced that certain regions of the Roman world (such as the Tunisian Sahel, then well-irrigated and fertile) produced, exclusively for export, one of the three principal riches of Mediterranean agriculture: wheat, wine, or oil. When the market was depressed or trade was interrupted, the patrimony survived; estates could fall back on a subsistence economy. Landlords were careful not to plant all their land in wheat or grapes, for these were speculative and costly crops. Part of every estate was left forested, for forests cost nothing to keep up and served as a kind of savings bank. One proverb described a fool who does everything backward by saying that he was "like a man in debt who sells his woods instead of his vineyards." The important thing was to own land, which would always maintain its value. It was not necessary to grow crops. Was there any need to waste time overseeing slaves, agricultural laborers, and sharecroppers, amusing as this activity may have been? Cato, according to Plutarch, came to "see farming as a diversion, as much as, if not more than, a source of income." Caring little for amusement, he preferred productive but uncultivated real estate, which did exist: "fish-stocked ponds, thermal springs, fulling mills, natural grazing land, forests." From these he "drew an income that was not subject to the hazards of the weather."

---

No matter how the patrimonial enterprise was organized, the important thing was to run it as a "good father" should.

*Investment*

This expression, less patriarchal than it may seem, survives in modern commercial law, where it is used to describe the sound management of publicly owned corporations. The paterfamilias was supposed to be "honest and diligent," according to Roman jurists, and Cicero and Seneca held that it was a merit for a man to increase his patrimony. The Romans devoted some thought to what they meant by "diligence" in this context: a paterfamilias worthy of the name could not rest on his laurels and merely pass on to his heirs an undiminished patrimony. He was advised to invest wisely, weighing the possible gains against the costs of investment.

In the final book of the *Digest* the jurist Paulus distinguishes among "necessary expenditures, which prevent a good from perishing or losing its values," expenditures on amenities such as gardens, paintings, and marble decorations, and "useful" expenditures (what we would call investments), which "might not have been made without causing the property to lose its value but which improve it by producing more income," such as "planting more vines than necessary to maintain a vineyard in good condition" or adding docks, a mill, or a bread oven to a property, or, again, "putting slaves out to apprentice." Paulus points out that the cost of these investments should not ultimately reduce the net income of an estate. For jurists, who frequently had to resolve questions of this kind, the problem was to determine who had the right to decide on an investment, and when. Justice required that such an important decision be taken by no one but the legal owner of the property. A guardian's only duty was to deliver to his ward an undiminished estate, but the duty of a paterfamilias was different, namely, to increase the size of the family patrimony.

A guardian was not supposed to show zeal. It was not his place to make investments whose risks would be borne by his ward; nor was he to offer generous gifts in his ward's name, even to enhance the child's reputation. The guardian's primary duty was to sell perishable goods (furnished houses, which could catch fire, and slaves, who might die) and invest the proceeds in sure properties: real estate and gold to be lent out at interest. (Hoarding was to be avoided at all cost, and for a guardian to ignore this dictum suggested, as for the servant of the Gospel, a lack of diligence.) Such a do-nothing attitude was to be avoided by the paterfamilias, however. Nothing could be further from the truth than to imagine that the paterfamilias simply served as guardian of the family for-

tune, which actually belonged to his posterity, or that he was merely the temporary beneficiary, the "usufructuary," of a property over which the family dynasty as a whole enjoyed eminent domain.

Under Roman law, moreover, the "beneficial occupant" of a property was entitled to make investments, to "improve" the property, as though he were the family head. The husband who administered his wife's dotal property enjoyed the same right. In Book XXIII of the *Digest* the jurist Javolenus tells of a man who had established marble quarries on his wife's dotal estates. He divorced and, as was customary, the woman reclaimed her dowry. Should she not be obliged to reimburse her ex-husband for the costs incurred in establishing the quarries, which increased the value of her property? Jurists of the old school answered no, because the expenditure was not "necessary," and, far from "improving" the estate, the husband had pillaged it of its underground supply of marble. But to this argument Javolenus retorts that merely "useful" expenditures are permissible, even on dotal property. He adds one proviso: that the quarry be one in which the supply of marble is not exhausted but "continues to grow." In that case the wife

A press for oil or wine, this time with a vertical shaft. The capstan was obviously known; the crank was not invented until the Middle Ages. (Aquileia, Archaeological Museum.)

would not have lost anything, since the husband did nothing but harvest the quarry's fruits. (The notion that marble and gold grow like plants is common to many peoples; it forms the basis of Roman law on mines and quarries.)

Reading between the lines, we can interpret what the usufructuary was allowed to do as a clue to what every good paterfamilias was required to do if he wished to be considered a good administrator of his estates. Unlike the paterfamilias, the usufructuary was certainly not allowed to alter the use to which an estate, or part of an estate, was put. He could not replace ornamental gardens with productive plantations, for example. This restriction aside, he was allowed, as Ulpianus observes in Book VII, "to improve the situation of the property," by establishing stone, sand, or chalk quarries (chalk was used to starch clothing and give it luster), or by extracting gold, silver, sulfur, and iron from mines "that the paterfamilias had dug or might have dug." Certain conditions had to be met, however. The mines had to bring in more than the vineyards or olive trees they replaced. The underground resources must not be depleted during the period of beneficial occupancy. Finally, the new investment must not be so costly as to ruin the estate, and overall income, allowing for the cost of additional labor, must not be diminished.

## The Business Mentality

These revealing texts show that the contrast often drawn between capitalist rationality, which allegedly seeks to maximize profits, and "patrimonial rationality," which allegedly aims simply to transmit wealth undiminished from generation to generation, is beside the point. The Romans sought to increase their patrimony wherever possible and put themselves ahead of their posterity. To say that a capitalist firm has no strategy other than to maximize profits is like saying that politics is the art of acquiring new territory. In reality, the policies of a modern corporation are as complex as those of a modern state and as variable from one company to another as the foreign policy of Sweden is different from the foreign policy of a great empire. Just about as worthless is the academic claim that the Romans were a nation of peasants. Roman notables were entrepreneurs who aimed to get rich. They did not amass acres as misers amass gold. They invested, took risks, and speculated. Their penchant for profit was an ethnic feature that distinguished them from many other nations. Nations with similar economic structures and class interests may still exhibit quite different drives, just as some ethnic groups are more hard-working, more artistic, or more bellicose than others. The facts are the facts; such different "mentalities" cannot be manufactured or produced at will. Economists who have tried to develop certain Third World economies have learned to their sorrow that knowledge of econometrics is not enough, and that simply creating economic opportunities cannot ensure that people will actually avail themselves of those opportunities. Attitudes cannot be shaped at will. Roman economic attitudes were very aggressive. To know what a Roman paterfamilias was really like we should look not at economic structures or obvious class interests but at attitudes, the real independent variable in this equation. A wealthy Roman had the soul of a businessman and knew a great deal about making money. Obviously this had positive consequences for the level of production. As for the distribution of wealth, that is another question.

To conclude, let me say simply that this Roman talent for business was strengthened by a rather surprising circumstance. Like the Jews, the Greeks, and the Chinese, the Romans were not just farmers, generals, and soldiers, but also the people of a *diaspora*. In the last two centuries before Christ and even earlier they fanned out through the Greek Orient, into Africa, and out to the very limits of the civilized world as traders and bankers as well as planters. Taking advantage of their political influence, they seized the good land of Africa and central Turkey and soaked up the profits of Greek commerce. The city of Rome sheltered numerous Greek intellectuals of whom their Roman counterparts were jealous, while Mytilene and Smyrna were full of Italian businessmen, whom the Greeks had excellent reasons to hate.

Death scene, ca. A.D. 100. Weeping women beat their breasts. The torches were kept burning even during the day. At the feet of the deceased are three tablets containing his will. Seated, at right, slaves freed by the dead man's will wear the Phrygian cap as a sign of freedom. (Rome, Vatican Museums.)

# ✍ Public Opinion and Utopia

THERE we have it—a composite portrait of the ideal Roman: a male, free and born that way, wealthy but not newly wealthy, well-bred, even cultivated, a businessman, proud of having held political office, and yet fundamentally a man of leisure. Like the various details of his fine clothing, each of our specimen individual's features is a legacy of the Greek and Roman past. There was no need to coerce people to accept this ideal; it was taken for granted.

Funerary art, less concerned with the hereafter than with what a man had been on earth, cast this imposing image in terms comprehensible to all. Depending on the whim of the stonecutter and the preference of the buyer, tombs emphasized varied aspects of men's lives. Opulence was represented by showing the deceased poring over his accounts or accepting the homage of his farmers or tending his shop or cutting wheat with that recent marvel of human ingenuity, the mechanical reaper. On a woman's tomb luxury might be symbolized by picturing the noble lady seated in a high-backed chair or in front of a mirror held by one slave while selecting jewels from a casket held by another. Images were often little more than emblems: an umbrella sculpted on the side of a tombstone told passersby that the woman buried there had had a slave to hold her umbrella and the leisure to go strolling. Or a woman making her toilette might raise her hand in homage to a statue of Venus, symbol of marriage, presented to her by a maid, who had taken it from the household repository of pious images (*lararium*). Senators' sarcophagi juxtaposed images of private and public life. In the center of one, we might see the late senator taking his wife's hand. On the sides, in a general's armor, he could be shown seated on a dignitary's low folding chair, accepting the surrender of barbarian chieftains he had

Detail of sarcophagus, 2nd century(?). The woman honors the religious statue of Venus with a gesture of her hand. This sculpture comes close to the reality of Roman religion. (Arezzo Museum.)

Physician, seated, examines his patient, a naked child who stands before him, 2nd–3rd century. In the background are the doctor's two assistants or pupils. Though slaves, they will succeed him if he emancipates them. (Rome, Vatican Museums.)

vanquished (or might have vanquished, given his high office). Other tombal reliefs depict money being distributed to his fellow citizens at his behest or a gladiator fight paid for by the late dignitary. The dead man's rank is suggested by the number of fasces carried by the lictors, those apparitors and executioners who preceded him everywhere during his year of public life. Rome had no penal law, so every important dignitary had the right to use force as he saw fit.

Every person had his or her role. On the left face (the most honorable) of the tombstone the husband is shown practicing his profession: he examines his patient, who stands naked and at attention before the physician. On the right face, the wife exhibits the feminine virtue of piety: followed by slaves, she goes to raise her hand before the image of some god in gratitude for a favor granted; a slave holds up a sign on which her mistress has had a description of this favor inscribed. In other words, some tombs commemorated not the opulence, leisure, rank, or profession of the deceased but finer aspects of character such as piety (for women) or cultivation (for men). A woman burns a few grains of incense in homage to a god, say, or a man seated in his armchair reads a book (a scroll) or holds a rolled scroll in his hand as proof that he has completed the studies that capped preparations for entry into good society.

Little about these images was egalitarian or individualistic. Originality, pride, cheerfulness, grace, and lightness of touch are not conspicuous among Roman traits. Their funerary art underscores this in a ponderous way. Roman society was unequal in fact and inegalitarian in its distinction of "orders" (akin to the "three estates" convoked by Louis XVI just prior to the French Revolution). People were constantly and visibly reminded of the differences between individuals. One showed laudable "frankness" (*parrhesia*) by speaking insultingly to people of the lower orders. The "friends" of great personages were categorized into distinct, and unequal, groups. (This was true even of the "friends" of the Gracchi, two celebrated social reformers of the old Republic.) No great man ever went out without a cortege. When he visited a town that had named him its "patron" because of some public benefaction, he made a formal public entry. "Yesterday I had to dinner people of higher rank than you," Trimalchio proclaims to his guests. He can be faulted only because, coming from a vulgar freedman like himself, his words are an outrage; he has invited above his station. Simple folk were especially susceptible to the "simplicity" that a few of the powerful had the knack of affecting. "That most respectable dignitary returned our greeting," said one. Commoners were expected to address their betters with humility. Every gesture contributed to what Ramsay MacMullen has called the "explicit expression of status."

---

*The Individualism of the Law*

These obvious signs of status were confirmed by no less explicit moral ideas, which now reinforced, now mitigated, status differences. People might, for example, praise their governor for his "mildness." Everyone was judged by his scrupulousness in performing public and private duties. "The tyranny of opinion—and what opinion!—is as beastly in the small towns of France as in the United States," wrote the individualist Stendhal, who had in mind the puritanical America of his day. Pagan civism was perhaps no less harsh in its judgment of private behavior than the small-town puritanism reviled by Stendhal.

Rome, reputed to be the mother of law, is supposed to have been a government of laws, a state where no one could be obliged to do what was not prescribed by law and where public justice supplanted arbitrary private justice. Roman law can fairly be called individualistic. Both sexes enjoyed the same freedom to divorce, property could be freely alienated, and testators enjoyed a large measure of freedom. No religious belief was enforced; each city had its preferred gods, and each individual had his or hers. The secular arm left it to the gods themselves to avenge any insults—if they could—and the only respect the citizens of a city were required to show its gods was to observe their holidays by not working. The right to change place of residence or line of work was uncontested. An easygoing indulgence of sexual sins, even when committed by women, was erected into doctrine by the Senate itself. Yet, as Bleicken has remarked, this liberalism was a "tacit consequence of an aristocratic idea of private life," and Rome, like Greece, never incorporated formal guarantees of freedom into its law. The law in fact was regarded as a mere codification of the duties imposed by family piety, loyalty, wealth, and status.

"Private" (the antonym of "public") was a common Latin adjective, but its meaning was negative: it characterized those things that an individual might do without failing of the duties required of a man holding public office. There was no rec-

Physician's wife carrying a basket of flowers to a god. The slave, carrying a sign, raises his hand to his forehead in a salute to the god.

Silver coin from time of
Domitian. Diameter: 19 mm.
With this coin one could enjoy
an entire day of modest luxury.
Gold coins were used for major
purchases and international
trade.

ognized sanctuary in private law; there were boundaries which
the law did not transgress, but it was under no obligation not
to transgress them. Am I making a mountain out of a historical
molehill? No doubt, but the fact remains that the absence of
guarantees left the door open to all kinds of dangers. Like
storms, these dangers descended briefly on Rome, the blood-
iest episodes being the persecution of the Christians and
Manichaeans.

In addition, certain emperors attempted to enforce their
own notions of moral order. Roman sovereigns, unlike their
Chinese and Japanese counterparts, did not have what Maurice
Pinguet has called "the old Confucian habit of measuring
power by moral order." Some, such as Augustus, Domitian,
the Severi, and Constantine, did try to correct morals by
decree. Augustus instituted severe measures against adultery
by women (severe in appearance, at any rate). Domitian compelled men to marry their mistresses, had buried alive one
vestal virgin who violated her vow of chastity, and forbade
satirical poets to use obscene language. The Severi made adultery by the husband a crime and abortion an offense against
both husband and fatherland. Constantine's legislation swept
away a lax aristocratic ethic and substituted strict moral laws,

Sarcophagus, 2nd century. The three virtues of a nobleman. Left: Clemency. As a general, he conquers and pardons barbarians (behind him are the Fatherland and, with bare leg and breast, Courage). Center: Piety. He sacrifices an ox. Right: Concord between man and wife (dressed as a bride), in the presence of Venus and Cupid (with torch). A Grace, with bared shoulder, touches the bride's hand. (Mantua, Ducal Palace.)

more popular than truly Christian in origin. This moralism was quite unusual. Greek and Roman lawgivers could attempt to revolutionize society by decree. Imprudent, they were not always careful to avoid lagging too far behind or moving too far ahead of actual mores. The ancients did not regard the city as a product of natural social forces, but rather held that it was an institution created by law, which could decay if not protected by the lawgiver against its natural enemies. The citizen, they believed, is a reprobate in need of discipline. Thus, the main purpose of moral reform was to prove that the reigning emperor was indeed a master, who, not content to establish public order, which private vice scarcely threatened, sought also to regulate the moral conscience of each individual. Once this idea had been driven home, the revolutionary new laws ceased to be enforced and were forgotten under the next emperor. Only the code of Constantine endured, leaving its mark upon the Middle Ages.

These brief tempests may be safely forgotten. In normal times civil law accurately reflected Roman mores. Law and morality were linked by an umbilical cord that was never

*Did Roman Law Exist?*

Bronze coin with head of
Severus. Diameter: 28 mm.
With this coin a slave could
buy his daily bread and
escape death by starvation.

Reverse of same coin: each of
the three figures (gold, silver,
bronze) holds a horn of plenty
and a pair of scales.

really cut. Although technically complex, Roman civil law
was more verbal than conceptual, and scarcely deductive. It
afforded professional students plenty of opportunity to demonstrate their virtuosity. Did it enable ordinary people to obtain justice, however? Did it enforce respect for the rules when
people violated them and oppressed their neighbors? In a society as unequal and inegalitarian as the Roman, it is obvious
that formal rights, however clear, had no reality, and that a
weak man had little to gain by going to court against powerful
enemies. But even when the law was not simply violated, did
it provide means of enforcing people's rights? One example
will suffice, I think, to show that the public authorities did
not so much supplant private vendettas as organize them.

Suppose I lend money to someone who decides not to
pay me back. Or, better still, suppose that all I own in the
world is a small farm, to which I am attached because my
ancestors lived there and the country is pleasant. A powerful
neighbor covets my property. Leading an army of slaves, he
invades my land, kills those of my slaves who try to defend
me, beats me with clubs, drives me from my land, and seizes
my farm. What can I do? A modern citizen might say, go to
court (*litis denuntiatio*) to obtain justice and persuade the authorities to restore my property (*manu militari*). And this was
indeed what would have happened toward the end of antiquity, when provincial governors finally succeeded in imposing
their ideal of public coercion. But in Italy in the first two
centuries A.D. events would have taken a different turn.

For one thing, the aggression against me by my powerful
neighbor would have been considered a strictly civil offense;
it would not have been covered by a penal code. It would
have been up to me, as plaintiff, to see to it that the defendant
appeared in court. In other words, I would have had to snatch
the defendant from the midst of his private army, arrest him,
and hold him in chains in my private prison until the day of
judgment. Had this been beyond my power, the case could
never have been heard (*litis contestatio*). But suppose that I did
manage to bring the defendant into court and, thanks to the
intervention of a powerful man who had taken me on as client,
succeeded in obtaining justice, meaning that the court declared
the law to be on my side. It then would have been up to me
to enforce that judgment, if I could. Was I obliged to recapture
my ancestral farm by myself? No. By an inexplicable twist in
the law, a judge could not sentence a defendant simply to

restore what he had taken. Leaving my farm to its fate, the judge would authorize me to seize my adversary's chattels real and personal and sell them at auction, keeping a sum equal to the value placed on my farm by the court (*aestimatio*) and returning the surplus to my enemy.

Who would have considered recourse to a system of justice so little interested in punishing social transgressions? Most likely two types of people. When powerful, stubborn men quarreled over a piece of land, both parties wished to be judged to have the better case by the many Romans who followed trials in the courts because they found chicanery or legal eloquence to their taste. Such men would have settled their dispute in the courts, as they might have settled it at other times in history in a duel before witnesses. Or a creditor might bring suit against a debtor in default, who was scarcely in a position to put up a fight. The creditor would already have seized the debtor, who might at first have attempted to hide. Ulpian tells of one debtor who stayed away from the public market in order to avoid running into his creditor. When he saw him, he quickly hid behind the columns of the courtyard or one of the many kiosks in the marketplace. Recourse to the law was therefore just one of many possible moves in the social game,

Painting of a dispute before a judge. This is the work of a talented artisan, whose hand captured the movement and tension of the figures. At issue in this lawsuit is a large amphora of oil that has been broken; the two pieces of the amphora can be seen at the orators' feet. (Ostia, Archaeological Museum.)

and some people begged that it never be used against them: *Juris consultis abesto,* "No lawyers in this business!"

Apart from its strategic uses, the law formed part of the substance of the old Roman culture. To have recourse to law, to make learned use of the ins and outs of civil law, was sophisticated behavior. Consider the following example. In

Tomb of the Haterii, ca. A.D. 100. The family tomb, which resembles an overdecorated temple, celebrates its own construction. Above the temple the sculptor has represented another scene, for which he could find no other place. The machine on the left is a marvel of human ingenuity, which the family was proud to display on its tomb. (Rome, Vatican Museums.)

theory, no Roman woman could take a case to court without a male representative (although this rule of law was honored mainly in the breach). A non-Roman inhabitant of the Empire, a Greek or Egyptian woman, say, had even less right to take her case to court. Yet the papyri tell us that many such women went to court anyway. What was the rule? We are obliged to admit that there was none. And we discover, too, that many Roman women chose male representatives even though it was not strictly necessary. Although there was no rule, there were elegant, or perhaps pedantic, ways of going about things.

Obscurely baffling, Roman law was marked by survivals of popular and private justice. Even under the Empire it was not unusual to see justice meted out in the streets. The simplest way to force a debtor to pay up was to surprise him at home and provide him with an "escort" (*convicium*). The man was heaped with ridicule, and mocking songs were sung, with choruses demanding that the debt be paid. The jurists required only that the debtor not be stripped naked and that the words of the songs not be obscene. The sensibilities of the community, called to witness, had to be respected. The debtor, for his part, sought to win the public's pity. He dressed in mourning garb and stopped cutting his hair as a sign of dereliction.

Fear of public opinion played a large role in private life, of which the public considered itself a legitimate judge. In small towns anyone who braved public opinion was hounded and mocked. He was seized, placed in a kind of hearse, and followed by a laughing and crying crowd of "mourners" before being allowed to escape. Even the dead were insulted in this way if their wills did not meet with public approval. Such greetings were also in store for stingy heirs who offended the crowd by not footing the bill for the gladiator fights expected when a notable died. In one Ligurian town the plebs halted the funeral cortege of a former officer in the town square. His family was able to take his body to the pyre only after promising to pay for a memorial spectacle.

View upon leaving Pompeii, just outside the city gates, on the road to Herculanum. The first of a row of tombs, all in the form of altars, is decorated with the image of a ship.

The many, in other words, arrogated to themselves the right to judge the conduct of each individual. Whether notable, plebeian, or senator, no Roman was allowed an intimate life all his own. Anyone could address anyone else and judge anyone else. The least important citizen could address the "public," which after all consisted of other citizens like himself. Any man willing to play the fool, for instance, could play

### The Publicity of the Tomb

A deceased couple depicted as Mars and Venus, after A.D. 120. Since the dead, like gods, were venerable and invisible, funerary art often immortalized them as gods in an act of hyperbole that only archaeologists have taken literally. The husband, who must have been a good senator, was prouder of his military functions than of his civic ones. Just as many a contemporary of Napoleon III contrived to resemble the emperor, this senator resembled his emperor, Hadrian. His wife refused to play Venus in the nude; other women were bolder. (Paris, Louvre.)

to the gallery. Nowadays of course we have subway graffiti, a forum anybody can use to tell everyone else what's on his mind or whom he loves or simply to record his name and the fact that he exists. It was no different with the citizens of Pompeii. The walls of that small city, like so many others, are covered with graffiti left by strollers for the amusement of other strollers.

Oddly enough, a similar kind of publicity was fashionable in the ancient equivalent of our modern cemeteries: the roadside. The land abutting the Roman highways belonged to no one, and it was here that the Romans placed their tombs, on the outskirts of their cities. No sooner did a traveler pass through the city gates than his eyes were drawn to tombs flanking the road. A tomb was meant to be viewed not by a person's family and close friends but by everyone. The grave, underground, was one thing, and was honored each year by family memorial services. The tombstone with the epitaph was something else again; it addressed itself to passersby. We must not imagine that Roman epitaphs resemble modern ones, which speak to heaven alone. A typical Roman epitaph was cast in the following pattern: "Read, passing friend, what role I played in this world . . . And now that you have read, have a pleasant journey." And the passing reader inscribed his reply on the tomb: "You take care, too." We know for a fact that when a Roman felt like reading a little, he took a walk outside the city. Epitaphs were easier to read than the cursive script of books. Nothing will be said here about two later developments: the necropolis and the pagan catacomb.

The roads leading out of Roman cities, with their double rows of memorial billboards, were like some Broadway of the beyond. Certain epitaphs sought to captivate the traveler's attention, to distract his eyes from neighboring monuments. They offered rest and recreation within the cemetery walls. None spoke of the suffering of the bereaved; all mentioned the social role of the deceased and his faithful discharge of duties toward family and friends. To make dinner conversation about one's host's tombstone was not a social gaffe likely to bring morbid thoughts to his mind. He would have been reassured, rather, that his dignity and virtues would remain in the public eye after he was gone. Some men were not averse, after a few drinks, to reading their own epitaphs, composed by themselves as carefully as they composed their wills. There was no better way for a city to show gratitude to a benefactor than to detail the official honors that would grace his funeral.

One lady was delighted to learn that her fellow citizens planned to donate saffron (then valued as a perfume) to scent the pyre on which she was to be cremated.

Archaeologists have recovered some 100,000 Roman epitaphs, and MacMullen has noted that they became all the rage around the first century A.D. and began slowly to die out in the third century. This is not surprising, for Roman epitaphs reflected not some fundamental idea of death but the reign of public rhetoric. Epitaphs were not limited to the great. Simple private individuals may not have been public figures, but they did live in the public eye, watched by their peers. Some therefore left the public a message in their epitaphs as well as their wills: "I lived meanly so long as it was given me to live, and I advise you to enjoy yourself more than I did. That's life: you get this far and no farther. I never heeded the advice of any philosopher. Beware of the doctors: they are the ones who killed me." The deceased draws from his life a moral for the living. The hereafter, rarely mentioned in these epitaphs, has been the object of too much attention from historians influenced by Christianity, who fail to recognize the public function of ancient tombs. In some cases epitaphs were used to censure. From the grave people castigated those who had done them wrong. One patron damned an ungrateful freedman, calling him a highway robber. A father announced to all the world that he had disinherited an unworthy daughter. A mother accused another woman of poisoning her son. For us, to engrave such words on a tombstone would be an affront to the majesty of death. But the Romans washed their dirty linen in public. In Pompeii, on the Nocera road, one epitaph expresses the hope that a wicked friend will feel the wrath of the gods of heaven and hell.

---

*Public Censure*

Public censure of private conduct was heard everywhere, and reminders of the rules of conduct were ubiquitous. The air was heavy with calls to order, with an insistence on respect for the rules. One notable in Pompeii had the following maxim painted on the wall of his dining room: "Kindly restrain your quarrelsome words, if possible. If not, get up and go home. Keep your sweet eyes and lewd looks from straying to other men's wives and let chastity shine in your face." The guests did not consider these admonitions insulting. They felt, rather, that virtuous mottoes graced their respectable company. The Romans burned enough incense to virtue to kill an ox. Ovid, a delicate poet forced to endure the tragedy of exile, paid tearful homage to the devoted wife he left behind in Rome; she did not betray him. Eulogizing himself, Horace lays his cards on the table: as a young man, thanks to his father's admonitions, he had been no one's catamite. Statius, in praising the late wife of his patron, says that she was so modest that she never would have betrayed him for anything in the world, not even a large sum of money. It was a compliment to praise a woman for not selling herself or an adolescent for not having been kept. The same Statius congratulates one adolescent for not participating, though an orphan, in ephebic loves. However vigilant the censors, the praise was crude.

Skeletons were eagerly let out of closets. When it came to countering vice with virtue, the slogan was, "anything goes." Statius, continuing his panegyric, tells us that the same adolescent, his protector, ran into some difficulties; his mother tried to poison him, but the emperor had sent her to prison. If the poet passed judgment in public so clumsily, it was only because public opinion had preceded him. The collective conscience commented, as shamelessly as it pleased, on anyone's life. This was considered not gossip but legitimate censure, *reprehensio*. Every marriage, divorce, and will was weighed in the balance, as Cicero's letters show and as Pliny's, written only in order to be published, show even more. Pliny's correspondence, in fact, was intended to serve as a manual for the compleat Roman senator, with the author as prime example. Whenever Pliny mentions a will or a divorce, he carefully details what people thought, and, if public opinion was divided, he decides which side was correct. The ruling class felt it had the right to govern the private lives of its members, in the interest of all. Those who braved public opinion faced ridicule. Insulting songs (*carmen famosum*) were quietly circulated, and pamphlets (*libelli*) passed from hand to hand, heaping obscene insults and sarcasm upon the deviant in order to demonstrate that public opinion was more powerful than any man. When one senator decided to marry his mistress, Statius, his protégé, dotted the i's: "Let the lying insinuations in the pamphlets be silenced. This illicit love has just submitted to the laws of Rome, whose citizens have now seen with their own eyes the kisses they used to jabber about." There was a great deal of cant in this civic puritanism, which was quick to denounce anyone who did not conform. An entire literary genre, satire, has its roots here.

No one was exempt from justifying his private life before the bar of public opinion, not even the emperors, or at any rate not the "good" emperors. When Claudius learned of Messalina's misconduct, he harangued the imperial guard, detailed his wife's infidelities, and promised the guardsmen that "he would never remarry, for marriage had turned out so badly for him." When Augustus learned of his daughter's and then of his granddaughter's mischief (both pretended to live as great ladies rather than as exemplary members of the reigning family), he listed their offenses in a message to the Senate and a manifesto (*edictum*) to the people. The "bad" emperors turned this public censure upside down: they paraded their mistresses and catamites to show that a potentate stands above public opinion.

A paterfamilias worthy of the name avoided criticism by soliciting advice from friends and peers, seeking their approval in advance for any important private decision, whether it be to punish a son in accordance with paternal authority or to free a young slave or to marry or to repudiate a wicked wife or to remarry or to commit suicide (for otherwise a suicide might be accused of cowardice). To the same council of friends men laid out insults they had suffered. One man, unjustly disinherited by his brother, publicly read his brother's will along with his own; the contrast between the two aroused general indignation. The council of friends had something of a formal quality, and in old families when one quarreled with a friend and no longer wanted his presence on the council, it was necessary to notify him officially of that fact (*renuntiare amicitiam*).

There was no conspiracy of silence within the governing class. Public and private wrongs were set forth for all to see. Pliny, who held himself up as a model of sophisticated virtue, denounced his peers' foolishness or, rather, their flaws (no one in Rome was mortified by being made to look a fool) and published passages from private letters that led to the downfall of one overly greedy governor. In senatorial tones Seneca detailed the sexual perversions that prevented one of his peers from being named consul. Members of the governing class did not hesitate to slander their peers because they never spoke as private individuals. Every citizen was to some degree a public man, an activist. The legitimacy accorded to public opinion resulted in a rather odd "freedom of the [oral] press." People were permitted to accuse a late emperor of tyranny and of wanting to suppress the frankness (*parrhesia, libertas*) of noble opinion, provided that they were careful to add that the reigning emperor was anything but a tyrant. Hence reigning emperors were praised as freely as their predecessors were damned.

---

*Moral Authority*

A senator was not a man like other men. Whatever he said was public and was supposed to be believed. He judged the public and private actions of his peers, in much the same way that our generals and diplomats award merits and demerits in their memoirs to fellow generals and statesmen. The governing class ruled legitimately, not so much by virtue of the official titles held by its members as in the name of a class "authority" (*auctoritas*) that was "naturally" theirs: that was the way things were. This authority pertained to private morals as well as public life. A senator was entitled to say how any citizen worthy of the name ought to live. If the senator was also a historian or philosopher, his books were not read in the same way as the books of mere mortals. If a historian, he would have been expected to say what people ought to think about the Roman past, in order to drive home the political, moral, and patriotic verities of which the Senate was the conservatory or academy. Historians of more humble origin would loyally repeat this edifying version of history. Or, being themselves insignificant, they would, with all due respect, content themselves with a valet's view of great affairs, regaling their readers with anecdotes about the private lives of the great. A senator who was also a philosopher, like Cicero or Seneca, had the exclusive right to explain how philosophy applied to politics and to scour the books of wisdom for traces of old Roman principles, which it was the duty of the senator to uphold.

Every noble was expected to be a man of gravity, since he was already a man who carried weight (*gravis*). He was not supposed to make jokes in public; to have done so would have been a travesty. Still, there was a time for seriousness and a time to let oneself go (*non intempestive lascivire*). A senator who knew how to make jokes and be simple in private was especially praiseworthy. Private life was the proper place for humor. Scipio, so rigid in public, showed himself quite "civil" with his intimates. Rome had a long tradition of aristocratic sophistication; censure had long since ceased to be mordant and become needlingly ironic. The satires of the noble Lucilius retain something of the esoteric quality of works addressed to

"insiders." His mocking allusions are delicate without sacrificing any of their bite. This same Lucilius laughed along with
Scipio and other peers. When they were together in their rural
villas, the stiffness imposed by the rigid aristocratic code of
behavior was no longer necessary, and these august personages
indulged in one of the children's games of the time: chasing
one another around the dinner beds. Their notion of private
civility allowed them to behave much like overgrown children
(*repuerascere*).

In doing so these nobles behaved, however briefly, much
as the common folk behaved all the time. Ordinary people
could sing in public as they harvested grapes or did the mend-
ing. Seneca said, "A poor man laughs more often and more
heartily." The Romans did not share the haughty elegance of
the Greeks, for whom distinction of manners was an important basis of public life and private attitudes. Two centuries
before the birth of Christ, Rome, which had always been a
semi-Hellenized city, entered for the first time into diplomatic
relations with the Hellenistic kingdoms, at that time still the
world's leading power. A Roman ambassador who found himself in the presence of Antiochus the Great, the most famous
man of his day, could express his high conception of his
Roman fatherland in no other way than by holding himself
stiffly, in consequence of which his words were deemed of-
fensive. The king made the ambassador understand how little
he was impressed by such haughty, half-barbarian manners,
but added that he forgave him because he was so young—and
handsome.

Rome, whatever has been said about it, was a state that
obeyed not laws but orders from its governing class—*pace* the
many sociologists who will find this assertion difficult to accept. Roman public law itself becomes clearer as soon as one
ceases to look for rules and accepts the fact that everything
depended on the relative strength of the various parties in
contention. What is even more curious is that Rome was in
no sense a traditionalist state, governed in the English manner
by respect for custom. Roman institutions were a jumble and
remained remarkably fluid throughout Roman history. Rome
was an authoritarian state unconstrained by rules. Much has
been made of Roman "good faith," but Roman loyalty was
to a man, not to a pact. Much has also been made, and still is
made, of "ancestral customs" (*more majorum*), but the claim is
specious: custom enjoyed no authority in Rome. Custom was
invoked only in connection with public institutions. Only the

This Roman bronze is a copy,
one-third scale, of an ancient
Greek statue of an athlete. But
the copyist has added a horn of
plenty in the left hand and
what may have been a wreath
in the right, thus turning the
idle beauty of the nude into a
Bonus Eventus. (Paris, Petit
Palais, Dutuit Collection.)

great, alone authorized to talk politics, mentioned it. And it was invoked only as an objection, that is, only when it was about to be violated. Ancestral custom was adduced in order to prevent a rival from introducing an innovation advantageous to himself or as grounds for doing something unusual. (One could always argue that the new was really a return to some forgotten custom.) In any case, current custom was explicitly cited in opposition to ancestral custom; the one was no less worthy of mention than the other. Whether ancient or recent, custom served only as an argument. It could be used to justify whatever one pleased.

| | |
|---|---|
| *Popular Wisdom* | Public life was ruled by the will of the governing class, and private life by fear of what the governing class would say. Public opinion was internalized in the form of self-restraint and occasionally revealed itself in public outbursts of shame. Such shame was considered honorable. As we saw earlier, one wicked master, ashamed of having mistreated his slaves, begged Galen to whip him. In Sparta when the sage Apollonius accused a wealthy shipowner of neglecting public affairs and thinking only of enriching himself, he burst into tears and immediately changed his ways. |

People were as obsessed with superstitions as we are with Freudian slips. In the ancient world, astrology, considered a scientific doctrine, was part of high culture and enjoyed the same respect among the cultivated as does psychoanalysis today. Maecenas and Tiberius never did anything without consulting their astrologers. Dreams, too, were taken as omens. The issue was very controversial. One high official, a most learned man, had a dream one day that seemed to presage his losing a case in court. He begged a senator with whom he was friendly to postpone the hearing. The senator asked him to think it over: dreams could no doubt be meaningful, but their meaning was often ambiguous. Another high official experienced what was not a dream but a true apparition: he was walking in a courtyard when a giant figure appeared before him. It was Africa, with the feminine features ascribed to her by painters and sculptors, and she revealed that one day he would enjoy the good fortune of being named governor of the province Africa. This came to pass. Another fashionable topic concerned the existence of ghosts. When the philosophers were consulted, they said that this came down to the problem of the immortality of the soul: if the soul is immortal, ghosts are possible.

The "evil eye" was widely feared. To protect against its spell people placed a painting or sculpture of a phallus, scorpion, or some other penetrating creature in their doorways; these were supposed to put out the evil eye. Fear of the evil eye was essentially fear of the jealousy of neighbors or hatred of rivals: *Rumpere, invidia!* is the legend found alongside one phallic charm.

Such were the shames, fears, and phobias of the rich. The private life of the common folk was governed by custom, which had been erected into a kind of philosophy, a popular oral doctrine comparable to that of the Old Testament's Book of Proverbs.

Senatorial opinion reminded people at every opportunity of what they ought to do. Popular wisdom, on the other hand, taught that "the wise man does this, the madman that." The man of the people instructed his children by expounding the faults of others and painting a diptych of good and evil, or prudence and imprudence in private dealings. Aristocratic behavior did not claim to be based on any philosophy; it was a law unto itself. Proverbs were good for the common folk. The wealthy freedman who was father to the poet Horace sent his son to school to obtain the liberal education that he, the father, lacked; personally he instructed the boy in the teachings of popular wisdom. In order to encourage his son to shun vice and adultery, he cited the case of a man who had been caught red-handed and lost his reputation. To teach the principles of prudent management he told of another man who had ended his days in poverty. The common man had as much to fear from imprudence as from immorality. "How can you fail to see that an action is either immoral or unprofitable when the man who commits it gains nothing but condemnation for his efforts?" As a positive example, Horace's father cites a great man who, having been named to a jury, is officially recognized as good: "There is an authority." When he grew up to become a poet and thinker, Horace sensed a kinship between the oral but explicit doctrine he had heard from his father and the express, written lessons of philosophy. Many others sensed the same kinship. An epitaph such as "He never took lessons from any philosopher" or "He learned the venerable truths on his own" expresses not disdain for culture but the claim that popular culture and high culture are equal. The man buried here, the epitaph claims, needed no philosophy to live as a philosopher, to know what was good and useful.

*Softness*

Apart from this proverbial wisdom of the people, Rome had an oral tradition of common sense, a tradition shared by all classes of society and pertinent to every sort of problem. It was a veritable philosophy, like Marxism or psychoanalysis, the two varieties of common sense most prevalent in the West today. Like Marxism and psychoanalysis, Roman oral doctrines could explain and demystify anything. They demonstrated that the reality in which people lived was radically distorted, that it should have been other than what it was, and that all ills, public and private, stemmed from this state of affairs. The fault lay not with class society but with some fundamental defect shared by virtually all men: softness, perhaps, or extravagance. Everyone took these facts for granted, and philosophers claimed to derive them from their doctrines or, in perfect good faith, bolstered their doctrines with the teachings of common sense. For at least half a millennium the Greeks and the Romans lived convinced that their society was decadent; "Roman decadence" was a familiar topos. Oral philosophies are accidents of the history of ideas, not some sort of immutable functional reflection of reality. They are free creations, and each stands in a different relation to reality. Some are conformist, others demystifying.

Softness destroys individuals and dooms societies, which are mere aggregates of individuals. But what is softness? Not so much a specific defect as a symptom, a clue to analysis of the psyche. At first sight it seems to be but one defect among others, perhaps no more than a set of not very virile traits: an effeminate way of speaking, affected gestures, a slow way of walking, and so on. But the Greeks and Romans subjected these details to puritanical scrutiny and attached undue importance to them. They held that this visible softness was a symptom of a more deep-seated softness, a profound weakness of character. Like a weakened organism unable to resist infection, a character that lacked resistance was in danger of succumbing to every vice, even, and perhaps primarily, those vices bearing the least resemblance to the soft character. Thus, softness was the cause of luxury and lasciviousness, for which there was a single word (*luxuria*) and which consisted in denying oneself nothing and believing that "anything goes." In the Roman Empire a man who loved women too much, who made love too often, gave proof that he was effeminate. How could one combat softness? By struggling against its root cause: indolence. Not that the Romans believed that "the Devil finds work for idle hands"; nor did they share the modern notion that man has an excess of energy, which he will expend in sex if he does not invest it in work. The Romans held that indolence is the grandmother of vice, because an idle character will lose its muscle tone, will "break training," so to speak, and become vulnerable to the diseases of the soul. The Greeks and the Romans subscribed to a kind of machismo, condemning pleasure, dancing, and passion with clerical strictness and casting a pall of suspicion over solitary pursuits. During brief periods, whenever an emperor or public opinion succumbed to an excess of moral fervor, certain types of private behavior were not tolerated.

---

Another philosophical anthropology hinged on the notion of extravagance, or excess, rather than softness. This enabled the Romans to condemn man as he was and the world as it was, in their very principle. Man may be a creature of reason, but all men are mad. Delusions of grandeur drive men to want more than they can ever use. Excess is thus the root cause of ambition and greed, which in turn are the causes of luxury, conflict, and decadence. This idea was central to the philosophy of Horace, which consisted not, as some have said, in recommending that the wise stick to the happy medium in all things, but in deploring the fact that such obvious advice is never heeded, that fate has arranged things so that there is a radical flaw at the heart of every man. Against this universal flaw, a highly systematic philosophy fought with energy born of despair.

*Excess*

Proponents of this philosophy sought to show in a new light the most widespread form of excess: greed, the desire for wealth. It is enough, they argued, for a man to be comfortable. What is the good of a man's wanting more than he needs in order to live without working? But humans are foolish enough not to be content with what they have, and to want to live like millionaires. Clearly the conception of poverty invoked here is one that seems rather peculiar to us. What was the point, Galen asked, of owning fifteen pairs of shoes? Two were enough. With a house, a few slaves, and suitable furniture, one could live happily. From Prodicos to Musonius and beyond, all the philosophers delighted in making paradoxical praise of "poverty." Pleasure in this paradox was quite widely shared. We find it in the theater, a popular pastime, where the public expressed its approval. Seneca tells us that

Banquet on a Greek tomb. A Roman epitaph explains the meaning of such images: the deceased, sorry to have led a mean life, wished to be depicted at least on his tomb at a feast. "But what good is it to the dead to be shown feasting? They would have done better to have lived that way." (Avignon, Calvet Museum.)

audiences applauded tirades against the miserly and greedy, who harm themselves with their passion for more. Greek economists taught that the real goal of production ought to be autarchy, which involved reducing needs to the point where one was no longer dependent on the economy. This ideology has persuaded some recent historians of the ancient world that the ancients did not care about production and that therefore the economies of Greece and Rome must not have been very highly developed. Such a view reflects a fundamental misunderstanding of the oral philosophy of excess, which did not describe reality but condemned it.

We must know how to make do with little, said Epicurus. But, he added, if need be. Whether condemning wealth or softness, the oral traditions of the ancients had but one goal: to protect the individual by censuring those weaknesses and appetites that left him vulnerable to life's tempests. The ancients were critical of anyone who hoisted too much sail in heavy weather. They used philosophy as a tranquilizer. If excess makes an individual vulnerable, religion, proverbs, and eschatological speculation bring tranquillity. And if theory condemns softness, reality offers an abundance of pleasures.

The common people condemned avarice above all, avarice being defined as the accumulation of wealth without enjoyment. But if a wealthy man—a prince or object of public adulation—indulged himself ostentatiously and made a great show of banquets, mistresses, and favorites, people regarded him with a fair degree of sympathy; the simple pleasures of the bed and dinner table everyone could understand. Reassured plebeians consoled themselves with the belief that the powerful were made of the same stuff as themselves.

Hercules and Bacchus, second half of 1st century. These colossal statues, carved from very hard stone (whence their smooth finish) were found in the imperial palace in Rome. The old satyr who grabs Bacchus is larger than life. Hercules represents virtuous, civilizing power; Bacchus, whose face would not be out of place on a statue of Venus, represents pleasure and wild abandon. (Museum of Parma.)

# ✒ Pleasures and Excesses

"**B**ATHING, wine, and Venus wear out the body but are the real stuff of life," a proverb warns. In Sparta—yes, Sparta—the following epitaph commented on an erotic relief that graced one tombstone (such things were not unknown):

> This is what is called a temple.
> This is where your mysteries lie.
> This is what a mortal must do
> When he sees where life ends up.

To everything there was a season, and pleasure was no less legitimate than virtue. One picture is worth a thousand words: the ancients liked to show Hercules in moments of weakness, spinning at the feet of his mistress Omphale or drunk on wine, barely able to stand, his eyes distracted and face alight. Besides pleasures, there were marvels: spectacles, the grandeur of public buildings, the size of a city. People also marveled at the miracles of technology; in the theater scenic machinery enchanted spectators with its ingenuity. Geographic maps and plans of cities and buildings were quite common, less cause for astonishment than home computers today. The engineer's art was held in high esteem by civilian and military authorities and admired by the people. Major projects such as canals and roads struck the imagination as grand exploits; Nero's engineers undertook to cut off the isthmus of Corinth by digging a canal. Technology in this period did not pretend to dominate and revolutionize nature, as it does today, but in isolated areas the ancients were capable of amazing feats—miracles, as astonishing as the feats of nature. Among them were the siphon (which enabled aqueducts to span valleys) and the sundial. In the first century B.C. the sundial was all the rage; every city wanted one. Emperor Nero, well aware of the value of amazement, contrived to reign as, much later, the princes of the Renaissance would

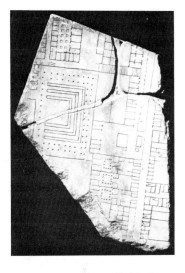

A fragment of an official plan of Rome, engraved on marble ca. 210. Part of what filled the space between the monuments: a street lined with shops and multistory buildings and, side by side, three houses with patios (the three dotted rectangles). The plan, which shows domestic interiors as well as outside walls, celebrated the immensity of the city and human domination of space thanks to the surveyor's art.

do—as *artifex,* a word meaning both "artist who creates spectacles" and "engineer." He was unfortunately overthrown, because the notables and the nobility preferred urbanity, at least in an emperor.

Urbanity required savoir-vivre. A well-bred man (*pepaideumenos*) exhibited neither baseness nor presumptuousness in the company of his peers, and every noble, every notable, was well-bred by definition. Respect for others was to be shown with liberal ease; the deference due a superior was to be offered with familiar simplicity, the mark of the free man's civic pride. Let "barbarians stand petrified before kings" and the superstitious tremble before the gods like slaves before their masters. In the eyes of the governing class "liberty" reigned, and the reigning sovereign was a "good emperor" so long as he adopted a liberal tone with citizens of the upper class, gave orders as though speaking to equals, avoided acting like a living god or barbarian potentate, and refused to take seriously his own divinization, a concession to the religious enthusiasms of the masses. The political style of the High Empire was one of conviviality. Public men, it was felt, should be as free and easy with one another as the participants in Cicero's philosophical dialogues, and religious life should be conducted in the same liberal atmosphere. Nothing could be farther removed from Christian relations with the divine, based as they were on the model of the family. Filial love for the Father must have struck the pagans as distastefully intimate and servilely humble. It probably seemed plebeian.

Sarcophagus. Couple banqueting, their children at their feet. The lady, who is interested in music, sits in a handsome armchair, but her lord and master is entitled to a dining couch. Slaves serve an abundance of dishes. (Rome, Vatican Museums.)

Even in politics, the style of interpersonal relations between the emperor and his subjects was frequently much more important than actual political or economic decisions or the manner in which power was shared. Here again it is hard to differentiate between public and private life. Emperors were toppled because of private immorality or because of what they thought privately about the people they governed. The prince's private misconduct obviously did no harm to political or material interests, but it was humiliating to Roman notables to think that their emperor entertained megalomanic or immoral ideas, which offended their sense of honor.

Gold coin. Weight: 8 grams. Depicted is Emperor Augustus, given the profile of a young god by a Greek engraver.

Our impression of the ancient world prior to the "decadence" of the late imperial period—an impression of classicism, humanism, clarity, reason, and liberty—comes from the thin veneer of style that graced private relations within the governing class. The style of private letters and prose generally, including epitaphs, reflects the same values. Our impression is also shaped by Roman art, with its taste for realism. As Ernst Gombrich has written, the catacomb painters and medieval sculptors who recreated the "Bible in images" represented the elements and content of legend in a conventional montage. By contrast, classical pagan art consisted of momentary images—snapshots—of legends that presumably everyone knew: man and the real stood on a footing of equality. Portraits of the emperors from late antiquity depict the sovereign with the traits of a mystic or a Mussolinian hierarch. But imperial portraits from the period of High Empire show the prince with the head of a handsome young man, an intellectual, or a respectable gentleman. His features are individualized; his head is that of a man like other men. There is nothing ideological or didactic about these busts.

For those who subscribed to the liberal ideal, friendship rather than passion epitomized the desirable qualities of reciprocity and inward freedom. Love is slavery, but friendship is freedom and equality. This despite the fact that in reality the word "friendship" often (though not always) meant "clientage." Did people really have more friends then than they do now? I don't know. But friendship was talked about far more often than we talk about it today. Frequently, though, a culture speaks not of what really exists but of imaginary solutions to its real contradictions. (The Japanese do not commit suicide more often than Westerners, but they talk about it much more.)

In late antiquity everything changes. Rhetoric turns dark and expressionistic, and the style of politics becomes authoritarian and sublime. The exaggerated tone of the Late Empire, so extreme that it is almost a caricature, is responsible for the period's reputation as "decadent." For a long time historians, misled by this, believed that the population of the Empire, urban life, production, the monetary economy, and the authority of the government all suffered a serious decline. Such is the power of style to deceive.

## The Urban Ideal

The style of the first two or three centuries of the Empire was one of urbanity and urbanism. The notables, as we know, were a nobility of the cities, who visited their rural estates only during the heat of summer. As for nature, these city folk appreciated only its agreeable aspects (*amoenitas*). They explored its wild depths in cumbrous hunting parties only to prove their *virtu,* or courage. The nature they loved was "humanized" with parks and gardens; a landscape made a better composition if the site's possibilities were exploited by, say, placing a small sanctuary on a hilltop or at the end of a spit of land. Men were fully themselves only in the city, and a city was not so much a place of familiar streets and bustling, anonymous crowds as an array of material conveniences (*commoda*) such as public baths and buildings, which lifted the spirits of residents and travelers alike and made the city much more than just a place where numbers of people lived. Pausanias asks: "Can one call 'city' a place that has neither public buildings nor gymnasium nor theater nor square nor water to supply a single fountain, and where the people live in huts, small shacks (*kalybai*) perched on the edge of a ravine?" Romans did not really feel at home in the country. To feel at home they needed a city, in particular a city surrounded by ramparts. This is a trait of the Roman psychology: walls were a city's finest ornament, defining the space of the communal home. Nowadays, even if we do not live in fear of thieves, most of us lock our doors at night. Similarly, walled cities locked their doors at nightfall, and nocturnal comings and goings were suspect. Would-be miscreants did not dare apply to the night watch for the keys to the city gates and were forced to enlist the aid of accomplices, who might lower them in baskets from atop some poorly guarded section of the city wall.

## Banquets

Walls were a sign of civility, banquets a ceremony of civility. The moment Horace arrived at his beloved country retreat he invited a woman friend to join him for dinner, most likely a freedwoman, a well-known singer or actress. Banquets were occasions for the private man to savor his accomplishments and show off to his peers. The banquet was as important to the Romans as the salon to the eighteenth-century French aristocracy, as important even as the court of Versailles to the seventeenth-century nobility. The emperors kept no court. They lived in their "palace," on the Palatine Hill, much as the nobles of Rome lived in their private villas, with only slaves and freedmen for company (which of course meant that the palace housed the various ministries of government). When night came, however, the emperor dined with his guests, senators and others whose company he relished. The time of public "honors" and "government" of the patrimony was over. Now the private man could relax at table. Even the poor people (*hoi penetes*), nine-tenths of the population, had their nights of revelry. During a banquet the private man forgot everything but his "profession," if he had one. Those who had vowed to devote their lives to the pursuit of wisdom celebrated not as the profane did but as philosophers.

There was an art to banqueting. Roman table manners were apparently less elaborate and formalized than ours, however. People dined with clients and friends of all ranks, and

Silver pieces, found at Boscoreale, before A.D. 79. Rarely has the average of any art reached as high a level of good taste as in Late Empire embossing. (Paris, Louvre.)

Banquet on a Syrian tomb, 2nd century. (Museum of Beirut.)

protocol was strictly observed in the assignment of "dining couches" around the pedestal table that held the platters of different dishes. Without couches there could be no real feast, even among the poor. Romans sat up to eat only at ordinary meals (with simple folk, the mother stood and served the father seated at table). Roman cooking strikes us as a mixture of oriental and medieval. The food was quite spicy and covered with complicated sauces. Meat was boiled more often than it was braised or roasted, so that it was bloodless, and served sugared. Romans preferred their food in the sweet-and-sour range. As for drink, there was a choice between wine with a flavor something like marsala and a resiny wine such as one might drink in Greece today, both diluted with water. "Make it stronger!" the suffering erotic poet orders his cup-bearer. The trickiest part of the evening, and the longest, was that set aside for drinking. Early in the dinner people ate without drinking. Later they drank without eating: this was the banquet in the strict sense of the word (*comissatio*). More than a feast, the banquet was a festival, and each man was expected to hold his own. As a token of festivity guests wore hats with flowers, or "wreaths," and were perfumed, that is, anointed with fragrant oil (alcohol was unknown, so oil was used as a solvent for perfumes). Banquets were unctuous and brilliant, as were nights of love.

The banquet was more than just a meal. Guests were expected to express their views on general topics and noble

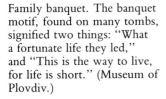

Family banquet. The banquet motif, found on many tombs, signified two things: "What a fortunate life they led," and "This is the way to live, for life is short." (Museum of Plovdiv.)

subjects or to give summaries of their lives. If the host had a domestic philosopher or tutor on his staff, he would be asked to speak. Between dishes there might be music (with dancing and singing), by professional musicians hired for the occasion. At least as much a social manifestation as an occasion for eating and drinking, the classical banquet gave rise to a literary genre, the "symposium," in which men of culture, philosophers, and scholars (*grammatici*) held elevated discussions. Ideally the banquet hall was supposed to resemble not a dining room but a literary salon; when this happened, confusion with popular merrymaking was no longer possible. "Drinking," then, meant the pleasures of good company, culture, and in some cases the charms of friendship. Thinkers and poets found it perfectly possible to philosophize about wine.

---

Ordinary folk enjoyed one another's company in less ostentatious ways. They had taverns and "colleges," or confraternities. As in Moslem countries today, men met friends at the barber, the baths, or the tavern. In Pompeii taverns (*cauponae*) were numerous. There one met travelers, had food warmed (not all the poor had ovens at home), and flirted with bejeweled waitresses. Amorous taunts are recorded on the walls. These popular customs were considered bad form by the nobility, and a notable seen lunching in a tavern risked tarnishing his reputation. Street life was disreputable. One old philosopher was so immoderate in his desires that he never went out without money, people said, so that he could buy any pleasure that he happened upon. The imperial government waged war for four centuries against the taverns to keep them from serving as restaurants (*thermopolium*), for it was considered morally healthier to eat at home.

As for the *collegia,* or confraternities, the emperors were suspicious of them, since they were places where numbers of men gathered for purposes that were hard to define. Rightly or wrongly, government feared their potential power. In principle, the collegia were free, private associations, whose members were free men and slaves who practiced a common trade or worshiped a common god. Nearly every city boasted one or more. In one town, for example, there was a weavers' association and a college of worshipers of Hercules. A neighboring town was home to a blacksmith's confraternity and an association of clothing merchants who worshiped Mercury. Each confraternity was confined to a single city. Members

*Confraternities*

Funerary relief. The deceased, who served drinks in life, is shown with two customers seated at a table. (Ostia, Archaeological Museum.)

lived in the town and knew one another. All were men; no women were admitted. Finally, all the collegia, whether religious or professional, were organized along the same lines as the city itself. Each had a council, magistrates who held office for a year at a time, and benefactors, who were honored with handsome declarations patterned after the honorary edicts issued by the city council. In sum, the collegia were make-believe cities. They served religious and professional purposes, and their members were common people from a particular city or town.

Why did people join such groups? Why did the carpenters in one town or the worshipers of Hercules in another feel the need to band together? One thing is certain: the colleges were nothing like modern trade unions, nor were they workers' mutual aid societies. They offered men a place to meet and to enjoy one another's company, away from women. If a college was religious in character, honoring its god provided a pretext for staging a banquet. If professional, it brought together men working in similar trades; cobblers liked to talk to other cobblers, carpenters to other carpenters. Each new member paid an entry fee. Coupled with gifts from benefactors, these dues enabled college members to stage joyous banquets and buy members decent burials (which were also followed by banquets). Slaves joined colleges to ensure that they would not be buried like dogs. In this there is a strict parallel with the workers' and religious confraternities of early modern Europe. In Florence, Davidsohn tells us, religious and craft confraternities were associated with worship of the Virgin or a saint. Members' funerals were celebrated with much pomp, and a cortege followed the deceased member's body to the collective tomb the confraternity had built at its own expense. Early modern confraternities were renowned for their immoderate love of banquets, often held to honor founding members who had donated money for toasts to be drunk in their memory; Roman collegia seem to have been no different. The two things that interest the collegia, Saint Cyprian wrote, are banquets and burials. In a few cases the zeal for banqueting required no pretext; at Fano on the Adriatic there was a confraternity of *"bons vivants* who dine together."

Collegia proliferated to the point where they became the center of plebeian private life. Not surprisingly, the imperial government viewed them with suspicion. And not without reason, for any association tends to acquire purposes beyond its officially stated aims, beyond even its unconscious desires.

When men come together for whatever reason, their conversation will quite naturally range over matters of common interest. At the end of the Republic, candidates for election sought the support of colleges as well as cities. Later, in the politically troubled city of Alexandria, religious colleges met and, "under the guise of taking part in some sacrifice, people drank and in their drunkenness talked nonsense about the political situation." After "talking nonsense" long enough they took to the streets, egged on by a notable who defended the privileges of the city's Greeks against the Roman governor and who, by means of generous donations, had secured for himself the position of president of these religious groups, the ancient equivalent of our political clubs.

More numerous, however, were the clubs where people went merely to drink with friends. The need for association was so great that groups formed even within households and, under the guise of piety, in the finest society. The slaves and freedmen of one household, or the sharecroppers and slaves of an estate, might band together in a college, pay dues to cover members' burial costs, and show devotion to the master's family by erecting a small domestic sanctuary in honor of the protective deities of the household or estate. These colleges also mimicked the political organization of the cities.

---

*Bacchic Ideology*

In the cities themselves, as we saw earlier, wealthy benefactors paid for public feasts. Banquets were important occasions, rituals of conviviality and drink. Some were held at fixed intervals, others on special occasions; eagerly anticipated, they added solemnity to pleasure. Funerals, too, were important occasions for which people prepared diligently. The worship of Bacchus symbolized and glorified Roman attitudes toward both feasting and death. "Worship" may be too strong a word. Even if people naively believed in the existence of Bacchus, they never worshiped this god, who was famous mainly from his legends. Certain mystical sects held that he was a truly great god, but most Romans, when they felt the need of divine protection, worshiped deities considered more authentic than Bacchus, to whom no shrines were erected. Yet the legend of Bacchus was more than a legend. Bacchic imagery was ubiquitous, and its meaning was obvious. Images of Bacchus are found in mosaics, in paintings that hung on the walls of houses and taverns, on dishes, and on household objects of all sorts, to say nothing of sarcophagi. No other

Mausoleum of Igel, near Trier,
ca. A.D. 200. Servants of the
Secundini family, which owned
land and engaged in wholesale
trade, prepare drinks for their
masters.

A servant prepares drinks for
his masters. Note the style of
the furniture; the table leg
features a lion's head.

image was as widely disseminated, not even that of Venus. Bacchic imagery was appropriate anywhere because it evoked only pleasant associations. The god of pleasure and sociability, Bacchus was always accompanied by a train of tipsy friends and ecstatic female admirers; pleasant excesses of all sorts lay in store for them. A benevolent, civilizing god who soothed the mind, Bacchus won peaceful victories in every corner of the world. He was clever enough to calm the fiercest tigers, who hitched themselves like lambs to his chariot. His admirers were as beautiful, and as lightly clad, as his lovely mistress, Ariadne. Bacchic imagery certainly had no religious or mystical significance, but it was not merely decorative, either. It affirmed the importance of sociability and pleasure, on which it bestowed the blessings of the supernatural. It was an ideology, an affirmation of principle. Against this was set the image of Hercules, symbol of civic and philosophical "virtue."

Bacchus, emblematic of a principle, was one god the people did not doubt. His worshipers banded together in popular confraternities, whose chief concern (proved by their regulations) was to drink toasts in honor of this amiable deity. In the Middle Ages people no less joyously worshiped certain

Triumph of Bacchus, mosaic from Susa, 2nd–3rd century. Victory crowns the god on his chariot, as *putti* ride lions. In contemporary theater the triumph of Bacchus was a subject of (pyrrhic) dance, as were Venus and the Graces, Nymphs, and Seasons, according to Philostratus and Athenaeus. Only rarely did mosaics depict pious images; the gods most often represented were Venus and Bacchus, and their style was mythological. (Tunis, Bardo Museum.)

Funerary relief, 1st–3rd century. Young woman idealized as bacchante. Crowned with ivy, the plant of her god, the seated bacchante or maenad dreamily teases a goat, which strains against her restraint. She supports herself with one arm, whose tension reveals the energy dormant within her. This melancholy masterpiece poeticizes death; it does not suggest that hope was vested in the hereafter. (Rome, Museum of the Baths.)

saints from the *Golden Legend*. To the cultivated, the Bacchus legend was a pleasant fancy; the god might exist, or he might be one of the many names of the godhead, or he might be a superhuman individual who had lived in the distant past and whose legend was based on authentic exploits. These beliefs were enough to encourage speculation about the god, and a few sects formed for the purpose of worshiping him: small, isolated groups in which exalted piety and authentic religious fervor coexisted with more worldly attitudes. To understand this mixture of snobbery and salon mysticism, we need only think of the early days of Freemasonry, in the time of *The Magic Flute*. Like Freemasonry, the Bacchic sects had secret rites, initiation rituals (or "mysteries"), and a hierarchy from which women were not excluded. Archaeologists have happened upon the actual site used by one of these mystery sects only once or twice. Nevertheless, I feel I ought to say a word about them, because sects, popular and otherwise, were a feature of the age, and religious fervor was no less important than the need for sociability. The speculations of these mystery sects contributed to the spiritual revolution of late antiquity.

## Festival and Religion

Feasting and piety could coexist in sects and confraternities because festival was an integral part of pagan religion. A cult was nothing more than a festival, which pleased the gods as much as it pleased the men and women who took part. All religions are likely to confound spiritual emotion with formal ritual; untroubled by the confusion, the faithful find sustenance in both. Was wearing a wreath in antiquity a sign of feasting or religious ceremony? How can we tell? Piety meant honoring the gods as they deserved. Religious festivals yielded a twofold pleasure: besides enjoying oneself, one did one's duty. The pagans never asked the faithful how they "really" felt; hence we have no way of knowing. Paying homage to the gods was a solemn way of enjoying yourself. Fortunate were those who, more than others, felt the presence of divinity and whose souls were moved.

The principal rite of every cult was of course the rite of sacrifice, which people attended in a contemplative mood. It is important to bear in mind, however, that in a Greek or Latin text the word "sacrifice" always implies "feast." Every sacrifice was followed by a dinner in which the immolated victim was cooked on the altar and eaten. (Great temples had kitchens and offered the services of their cooks to worshipers

who came to sacrifice.) The flesh of the victim went to the participants in the ritual, the smoke to the gods. Scraps from the meal were left on the altar, and beggars (*bomolochoi*) spirited them away. When sacrifice was made not on a household altar but at a temple, the custom was to pay for the priests' services by leaving them a set portion of the sacrificial animal; temples earned money by selling this meat to butchers. (When Pliny the Younger wishes to inform the emperor that he has eradicated Christianity in the province of which he is governor, he writes: "The meat of sacrificial animals is on sale once more," proving that sacrifices have resumed.) Which was it: Did people eat sacrificial victims or did they sacrifice animals they wanted to eat? That depends. The word for a man who made frequent sacrifice (*philothytes*) came to mean not a devout person but a host who gave good dinners, an Amphitryon.

The religious calendar, which varied from city to city, was filled with festivals, days when no one was required to work. These occurred at irregular intervals throughout the

Ornamental relief. The driving rhythms of the double oboe and tambourine set the pace of the march. The panther skin and long cane topped with pine cone are the insignia of Bacchus. (Madrid, Prado.)

year. (Incidentally, the week, a period of astrological rather than Judeo-Christian origin, did not come into common use until the end of antiquity.) On feast days people invited their friends to sacrifices in their homes; such invitations were considered a greater honor than mere dinner invitations. Vapors of incense spewed forth from many houses on these great occasions, according to Tertullian. Among the important holidays were the national feasts of the emperors, the festivals of certain gods, New Year's Day, and the first day of each month. A custom cherished by Romans wealthy enough to practice it was that of sacrificing a piglet on the first of the month in honor of the household gods, the Lares or Penates. Once a year the birthday of the paterfamilias was celebrated with genuine fervor. On that day the family feasted in honor of its protective deity, or *genius*. (Each individual had, as it were, a divine double, or genius, whose existence had little consequence other than to allow people to say "May my genius protect me!" or "I swear by your genius that I have carried out your orders.") The poor sacrificed less costly animals. If Aesculapius cured them of some malady, they sacrificed a chicken at his temple, and then returned home to eat it. Or they might place a simple wheat cake on the family altar (*far pium*).

A simpler means of sanctifying a meal was what Artemidorus, I think, called "theoxenies"; one invited the gods (*in-*

Sacrifice of a bull, a ram, and a boar, first half of 1st century. Officiating at the altar is a veiled figure, probably an emperor. The animals are ready, and the scene will soon resemble a slaughterhouse, a butcher-shop, or a barbecue. (Paris, Louvre.)

Diana the archer. Hellenistic art. Common women prayed to the mother of Diana to give them daughters just as beautiful. (London, British Museum.)

*vitare deos*) to dinner by removing their statuettes from the house's sacred niche and placing them in the dining room during the meal, as platters of food were heaped in front of them. After dinner the slaves feasted on these untouched dishes. This custom probably explains the following lines from Horace: "O nights, O dinners of the gods at which my friends and I ate before the household genius, and I gave my excited slaves consecrated dishes to eat." If the slaves were excited, it was the feast that excited them, and this was as it should be. Peasants, too, celebrated seasonal festivals according to a rustic calendar. With gifts formally offered by sharecroppers, the great landlord of a district used to sacrifice a tithe of the soil's produce to the gods of the fields, after which everyone ate, drank, and danced. Then, at nightfall, as Horace states explicitly and Tibullus implies, people had the right, even the duty, to make love as a fitting end to a day in which they had enjoyed themselves while honoring the gods. Someone once reproached Aristippus, a philosopher and theoretician of pleasure, for leading a life of indolence. "If it is wrong to live like this," he replied, "why do people do it for the gods' feasts?"

## The Baths

In addition to the enthusiasms and delights of the religious calendar, there were other pleasures with nothing sacred about them that could be had only in the cities. These were among the benefits (*commoda*) of urban life, the product of public benefaction, or evergetism, and included public baths, theaters, chariot races at the Circus, and fights between gladiators or hunters and wild animals in the arena of the amphitheater (or theater in Greek areas). Baths and public spectacles cost money, in Rome at any rate (we know little about the subject, and it seems likely that generosity of benefactors had some influence on the price of admission), but the cost was in any case modest. Free seats were reserved at every show, and lines began forming the night before. Free men, slaves, women, children—everyone had access to the baths, even foreigners. When gladiators were on display, people flocked to the cities from great distances. The better part of private life was spent in public establishments of one kind or another.

The baths were not for cleanliness. They offered an array of pleasures, rather like our beaches. Christians and philosophers denied themselves these pleasures. Not so soft as to lust after cleanliness, they bathed only once or twice a month. A philosopher's dirty beard was proof of the austerity on which he prided himself. No rich man's house (*domus*) was without a bath, which occupied several specially prepared rooms, with heating under the floor. And no city was without at least one public bath, supplied, if necessary, by an aqueduct, which also carried water to the public fountains. (Door-to-door water delivery was still a corrupt business monopolized by criminals.) The gong (*discus*) that announced the opening of the public baths each day was a sweeter sound, Cicero says, than the voices of the philosophers in their school.

For a few coins the poor people could spend several hours a day in a luxurious setting provided by the authorities, the emperor, or the city notables. Along with complex installations, including hot and cold baths, there were promenades and fields for sports and games. (The Greco-Roman bath was also a gymnasium and in Greek regions was still called by that name.) The two sexes were separated, at least as a general rule. Excavations at Olympia allow us to follow the evolution of the baths over more than seven centuries. Originally modest, functional buildings, with a cold pool, hot slipper baths, and a steam bath, the "therms" eventually developed into pleasure palaces. A well-known quip calls them, along with the amphitheaters, "cathedrals of paganism." Beginning in the Hellenistic era, their role expanded from one of facilitating cleanliness to one of making life as pleasant as possible. The great novelty (which dates from around 100 B.C. in Olympia and earlier still at Gortys in Arcadia) was the heating of the basement and even the walls of the building. Large numbers of people were offered an enclosed place that was always warm. At a time when, no matter how cold it became, people had no source of heat at home other than braziers and wore overcoats in the house as well as in the street, the baths were a place to keep warm. Ultimately in the baths of Caracalla the Romans introduced "climate control" throughout the building by means of convection. There was another kind of evolution in the baths: from functional edifice to dream palace, with sculptures, mosaics, painted decor, and sumptuous architecture making the splendor of a royal residence accessible to all. Life at the baths was like life at the beach in summertime; the greatest pleasure was to mix with the crowd, to shout, to meet people, to listen to conversations, to spot and tell stories about odd characters, and to show off.

The wind of musical abandon effaces differences and stirs the most splendid drapery. (Rome, Vatican Museums.)

*Spectacles*

Passion for the races at the Circus and the fights at the arena, Tacitus complained, rivaled the study of eloquence among young men of good family. These spectacles were of interest to everyone, including senators and philosophers. Gladiators and chariots were not pleasures for the plebs alone. Criticism of them, usually by Platonic philosophers, smacked of that conventional utopian wisdom that we have learned to recognize. In the theater the plays known as pantomimes (a kind of opera; the word has since changed its meaning) were attacked for encouraging "softness" and occasionally prohibited. The gladiator shows were different. Infamous as they were, they at least had the merit of fortifying their spectators' courage by inuring them to the sight of blood. But even gladiator fights and chariot races had critics, who charged that such spectacles typified the human tendency to complicate life unnecessarily and waste time with frivolities. In Greek parts of the Empire intellectuals condemned athletic competitions for the same reason; to which other intellectuals responded that athletes offered lessons in endurance, moral strength, and beauty.

Intellectuals, along with everyone else, attended these spectacles. Cicero, who liked to say that he spent show days writing books, was one of the crowd and reported the events to his noble correspondents. When Seneca felt the shadow of melancholy steal across his soul, he headed for the amphitheater to cheer himself up. Maecenas, a sophisticated Epicurean noble, inquired of his client Horace about the program of the fights. But Marcus Aurelius, good philosopher that he was, found one fight pretty much like another and went to see the gladiators only to fulfill his duty as emperor. The passions of the public were engaged, however, and wealthy youths and honest yeomen divided into rival factions backing one actor or racing team or group of gladiators against another. The enthusiasm sometimes spilled over, but the ensuing riots concealed no ulterior political motives or class divisions. Occasionally it was necessary to exile an actor or chariot racer who had stirred the passions of the crowd for or against him.

In Rome and other Italian cities spectacles were the great drawing card. In Greek areas, by contrast, athletic competitions were. Greeks flocked not only to great games (*isolympicoi, periodicoi*) and lesser games (*stephanitai*), which were associated with fairs, but also to minor games (*themides*). The Greeks enthusiastically borrowed gladiatorial combats from

Rome. 3rd century(?). This *bestiarius,* or animal-fighter, defended himself against bears with pick and whip. (Copenhagen, Ny Carlsberg Glypotek.)

the Romans. Athletes, actors, racers, and gladiators were stars. The theater set fashion, and many popular songs were first heard on the stage.

The role of spectacles and competition in ancient life at first seems surprising. The most distinguished individuals, even public officials, confess a passionate interest in these events without the slightest embarrassment. Rather than build dams or docks, cities and their benefactors ruined themselves building aqueducts (to supply water to the public baths), theaters, and gigantic amphitheaters. This passion can be understood. Public spectacles were not dependent on individual tastes (as opposed to policy), nor were they leisure activities (as opposed to the more serious and laborious parts of life). Hence it is wrong to draw a parallel with our Olympic Games or World Cup Soccer or World Series. The ancients did not distinguish between popular and elite sports, and spectacles were public institutions, organized (and sometimes financed) by government authorities. In a period in which idleness was an ideal, no contrast was drawn between pleasure and work; nobles and plebeians alike took public spectacles seriously.

Philosophers charged that the passions aroused by these spectacles were excessive, and Christians agreed: "The theater is lasciviousness, the Circus, suspense, and the arena, cruelty." As critics saw it, the cruelty belonged to the gladiators themselves, who volunteered to commit murder and suicide. All were volunteers; otherwise they would have put on a poor show. The criticism that occurs to us—that the spectators must have been sadists—never occurred to any Roman, philosopher or not. The gladiators brought Rome a strong dose of sadistic pleasure of which people fully approved: pleasure at the sight of bodies and at the sight of men dying. Gladiator fights were not mere fencing matches with actual risks. The whole point was to witness the death of one of the combatants or, better still, the decision whether to slit the throat or spare the life of a fallen gladiator who, exhausted and frightened for his life, was reduced to begging for quarter. The best fights were those that ended in exhaustion, with the life-or-death decision made by the patron who had paid for the show, in conjunction with the public. Innumerable images on lamps, plates, and household objects reproduced this great moment. And the patron boasted of having decided a man's fate: the cutting of the gladiator's throat was depicted in mosaic, painting, or sculpture and placed in his antechamber or on his tomb. If the patron had purchased from the imperial treasury men sen-

Detail of sarcophagus, 2nd century(?). Boxers: an evocation more literary than biographical of Greek athletic competition and educational methods. (Rome, Torlonia Collection.)

tenced to death in order to have them executed during the intermissions in the fights, he also had the artists show these prisoners being thrown to wild beasts. After all, he had paid for them. In Greek regions the death of a boxer during a match was not a "sports accident." It was a glory for the athlete to die in the arena, just as if he had died on the field of battle. The public praised his courage, his steadfastness, his will to win.

It would be wrong to conclude that Greco-Roman culture was sadistic. People were not convinced that watching suffering was pleasurable; they were critical of those, such as Emperor Claudius, who took obvious delight in viewing the slaughter, rather than adopting an objective attitude as if witnessing an exhibition of courage. Greek and Roman literature and imagery are not generally sadistic. In fact the contrary is true, and when the Romans colonized a barbarian nation their first concern was to prohibit human sacrifice. A culture is a tissue of exceptions, whose incoherence goes unnoticed by those involved in it, and in Rome spectacles were such exceptions. Images of victims occur in Roman art only because the victims died in spectacles that were sacred institutions. In our own time sadistic images, justified on patriotic grounds, occur in war films but are condemned elsewhere. Our pleasure in such things must be unwitting. The Christians were more critical of the pleasure than of the atrocity of the institution.

## Desire and Passion

Similar incoherences and baffling limitations are found in every century. In Greco-Roman culture we find them associated with another pleasure: love. If any aspect of ancient life has been distorted by legend, this is it. It is widely but mistakenly believed that antiquity was a Garden of Eden from which repression was banished, Christianity having yet to insinuate the worm of sin into the forbidden fruit. Actually, the pagans were paralyzed by prohibitions. The legend of pagan sensuality stems from a number of traditional misinterpretations. The famous tale of the debauches of Emperor Heliogabalus is nothing but a hoax perpetrated by the literati who authored that late forgery, the *Historia Augusta*. The legend also stems from the crudeness of the interdictions: "Latin words are an affront to decency," people used to say. For such naive souls, merely uttering a "bad word" provoked a shiver of perverse imagination or a gale of embarrassed laughter. Schoolboy daring.

What were the marks of the true libertine? A libertine was a man who violated three taboos: he made love before nightfall (daytime lovemaking was a privilege accorded to newlyweds on the day after the wedding); he made love without first darkening the room (the erotic poets called to witness the lamp that had shone on their pleasures); and he made love to a woman from whom he had removed every stitch of clothing (only fallen women made love without their brassieres, and paintings in Pompeii's bordellos showed even prostitutes wearing this ultimate veil). Libertines permitted themselves to touch rather than caress, though with the left hand only. The one chance a decent man had of seeing a little of his beloved's naked skin was if the moon happened to fall upon the open window at just the right moment. About libertine tyrants such as Heliogabalus, Nero, Caligula, and Domitian it was whispered that they had violated other taboos and made love with married women, well-bred maidens, freeborn adolescents, vestal virgins, or even their own sisters.

Pompeii, so-called Centenary House. Painting found in an out-of-the-way room of a house whose decoration ranks among the finest in Pompeii. For reasons of modesty the servant has not removed her final layer of clothing. (Naples, Archaeological Museum.)

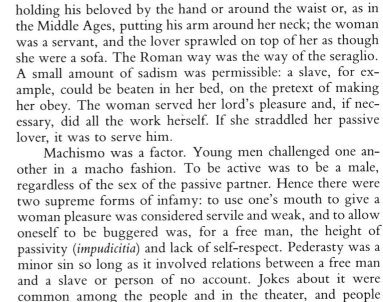

This puritanism went hand in hand with an attitude of superiority toward the love object, who was often treated like a slave. The attitude emblematic of the Roman lover was not holding his beloved by the hand or around the waist or, as in the Middle Ages, putting his arm around her neck; the woman was a servant, and the lover sprawled on top of her as though she were a sofa. The Roman way was the way of the seraglio. A small amount of sadism was permissible: a slave, for example, could be beaten in her bed, on the pretext of making her obey. The woman served her lord's pleasure and, if necessary, did all the work herself. If she straddled her passive lover, it was to serve him.

Machismo was a factor. Young men challenged one another in a macho fashion. To be active was to be a male, regardless of the sex of the passive partner. Hence there were two supreme forms of infamy: to use one's mouth to give a woman pleasure was considered servile and weak, and to allow oneself to be buggered was, for a free man, the height of passivity (*impudicitia*) and lack of self-respect. Pederasty was a minor sin so long as it involved relations between a free man and a slave or person of no account. Jokes about it were common among the people and in the theater, and people boasted of it in good society. Nearly anyone can enjoy sensual pleasure with a member of the same sex, and pederasty was not at all uncommon in tolerant antiquity. Many men of basically heterosexual bent used boys for sexual purposes. It was proverbially held that sex with boys procures a tranquil pleasure unruffling to the soul, whereas passion for a woman plunges a free man into unendurable slavery.

Thus, Roman love was defined by macho domination and refusal to become a slave of passion. The amorous excesses attributed to various tyrants were excesses of domination, described with misleading Sadian boldness. Nero, a tyrant who was weak more than cruel, kept a harem to serve his passive needs. Tiberius arranged for young slave boys to indulge his whims, and Messalina staged a pantomime of her own servility, usurping the male privilege of equating strength with frequency of intercourse. These acts were not so much violations as distortions of the taboos. They reflect a dreadful weakness, a need for planned pleasure. Like alcohol, lust is dangerous to virility and must not be abused. But gastronomy scarcely encourages moderation at table.

Amorous passion, the Romans believed, was particularly

Nymph attacked by satyr, 1st–2nd century. Decorative excess was well suited to scenes in which creatures of fancy made love, drank, or listened to music with Edenic ease. (Venice, Archaeological Museum.)

to be feared because it could make a free man the slave of a woman. He will call her "mistress" and, like a servant, hold her mirror or her parasol. Love was not the playground of individualists, the would-be refuge from society that it is today. Rome rejected the Greek tradition of "courtly love" of ephebes, which Romans saw as an exaltation of pure passion (in both senses of "pure," for the Greeks pretended to believe that a man's love for a freeborn ephebe was Platonic). When a Roman fell madly in love, his friends and he himself believed either that he had lost his head from overindulgence in sensuality or that he had fallen into a state of moral slavery. The lover, like a good slave, docilely offered to die if his mistress wished it. Such excesses bore the dark magnificence of shame, and even erotic poets did not dare to glorify them openly. They chose the roundabout means of describing such behavior as an amusing reversal of the normal state of affairs, a humorous paradox.

Petrarch's praise of passion would have scandalized the ancients or made them smile. The Romans were strangers to the medieval exaltation of the beloved, an object so sublime that it remained inaccessible. They were strangers, too, to modern subjectivism, to our thirst for experience. Standing apart from the world, we choose to experience something in order to see what effect it has, not because it is intrinsically valuable or required by duty. Finally, the Romans were strangers to the real paganism, the at times graceful and beautiful paganism of the Renaissance. Tender indulgence in pleasures of the senses that became, also, delights of the soul was not the way of the ancients. The most Bacchic scenes of the Romans have nothing of the audacity of some modern writers. The Romans knew but one variety of individualism, which confirmed the rule by seeming to contradict it: energetic indolence. With secret delight they discussed senators such as Scipio, Sulla, Caesar, Petronius, and even Catiline, men scandalously indolent in private yet extraordinarily energetic in public. It was an open secret among insiders that these men were privately lazy, and such knowledge gave the senatorial elite an air of royalty and of being above the common law while confirming its authentic spirit. Although the charge of energetic indolence was a reproach, it was also somehow a compliment. Romans found this compliment reassuring. Their brand of individualism sought not real experience, self-indulgence, or private devotion, but tranquilization.

Stucco roof of a large villa, which probably dates from slightly before the birth of Christ. Slimly elegant figures perform ambiguous rites. In the unarticulated spaces of an idealized landscape we count fewer trees than buildings of uncertain purpose, whose design is a fanciful extension of the exoticism of Alexandrian palaces. (Rome, Museum of the Baths.)

# ✑ Tranquilizers

HOW can individual anxieties about life be alleviated? This was the primary question for the various forms of wisdom that we call "ancient philosophy," as it was for religion, which generally did not aim to secure salvation in the hereafter. Indeed, the very existence of a hereafter was often denied, or else the other world was such a vague concept that it implied little more than the peacefulness of death, the tranquillity of the grave. Philosophy, religion, and the afterlife aroused precious little anxiety. What is more, the boundaries of their respective provinces were so unlike what they are today that the three words meant something quite different from what we imagine. Who am I? What should I do? Where am I headed, and have I any reason for hope? There is nothing natural about these modern questions; they derive from their Christian answers. Ancient philosophy and religion managed to get along without asking them. The problem of the ancients, with its various subdivisions, was different.

For us, philosophy is an academic subject and a part of our culture. Students study it and educated people are curious about it. Our religion is an amalgam of spiritual practices, moral precepts, and thoughts about the afterlife. The notion that after life there is nothing strikes us as eminently irreligious. For the ancients, however, moral precepts and spiritual practices were an essential part of "philosophy," rather than religion, which had very little to do with ideas about death and the hereafter. Sects existed, but they were philosophical sects, which furnished disciples with credos and rules of good behavior. One became a Stoic or an Epicurean and lived more or less faithfully, according to the convictions of one's sect— much as one might become a Christian or a Marxist today (thereby incurring a moral duty to live the faith or engage in active political work). Ancient China offers a useful parallel. There Confucianism and Taoism, doctrinal sects, offered theories and ethical systems to anyone who cared for such things. Another parallel is with modern Japan, where a man can take an interest in a Buddhist sect, yet still observe, like everyone else, Shinto religious practices. He may marry according to the Shinto rite but die and be buried according to Buddhist rite, implicitly accepting consoling Buddhist beliefs about the afterlife to which he devoted scarcely any thought during his lifetime.

## The Nature of Divinity

The paganism of the Greeks and Romans, though a religion without salvation or afterlife, was not necessarily indifferent to man's moral behavior. What has misled some historians is that this religion, without theology or church, was, if I may put it this way, more an à la carte religion than a religion with a fixed menu. If an established church is a "one-party state," then paganism was "free enterprise". Each man was free to found his own temple and preach whatever god he liked, just as he might open an inn or peddle a new product. And each man made himself the client of whichever god he chose, not necessarily his city's favorite deity: the choice was free.

Such freedom was possible because between what the pagans meant by "god" and what Jews, Christians, and Moslems mean, there is little in common but the name. For the three religions of the Book, God is infinitely greater than the world which he created. He exists solely as an actor in a cosmic drama in which the salvation of humankind is played out. The pagan gods, by contrast, live their lives and are not confined to a metaphysical role. They are part of this world, one of three races that populate the earth: animals, which are neither immortal nor gifted with reason; humans, who are mortal but reasonable; and gods, who are immortal and reasonable. So true is it that the divine race is an animal genus that every god is either male or female. From this it follows that the gods of all peoples are true gods. Other nations might worship gods unknown to the Greeks and Romans, or they might worship the same gods under different names. Jupiter was Jupiter the world over, just as a lion is a lion, but he happened to be called Zeus in Greek, Taranis in Gallic, and Yao in Hebrew. The names of the gods could be translated from one language to another, just like the names of planets and other material

Mosaic, Pompeii. Enjoy life while there is still time. The measuring instrument (a square with level) indicates that death is the great leveler and gives the true measure of all things. (Naples, Archaeological Museum.)

things. Belief in alien gods foundered only where it was the product of an absurd superstition, something that smacked of a fantastic bestiary. The Romans laughed at the gods with animal bodies worshiped by the Egyptians. In the ancient world religious people were as tolerant of one another as are Hindu sects. To take a special interest in one god was not to deny the others.

This fact was not without consequence for man's idea of his own place in the natural order. Imagine a circle, which represents the world according to the religions of the Book. Given man's importance in the cosmic drama, he occupies at least half the circle. What about God? He is so exalted, so awesome, that he remains far above the circle. To represent Him, draw an arrow, pointing upward from the center of the circle and mark it with the sign of infinity. Now consider the pagan world. Imagine a sort of staircase with three steps. On the lowest step stand the animals; on the next step, humans; and on the third step, the gods. In order to become a god, one did not need to rise very far. The gods stood just above humans, so that it often makes sense to translate the Latin and Greek words for "divine" as "superhuman." Epicurus, according to one of his followers, "was a god, yes, a god," by which he meant a superhuman genius. This explains why the cosmos was characterized as "divine"; things occurred that were superhuman, that no human could cause to occur. This also explains why it was possible to apotheosize kings and emperors. The practice was ideological hyperbole, perhaps, but not absurd. The emperor simply moved up a notch; he did not go soaring off toward infinity. Given this conception of divinity, the Stoics and Epicureans were able to ask disciples to aspire to become sages, that is, mortal equals of the gods, "supermen."

Human beings entered into relations with both the lower fauna and the divine fauna. Because the gods were superior to men, men were obliged to pay them homage, to offer the same respect (*colere, timan*) offered to superior men, to sovereigns. The gods had their own ways and their own shortcomings; it was not amiss to smile respectfully at them, much as one might be amused by the behavior of some foreign potentate, wealthy enough to indulge his every desire. People joked about the innumerable loves of the great Jupiter much as the subjects of libertine kings joked about the royal loves, while showing proper fear of and respect for the throne. Joking about the sacred requires simple faith. Relations between

The "great cameo of France," probably A.D. 17. This is neither the most beautiful nor the least boring of ancient cameos, but it is the largest (12 inches). Depicted are members of the dynasty founded by Augustus, apotheosized or in glory. The piece traveled from the imperial treasury of Rome to that of Byzantium and finally to the Sainte-Chapelle in Paris, where it was brought by pillaging crusaders. (Paris, Bibliothèque Nationale, Cabinet des Médailles.)

Ephesus. One of two temples to the apotheosized Hadrian, donated by a public benefactor in A.D. 118, with graceful and sumptuous floral decoration. The prettiness of the facade results from the violation of a rule to which our eyes are unwittingly accustomed: rather than a straight lintel supported by two round columns or an arcade supported by two rectangular pillars, we have here an arcade on columns, imitating eastern models.

men and gods were reciprocal. A believer who promised Aesculapius a cock in return for a cure hoped that the divine race would honor its contracts as faithfully as men of good faith honored theirs. Sometimes they were disappointed: "Is that what you call honest dealings, O Jupiter!" When men were disappointed in the gods, they criticized them, just as we criticize the government: "Jupiter, have pity on this sick girl. If you let her die, you'll be blamed." When the beloved prince Germanicus died, the Roman mob demolished temples, as demonstrators today might stone an embassy. People could turn their backs on the gods: "Since the gods did not spare me, I will not spare them either," wrote one furious unfortunate.

---

*Relations with the Gods*

Relations between men and deities resembled relations between ordinary men and such powerful brethren as kings or patrons. A man's first duty to a god was to salute the god's image. The most common form of prayer involved flattering the god's power: "Help me, Jupiter, because it is in your power." If the god did not help, he risked incurring suspicion that he was less powerful than he seemed. Some people sought to wear the gods down (*fatigare deos*), to overcome their haughty indifference with endless prayers. They "frequented their temples" and went every morning to hail the gods, as clients hailed their patrons. Special homage was paid to the god of the temple near one's home, for a powerful neighbor was the best and most natural protector a person could have. With liberal grace and serene naiveté, the pagans modeled relations with the gods on political and social relations among themselves. It was the Christians who substituted the paternal model, basing relations with God on relations within the family, which is why Christianity, unlike paganism, would be a religion of obedience and love. The genius of Saint Augustine, the sublimity of Saint Theresa—these were extraordinary elaborations of the familial model. And so was Luther's anguish over the arbitrariness of the all-powerful Father. Pagans of sound mind rejected still another model of divine relations: the servile model. The man who constantly trembled with fear at the thought of the gods, as though they were capricious and cruel masters, projected an image unworthy of the gods and unworthy of a free man. Such fear of the gods (*deisidaimonia*) was what the Romans meant by "superstition." They left it to the Oriental masses, accustomed to bow down to potentates, to conceive of piety as a matter of declaring oneself the slave or servant of a god. At bottom the classical relation between man and god was noble and free, one of admiration.

True piety meant thinking of the gods as benevolent, just, and providential, like good supermen. Not all men achieved this, because every man's character affects his behavior with the gods. Some held that a god is only as good as his word; they offered a contract—"Cure me and I'll give you an offering"—and paid up only if their prayers were granted. Others believed that the gods were as unscrupulous as themselves: "Make me richer than my neighbor," they asked. They did not dare to utter such a wish out loud, in front of other worshipers, so they wrote it down and left the sealed document on the altar. The truly devout were more scrupulous, knowing that the gods have always preferred a humble cake offered by a pure heart to the costliest of sacrifices. If they multiplied their solemn vows and turned to the gods whenever they were in difficulty, it was out of love, not self-interest. A pious man liked to be in contact with divinity as often as possible: prayers, pilgrimages, apparitions of the gods in dreams all served. Piety lay not in faith, works, or contemplation but in a whole range of practices that seem self-interested only because the beloved god-patron was a protector.

Two serpents, symbols of the Lares, and an altar, indicating that they were worshiped. These symbols were borrowed from Greece, where many homes had live but quite harmless serpents as tutelary deities. (Ostia, Archaeological Museum.)

Illness, travel, and childbirth were occasions to prove one's loyal confidence in one's protector.

Some of these practices were consecrated by tradition. What was the mark of an impious man? A little-known passage in Apuleius tells us: "He never made solemn vow to any god, never went to temple. When he passed a chapel, he would have thought it a sin to bring his hand to his lips to signify adoration. Not once did he offer the gods of his estates, who fed and clothed him, first choice of the harvest and of the increase of his flocks. On the grounds of his country seat there is no chapel, no place consecrated to the gods, no sacred wood." A pious man behaves quite differently. When traveling, he "stops when he passes a chapel or sacred wood and composes a vow, places a piece of fruit on the altar, and sits for a moment with the gods." The gift and the vow, the exchange of divine protection for man's gift, are as important as prayer. If God is a father, there is little to do but pray to him. But if the gods are patrons, one can offer them gifts and receive gifts in return, symbolizing a friendship between unequal partners, each with a life of his own; indeed, there would be no reason for men and gods to enter into relations at all were such relations not in the interest of both parties. If the human partner behaved any more humbly, he would not be acting like a free man. People smiled when women went to temple and told the goddess Isis their troubles. Such intimacy with the gods was plebeian. A free man knew how to maintain a proper distance between himself and other men and between himself and the gods. He did not abase himself before his deity. Leave it to the common people to spend all day in the temples waiting on their gods like slaves, behaving like valets and hairdressers before the statues of their deities.

These private religious practices, reminiscent of the popular cults of the saints in the Middle Ages, were reassuring in two ways. People with little or no religious disposition, who in another society would have been nonbelievers, sought in relations with the gods a sort of magic tranquilizer for the dangers and sorrows of real life; for them pious practices were the equivalent of a good-luck charm or amulet. For those of religious bent, these practices facilitated contact with "another" reality. The divine devalued the real by suggesting the existence of another realm. The closer one came to this other world, the smaller reality seemed; the real ceased to be man's only concern. In private letters, numerous examples of which have been found in Egypt, there was much talk of the gods

Bronze statuette. Not an exhibitionist but the god Priapus himself, quite male despite his feminine hair style and clothing. His divinity was limited to his power to chase away thieves, whom he frightened by his obscenity. This statuette was intended to make people laugh and to ward off the evil eye by means of indecency. (Paris, Petit Palais, Dutuit Collection.)

(although the divinity of the emperor is never mentioned). Detailed and complex, religious rites were performed with great care in a meditative spirit. Innumerable bas-reliefs depict worshipers, both male and female, making offerings to the gods. If we knew nothing of the pleasure that pagans took in performing these rites, we could no more understand these sculptures than an asexual being can understand an erotic film.

The tranquilizer of magic was hardly distinguishable from the tranquilizer of religion. Magical and religious acts and symbols were commonly confounded. ("Religion" is one of those paradoxical things whose essence is confusion.) A country chapel evoked the possibility of supernatural aid. The simplest religious act, such as pouring onto the household altar the first drops from a cup one was about to drink from (*libatio*), proved that the utilitarian was not everything. The emperor himself was worshiped in private and had his place in every household's niche of sacred images. Was this because

Left: Pompeii: bacchante sacrificing on an altar before a statue of Bacchus. Most Bacchic images are of no religious significance, but some embellished the sacred meeting place of a sect or the private home of a Bacchic priest. (Naples, Archaeological Museum.)

Right: Small bronze: female worshiper pouring a libation. An authentic pious image, as opposed to an image of fantasy or myth. The woman's left arm hangs submissively at her side. (Paris, Petit Palais, Dutuit Collection.)

people considered him a god? No. Nobody made vows to him and no one imagined that this mortal had the power to cure illness or recover lost objects. Was it mere religious camouflage for patriotic obedience? No. Was it a cult of personality for a charismatic dictator? Not that either. In drinking a toast to the emperor's sacred image after dinner, a man raised himself to the level of that ineffable otherness, proof of whose existence lay in the fact of its veneration.

*"The Gods"*

Small bronze. Tutelary deity of city, or City apotheosized. Another authentic pious image, with little to satisfy the fancy or the taste for art. This image of the City wears a crown in the form of a rampart. The goddess prepares a libation: in a kind of shorthand, the artist has depicted her making the gesture actually made by her worshipers. (Paris, Petit Palais, Dutuit Collection.)

Private religion played a third role (although not as well as philosophy or, later, Christianity): it was the impartial guarantor of a system of ethics and of interests that wished to appear disinterested. Thus far we have considered religion only in relation to the various individual gods of the pantheon—Jupiter, Mercury, Ceres, and so on. Yet the Greeks and Romans referred just as often to "the gods" as a group. Or, rather than use the plural, they sometimes spoke of the "divine" in the neuter or even of "god," that is, of god in general (just as a philosopher might say "man") or even "Jupiter." The plural "gods" and these various synonyms meant something quite different from the sum of all the individual gods. "The gods" had a function, and virtues, that each single god lacked, or at least did not always have. Only individual gods were honored by cults; "the gods" were not. But their will was cited; it was hoped that "the gods" would not fail to be providential, reward their friends, and avenge themselves against their enemies. "The gods" loved virtuous men and would ensure the victory of the just cause. They will punish my persecutor, said one oppressed man; they will punish that scoundrel in the afterlife, they will not allow such crimes to go unpunished. "The gods" will protect our city. "The gods" were Providence to every hope. It was commonly said that "the gods" governed events or that they had arranged the world for man. In truth, no one had any very clear idea how they went about doing these things, but there was no need to wonder about it. The gods' intervention was recognized and anticipated only where laudable and desirable, and no attention was paid to anything else. To say that an event had been brought about by the hand of the gods was just a way of saying that it was undeniably praiseworthy and that Heaven itself ratified this objective judgment. With "the gods" in the plural, paganism had its Providence, which it adduced but did not worship.

What is more, not only "the gods" (or Providence) but also those good supermen, the individual gods of the pantheon, promoted good morals. They were for virtue and against crime. To be sure, the divine race existed for its own sake and was not defined in terms of its role as lawgiver or avenger. But gods were like good men: they approved virtue and hated vice, and the wicked, who imputed to the gods an immorality all their own, would one day learn this lesson, to their sorrow. There is my considered answer to the highly controversial but ill-posed question, Was paganism an ethical religion in the same sense as Christianity? The gods liked men to behave piously toward them. Because they profited from what men offered them? No, but because piety is a virtue and gods like virtue, just as men do. "I alone survived," says a man who survived a shipwreck, "because I am a pious man." A little later he rectifies this: "I alone was saved because never in all my life did I do anything wrong." The gods, as I said earlier, were a divine species of fauna, males and females whose genealogies and adventures formed the subject of myths set in an imaginary time, prior to and different from our own. In the present, however, time has come to a halt for them; they do not age any more than the characters in our comic strips. These fictional beings also played the role of metaphysical divinities, of Providence and the Good, and had done so since the time of the Homeric poems. Here popular religion, which I have been describing, and the religion of the cultivated class, the wealthy elite, had come to a parting of the ways several centuries earlier. The elite could believe in a metaphysical divine but not in the gods of the mythological pantheon, from which, however, they found it impossible to divorce themselves entirely.

---

Irreligion was unknown among the Roman populace. The people never ceased to believe and to pray. But what might a cultivated Roman, a Cicero, a Horace, an emperor, a senator, a notable, have thought about the phantasmagoria of the ancestral gods? My answer is categorical: he did not believe in them at all. He had read Plato and Aristotle, who four centuries earlier had already ceased to believe. Virgil, an exquisitely religious soul, believed in Providence but not in the gods of his own poems—Venus, Juno, or Apollo. Cicero and the solemn encyclopedist Pliny could not find enough sarcasms to heap upon the gods. These ethereal beings, they

*The Religion of the Educated*

Pompeii. Because inlaying was considered a minor art, the artist felt free to portray this touchingly familiar scene. Despite the difficulty of cutting marble, Hellenistic craftsmen produced remarkably fluid images. At least seventy other examples of this Venus undoing her sandal have survived. (Naples, Archaeological Museum.)

wrote, have human figures, if the sculptors and naive believers are to be trusted. Are we to believe, then, that inside their bodies we find a stomach, intestines, and sexual parts? What, pray tell, do the blessed immortals do with these organs? The beliefs of the governing class deserve a separate chapter in every history of Roman religion. Such a chapter would treat not Mercury or Juno but perhaps "Providence, Chance, or Fate"—not a bad title. For that was the crux of the religious problem. Should one believe in Providence, as did many pious and cultivated souls and followers of the Stoics? Should one believe in Fate, as did those who studied physics and astronomy (which included astrology)? Or was there nothing in the confusion of this world but Chance, as many impious people held, thereby denying the existence of any kind of Providence? But all educated people smiled at the women of the lower orders who worshiped the goddess Latona in her temple, believed that she looked as the sculptor depicted her, found her happy to have a daughter as beautiful as Diana, and wished that their own daughters were as pretty. In the senatorial order, guardian of the public religion and breeding ground of its priests, the consecrated doctrine was one of amused skepticism regarding official religious ceremonies and naive popular beliefs.

Yet if it was impossible to believe in the strict letter of the old religion, it was just as impossible to dispense with it entirely, not because it was the official creed, believed in by the populace, but because it contained a kernel of truth. Polytheism gravitated not so much toward monotheism (which historical accident would later bring to the fore) as toward the simplicity of abstraction (and it is of the essence of abstract words that they are used only in the singular). Providence and the Good were subjects about which philosophers discoursed at length. A cultivated man might have stated his beliefs more or less as follows: "Providence exists, as I want to believe. The kernel of truth in all these fables about the gods must lie therein. But is there any other reality to Apollo or Venus? Are these names of the one God? Emanations of the Godhead? Names for his virtues? An abstract principle, yet at the same time a living thing? Or nothing but a meaningless fable?" There was certainty on the essential point, divine Providence, but doubt about everything else. It was therefore permissible to participate in popular religion, partly out of condescension, for the fables tell the truth in a naive, thus false, language, and partly out of intellectual prudence, for who knows if

Apollo, despite the legends that surround him, is not just a name but an Emanation. It was possible to use the language of the old religion without seeming ridiculous. When the skeptic Horace just missed being crushed by a falling tree, he thanked the gods of the pantheon according to the traditional forms. Though sure that he owed his salvation to the God-head, he did not know how to thank that abstraction by other than the venerable ceremonial means. When he saw his maid offer a cake to the protective geniuses of his house, he understood that she dimly sensed the conclusion to which he eventually came: atheists notwithstanding, the Hazards of the World are also a Providence whose will it is that we conform to the Good.

---

*The Second Paganism*

We have seen what the common people, on the one hand, and the cultivated class, on the other, thought about the gods. But around A.D. 100, speaking very roughly, there occurred a transformation similar to that which we have witnessed in other areas. The old paganism was internalized and modernized and ceased to be beneath the notice of cultivated men and women. Do not confuse this development with the more recent conflict between Catholicism and the Enlightenment. Antique irreligion was not an episode in the allegedly eternal wars between enlightenment and obscurantism, or between freedom of thought and the authority of the church. It hinged on the question of whether religion was or was not culturally respectable. Pagan religion oppressed no one. The question was whether, for an educated person, it was ridiculous, beneath contempt.

I am using the word "culture" in a very simple sense: "to be cultivated" meant "not to think like the common folk." Culture was a privilege, along with wealth and power. This is not true in all societies. In Homer's day leaders talked, thought, prayed, danced, and even dressed like their followers, whose beliefs they shared. But Hellenistic and Roman society was quite different from Homeric society: it was riven by a cultural divide. For Cicero, religion was an amalgam of foolish superstitions, good for the uneducated. How could anyone believe, naively, that Castor and Pollux had manifested themselves to a citizen in the Via Salaria, or that Apollo hovered in the heavens with a silver bow?

That is not all. A cultivated man usually attaches too much importance to words. He expresses his opinion and imagines that his words correspond exactly to his actions (just as sociologists take the answers that people give to their questionnaires as an authentic representation of their thinking). The religion of the common people was not easily expressed in words, however. A common man who prayed fervently to Apollo rarely thought, while praying, of the god's silver bow or the puerile myths about his loves and exploits. If questioned, however, he would speak of those legends, docilely repeating what he had been told. The educated judged the uneducated on the basis of these naive responses, attaching greater importance to words than to the secrets of the heart.

When paganism began spontaneously to modernize itself around A.D. 100, it ceased to be a mythological religion and began to prefigure the Christian relation to God. Relations between men and gods ceased to be those between two living species, two kinds of fauna each with a life of its own, and became those between a monarch and his subjects. This monarch was either a single, providential god or a collection of providential gods, all of which resembled one another and may have been nothing more than several names for one god. These gods were interchangeable, and all wore the providential uniform. They lost their mythological biography and personal traits. All fulfilled the same function: to govern, counsel, and protect men and rescue them from the grip of blind Fortune or Fate. It was not ridiculous to believe in such gods.

The gods no longer existed in a realm of their own; their existence corresponded to the function of governing individual human beings. And individuals began to count docile obedience to the sovereign gods as a virtue. I do not think that this docility was adopted from the ancient Orient, long habituated to humbling itself before potentates. There is nothing servile about it. The believer did not seek to abase himself but to exalt the sovereignty of the divine. There was nothing capricious or venal about the providence of the gods, which became one with justice and reason. People no longer curried favor with the gods by promising sacrifices. In the old paganism the worshiper took the initiative and offered the god a bargain: "If you see to it that I have a good journey to Alexandria, I'll make you a sacrifice." In the new paganism the initiative belonged to the gods themselves, who gave orders (called "oracles") to the faithful for their own good: "Go to Alexandria without fear, then offer me a sacrifice." People felt happy and reassured because they lived under the protection of a sovereign deity.

Pompeii, tomb of a woman. The ship of life has arrived at its destination, and the sailors furl the sail.

Finally the new paganism ceased to be institutionalized. It was much more informal than the old paganism. Each person could shape religion as he pleased. In the past, when someone wished to know the will of the gods, he sought out a priest or oracle: a legitimate institution. Now, the orders of the gods were conveyed to individuals in all sorts of ways, outside official channels. They came in dreams, in ominous incidents, in vague presentiments, and so on. Divine commandments were seen everywhere. The boundary between ordinary life and the divine became fluid. The gods traveled everywhere, without stopping at the official customs stations. In addition, a whole literature of popular piety made its appearance. Some of these books were best-sellers that helped to modernize and "spiritualize" popular religious practices.

---

*The Afterlife*

One concern is curiously absent from these musings on religion: the afterlife, the immortality of the soul. The Romans devoted little more thought to this subject than do most of our contemporaries. The Epicureans did not believe in the immortality of the soul, Stoics did not believe in it much, and the official religion for the most part avoided the question. Beliefs about the afterlife were a subject separate from religion. The most widely held opinion, even among the lower orders, was that death is nothingness, eternal sleep. The vague notion that Shades survived somewhere after death was, it was often repeated, nothing more than a fable. To be sure, numerous philosophers had speculated in great detail about the survival of the soul and its fate in the hereafter, but these speculations remained the property of small sects. No generally accepted doctrine taught that there is anything after death other than a cadaver. Lacking a common doctrine, Romans did not know what to think; consequently they assumed nothing and believed nothing.

By contrast, funeral rites and funerary art made all sorts of affirmations to allay the anxieties that attend the anticipation of death. Even if people did not strictly believe these affirmations, they appreciated the consolation they contained. A sarcophagus found at Simpelveld, extensively carved on the inside, showed nothing less than a domestic interior in which the deceased lay on her bed, propped on one elbow. The Fates cut the thread of life, but the tomb, this tomb in particular, spun it out indefinitely, embroidering on the metaphor of eternal rest: everything continues after everything has ceased,

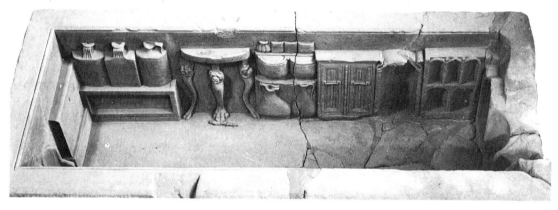

Sarcophagus found at Simpelveld. Note the furniture. (Leyden, Museum of Antiquities.)

and nothingness assumes the comforting form of monotony. On many children's tombs a sleeping *putto* equivocates between sleep and death. Images of ships or of travelers on horseback or in carriages, which appeared on many tombs, illustrated not some voyage in the hereafter but the voyage that is life in this world. The natural end of that voyage is the port or roadside marker that is death. It was consoling to think of death as a time of rest after a long journey. A more resigned attitude was that life is after all but a brief voyage. On some sarcophagi in fact a comparison was made between life and the Circus races: the chariots race seven laps around the course and then are gone.

The Romans had their feast of the dead, which lasted from February 13 to 21. During this period they left offerings at the graves of their loved ones. But they no more believed that the dead ate these offerings than we believe that the dead admire or smell the flowers that we place on their graves. In

Greece people had long placed in graves terra-cotta figurines, tanagras, representing Cupids, Victories, or Sirens. Everyday religion had little to say about these funerary geniuses, so special beliefs pertaining particularly to funerals were created. Distinct from other beliefs, these were viewed, in the absence of more substantive teachings, as circumstantial rather than universal truths. By the time of the Roman Empire they had fallen into oblivion. Greek tombs, like their Roman counterparts, now contained only small objects of homage such as lamps, mirrors, and vials of perfume. Consoling ideas about the afterlife stemmed from the desire to believe, not from the authority of an established religion; they therefore lacked the coherence of dogma. As Rohde has observed, a single epitaph could simultaneously exhibit perfect incredulity and sublime hope. A problem of interpretation confronts anyone who would move from ancient images to ancient mentalities, however. What an image represents often matters less than the sphere to which it belongs. A Bacchic bas-relief on a tomb indicates not so much belief in Bacchus as the existence of a sphere of religious ideas—nothing more precise. Consider a modern analogy. Many sixteenth- and seventeenth-century religious paintings exhibit quite secular attractions: saints who are too pretty by far, sometimes depicted in a state of semi-nudity. Yet any viewer, even a *philosophe* or libertine, would have recognized these as religious paintings and assigned them to a sphere higher than that reserved for Boucher's nudes.

Bacchus, that happy deity and marginal character who lent himself to every innovation, a god who belonged primarily to mythology and was ignored by common religion

Life is a circuit of the track. (Naples, Archaeological Museum.)

and whom imagination could bend as it pleased, was the favorite god of graveside theology. His legend and rites were depicted on numerous sarcophagi, and especially on the tombs of children. The death of a youngster called for consoling poetization. One adolescent's epitaph reads: "He was kidnaped by Bacchus to become his initiate and companion." Only occasionally are these the sarcophagi of initiates of some Bacchic sect, and their decoration does not reflect the convictions peculiar to such sects. Nor do they illustrate, as some have alleged, the existence of a widespread Bacchic religion. Yet these figures are not just decorative. People were never sure just how much truth there might be in any of these fables or sectarian doctrines. Bacchus, god of the hereafter, was a consoling "maybe" about whom everyone had heard.[2]

Epitaphs and funerary art tactfully suggested none but consoling ideas. But Plato, Epicurus, Lucretius, and others repeatedly tell that the souls of the dying were often troubled by memories of their sins and crimes and anguished at the thought of soon having to appear before the gods, who would punish them. To us, such statements seem comprehensible. What dying people feared was not punishment in the underworld, a mythological fantasy that no one took literally. It was "the gods" who frightened them, for everyone knew that the gods were just, providential, and vengeful, even if they did not ask exactly how these qualities manifested themselves. The gods were there to avenge human conscience. Valerius Maximus writes: "That scoundrel died with thoughts of his perfidy and ingratitude on his mind. His soul was torn apart

A child died so young that his life's journey ends (left) as it began (right), on his mother's knees. (Rome, Museum of the Baths.)

as by a torturer, for he knew that he was passing from the gods of heaven, who hated him, to the gods of the underworld, who execrated him."

I do not believe that Lucretius, an Epicurean, exaggerated the torment of the dying in order to make his sect's tranquilizing philosophy seem more essential. He simply told the truth: paganism, a religion of festival, had an ethical component, which aroused anxieties that it could not allay because it was not a soteriological religion that could reassure the faithful by organizing their lives in this world on the pretext of securing salvation in the next. Those seeking to learn how to live in this world had to turn to the philosophical sects: the Stoics, the Epicureans, and others. The wisdom these sects offered promised to free individuals from anxiety and make them happy—that is, tranquil.

---

*Philosophical Sects*

In a famous book, more learned than perceptive, Max Pohlenz expressed astonishment that the philosophy of the ancients, unlike that of the moderns, based moral obligation on the self-interested grounds of happiness. In this he displayed an odd lack of historical sense. It is hard to see how the ancients could have done otherwise, for what they meant by philosophy did not take for its aim, as Kant took for his, establishing the possible grounds of morality. The aim of ancient philosophy was to provide individuals with a method for obtaining happiness. A sect was not a school where people came to learn general ideas; they came looking for rational means of achieving tranquillity. Morality was among the remedies prescribed by certain sects, who gave reasoned justifications for their prescriptions. This has confused modern students of the subject.

The Epicurean and Stoic sects offered adherents a formula based on the nature of the universe (that is, philosophically grounded), whose purpose was to enable them to live without fear of men, gods, chance, or death, to make individual happiness independent of accidents of fate. In summing up their aims, both sects declared that they wished to make men as tranquil as the gods, their mortal equals. The differences between the two sects lay in subtleties, and in the metaphysics used to justify their remedies. Stoicism (not to be confused with what Vigny calls by that name) prescribed mental exercises by means of which a man might maintain his mind in a state where nothing could harm it. Epicureanism held that

Tomb of a physician, 3rd–4th century. He is not, as was once thought, reading a medical treatise but rather his classics; however narrow his profession, he is a cultivated man. (New York, Metropolitan.)

man's chief need was to free himself of illusory anxieties. Both sects were contemptuous not only of death but also of vain desires, desires for money and honors, perishable goods that cannot promise unbreachable security. The Epicureans taught that man should liberate himself from false needs; they recommended living on friendship and cold water. The Stoics argued that their method was based on reason and Providence, while the Epicureans, with their atomism, allayed fears born of superstition. The Stoics believed that human beings feel innate affection for their families and cities, so that if duties toward these are neglected, feelings of incompleteness and unhappiness result. The Epicureans, on the other hand, held that human happiness requires us to abide by only those pacts that we ourselves have ratified out of deliberate, self-interested calculation. Both sects held that a man who, because of illness or persecution, found it impossible to lead a humane life in his body or his city could reasonably resort to suicide; indeed, suicide was the recommended remedy in such situations.

The sects did not barrage their members with moral precepts; they promised happiness. Would a literate man have made a free choice to join a sect had he not been seeking personal advantage? Stoicism and Epicureanism were intellectual faiths. They asked how man might be made heroic, how he might be delivered from his anxieties and vain desires. And

Sarcophagus, traces of polychrome, 2nd century. Bacchantes and musicians. Silenus and Pan precede Bacchus, left, in chariot drawn by centaur. The human figures are overcome by rapture or ecstasy; the animals, similarly overwhelmed, lie on the ground. (Rome, Museum of the Conservators.)

they answered: by intellectual persuasion. If a man's intellect is supplied with good reasons, his will will follow. It is hard to see what authority a "director of conscience" might have exercised in the ancient world other than that of persuasion, for his followers were not subject to his discipline.

There was a clear difference between the sects and the schools. All people of good society had been to school in their youth and studied rhetoric. A few, at some point in their lives, "converted" (this was the word they used) to the doctrine of some sect. Besides a handful of wealthy converts who lived lives of leisure, sects also included a handful of converts of more modest station. These men had little income and were obliged to supplement their meager resources by accepting positions as tutors in noble households, becoming clients of powerful lords, or making careers as itinerant lecturers. They took vows of devotion to philosophy, proof of which could be seen in their austere clothing—almost the uniform of the philosopher. For the rich, who did not earn their daily bread from their devotion, the degree of commitment to the sect varied. Only the truly convinced carried the consequences of their profession of faith to the point of wearing philosophical garb and long, ill-kempt beards. Most well-to-do converts were content to change a few symbolic details in the way they lived, to read the works of their sects' authors, and to keep a philosophy tutor around to teach them the dogma of the faith and advertise the spiritual elevation of the household.

Why did these wealthy converts hesitate to commit themselves fully to the wisdom of their sect? They frequently claimed that they did not have the time, that managing their property or tending to the duties of office demanded too much of them. In any case, as Seneca pointed out, the important thing was that they should devote their thoughts to the sects' teachings, surround themselves with friends who were philosophers, and spend their leisure hours in conversation with the philosopher they kept on call. To one high official attracted to Stoicism, Seneca recommended simply reading and doing mental exercises, avoiding practices that he, Seneca, considered more ostentatious than sincere, such as wearing the philosopher's garb and beard, refusing to eat from silver plates, and sleeping on a mattress on the floor. Nevertheless, many people were quite serious about changing their lives, and some even succeeded in doing so.

*The Influence of Philosophy*

Simple people made fun of the converts and noted the contrast between their avowed convictions and the way they lived—their opulence, their groaning tables, and their mistresses. These jibes were dictated by envy, for philosophers as a human type enjoyed a considerable measure of admiration and authority. A senator could, without losing caste, dress and write as a philosopher, and so could an emperor. No Roman writer, poet, or scholar played the role of public conscience, which was reserved for the philosophers, provided only that the way they lived, their exterior trappings, proved that they lived in accordance with their teachings. Philosophers were permitted to administer public rebukes and to give advice; one of their functions was to give high moral counsel to the cities they visited. When Saint Paul preached in the Areopagus of Athens, he was following their example. In essence, the philosophers constituted a lay clergy, and the mockers told merry tales about them similar to those told about the ways of the clergy in the Middle Ages. One senator, condemned to death, went to meet his fate in the company of his domestic philosopher, who continued to exhort him right to the very end. Another, on his deathbed, engaged in learned conversation with a philosopher of the Cynical sect. Still another great personage, gravely ill, heeding the advice of a Stoic that he commit suicide, let himself die of hunger.

Every convert to a doctrine became a propagandist for the faith and sought to attract new members. One prospect might prove refractory, but another was not hopeless, there was still a chance of winning him over. The words "conversion," "dogma," and "heresy" were borrowed from the philosophical sects by the Christians. Stoicism, Epicureanism, Platonism, Cynicism, Pythagoreanism: each sect continued the doctrine of its founder and remained, or believed that it remained, faithful to his dogmas. The idea of an unfettered search for the truth was anathema. The doctrine was passed on from generation to generation as a sacred treasure, and each sect engaged in ardent polemic with its rivals. The sometimes considerable modifications these doctrines incurred over the course of centuries were introduced unwittingly. The sects were associations of believers who entered into them freely; although there was no hierarchy or organization, nonetheless they were "sectarian" in their beliefs. Besides being unorganized, these sects differed from the Christian churches and sects in one major respect: they did not assume that one day their truth would or could impose itself on all mankind. They believed that only a handful of the fortunate would ever see the light. They did not seek to save mankind in spite of itself. In other words, their universalism was not imperialistic.

The dogmas of the sects served as rules of life for the

Sarcophagus said to be of Plotinus, late 3rd–4th century. The deceased, a man of letters, who must have been a celebrity, sits in the center, a bundle of books at his feet. Around him are relatives or disciples. At either end a Sage stands guard, setting this uncommon family or group of disciples apart from the common run of mankind. Chronological objections have been raised to the identification of this tomb as that of Plotinus. Every age boasted more than one celebrated man of letters. (Rome, Vatican Museums.)

handful of believers who considered themselves members. As Pierre Hadot has shown, an ancient philosophy was not constructed to be interesting or true but to be put into practice, to change lives, and to be profoundly assimilated through intellectual exercises, which would serve as the model for the spiritual exercises of Christianity. These exercises were to be practiced every day: "Remind yourself constantly of the truths that you have often heard and even taught yourself." Members were supposed to meditate upon the sect's dogmas and apply them to everyday events; they were supposed to look for occasions to think about these dogmas, to recapitulate the verities, to repeat them silently in the presence of others and aloud to themselves; and they were supposed to attend public lectures and to give lectures themselves. Spiritual exercises were also supposed to be recorded in writing. According to Hadot, the *Meditations* of Marcus Aurelius are not, as was long believed, the emperor's intimate diary, a collection of random thoughts and free speculation, but the product of methodically following a typical three-point plan of meditation.

The influence of sectarian doctrine was not limited to members of the sect. It extended to many different aspects of social, to say nothing of political, life, although the significance of many points of doctrine changed as its scope of application widened. Stoicism became an ideology of right-thinking people, universally respected. The Stoics were such vigorous conformists that people mistook them for original thinkers. More generally, philosophy ceased to be a method for living and became an object of intellectual curiosity among cultivated people. It was little more than culture and ideology to a man like Cicero, who lived as a lettered senator rather than a philosopher. Philosophy played a considerable role in his intellectual life and almost no role at all in his personal life. No man could claim to be educated without some knowledge of sectarian dogma. Physicians and architects were divided over the question whether their arts should be philosophical or strictly empirical. Above all, the philosophical doctrines provided the raw material of rhetoric. A student or amateur of rhetorical art could shine by decking his argument out in philosophical dress. Teachers of eloquence taught apprentice orators which doctrines were most useful to study. Philosophy ended up as part of cultural life, incorporated into its ceremonies and works, and people flocked to hear the eloquent public lectures given by leading thinkers. It became an essential ingredient of that *paideia* that literate men held up as the ideal of their idle lives. On tombs, the image of a man of letters reading might equally well represent a philosopher, an amateur of belles-lettres, or a rhetor. The distinctions were irrelevant. For the ancients, a man's study was a sanctuary of private life. It was furnished with the works of writers and thinkers and decorated with their busts or painted portraits.

The degree to which the lettered class, including those of its members not enticed by the sects, was imbued with philosophical notions can be gauged by its capacity to reflect upon itself. Philosophy's success is demonstrated by the frequency of philosophical suicide. A senator who learned that the emperor was about to charge him with some crime and sentence him to death might choose to end his own life. Or a sick or elderly man might choose to die a decent death, one less painful than if he waited for nature to take its course. Suicide was accepted, even admired. The courage of the man who decides to end his suffering and accept eternal rest was extolled by the philosophers, for the suicide proved the truth of the philosophical notion that what matters is the quality and not the quantity of the time that one lives. Private life took refuge in self-mastery, in both senses of the term: having the strength to control the course of one's life, and granting oneself the sovereign privilege to do so rather than leaving the decision to nature or to a god. Suicide and eternal peace symbolized the ideal of private tranquillity, to be achieved by renouncing illusory riches.

---

The ancients sought not to retreat from social and ethical norms but to "care for the self," achieving security at the cost of pruning back the ego. In other societies private life later came to mean secession from public life, or sailing life's seas as a solitary mariner—or a pirate—tossed by the winds of individual desire, fancy, and fantasy.

*Care of the Self*

It is narcissistic and self-indulgent to give free rein to desire, fancy, and fantasy. Smiles are rare in Greco-Roman art. Tranquillity was bought at the price of tension and renunciation—hallmarks of the ancient world as much as of the world of the samurai or of Queen Victoria. The beliefs of the ancients may seem somewhat superficial. Their moralists, thinkers, and poets seem naive in their overestimation of the possibilities of self-censorship and facile in their underestimation of the potency of the censored material; they take a narrow view of man. The simplest example is probably the

most convincing. "Every person has his secret; in reverie, unbeknown to others, he finds peace, freedom, sorrow. There is a solitude between friends, between lovers, between all human beings." So simple a judgment would have been unthinkable in antiquity. To be sure, the second century witnessed the emergence of a new, subjective style that introduced a note of hypochondria and affectation. Aelius Aristides is obsessed with his health; Fronto exchanges letters of the tenderest (and most unequivocal) sort with his pupil Marcus Aurelius; and Herodius Atticus makes a ritual of sorrow of his quite sincere grief. With the help of culture every spark of spontaneity was converted into doctrine and artifice. Prisoners of their aristocratic civism and haughtiness, the cultivated had no escape other than philosophy, which imprisoned them even more closely in prudence and self-mutilation. They completely lacked the ability to "rework, in consciousness, the broadest possible range of experience"; this adventurer's ideal would have seemed unnatural. Our modern passion is to "have an experience" in order to taste its flavor and judge its effects; such an idea apparently never occurred to the Romans. As

Masterpiece of an identified workshop, ca. A.D. 200. At the extreme left, the handsome shepherd Endymion has fallen asleep. The amorous Luna, haloed by her veil, descends majestically from her chariot to gaze at him. At right, winged Zephyr is frozen at the sight of such a handsome man. Upper left, Morphius pours poppies on Endymion. At right, the rustic scene situates Luna's loves in the innocence of pastoral. (Genoa, Doria Palace.)

Heidegger says, the Greeks went to the games at Olympia because they were interesting and an institution. None of them said, "This is an experience that I absolutely must have." Indeed, to want to explore the unknown was considered a vicious temptation, something to be feared, and was called "curiosity." This was the vice to which those who indulged in magic were prone, and it always ended badly.

Accordingly, no ancient, not even the poets, is capable of talking about himself. Nothing is more misleading than the use of "I" in Greco-Roman poetry. When an ancient poet says "I'm jealous, I love, I hate," he sounds more like a modern pop singer than a modern poet. The modern singer and the ancient poet do not recount their loves and sorrows; rather they set Jealousy and Love on a stage. When an ancient poet says, "Wealth means nothing to me," he is stating what one ought to think about wealth. He speaks in the name of all and makes no claim that his readers should be interested in his own personal state of mind. To talk about oneself, to throw personal testimony into the balance, to profess that personal conviction must be taken into account provided only that it is sincere is a Christian, indeed an eminently Protestant idea that the ancients never dared to profess.

Paganism was something more than this and continues to inspire dreams. With censorship came elegance. The art, the books, even the writing of the ancients were beautiful. Compare a Greek or Latin inscription of the first century, done in a style worthy of our greatest typographers, with an inscription of the Late Empire or Middle Ages. The decline began in the second century. The world became increasingly ugly to look at, while inwardly man ceased to avert his eyes from his own unstylized suffering, impotence, and abysmal depths. He ceased to be an elegant fool, a purveyor of empty advice. Christianity placed its bets on the less constricted, less sophisticated anthropology that it invented in the psalms. This would prove more comprehensive and popular, but also more authoritarian. For fifteen centuries pastoral authoritarianism, ecclesiastic government of souls, would arouse greater appetites and more revolts and, all things considered, shed more blood than class struggle or even patriotism had ever done.

## The Imagery of Death

The Roman Empire was the property of an urban nobility, if not by right of blood then at least by the fact of wealth and by virtue of an aristocratic cast of mind cloaked in civic trappings. As besotted by vanity as any of Saint-Simon's contemporaries, Roman notables hesitated for quite a long time between the old ideal of *homo civicus* and the new ideal of *homo interior*.

Sarcophagus, 2nd century or first half of 3rd century. Castor and Pollux, wearing conical hats, kidnap two beautiful women, whose attendants flee. Two warriors attempt to do battle with the armed companions of the two heroes. (Rome, Vatican Museums.)

As proof of this, let me point, paradoxically, to imagery from which Frantz Cumont's many disciples have drawn precisely the opposite conclusion: the mythological images decorating the sumptuous sarcophagi of the wealthy. May they be the last images that the reader takes with him from the ancient city! From the second century A.D. wealthy Romans

chose to be buried in sarcophagi decorated with bas-reliefs. There was nothing morbid about these decorations, which represented a wide variety of myths. Their style, even less morbid than their subject matter, has the conventional academicism of the "ancients," the graceful, serene humanism of the Greek arch. When a sculptor gives pathetic animation to one of his figures, the emotion that comes through is that which a good storyteller imparts to his tales. These funerary decorations speak of subjects other than death and the deceased. A good example, on display in the Louvre, is the nude Diana surprised in her bath by the indiscreet hunter Actaeon, whom the chaste goddess thereupon has her dogs devour.

What are such graceful, if gratuitous, images doing on a tombstone? Nothing is easier or more tempting than to interpret symbolism. Cumont ascribed eschatological significance to this mythology. Statues in the Louvre of Jupiter abducting the handsome Ganymede to heaven, where he will serve as the god's pet, and of Castor and Pollux abducting the daughters of King Leucippus are described as allegories depicting the immortal soul being wafted off to heaven. The trouble is that such ingenious interpretations can be invented for only some of the myths represented on tombs, and not necessarily those that occur most frequently. Not to mention the fact that they clash with the style.

If the mythological decorations on the sarcophagi are not symbolic, must we conclude that they are simply decorative? No. Iconography in the manner of Panofsky has limits; the meaning of imagery is not just conceptual or doctrinal. The mythology on the sarcophagi did not only fill space; it plunged viewers into an unprosaic, nonrealistic atmosphere. It matters little which myth is represented; the point is that the Romans fled death through myth. The beautiful imagery of mythology (so unlike the pathos in the portrait art of the same period) was a way of aestheticizing death, of avoiding melancholy. In this respect the imagery is pregnant with meaning. It was the last flowering of the Apollonian spirit of ancient Greece. How does the viewer react to a sarcophagus with mythological decoration? The fear of death is eclipsed by a sense of the marvelous, the fabulous, and the voluptuous, by thoughts of carnal humanity. Costly, richly decorated tombs and moral ease in the face of the afterlife were privileges that went together. Refined Apollonian sentiments coupled with self-imposed censorship; self-satisfied wealth confused with virtue; conscious but secretly puritanical quietism and aestheticism: in these things a whole world stands revealed.

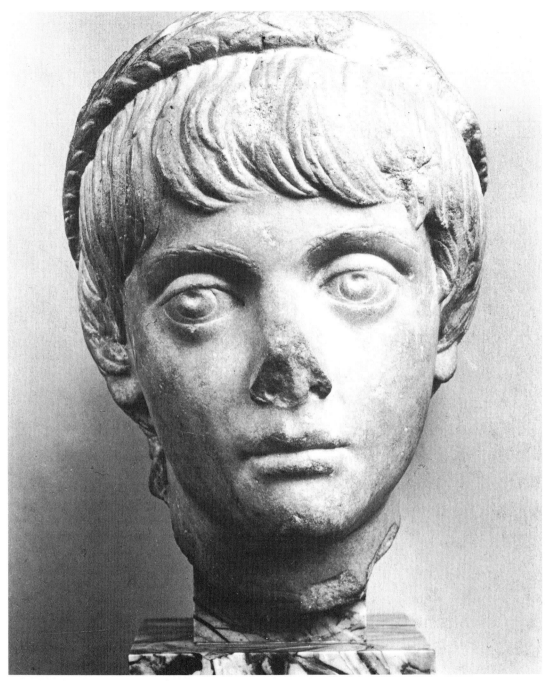

Bust of a young pagan prince, late 2nd century. It is notable not only for its polished surfaces and sharp outlines but also for a face consumed by inner reflection. This inwardness is the way the late pagan nobility wished to appear, and it remained among the official styles of the Christian era. (Paris, Louvre.)

# 2

# Late Antiquity

Peter Brown

# ✦ Introduction

IN four centuries, between the reigns of Marcus Aurelius (161–180) and Justinian (527–565), the Mediterranean world passed through a series of profound transmutations that affected the rhythms of life, the moral sensibilities, and the concomitant sense of the self of the inhabitants of its cities, and of the countryside around them. During the late antique period there was a slow shift from one form of public community to another—from the ancient city to the Christian church. The life of the individual, the life of the family, even matters as intimate as the perception of the body itself came to be seen in relation to changing social contexts, associated with the rise of new forms of community.

Marcus Aurelius offering incense at the start of a sacrifice. Behind the emperor an old man stands for the Senate. In the background is the Temple of Jupiter Capitoline, god of state. (Rome, Museum of the Conservators.)

Tomb, 2nd–3rd century. Although the man buried here lived in remote if urbane Germania, he nevertheless found a sculptor of the right school to execute his tomb. The master wears a magnificent costume and holds a scroll; the lady is slender, and the child knows what pose to strike. The foliage is rich, but the sculptor has chosen not to render the folds of the robes, which are sketched in a merely "decorative" manner. (Trier, Landesmuseum.)

# ☙ The "Wellborn" Few

IN order to measure the nature and extent of the transformation that began with the "civic" man of the age of the Antonines and ended with the good Christian member of the Catholic Church of the Western Middle Ages, the theme must be allowed to wander, like a winding river, throughout the length and breadth of Roman Mediterranean society. It washes past many banks, touching on issues as intimate and as "private" (in the modern sense) as the changing meaning of marriage, of sexuality, of nudity. Yet during these centuries the river was fed by a concern largely alien to modern persons. Whether it be in the life of the notables of an Antonine city or in the habits of a late Roman Christian, we meet at every turn an ancient sense of need for a public community—for a community in which the experiences of the private individual were permeated at every level by the values of the community and were frequently expected, in ideal conditions, to be totally transparent to these public values. The way men and women in specific social contexts in the Roman world guided their lives in the light of changing notions of the public community to which they sensed they belonged provides insight into the history of the private life of Western Europeans.

Certain features of the Mediterranean world remained surprisingly constant throughout late antiquity. Topographically, we will seldom leave the cities. Each city was a little world of its own, defined by an intense awareness of its own status vis-à-vis that of its neighbors. "Daddy," asked a little boy in a third-century joke book, "do other cities have a moon as big as ours?" Status demanded an enduring and intimate connection with the city. In our joke book, a rich landowner altered the numbers on the milestones on the road leading to his country villa, in order to lessen the distance between his

Page from a manuscript of Virgil, 4th or 5th century. The illustration is not all appropriate to the text it accompanies, and the manuscript is a failed work of art. (Rome, Vatican Library.)

Villa of Piazza Armerina, first half of 4th century. The undressed woman wears a brassiere and artfully shields her lover from a frontal view. And for good reason, because the lover is probably Priapus, identifiable from the fruits carried in the fold of his raised garment and from the woman's wig that he often wore.

properties and *his* city! For all classes the anonymity of a modern city was almost totally absent. A woman whose husband had been crucified was advised by the rabbis to leave town—unless the city were as big as Antioch. The norm against which the elites measured their actions was the face-to-face society of the city.

In every city a crushing sense of social distance between the notables, the "wellborn," and their inferiors was the basic fact of Roman Imperial society. The most marked evolution of the Roman period was the discreet mobilization of culture and of moral grooming to assert such distance. The upper classes sought to distinguish themselves from their inferiors by a style of culture and moral life whose most resonant message was that it could not be shared. They created a morality of social distance that was closely linked to the traditional culture of the cities. At the very center of this culture and its attendant morality was the need to obey the rules for interchange between upper-class citizens in conducting the public business of the city.

Education gave the child to the city, not to the school. Physically, the *pedagogus* began by leading the seven-year-old boy from his house to the forum, where his teachers sat, in ineffectively screened-off classrooms abutting on this main center of urban life. Here he would be absorbed into the peer group of young men of similar status. He would owe as much to that peer group as to his teacher. The contents of this education and the manner and the place in which it was communicated aimed to produce a man versed in the *officia vitae*—in those solemn, traditional skills of human relations that were expected to absorb the life of the upper-class male.

A literary education was considered part of a more intimate and exacting process of moral grooming. It was firmly believed that the meticulous internalization of the literary classics went hand in hand with a process of moral formation: correct forms of verbal interchange manifested the upper-class citizen's ability to enter into the correct form of interpersonal relations among his peers in the city. A studied control of deportment, quite as much as of language, was the mark of the wellborn man on the public stage. Behavior which today we might dismiss as irrelevant—the careful control of gestures, of eye movements, even of breathing—was scrutinized for signs of successful conformity to the moral norms of the upper classes. The unbroken succession of laudatory epithets lavished on notables in the gravestones of Asia Minor from the Hellenistic age to the reign of Justinian betrays more than wishful thinking. The central role of adjectives stressing controlled and harmonious relations with peers and city, to the almost total exclusion of all other values, betrays the oceanic weight of expectations that pressed upon the successful male.

---

*Social Distance*

What could almost be called "moral hypochondria" formed a firm barrier between the elites and their inferiors. The harmonious person, groomed by long education and shaped by the constant pressure of his peers, was thought to live at risk. He was exposed to the ever-present threat of "moral contagion" from anomalous emotions and actions, inappropriate to his own public status though acceptable in the uncultivated society of his inferiors. I use "hypochondria" advisedly, for this was the age of great doctors—most notably, the doctor Galen (A.D. 129–199)—whose works circulated widely among the wellborn.

A specific body image, formed from a conglomeration

Mosaic of Susa, 2nd–4th century. Virgil seated on throne, holding a copy of the *Aeneid*, flanked by two Muses. The only image of a writer ever found on a mosaic features the greatest writer of all. Was this because the owner genuinely liked Virgil's poetry, or because, for all his reverence for culture, he did not go so far as to judge for himself the ranking of authors in the classical hierarchy?

Bronze tokens, showing various sexual positions on one side and numerals on the other. They must have been used in some sort of game.

of notions inherited from the long past of Greek medicine and moral philosophy, was the physiological anchor of the moral codes of the wellborn. In this model personal health and public deportment converged with the utmost ease. In it the body is represented as a delicately maintained balance of complementary humors, whose health was upset by excessive losses of needful resources or by excessive coagulations of detrimental surpluses. The emotions that were held to disrupt or deplete the carefully balanced deportment of the well-groomed man could be traced in large part to the effects of such imbalances. The body, therefore, was regarded as the most sensitive and visible gauge of correct deportment; and the harmonious control of the body, through traditional Greek methods of exercise, diet, and bathing, was the most intimate guarantor of the maintenance of correct deportment.

The status-based, inward-looking quality of a morality rooted in an upper-class need to demonstrate social distance by means of an exceptional code of deportment is immediately apparent in the moral concerns of the Antonine age. Relations with social inferiors and sexual relations, for example, are regulated in terms of an exacting code of public deportment. To beat a slave in a fit of rage was condemned. This was not because of any very acute sense that an act of inhumanity against a fellow human being had been committed, but because the outburst represented a collapse of the harmonious image of the self of the wellborn man, and had caused him to behave in a manner as uncontrolled as a slave.

Similar concerns determined attitudes toward sexual relations. Homosexual and heterosexual love were not distinguished. What was perceived as an underlying continuity between the two was the fact of physical pleasure. Sexual pleasure as such posed no problem to the upper-class moralist. What was judged, and judged harshly, was the effect of such pleasure on the public deportment and social relations of the male. Any shame that might be attached to a homosexual relationship resided solely in the moral contagion that might cause a man of the upper class to submit himself, either physically (by adopting a passive position in lovemaking) or morally, to an inferior of either sex. The relations of men and women were subject to the same strictures. Inversions of true hierarchy through oral sexuality with a female partner were the most condemned and, not surprisingly, the most titillating, forms of collapse before the moral contagion of an inferior, the woman. Fear of effeminacy and of emotional dependence, fears based on a need to maintain a public image as an effective upper-class male, rather than any qualms about sexuality itself, determined the moral codes according to which most notables conducted their sexual life.

The fear of social subservience to an inferior was subtly buttressed by physiological anxiety. A man was a man because he moved effectively in the public world. He did this because his fetus had "cooked" more thoroughly than had a woman's in the hot womb; his body, therefore, was a reservoir of the precious "heats" on which male energy depended. Although the difference between men and women might be securely fixed, in the case of the woman by the low ceiling of her heat and the consequent frailty of her temperament, there was no such security for the active man. His heat could be lost. Excessive sexual discharge might "cool" his temperament; such a drain on his resources would be betrayed with merciless precision in a loss of momentum on the public stage. That orotund voice of the public man that Quintilian and his con-

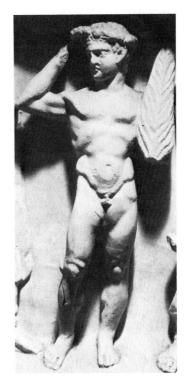

Detail of sarcophagus, 2nd century. This was either imported from Greece or done in imitation of Greek work. After winning a gymnastic contest, the ephebe dons the wreath that is the prize of victory and is awarded the palm by the man in charge of the games. (Rome, Vatican Museums.)

Marble marquetry, after 331. A solemn parade crosses Rome, headed for the Circus. Riding in the ceremonial chariot is the consul who will preside over and pay for the races, followed by the four chariot drivers who will compete. So many chariots are shown in profile in ancient art that it is interesting to see one head on. The frontal view results in a perspective that has been called "the exploded chariot"; even the wheels are splayed apart like the pages of a book.

temporaries so dearly loved to hear echoing through the noisy public spaces of the city was the fine fruit of a masculinity carefully preserved by "abstinence from sex." The very real puritanism of the traditional moralities of the upper classes of the Greek and Roman worlds rested heavily on those who subscribed to them. Such puritanism did not rest on sexuality; it rested on sexuality as a possible source of moral contagion. For sexual indulgence could erode, through the effeminacy that could result from excessive sexual pleasure with partners of either sex, the unchallenged superiority of the wellborn.

Hence the unquestioning particularity of the sexual codes of the age. They did not apply to everyone. The notables might tend to subject themselves and their families to a code of dour masculine puritanism, closer to that still current in Islamic countries than to the puritanism of modern northern Europe. Yet, having drawn the carapace of deportment around themselves, they found themselves all the more free to exhibit the other side of their public selves: their *popularitas*. In their relations, as givers of the good things of urban life, to their inferiors, they lavished on those assumed to have cruder pleasures than themselves a succession of displays, amenities, and paintings that flatly contradicted, in their cruelty and frank obscenity, the orderly self-control these men had arrogated to themselves as the badge of their own superior status in the city. Highly cultivated aristocrats patronized the appalling bloodshed of the gladiatorial games in the Greek cities of the Antonine age. Nor did the rise of Christianity greatly change this aspect of their public life. If a modern reader remembers anything about the emperor Justinian, it is likely to be Procopius' portrait of the youthful career of his wife, Theodora: a striptease dancer in the public theater of Constantinople, geese used to peck grain from her private parts in front of an audience of thousands of citizens. What is important to bear in mind is the venomous precision of this sketch. Here was a woman of the people, to whom upper-class codes of moral restraint did not apply. Theodora is the exact inversion of the respectable upper-class wives (soberly shrouded and even secluded in Constantinople, by that time). Yet, as notables, the husbands of such respectable ladies had for centuries donated just such performances, to the everlasting glory of themselves and of their city.

Nor is there anything surprising in the long survival of indifference to nudity in Roman public life. This was not a society bound together by the implicit democracy of sexual shame. Athletic nudity remained a mark of status for the wellborn. The essential role of the public baths as the joining point of civic life ensured that nudity among one's peers and

Mosaic of gladiators, dead and alive, with their names, 4th century. The patron who paid for the combat wished to preserve the names of the stars who fought and died at great expense to himself. Never were gladiatorial combats more deadly than in the 4th century, when sadism and munificence were at their peak. (Rome, Villa Borghese.)

in front of one's inferiors was a daily experience. The codes of deportment, as we have seen, reached down into the body itself; as a result, the clothes of the upper classes of the Antonine age, though expensive, lacked the ceremonial magnificence of later ages. How a man carried himself, in the nude or otherwise, was the true mark of his status—a mark all the more convincing because understated. As for women, the social shame of exposure to the wrong person, rather than the fact of exposure itself, was the principal anxiety. Nudity before one's slaves was as morally insignificant as nudity before animals; and the physical exposure of the women of the lower classes was yet another token of their disorderly inferiority to the powerful.

## Empire and Order

In the cities of the Antonine age the facts of power weighed with all the unperceived mass of an atmosphere on the upper-class subjects of a world empire. However intimate the life of the average city might be, Rome was an empire, one founded on and protected by violence. The cruelty of the gladiatorial games was put on display as part of the official celebration of the Emperor in every great city of the Mediterranean. Such displays made plain the bloodthirsty will to rule of the Italian elite. Even the games played by the humble, as they tossed dice on the edges of the forum, were games of war. The moves designated on the counters were: The Parthians are killed; the Britons are conquered; the Romans can play. There was no disguising the fact that small-town politics, which had remained the principal school of character of the notables in every region, were now played out "beneath the boots": that is, they were subjected to constant intervention by the Roman governor, flanked by his military guard of honor, in the strong leather boots of the legionary. If the life

The deceased at the hunt, 4th century. A crew was needed to place the nets, hundreds of meters long (visible at the right). (Rome, Museum of the Conservators.)

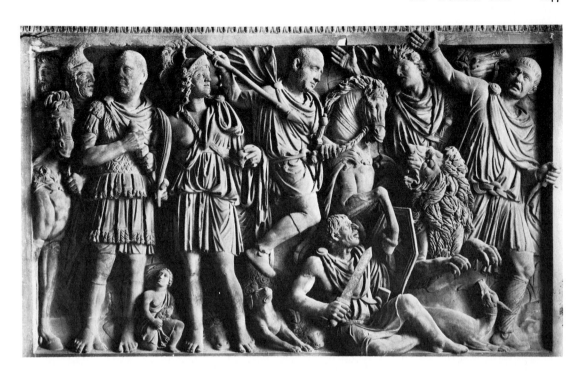

of the cities was to continue, the discipline and the solidarity
of the local elites and their ability to control their own dependents had to be mobilized with greater self-consciousness than
ever before. A sense of public discipline had to reach deeper
into the private lives of the notables as the price for maintaining the status quo of an imperial order. Accordingly, a profound mutation in the attitude toward the married couple took
place during the course of the second century A.D.

In the Late Republic and early Empire the womenfolk of
public men had been treated as peripheral beings, who contributed little or nothing to the public character of their husbands. They were considered "little creatures," whose behavior and relations with their husbands were of no real concern
to the all-male world of politicians. They might sap the characters of their males by sensuality; they might even inspire
them to heroic improvidence through genuine love; they frequently emerged as strong resources of courage and good
counsel in difficult times. But the married relationship in itself
carried little weight on the public stage. Much of what we call
the "emancipation" of women in upper-class Roman circles in
the Early Empire had been a freedom born of contempt. The
little creatures could do what they liked, as long as it did not

Sarcophagus, 3rd century.
Mounted on a horse, the deceased, a cavalry officer, fights
with a lion. Left, the officer
again with one of his troops.
Right, his men take part in a
hunt. One of the army's official
missions was to hunt wild animals, both to ensure the safety
of the population and to capture animals for combats in the
arena. Behind the officer, bare-
breasted, stands Valor. (Rome,
Palazzo Mattei.)

Statue of a woman, based on an ancient Greek model, 1st or 2nd century. Note the majestic elegance of the pose and the robe. The left hand is veiled, for reasons of distinction, not modesty: in Greece it was considered elegant, even for orators, to leave the hands underneath one's clothing rather than to make grand gestures. The right hand and face are modern restorations. (Rome, Vatican Museums.)

interfere with the serious play of male politics. Divorce was quick and simple; adultery, though it might unleash occasional savage revenge on wife and lover, in no way affected the husband's public standing.

In the age of the Antonines the sense of the relative neutrality of upper-class marriage arrangements collapsed. The *concordia,* the *homonoia,* of the good marriage was now brought forward (often as a conscious revival of the imagined discipline of the archaic Roman past) to act as a resonant new symbol of all other forms of social harmony. Where the coins celebrating the crucial Roman political and social virtue of concordia had previously shown male politicians joining their right hands in alliance, with Marcus Aurelius it is his own wife, Faustina the younger, who appears on the coins associated with concordia. Young couples in Ostia are expected to assemble to offer sacrifice, "by reason of the exceptional concord" of the imperial pair. A little earlier, in *Advice on Marriage,* Plutarch had described how the husband should use the skilled personal guidance associated with the philosopher to bring his young wife, still thought of as a kittenish little creature more interested in her partner's sexual vigor than in his philosophical gravity, into line with the public deportment of the upper-class male. Marriage was to be a victory of the *mission civilisatrice* of the deportment of the wellborn along the disorderly fringe of their own class: their womenfolk. The contours of public eminence were that much more sharply drawn by including even women in the charmed circle of upper-class excellence. As a result, the married couple came to appear in public as a miniature of civic order. The *eunoia,* the *sumpatheia,* and the *praotes* of the relations of husband and wife echoed the expectations of grave affability and unquestioning class loyalty with which the powerful man both lovingly embraced and firmly controlled his city.

The role of the philosopher and of the moral ideas generated in philosophical circles in the second century must be seen against the tense background of a need for closer solidarity among the upper classes and for more intimate means of control over their inferiors. The philosopher, "moral missionary" of the Roman world, claimed to address humanity as a whole. He was "the teacher and leader of men, in all things that are appropriate to men according to nature."[1] In reality, he was no such thing. He was the representative of a prestigious counterculture within the elite, and he originally addressed his elevating message to members of that elite.

Carthage, 1st century. Mother Earth or Italia. (Paris, Louvre.)

The philosopher had never seriously considered addressing the masses. He had reveled in the high moral status that came from preaching to the unconvertible among his peers. Philosophers had attempted to persuade the self-confident rulers of the world to live up to their own codes; in so doing, they had urged them to look beyond the narrow confines of their immediate social horizons. In Stoic exhortation the upper-class man was urged to live according to the universal law of the *cosmos,* and to attempt to rise above the brittle particularities and hot passions of mere human society. Such preaching had the effect of adding qualifications, reserves, additional dimensions, even consciously paradoxical a fortiori elaborations to well-known moral codes; "also" and "even" recur with telltale frequency. The public man was to think of himself as a citizen not only of his city but "also" of the world. The confirmed bachelor philosopher was to feel that "even" he should recognize the new status accorded to marriage, "for such a union is beautiful." The married man was to expect "even" himself to shun infidelity to his wife—"no, *not even* [!] with his own maidservant . . . a thing which some people consider quite without blame, since a master is held to have it in his power to use his slaves as he wishes." Behind his public face the public man was to be aware that, apart from the expectations of his peers, his inner motives were known "also" to the still presence of his guardian spirit.

As spokesman for the counterculture of the wellborn, the philosopher enjoyed a paradoxical position as both buffoon

Mosaic at Piazza Armerina, first half of 4th century. These ladies, whose attire barely preserves their modesty, are featured in a spectacle intended to titillate.

Lateral face of sarcophagus, 2nd century. Socrates with a Muse. He is doing the talking; she is his friend rather than his inspiration. (Paris, Louvre.)

and "saint of culture." Though their works bulk large on the shelves of modern libraries, it is far from certain that such works rested in great numbers on the shelves of the public men of the philosophers' own times. Papyrus fragments found in Egypt show that it was Homer who remained the true "mirror of the soul" of the Greek gentleman; the *Iliad* and the *Odyssey* can be reconstructed many times over from the debris of the shelves of the notables throughout the whole length of our period. Of the philosophical moralists of the second and third centuries, not a fragment in papyrus has survived. Competitive, logic-chopping, hopelessly otherworldly, when not hypocrites, hiding lust and ambition beneath their coarse cloaks and long, shaggy beards, the philosophers were fair game for the scorn of the majority. Frescoes flanking the seats of a public toilet in Ostia show these philosophers, self-styled masters of the art of living, offering their seated clients stern, gnomic counsels on the correct manner of defecation!

Yet *verba volant, scripta manent*: the philosophers' preaching had only to be transferred from its original, highly specific and class-based context and placed among a different social group, with a different social experience and significantly different moral preoccupations, for the "even's" and "also's" of philosophical exhortations to the upper classes quietly to drop away. What the philosophers presented as further refinement, tentatively added to an ancient and inward-looking morality of the elite, became, in the hands of Christian teachers, the foundation for the construction of a whole new building that embraced all classes in its demands. Philosophical exhortations, originally addressed to upper-class readers by writers such as Plutarch and Musonius, were drawn upon by Christian guides of the soul such as Clement of Alexandria in the late second century and passed along to respectable urban tradesmen and artisans. Philosophical exhortations enabled Clement to present Christianity as a truly universalist morality, rooted in a new sense of the presence of God and the equality of all men before His Law.

The surprisingly rapid democratization of the philosophers' upper-class counterculture by the leaders of the Christian church is the most profound single revolution of the late classical period. Anyone who reads Christian writings or studies Christian papyri (such as the texts found at Nag Hammadi) must realize that the works of the philosophers, though they may have been largely ignored by the average urban notable, had drifted down, through Christian preaching and Christian speculation, to form a deep sediment of moral notions current among thousands of humble persons. By the end of the third century they had been made available to the inhabitants of the major regions of the Mediterranean, in the languages current among the lower classes in those regions: Greek, Coptic, Syriac, and Latin. In order to understand how this could happen, we must go back in time a few centuries and consider a very different region: the Palestine of Jesus. Then we must retrace our steps through very different segments of Roman society, to follow the growth of the Christian churches from the mission of Saint Paul to the conversion of Constantine.

Sarcophagus, 3rd century, found at Acilia. As Bernard Andreae has shown, this was the sarcophagus of a consul. The elderly man wearing a crown visible to his right stands for the Senate. He looks toward the consul and with a gesture of the hand invites him to inaugurate his consulate with a solemn procession. Hence the young man with shaved head who is dressed in a toga is the consul's son. He will march in the parade and one day follow in his father's footsteps. (Rome, Museum of the Baths.)

The Good Shepherd with his Pan's pipe leads a stray lamb into his paradise. This shepherd tended no earthly flock but watched over the dead in a bucolic Eden; birds emphasize the scene's idyllic nature. 3rd century. (Rome, vault of the Catacomb of Saint Priscilla.)

# Person and Group in Judaism and Early Christianity

T O move from the elites of the age of the Antonines, in the second and early third centuries A.D., to the world of later Judaism, of the second century B.C. onward, is to leave behind a morality securely rooted in a sense of social distance and enter the world of an afflicted nation. The very survival of the group as a whole held the center of moral anxiety.

The continuance of the traditions of Israel, the continued loyalty of Jews to those traditions and to each other, was the common, central issue for Jewish figures as various as the followers of Jesus of Nazareth, Saint Paul, and the later rabbinic sages—not to mention the communal experiments of the Essenes and the Qumran community. Seldom in the history of the ancient world are we confronted with such an explicit sense of the need to mobilize the whole of the self in the service of a religious law, and of the concomitant need to mobilize to the full a sense of solidarity between the members of a threatened community.

"But now the righteous have been gathered,
and the prophets are fallen asleep,
and we also are gone from the land,
and Zion has been taken from us,
and we have nothing now save the Mighty One and His
    Law."[2]

Even more unique in ancient literature is the clear and persistent expression of the underside of this concern for loyalty and for solidarity, an unrelieved anxiety that the participants will fail to give the whole of themselves to so demanding a venture. For only by such total loyalty could the affliction of Israel be reversed:

"If, therefore, we direct and dispose our heart,
we shall receive everything that we have lost."

The "heart" upon which such great hope must turn became the object of profound and somber scrutiny. Much as engineers, faced with the sagging mass of a building, are driven to concentrate on the most minute flaws, to pay attention to hitherto unexamined crystalline structures in the metals that support it, so late Jewish writers came to peer intently into the human heart. Like engineers, again, concerned with the fatigue and breaking points of metals, they noted with particular precision and concern the "zones of negative privacy," those dangerous opacities in the heart that threatened to exclude the demands of God and of fellow Jews (or fellow Christians) upon the whole of the self.

What emerged from these centuries of anxious concern for the solidarity of a threatened group was a sharp negative sense of the private. What was most private in the individual, his or her most hidden feelings and motivations, those springs of action that remained impenetrable to the group, "the thoughts of the heart," were looked to with particular attention as the possible source of the tensions that threatened to cause fissures in the ideal solidarity of the religious community.

This was a distinctive model of the human being. The starting point was the heart, presented as a core of motivation, reflection, and imagined intentions, that should ideally be single, simple—translucent to the demands of God and its neighbors. The heart of course was more habitually observed to be double. The double-hearted cut themselves off from God and their neighbors by retiring into those treacherous zones of negative privacy that screened them from such demands. Hence the sharpened features of the relations of the Jew, and later of the Christian, to the supernatural world. Shielded by "negative privacy" from the eyes of men, the heart was held to be totally public to the gaze of God and His angels: "When one commits a transgression in secret, it is as though he has thrust aside the feet of the Divine Presence."[3]

In the first century A.D. this model was supported, if with widely varying degrees of urgency and abruptness, by the belief that through the action of God a social state presently governed by the abrasive opacities of double-heartedness would give way, among a true remnant of Israel, to a time of utter transparency to each other and to God. In such a true, redeemed community, the tensions of the "evil heart" would have been eliminated. Backed by a sharpened belief in the Last Days and the Last Judgment, this high hope affirmed that a

Ivory tablet, 5th or 6th century. Height: 7 inches. Christ offering benediction, surrounded by the twelve apostles and flanked by Saints Peter and Paul. The eight books in the box are the four Gospels and the four great prophets. The perspective is reversed: the foreground figures are smaller than the background ones. The rather harsh style is that of a copyist working from an unknown model. (Dijon, Museum of Fine Arts.)

Ivory in high relief. Height: 6 inches. Preaching of Saint Paul, or possibly of Saint Mark, legendary founder of the Church of Alexandria; here he may be surrounded by 35 of his successors as head of that church. If that assumption is correct, the work would date from 607–609, and the city would be Alexandria. (Paris, Louvre.)

state of total solidarity and of openness to others was the predestined and natural state of social man—a state lost in the sad course of history, but to be regained at the end of time. Many groups believed that the ideal conditions that would be achieved at the end of time might be foreshadowed in a present religious community. A group such as the early Christian community believed in the present coming of the Holy Spirit upon the true remnant of Israel. Its adherents could expect to experience, if in the hauntingly transient form of possession, those solemn moments when the "hidden things of the heart" would stand revealed, as the community of the "saints" stood undivided, their hearts unveiled, in the very presence of God.

This is the vision of solidarity and, consequently, of the total permeability of the private person to the demands of the religious community that came to haunt the ancient world in its last centuries.

When we talk of the rise of Christianity in the cities of the Mediterranean, we are speaking of the destiny of an exceptionally labile and structurally unstable fragment of sectarian Judaism. The mission of Saint Paul (from about A.D. 32 to about A.D. 60) and of similar apostles had consisted of gathering the Gentiles into a new Israel, made available to them at the end of time by the messiahship of Jesus. In practice, this new Israel was formed among pagans who had been attracted, with varying degrees of commitment, to the influential Jewish communities of the cities of Asia Minor and the Aegean and to the large Jewish community in Rome. In its view of itself, the new Israel was a "gathering in": Jesus, as Messiah, had broken down previous "walls of division." Paul in his letters recited the traditional catalogues of opposed groups of persons—Jew and Gentile, slave and freeman, Greek and barbarian, male and female—in order to declare that such categories had been eradicated within the new community. The sole initiation into the group—a single purificatory bath— was presented by Paul as a stripping away of the garments of all previous social and religious categories, and the putting on of Christ, by which Paul meant the gaining by each believer of a single, uncompartmented identity, common to all members of the community, as befitted "sons of God" newly adopted "in Christ."

This potent mirage of solidarity flickered on the horizons of bodies of men and women whose position in Roman society made the achievement of such solidarity a hope destined to remain forever unfulfilled and, for that reason, all the more poignantly central to their moral concerns. The early Christian converts lacked the social situation that would have made Paul's mighty ideal of undifferentiated solidarity "in Christ" possible. The patrons and disciples of Paul and his successors were not simple souls, nor were they the humble and oppressed of modern romantic imagination. Had they been so, his ideals might have been realized more easily. Rather, they were moderately wealthy and frequently well traveled. As a result, they were exposed to a range of social contacts, of opportunities for choice and hence for potential double-hearted conflict, on many more issues than were, for instance, the rural poor of the "Jesus Movement" of Palestine or the members of the sedentary and enclosed Jewish settlement at Qumran. To "follow Jesus" by moving from village to village in Palestine and Syria, to "choose the Law" by abandoning "the will of their own spirit" in a monastic grouping perched on the edge of the Judaean wilderness, exposed believers to a range of choices mercifully more restricted than those experienced by the men and women of the "gatherings of the saints" in large and prosperous cities such as Corinth, Ephesus, and Rome. In the history of the Christian churches in the first and second centuries A.D. we are looking along a rich vein of human material notably different from that known to us either among the wellborn of the cities or among the villagers of the Gospels.

We need look only at the Roman Christian community of around A.D. 120, as it is revealed in the visions collected in the *Shepherd* of Hermas, to see what this could mean. Here was a religious group where everything that a student of ancient religion could have predicted as capable of going wrong in a "Pauline" urban community had indeed gone wrong. Hermas was a prophet obsessed with preserving a single-hearted solidarity among the believers. He wished poignantly for a childlike innocence of guile, of ambition, of double-hearted anxiety among his community. Yet Hermas' fears reveal a group whose very sins were a measure of its

Detail of pagan sarcophagus, before A.D. 275. Many pagan sarcophagi represent images of paradise borrowed from early Christianity. (Rome, Museum of the Baths.)

success in society. The church in Rome was supported by rich patrons, whose contacts with the pagan community at large had provided protection and prestige. The hearts of the influential Christians were predictably divided between the demands of solidarity and open-hearted dealing among the faithful, and concern for the conduct of their business ventures (hence with their contacts with pagan friends). The wealth of their households and the success of their sons preoccupied them. Hermas had no doubt that such persons, though a source of anxiety and of double-hearted tension, played a crucial role in a well-to-do Christian community: they were the solid, dry wood over which the vine of a prosperous and highly articulate religious community scrambled abundantly.

The prophet himself, Hermas—"patient, not given to indignation, always with a smile"—was no simple soul. He was a successful and sophisticated slave in an urban household. He had been disturbed by sexual attraction for his mistress, who, though a good Christian woman, still expected Hermas, as her slave, to help her naked out of the Tiber after her bath! He had witnessed the ravages of guile and double-hearted dealings among rich Christian patrons, among priests, and among rival prophets. Yet he couched a large part of his message against the backdrop of a classical Arcadian idyll, for this denouncer of the double-hearted contagion of wealth experienced his visions in a well-trimmed little vineyard property, which he happened to own in the residential countryside just outside Rome! As Ortega y Gasset has said, the virtues we do not possess are those that mean most to us. Much of the history of the early Christian churches is the history of an urgent search for equilibrium among those whose ideal of single-hearted loyalty to each other and to Christ was constantly eroded by the objective complexity of their own position in Mediterranean society.

---

*Early Christian Morality*

Paul wrote the community at Corinth, possibly in the spring of A.D. 54: "God is not the author of confusion, but of peace, as in all the churches of the saints." As so often, Paul was writing to impose his own interpretation (in this particular case, to stress the need for prophecy in languages intelligible to all) on a situation of insoluble complexity. As we have seen, the Christian churches in the cities depended on respectable and well-to-do households, members of which might welcome certain rituals of undifferentiated solidarity. But life in

Arycanda (Lycia). In 311–312, a year before the triumph of Christianity, delegates from one province asked the emperor to make those "atheists," the Christians, stop violating the rules of piety. To that end, they were to be forbidden from engaging in their execrable practices and ordered to worship the gods. (Museum of Istanbul.)

an urban environment, unless lived permanently among the totally uprooted and marginal—which was not the case in the Christian urban communities of the first, second, and third centuries—could not be based upon such high moments. If singleness of heart was to survive in the Christian churches and be seen to survive before a suspicious pagan world on the relentlessly public stage of everyday life in the city, it could survive only if caught in the fixative of a group life consciously structured according to habitual and resilient norms.

Hence the paradox of the rise of Christianity as a moral force in the pagan world. The rise of Christianity altered profoundly the moral texture of the late Roman world. Yet in moral matters the Christian leaders made almost no innovations. What they did was more crucial. They created a new group, whose exceptional emphasis on solidarity in the face of its own inner tensions ensured that its members would practice what pagan and Jewish moralists had already begun to preach. That singleness of heart for which a man such as Hermas yearned would be achieved in the successful community of Rome less through the undifferentiated workings of the Spirit, than by the intimate discipline of a tight-knit group, whose basic moral attitudes differed from those of their pagan and Jewish neighbors only in the urgency with which such attitudes were adopted and put into practice.

It is important to note at the outset the crucial difference between the widespread morality adopted by the Christians and the codes of behavior current among the civic elites. Much of what is claimed as distinctively "Christian" in the morality of the early churches was in reality the distinctive morality of a different segment of Roman society from those we know from the literature of the wellborn.

It was a morality of the socially vulnerable. In modestly well-to-do households the mere show of power was not available to control one's slaves or womenfolk. As a result, concern for intimate order, for intimate restraints on behavior, for fidelity between spouses and obedience within the household acted out "in singleness of heart, fearing God," tended to be that much more acute. Obedience on the part of servants, fair dealings between partners, and the fidelity of spouses counted for far more among men more liable to be fatally injured by sexual infidelity, by trickery, and by the insubordination of their few household slaves than were the truly wealthy and powerful. Outside the household a sense of solidarity with a wider range of fellow city-dwellers had developed, in marked contrast to the civic notables, who continued throughout the period to view the world through the narrow slits of their traditional "civic" definition of the urban community. A sense of solidarity was a natural adjunct of a morality of the socially vulnerable. There was, therefore, nothing strange, much less specifically Christian, in the inscription on the undoubtedly pagan tomb of an immigrant Greek pearl merchant on Rome's Via Sacra: "[Here] lie contained the bones of a good man, a man of mercy, a lover of the poor."

Trajan cancels the tax debts of the poor. Date: under Trajan or Hadrian. Poor citizens (as shown by their clothing) deposit the tablets on which their debts are recorded so that they can be destroyed. (Rome, Forum; now in the Curia.)

---

The difference in the attitudes of the upper classes and the average urban dweller toward giving and sharing affords a sharp contrast. The civic notables "nourished" their city; they were expected to spend large sums maintaining the sense of continued enjoyment and prestige of its regular citizens. If such nourishment happened to relieve some distress among the poor, this was considered an accidental byproduct of relief from which the civic body as a whole, the rich quite as much as the poor, benefited by virtue of being citizens. A large number of the city's inhabitants—most often the truly poor, such as slaves and immigrants—were excluded from such nourishment. These large sums were given to the city and its citizens to enhance the status of the civic body as a whole, not to alleviate any particular state of human affliction among the

*A Morality of the Vulnerable*

poor. Individual donations could be magnificent displays of fireworks celebrating great occasions—the power and generosity of the patrons, the splendor of the city. The idea of a steady flow of giving, in the form of alms, to a permanent category of afflicted, the poor, was beyond the horizon of such persons.

Among the socially vulnerable it was a matter of daily perception that a relationship did exist between the superfluity enjoyed by the modestly well-to-do and the lack of means experienced by their poorer neighbors. Such an imbalance could be remedied, or at least muted, by the redistribution of very small sums, such as were within the reach of any modest city household or of any comfortable farmer among the rural poor of the countryside. It had long been obvious also to the Jewish communities, as it would be to the Christians, that among small men the maintenance of a margin of financial independence in a hostile world was possible through a small measure of mutual support. By offering alms and the chance of employment to the poorer members of their community, Jews and Christians could protect correligionists from impoverishment, and hence from outright vulnerability to pagan creditors or pagan employers. It is against this social background that we can begin to understand how the practice of almsgiving to the poor soon became a token of the solidarity of threatened groups of believers. The eventual replacing of a model of urban society that had stressed the duty of the wellborn to nourish *their* city by one based on the notion of the implicit solidarity of the rich in the affliction of the poor remains one of the most clear examples of the shift from a classical to a postclassical Christianized world. This shift was under way by the second century A.D. among the Christian communities.

Even without the intervention of the Christian churches, we can detect the slow rise, alongside the civic codes of the notables, of a significantly different morality, based on a different world of social experience. By the early third century, long before the establishment of the Christian church, aspects of Roman law and of Roman family life were touched by a subtle change in the moral sensibilities of the silent majority of the provincials of the Empire. Respectable wedlock was extended to include even slaves. Emperors posed increasingly as guardians of private morality. Suicide, that proud assertion of the right of the wellborn to dispose, if need be, of his own life, came to be branded as an unnatural "derangement."

The Christian church caused this new morality to undergo a subtle process of change by rendering it more universal in its application and far more intimate in its effect of the private life of the believer. Among Christians a somber variant of popular morality facilitated the urgent search for new principles of solidarity that aimed to penetrate the individual ever more deeply with a sense of the gaze of God, with a fear of His Judgment, and with a sharp sense of commitment to the unity of the religious community.

*The Democratization of Moral Codes: Sexual Behavior*

To appreciate the extent of the changes in moral ideals brought about within the churches we need only consider the structures of marriage and sexual discipline that developed in Christian households during the course of the second and third centuries. Galen was struck by the sexual austerity of the Christian communities in the late second century: "Their contempt of death is patent to us every day, and likewise their restraint in cohabitation. For they include not only men but also women who refrain from cohabiting all their lives; and they also number individuals who, in self-discipline and self-control, have attained a pitch not inferior to that of genuine philosophers."[4]

On the surface the Christians practiced an austere sexual morality, easily recognizable and acclaimed by outsiders: total sexual renunciation by the few; marital concord between the spouses (such as had begun to permeate the public behavior of the elites, if for very different reasons); strong disapproval of remarriage. This surface was presented openly to outsiders. Lacking the clear ritual boundaries provided in Judaism by circumcision and dietary laws, Christians tended to make their exceptional sexual discipline bear the full burden of expressing the difference between themselves and the pagan world. The message of the Christian apologists was similar to that of later admirers of clerical celibacy, as described by Nietzsche. They appealed to "the faith that a person who is an exception on this point will be an exception in other respects as well."[5]

It is important to understand the new inner structures that supported what on the surface seemed no more than a dour morality, readily admired by the average man. The commonplace facts of sexual discipline were supported by a deeper structure of specifically Christian concerns. From Saint Paul onward, the married couple had been expected to bear in their own persons nothing less than an analogue in microcosm of the group's single-hearted solidarity. Even if these might be

Rome, bas-relief reused on Constantine's Arch. Marcus Aurelius distributes family allowances to needy citizens, not out of charity but in order to sustain the citizenry. The distinction between citizens and noncitizens was gradually giving way to a distinction between the upper class and the common folk. One inscription refers to "plebeians, free or unfree." In this relief, however, we see only citizens. The one in the center owned a toga, or ceremonial costume; the other two are dressed as plebeians. The woman wears the robe of the female citizen, which extends to the feet.

dangerously confused by the workings of the Holy Spirit, in the undifferentiated "gatherings of the saints" the proper relations of husbands and wives, of masters and slaves, were reasserted in no uncertain manner within the Christian household. These relations were invested with a sense that such fidelity and obedience manifested in a peculiarly transparent manner the prized ideal of unfeigned singleness of heart. With the moral gusto characteristic of a group that courted occasions on which to test its will to cohesion, Christian urban communities even abandoned the normal means which Jewish and pagan males had relied upon to discipline and satisfy their wives. They rejected divorce, and they viewed the remarriage of widows with disapproval. The reasons they came to give, often borrowed from the maxims of the philosophers, would have pleased Plutarch. This exceptional marital morality, practiced by modestly well-to-do men and women, betrayed an exceptional will for order: "A man who divorces his wife admits that he is not even able to govern a woman."[6]

It was quite possible for Christian communities to settle down into little more than that. Marital morality could have been presented as a particularly revealing manifestation of the will of the group to singleness of heart. Adultery and sexual scheming among married couples could have been presented as the privileged symptoms of the "zone of negative privacy" associated with doubleness of heart. Without the tolerant space accorded by the ancient city to the upper-class males in which to work off their adolescent urges in relatively free indulgence in sexuality, young people would have married early, as close to puberty as possible, in order to mitigate through lawful wedlock the disruptive tensions of sexual attraction. Women and, it was occasionally hoped, even men would be disciplined by early marriage and by a sense of the piercing gaze of God penetrating into the recesses of the bedchamber. By avoiding remarriage the community could assure for itself a constant supply of venerable widows and widowers able to devote time and energy to the service of the church. Less exposed than notables to the tensions associated with the exercise of real power—bribery, perjury, hypocrisy, violence, and anger—these quiet citizens "of the middling condition" could show their concern for order and cohesion in the more domestic sphere of sexual self-discipline.

The disturbing ease with which the sexes mingled at ritual gatherings of Christians remained distasteful to respectable pagans, and strangers avoided speaking to Christians for that reason. A Christian contemporary of Galen actually petitioned the governor of Alexandria for permission to allow himself to be castrated, for only by such means could he clear himself and his correligionists from the charge of promiscuity! On a more humble level, the difficulties in arranging matches for young people, especially for Christian girls, in a community

Detail of Christian sarcophagus, 5th century(?). The miracle of the loaves. (Rome, Museum of the Baths.)

anxious to avoid marriage with pagans ensured that issues of sexual control would be treated with an intensity greater than that of more settled communities. It also meant that the resulting morality would be much more apparent to outsiders and applied much more rigorously to believers.

*From Control to Continence*    Such pressures go a long way to explain the moral tone of the average late antique Christian community. What they cannot explain is the further revolution by which sexual renunciation—virginity from birth, or continence vowed at baptism, or continence adopted by married couples or widowers—became the basis of male leadership in the Christian church. In this, Christianity had made *il gran rifiuto* (the great renunciation). In the very centuries when the rabbinate rose to prominence in Judaism by accepting marriage as a near-compulsory criterion of the wise, the leaders of the Christian communities moved in the diametrically opposite direction: access to leadership became identified with near-compulsory celibacy. Seldom has a structure of power risen with such speed and sharpness of outline on the foundation of so intimate an act of renunciation. What Galen had perceived at the end of the second century would distinguish the Christian church in later centuries from both Judaism and Islam.

It is claimed that a disgust for the human body was already prevalent in the pagan world. It is then assumed that when the Christian church moved away from its Jewish roots, where optimistic attitudes toward sexuality and marriage as part of God's good creation had prevailed, Christians took on the bleaker colors of their pagan environment. Such a view is lopsided. The facile contrast between pagan pessimism and Jewish optimism overlooks the importance of sexual renunciation as a means to singleness of heart in the radical Judaism from which Christianity emerged. The possible origins of this renunciation may be diverse in the extreme, but they do not in themselves explain why sexual renunciation rapidly became a badge of specifically male leadership in the Christian communities of the second and third centuries.

We must ask not why the human body could have come to be treated with such disquiet in late antiquity, but the exact opposite. Why is the body singled out by being presented so consistently in sexual terms—as the locus of imagined recesses of sexual motivations and the center of social structures thought of sexually—as being formed originally by a fateful sexual drive to marriage and childbirth? Why was this particular constellation of perceptions about the body allowed to carry so huge a weight in early Christian circles? It is the intensity and the particularity of the charge of significance that counts, not the fact that this significance often was expressed in terms so harshly negative as to rivet the attention of the modern reader, who is understandably bruised by such language.

The division between Christianity and Judaism was sharpest in this. As the rabbis chose to present it, sexuality was an enduring adjunct of the personality. Though potentially unruly, it was amenable to restraint—much as women were both honored as necessary for the existence of Israel, and at the same time were kept from intruding on the serious business of male wisdom. It is a model based on the control and segregation of an irritating but necessary aspect of existence. Among the Christians the exact opposite occurred. Sexuality became a highly charged symbolic marker precisely because its disappearance in the committed individual was considered possible, and because this disappearance was thought to register, more significantly than any other human transformation, the qualities necessary for leadership in the religious community. The removal of sexuality—or, more humbly, removal from sexuality—stood for a state of unhesitating availability to God and one's fellows, associated with the ideal of the single-hearted person.

The Three Children of Israel, 7th–8th century. The arched doorways were for loading wood into the pyre. The Jews are wearing Phrygian caps because they were Orientals. (Verona, Crypt of Santa Maria.)

Fresco, 10th century. Pope Sylvester (314–355). This contemporary of Constantine witnessed the triumph of Christianity and the founding of Saint Peter's in Rome. (Rome, Museum of Saint Paul's Outside-the-Walls.)

# ❧ Church and Leadership

T HE rise of a celibate male leadership in the Christian church brings us to the reign of Constantine and beyond. From the earliest period, the many forms of this celibacy had a drive to create a firmly delineated "public" space in the midst of the loose confederation of households that made up the Christian community. This was public space created in the bodies of the leaders themselves. Celibacy, however entered into, for the Christian community meant removal from what was held to be one of the most private sources of motivation and the dismantling of one of the most private social bonds on which the continuity and the cohesion of normal society depended. Its effect was to place the society of the Church, ruled and represented in public by celibate males, over against the society of the world, in which double-hearted pride, ambition, and the stubborn solidarities of family and kin group raged unchecked.

Such celibacy tended to take the form of postmarital abstinence from sexual relations. It was usually adopted in middle age and would later be imposed on priests after the age of thirty. This form of celibacy came to be expected as the norm for the average urban clergyman in the late antique period. It was not a spectacular renunciation. Sexuality was considered by ancient men to be a volatile substance, rapidly used up in the "heats" of youth. The grim facts of mortality in an ancient society ensured a constant supply of serious-minded widowers, who were available by their early middle age, "all passion spent," free to indulge in the more public joys of clerical office. In such a way celibacy demarcated quite unmistakably the existence of a class of persons who were central to the public life of the church, precisely because they were permanently removed from what was considered most private in the life

Gold medallion, ca. A.D. 330. Constantine and his imaginary companion, Alexander the Great. An autocrat who had one of his sons and one of his wives put to death, Constantine assumed the role of head of the Catholic Church. On the eve of their victory, the Christians were a minority, but an active and concentrated one.

of the average Christian layman in the world. Incorrectly remembering Hermas' *Shepherd* a hundred years later, Origen would speak of the "married," no longer simply of the rich, as the solid, unproductive wood over which vine of the church scrambled.

Celibacy, in the strict sense of entering into a state of permanent sexual abstinence, was unusual for public men in the Roman world. Thinking of himself as a man in his prime, whose social status gave him unthinking access to sexual satisfaction, Augustine admitted in Milan that, for all the high influence and access to the great that he envied in Ambrose, the Christian bishop, "his celibate state seemed a most hard thing to endure." For active men to come to create a "public" space in their own bodies through the renunciation of marriage, such public space had to be palpable (even attractive) and the community's need for a public space defined in this drastic manner, in the persons of its leaders, had to be very urgent indeed.

This was certainly the case for the Christian church of the third century. By A.D. 300 this church had become a public body in all but name. In 248 the church of Rome had a staff of 155 clergy and supported some fifteen hundred widows and poor. Such a group, quite apart from the regular congregation, was as large as the city's largest trade association. It was an enormous assemblage in a city where the average cult-group or burial club could be numbered in scores, not in hundreds. More revealing, perhaps, Pope Cornelius had paraded these impressive statistics as part of his claim to be regarded as the legitimate bishop of the city. Cyprian, who supported him, was careful to stress the "moral delicacy of virginal continence" with which Cornelius had shrunk from seizing high office. With such impressive responsibilities and resources at stake in every major city of the Empire, celibacy and the language of power had to be seen as one on the wider stage of Roman urban life. By being celibate and detached from the world in this manner, by the end of the third century the Christian bishops and clergy had become an elite equal in prestige, in the eyes of their admirers, to that of the traditional elites of urban notables.

It is to such a church, now firmly controlled by such leaders, that the conversion of the emperor Constantine, in 312, gave a fully public standing that proved decisive and irreversible in the course of the fourth century.

Glass on gold, Christian era. A family heirloom with no religious overtones; the sumptuously costumed couple receive victors' crowns, an omen of prosperity.

The empire that Constantine ruled as a declared Christian, from 312 to 337, was profoundly different from the classical urban society of the age of the Antonines. The huge fact of world-empire, present from the very beginning, finally was brought home to the cities. After 230 perceptible increases in taxation were necessary to maintain the unity and defense of the empire. In ancient conditions such increases meant far more than an increase in the proportion of the surplus appropriated by the imperial government. Upper-class society itself

Mausoleum, 3rd century. Images of wealth. Above: noble leisure (the master returns from a rabbit hunt). Below: running the estate (the master consults the account book in the presence of his paymaster and a sharecropper). (Trier, Landesmuseum.)

Ivory Diptych (right-hand portion), ca. A.D. 400; height: 12 inches. When a noble was awarded a high-ranking position, he had the fact recorded on an ivory tablet. Above, Rufius Probianus, named vice-prefect (of Rome?), sits on a throne, flanked by secretaries. With his hand he makes the "orator's gesture," which indicates that he is speaking, or that he has the right to speak, while others only have the right to listen. Below, two well-dressed lawyers (one holds a petition in his hand) raise their hands to beg the official's attention, as schoolchildren do in class and as the Greeks did to attract the attention of a god. (Berlin, Staatsbibliothek.)

had to be restructured so as to gain unimpeded access to that surplus. Old-fashioned local exemptions and the old-fashioned reluctance to injure the status of the rich by direct taxation were set aside. Direct intervention in the affairs of the cities became the norm for the imperial administration.

Such taxation did not cause the cities to disappear; still less did it eliminate the traditional elites. The elites merely changed their structure. Those who now wished to dominate society did so by combining their former positions as local notables with new roles as servants of the emperor. With the towering advantages of access to the imperial administration behind them, they came to consider themselves that much less fellow citizens, competing with a circle of equals in the traditional manner to nourish their "most sweet city." They were the *potentes,* the men of power, who controlled their cities in the name of the distant emperor in a manner that was far more blatant and much less sensitive to the delicate restraints of the diffused peer group of the wellborn. We noted in the age of the Antonines the enormous pressure brought to bear on the average civic notable by the insistence on a shared culture, and especially on a shared morality of social distance. By emphasizing the unbridgeable differences between their own class and everyone else, the Antonine wellborn had been able to consider themselves part of a group of interchangeable members of an elite. In the second and early third centuries this emphasis had effectively masked growing inequalities among the upper classes and the outright dominance within the upper class of those whose status depended on the service of the emperor. By the end of the third century these facts came to be accepted as the basic pattern on which Roman society had to be organized, if it was to survive. The later Roman Empire was a society explicitly dominated by an alliance of the servants of the emperor and of great landowners, who collaborated to control the taxpaying peasants and to assert law and order in the cities. The dominance of the few at the expense of their wellborn peers was stated unambiguously by the potentes of the reign of Constantine and his successors. Codes of behavior for the public man changed dramatically. Viewed by the sober eyes of men who liked to remember the older codes, the public man as *potens* came to blossom indecently. The discreet, uniform dress of the classical period, common to all members of the upper classes (think of the toga, heavy with overtones of the unchallenged dominance of a class of interchangeable *nobiles*) was abandoned in favor of the use of dress as a heraldry, designed to show hierarchical divisions within the upper classes. These new robes ranged from the billowing silk gowns of senators and the uniform-based dress of the imperial servants, embroidered with panels that indicated precise official ranks, to the studiously faceless tunic affected, in an equally explicit manner, by the Christian bishop. Previously it had been the body itself, its deportment in public and frequently, in the public baths, in the nude, that had given the most clear signals of natural membership of a distinctive class. Now the body was swathed in its owner's rank, in the form of heavy, close-fitting dress, each of whose ornaments spoke explicitly of a position in a hierarchy that culminated at the imperial court.

As for the city, in most regions of the Empire economic conditions ensured that it would no longer be an expanding site, a stage on which the competitive urges of the notables could express themselves in ever more lavish buildings, spectacles, and forms of public largesse. These aspects of the city did not vanish, however. They were maintained, often splendidly, in the great imperial residences at Trier, Sirmium, and, above all, Constantinople, as well as in major cities such as Rome, Carthage, Antioch, Alexandria, and Ephesus. But the splendor of the cities was now maintained by the Emperor, and on his behalf by the potentes. From being a vivid stage for the deployment of local energies in its own right, the city had become instead a microcosm of the ordered security of the Empire as a whole.

The fourth-century city was no pale shadow of its classical past. Much of its public decor had been carefully maintained, including the imposing facades of old pagan temples. In a surprising number of cities the imperial government continued to provide a privileged supply of foodstuffs, access to which was strictly limited, as in previous centuries, to citizens, irrespective of personal wealth or poverty. Similar supervision maintained vast public baths in all major cities. The circus, the theater (many altered at this time to accommodate ever more grandiose displays, such as water battles and wild beast hunts), and, most notoriously in Constantinople, the hippodrome replaced the ancient spaces traditionally associated with pagan public worship as the places where the loyalty of the city to its rulers, and so to its own survival, was solemnly expressed. The numinous associations attached to the proper performance of serious ceremonies clustered around such gatherings with as much intensity as in the religious ceremonies of pagan times. In Trier, Carthage, and Rome—all menaced and mauled by barbarians in the fifth century—the populace remained convinced that the performance of solemn circus games had effected, through their mysterious occult power, the continued survival of their city.

The potentes appeared less frequently in the forum. They now tended to dominate their cities from opulent palaces and country villas, set a little apart from traditional centers of public life. Rather than retreats from public life, however, these residences were the forum made private. The private rooms of the women's quarters were flanked by large halls for ceremonial receptions, often with an apse at one end. The small banquets held here were solemn gatherings of the inner group that ruled the city, very different from the magnificently indiscriminate civic banquets of clients, freedmen, friends, and fellow citizens on which, three centuries before, the younger Pliny had lavished his supplies of studiously indifferent cheap wine. Many of the masterpieces of classical statuary that once had stood in or around the temples and the forums came to rest in the extensive courtyards and entry halls of such palaces. They were tokens of the right of the potentes to absorb and preserve, on their own terms, the best of the classical city. Such men and their dependents would have to be persuaded that the Christian bishop and his fast-growing religious community could offer an alternative to their own vision of an urban world restored and maintained through the frank exercise of their own power and that of their master, the emperor. It was far from certain in the course of the fourth century that the new Christian church could impose its own peculiar notions of community on the ancient city in this, the last, carefully restored stage of its long existence.

| Church and City in the Fourth Century | The Christian bishop and his church were only one element in the new urban scene. Many churches might be magnificently constructed through imperial gifts, according to a new imperial design. The basilica was a building with heavy associations of the audience hall of the Emperor—and so of the judgment seat of God, invisible emperor of the world. The clergy might receive exemptions and privileged allocations of food. The bishop had access to the governors and the potentes, in intervening, above all, for the poor and oppressed. (Although, Augustine remarked, he often was kept waiting for hours on end in the entrance hall of the great, while more |

The grace of hesitation. With curls in the style of the time, does this woman of Pompeii represent the cultivated woman or is she an imaginary portrait of the ideal poetess? The Romans were fond of pictures of women writing. The left eye is higher than the right by a convention of perspective, indicating that the face is shown slightly in profile. (Naples, Archaeological Museum.)

This marble Venus was found at Pompeii in the Temple of Isis, a chaste goddess; but Venus was also the goddess of marriage. It was common to give an image of one god to another as an offering. The jewelry is of gold, and the hair was painted blonde, as traces of paint indicate. Naked parts of the body were left in natural color of the marble. The gold on the chest is for modesty's sake and does not represent some sort of lingerie. The goddess is twisting her hair and is therefore emerging from the bath. Ancient art portrayed frozen moments of time; it did not attempt to indicate the moral significance of an image by abstracting from real time. (Naples, Archaeological Museum.)

Pompeii, House of the Vettii, before A.D. 79, perhaps before 62. In one painting the young Hercules strangles two serpents. In the other King Pentheus, enemy of Bacchus, is torn apart by the Bacchantae. The paintings are placed on protruding walls with paneled ceilings supported by slender columns. In the corner the room seems to look out onto fantastic constructions, shown in perspective.

Wings. Mosaic from Pompeii. The theater was religious, as were all festivals, which explains the presence of garlands and sacred bandelets. Two actors in hide loincloths play satyrs; one wears a goat mask. The play is a "satyric" farce, a classical genre. Another actor selects a female mask. (Naples, Archaeological Museum.)

Grounds of the villa of Hadrian at Tivoli (ca. A.D. 125): fanciful architecture in a rural setting. The statues were excellent replicas of old Greek masterpieces. The pool lay between two hills, one of which was equipped with additional colonnades, cupolas, and a tree-filled park.

Detail of a floor mosaic, 4th century. The man is distributing bread from a full basket. (Aquileia, Cathedral.)

Theotecnos, Nonnosa, and Hilaritas, 5th century. (Naples, Catacombs of Saint January.)

Thysdrus: House of the Months. Mosaic of the Muses: from left to right and bottom to top, Euterpe and Clio, Terpsichore and Calliope, Urania and Erato. (Museum of El Jem.)

Bulla Regia. Mosaic in the triclinium of the House of the New Hunt.

Bulla Regia: House of the New Hunt. Ornamental foliage framing the hunting mosaic in the triclinium.

Utica: House of the Cascade.

Gilt silver clasps with filigree and almandine ornamentation. 7th century.
(Strasbourg, Archaeological Museum.)

Fresco, 12th century, depicting Clovis, King of the Franks, being treated by Saint Severinus. (Château-Landon, crypt of Saint-Séverin.)

**Psalter, late 11th century, Constantinople. Miriam, sister of Moses, leads women in a dance. A group of musicians is visible in the center. (Rome, Vatican Library, Greek 752.)**

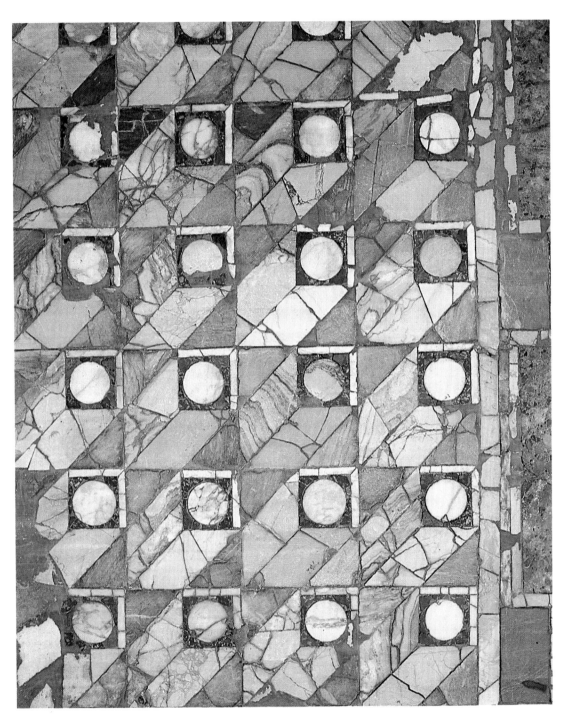

Mosaic of colored stones from a palace at Divanyolu, 9th–10th century. (Museum of Istanbul.)

Danielis travels by litter from the Peloponnese to Constantinople to visit her former protégé, now Emperor Basil I. Her servants deliver gifts to the emperor. The bottom sequence of figures shows Danielis in her old age visiting Constantinople and offering gifts to the young Leo VI. (Madrid, National Library.)

Octateuch (eight books of the Old Testament), 11th century. At left, Rebecca laments her sterility, while her husband prays to heaven. At right, Rebecca gives birth in seated position. Esau is lying on the ground, as the midwife delivers Jacob. (Rome, Vatican Library, Greek 747.)

important figures were admitted ahead of him.) Impressive though the fourth-century church might have appeared, it was marginal to the *saeculum,* a world whose main structures had evolved beneath the huge ancient pressures of power and the need for security and hierarchy. Christianity, even though now the nominal faith of the powerful, was peripheral to that saeculum.

The Christian community remained united by its distinctive mirage of solidarity. This solidarity could now be expressed in full public view by the ceremonies that took place in the basilica of the bishop. Though no longer a "gathering of the saints," the Christian basilica remained a place where the structures of the saeculum were pointedly absent. Secular hierarchy was less clear within the basilica than in the city streets. For all the new prominence of the clergy, for all the careful segregation of men and women (on most occasions onto different sides of the basilica's great aisles), for all the continued ability of the powerful to shine among the drab mass of their inferiors in spectacular Sunday clothes (now piously embroidered with scenes from the Gospels)—the Christian basilica remained the scene of a coming together of men and women of all classes, equally exposed, beneath the high chair of the bishop in the apse, to the searching eye of God. John Chrysostom made himself exquisitely unpopular in Constantinople by his habit of following with his eyes individual great landowners and courtiers as they strode in and out of the basilica during his sermons, marking them out by such a penetrating and public glance as the actual perpetrators of the sins and social wrongs he was denouncing. The old freedom of speech of the philosopher as critic of the great was now brought to bear on an entire urban community, gathered by its clergy into the audience hall of God. A community led in this manner, by such persons, was bound to attempt to transform the ancient city into a community shaped in its own, largely unfamiliar image.

In the eyes of these leaders the church was a new public community held together by repeated emphasis on three themes, each of which received a sharpness of focus hitherto lacking in the ancient world: sin, poverty, and death. Those three dark, seemingly faceless notions, closely interlocked, ringed the horizon of the late antique Christian. Only by coping with them in a manner laid down in no uncertain manner by the clergy could the average man or woman gain that "city of God" whose palpable joys still speak to a modern

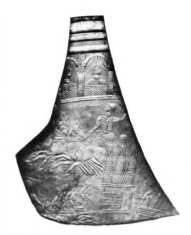

Fragment of an engraved cup, 4th century. In front of the viewing stand, a chariot rounds a marker with three staffs and balls. (Trier, Landesmuseum.)

So-called Temple of Bacchus at Baalbek, mid-2nd century. This temple, with its high foundation, is Roman in type, but the columns are exceptionally tall. The architecture of Roman Syria is notable for its large scale, its splendor, and (except for Palmyra) its originality.

visitor in the sheer sensual delight of late antique Christian mosaics and in the stilled, ever-beautiful faces of the saints. For on the mosaics they could see the saints—men and women acceptable to God and placed by Him, not in some ethereal and antiseptic afterlife but in the ancient "Paradise of delights," in "a grassy place by refreshing waters, whence pain and suffering and groaning are fled."[7]

*Sin and Community*

    The Christian basilica housed a gathering of sinners equal in their need for the mercy of God. The firmest boundaries within the group were those drawn by sin. One should not underestimate the element of novelty in such a definition of the community. Matters that might be as deeply private to the individual as his or her sexual mores or his or her opinions on Christian dogma could be adjudged by members of the clergy as grounds for a resounding public act of exclusion from the church. A public system of penance remained current throughout the period. Excommunication involved public exclusion from the Eucharist, and its effects could be reversed only by an equally public act of reconciliation with the bishop. Thus, in a fourth-century basilica public solidarity was linked to the issue of sin and to the even more interesting "thought crime" of heresy with a clarity that would be blurred in later ages. Access to the Eucharist involved a series of visible acts of separation and adhesion. The unbaptized were shepherded out of the building when the main liturgy of the Eucharist began. The ceremony began with the gesture of the believers in bringing offerings to the altar-table. In the final solemn advance of the faithful to participate in the "Mystical Supper," the only fixed hierarchy within the Christian group was made clear: bishops and clergy first, then the continent of both sexes, and, last of all, the married laity. In a specially designated area at the very back of the basilica, furthest from the apse, stood the "penitents," those whose sins excluded them from active participation. Ideally humbled, dressed beneath their status, their beards unshaven, they waited in full public view for the public gesture of reconciliation with their bishop. Occasionally the hierarchy of the saeculum and the democracy of sin would clash, with memorable results: in Caesarea, Basil refused the offerings of the heretical emperor Valens; in Milan, Ambrose kept the emperor Theodosius among the penitents—the ruler of the world stripped of his robe and diadem—for having ordered the massacre of the people of Thessalonica.

The poor were ever-present. The crippled and indigent, vagrants, and immigrants from an often afflicted countryside, hordes of them squatted at the doors of the basilica and slept in the porticoes surrounding its outer courtyards. The poor were spoken of always in the plural. They were described in terms that bore no relation to the earlier classification of society into citizen and noncitizen. They were the faceless human refuse of the ancient economy. It is precisely this anonymous quality that brought them into sharp focus as the remedy for the sins of the more fortunate members of the Christian community. Alms to the poor were an essential part of the prolonged reparation of penitents and the normal remedy for lesser, venial sins—sins of idle, impure thoughts and of minor self-indulgence—that did not require public penance.

The abject condition of the poor carried a heavy charge of religious meaning. They stood for the state of the sinner, in daily need of the mercy of God. The symbolic equation of the poor with the afflicted sinner, abandoned by God, recurred insistently in the language of the Psalms that formed the backbone of the church liturgy, and especially of its ceremonies of penance. Without such symbolism the leap of empathy simply would not have occurred, by which the urban dweller, accus-

*Solidarity and the Poor*

Mosaic, 4th century. A noble has had one of his villas depicted here. Its central courtyard is surrounded by a long loggia flanked by two majestic towers. The facade of the main building is roofed by small concrete cupolas, like the Baths of the Hunt at Lepcis. (Tunis, Bardo Museum.)

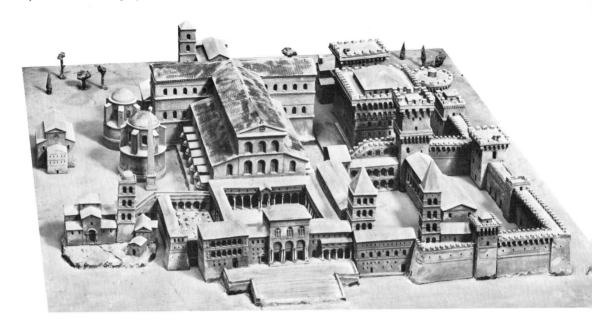

Marcelliani model of the medieval Vatican. The great edifice that is the left half of the model is the original Saint Peter's Basilica, construction of which was begun around 325. Every city had at least one "basilica," or official meeting hall, as did every palace.

tomed to perceiving such unpleasant human debris as little more than menacing exceptions to the rule of the ancient civic community of fellow citizens, came to accord to the poor a privileged status as symbols of the afflicted condition of mankind, his own sinful self included. Almsgiving became a potent analogue of the relation of God to sinful man. The whining of the beggars as the worshipers entered the basilica to pray were overtures of their own, desperate appeals to the mercy of God. "When thou art weary of praying," said John Chrysostom, "and dost not receive, consider how often thou hast heard a poor man calling, and hast not listened to him." "It is not for stretching out thy hand [in the *orans* gesture of prayer] that thou shalt be heard. Stretch forth thy hand not to heaven, but to the poor."[8]

The very anonymity of the poor helped maintain a sense of the undifferentiated solidarity of sinners in the church. The civic ideal that the great were under an obligation to give largesse pressed in upon the Christian church; for the civic ideal also implied that largesse made manifest the right of the powerful to control their community. After all, few basilicas would have been built without such a reflex. The most spectacular were gifts of the emperor or of leading clergymen. They were the acts of men who had every intention of making it clear, in the old-fashioned way, that they were the ones who

had a right to nourish, and so to control, the Christian con-
gregations who assembled in them. The names of those who
brought offerings to the altar were read aloud in the solemn
prayers of offering that preceded the Eucharist; frequently
these names were acclaimed. Only the notion of sin could
flatten the profile of so confident and high-pitched a pyramid
of patronage and dependence. What the bishops emphasized,
therefore, was the fact that every member of the Christian
community had his or her own sins; and that, given as alms,
any sum, however small, would be welcome to the truly poor.
As a result, the obtrusive outlines of patronage by the great,
expressed in stone, mosaic, silken hangings, and blazing candelabra, in the manner of the old civic munificence, were
veiled in the slight, but steady drizzle of daily almsgiving by
the sinful average Christian to the faceless afflicted.

The helplessness of the poor made them ideal clients for
a group anxious to avoid the tensions caused by real relations
of patronage to real clients. Of all the forms of patronage to
which the clergy had long been exposed, the most perilous,
and the most ignominious in the eyes of outsiders, was their
dependence on wealthy women. From Cyprian onward, poverty and the role of influential women in the church were
closely related. The wealth of many virgins, widows, and
deaconesses created ties of patronage and of humiliating obligation between the clergy and women who, by the end of
the fourth century, were leading members of the senatorial
aristocracy. Such wealth, and the patronage associated with it,
could be safely expended on the poor, for, as any ancient man
knew, the poor could offer nothing in return; their support
counted for nothing. Furthermore, strict codes of segregation
between the sexes had blocked access by women to public
power within the church. Any breach of these codes caused
studiously nurtured scandal whenever there was a threat that
influence in the church might come to be wielded by women
on the strength of their wealth, culture, or superior courage.
Such taboos, however, did not apply to a woman's public role
as patroness of mere human wreckage. As patronesses of the
poor, through almsgiving and through care of the sick and of
the stranger in hostels, well-to-do women came to enjoy a
real degree of public status in cities all over the Mediterranean
that was exceedingly rare in any other aspect of the hierarchical, male-dominated public life of the powerful in the Late
Empire.

As patron of the poor and protector of influential women,

The deceased Comminia, 4th
or 5th century. This figure, in
the Christian (and pagan) attitude of prayer, represents
Comminia, her immortal soul,
and prayer itself. (Naples,
Catacombs of Saint January.)

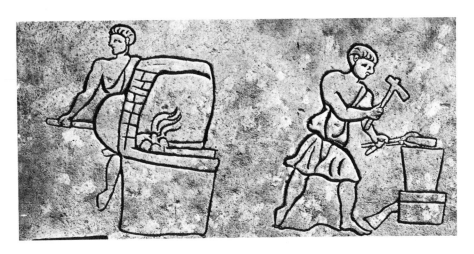

Rome, tomb of a blacksmith
in the Catacomb of Saint
Domitilla, 4th–5th century.
The use of engraving, less
costly than relief, represents a
democratization of funerary art.
(Rome, Christian Museum of
the Lateran.)

whose energies and wealth he could direct into the service of
the church by acting as the spiritual director of large groups
of widows and virgins, the bishop rose to prominence in the
fourth-century city. He publicly associated himself with precisely those categories of persons whose existence had been
ignored by the ancient, "civic" model of the urban notables.
In the words of the *Canons of Saint Athanasius:* "A bishop that
loveth the poor, the same is rich, and the city, with its district,
shall honor him." One could not have asked for a more
pointed contrast to the civic self-image of the notables of two
centuries earlier.

The Christian community, growing up parallel to the
ancient city, though far from dominant within it in the fourth
century, had created through its public ceremonies its own
sense of a new form of public space, dominated by a new type
of public figure. Celibate bishops, largely supported by celibate women, based their prestige on the ability to nourish a
new category: the faceless, profoundly anticivic rootless and
abandoned poor. In the fifth century Mediterranean cities came
to be touched by further crisis. The crucial generations immediately preceding and following A.D. 400 were noted
equally for urban catastrophes, such as the sack of Rome by
the Visigoths in 410, and for the emergence of influential
bishops, such as Ambrose at Milan, Augustine at Hippo, Pope
Leo at Rome, Chrysostom at Constantinople, and Theophilus
at Alexandria. These bishops ensured that the restored facade
of the late Roman city would collapse upon itself, leaving the
Christian bishop with his noncivic definition of the commu-

Part of an ivory diptych; height: 12 inches. It commemorates the consulate of Flavius Felix in 426. He holds a scepter with an eagle on top as an insignia of his rank and wears a long tunic, a dalmatic on top, and over all, a sumptuously embroidered toga. We have moved from the age of draped garments to that of sewn garments with gold and silver embroidery. (Paris, Bibliothèque Nationale, Cabinet des Médailles.)

Funerary mosaic, 5th century(?). In Spain and Africa such mosaics cover the gravestone, almost level with the ground. Legible are the name of the deceased, his age, and the month and day of death but, as in this case, not always the year. The important thing was the date on which the anniversary of the death should be celebrated. (Tunis, Bardo Museum.)

nity free to act as the sole viable representative of urban life around the shores of the Mediterranean.

*The Impact of the Afterlife*

Outside the cities stretched the quieter final solidarity of the Christian graves. To walk from the pagan into the Christian rooms of any modern museum is to pass into a world of clear standard meanings. The haunting richness of the upper-class sarcophagi of the second and third centuries—over whose message scholars will long continue to labor, in large part because they are so resolutely idiosyncratic—gives way to a limited repertoire of clearly recognizable scenes, found with few variations on all Christian tombs. The amazing variety of pagan funerary inscriptions and pagan funerary art testifies to a society with few common meanings about death and the afterlife. The grave was a magnificently private place. The dead person, supported by his traditional groups—family, peer group, burial associates, even, in the case of the great, his city—had to make the meaning of his own death clear to the living. Hence the extraordinary proliferation of burial clubs among the humble, the crucial role of the family mausoleum among the well-to-do, and the almost bizarre diversity of the statements of the deceased or about the deceased. (Recall the Greek notable Opromoas, who covered his tomb with the letters of praise for his civic generosities, written about him by Roman governors, or the lines of a humble stoneworker, apologizing for the quality of the verses on his epitaph!) Such tombs are the joy of any reader of Greek or Latin epitaphs, but they are the despair of any historian of religion who might wish to elicit from them a coherent doctrine of the afterlife. In the pagan world of the second and third centuries no widespread religious community had intervened to muffle the variety of so many private voices from the grave.

With the rise of Christianity the church came gradually to intrude between individual, family, and city. The clergy claimed to be best able to preserve the memory of the dead; their Christian doctrine about the afterlife made clear to the living the meaning of the passing away of the deceased. Traditional graveside ceremonies continued to be performed, but they were not enough. Offerings at the Eucharist ensured that the names of the dead would be remembered in prayer in the Christian community as a whole, presented as the larger, artificial kin group of the believer. Annual feasts in memory of the dead and for the benefit of their souls—given, as always,

Detail of Christian sarcophagus, 4th century. For centuries funerary art showed husband and wife half turned toward each other, half toward the spectator. (Rome, Lateran Museum.)

to the ever-available poor—took place in the courtyards of the basilicas and even within their walls. The church rather than the city now made manifest the glory of the departed. Once brought within the precincts of the basilica, the democracy of sin was made to stretch beyond the grave in a manner inconceivable to pagans. The clergy could refuse the offering made on behalf of unconverted family members, of unrepentant sinners, and of suicides.

A new sense of holy ground drew the dead into the shadow of the basilicas. Large Christian cemeteries, administered by the clergy, had existed in Rome since early in the third century. They included carefully engineered subterranean galleries, designed to provide burial for the poor in great numbers. The graves of the poor, cut in ledges one above the other in the catacombs, remain to this day as silent witness of the clergy's determination to act as patrons of the poor. Even in death, the poor are mobilized. The rows of humble graves, placed at a decent distance from the mausoleums of the rich, represented the care and solidarity of the Christian community.

At the end of the fourth century the spread of the practice of *depositio ad sanctos,* the privilege of being buried in near proximity to the shrines of the martyrs, ensured that if the Christian community demanded a hierarchy of esteem among its members the clergy, who controlled access to such shrines, would emerge as the arbiters of that hierarchy. Virgins, monks, and clerics are buried closest to tombs of the martyrs in the cemeteries of Rome, Milan, and elsewhere. These, the new elites of the urban church, are followed by the humble laity, rewarded for good Christian behavior: "Probilianus . . . for Hilaritas, a woman whose chastity and good nature was known to all the neighbors . . . She remained chaste for eight years in my absence, and so she lies in this holy place."[9]

The dead, absorbed into the Christian churches in this highly visible manner, were imperceptibly removed from their city. In order to establish the repose and continued renown of their dead, the Christian family dealt only with the clergy. Civic forms of testimony were disregarded. Only among the old-fashioned in small Italian towns was the anniversary of a public figure still made the occasion of a large public civic banquet for the notables and their fellow citizens. Petronius Probus, greatest of the fourth-century Roman potentes, was mourned publicly by the imperial court as a "first citizen." But after that his memory was entrusted to the shrine of Saint

Statuette of an empress, ca. 380(?). The polished appearance results from more than just the use of marble and the illusion of scale. Under the cloak, folded in the Hellenistic manner, we glimpse the long, gold-embroidered scarf worn by empresses as early as the 3rd century. (Paris, Bibliothèque Nationale, Cabinet des Médailles.)

Painting from an imperial reception hall, before 326. The aureole or nimbus indicates a princess, or perhaps an allegory; crowned with laurels, the woman is showing her jewels as a sign of prosperity. (Trier, Episcopal Museum.)

Mosaic, portrait of Saint Ambrose, 5th century. Here we see the melancholy man of action, a small, aloof, cultivated man whom Saint Augustine managed to see only in church on Sundays, a bishop whose policy relied on acts of violence calculated to look like caprices. (Milan, Church of Saint Ambrose.)

Peter. His splendid marble sarcophagus proclaimed Probus' new intimacy with Christ in the court of Heaven. And so the great man lay, some yards from Saint Peter himself, until sixteenth-century workmen found his sarcophagus, filled with the strands of gold woven into his last robe. As for the clergy and other holy dead, the mosaics show them far from the ancient city. They tread the enamel-green grass of God's Paradise, beneath the Eastern palms, surrounded by a most unclassical group of peers: "and now among the Patriarchs [he lives], among the Prophets of clear future sight, among the Apostolic company, and with the Martyrs, mighty men of power."

Rome, Santa Maria Maggiore, ca. 435. Only the floor, the baldachin, and the altar are recent; the ceiling imitates the ancient style. With a grace more imperial than sacred, it could pass for a pagan civil basilica. This is a masterpiece in the antique style, with its harmonious precision of proportions. A frame in relief once surrounded each mosaic, between the columns and the windows; these reliefs varied the flatness of the upper sections without cutting them in two by interposing a continuous horizontal projection.

# ✒ The Challenge of the Desert

THE rise of monasticism in the course of the fourth century brought a new element into the moral and social attitudes of the late antique Christian world. Constantine on one occasion wrote Saint Anthony, older than the emperor by almost a generation. Anthony, who had abandoned his village in the Fayum the year the emperor was born and was long settled in the outer desert of Egypt, was unimpressed. Pachomius, too, had established his first monasteries some years before Constantine became emperor in the East. The Constantinian dispensation, so notable in the cities, was a recent phenomenon compared to the world of the ascetics. The monks—*monachoi,* or "lonely ones"—drew on a very different, almost archaic, Christian tradition. Their spiritual and moral attitudes were nourished by the experience of a predominantly rural environment, very different from that of the urban Christians. In the fourth century the monks of Egypt and Syria enjoyed a *succès d'estime et de scandale* throughout the Mediterranean world. Athanasius' *Life of Anthony* appeared immediately after that saint's death in 356. Between 380 and 383 John Chrysostom withdrew, for a short but formative period, to live among the ascetics in the hills outside Antioch. "Journey in thought to the mountaintop on which Christ was transformed" remained the poignant dream of that most city-bound of Christian rhetors. In August 386 the story of Saint Anthony shocked Augustine out of his desire to marry and launched him on a trajectory that within a few years would lead to his ordination as bishop of Hippo, where he remained for the remaining thirty-five years of his life. By the end of the fourth century the role of the Christian church in the cities had been overshadowed by a radical new model of human nature and human society created by the "men of the desert."

Saint Paul the Simple. Menology of Basil II, 11th century. (Rome, Vatican Library.)

The prestige of the monk lay in the fact that he was the "lonely one." He personified the ancient ideal of singleness of heart. He had renounced the world in the most starkly visible manner possible. By an act of *anachôrésis,* he had moved away to live in the desert: he was an anchorite, a man defined by this single elemental move. Individual hermits or groups of hermits settled on the tracts of useless (though by no means always hostile) land that flanked the towns and villages of the Near East. They were known as the men of the *erémos,* of the desert, our "hermits." This desert had always been the ever-present antithesis of the life of the settled world. Those who moved into it often remained within sight and walking distance of the settled communities that they had abandoned; they soon came to serve the villagers as heroes and spiritual guides.

The monks moved in a marginal zone, clearly perceived as shorn of the habitual supports and definitions of organized life in society. They had settled on the social equivalent of an Antarctic continent, reckoned from time immemorial to be a blank space on the map of Mediterranean society—a no-man's-land that flanked the life of the city, flouted organized culture, and held up a permanent alternative to the crowded and relentlessly disciplined life of the villages.

In doing this, the individual monk had set himself free to achieve, in the face of God and among his fellows, the ideal of singleness of heart. Unriven by the tensions of settled so-

ciety, slowly and painfully purged of the murmurous promptings of demons, the monk longed to possess "the heart of the
righteous," a heart as unfissured, as clear of the knotted grain
of private, doublehearted motivation, as the solid, milk-white
heart of the date palm.

Admirers did not doubt that the monk, as "lonely one,"
had recaptured a touch of the original majesty of man. Centuries of speculation about the "glory of Adam" gathered
around his person. He stood, as Adam had stood, in single-
hearted worship of God in Paradise. The bleak, asocial landscape of the desert was a distant image of Paradise—the first,
the true home of humankind, where Adam and Eve had dwelt
in full majesty, before the subtle and overpowering onset of
the doublehearted cares of human life in settled society, before
marriage, physical greed, the labor of the earth, and the grind-
ing cares of present human society robbed them of their original serenity. Totally singlehearted, therefore joined with the
angelic hosts in unfailing and undivided praise of God, the life
of the monk mirrored on earth the life of the angels. He was
an "angelic man": "Often He showed me [said old man A-
nouph] the hosts of angels that stand before Him; often I have
beheld the glorious company of the righteous, the martyrs
and the monks—such as had no purpose but to honor and
praise God in singleness of heart."[10]

The monastic paradigm drew on the more radical aspects
of the pagan philosophic counterculture, most notably on the
magnificently asocial lifestyle of the Cynics, and on a long
Judeo-Christian past. Its originality lay in its dramatic shift of
viewpoint. It equated the world with a clearly identifiable
phenomenon—settled society as it existed in the present—and
it viewed that society as transparent to a sense of the true, that
is, of the "angelic," ordering of man's first estate. Behind the
preaching of a man such as John Chrysostom, in his sermons
around 382 *On Virginity,* we can sense the excitement of John's
monastic vision of a human race standing on the threshold of
a new age. The life of a city such as Antioch, the facts of
sexuality, of marriage, of childbirth, solid and immemorial as
they might seem, even to conventional Christians, appear now
as no more than a confused eddy in a stream that was slipping
fast from Paradise toward the Resurrection. Society, like human nature as adjusted to its demands, was an unplanned and
impermanent accident of history. "The present time draws to
its close; the things of the resurrection now stand at the
door."[11] All human structures, all human society—all "arts and

Detail of floor mosaic, 4th century. Not, as the guides would
have it, the devil sticking out
his tongue, but a cool Wind,
which complements the other
symbols of paradise visible in
the mosaic: flowers, river, and
a brimming pitcher. (Aquileia,
Cathedral.)

buildings," "cities and households"—even the socal definition
of men and women as sexual beings destined for marriage and
reproduction, were soon to come to rest in the vast hush of
the presence of God. Those who had adopted the life of the
monks and virgins on the edge of the city had anticipated the
dawn of man's true nature; they were "ready to receive the
Lord of Angels." That moment of rapt adoration at the high
moment of the liturgy of the Eucharist (as celebrated in Antioch), when the faithful joined their voices with those of the
angels in chanting "Holy, Holy, Holy" to the King of Kings
as He approached unseen to the altar, revealed for an instant
the true, undivided state of man. City, marriage, and culture,
the "necessary superfluities" of settled life, were but a passing
interlude compared with that clear state, shorn of the "cares
of this life." The monks on the hills outside the city strove to
make that moment last for a lifetime.

---

*Desert and Society*

Christian monasticism aimed to create a world stripped
of familiar structures. The compartmentations, the hierarchies,
the sharp distinctions on which the life of the city continued
to be based, had been blurred and softened, by the impressive
communal rituals within the Christian basilicas. But these
basilicas remained encapsulated spaces within the solid structures of the city. Social structures might be held in suspense
at high moments, but they were never banished entirely from
the minds of the believers, who would step out of the basilica,
once the ceremonies were over, to find themselves in the hard
world of the late antique city. Men like John Chrysostom now
wished all these to vanish in the growing radiance of a new
age. The dawn light of the "things of the Resurrection" already
played on the little settlements of "angelic men" on the hills
around Antioch; it might slip down to bathe the sleeping city.
This was Chrysostom's lifelong dream. He died in 407, in
exile—broken by the power of the world. Yet the acceptance
of monasticism by so many leading Christian figures betrayed
a sense of the vulnerability of the cities, as these had been
restored in the generation of Constantine. The fifth century
was marked by barbarian invasion in the West and dogged
organization of rising population and a consequent rising
misery in the East. The newly created structures of the late
Roman cities were yet further weakened as the radical monastic view of the world helped the articulate leaders of the
Christian community to make plain the demise of the classical

city. The monks and their admirers were the first Christians of the Mediterranean to look beyond the ancient city. The monks saw a new society. Their personal preoccupation with new forms of personal discipline, which included the renunciation of sexuality, ensured that a very different flavor would be instilled into the private life of the Christian family within that society.

Coptic monastery of Saint Simeon, west of Aswan, in the desert. Cells are clustered inside a fortified wall. Founded in the 4th century, the building shown here is the result of 15 centuries of additions and modifications.

## City and Countryside

In the monastic paradigm the city itself lost its identity as a distinctive cultural and social unit. In many parts of the Near East the rise of the monks marked the end of the splendid isolation of the Hellenistic city from its surrounding countryside. City-dwellers who trooped out to seek the counsel and blessing of the holy men established in the neighborhood tended to meet there village illiterates, who could speak, at best, pidgin Greek. Throughout the Mediterranean region the monks joined the faceless poor in forming a new universal class, without ties to city or countryside because equally dependent on the mercy of God in either. The symbolism of the poor as dark mirrors of the abject condition of man was immensely heightened by little colonies of voluntary poor, which flanked the cities. The actual poor did not benefit, for

*Vaticanus latinus* 1202, 11th century: An example of the lewdness which Saint Benedict of Norcia saw in Rome and which induced this Umbrian influenced by eastern monasticism to leave that city. He retired at first to Subiaco, to the ruins of the villa built by Nero in a beautiful rural setting. Later he founded the famous Monastery of Monte Cassino. The naked Venuses that were celebrated in ivory and silver as late as the 6th century here represent sin.

the laity preferred to give alms to the monks, the "ceremonial poor," whose prayers were known to be effective, rather than to the noisy and repulsive beggars surrounding the basilicas. The monks functioned much as a chemical solution functions in a photographer's darkroom: their presence brought out with greater sharpness of contrast the new features of a Christian image of society. This was an image that ignored the cities, by ignoring the old divisions of town and countryside, citizen and noncitizen, and concentrated on the universal division of rich and poor in town and countryside alike.

Take, for example, the Egyptian provincial city of Oxyrhynchus, which until the end of the third century had enjoyed a privileged supply of food. This supply was allotted to those who, irrespective of wealth or poverty, could claim descent from the citizen class, and the genealogies recorded to establish these claims go back to the very beginnings of the Roman urban order in Egypt. By the end of the fourth century, however, the city was ringed around with populous monasteries and convents, and the ancient structures had been definitively eclipsed. As Christians, the notables now competed to lavish charity on the poor and the strangers rather than on "the most resplendent city" of Oxyrhynchus.

The Christian notable is now the *philoptôchos*, "lover of the poor," no longer the *philopatris*, "lover of his home town"—though it is still on bended knee that the humble man must approach him. Although the misery of the poor had been revealed by Christian symbolism of sin and its reparation, they had not gone away. They shivered in the cold desert nights, as they crowded around the basilica for a Sunday meal, provided now by the monks, "on behalf of the souls" of the "most resplendent families," who still controlled the city of Oxyrhynchus and the surrounding countryside. These families no longer felt the need to express any special love for their city, as if it were any different from the mass of humble persons, whom they controlled in town and country alike. As "lovers of the poor," the great patronized the afflicted equally, whether they had been born in the city or in the countryside.

## A New Education

Monasticism not only destroyed the particularity of the city; it threatened to weaken the city's hold on its notables at one of its most intimate points: it challenged the role of the public spaces of the city as the principal locus for the socialization of young males. It would be misleading to treat the

monks as if they were without exception illiterate heroes of an anticulture. Many converts to asceticism were educated men, who had found in the desert—or in the idea of the desert—a simplicity on the other side of great sophistication. In the hands of a Basil of Caesarea or an Evagrius of Pontus, techniques of moral grooming, standards of deportment and of spiritual discipline, previously practiced only by the elites of the cities, flowered with new vigor in the monasteries.

Nor was such a culture for mature men only; by the middle of the fourth century monastic settlements were being recruited from among the very young. Quite well-to-do village and urban families dedicated their children to the service of God, as often as not to keep the family heritage together, unburdened by excessive sons—and especially by surplus daughters. These very young monks did not simply vanish into the desert. They tended to reappear some years later, and even in the cities, as members of a new elite of abbots and clergymen of ascetic training. The monastery, therefore, was the first community prepared to offer a fully Christian training from boyhood up. The monks demanded that their young hermits absorb a literary culture based entirely on the liturgy and the Bible. Monastic practice sharpened existing codes of behavior, by basing the formation of young boys and girls on the slow penetration of their souls with dread "certainty of the Presence of the Invisible God." In its content and, even more, in the emotions to which it appealed, this process of socialization, as advocated in ascetic circles, spelled the end of

*Codex Sinopensis* on purple leaves, 6th century. In this case the decline of ancient academicism resulted in something other than clumsiness or naiveté: a lively theatrical talent is evident. At right is the prison where John the Baptist has just lost his head (the scene is agitated, and it is clear that a deed has just been done). At left, the head is brought to Herod Antipas, Herodiad, and Salome (wearing wigs), in the midst of a banquet. (Paris, Bibliothèque Nationale.)

the ideal of education by the city. For until the end of the fourth century it had been taken for granted that all boys, pagan and Christian alike, should be exposed to the magnificently noisy, articulate, and extroverted "shame culture" of competing peers, associated with the ancient rhetor's classroom on the edge of the forum. Now this could fall silent.

That so drastic a new model of education had so little effect on the public grooming of the younger members of the upper classes in this period is a telling symptom of the vigor of the late antique city. The educational ideals of the city were by no means absorbed by those of the monastery. Yet the monasteries clearly revealed a fissure that might open up at any later time between the city and the Christian households within it. The ancient city, whose intimate disciplines had molded the private and public identities of its upper-class members for centuries, threatened to dissolve into a mere confederation of families, each of which ensured for itself, in collaboration with clergymen or even with monks who lived at some distance from the city, the true—that is, the Christian—grooming of the young male.

Reading the sermons of John Chrysostom, we receive an impression of the doors of the Christian household slowly closing in on the young believer. His adolescence no longer belongs to the city. A classical culture, the privileged tool of interchange between upper-class peers, might continue to be instilled in him by schools at the traditional center of the city. But it was already a "dead" culture, derived from ancient texts, still held to be necessary for correct writing and speaking, but whose connection with daily life had been severed. The young Christian's code of deportment no longer derived from the same source that it would have two centuries earlier. The deportment of the Christian believer is now revealed most clearly in the lifestyle of the monk. This amounted to an education in the fear of God, which could be observed in contemporary monastic circles to cut far deeper into the personality than did the old-fashioned civic fear of incurring shame in the presence of the wellborn. It was mediated in an environment that was more intimate and more stable than that provided by the upper-class youth group. Chrysostom saved the young Antiochene boy from the city, in order to hand him over to the subtle dread of his own father. Chrysostom, a great psychologist of religious awe, now saw the fear of God, instilled every day in the growing boy by the weighty

Painted glass, 5th century(?). Two women in court costume with a young prince, all Christians; we do not know who they are. (Christian Museum of Brescia.)

presence of the Christian father, as the basis of a new, and Christian, code of deportment.

At a stroke, we glimpse early Byzantine Antioch as it could yet be. No longer a Hellenistic city, the behavior of its leading citizens is no longer subtly molded by codes derived from life in ancient public centers. The ancient public spaces are ignored. Theater and forum are absent. Winding, narrow lanes lead back and forth from great religious gatherings in the Christian basilica, to secluded courtyards in whose screened privacy the believing father passes on to his sons the religious art of the fear of God. It is a glimpse into the future, to the Islamic town.

Yet the glimpse is misleading. Passing from the sermons of John Chrysostom to the epitaphs of his contemporaries, in Greek and Latin, we catch a very different sight of the urban Christian. He had remained to the end a man of public space. If no longer a "lover of his town," he was instead a "lover of the people of God," or a "lover of the poor." Apart from a few gravestones of monks and clergymen, hardly a single inscription stressed the intimate motive force of the fear of God in the Christian believer. The Christian layman had remained an ancient man, gloriously sensitive to those ancient adjectives that acclaimed his relations with his fellows. He was far less concerned to lay bare for posterity motives that we know to have caused his heroes, the monks, to sigh and shudder throughout their lives in salutary dread.

Silver wedding casket (detail), found in Rome, 379–382. Intended as a gift for a Christian bride, Prospecta, the casket is carried into the groom's home. (London, British Museum.)

## Asceticism and Marriage

Of all the aspects of the life of the settled community upon which the monastic paradigm laid a vast, impalpable burden, the most intimate was that associated with marriage, with intercourse within marriage, and with the role of sexuality. The Christian household might be expected to close its doors to the forum and the theater as places for the grooming of the young; but it was called upon to open the doors of the bedchamber to a new awareness of the nature of sexuality, developed among the continent "men of the desert." The varying degrees to which such households opened that door— or, to be more precise, were expected to do so by their bishops, clergy, and spiritual advisers—takes us to the beginning of the contrast between the Christian societies of Byzantium and of the Catholic West throughout the Middle Ages.

Sarcophagus of Junius Bassus, ca. 359. In this consecrated rural setting and a dignified atmosphere, Adam and Eve feel shame for the sin they have committed. (Rome, Vatican Grottoes.)

# ❧ East and West: The New Marital Morality

THE monastic paradigm had placed a question mark after marriage, sexuality, and even the differentiation of the sexes. In Paradise, Adam and Eve had been asexual beings. Their decline from an "angelic" state of single-hearted worship of God was assisted, if not directly caused, by a decline into sexuality. This decline into sexuality started the fatal slide of men and women into a world of double-hearted cares associated with marriage, with childbirth, and with hard labor to support hungry mouths.

The story of the Fall of mankind, in the persons of Adam and Eve, was held to be a faithful mirror of the soul of the contemporary ascetic, trembling on the brink of commitment to the dire restraints of life "in the world," and summoning up the resolution to opt for the "angelic" life of the monk. For in the cramped world of the Near Eastern villages, as among the dour households of the urban Christians, entry into the world began, in practice, with a parentally arranged marriage for the young couple in their early teens.

Told in this radical form, as pointing the road to a Paradise Regained in the desert, monasticism threatened to wash away some of the firmest supports of settled life in the eastern Mediterranean. It implied that married Christians could not hope to enter Paradise, which was accessible only to those who in this life had adopted the sexual abstinence of Adam and Eve before their fall into sexuality and into marriage. If the life of the monk was thought to foreshadow the paradisiacal state of an asexual human nature, then man and woman—as monk and virgin, their sexuality eliminated by being renounced—might yet wander together over the bleak mountainsides of Syria, as Adam and Eve had once stood, upon the flowering slopes of Paradise, untouched by gender and by its present, disturbing sexual ache.

One of six surviving diptychs of Anastasius. Consul in Byzantium in 517, he holds the handkerchief that he will throw down to signal the start of a race. He also staged animal hunts. Here one of the hunters is bitten by a hyena, and others attempt to lasso lions. (Paris, Bibliothèque Nationale, Cabinet des Médailles.)

The threat of an obliteration of gender, with a resulting indifference to sexuality as an element to be feared in the relations of men and women, was the *Grande Peur* (Great Fear) of the fourth-century Eastern world. It provoked immediate reactions from monks and clergy alike. A shrill misogyny is the modern reader's first impression of much monastic literature. The citation *All flesh is grass* was interpreted as meaning that men and women, as indelibly sexual beings, were permanently liable to instantaneous combustion! The good monk was supposed to carry even his own mother across a stream, carefully shrouded in his cloak, "for the touch of the flesh of a woman is as fire." Behind such bruising anecdotes lies the incessant challenge of a radical alternative. In radical Christian ascetic groups, denial of the value of marriage tended to go hand in hand with a denial of sexuality itself. This, in turn, implied a denial of the division between the world and the desert. For those whose feet already trod the slopes of Paradise in this life, by opting for the "angelic" existence of the monk or the virgin, might pass with eyes as innocent as those of a child through the countryside, through the villages, and through the crowded towns, mingling unrestrained with men and women alike. Athanasius had to challenge the followers of Hierakas on this issue in Egypt. Hierakas, a revered ascetic thinker, had doubted whether married persons had any place in Paradise and, at the same time, expected his austere followers to be ministered to with impunity by virgin female companions. Chrysostom preached against "spiritual partnerships" of monks and virgins within the city of Antioch. Later the stirrings of the Messalian monks, monks devoted to wandering and perpetual prayer and notoriously indifferent to the presence of women in their shabby ranks, became endemic in Syria and in eastern Asia Minor.

As a result of the need to contain the radicalism implicit in the monastic paradigm, the eastern Mediterranean became a society explicitly organized, in a shriller manner than ever before, in terms of a democracy of sexual shame. All persons, from the married heads of upper-class families to the heroic men of the desert, were expected to share a common code of sexual avoidance, irrespective of class and profession. In Antioch, Chrysostom even dared attack the public baths, social gathering point par excellence of civic upper-class society. He criticized aristocratic ladies for exposing themselves before the eyes of troops of servants, their softly nurtured flesh draped only in the heavy jewelry that was the mark of high status.

In Alexandria even the scanty dress of the poor was thought to create distressing fantasies in the believer, in a manner inconceivable in previous centuries where such exposure might be treated as contemptible but was hardly feared as a source of automatic moral danger.

As for members of married Christian households in the eastern Mediterranean, in this and in later periods, we are faced with a paradox. The heroes and spiritual advisers of the *kosmikoi,* "the men in the world," tended to be "men of the desert." The kosmikoi dearly loved to walk out to visit them or to receive them into their houses, their very bodies exuding the "sweet smell of the desert." As we have just seen, the monastic literature produced by the men of the desert generated an exceptional amount of overt anxiety on the issue of sexual avoidance. It presented the sexual drive as potentially operative, for the bad, in all social situations between men and women. Yet, beyond that, the concern of the men of the desert with sexuality followed lines that were strictly parallel to those of the married men in the world.

The spiritual masters of the desert, most notably Evagrius and his Latin exponent, John Cassian, came to treat the fact

Syrian relief, ca. 200. The Syrian woman is invisible beneath her veils; the Syrian goddess has become a nude Venus. Below, Astarté-Venus, goddess of nature, and her lover, Adonis, oriental god of rebirth, here stylized as a Greek hero. At the left is a model of a round temple offered by the couple; above and below can be seen a schematic representation of folds in the temple curtain. (Paris, Louvre.)

of sexuality as a privileged sensor of the spiritual condition of the monk. Sexually based imaginations, the manifestation of sexual drives in dreams and through night emissions, were examined with a sensitivity unheard of in previous traditions of introspection, and in a manner entirely independent of any opportunities for contact with the other sex. To see sexuality in this manner was a revolutionary change of viewpoint. From being regarded as a source of "passions," whose anomalous promptings might disrupt the harmony of the well-groomed person if triggered by objects of sexual desire, sexuality came to be treated as a symptom that betrayed other passions. It became the privileged window through which the monk could peer into the most private reaches of his soul. In the tradition of Evagrius, sexual imaginings were scrutinized minutely in and of themselves. They were held to reveal concretely (if shamefully) the presence in the soul of yet more deadly, because more faceless drives: the cold cramp of anger, pride, and avarice. Hence the abatement of sexual imaginings, even the modification of night emissions, was closely observed as an index for the monk of the extent to which he had won through to a state of single-hearted translucence to the love of God and of his neighbors. "For you have possessed my innermost parts," wrote Cassian, reporting the discourse of Apa Chaeremon. "And so he shall be found in the night as he is in the day, in bed as when at prayer, alone as when he is surrounded by crowds."[12] The slow remittance of the lingering, intensely private meanings associated with sexual dreams heralded the passing away from the soul of those far greater beasts, anger and pride, distant echoes of whose heavy tread appeared in the form of sexual fantasies. With this the monk had closed the last, razor-thin fissure in the single heart.

The doctrine of sexuality as a privileged symptom of personal transformation was the most consequential rendering ever achieved of the ancient Jewish and Christian yearning for the single heart. In the hands of an intellectual such as Evagrius, it was the most original approach to introspection to come from the late antique world. Yet it scarcely touched on the experience of the laity. The doors of the Christian household, which we have sensed closing silently between the young Christian and the claims of his city as the source of moral guidance, closed also against the strange new sense of sexuality developed, among themselves and for themselves, by the men of the desert. The marital and sexual morality of the early Byzantine Christian was dour; but little in it seemed

Ivory plate. A bearded Christ is flanked by Peter and Paul and scenes from New Testament. (Paris, Bibliothèque Nationale, Cabinet des Médailles.)

problematic. Its rules provided a clear guide for those young persons who wished to remain in the world. Throughout the Byzantine Near East the norms of married life were as familiar, and as seemingly unshakable in their own way, as were the structures of secular law and administration that still ringed the Near East in the age of Justinian with the sense of an Empire, with frontiers "firm as statues of bronze."

In Eastern Christian morality the facts of sexuality were not communicated by the clergy as fraught with any particular sense of mystery. Either one lived with them, as a married person, in the world, or one abandoned them, in order to soak the body in the "sweet smell of the desert." The latter choice was best made at an early age; the age of stormy, middle-aged conversions to the ascetic life had passed. By A.D. 500 it was important that the young man, and especially that the very young girl, should make up their minds for or against continuing to live as a married person in the world, before the heavy social restraints of betrothal came to weigh in on them in their early teens. Uncertainty after that point could lead only to the disruptive consequences of an unsatisfied yearning for the desert in later, married life. Very often the choice that one of the parents might have made was postponed

Convent of Saint Simeon (Qal'at Saman), ca. 470. Thirty-odd miles northwest of Aleppo, this was a masterpiece in a severe style, monumental yet airy, in which the language of ancient architecture was still alive.

for a generation, by being passed on to one of the children. The sixth century is a century of child saints, of infant recruits to the ascetic life. Martha, the pious mother of Simeon the Younger of Antioch, raised her son to become a famous stylite, or pillar-squatting, saint (at the age of seven!) because she herself had been married off against her will to a newly arrived artisan-colleague of her father. Young Simeon was a substitute for Martha's own yearning for sanctity, cut short, as was so often the case, by an arranged marriage.

Women in the eastern Mediterranean were shunned more carefully than before. Ancient imaginative boundaries between the sexes were reemphasized, including the exclusion of menstruating women from the Eucharist. Yet in Byzantine cities most people lived in close quarters, usually off a single central courtyard; sexual segregation must have been largely notional. The architecture of the harem, of a totally separate living quarter for women, had not yet appeared in the Christian cities of the sixth-century Near East. Among the males it was known that the "heats" of youth could be discharged through premarital sex. The only contribution of the ascetic tradition on this point was a tendency to ask even male penitents if they had "lost their virginity," and under what circumstances. It

Reliefs on wooden doors, ca. 432. One of the most ancient images of the crucifixion. Christ's cross, almost never depicted in early Christian art, does not appear. The noble architecture in the background, historically ridiculous, makes the scene unrealistic and represents, inaccurately, the church with three entries built by Constantine at Calvary. (Rome, Church of Santa Sabina.)

would have been a very strange question indeed to ask three hundred years earlier of a man for whom "virginity" was the exclusive concern of his sisters and daughters.

---

*Byzantine Realities*

Early marriage was proposed for the young of both sexes as a breakwater that could shield Christian men from the choppy seas of adolescent promiscuity. Yet even such a moralist as Chrysostom could see little problematic in the act of sex within the stilled waters of lawful wedlock. Ancient restrictions still hedged in the act of intercourse, but they were largely concerned with when or how it should be performed. The time-honored imposition of withdrawal from the woman in times of menstruation and during pregnancy had been compounded by the obligation to abstain during church fasts and festivals. When permitted, however, the intercourse between married partners was taken for granted. What is more, medical opinion continued to assert that only through a passionate and pleasurable discharge, experienced by both the man and the woman in a hot act of love, could the conception of the child be guaranteed and, with it, the quality of its "temperament"— that balance of hot and cold humors that might make it a boy or a girl, a healthy or a morbid character.

Let us look back at the world of the early Byzantine men in the world, flanked now, if at a safe distance, by the imposing men of the desert. We see the outlines of a very ancient urban society in its final days.

Beyond the doors of the basilica and the gates of the Christian household, the city had remained stridently profane and sexually undisciplined. In the city, although it might now be supported by Christian notables in the name of an ostentatiously pious Christian emperor, nude girls of the lower classes continued to delight the upper-class citizens of Constantinople; they splashed in great aquatic spectacles in Antioch, Gerasa, and elsewhere. In the "Blessed City" of Edessa, oldest Christian city in the Near East, pantomime dancers still whirled sinuously in the theater. A nude statue of Venus stood outside the public baths of Alexandria—allegedly causing the robes of adulterous ladies to blow up over their heads—until it was finally removed, not by a bishop but by the local Muslim governor, at the end of the seventh century. As late as 630 in Palermo three hundred prostitutes rioted against the Byzantine governor as he entered the public baths. (We know of the incident only because the governor, a good Byzantine

Detail of sarcophagus, 4th century. Adam and Eve after the Fall, facing eviction from Eden. (Velletri, Communal Museum.)

who expected the clergy to do their duty by their city, had met clerical demands by appointing the bishop Imperial Inspector of Brothels—thereby earning the rebuke of a shocked Western pope!) What remained of the ancient city in the Byzantine East had evidently not rallied in all its aspects to the moral codes exemplified for the laity by the monks.

*Laity and Clergy in the West*

In looking at the problems posed by sexuality, not from the "desert" and the "world" of Byzantium but through the eyes of Augustine, the Catholic bishop of Hippo, and of subsequent Latin clergymen, we can sense the outlines of another, different world that would form around the bishops of the Catholic Church in the provinces of the post-Imperial West.

The monastic paradigm, based on a sense of the presocial

and presexual glory of Adam and Eve, did not haunt the urban bishop of the Latin West as it so plainly tantalized and disturbed the bishops of the eastern Mediterranean. With Augustine, its basic assumption was firmly abandoned. Human society, including marriage and sexuality, was by no means a second best, interim stage of humanity, rendered impalpable by nostalgia for a lost "angelic" majesty of man. For Augustine, Adam and Eve had never been asexual beings. They would have enjoyed in Paradise a full marital existence; the joys of continuity through children would have been granted to them. Augustine saw no reason whatsoever why such children should not have been begotten and conceived by an act of intercourse accompanied by sensations of solemn and sharp delight. Paradise, for the bishop of Hippo, was no shimmering antithesis to life "in the world," but a "place of peace and harmonious joys"—that is, not the absence of settled society, as the desert was, but settled society as it should be, shorn of the tensions inherent in its present condition. Paradise and the experience of Adam and Eve there provided a paradigm of social, even sexual, interchange, against which to judge—and, given the fallen condition of man, find wanting—the most intimate sexual deportment of the married laity. For if Paradise could be presented as a fully social state, a shadow of Paradise Regained could be seen not only, as in Byzantium, in the vast silences of a desert, at a distance from organized human life, but even in the solemn hierarchy of service and command, within the basilicas of the Catholic church in the cities. Part of this Paradise Regained would be associated not just with the clear-cut, public abandonment of marriage for the desert, but with the intensely private endeavor of married couples to equate their own sexual behavior to the harmonious innocence first exemplified, in married sexuality, by Adam and Eve.

In such a view sexuality ceased to be an anomaly whose importance faded into relative insignificance when compared with the far greater anomaly of man's sad decline from the angelic state. Unlike Evagrius and John Cassian, therefore, Augustine could not hope to see sexuality fade away from the imagination of a single-hearted few, schooled in the vast solitudes of the desert. Nor could he follow the Byzantine householder and his spiritual guides in treating sexuality within marriage as of little interest, provided that it was entered into within traditional forms of social restraint. As long as sexuality was dwarfed by a sense of the vast sadness of mortality, it posed few problems. It was possible for John Chrysostom and other Greek bishops to present intercourse as no more than an untidy, but necessary, means of securing continuity through the begetting of children. Chrysostom indeed could acclaim it as a positive boon, which had been granted by God to Adam after his Fall, so that human beings, fallen from their angelic majesty into death, could seek a fleeting shadow of eternity through begetting children. For Augustine, by contrast, sexuality was as intimate a symptom of the Fall of Adam and Eve as was mortality; its present, uncontrollable nature resulted from the Fall as immediately and as surely as did the chill touch of mortality.

*Concupiscence*

The anomaly of sexuality lay in its concrete experiences, which registered with sad precision the gulf between sexuality as it might have been enjoyed by Adam and Eve, had they not fallen, and the sexuality of the present, fallen Christian married couple. With the flair of an old rhetor presenting his findings as a statement of the obvious, known to all men of feeling and intelligence, pagan and Christian alike, Augustine elucidated those aspects of intercourse that seemed to betray a deep-seated dislocation of will and instinct. Erection and

Silver plate, 6th century A.D. Diameter: 12 inches. Venus and Adonis. This Venus, whose small bust emphasizes her full hips, reflects a taste for realism that classical canons had consigned to the minor arts. The male nude is well built. The pillar is a clumsy means of breaking the symmetry. The draftsmanship lacks precision, but the boldness is impressive. These are not idealized creations but two magnificent specimens of humanity. Byzantine work. (Paris, Bibliothèque Nationale, Cabinet des Médailles.)

Syrian plaque, 6th century.
One of the two Saints Simeon,
seated atop the column, around
which a serpent has wrapped
itself. The ladder symbolizes
the difficulty faced by the soul
in ascending to heaven. Images
of the two stylites were among
the first to attract cults.

orgasm hold his attention, for the will seemed to have no access to either, in that neither could the impotent (or frigid) summon up such a sensation by an act of will nor, once summoned, could such sensations be controlled by the will. For Augustine these were vivid and apparently irreversible tokens in all human beings, men and women, married and continent, of the wrath of God against the pride of Adam and Eve in cutting themselves off from the will of God. An ageless, faceless, and protean "concupiscence of the flesh" capable of manifesting itself in such very precise symptoms in the intercourse of married persons and requiring constant moral vigilance also among the continent, was the sign of a fateful dislocation of the former harmony of man and God, of body and soul, of male and female, enjoyed by Adam and Eve. They had lived in Paradise not as asexual celibates but as a fully married human couple, and so as much an embryonic human society as any Christian householder of Hippo. The juxtaposition of an ideal human married state with the actual married life of the lay person was a comparison as potent and as pointed as it was invidious to the average couple.

Such views, or variants of such views, have become so much a part of the bloodstream of Western Christendom, that it is important to step back a little in order to sense their first strangeness and to appreciate the particularity of the situation that led Augustine and his successors to modify, in so significant a manner, the monastic paradigm that they had inherited from the East.

For the Christian layman nothing less was at stake than a new interpretation of the meaning of sex. The new interpretation implied the obsolescence of the codes of deportment rooted on a specific physiological model of the human person. Both the codes and the physiology had conspired in the Antonine age to harness the energies of sexual passion to a specific model of society. The doctors and moralists of the period had attempted to absorb sexuality into the good order of the city. They had taken for granted that a vigorous discharge of "generative heat," mobilized throughout the body as a whole in both man and woman and accompanied by clear sensations of physical pleasure, was a sine qua non of conception. Conception and passion could not be disjoined. The only problem for the moralist was that such passion should not sap the public deportment of the male by being indulged in frivolously or excessively in private. Furthermore, it was widely believed that intercourse that took place according to norms of decorum that were in some manner continuous with public codes of deportment would produce better children than would intercourse in which such norms had been flouted, whether by oral foreplay, by inappropriate postures, or by access to the woman in menstruation. In such a way, the sexual act might be presented as the most intimate token of the "morality of social distance" associated with the maintenance of the codes of public decorum specific to the upper classes.

Augustine dismantled this model; his views implied nothing less than a new body image. Sexual passion was no longer presented primarily as a diffused and mindless bodily "heat" brought to a peak in intercourse. Attention was focused instead on precise zones of specifically sexual feeling: for men, the nature of the erection and the precise quality of the ejaculation. These were weaknesses in which all human beings shared equally. As a result, the more brutal forms of misogyny were muted, in Augustine's thought at least, if not in day-to-day practice in the early medieval West. It was less credible to claim that women had more sexuality than men, or that they sapped men's reason by provoking them to sensuality. Men were as passive to deep-seated sexual frailty, in Augustine's opinion, as were women. Both bore in their unruly bodies the same fatal symptom of the Fall of Adam and Eve. The fact of the swamping of the conscious mind in orgasm for both parties eclipsed the ancient Roman dread of "effeminacy," of a weakening of the public person through passionate dependence on inferiors of either sex.

The surprisingly tenacious belief that upper-class decorum in bed might contribute to the begetting of "well-conceived" children—healthy, biddable, preferably male—was superseded by a new sense of the sexual act as a moment of inevitable disjunction from the rational, which meant in effect from the social, aspects of the person. The "concupiscence of the flesh," as revealed in the sexual act, was a streak of the human person that defied social definition and could only be touched externally by social restraint. For the layman and laywoman normal restraints on intercourse, which had been largely of an external, social nature, had to include a new sense of a fissure deep within the texture of the act. Ultimately God created and formed the child; the sexual act by which the partners provided the material for His creative act owed nothing whatsoever, even in the most remote manner, to the subtle and penetrating disciplines of the city.

Whether such bleak and novel thoughts cast a chill over

the sexual relations of late Roman couples in the West is an entirely different matter. One suspects that they did not. This in itself is silent testimony to the strength of the ancient ways of life, in the face of Christian clerical leadership. Christian couples continued to believe their doctors: in any case, only a hot and pleasurable act of love could give them the children that justified the act of sex in the eyes of the celibate clergy. Christians were careful to avoid intercourse on forbidden days, as laid down by the church: mainly on Sundays, in Lent, and on the vigils of great feasts. They feared the genetic effects of such lapses from the new code of public decorum. Yet Augustine's emphasis on the venial sin inherent in married intercourse, though stated by him without a hint of prurience and with far greater moral tolerance than usual among late antique writers (who usually condemned out of hand all acts of sex that were not consciously entered into with the express purpose of begetting children "for the city"), did imply a sense of inappropriateness in the sensuality of married love. In the very different society of the high middle ages clergymen could believe that married love might be consciously controlled so as to minimize these inappropriate aspects, by deliberately modifying subjective enjoyment in intercourse, through controlling, for instance, forms of caress and endearment. The Augustinian doctrine had opened a crack in the door of the Christian household, such as no Byzantine had ever dreamed of opening: and through that crack many a cold wind would blow, from the canonists and their readers, the father-confessors of the later Middle Ages.

| Clergy, Laity, and the Catholic Church | Augustine's views imposed an ascetic's rigor and an ascetic's awareness of human frailty on the humble householders in the world. He joined world and desert in the Catholic Church. In this he would be followed, in the silent rise of the Catholic Church in western Europe. The urban Catholic bishops of Gaul, Italy, and Spain, rather than the "men of the desert," became the arbiters of the monastic paradigm as it had been subtly and irreversibly modified by Augustine to embrace even sexuality in the world. In this form, the desert enters the city, and it does so from above. Desert and world no longer operate parallel to each other, as remained the case in Byzantium. Instead we have a new hierarchy, in which a continent clergy, frequently trained, as were Augustine's clergy, in urban monastic communities, came to govern the |

laity, largely by means of disciplining and advising them on the perpetual, shared anomaly of a fallen sexuality.

Apart from this one, clear hierarchy, we see a social structure flattened beneath the gaze of the old bishop of Hippo. Men and women, the wellborn and their inferiors, the "men of the desert" as inescapably, if less luridly, as the married "men in the world," were all held to share in a universal and aboriginal weakness in the form of a sexual nature inherited in its dislocated form from Adam and Eve. No renunciation could raise a person above it; no studiously internalized code could do anything more than contain it. This dislocation was presented as a privileged, because a singularly intimate and apposite, symptom of the human condition. Man as a sexual being had become the lowest common denominator in the great democracy of sinners gathered into the Catholic Church.

Around 1200 a minor writer of confessional manuals declared: "Of all the battles of the Christians, the struggle for chastity is the most great. There, combat is constant and victory is rare. Continence, indeed, is the Great War. For, as Ovid says . . . and as Juvenal reminds us . . . Claudian also . . . As do Saint Jerome and Saint Augustine."[13]

In all later writings of the Latin church, it is notable how the vivid love poetry of ancient Rome and the somber warnings of the Christian writers of the late antique period blur together. They communicate a strange sense that it is sexuality and not, as for Byzantines, haunted still by the mirage of a Paradise Regained in the deep desert, the darker and more faceless pride and violence of the world that has become the privileged concern, the horror, and even the delight, of the western European.

Tombstone, 5th century. Baptism was most commonly administered when a person reached adulthood. Water was poured over him, in this case by a dove representing the Holy Spirit. As usual, the baptized person is shown smaller than the other figures. (Aquileia, Christian Museum of Monastero.)

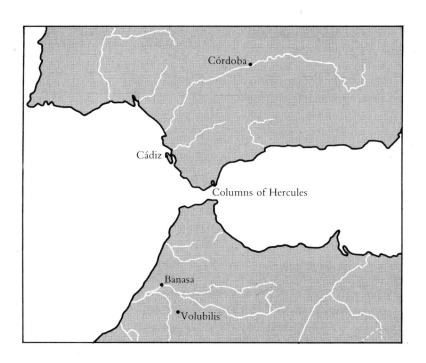

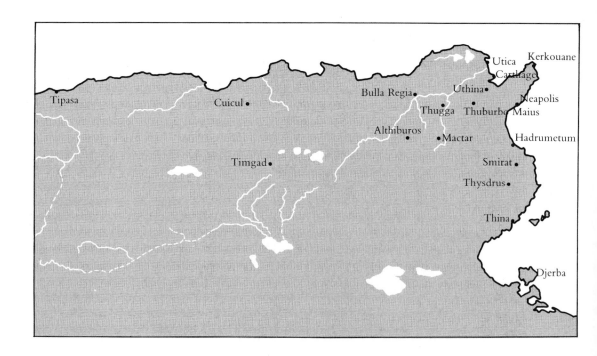

# 3

# Private Life and Domestic Architecture in Roman Africa

Yvon Thébert

Fresco in a Roman *domus*. (Rome, National Museum.)

# The Roman Home

## A Foreword by Paul Veyne

ROMAN houses, except for the homes of a few privileged individuals, had no running water. Aqueducts supplied water for public fountains and baths.

Except for an equally small number of privileged individuals, no one, citizen or foreigner, was allowed to travel about any city on horseback or in a carriage; to do so would have been an affront to the city's dignity. The ruts visible today in the streets of Pompeii were traced by chariots carrying building materials and merchandise, as well as by the occasional ritual chariot used in religious processions.

There was little glass. Windows were closed by shutters, often articulated, or by latticework in stone or terra-cotta. People either went cold or shut themselves up in darkness or stayed within the brief circles of intense light cast by innumerable oil lamps.

Chimneys or fireplaces did not exist in Rome. The warmth of a hearth on which a great fire roared, its smoke funneled through a hole in the roof, was paradoxically praised as one of the great amenities of rude rural winters amid snow-covered fields. In parts of the Empire efficient heating systems were developed for country houses (as at Pergamum in Turkey, according to a detailed account by Galen); but in the cities of Italy winters were as they are today. Then as now people wore overcoats indoors and went to bed fully clothed. (Erotic poets complained about lovers so cruel that they refused to take off their coats in bed.) But inside city homes braziers burned. Incapable of heating whole rooms, they at least offered comforting warmth to anyone who drew near.

Latrines were communal. According to a vulgar anecdote about the poet Lucan, he found his heroes in the common latrines of the emperor's palace. Those used by men were larger and grander than the ones used by women (as in the temple of Aesculapius at Pergamum or the magnificent villa recently discovered at Opluntis—Torre Annunziata as it is now known—near Naples).

Roman homes contained little furniture. Our poetic array of standard furnishings, those works of architecture in the small that we call armoires, commodes, and cupboards, "ancient sideboards with plenty of stories to tell," were rarely found. There were a few beds for sleeping and eating; small, round tables on three-legged stands; a few wardrobes and closets—that was all. Some of this furniture was made of wood (a few meager relics survive in Herculanum and England), some of stone, marble, and bronze. And there were candelabra. Roman furniture resembles our lawn furniture more than the furniture inside our homes.

The private architecture of the well-to-do—the *domus,* more a noble town house than a "home"—was one of the finest creations of Greek and Roman art. A dwelling was above all an empty space; this could be sensed as soon as you reached the heart of a building, and in some cases as soon as you crossed the threshold. You passed through a series not of enclosed rooms but of open spaces: a covered courtyard, an open courtyard with a portico, and a garden with fountains. There was more empty space than filled space. Open space yielded perspective views. The Samnite House at Herculanum reveals its internal structure at first glance; we breathe freely inside its empty volume. Around this void are scattered rooms whose small size is surprising. People withdrew into these cells to sleep or to read, but they lived in the central spaces, with dining rooms open along their entire length, like boxes from which one of the four walls has been removed.

Whether a dwelling belonged to a wealthy man or a not-so-wealthy man, its floors, walls, and ceilings were covered with mosaics in vivid colors, with stucco, and with paintings of decorative and mythological subjects. Fantastic trompe l'oeil architecture created imaginary spaces in the walls. To us these rooms resemble not splendid princely apartments but the riotous colors of a puppet theater. Imagination is in charge here, not pomp. Some of it seems in atrociously bad taste (fountains of mosaics encrusted with shells), some, for all its boldness, is opulently harmonious. When we consider what Roman society was like, with its clientele system and ponderous civism, nothing seems more unlikely than these domestic feasts of imagination and color. There is no point looking for allegorical meaning; people savored the feast without worrying about its ingredients. Besides all this, there were interior sculptures, half-life-sized. Our museums are full of them.

Unused space was another luxury. The essence of this architecture lies in the wedding of vast, open spaces with small, private rooms without the use of narrow corridors. The central space created these side chambers. At Paestum a modest gentleman who owned at most two or three slaves probably occupied a "small" home of about 1,000 square feet, with a kitchen and three small rooms. But these rooms are cut out of the sides of a wide patio, an empty space that takes up most of the house. The visitor who knocked at the door of this house (with his foot, as was the Roman custom) entered directly into this vast, open space, which informed him at once that the occupant was not a plebeian. Toward the end of late antiquity, in the third or fourth century A.D., the magnificent villa at Montmaurin in southwestern Gaul (whose remains deserve more visitors than they receive today) was composed of a series of empty spaces around which was arrayed a pleasant labyrinth of small rooms and staircases where the mind can wander without ever feeling lost. Eventually, in the depths of the building, one comes to the sanctum sanctorum, a minuscule room in which the master of the premises sat enthroned.

Whether at Ephesus in Turkey or Karanis in Egypt, modern visitors are invariably surprised by the ubiquitous presence of art and images. There is yet another shock: reliefs and statues were always painted; the ideal of ancient sculpture was the painted plaster statue of France's village churches. Ancient cities were never white. In Pompeii the columns of one temple were painted yellow and white, the capitals red, white, and blue. The Parthenon was painted to cover the marble sheen, and what we now call the Pont du Gard was painted red.

# ✍ Some Theoretical Considerations

WHAT can we learn about private life from the study of domestic architecture? In attempting to answer this question, I shall restrict myself to a well-defined class of dwellings in Roman Africa: the urban homes of the ruling class. Given the current state of our knowledge and my desire to avoid repeating generalities, these limits are necessary. Roman Africa is a fruitful area for study, since it was one of the most important provinces of the Empire. By concentrating on a precise geographical area I hope to elucidate general principles valid for the Empire as a whole, as well as regional peculiarities, of lesser importance perhaps but useful for gaining a better idea of everyday life.

My aim is not just to understand private life by studying the place in which much of it took place. Architectural investigation offers a method of inquiry, not a theory of private life. Yet we cannot dispense with such a theory if we wish to understand what the ruins have to tell us. Domestic architecture was not static; it evolved over time. The architecture and decoration of private dwellings in the classical Greek city were quite modest. Majesty and luxury were qualities the Greeks considered appropriate only to the public sector, the city, which involved both individual and community, private and public. Here the individual owed everything, including his status as a Roman subject entitled to lead a private life, to membership in the political community. In the Hellenistic era the classical city emerged from a crisis changed in ways that can easily be interpreted as the result of a remarkable extension of the private sphere at the expense of the public. Along with other changes, homes became increasingly luxurious, and people began to amass private collections of art, a development that paralleled the transformation of the work of art into a commodity.

How are we to interpret these changes? Should we opt for an evolutionary view, according to which what we are witnessing is the emergence of private life as such? To adopt such a view would be to argue that the Hellenistic era marked a key moment in a lengthy historical process: the slow development of the private vis-à-vis the public sphere. The ebb and flow of this process could be traced over many centuries. The problem is not quantitative but qualitative, the question being not to measure the relative importance of public versus private but to describe how the spheres were related, how each defined the other. It is not true that the private sphere had to struggle for its very existence against public constraints, but it is true that society determines what private life will be like. Private life is a product of social relations and a defining feature of every social formation. Hence private life is subject, from time to time, to radical redefinition; to attempt to trace its history as a matter of continuous evolution, independent of sharp discontinuities in other areas of social life, would be misleading. It is particularly risky to take our current conception of private life as a starting point and to trace its genealogy by interpreting the past in the light of what we now believe. If we adopted such an approach, we would very likely find that "private life" did not begin until quite recently. But this "finding" would be anachronistic, the result of misapplying modern bourgeois notions to the past.

Nor is a strictly psychological approach adequate. By "psychological approach" I mean one that begins with the assumption that every individual has an "identity" that can be characterized in terms of his "strategies" toward the outside world. In this way of looking at things, the public/private dichotomy is replaced by two other dichotomies: individual/society and internal/external. The result is that the social determinants of individual psychology are not taken into consideration. My own view has much in common with the approach taken by sociologists such as Erving Goffman, who deny that internal psychological states are the decisive determinants, and who emphasize the interaction between public and private, which can be elucidated through the study of "practices."

These theoretical considerations have had an important impact on my work. I hold that the organization of domestic space is not determined by autonomous private needs but is, rather, a social product. This same view is present in the only comprehensive meditation on architecture that antiquity has left us, that of Vitruvius. Vitruvius asserts that there is a connection between the floor plan of a house and the social status of its owner. Even more significant, he states that the house came into being not in response to individual needs but as a consequence of social organization. When men finally learned to tame fire and gathered together around its warmth, they collectively invented both language and the art of building shelters.

A further consequence of the foregoing theoretical remarks is that domestic space is intrinsically unified. The Roman household was the scene of extremely diverse activity (diverse in appearance at any rate), some of which strikes us as eminently public in nature rather than private. The master of the house, for example, received large numbers of clients every day. Vitruvius himself uses the expression "public places" in referring to those parts of the dwelling open to outsiders; it will be convenient, when it comes time to discuss the various parts that went to make up a house, to use "public" and "private" in describing the various rooms. Different parts of any house are of course always "visible" to the public to a greater or lesser degree, but in the Roman house this difference of degree comes close to being a difference of kind. Yet it would be a mistake to suppose that a Roman house was an incoherent juxtaposition of two distinct areas, one essentially private, the other essentially public. That a place was made in the home for what came from "outside" was neither contradictory nor irrational. Indeed, architecture gives us a way of grasping the rather distended definition of private life current among the Roman ruling class. This distension explains why certain obviously social activities naturally took place inside private dwellings. The Romans behaved as they did because this was their way, not because they had no alternative or because private citizens usurped power that rightfully belonged to the public authorities.

The homes of African notables, like those of notables elsewhere in the Empire, sheltered several levels, several modalities, of private life. They were, as homes usually are, places to which the individual could withdraw, homes for the "family" in the narrow, modern sense of the term: the master of the house, his wife (who, in marrying, *convenit in manum*, that

*Modalities of Private Life*

is, came under the paternal power of her husband), and their children. The basic family structure showed a remarkable capacity to expand; even though paternal authority was considerably weakened by changing ways of life, the paterfamilias remained theoretically in charge of the many disparate elements that made up the household. Besides the master's wife, and possibly other relatives, there were servants and slaves, described as the *familia,* among whom one carefully distinguished the *vernaculi,* those born in the house. The vocabulary reveals how the family subsumed social relations that would have been regarded as extrafamilial in other periods. The same phenomenon is evident in relations between patrons and clients, which were closely modeled on relations between a father and his children, as well as in religious attitudes. Pagan priests were in fact compared with parents and disciples with children (Apuleius, *Metamorphoses,* XI, 21). The Christian sect, also modeled on the family, simply carried on a long tradition. In all of this we see the central role of the private sphere in Roman society from the final centuries of the Republic onward. Political life was concentrated in the home of Caesar or Pompey as much as, or more than, in the Senate. The wealth of activities in the home is explicable only in terms of the nature of the society. We see here a reflection of the new relations between public and private typical of the Roman world (where Senators were, after all, *patres*). These relations, which reflected the evolution of the Mediterranean world in general, became established in the late Republic and endured, in one form or another, to the end of the Empire.

In describing how the examination of domestic architecture can help explain the private life of African elites, and of imperial elites generally, I shall consider not only rich urban remains but also African literature, less abundant than Italian literature but also less exploited, at least from this point of view. I shall assume from the outset that African literary and African archaeological sources complement each other. This requires us to begin with the archaeological remains, the vestiges of the *domus,* that is, with the scattered and incomplete material record. In order to distinguish what is of general significance from what is unique, classification and comparison are essential. I shall look first at the concrete archaeological data before moving on to literary texts and comparisons with other provinces or even other periods. This approach has the advantage of confronting the facts directly, whereas the literary sources interpret private life as much as they describe it. I

shall turn for corroboration to the work of numerous researchers whose experience in the field has contributed to a revision
of earlier views of ancient society. Because these views were
based too exclusively on literary sources and idealizations,
every object was transformed into a work of art and treated
as if laden with symbolic significance. This "demythification"
of the past, though salutary, is not without risks. It sometimes
engenders hypercritical attitudes and can make scholars overly
cautious in interpreting the quality and significance of elite
dwellings. In studying domestic spaces I shall try to come to
grips with their true nature. To do this I must say something
about how owners shaped the designs of their homes. In this
regard ruins can be quite instructive.

Fig. 1. Kerkouane, house with columns.

# The Domestic Architecture of the Ruling Class

THE nature of the ancient Mediterranean world directly influenced the nature of the architecture favored by its elites. For centuries a cultural community had existed there, sustained by a massive flow of men, ideas, and merchandise. Greece and its colonies had long been the heart of this community, whose cohesion was strengthened considerably by changes that occurred in the Hellenistic period. Although conflict was continuous, the prevailing image is not that of a world divided into hostile blocs but that of a whole consisting of many individual parts, each shaped by the character of its relations with the overall community. This underlying unity is most clearly visible when we look at social elites, whose political choices it influenced directly and whose culture openly embraced a common civilization bearing the characteristic imprint of Greece.

The architecture of the African ruling classes illustrates this state of affairs. A major innovation in the history of Mediterranean dwellings was the introduction of a peristyle, or central courtyard surrounded by a row of columns, around which the various parts of the house were disposed. This Greek invention was soon copied throughout the Punic world, as is proved by the house with colonnade at Kerkouane, a city on Cape Good that was destroyed and abandoned around the third century B.C. (see fig. 1). African elites were immediately drawn to a style of building that enhanced their prestige by bringing into their private houses architectural composition on a scale previously reserved for public monuments.

The traditional Italic house with atrium, or entry hall with open central portion just off the vestibule, was unknown in Africa. This assertion, once controversial, has been confirmed by recent research. Quantitative data on the relative proportions of covered and open space show that the vast majority of African homes with colonnaded courtyards and vast, unroofed central spaces, should be classed as peristyle constructions. The ratio of covered to uncovered space depends not on the architectural character of the structure but simply on the space available. The table compiled by R. Etienne, based on his study of the wealthy northeastern district of Volubilis, reveals that the peristyles with the lowest proportion of uncovered area have the smallest total area; the converse is also true.[1] Size was the determining factor. Hence these colonnaded spaces can all be described as peristyles; there is no need to interpret even the smaller domestic courts as atria.

Purely architectural criteria would in any case be insufficient to prove that central courtyards were atria; the latter term suggests a very specific function. The location of the colonnaded courtyards in African dwellings and the relation established between the court and other rooms show that their role was not the same as that of the atrium. It is safe to conclude that the atrium did not exist in Africa, except perhaps for isolated instances without historical significance (because remote from the Italic origins of the form). This conclusion is bolstered by the evidence of African texts in which the word "atrium" appears only once, in the description of an eccentric structure (Apuleius, *Metamorphoses*, II, 4), as well as by the evidence of ruins.

The absence of atria in Africa proves that African domestic architecture was not a mere by-product of Italic architecture but stood in its own unique relation to the dominant culture of the Mediterranean world. Africans managed without atrium-equipped houses and did not await the Roman conquest to discover the peristyle. Africa's integration into the Roman world intensified a preexisting cultural relationship; it did not create the relationship.

## A Theoretical Architecture

African domestic architecture, like that of other Roman provinces, was the product of theoretical reflection. As such, it was distinguished from vernacular architecture—architecture without architects, if you will—which often creates quite different types of buildings in response to the same social demand. Vernacular architecture usually has no real program. The person commissioning the project states his desires in some vague way, generally referring to concrete examples close at hand. The result is a characteristic "regional" architecture, with builders improvising on the possibilities inherent in the locale: climate, availability of building materials, and so forth.

In the Roman era, however, architecture freed itself from local limitations and turned its attention toward social, aesthetic, and individualistic considerations. This resulted in a highly elaborate architectural theory, to which both architect and client referred in making proposals and plans. A long tradition of meditation upon the city and its component parts had great influence on the considerable investment devoted to urban improvement. Not only were existing cities frequently and extensively renovated, but new cities were constantly being founded. New cities were often planned in detail, down to specifying typical house plans, or at least indicating how much space was to be allocated for each individual dwelling.

Theories of the city directly influenced housing by dictating sites, dimensions, and orientations. This does not mean, however, that domestic architecture was subsidiary to urban planning in the large. Urban plans were not abstract designs; they went beyond just allowing for topography and the necessities of public life. From Hippocrates to Aristotle and Vitruvius, the correct orientation of buildings was considered important to the salubrity of a city and the health of its inhabitants; it had to be considered from the moment a city was founded and its overall plan laid down. The needs of individuals assumed an increasing importance in the minds of those concerned with urban design. Aristotle was still mainly interested in communal buildings. Vitruvius pondered all the elements that go to make up a city and dwelt at length on the problems of domestic architecture.

In addition to reflections on the city as a whole, there were theories appropriate to each type of monument. In the work of Vitruvius buildings are described for the general principles they embody. His description of a basilica he built in Fano follows, and illustrates, a general treatise on buildings of this type. Theory preceded building. Builders and clients adhered to a centuries-old tradition.

When it came to building a new dwelling or modifying an old one, the ancients were on firm ground. General principles governed the method of construction and orientation of buildings; rooms were classified by type, and for each type there were certain desirable proportions; aesthetic principles guided both the details of decoration and the construction of

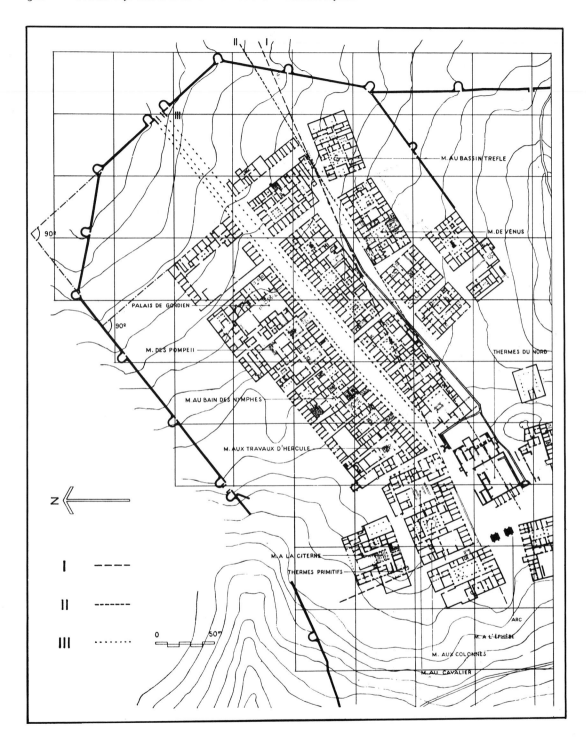

the colonnade. The remarkable unity of Mediterranean domestic architecture is a consequence of the social homogeneity and political cooperation of the region's elites. Everywhere the ruling classes built in order to live in the Roman manner, thereby symbolizing their participation in the government of the Empire and bolstering their prestige in the eyes of local clients.

The importance of architectural theory gave a decided ideological cast to domestic architecture. In the Late Republic the luxurious dwellings of powerful men were severely criticized by the senatorial majority, which clothed its political anxieties in the trappings of moral argument. Imagine the emotions stirred in Rome, in this conservative milieu, when Crassus and Scaurus first used marble columns in their homes! The size and luxury of private dwellings increased as political life became more personal and charismatic leaders emerged to rival the traditional *auctoritas* of the Senate. The domestic scene was transformed radically, and for centuries, by the new emphasis on luxury. The change affected the entire elite. While the homes of the most powerful men continued to be exceptionally large, even the most mediocre imperial notable required a house that reflected his rank and facilitated the transaction of business.

The theory of the city and its components was highly developed. Domestic architecture was urban architecture. In Africa, and most likely in Rome's other provinces as well, the elite never fled the city for the countryside. Although members of the elite did construct sumptuous *villae* on their country estates, they never deserted the cities in which their political fortunes, and hence their fate as individuals, were played out— at least not until some time after the end of antiquity, however broadly that term is construed. In deliberately neglecting the rural residences of the African elite, I am departing from the traditional approach to the subject but respecting the priorities of what I call the group's "spatial strategy." I am also allowing for the limits of the sources, for very few African villae have been excavated, and still fewer have been the subject of published works.

The nature of private space cannot possibly be described without taking account of the urban environment in which that space was situated. Consider a building's surroundings. Vitruvius himself insists that venerable architectural formulas must be modified in order to adapt a building to its surroundings; he suggests, for instance, modifying the usual propor-

Fig. 2. Volubilis, northeastern quarter (map by Hallier, Golvin, and Lenne, from R. Rebuffat, "Le développement urbain de Volubilis," *BAC,* 1965–1966).

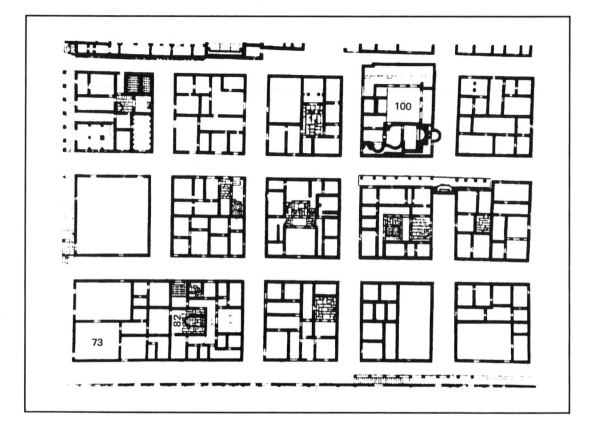

Fig. 3. Portion of map of Timgad colony. (E. Boeswill-wald, A. Ballu, and R. Cagnat, *Timgad, une cité africaine sous l'Empire romain* [Paris, 1905], p. 337, fig. 166.) The original layout included 132 square *insulae* measuring about 70 feet on a side. Walls that divided these blocks into lots can often still be made out. Insulae 73 and 82 were joined by appropriating what had been a public street. Insula 100 was enlarged by extension into the street.

tions of a room to improve its lighting. More broadly, the way a building functioned depended to a large extent on how the surrounding area of the city was laid out and equipped. Water-distribution systems and sewers had a considerable impact on daily life. Such things did not exist everywhere, and where they did exist, they rarely dated from the founding of the city. These vast public works greatly affected private comfort. It is difficult to evaluate the quality of urban housing properly without allowing for the availability of such public facilities as baths and latrines, which cities made available to residents. In this sense, public and private were not antagonistic but complementary. Housing cannot be isolated from its context.

How did individual houses relate to the city as a whole? It often seems that the city's essential structure was determined by its large public monuments, with private buildings filling the interstices. But relations between public and private construction were not always so one-sided. In Timgad and Cuicul, for example, the area inside the walls was razed, probably under the Severi, and new residential districts were erected. And it seems likely that dwellings in the northeastern corner of Volubilis (fig. 2) were not erected inside the area defined by existing city walls, but that the walls were erected at the behest of real estate promoters who hoped to make the district suitable for luxurious homes and thereby raise the value of their property.[2] In this case a major construction project, normally undertaken to bolster a city's prestige and defenses, was coopted by private interests, which subverted its fundamentally public significance. This is a striking illustration of the changes that occurred between classical and imperial times. By the time of the Empire the private sphere had expanded to such a degree that it simply subsumed, as though by right, what previously had been a matter for communal decision.

Little is known about the way in which houses related to the streets on which they stood. It has not been possible to reconstruct the full elevation view of any house facade. We do not know how many windows there were, what size they may have been, or where they were located; in most cases we do not even know how they closed. Nor do we know how windows were used. Were they kept open or closed? Did people stand at the window or on a balcony? Were facades decorated on feast days? Answers would shed interesting light on the relation between domestic space and street life, but the texts are silent.

Archaeology, however, does tell us something about the relation between public and private space. Street and interior communicated by means of porticoes rather than through a simple doorway abruptly penetrating a facade. As an architectural device, the portico is ambiguous: a transitional volume, it can be either an essentially public space or a decisively private one. The brief portico before the principal entry to the House of Sertius in Timgad (fig. 24), for example, is part of the house, an embellishment of its entryway. On the other hand, when great colonnades, paralleling and broadening the street, were built in conjunction with some ambitious plan of urban redevelopment, their role was essentially public, as can be seen from their architectural coherence and function, namely, to facilitate pedestrian traffic. Colonnades established a unified idea of the city, which relegated compartmentalized private space to a position of secondary importance.

A closer look at the vast porticoes that bordered city

streets reveals their architectural ambivalence. Their homogeneity is never perfect, even along a main artery such as the *decumanus maximus* in Volubilis, where the rhythm of intercolumniation changes in front of the House of Hercules' Labors (fig. 30). Great arches rest on nine pillars in a composition clearly related to the house. To the right of the walls that delimit where the house begins, even larger pillars are turned in such a way as to support arches perpendicular to the axis of the street. Aesthetically this space is attached to the house, to whose boundaries it hews closely. Functionally the cut is secondary. It does not destroy the coherence of the whole or rule out the use of another portico as a complement to that provided by the street. The ambiguity to which this public space was subjected was not without significance, however: in a parallel street, the House of the Train of Venus was able to annex this space, impeding public circulation to a degree (fig. 27: first entry vestibule V. 1 and room 19, which served as a dressing room for the building's baths). Something similar seems to have been done in Cuicul at the House of Europa (fig. 20). The extension, probably during remodeling, of part of one room out to the paving of the great *cardo* interrupted the portico that paralleled that major thoroughfare. What was left of the colonnade does not seem to have been annexed completely. Yet the carving up of the portico, whose public function depended on its continuity, had the effect of making it an annex of the building, integrating it decisively into the facade.

## A Unitary Architecture

What was the meaning of this device? Domestic architecture has specific properties of its own, related to the kinds of needs it must satisfy, but these cannot be properly understood unless we appreciate the close connection between public monuments and private dwellings. Such a connection had a long history (republican villas in Italy were in many ways strikingly similar to official buildings, even down to the terminology used by contemporaries to describe them), and it survived as a vital tradition under the Empire. Mosaics are a good example. The same geometric motifs were used in constructions of all sorts. Certain complex patterns enable us to appreciate the impact of official art on domestic decoration. In the home of Asinius Rufinus at Acholla, for example, G. Picard has shown how the contemporary mystique of the emperor (Commodus' claim to be the Roman Hercules) influenced the

choice of themes.³ The mosaic of the *triclinium* illustrates the labors of Hercules, who is represented as a type created under the reign of Commodus, known to us from coins of the period. No doubt the emperor had dedicated a statue to his favorite divinity, and this statue inspired the mosaicist of Acholla.

The unity of public and private was no less important in architecture, all aspects of which evolved in similar ways. In the Late Empire houses and monuments were increasingly likely to incorporate multiple apses or to replace the traditional architrave with arches supported by columns. Architecture and decoration were so coherent that, in the absence of inscriptions, it can be difficult to identify remains. Indeed, in some public buildings—for example, official residences, buildings designed to house official guests of a city, and buildings used by *collegia,* or confraternities, as centers of sociability— the needs that had to be met were quite similar to those that had to be met in a private home. The profound unity of architecture in this period is evident in the many debates that have raged over whether certain buildings were public or private. Occasionally these controversies have yielded satisfactory interpretations, as in the case of the House of the Asclepiae at Althiburos (fig. 17). This ambitious building was

Fig. 4. Timgad: street bordered by colonnades and broad sidewalks in one of the new neighborhoods built on the western outskirts of the town. This was the road to Lambesi, which veered northward, disrupting the original orthogonal city plan. The arch, which dates from the Severian era, once marked the entrance into Trajan's colony, but the city grew in such a way that it later occupied the center of town. The milestones marking the beginning of the highway are under the arches.

well suited to communal use, and the presence of a late mosaic depicting a sort of basket bearing the inscription "Asclepia" suggested, or so it was thought, that the building had at some point changed its function, perhaps serving to house the cult of Aesculapius. The correct interpretation of the object bearing the inscription (which is in fact an agonistic crown awarded to the winner of games of which Asclepius was the patron) has made this hypothesis superfluous.[4] This house never ceased to be used by private owners, one of whom chose to commemorate a victory in one of the many athletic competitions held throughout the Mediterranean region.

The private basilica of the House of the Hunt at Bulla Regia enables us to see how domestic architecture was affected by the problems encountered and solutions worked out in other types of construction. (The excavation of the insula of the House of the Hunt, in Bulla Regia, to which I refer several times, was carried out by R. Hanoune, A. Olivier, and Y. Thébert.) The building, which dates from the first half of the fourth century, was built according to a plan that combines an apse, a transept (whose crossing was emphasized by the

Fig. 5. Thugga: house with peristyle at the foot of the Capitol (House with Two Fountains).

use of molded columns), and a long nave flanked by dependencies occupying the place that, in a civil or religious basilica, would have constituted the lateral naves (figs. 7, 8, 9). These rooms, laid out in a series and for the most part communicating with the central nave, made it possible for traffic to move about the building in much the same way as in buildings with three naves. The whole, designed at one time, is perfectly coherent and easily reconstructable, in spite of numerous late reworkings.

Because several parts of this building call to mind identical solutions adopted in the earliest Christian churches, we are confronted with one of the most difficult problems in the history of ancient architecture: the origins of the early Christian basilica, which was based on the combination of a rectangular hall divided into naves (the higher central nave receiving its light from above the roofs of its lateral annexes), an apse, and various secondary components, one of the most typical being a transept.[5] Though the literature on this subject is abundant, much of it is based on an erroneous way of posing the problem. Some scholars have been misled by a desire to assert the originality of Christian architecture. Others, rejecting this approach, have focused their attention on finding antecedents for later styles and discovering influences of earlier ones. The truth lies elsewhere.

Despite protestations of originality, it is obvious that Christian monuments drew largely on solutions worked out by architects of preceding centuries. The use of the apse for the purpose of glorification was one of the most common themes of civil and religious architecture from the early days of the Empire. So was the creation of a vast meeting space by juxtaposing several naves, some more important than others. The manipulation of these architectural elements formed part of a still-living tradition, and important innovations were introduced during the Late Empire. But these innovations were not animated by Christianity. They have to do with a broader evolution in architecture, directly related to changes in social relations. Cult buildings in the Late Empire were constructed according to the same principles that governed the construction of other kinds of buildings. "Christian architecture" can refer only to buildings designed to serve the Christian cult and hence fitted out in a certain way; the term does not designate any original tendency in architecture that created new forms or building plans.

The private basilica at Bulla Regia illustrates this point

Fig. 6. Bulla Regia (map by H. Broise, from A. Beschaouch, R. Hanoune, and Y. Thébert, *Les ruines de Bulla Regia* [Rome, 1977], fig. 3). 12: house no. 3 (see fig. 40); 18–19: insula of the hunt (see fig. 8: the regular shape of this insula contrasts with other lots); 23: House of the Fisherman (whose west wing encroaches on the street). Peristyles have been identified in houses numbered 10, 11(?), 12, 13, 17, 18, 19, 21, 22, 23, 25, 28, 36, and 37. Private baths have been identified in houses 9, 18, 23, 25, 28, and 37(?).

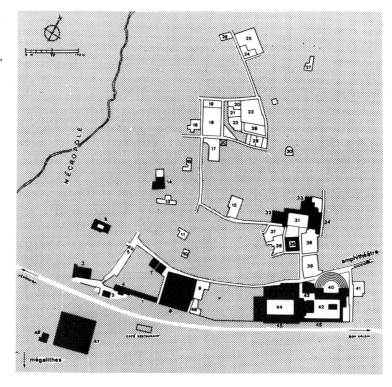

especially well. Part of it is built according to a cruciform plan, which in Christian architecture takes on symbolic meaning. There is no archaeological evidence of any previous transept in a pagan basilica, notwithstanding the text in which Vitruvius describes "chalcidica," that is, transverse annexes used to balance certain architectural compositions. The first known examples of basilicas with transepts are the religious constructions of Constantine in Rome and Constantinople. Accordingly, some scholars have held that basilicas with transepts were a specifically Christian variant on the basilica theme, incorporating the grandiose symbol of a cross.

The debate was misconceived from the start. Around 380, Gregory Nazianzen, describing the Constantinian Church of the Holy Apostles at Constantinople, was the first to point out its resemblance to a cross. Because the cult of the cross was spreading at about the same time, this comparison met with stunning success, as is illustrated in the West by the constructions undertaken by Bishop Ambrose of Milan. But Eusebius, who described the same church fifty years before Gregory, failed to note the parallel. The chronology of the

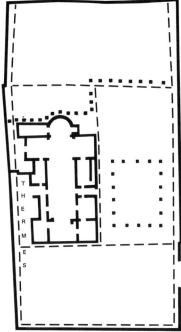

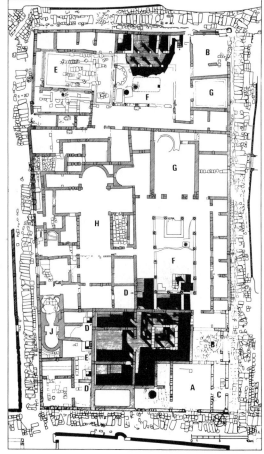

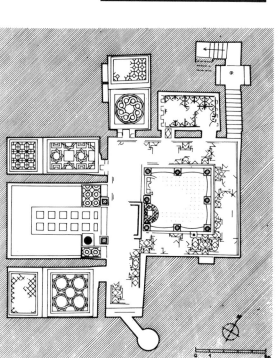

Figs. 7, 8, 9. Bulla Regia, insula of the hunt and southern basement (plans by A. Olivier, from *Ruines de Bulla Regia,* figs. 44, 46). A: courtyard for wagons; B: vestibule; C: stairway leading to upper stories; D: bedroom; E: triclinium; F: peristyle; G: exedra for reception; H: private basilica; I: latrines; J: baths. The drawing in the upper left corner of the page is a hypothetical sketch of the original location of the basilica and the large peristyle. The line of squares shows the boundaries of the lot in the Hellenistic period; the dotted lines show the gap between the House of the Hunt, to the south, and the House of the New Hunt.

Fig. 10. Bulla Regia, insula of the hunt seen from the south-west.

symbol's discovery suffices to refute any attempt to explain the development of the cruciform plan in religious terms. The process was in fact the reverse: a Christian interpretation was applied to an architectural theme that originally had no such significance.

The dating of the basilica at Bulla Regia confirms this argument. Among the Constantinian monuments and other examples of cruciform Christian basilicas from the fifth or possibly sixth century, none exhibits a construction of the type found at Bulla Regia. It is noteworthy that this gap should have been filled in part by a building that can be classed as domestic architecture. This fact points up the need for comparison between the use of the transept in paleo-Christian architecture and its use in aulic monuments and other kinds of architecture. Such a comparison reveals that the transept solved a problem of circulation during ceremonies, whether processions of the faithful around relics or deployment of the clergy around the altar or dignitaries around the sovereign. At Bulla Regia the problem was the same—the parade of the *dominus* before his dependents—and the architectural solution was identical, down to the proportions. The projecting parts of the transept formed two squares, a solution also attested in

Christian architecture, and possibly in the imperial palace at Ravenna.[6]

The most striking feature of these monuments is the way in which space is quartered by the introduction of a transverse axis that cuts across the long nave. This quartering creates a convergence toward a central point, around which the building's volumes are articulated. This spatial structure, which singles out one place as special, as dominant over other spaces to which participants or spectators are confined, is diametrically opposed to the spatial arrangement of, say, a chamber of deliberation, which requires not only a central plan but also spatial unity. The cruciform plan reflects submission to the emperor, bishop, or aristocrat. Onlookers are grouped together in the long naves, where they can do nothing but look straight ahead, into the apse. The transept reinforces this focusing of attention and eases the task of arranging dignitaries in a hierarchical fashion. Comparable needs led to parallel architectural solutions, which drew upon an already elaborate repertoire of techniques and modified them to meet requirements that were not new but had become essential. The construction of Bulla Regia shows that even so characteristic a solution as the basilica with transept was not peculiar to religious bulidings. It is remarkable proof of the unity of architectural production.

---

## A Dynamic Architecture

When we consider the domestic architecture of Roman Africa, we discover centuries of profound change that were not without impact on the setting of private life. Changes in plan, volume, and decoration modified domestic interiors, sometimes requiring extensive renovations. The very outline of the building might be altered, adding enough new space to permit a complete redesign of the internal organization.

A house's location affected its design. Some quarters of the city were densely populated; others, on the outskirts, developed slowly. The contrast was particularly striking in cities developed as colonies. Here, a grid of streets in the city center marked out islands (*insulae,* or blocks) for construction. This arrangement was not suitable for building large houses, so in such cities the larger homes were built in outlying districts, where there were fewer design constraints.

Timgad is a good example (see fig. 3). In this colony, founded by Trajan in A.D. 100, the original territory of the city was divided into squares of about 4,000 square feet. Only

Fig. 11. Bulla Regia, House of the Hunt viewed from the south. Foreground: secondary peristyle and basement. Background: principal peristyle.

the forum and a few large public monuments exceeded this size, covering several insulae. Private housing, which occupied about three-quarters of the land thus divided, had to respect the grid of streets. In some cases insulae were further subdivided into lots assigned to individual owners. This layout, which reflected a relatively homogeneous social composition, proved inimical to the development of great houses, though a few made their pretensions clear by adding modest peristyles.

Some great houses reached proportions ten times the size of the city's central insulae. Their magnificence could flourish only in outlying districts, which soon developed beyond the original walls. Some homes were even built where the wall had stood before it was razed by real estate speculators. J. Lassus has studied this coopting of public space—urban fortifications—by private interests for the benefit of certain wealthy individuals.[7] Throughout the western section of the enclosure, which became a central zone when the city stretched westward, a strip of land 70 feet wide was placed at the disposal of well-to-do residents. The constraints imposed by the original grid were forgotten. Rather than extend existing streets to impose a pattern on the newly liberated space, those in charge of the city let the streets end where the new territory began. Thus, the growth of the city led to social differentiation of its districts. The sumptuous houses of notables (see, for example, figs. 24, 25) were not erected in the original city, hemmed in as it was by a grid of streets that imposed social homogeneity. Instead, the wealthy arrogated to themselves the spaces freed by the destruction of the city's walls, and they made sure that those spaces would not be subject to the communal constraints imposed on the old central district (fig. 4).

It is unusual to be able to trace the evolution of an African city so closely. But Timgad was not unique. The central portion of Banasa in Morocco is laid out according to an orthogonal grid, which probably dates from the Augustan period, when the colony was founded. What ensued was quite similar to what happened in Timgad: most of the great houses were located on the outskirts, outside the original checkerboard.

Development patterns in cities that were not originally laid out according to orthogonal patterns were not fundamentally different. Here, however, the city structure was more flexible, and over the course of time luxurious homes were constructed near the city center. This occurred in Thugga (fig. 5) and in Bulla Regia (fig. 6), where houses large enough for their rooms to be arrayed around a peristyle were built close to the forum. Yet these centrally located dwellings cannot compare in size with the grandest African homes.

It is impossible to say why the homes of the wealthy were located where they were without taking into account each city's history. In bustling cities well-to-do quarters grew up on the outskirts of the center, no matter how it was laid out. Volubilis, which never had a strict orthogonal plan, was quite similar to Timgad in this respect. Over the centuries urban dwellings in the old city remained rather small; peristyles were rare. Here, too, the great houses were built on the outskirts, in particular in the northeastern corner (see fig. 2), which was developed in such a way as to allow each owner at least 12,000 square feet. Rather than renovate the densely populated central city, the bourgeoisie transformed a suburban area into a fashionable quarter.

Fig. 12. Bulla Regia, House of the Hunt, peristyle of basement viewed from the east.

In smaller, less vital cities the situation was quite different, and local elites were forced to find space for themselves within the old city. The well-to-do bought land and built houses

wherever they could and were forced to accept the inconvenience of irregular lots, sometimes too small for their grandiose ambitions.

It is in this context that I shall discuss a curious problem of domestic architecture over which a great deal of ink has flowed: the multistoried basements found in several sumptuous houses at Bulla Regia (figs. 9–12). In itself there is nothing extraordinary about this type of construction. The design was not uncommon in Roman architecture; though rarely used in flat terrain such as is found in Bulla Regia, it was often employed elsewhere. The fact remains that Bulla Regia is the only Roman city known to exhibit so many examples of an architecture in which the occupant increased the amount of space available to him by digging down into the earth.[8] Although the climatic advantages of such construction are obvious, they are not in themselves a sufficient explanation. Many other places with equally hot summers or cold winters have no comparable architecture. The theory that a local school of architects existed, though interesting, only shifts the focus of the problem: Why this school in this place? The only possible answer seems to be that local elites, confronted with a stagnating city, resorted to this solution in order to find more space. Such costly work would not have been undertaken had there been any way to avoid it. Excavations on the city's periphery have shown that growth remained confined inside the old walls, even though the city's dynamic elite sent several of its members to the Senate in Rome. No outlying district of any size developed, and the ruling class, unable to move into growing new districts, was forced to turn to subterranean construction.

This history illustrates some of the general principles that governed the development of African cities. In growing cities the elite, in search of more space, tended to build homes on the outskirts. In less expansive cities districts were less sharply differentiated, and sumptuous homes had to be constructed in relatively static areas. But the static nature of the old urban centers should not be overestimated. Throughout the centuries renovations were of course carried out. The simplest and most common was to combine several smaller properties into a single large one. In Bulla Regia the insula on which the House of the Hunt stands shows traces of an earlier subdivision into four equal rectangular lots (fig. 7). Two of these, oriented east-west, were situated on the extremes of the insula; the other two, oriented north-south, occupied the central portion.

Unlike previously discovered blocks, with irregular outlines traced by streets laid out according to no particular plan, the block on which the House of the Hunt sits was traced by a strict orthogonal design. Excavations have shown that this plan was adopted under a Numidian monarchy in the Hellenistic era and that it extends into the western quarter of the city, though at present it is not possible to say precisely how far (see figs. 6, 10).

Thus, this section of the city underwent renovations in the Hellenistic period. (It was not virgin territory at the time the orthogonal plan was instituted.) The principles adopted were of Greek inspiration, and the strictness of their application is reminiscent of the strict layouts of later Roman colonies, although the historical context is quite different. The original lots, about 5,000 square feet, were just large enough to permit a small peristyle, and the remains of a house that once occupied the southernmost lot show that at least one was actually built. For three centuries the Hellenistic grid of streets traced the space available for housing. It was not until the Severian period, probably around the beginning of the third century, that the southern lot and the central eastern lot were joined. This made it possible to alter the plan of the building. A large peristyle was erected to the north, while a smaller peristyle opened the southern part of the building to the air. The desire to expand was constant over a long period of time and reflected real needs. Around the middle of the fourth century the owner of the property managed to acquire the second central lot, only a small portion of which was ceded to the owner of the lot to the north. This further extension provided the space to build private baths and a basilica. In a century and a half the size of the building tripled, and its plan was completely revised. A veritable domus, nearly 15,000 square feet in size, was created in a district of the city that had long been populated, quite close to the center of town.

Renovation of buildings in dense urban centers was often effected by similar means. In the original center of Volubilis, where the average building covered 5,000 square feet, the House of Orpheus was the only large building; it covered more than 20,000 square feet created by joining four or five separate lots. Room was found for a number of imposing houses in the heart of Cuicul: the House of Europa, which covers nearly 14,000 square feet, preserves traces of the original lots combined to create the plot on which it stands (fig. 20).

Owners who wished to expand their property encroached

on the street, often impeding the flow of traffic. The excavation of the House of the Hunt insula has revealed in detail how the property grew. Because the final state maintained the regularity of the original site, it had been assumed that the expansion must have been carried out at one time or at least that the relocation of each wall had been accomplished in a single operation. On the contrary, a number of successive operations were involved. Apparently the owners took advantage of a repaving of the street (after its level was raised to permit the installation of a drainage system) to relocate the walls of the building. The recesses that had enlivened the facade were gradually absorbed into the building, until the original plan was finally reconstituted on a larger scale. The extension of the building toward the street was not unplanned, and the whole operation seems to have been carried out in concert with the local authorities. One indication of this is the abortive attempt by the owner of the House of the Hunt to set up a pool as part of his private baths on the land where the street to the west was located. This occurred fairly late, well into the fourth century at the earliest. But the pool was carefully filled in, probably after strenuous protests by the authorities. Down to the fourth century at least, it seems that the local authorities were powerful enough to control such alterations to the city plan, especially in major, planned improvements. At Utica, for example, the facades of several insulae were moved toward the street without altering their alignment.

Yet there can be no doubt that renovations could go only so far in altering petrified central city districts. Study of the expansion of the insula on which the House of the Hunt stands shows that, five centuries after the Hellenistic grid was first laid down, the size of the lot had increased by only 2,000 square feet, about 10 percent of the original area. A more promising alternative was to annex the entire street. This not only made for increased public space but also allowed properties previously separated by the roadway to be connected. Such an expedient wreaked havoc with city plans. In Bulla Regia the expansion of the House of the Fisherman transformed a small street into a dead end; pedestrians ran into a wall behind which stood the expanded building. In the central portion of the colonial city Timgad (see fig. 3) such joining of lots by annexing the streets between them was the only way to augment by any considerable amount the size of a piece of property.

From the beginning Roman law was concerned with the

legal aspects of the relation between public and private space, essentially because of the need to give due consideration to the respective rights of neighbors owning adjoining properties. The role of the state increased after the establishment of the Empire, as is shown by the senatus-consult of 45 or 46 dealing with real estate speculation in Rome. A new notion of the public interest, as opposed to the interests of private property owners, was gradually developed. By the Late Empire, when this process was complete, legislation reflecting a complex new relationship between individual rights and central government prerogatives had been enacted.[9] Certain measures advance the claim that the government's rights are preeminent. By the late fourth century there was an explicit procedure for expropriation of property needed for public use.

The situation was not as simple as this piece of legislation suggests. Many other measures show the authorities on the defensive, as individuals improperly moved into or adjacent to public buildings, which were disfigured by the addition of board walls or improvised masonry. Ulpian, a jurist of the Severian era, held that the judgment whether to fine or expel private individuals who encroached on public property should be made by the provincial governor, who was charged with handing down a decision consonant with the interests of the city in question. A document dating from 409 illustrates the defensive battle being waged by the central government on its own turf: "Any site in the Palace of Our City [Constantinople] which has been occupied improperly by private buildings must be restored forthwith by demolition of said buildings. The aforesaid Palace shall not be restricted by private walls, for the government is entitled to open spaces isolated from all other property" (Codex theodosianus, XV, 1, 47). The general trend is clear, though it is not uniform: private property was not overwhelmed by governmental authority. The texts of the laws, about whose efficacy and scope of application little is known, provide no clue to the attitudes of the local authorities, alluded to in certain passages of the imperial laws (Codex theodosianus, XV, 1, 33, 37, 41). The terms of the relation between private property and the public domain were set by each individual city, based on local understandings and the local power structure, which varied considerably from place to place and time to time. Conflicts are rarely documented. One inscription from Pompeii, dating from the time of Vespasian, mentions a tribune who ordered restitution of public lands usurped by private individuals. In general, our only knowledge of such incidents comes from archaeology. The history of the House of the Hunt at Bulla Regia, with its successful but limited encroachments on public property and its occasional attempts, thwarted by the authorities, to exceed these limits, suggests how complex such affairs could be.

*Domestic Interiors*

Did the well-to-do live, like the French aristocracy, in buildings whose interiors changed very little over long periods of time? To be sure there was continuity. Many walls were constructed and left unaltered for centuries, and the essential lines of a house remained fixed in many cases for very long periods. This applies particularly to houses designed in one period and erected on large plots. Improvements, such as mosaic decorations, might be left untouched for many years. Older houses often contain mosaic floors laid at many different times. Even precious items of furniture seem to have been transmitted from generation to generation either by inheritance or through a developing trade in works of art. This has been revealed through study of Moroccan bronze furnishings, for example.[10] Archaeologists note that fragments of luxury objects, many quite old, have been found in late strata of excavation sites, which correspond to the period when cities were abandoned. In one room of the House of the Train of Venus at Volubilis (fig. 27:11) archaeologists have found various fragments, probably from the same bed, among which are two particularly interesting bronze ornaments. One, a splendid mule's head, dates from the first century; the other, a head of Silenus, is of mediocre quality and dates from a later period. Here is a concrete example of the extended use of a precious object. The bed was evidently repaired by a local bronzemaker, whose style differed radically from that of his predecessors.

This continuity should not be allowed to mask an important reality. Domestic interiors were frequently remodeled, in ways that only careful excavation can uncover. Who could guess at first glance that the great peristyle of the House of the Hunt at Bulla Regia, with a large exedra in the central part of the northern colonnade (fig. 8), underwent extensive alterations? Originally, no room extended to the east. The court (enclosed by 6 x 5 columns rather than 6 x 4 as it is now) and the porticoes occupied the entire width of the newly annexed lot. The space needed for the rooms of the east wing was not obtained until later, thanks to a reduction in the size

Fig. 13. Bulla Regia, House of the Hunt, peristyle of basement viewed from northeast.

of the court of the peristyle coupled with a relocation of the east facade, which was extended into what had been the street.

In fact, not a single house escaped some changes in detail—a change in the shape of a room, say, or a modification affecting the flow of traffic. Some renovations were so extensive that they changed the character of the house entirely. In the second half of the fourth century the owner of the House of the Hunt at Bulla Regia had a basement built, of relatively small size, nevertheless requiring the temporary destruction of much of the northern wing (figs. 8, 9). At the same time he had most of the mosaics on the ground floor replaced. Thus, not just the architectural organization but even the decor of the house was changed drastically.

Given the frequency and scope of renovations to houses, it is reasonable to ask how the work was planned and carried out. This can be answered by studying the remains of buildings. The basement of the House of the Hunt at Bulla Regia was built in the Severian era according to a rather simple plan (fig. 9). It includes a small, square, underground peristyle consisting of eight columns (fig. 13). Rooms were added on two sides only: to the north, where the access stairway was situated, and the main wing, to the west. The composition of the main wing was traditional, simple and classical. A large hall with three bays (a triclinium, or dining room) is flanked by two bedrooms, whose doors, slightly eccentric with respect to the bedrooms' axes, continue the tripartite composition of the dining room. The plan is thus based on principles of hierarchy and symmetry. The construction, however, reveals disturbing irregularities, the most striking being the way in which the peristyle is linked to the west wing. These two essential elements are slightly askew, so that the principle of symmetry, which underlies the design of the main wing, has been flouted in establishing the relation of that wing to the colonnade; there is a gap that considerably weakens the overall effect.

What are we to make of such an irregularity? Does it mean simply that the owner or his workmen cared little about the details of actual construction? Or did they fail to understand the classical architectural design, perhaps, since we are in Africa, because they were provincials? The problem is interesting to ponder in the light of a number of recent studies of the ancient way of life.

The authors of these studies begin with the assumption that not every antique object was a work of art; they try to define more precisely what is meant by "artisanal production." This approach is undoubtedly correct insofar as it rejects an overly aesthetic conception of antiquity, but it can be carried to extremes. To compare, say, a mosaic floor to a modern carpet or wallpaper mural is an effective way of demystifying the mosaic craft, but it glosses over basic differences and causes us to lose sight of the adaptability of the artisans involved. The repetitive nature of ancient architecture and decoration has no obvious interpretation. It may have more to do with identical needs of members of the ruling class than with the mechanical nature of the work. These same authors underestimate the role of the client in shaping the work. Given the repetitive nature of the work, it is argued, the client was concerned at most with the overall outlines of the plan and decor. Whether for lack of interest, incompetence, or lack of opportunity, the property owner, we are told, had no effective influence over the work he financed. Taken together, these arguments, if true, destroy the notion of an "architectural program," which assumes that the owner knows what he wants and monitors the work closely and that the artisans engaged to do the job are not very adaptable and do only what they are told. Accordingly, there is no reason to analyze the irregularities in the basement of the House of the Hunt; we have only to note that they exist and how they affected the quality of life.

Excavation of the House of the Hunt, however, has revealed the true reason for its structural irregularities. The basement was actually created from a previously existing underground chamber, which was entirely redesigned. The present peristyle stands on the site of the original rooms, which opened to the west, along the western portico. The northern and western wings are for the most part new creations. All this explains the reason for the major distortion: the offset of the axis of the triclinium with respect to that of the peristyle. The logic of the renovations is now clear. Taking account of what was already in place, the owner calculated what it would cost to make the desired renovations. Balancing his desires against his costs, he decided on the compromise that offered the best quality–price ratio.

Careful examination of the architecture and decor shows that the owner was concerned to diminish as much as possible the irregularities imposed by the reuse of the previously existing walls. In order to bring the two main axes into the closest possible alignment, the northern bedroom was made smaller than the southern one, which made it possible to shift the triclinium as much as possible toward the north. For the same reason the northern portico is wider than the southern one, which helps to bring the colonnade closer to its ideal position. In front of the central bay of the triclinium, moreover, the geometric mosaic that decorates the porticoes was interrupted to make room for a picturesque scene, today in ruins. The northern border of this painting is slightly oblique, so as to link the pillar of the triclinium to the column of the peristyle as harmoniously as possible. Furthermore, although certain irregularities resulting from the reuse of the old walls (such as the shortening of the southern end of the western portico) were allowed to remain, other defects were deemed intolerable and rectified at the cost of major reconstruction. Thus, the southern wall of the peristyle was entirely reconstructed so as to give it a regular shape. Excavation has uncovered, buried in the earth, the wall of the original basement, whose oblique orientation was unacceptable.

Fig. 14. Thugga, entry porch of the *trifolium* house.

In this case there is no evidence of incompetence, indifference, or provincialism. The owner evidently attempted to carry out a program that consciously incorporated contradictory requirements and strove to achieve the best possible compromise. The final solution is symbolized by the way in which the west wing and the peristyle were ultimately linked. Since it proved impossible to bring the two axes into line, the builders manipulated the spaces so as to link the two volumes along a diagonal running from the northeastern corner of the peristyle to the southeastern corner of the triclinium and passing through two of the corner columns. Although the strict symmetry principle had to be abandoned, the design was nevertheless rigorous and yielded rewarding optical effects. This example makes it clear that no judgment of the quality or significance of domestic architecture can be based on appearances alone. Many inconsistencies can be explained in terms of difficulties of construction or by the need to make the best quality–price ratio.

A similar analysis could be given of the basement of the house next to the House of the New Hunt, which was built a century and a half later (fig. 9). And J.-P. Darmon in *Nymfarum domus* has noted how architect and mosaicist cooperated in the construction of the House of the Nymphs at Neapolis. The architect was careful to shift the axis of the colonnade slightly off center, while the mosaicist introduced subtle distortions into the pavement in order to create the illusion of a rectangular peristyle when the space was in fact trapezoidal. Ruling-class homes were not turned out mechanically and did not suffer from repetitiousness, lack of planning, or inability to adapt construction to its context. Houses were planned, some more elaborately, some less, and their owners played a key role in the design, which reflected their needs and their financial resources.

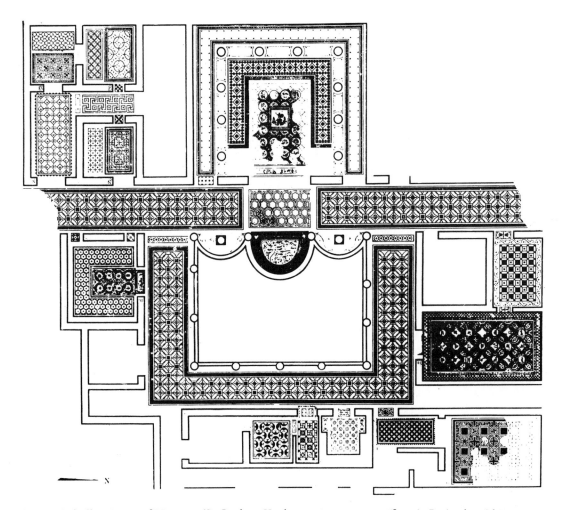

Fig. 15. Acholla, House of Neptune (S. Gozlan, *Karthago,* 16, 1971–1972, fig. 2). Peristyle with *oecus* to the west, triclinium to the south, and bedrooms abutting antechambers or corridors in the southwestern corner.

# ᚽ "Private" and "Public" Spaces: The Components of the Domus

ALL the interior spaces of the domus belonged to the sphere of private life. Individuals could dwell in a house in many different ways, however, ranging from isolation to the receiving of large numbers of visitors with whom the owner was not on intimate terms. Living space varied, with some parts closed to the outside world, others not. It is therefore convenient, if not strictly accurate, to use the terms "public" and "private" in characterizing different parts of the domus.

How did the house communicate with the street? Many larger houses had several entryways, but there was always a main entrance, symbolically and concretely the point of transition from outside to inside. It was here that Trimalchio posted the sign stating, "any slave who leaves without orders of the master will receive one hundred lashes." The sources attach many meanings to the main entrance. A plaintiff attacking the behavior of one family charged that songs were shouted beneath the windows of their house and the door was often kicked open; the fact that the home was not respected proved it was nothing but a hovel (Apuleius, *Apol.*, LXXV). In the many thefts recounted in *Metamorphoses,* the entrance gate determines success or failure. Once this barrier was surmounted, there was no way, short of mobilizing the neighborhood, to prevent thieves from pillaging a home. The gate protected property as it protected morality.

Builders took particular care with this strategic point. The importance of the main entrance was usually emphasized by the construction of a porch consisting of a roof supported by two columns. This created an ambiguous space, often projecting into the street, that was not really a part of the house's interior. The true dividing line was marked by the door or

*The Relation of Inside to Outside*

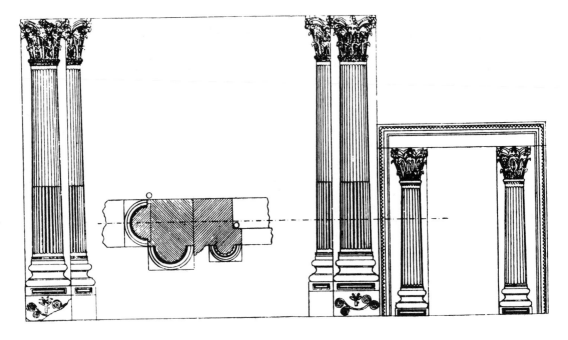

Fig. 16. Volubilis, entrance
of the House of Hercules
(Etienne, *Quartier nord-est,*
plate xxxiii).

gate, and the transition from street to house was often arranged in a complex manner (fig. 14). Usually there was not
one gate but two or even three, with a clear hierarchy. A vast
central bay was closed by a double gate, flanked by one or
two smaller gates. But we must not assume that the large gate
was for carriages and the smaller ones for pedestrians. The
pattern of wear on the threshold and the organization of the
rooms inside refute the notion that any vehicle ever passed
through the main gate. The use of this entryway varied from
time to time. As a rule, only one of the smaller gates was
used, the small size of the entrance underscoring the division
between the outside world and the house proper. At certain
times, however, the main entrance was opened wide—probably when the owner gave a reception of some importance,
and perhaps also in the morning, to indicate the moment when
he was ready to receive his clients' homage.

The functions of the entrance were complex. Symbols of
the owner's ambitions, entrances were the focus of much
architectural attention. Many who never actually entered
wealthy houses were aware of their owners' opulence from
the magnificence of their entrances. In a well-to-do section
like the northeastern quarter of Volubilis, splendid entrances
were the rule. Two embedded small columns frame the sec-

ondary entrance of the House of Hercules' Labors (fig. 16). The entire composition is framed by moldings. The main entrance is flanked on either side by twin embedded columns. The design informs the passerby that this is a wealthy home and, depending on the time of day and the positioning of the gates, tells the person about to enter how he must present himself.

After passing through the main entrance, the visitor finds himself in the vestibule. This transitional space, although part of the house proper, is one in which the visitor is still subject to scrutiny. His view of the house is limited, and the vestibule is under the watchful eye of a guard: the *ianitor* is often mentioned in the texts, and many ruins include a small room, directly off the vestibule, which is clearly where the slave posted as guard watched those who came and went. The vestibule was a transitional space in another sense: it was supposed to herald the sumptuousness in store for the visitor. When Apuleius describes the Palace of Psyche (an imaginary palace, but nonetheless valuable for our purposes), he states that its divine nature strikes the eye as soon as one enters (*Metamorphoses,* V, 1). The magnificence of a house was supposed to be on display from the moment one crossed the threshold. Vitruvius numbers the vestibule among those rooms that should be spacious and magnificent, and the remains of wealthy homes fully bear out this precept. In most great homes in fact the vestibule is one of the largest rooms. Frequently it opens onto the peristyle via a spacious triple bay that reflects the threefold entryway. Sometimes the nobility of the vestibule is enhanced by a small colonnade, as in the House of Castorius at Cuicul (fig. 19) or that of Sertius at Timgad (fig. 24). One of the most striking of all such entrances is found at Althiburos, in the House of the Asclepiae (fig. 17). Behind a gallery nearly 70 feet long, set between two projecting front rooms, are three vestibules, one for each of the three entries. The main vestibule leads into the central hall, located on the building's axis of symmetry. Covering nearly 700 square feet, it is the largest covered room in the building. The care taken in its decoration is in keeping with its magnificence. The walls are decorated with marble panels, and the floor is covered with a mosaic featuring a large marine composition, whose quality and complexity attest to the room's importance. The two side vestibules are actually annexes to the main vestibule. Each incorporates an uncovered pool between it and the central vestibule and amounts to little more

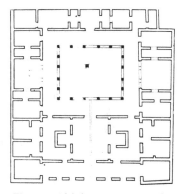

Fig. 17. Althiburos, House of the Asclepiae, original plan (M. Ennaifer, *La cité d'Althiburos* [Tunis, 1976], plan v). Behind the front gallery are three doors, the largest of which leads to the vestibule, the two others to porticoes flanking pools. The courtyard of the peristyle is a garden. Triclinia are to the left and right. At the northern extremity is an exedra with a mosaic depicting an agonistic crown.

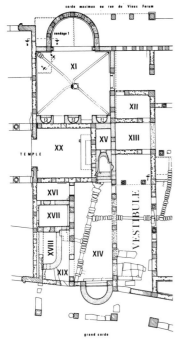

Fig. 18. Cuicul, House of the Ass (Blanchard-Lemée, *Quartier central*, fig. 4). XII–XIII: annexes of vestibule; XIV through XIX: baths built when building was extended to the north at the expense of a temple, whose *cella* (XX) is squeezed between the baths and room XI, decorated with a nymphaeum that abuts the podium of the sanctuary as well as an apse extending into the street. This is typical of the way private construction usurped public space.

than a walkway offering access to side rooms at either of the building's extremes. This symmetrical composition extends over the building's entire width.

In discussing the relation of exterior to interior, it is not enough just to call attention to the care taken in designing the place where the transition from one to the other was effected. For within the domus itself there were enclaves, often including an area, accessible by wagons, used for the owner's business activities. Household provisions were unloaded here (see figs. 8, 26, 29). Many houses also had shops along their outside walls. These could be used by the owner of the house to sell his own products, as is clear in cases where shops communicated directly with the domus, or rented to outsiders (see figs. 28, 29). They are architecturally complex: integrated into the building (especially where symmetrically arrayed on either side of the entry vestibule), they nevertheless functioned independently. Often they served both as shops open to the public and as private residences for the shopkeeper and his family.

There was another type of enclave inside the domus: apartments rented to people who were not members of the owner's household. This practice is often mentioned in Roman sources and well attested in Africa. Apuleius was accused of making nocturnal sacrifices in a domus where one of his friends rented an apartment (*Apol.*, LVII). In practice, it is difficult to recognize from the remains of buildings which parts were rented to tenants. Texts and inscriptions suggest that apartments were usually located in upper stories, so the presence of stairways easily accessible from the street suggests that a building may have contained independent rooms suitable for renting. When the upper stories have been destroyed, however, this hypothesis is difficult to verify. What, for example, was the purpose of the staircase that led up from the southeastern corner of the House of the Hunt at Bulla Regia (fig. 8)? Did it lead to terraces? Or to separate apartments? Its location, close to both the vestibule and the wagon entrance, meant that it would have been accessible to tenants without affecting the owner's privacy; but this argument is hardly convincing. On the other hand, we can say with some confidence that rooms in the northeastern corner of the House of Coins at Volubilis (fig. 28) were intended for rental. This vast building occupied an entire insula, and the small apartment in question was almost surely part of it. It was set up for independent access from the street to the north via corridor 36, which served rooms 1 and 16, the first of which had a window opening onto the street. Room 15 seems to have contained a staircase offering direct access to the street east of the building. Two ground-floor rooms and three upper-story rooms were thus available for rental. Also in Volubilis, next to the vestibule of the house to the west of the governor's palace, a staircase leads to the street through one of the three doors (fig. 29). In all probability it led to rental apartments above the shops which, together with the entry vestibule, formed the facade of the building. Rooms of very different status often stood cheek by jowl. The house was in contact with the street only through its vestibule, which like an antenna probed the outside world, completely surrounded by rooms to let. We can only assume that the corridor that served the upper-story rooms, which must have been situated above the southern portico, was lighted by high, narrow windows so as to protect the privacy of the courtyard below.

---

*The Peristyle*

The peristyle was the heart of every wealthy residence. The central court, open to the sky, allowed air and light into neighboring rooms, but it was the colonnade surrounding the courtyard that made the peristyle the ideal place for developing architectural ideas of some magnitude (see fig. 31). Where space was lacking, an owner might have to settle for an incomplete peristyle, eliminating one or two porticoes. Usually, though, owners preferred to allocate as much of the available space as possible to the peristyle. In the most ambitious houses the peristyle attained vast dimensions: more than 3,500 square feet in the House of the Asclepiae at Althiburos or the Peacock House at Thysdrus, more than 5,000 square feet in the House of the Fisherman at Bulla Regia, and around 6,000 square feet in the House of the Laberii at Uthina.

Analysis of the peristyle turns out to be a more exacting task than it appears at first glance. It is customary today to maintain that the peristyle was the heart of the public portion of the house, that this spacious area was where visitors were received. This claim is corroborated by house plans, for the peristyle is frequently accessible directly from the vestibule, and most of the reception rooms are arrayed around its boundary. Hence it would seem that this space served as a complement to the rooms in which guests were received.

Such an interpretation suggests a sharp contrast between the African house, with its peristyle used for receiving guests, and the type of house found in Pompeii, with the traditional atrium on the facade used for the same purpose and the peristyle located at the other end of the building, ostensibly serving mainly to enhance the beauty of the house's private portions. This contrast is, I think, too stark. A distinction must be drawn between two types of visitors: ordinary clients who came to pay respects and receive their sportulae (distributions of food and other gifts), and other guests who were received privately by the master. Although the atrium of the Pompeiian house was well suited to receive clients, it was not useful for receiving distinguished visitors, who would have been entertained in one of the dining rooms or salons off the peristyle. It is therefore wrong to draw a sharp contrast between the atrium and the peristyle of the Pompeiian house on the grounds that the former belonged to the "public" portion of the house and the latter to the "private" portion.

Did the absence of an atrium in the African house make the peristyle a much more public space? If so, clients would have been received there; but there is no evidence for this either in the texts or in the arrangement of space, which would scarcely have lent itself to such assemblies. The functions of the atrium were filled in the African house by other rooms: by the private basilica, about which I shall have more to say presently, and by the vestibule. We have seen that the vestibule was generally an ample room. It is likely that it inherited at least some of the functions of the atrium, although there is no persuasive proof of this assertion. A glance at the plans of many of these houses shows that their vestibules would have been suitable as sites for the salutation ceremony. In the House of the Ass at Cuicul the long vestibule ends in a sort of exedra marked off by two columns, behind which stood two rooms that might have served as storerooms for food handed out to clients. Vestibules were especially large in houses built on plots formed by combining a number of smaller lots. Rather than gain additional space by staying with a single entry, several entrances were kept in these houses. Some of the vestibules seem far too large to have served as mere anterooms. How else can we explain in the House of Europa at Cuicul the large southern vestibule, far from the central part of the building and not linked to the peristyle in any straightforward way (fig. 20:1, 26)? Despite the tiled floor, it cannot have been an uncovered room. The size of the triple doors and the fine molding around the bays show that it was an important place. Although the building has not been studied in sufficient detail to warrant any firm opinion, it seems likely that this was not

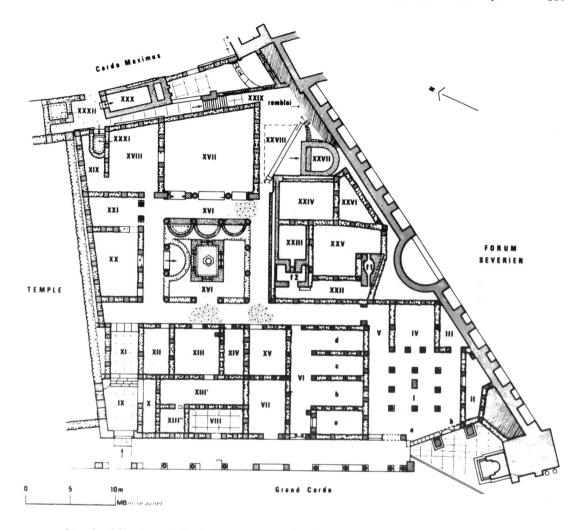

an earlier building's original entrance, retained when two neighboring houses were combined, but an entrance constructed when the joining of the properties made space available. This vestibule apparently served as a waiting room for clients; it has all the necessary appurtenances, and the stairs that face the door could have served as a dais on which the master might have stood or made his formal entrance. It would be helpful if we knew more about the room located just north of this vestibule, which communicated with the street through two entries. (The portico in front of it rules out the possibility that the larger of the gates was a carriage entrance.) The fact that the floor was tiled does not prove that

Fig. 19. Cuicul, House of Castorius (Blanchard-Lemée, *Quartier central*, fig. 62). At 15,000 square feet, this house, built to a "bayonette" plan, was the largest in central Cuicul. I: vestibule (possibly the peristyle of an older building); IX: vestibule (adjoining porter's lodge [?], X); XVI: peristyle; XVII: triclinium with three-part bay and doors; XXII–XXVIII: baths with latrines; XXX–XXXII: baths built later.

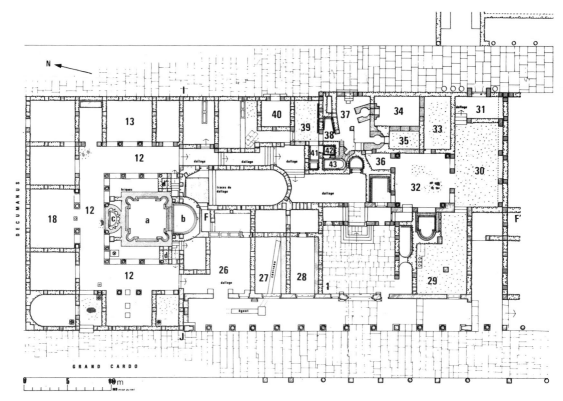

Fig. 20. Cuicul, House of Europa (Blanchard-Lemée, *Quartier central,* fig. 49). This house, covering some 14,000 square feet, stands on several lots (note subdivision walls I-J and F-F'). 1: vestibule with triple doors; 12: peristyle with courtyard filled with pools (a, b, c) and jardinieres (d and d'); 13: triclinium; 18: triclinium or exedra; 26: vestibule; 27–28: shops; 29–43: baths with latrines in 29.

this room was open to the elements. The space communicates with an inner room from which it is separated by nothing more than a row of stone vessels. These troughs, which were kept covered, would have been suitable for a room used for distribution of sportulae. If this hypothesis is correct, then the whole southwestern portion of the building, which included shops (fig. 20:27, 28, 46), would have been given over to "public" functions.

Thus, the African house was not without rooms located close to the street and, like the atrium, suitable for receiving certain visitors without disturbing the privacy of the rest of the house. The usual way of stating the contrast between the African and the traditional Italic house is therefore fundamentally wrong, since, on the one hand, the peristyle in the Pompeiian house was not used only by residents and, on the other hand, the African peristyle need not have been used to receive all visitors despite the absence of an atrium. This impression is confirmed by study of the rooms bordering the courtyard. Reception rooms are next to rooms used for completely different purposes, proof that the peristyle was not used solely as a public space.

The bedrooms, among the most private rooms in the house, are easily identifiable. The bed was often installed on a dais, raised slightly above the rest of the room; another device was the use of two different kinds of tile, with the simpler motif indicating the placement of the bed (see fig. 32). Hence it is easy to see where reception rooms and bedrooms were juxtaposed. Such an arrangement was commonplace. The Sollertiana domus in Hadrumetum has two bedrooms that occupy an entire wing of the peristyle (fig. 23:4, 6). At Acholla, in the House of Neptune (fig. 15), a suite of rooms occupies the northeastern corner of the peristyle, between two dining rooms. Three of the rooms in the suite are probably bedrooms, as is suggested by the use of two motifs in the mosaic tiling. The House of the Hunt at Bulla Regia provides a striking instance of this interspersing of public and private rooms (see figs. 8, 9). The building contains two *triclinia,* one on the ground floor, the other immediately below it on the basement floor. Both rooms, which open onto the building's second peristyle, are flanked by bedrooms.

The complexity of the peristyle is highlighted by the placement of rooms serving such different purposes around its periphery. The peristyle cannot, therefore, be characterized as a reception area. It was the scene of such diverse activities that one is forced to ask how they could have coexisted. I shall return to this question when we consider how the various parts of the house were related.

The ambiguity of the peristyle is evident, too, in the way it was built. Construction sometimes highlighted the utilitarian aspect. Some courtyards were made of packed earth, and often there was a well and holes for cisterns. The House of the New Hunt at Bulla Regia demonstrates such utilitarian construction. Usually, however, the colonnaded space was decorated, often with plants, suggesting a domestication of nature. There were many different approaches. Some courtyards were entirely paved with mosaics. This emphasized the architecture and deemphasized the plants, which were here limited to the potted variety. Still, water and vegetation were constant, and complementary, themes of decoration, sometimes to such a degree that the peristyle was transformed into a garden with fountains and pools (see figs. 33, 34).

Practically every peristyle of any size was embellished with fountains. One of the most common and simple devices was to place next to one of the porticoes a semicircular basin with holes pierced through its lip. These were not pressurized fountains, merely pools of water a few inches deep. There were probably fixtures for inserting a frame to support a trellis, which made for an intimate association of water and vegetation on a small scale.

The same theme was carried to much greater lengths, and many courts were filled with basins and pools. In the House of Europa at Cuicul three complex basins are complemented by two jardinieres (fig. 20:a, b, c, d-d). In the House of Castorius, four semicircular basins flank the porticoes, while the central space of the courtyard is occupied by a rectangular pool. In this arrangement the space left open for passage appears to have been quite limited. A more radical approach was to give the court entirely over to water. Consider the House of the Fisherman (fig. 9) at Bulla Regia.[11] In an immense peristyle, covering some 5,300 square feet, the court per se occupies some 2,700 square feet. This entire area (apart from a few places left open to allow air and light to penetrate to the floor below) is filled with basins separated by low walls, in which holes have been left to allow water to circulate. On top of these walls there are traces of the fixtures used to support wooden studs or small stone columns, some of which are still in place. It is easy to imagine these devices supporting a light framework decorated with hanging plants.

When it came to bringing water and plants into the heart of the house, the owner had a wide range of possibilities. He might opt for a single basin and a few potted plants, or he might turn his entire courtyard into a garden with fountains or even a watery fantasy upon which one gazed but did not enter. Even the decor emphasized the "natural" aspect of the peristyle. In the House of the Fisherman vestiges of paintings depict birds and plants, while a basin with several lobes to catch the overflow was decorated with a mosaic of fish. In the Villa of the Aviary in Carthage the mosaic of the porticoes depicts various animals among the flowers and fruits. Frequent remodeling reveals changes in taste, but there are too few detailed studies to warrant the conclusion that owners devoted increasing amounts of space to such artificial natural decor. However that may be, no African house was without a peristyle decorated in this manner.

The charm of the peristyle obviously would have enhanced the private lives of the residents; its magnificent decor was just as obviously intended for the eyes of visitors. Evi-

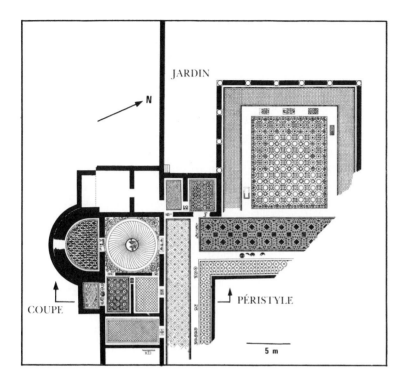

Fig. 21. Hadrumetum, House of the Masks (L. Foucher, *La maison des masques à Sousse* [Tunis, 1965]). West of the peristyle and separated from it by a garden and gallery is a vast triclinium. An exedra with apse is located south of the peristyle.

dence for the latter assertion lies in the way in which the decorative elements of the court were arranged. Usually the basins were placed along the axis of the reception hall. In the House of Castorius at Cuicul (fig. 19) three basins correspond to each of the three bays of the main reception hall. Sometimes the connection between the architecture of the peristyle and that of the large adjoining halls is closer still. The rhythm of the colonnade in the House of the Trefoil Basin in Volubilis was altered so that the columns would line up with the three bays of the large hall (fig. 26:9). This extreme case, in which the entire peristyle is subjected to the ceremonial necessities of reception, merely confirms an obvious fact: this space was intended to convey to visitors the owner's high status.

The peristyle was the perfect embodiment of the complexity of the private sphere. Embellished by a combination of architectural and natural effects, it was a space in which a variety of activities took place, from solitary pursuits to great receptions befitting the master's high social station—to say nothing of the work of the servants, for whom the peristyle served as passageway, work space, and water supply. Whenever domestic chapels have been located in African houses,

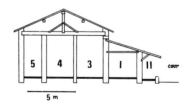

Fig. 22. Elevation view of southern wing of the House of the Masks, showing rooms lying to the east of the exedra (3–5) and the southern portico (1).

they have been found either in or close to the peristyle. In the House with Four Pillars, at Banasa in Morocco, the altar stood in a room just off the peristyle. In Libya, in the insula of Jason Magnus of Cyrene as well as in Ptolemais' House (with its D-shaped peristyle), a small chapel stands in the courtyard. An altar dedicated to the genius of the domus sat under one of the porticoes of the Wild Animal House at Volubilis, as well as the House of Flavius Germanus. The presence of a chapel did not "privatize" the use of the peristyle, however. In the House of Asinius Rufus at Acholla a cippus was dedicated by *cultores domus*, clients who participated in the domestic cult of the Asinii, the family that owned the house. The private cults were not limited to the family in the strict sense but included other "dependents." Hence it was entirely appropriate to place these altars in the peristyle, whose many functions reflected the many roles of religion.

## Reception Halls

Certain rooms were distinguished by size, architecture, and decor. Reception halls, often easy to spot, played a very important role in domestic life, since wealthy house owners were obliged to receive guests often and treat them handsomely. Meals were a favorite way of discharging this obligation, and no noble house is without one or more dining rooms (triclinia). The design of the mosaic often makes this room easy to identify: the central space was usually decorated with a choice motif; the space along the wall where the diners' couches were placed was more simply decorated. The importance of the dining room was often emphasized by its size and three access bays; it frequently was the largest and most sumptuous of the house's reception areas. The House of the Train of Venus at Volubilis has a triclinium (fig. 27:11) with three bays that measures 25.6 x 32.2 feet, larger than the court of the peristyle; it is decorated with a complex mosaic representing the navigation of Venus. In the new House of the Hunt at Bulla Regia (fig. 8) the dining room is the largest and most luxuriously decorated room; its central panel depicts a hunting scene surrounded by a rich foliated scroll that twines around the forequarters of various animals.

Complex architectural designs could make a room particularly sumptuous. Vitruvius describes vast dining halls that included an interior colonnade, which he called an *oecus*. This device was used in Africa, as evidence of the remains reveals. In the House of Masks at Hadrumetum (fig. 21), the triclinium, nearly 2,500 square feet in size, is separated by a row of pillars from a gallery some 8 feet wide that leads through a colonnade into a garden. The House of Neptune at Acholla (fig. 15) has a dining room of more than 1,000 square feet, whose couches were separated from a peripheral gallery by a colonnade.

The luxury of these rooms demonstrates the key role they played. The dinner ceremony, designed to display the host's wealth, was also an occasion to expound his philosophy and announce changes in his circle of friends or family. This is not the place to review information gleaned from well-known sources, most of which in any case concerns Italy or the eastern part of the Empire. The African sources tell us that in Africa as in Rome the triclinium was where the master of the house showed who and what he was.

The central propaganda theme was luxury. No attempt was made to conceal the equivalence of power and wealth, ostentatiously demonstrated in banquets. Let us follow the hero of Apuleius' *Metamorphoses*: "I found a large number of guests there when I arrived, the flower of the city, as befits the house of so great a lady. Sumptuous tables glamed with thuya and ivory, couches were upholstered with gold fabrics, and the drinking cups were enormous, varied in their elegance but all equally precious. Some were of glass with studious reliefs, others flawless crystal, still others gleaming silver or sparkling gold. Amber and other stones were miraculously hollowed out for drinking. In short, one saw everything, even the impossible. Several carvers, wearing splendid robes, skillfully presented copious dishes. Curly-haired young boys wearing fine tunics continuously offered old wine in cups each of which bore a gem" (*Metamorphoses*, II, 19, from the French translation by P. Valette). None of this is surprising, and without dwelling on the luxury of the architecture, the decor, or the furniture, I want to stress the social significance of the food served. Wine of good quality (signified, as today, by age and origin) was essential at a true feast. The food, too, had significance. A host like Trimalchio organized an entire ritual around every plate, whose presentation was turned into a kind of spectacle. In Africa fish was the preeminent sign of a rich table. And it was costly indeed: the edict of Diocletian states that on the average fish cost more than three times as much as meat, and, for an earlier period, we have Apuleius' remark about "gourmands whose fortunes are being swallowed up by the fisherman" (*Apol.*, 32). The problem of supply did not

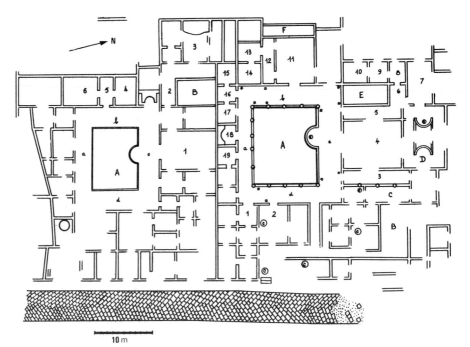

Fig. 23. Thysdrus: House of the Peacock to the north and so-called Sollertiana domus to the south (L. Foucher, *Découvertes archéologiques à Thysdrus en 1961* [Tunis, n.d.], plan 1). The House of the Peacock covers approximately 17,000 square feet. A: peristyle with courtyard garden (40.5 x 33.5 feet); 4: exedra (32.8 x 26.2 feet) with service doors; 7 and 11: triclinia; 3 and 5: corridors; C: small courtyard; D: small courtyard with fountain; E: small courtyard with garden; 9: bedroom (see fig. 32); 18: chapel(?). In the Sollertiana domus we see A: peristyle; 1: triclinium; B: secondary courtyard; 3: exedra; 4 and 6: bedrooms with adjoining antechamber 5.

arise in coastal cities, but it is remarkable that fish was eaten at all in the cities of the interior. The scarcity of fish is used by Apuleius in answering a charge that he practiced magic: "I was a long way inland, in the mountains of Getulia, where fish can be found, yes, thanks to Deucalion's flood" (*Apol.,* 41). Hence it is no accident that dining rooms and nearby corridors are often decorated with ocean scenes and representations of seafood. In the House of Venus at Mactar the decoration of the triclinium consists entirely of a catalogue of edible marine life, with over two hundred items initially: "the most important ancient work on marine fauna."[12] Marine life was not only decorative but reputedly prophylactic, capable of protecting a house against noxious influences. Beyond that, however, these maritime mosaics no doubt reminded viewers of luxurious meals past. Apuleius explains that, following the lead of the greatest names in Greek philosophy, he studied fish. He dissected and described various kinds and summarized and completed the work of his predecessors. He also coined Latin words to translate Greek terms. This scientific interest in classification and cataloguing is reflected in the mosaic at Mactar, where the various animals are represented so accurately that almost all have been positively identified by modern researchers. The illustrative plates accompanying Pliny's remarks on fish may have served as one source for this group of mosaicists. Was the culinary use of such scientific catalogues a vulgar perversion of philosophical speculation? No. Materialist and idealist interests coexisted in the noblest intellectual tradition. Apuleius himself reminds us that Ennius, a Hellenistic poet from southern Italy, wrote a poem celebrating seafood, in which he probably imitated earlier Greek poets. In this poem, for each fish he explains "where and how—fried or in sauce—it ought to be eaten to obtain the best taste" (*Apol.*, 39)

After this our attention turns naturally to the basins in the court of the peristyle—basins frequently decorated with marine motifs, a way of artificially bringing home the pleasures of the sea. This was not enough for some owners, however. Fish were raised in pools in a number of African houses. In the House of Castorius in Cuicul (fig. 19) small amphorae are embedded into the masonry of the central basin, a device indicating the presence of fish. The same device occurs in the House of Bacchus, also in Cuicul. The design of the tank in the House of Sertius in Timgad (fig. 24) is more complex. At the opposite end of the house from the main entrance on the *cardo maximus* a room opens onto the second peristyle

Fig. 24. Timgad, House of Sertius, with principal entry (formerly tripartite?) off the *cardo maximus*; tiled vestibule with central colonnade; baths in upper right-hand corner; from right to left: first peristyle with adjoining large room (triclinium?); second peristyle with pool and second triclinium (?) preceded by an anteroom. This building, which covers more than 25,000 square feet, was constructed on the site of razed walls, whose location is indicated by the dotted line (the rounded corner next to the second triclinium was the southwestern corner of the city wall).

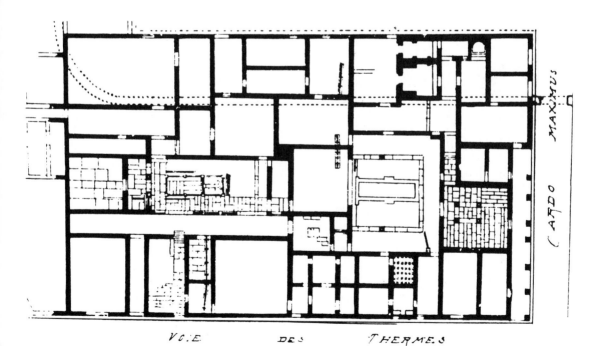

VOIE          DES          THERMES

Fig. 25. Timgad, House of the Hermaphrodite. On the left, underneath the portico bordering the *cardo maximus,* which separates this house from the House of Sertius, is a string of shops. From left to right we have the entry vestibule, which leads to a large hall adjoining an enormous room (36 x 25 feet) with triple bays at either end, undoubtedly a triclinium. The thick northern wall of the house follows the line of the old city wall.

through an antechamber with two columns. This may have been a triclinium. The court of the peristyle contains a basin consisting of two tanks, one on top of the other, with two holes to allow water to flow between them. Vessels, placed horizontally in the masonry walls of the basement, were designed as shelters in which the fish could spawn. These and many similar tanks found elsewhere were not just decorative ornaments but true fish hatcheries, which played an important economic role. In inland cities they enabled the host to offer his guests rare and highly prized fish dishes. These may have been but pale copies of the vast hatchery operations that occupied some Roman aristocrats to such a degree that Cicero called them *piscinarii*, or Tritons of the breeding tank. But the idea is the same, simply scaled down to suit local fortunes and conditions.

The dining room was more than just a place for the master of the house to display his wealth. It was used for more subtle—and significant—manifestations of domestic life. In Africa, as in the rest of the Roman world, women and even children had long attended banquets (see, for example, Augustine, *Confessions*, IX, 17, in which children are said to eat

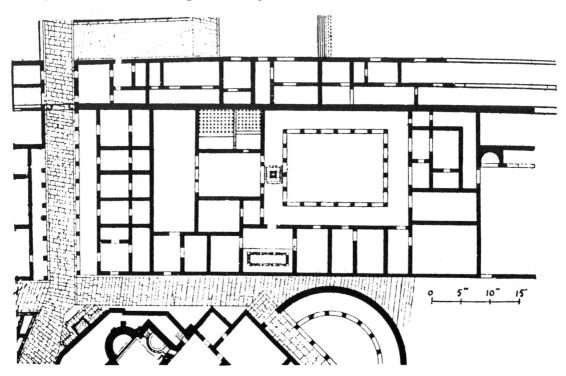

at their parents' table). Changes in family habits were reflected in the order of meals, which was strictly governed, even in the afterlife, as is shown by a funerary mosaic depicting a couple observing the usual etiquette at a banquet in the other world (fig. 37). The old custom had been that only men reclined at table; women sat upright. But this custom had been abandoned by all but the most conservative. When Apuleius first describes Milo, known throughout the city for greed and base manners, he shows him lying on a low couch preparing to eat, with his wife seated at his feet and the table empty. The slim pickings and poor furniture might be interpreted in any number of ways, but the positions of husband and wife remove all doubt (*Metamorphoses*, I, 32).

The meal also brought together the entire *familia*, or household. Slaves were sometimes allowed to eat dinner leftovers (*Metamorphoses*, X, 14); on holidays they were allowed to recline while eating, just like their masters. Dinners marked social differences but also brought together heterogeneous groups. It is no accident that banquets became an important social occasion in Christian communities and, in particular, an opportunity to practice charity. In Africa these communal dinners, often taken at graveside in honor of the deceased, assumed such importance that the ecclesiastical authorities were forced to take steps to curtail them.

The triclinium was an essential room, the reception room par excellence as well as a setting for important family occasions. Here the devout noble received the itinerant priests of the Syrian goddess for a sacrificial meal (*Metamorphoses*, IX, 1). Here the marvelous donkey that eats the same dishes as humans is taken to show off its talents; the first thing his slave attendant teaches him is to lean on his "elbow" and recline at table (*Metamorphoses*, X, 16–17). Here the bonds that hold the private realm together are most overtly displayed: marital ties, family ties, household ties, and ties of friendship. All of these relations were clearly manifest in mealtime ceremony. What is more, the master used the dinner stage to proclaim his conception of life. Space in the triclinium was coded space: the place where one sat signified rank, for the couches, and places on each couch, were hierarchically ordered, culminating in the master's seat on the right side of the central couch. To be *magister convivio* and preside over banquets was the role of the master (*Apol.*, 98). The guests were seated by a designated servant, the *nomenclator*, and the meal was served by specialized slaves, the *servi triclinarii*, each of whom was assigned a specific task. African artisans were careful to include these slaves in mosaics depicting banquet scenes.

Dinners were a visible affirmation of basic principles. Listen to the African Tertullian: "Our meal indicates the reason for its existence by its name, which is a word that signifies 'love' among the Greeks [*agape*] . . . Because it derives from a religious obligation, it is neither base nor immodest. We sit down at table [we do not recline] only after offering a prayer to God. We eat as much as hunger requires. We drink as much as sobriety allows . . . We converse in the manner of people who know that the Lord is listening . . . The meal ends as it began, in prayer. Then each person goes his own way . . . as though he had learned a lesson rather than eaten a meal" (*Apol.*, XXXIX, 16–19, from the French translation by J.-P. Waltzing). The same concern for propaganda through order is found two centuries later in Augustine: his friend Possidius reports that maxims engraved on the table are intended to elevate the conversation and that diners use silver utensils but earthenware dishes, not out of poverty but on principle.

These Christian attitudes derive without radical change from the dining art of earlier centuries. Even in pagan ideology the theme of temperance was developed in opposition to the association of social rank with sumptuous, not to say excessive, dining. When Erasmus in a later age praises "a table richer in literate conversation than in dining pleasure," he is merely repeating a favorite saying of the Romans, or at any rate of those Romans who thought of themselves as competent to pronounce on matters of the mind. Pliny the Younger, in praising the dinners given by the emperor Trajan, stresses the charm of the conversation and adds that the only diversions offered were music and comedies, as opposed to the dancers and courtesans so much in favor at African banquets. (A mosaic in Carthage shows them in action in the space delineated by the dinner tables.) When Apuleius seeks to discredit one of his detractors, he describes him as "a glutton, a shameless guzzler . . . a man who does not shrink from carousing at midday" (*Apol.*, 57). The accusation seems never to have grown stale. Another detractor is accused of having "devoured" an inheritance of three million sesterces, most of which ended up "in his stomach, frittered away on all kinds of revels," so that "all that is left of a fair fortune is a miserable scheming mind and an insatiable appetite" (*Apol.*, 75). Apuleius was too shrewd a man to have made such a charge unless it was likely to do some good.

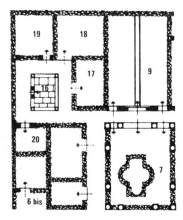

Fig. 26. Volubilis, House of the Trefoil Basin, built according to an axial plan (Etienne, *Quartier nord-est,* taken from plate xv). 7: peristyle with tiled courtyard; 9: triclinium (?) (36 x 24 feet); 16: secondary peristyle (25 x 23 feet), adjoining rooms 17–20.

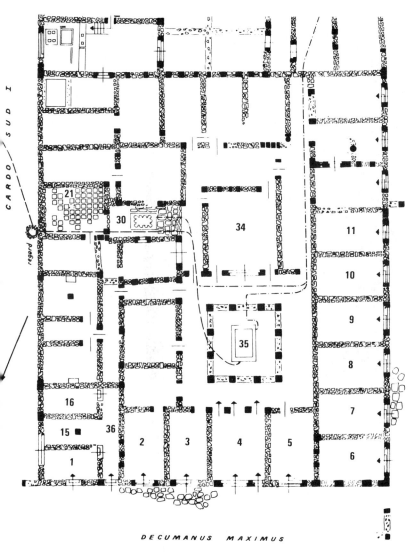

Fig. 27. Volubilis, House of the Train of Venus (Etienne, *Quartier nord-est,* plate XVII), axial plan. V1 and V2: double-entry vestibule (49.2 x 12.5 feet and 19.7 x 17.4 feet). Vestibule V1 and room 19 occupy space once belonging to a public portico that ran along the building's facade. 1: peristyle (45.9 x 42.6 feet); 9: exedra; 10: bedroom connected to peristyle by corridor-antechamber; 11: triclinium; 12: secondary courtyard with pool; 18–26: baths installed during remodeling at the time the public portico was annexed.

The dining room, which played a key role in domestic socializing, was a theater with its own conventions, its own code governing relations of husband to wife and master to guests. Guests were shown how the master lived and learned his opinions of the day's fashions. Every gesture, every dish, was of conscious significance. Reading how Juvenal or Martial, intellectuals always ready to engage in analysis and criticism, inform their guests in writing of the sophisticated, falsely modest menu of the dinner they are about to eat, with promises of properly moral, intellectual conversation, we see that there is no real difference between them and Trimalchio. For all these hosts the dinner is an occasion to teach, to preach a philosophy derived ultimately from the master's personal history. The dining room was all the more revealing because it was a dangerous place. As everyone knew, banquets often provided the occasion for the most audacious acts. This was the room where guests showed off, but it was also a room where certain types of behavior were proscribed. Martial promised his guests that on the day after one of his banquets they would not regret what they had seen or heard (X, 48). A citizen of Pompeii had maxims painted on the walls of his triclinium exhorting his guests to behave modestly and properly or risk being asked to leave. Augustine refused to serve wine to anyone who swore.

The atmosphere at Roman banquets ranged from the ascetic to the orgiastic. Augustine, in Book X of the *Confessions*, in the section dealing with the senses (X, 43–47), warns of the danger of taste: "For by eating and drinking we repair the daily decays of our body . . . But now the necessity is sweet unto me, against which sweetness I fight, that I be not taken captive; and carry on a daily war by fastings; often bringing my body into subjection . . . This hast Thou taught me, that I should set myself to take food as physic. But while I am passing from the discomfort of emptiness to the content of replenishing, in the very passage the snare of concupiscence besets me. For that passing is pleasure, nor is there any other way to pass thither, whither we needs must pass . . . Placed then amid these temptations, I strive daily against concupiscence in eating and drinking. For it is not of such nature that I can settle on cutting it off once and for all, and never touching it afterward, as I should of concubinage. The bridle of the throat then is to be held attempered between slackness and stiffness. And who is he, O Lord, who is not somewhat transported beyond the limits of necessity?"[13] For the sage, whether pagan or Christian, the act of eating is revealing precisely because it is both necessary and reprehensible. Recall that the only sin Augustine imputes to his mother is that of a somewhat immoderate, though quickly repressed, penchant for wine (*Confessions*, IX, 18). The social fact was inescapable: there was an art of eating, or, rather, a number of different ways of eating, none of which was innocent. And it was not, as in psychoanaylsis, after the fact that people became aware of the real reasons for their actions. The moral dangers of the table were well known and feared or accepted. This awareness preceded the unconscious acts of daring or bold speaking committed in the heat of a banquet. Some people were known to be unable to control themselves, which only enhanced the danger. Worse still, there were people who made "disorderly" behavior at banquets a way of life.

Although the dining room was the most important room for receiving guests, it was not the only room used for that purpose. From what we now know, we can say with certainty that at least one other room was used primarily for meetings with visitors: the exedra, generally smaller than the dining room but larger than other rooms and distinguished by a broad access corridor and fine decoration. Exedrae are often easy to identify. Opposite the dining room in the House of the New Hunt at Bulla Regia is an exedra that was originally attached to one of the porticoes of the peristyle by three bays (figs. 8, 38). The same arrangement was used in the House of the Hunt, where the exedra is even larger than the triclinia. The exedra is the largest room of the House of the Peacock at Thysdrus (fig. 23:4), which gives some idea of the importance attached to it by the owner. In the House of Masks in the same city the exedra is accented by an apse. The noble house in Africa rarely lacked an exedra.

Since the triclinium usually was reserved for the main evening meal, the master of the house needed another room in which to perform his social duties. The exedra of African houses served many of the same functions as the *tablinium* in the traditional Italic house. It was primarily the master's office. In the House of Fonteius at Banasa the mosaic floor of this room bears his name: s. FONTE(ius). When the master needed to escape from the daily bustle of the house, it was to this room that he retired. This was where he dealt with business matters and received friends. Discussions and lectures took place here. It is no accident that the decor of the exedra often alludes to intellectual or cultural activities: mosaics represent the Muses in houses in Althiburos and Thysdrus, and theatrical masks and a portrait of a tragic poet have been found in the exedra of the House of Masks at Hadrumetum (fig. 21). Culture was important in the social life of the elite. One model was the *vir bonus dicendi peritus* (gentleman skilled at speaking), to repeat Apuleius' characterization (*Apol.*, 94). Conversational and epistolary skills revealed a man's talents and moral qualities. The written sources mention other rooms used for cultural purposes, but unfortunately we do not know how to identify them in the archaeological remains. Apuleius, for ex-

Fig. 28. Volubilis, House of the Gold Coins (Etienne, *Quartier nord-est,* plate x), at 17,000 square feet one of the largest in the city, built to an almost axial plan. 1, 15, 16, and 36: independent apartments; 4: vestibule (19.5 x 16.3 feet); 2, 3, and 5: shops communicating with the house; 6–11: independent shops; 35: square peristyle (41 feet on a side); 34: triclinium (?) (24.2 x 21.3 feet) with two small service doors; 30: secondary courtyard with pool serving room 21 (18.3 x 14.1 feet), which is tiled with marble. To the south was a large area of workshops, including an oil factory and a bakery (not shown).

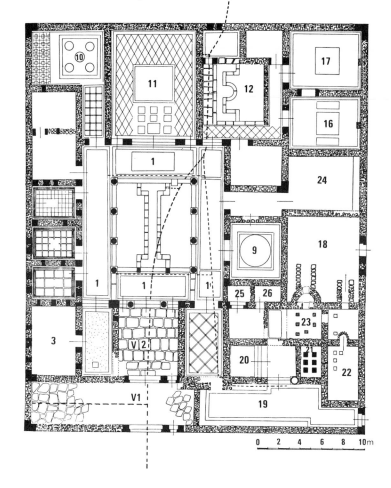

ample, describes a library, a room that could be locked and that was guarded by a freedman (*Apol.,* 87).

When it came to meeting with clients, the exedra, which was often located near the center of the house and, all things considered, rather modest in size, might not have been adequate. Clientele relations, which structured society by making each person the dependent of a more powerful neighbor with whom he exchanged services, were of great importance in Italy, as is attested by abundant evidence. All signs are that relations with clients were equally important in Africa. Apuleius married in the countryside in order to evade the patron's duty to distribute sportulae on his wedding day (*Apol.,* 87). Augustine reports that Alypius, one of his students in Carthage, was in the habit of paying his respects regularly to a senator.

These morning ceremonies, concrete expressions of the dependence of client on patron, were represented in art. One of the most significant examples is surely the mosaic of the noble Iulius from a house in Carthage (fig. 39). Paul Veyne has reinterpreted this mosaic,[14] so I shall confine my remarks to points relevant to my subject. The villa occupies the center of the composition, which is framed by scenes of preparation for a hunt and includes symbolic components. According to traditional interpretation, the four corners contain scenes illustrating the four seasons: winter (beating of the olive trees and duck hunting); summer (the grain harvest); spring (flowers); and autumn (the grape harvest and aquatic birds). But according to Veyne, the upper panel itself forms a coherent composition: the three standing figures are walking toward the woman in the center of the composition, bringing offerings. How can this spatial unity be reconciled with the temporal differentiation? By means of a symbolic interpretation. All the seasons are constantly bringing gifts. Similar symbolism occurs in the lower panel, which shows the noble couple ensconced in lush vegetation. He is seated with a stool under his foot, while she leans on her elbow next to a high-backed chair (cathedra), details indicating that the couple is actually inside the house. We are looking at an allegorical representation of the ceremonies in which dependents paid homage to their patron. What is symbolized is not simply clientele relations but economic dependence. There are the lord's coloni, peasants who were given a plot of land in exchange for a share of the produce. Here they are shown not paying rent per se but, according to Veyne's interpretation, bringing their masters the first fruits of the land, the forests, and the waters. (Corroboration of this religious dimension can be found in the fact that the mosaicist clearly indicates that the beating of the olive trees has only just begun, that the grain is still standing in the fields, and that the grapes are still on the vine.)

Examination of the xenia—representations of fruits, vegetables, and animals (familiar in Italic painting but a theme of African mosaic as well)—confirms Veyne's analysis. According to Vitruvius, such "still lifes" (which often contain not-so-still elements) depict the gifts that the master of the house bestows upon his guests. I have no reason to reject this interpretation, but it appears that in Africa (and it is unlikely that the phenomenon was purely local) these motifs carried a number of different meanings. The imagery often establishes a connection with the god Dionysus that transforms products of nature into symbols of fertility. This religious ideology is rooted, moreover, in a precise social context: the *xenia* are also, perhaps primarily, images of the first fruits offered to landlords by their coloni. Veyne's interpretation is bolstered

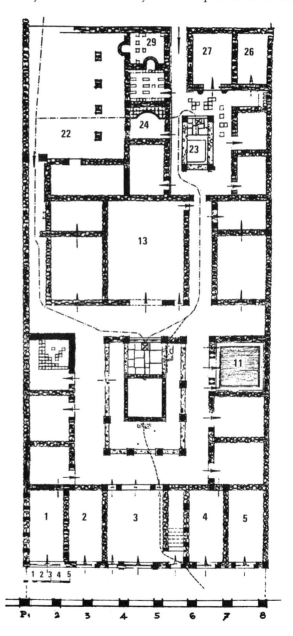

Fig. 29. Volubilis, house to the west of the governor's palace (Etienne, *Quartier nord-est,* plate VIII). Roughly axial plan. 1, 2, 4, and 5: shops (1 and 4 originally communicated with the house); 3: vestibule (24.1 x 19.6 feet) with triple bays leading to street and peristyle (the stairway probably served rented portions of the house); 11: exedra; 13: probably the triclinium, in this case especially large (38 x 26.2 feet), with service door at far end; 22: courtyard for wagons; 23: secondary peristyle serving dining room 27, whose entrance is set off by two embedded columns; 24: latrines (?); 26 and 29: baths (?).

by the floor of one of the bedrooms in the House of the Peacock at Thysdrus, whose four central tiles depict baskets filled with farm produce comparable to traditional *xenia* (fig. 32). These still lifes also symbolize the seasons, since each basket is filled with produce characteristic of one of the seasons. The message is the same as in the mosaic of Iulius, though here abstraction was preferred over allegorical social realism.

Such ceremonies, which occurred throughout the year, emphasized the power of the landlord, who alone was authorized to offer up to the gods the fruit of the community's labors. They also served as reminders of the rights of nobility. The colonate system frequently afforded the peasants a large measure of autonomy. Religion reasserted rights that the organization of labor tended to obscure or undermine. By according a leading role to the *dominus,* religion established his power beyond the reach of human controversy. In the mosaic of Iulius he is represented twice, once receiving visitors and once preparing to depart for the hunt. His wife also appears twice, and in a central role: receiving offerings. The peasant is clearly showing the master a scroll containing either a petition or his accounts. The master's wife is not relegated to the second rank. Is her presence essentially symbolic, signifying that she, too, is a landlord? Or is it a realistic portrayal of her functions, suggesting that she actually participated in these ceremonies designed to exalt the power of the nobility? An answer would throw a good deal of light on the nature of aristocratic marriage in the Late Empire, but unfortunately none is at hand. Whatever the woman's actual role, the mosaic shows that she did have a place in the management of the family estates. In this connection it is perhaps worth mentioning Apuleius' description of his future wife, "a businesslike woman [who verified] the accounts of farmers, ox-drivers, and lackeys" (*Apol.,* 87).

Great landlords needed rooms in their residences both for the daily visits of their clients and for other, less routine ceremonies. The exedra and the vestibule, as we have seen, were used for these purposes. R. Rebuffat has noted that in Tingitane it is common to find houses with a large room entered through a narrow door from the peristyle at a point close to the vestibule (see, for example, the House of the Train of Venus, fig. 27:3). He suggests that this was a storeroom for sportulae, a hypothesis which would confirm my own hypothesis that the vestibule was used for the reception of clients.

Some houses contained a room specifically set aside for ceremonial purposes having to do with patron-client relations; Vitruvius calls it the private basilica. I have already analyzed one of the most noteworthy examples of this type of room: the private basilica in the House of the Hunt at Bulla Regia, which, with its apse and transept (see figs. 7, 8), was well suited for public appearances by the *dominus*. There can be little question about the interpretation of the basilica in this case. The basilica, with its independent entry, occupies the better part of the new lot; nothing less would have been suitable. It is not always so easy to identify private basilicas. It is reasonable to assume that the long room near the secondary entrance of House Number 3 in Bulla Regia (fig. 40:B) is one. The presence of an apse, with sacred connotations that would have enhanced the master's image, is further evidence for this hypothesis. It is tempting to make a similar assumption about the large rectangular room in the House of Hermaphrodite at Timgad (fig. 25). Located near the main entrance, it communicates with the peristyle via the vast triclinium, separated from one of its two components by tripartite bays. What we have here may be a rather subtle architectural device, not without grandeur, for linking the peristyle with two different reception areas connoting two degrees of intimacy. Rather than cite other cases in which the interpretation of the architecture is open to doubt, let me cite a mosaic from Carthage that offers clear evidence of the presence of private basilicas in large houses. It depicts an ocean villa, one of whose parts is labeled *"bassilica."*

## Other Rooms

After the triclinium, few rooms are as readily identifiable as the bedrooms. They were among the more private parts of the house, and one might well apply to the noble African abode Corbin's description of the nineteenth-century bourgeois house, whose bedroom was a "temple of private life, an intimate space deep in the heart of the domestic sphere."[15] The sexual connotations of the bedroom were as obvious in Roman times as in other periods. It was here that the prevailing morality was most shockingly transgressed—a place of adultery, incest, and unnatural intercourse (Apuleius, *Metamorphoses,* IX, 20–X, 3, 20–22); opening the bedroom to strangers was the symbol of debauchery (Apuleius, *Apol.*, 75). Saint Augustine's words reveal the profoundly intimate nature of the *cubiculum.* In describing intense emotions, Augustine several times in the *Confessions* uses metaphors based on elements of domestic architecture, in which the bedroom is the most secret and personal of all the rooms in the house: "Then in this great contention of my inward dwelling, which I had strongly raised against my soul, in the chamber of my heart" (cum anima mea in cubiculo nostro, corde meo; VIII, 19). Or this prayer to God: "Speak Thou truly in my heart . . . and I will let them alone blowing upon the dust without, and raising it up into their own eyes: and myself will enter my chamber, and sing there a song of loves unto Thee; groaning with groanings unutterable in my wayfaring" (XII, 23).

The opulence and complexity of domestic architecture were often on display in the bedroom, for the lover "full of ardent hope" (Apuleius, *Metamorphoses,* VIII, 11) was not the only outsider who found his way there. It was customary to receive travelers, relatives, and people sent on the recommendation of a friend, so every noble house required guest rooms. These are quite difficult to identify in the ruins, but the sources prove that they did exist (for example, Apuleius, *Metamorphoses,* I, 23).

This brings me to the question of private baths. All the cities of Roman Africa were equipped with public baths. They played an important part in everyday life, being used not only

Fig. 30. Volubilis, House of the Labors of Hercules (Etienne, *Quartier nord-est,* plate IV). 1: vestibule (26.2 x 19.6 feet) with double bay facing the street (see fig. 16) and triple bay facing the peristyle (and a possible porter's lodge on the north side); 2: large reception hall (34.3 x 27.5 feet), triclinium or exedra, with four small service doors; 5: triclinium (23.6 x 16.4 feet) decorated with mosaic of Hercules' labors; 6 and 8–11: apartments with corridors and anterooms (note circular pool in room 10); 12 and 14: secondary entrances; 17–24: independent shops; 26–33: baths added during renovations.

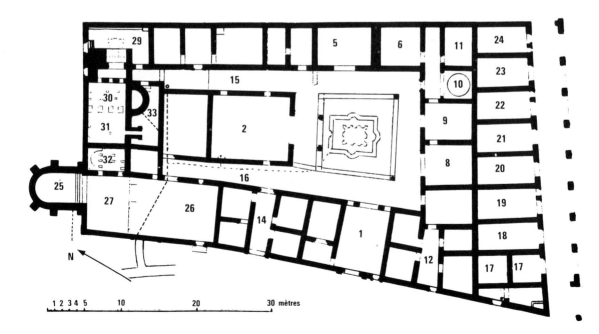

for bathing and related activities but also for physical exercise and intellectual activities. The public baths were a center of social life, if only by reason of their size, which made it possible to receive large numbers of users in rooms devoted to many different purposes. The pattern of use changed over time, and smaller neighborhood baths tended to be built as supplements to these vast edifices, possibly because the former were more convenient and accessible. There may also have been a change in customs, if we can believe the late Gallic author Sidonius Apollinaris, whose remarks appear to be applicable to Africa as well as to his native Gaul. He tells us that friends first gathered at a private home and then went to the baths, not to one of the large public baths but to a smaller establishment designed to respect each person's modesty (*Carmen*, XXIII, lines 495–499). The new attitude seems to reflect both the aristocratic need to stand apart from the crowd and a new, more modest attitude toward the human body.

These developments are relevant to understanding the proliferation of private baths in noble African homes. I feel justified in using the term "proliferation" because, although private baths had long been known, they seem to have become much more common in the late imperial period. Private baths were frequently added to existing houses or enlarged from smaller facilities, and eventually they became commonplace. Consider Bulla Regia: of the eight houses with peristyle that have been fully excavated, four were equipped with small baths. The baths of the House of the Hunt were built in the fourth century, at the same time as the private basilica.

The use of private baths tended to make the wealthy more independent of communal life, on which their comfort had earlier depended, at least in part. This development went hand in hand with increasing formalization of the social hierarchy. Could the man who in the morning sat enthroned in his private apse to receive dependents in the afternoon join those same dependents in the public swimming pool, without clothes to indicate his rank? Private baths made it possible to maintain the necessary social distance.

Some African houses were equipped with latrines, and for the same reason. In the House of the Hunt at Bulla Regia these were built after the first private baths (see figs. 8, 41). They replaced the original *frigidarium*, which was moved farther south. Similar two-hole latrines have been found in other houses; like public latrines, they could be used by more than one person at a time. But the group of persons admitted was now quite limited. The latrines were something new; previously chamber pots had to be used when it was inconvenient to go outside. The change probably reflects a new modesty, a new attitude toward bodily functions, sounds, and odors. Latrines in the House of the Hunt were supplied with a water flush that emptied directly into the sewer in the neighboring street. These architectural developments give us at best a limited idea of a change in ruling-class habits that is parallel, it would seem, to what Corbin dubbed the "deodorization" of the nineteenth-century bourgeoisie. The new attitude toward the body was directly related to the way in which power was asserted; henceforth there was greater distance between rulers and ruled and increasing hierarchy in social relations. The strictly regulated ceremonies in the private basilicas and the proliferation of private baths and latrines had a common cause. Once public acts became private, domestic space played an increasingly important role in public life; and, within the house, rooms were assigned increasingly specific functions.

In conclusion, I want to say a few words concerning parts of the home about which little is known. We do not know what many of the rooms found in the remains of African houses were used for. The service rooms, particularly kitchens, are hard to identify, which proves that they housed relatively simple operations and depended on large staffs to serve such magnificent meals. The sources tell us a great deal about this. Apuleius says that one of the master's most important jobs is to command the *familia* (*Apol.*, 98). The mistress of the house never went out without an escort of several servants (*Metamorphoses,* II, 2). A well-bred lady would have been served by several *cubicularii* (X, 28), and her husband would have employed several chefs (X, 13). Add the pedagogue (X, 5), and you gain some idea of the size of the household staff. But we know next to nothing about where in the house such people lived. The most favored servants probably lived in the upper stories, now in ruins. Two brothers, slaves who worked as chefs, lived in a small room (*cellula*), but it was large enough to house an ass in addition to themselves (Apuleius, *Metamorphoses,* X, 13–16). More commonly, servants kept their belongings in bags and slept on cots that could be moved as the occasion warranted. When Lucius, the hero of the *Metamorphoses,* is visiting a friend and needs to be alone in his room, the bed of the slave traveling with him is removed from the room and placed in another corner of the house (*Metamorphoses,* II, 15).

Fig. 31. Thugga, peristyle of trifolium house.

# &#x211B; How the Domus Worked

W E cannot understand how a building works without knowing how its parts are arranged. It has long been customary to distinguish three types of floor plan, based on the location of the vestibule relative to the peristyle and triclinium. When all three line up along a single axis we refer to an "axial plan." When the three axes are parallel but do not coincide we speak of a "bayonette plan." And when the vestibule is at right angles to the main axis of the house we have an "orthogonal plan."

*The Overall Arrangement*

This typology has little to do with the functioning of the house, and it is not as easy to apply as it might appear. There is sometimes little to distinguish between an axial and a bayonette plan. The house west of the Governor's Palace (fig. 29) has been described both ways. Other buildings are even harder to classify. The House of the Hunt at Bulla Regia (fig. 8) can be said to have an axial (or bayonette) plan if we focus on the vestibule, the secondary peristyle, and the triclinium—or an orthogonal plan if we focus on the vestibule, the principal peristyle, and the exedra. But this typology tells us nothing about the way in which the various components of the house relate to one another. In any case, the axial plan, broadly construed, was widely used in African domestic architecture. This arrangement of the principal public rooms of the house in a series seems to have been well suited to the reception of large numbers of guests.

The arrangement of public reception areas was an important aspect of house design. The public spaces established the overall shape of the house and determined the location of the more intimate rooms. The master's social requirements shaped the overall design, and architecture and decoration underscored the house's basic plan. Builders had at their disposal a repertoire of techniques in which sequences of architectural elements culminated in crucial points: columns or pillars (porticoes and tripartite bays), basins, and mosaics all reinforced the principal axes of the house. (Stairways were of secondary importance in African homes.) In the House of Neptune at Acholla (fig. 15) the relation between the bays of the *oecus* and the colonnade of the peristyle is underscored by the apses traced by the low walls of the courtyard. The principal axis, that of the dining room, is emphasized by the interruption of the portico mosaic—a new motif fills the hiatus—and by the treatment of the central basin, which is larger, deeper, and more ornate than the others. Many similar examples could be cited. Builders strove to emphasize the axis of one of the main rooms of the house and to exploit the ample colonnade of the peristyle. This type of sequence could be carried to grand proportions indeed in houses with an axial plan: the central axis became the backbone of the entire edifice. This is so in the House of the Train of Venus in Volubilis (fig. 27), where the visitor passed through two bipartite entries before coming to the tripartite compositions: two columns on dies outlined three bays opening onto the peristyle, whose colonnade, aligned with the walls of the vast triclinium, had three intercolumniations on the short side indicating the three entrances to the dining room. The composition was further enhanced by a long axial basin and by the mosaic floor, depicting animals in harness, which led to the central bay of the triclinium. The decoration, which grew richer as one penetrated deeper into the building (with a panel depicting the Navigation of Venus as the decorative centerpiece of the dining room), reinforced the ascending motif embodied in the architecture: the transition from a binary to a ternary rhythm, the greater size of the portico preceding the triclinium as compared with the three other porticoes, and the location of the largest room in the house at the far end of the composition. The entire house is arrayed around the central axis, which determined the residual spaces where other rooms might be located.

The routing of traffic through the house was perhaps the most important design consideration. Here the peristyle played an important part. The principal peristyle was frequently complemented by subsidiary areas that served the same purpose, sometimes true minor peristyles, sometimes

simple courts without colonnades, possibly embellished by a
fountain or garden. The rooms of the house were arrayed
around these primary and secondary central courts, and corridors often led to rooms situated some distance away. The
rooms of the house were rarely arranged in a series. Each was
independent of the others, accessible from the common areas
that bore the brunt of household traffic.

A few examples will help to clarify these general principles. In the original House of the Asclepiae at Althiburos
(fig. 17), all the rooms were accessible from the entry or
through the peristyle. In the House of the Peacock at Thysdrus
two galleries flank the vast reception hall, serving apartments
arrayed around the courtyards. In the adjacent Sollertiana Domus (fig. 23) the design is similar. Here an antechamber protected the privacy of rooms located just off a heavily trafficked
area like the peristyle (room 5 serves as antechamber to room
4 and bedroom 6). This arrangement is also found in the House
of the Labors of Hercules at Volubilis (fig. 30), where three
rooms (6, 10, 11) are isolated from the peristyle by an antechamber in the form of a corridor. In this huge house traffic
is also organized by two corridors (12 and 14) that link the

Fig. 32. Thysdrus, House
of the Peacock: mosaic in
bedroom 9 (see fig. 23).

Fig. 33. Utica, House of the Cascade. Peristyle with fountain-pool and garden.

peristyle to the street, and by two long galleries (15 and 16) flanking the large triclinium, the first of which leads to the bedrooms, the second to the private baths. Many houses in Volubilis contain secondary peristyles, which serve as central courts to more private sections of the house, often entered via corridors. The House West of the Governor's Palace (fig. 29) has a colonnaded courtyard (23) with basin that serves eight rooms. In the House with the Trefoil Basin (fig. 26) the two peristyles are linked by extending the southern portico of one to become the northern portico of the other, using a checkerboard plan that made the southeastern corner of the building independent of the rest of the house. In the House of the Train of Venus (fig. 27) a secondary courtyard with a basin of complex design (12) gives access to five rooms, two of which (16, 17) were decorated with beautiful mosaic floors and contained, on low brick columns, bronze busts of Cato and a crowned prince. The House of the Gold Coins, at 17,000 square feet one of the largest in Volubilis (fig. 28), had corridors running all around the triclinium and a small courtyard with basin and fountain (30) around which several rooms were placed.

The systematic use of peristyles, courtyards, and corridors ensured that all rooms would be independent of one another. Does this prove, as is often asserted, that great houses had a public portion (the reception rooms arrayed around the principal peristyle) and a private portion (apartments arrayed around a secondary central court)? The statement as such is not true. I have already called attention to the existence of many different kinds of rooms around the principal peristyle; those around the secondary courtyard were equally heterogeneous. The House of the Hunt at Bulla Regia (fig. 8) is a good example. Off the main peristyle is a single reception hall, while two large dining rooms open onto the two levels of the smaller peristyle. What is striking about this house is the way private rooms and reception rooms are interspersed around both central areas. In the houses in Volubilis just discussed the size and decor of certain rooms around the secondary courtyards suggest that they were not intended exclusively for the use of family members. The House of the Peacock and the Sollertiana Domus at Thysdrus (fig. 23:7, 3) reveal a similar design: a triclinium and an exedra are located off secondary courtyards.

Corridors and peristyles served not to separate "public" and "private" sections of the home but to permit the placing of different kinds of rooms next to each other by affording independent access. This subtle carving up of the available space shaped the way the domus worked.

---

The time of day affected the way in which different parts of the house were used. Clients visited in the morning; the master had guests to dinner in the evening. In between, a central area like the peristyle could be reserved for household and leisure activities. Although no traces of such a division of use remain, signs of other arrangements can still be observed in the ruins.

Roman houses, like modern ones, contained a great many doors. It was almost always possible to close off access to a room. In some well-preserved sites we can still see where doors were affixed to the masonry and sills or attached to wood frames whose mounting grooves are all that remain. Few entrances lack such devices. Even the vast bays of the great reception halls could be closed. The triclinium was opened for the evening feast, but the rest of the day this huge room was shut up, cut off from the rest of the house. There are even doors between flights of stairs, and traces of gates that controlled the flow of traffic between the porticoes and

*Subdivision of Interior Space*

the courtyard of the peristyle can be found. This systematic compartmentalization greatly increased the efficiency of the house, which was designed to facilitate independent access to all rooms.

Hangings were used in place of doors and above all to break up large volumes; traces of them are obviously harder to find than traces of doors. Drapes and curtains determined how a space like the peristyle was used. Curtains blocked spaces between colonnade columns and closed off porticoes (fig. 43). This efficient way of regulating light and heat also allowed the peristyle to be used simultaneously for different purposes without destroying its architectural unity, which derived essentially from the colonnade. It is easy to imagine the guests at a reception in the triclinium looking out through the open doors of that vast hall into the peristyle and enjoying the view, while curtains preserved the privacy of a wing of the court and prevented those not participating in the festivities from being disturbed.

The use of fabric hangings changed as society evolved.

Fig. 34. Thugga, "Omnia tibi felicia" house, peristyle: courtyard with mosaic floor surrounded by jardinieres.

As social relations became increasingly hierarchical, hangings were used to dramatize the importance of a house's owner. The higher a man's rank, the more hangings he had in his home, says Augustine (*Sermon,* LI, 5). The bishop of Hippo mentions the raised apse and throne draped with rich fabric on which the bishop sat, in a display of pomp comparable to that of a patron receiving his clients. Apuleius describes a ceremony of the Isiac cult in which white curtains are arranged on either side of the statue of Isis (*Metamorphoses,* XI, 20). It is clear that religious ceremonies, both pagan and Christian, as well as ceremonies in which aristocrats received the homage of their dependents, all grew out of the same matrix, the most sophisticated product of which was the complex ceremonial ritual that gradually developed around the sovereign, the center of late imperial society, who embraced both its political and religious aspects. This point is important for an understanding of private architecture. Draperies were no substitute, no mere convenient alternative to walls and doors, but key elements of architectural design. Curtains were not meant to be pushed aside as they are today. They barred the way, blocked passage. The curtain was the mask of all that was most powerful: the emperor, the godhead, the nobility. The sacred significance of curtains had great influence on the way they were used; it took less audacity to open a door than to raise a drawn curtain.

In the Late Empire the vast spaces of the traditional house were usually divided up. The existence of the peristyle was not fundamentally challenged, but it was divided in such a way that its functioning was altered. There were two complementary approaches: to separate the court from the porticoes and to interfere with the coherence of the galleries. The changes are evident in the decor. At the House of Neptune in Acholla (fig. 15) the floors on all four sides have the same geometric motif, but the composition was interrupted so as to separate the gallery in front of the oecus from the other three galleries. This decorative decision reflected other architectural choices: the gallery, which extended well beyond the peristyle, was separated from it in the same way. The decoration of the House of the Train of Venus in Volubilis (fig. 27) was similar. The mosaic floors of the porticoes broke the unity of the courtyard and emphasized the axial composition instead.

The architecture of the peristyle changed in even more striking ways. At a rather late but hard-to-pinpoint date a low wall was built between the columns of the colonnade, high enough to swallow up the lower portion of the columns. Usually this wall replaced a less substantial partition, which often consisted of nothing more than tiles standing on end, and underscored the separation between courtyard and galleries. Another device was to adorn the porticoes with niches, apses, sometimes even small rooms, considerably complicating a space that was once quite simple and allowing it to stand on its own. At the Sollertiana Domus in Thysdrus (fig. 23) the northern corridor has a small apse at one end; in the House of Dionysus and Ulysses at Thugga (fig. 42), one side of the peristyle has been hollowed out and filled with niches. The House of the Masks at Hadrumetum (figs. 21, 22) reveals still another approach: the uncovered portion of the peristyle is surrounded by a low wall and set below the porticoes, from which it is separated by a narrow gallery pitched at an intermediate height. This distinguishes the different parts of the peristyle from one another.

Culminating this evolutionary trend, rooms simply annexed the porticoes to which they were adjacent. The House of the New Hunt at Bulla Regia (fig. 8) is particularly instructive, because we can be fairly confident of the dates at which changes occurred. During the second half of the fourth century the owner changed the mosaic floors in the triclinium and adjacent portico. That both floors were changed was no coincidence. When the mosaic of the exedra was later altered, not before the end of the fourth century, the floors in the eastern and southern galleries were also replaced. The renovations were completed later, probably during the fifth century: the mosaic of the eastern corridor was extended at the expense of the southern floor, and the space thus obtained was enclosed by a wall pierced by two bays with doors. At the same time no doubt an identical partition was built at the other end of the peristyle, whose southern and western galleries are separated by a wall through which runs a bay framed by molded jambs on which hinge mountings are still visible. What was left after all this work was no longer a unified, central space (a court surrounded by porticoes onto which various rooms opened) but a series of compartmentalized volumes, the main rooms of which simply annexed the porticoes and used them as vestibules (see figs. 44, 45).

Examination of the relationship of the western portico to the court confirms this analysis. The two are separated by a high wall capped by a course of large stones that may have supported another, lighter partition. The openings onto the

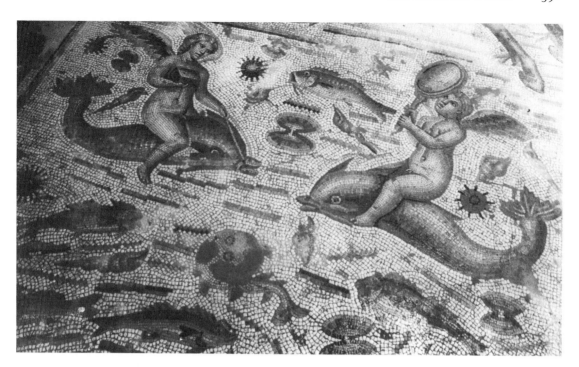

Fig. 35. Bulla Regia, House of
Amphitriton: detail of mosaic
in triclinium.

courtyard seemed unimportant enough that a trough of no
aesthetic value was placed in such a way as to obstruct the
space between two of the columns. Even the basin situated in
the second intercolumnar opening establishes no visual relationship with the courtyard: holes in its lip supported a trellis.
This apse-fountain was merely an annex to the portico, which
exploited the courtyard's light without establishing any link
with the open space beyond.

In a sense, if the house with peristyle represented an
advance over the house with just a plain courtyard, the evolution of the noble abode not just in Africa but in other
provinces as well tended to come full circle, back to the original conception. The gain was not negligible, however: the
colonnades remained, although encumbered as they were by
numerous enclosures, it was hard to appreciate their rhythm.
Significantly, the principal rooms obtained annexes that enhanced their majesty.

What is the meaning of this tendency to compartmentalize
domestic interiors? It may have been a response to the fact
that adjacent rooms served very different purposes. This answer is unsatisfactory, however. The available room played a
part. The peristyle was opulent architecture; it required a great

deal of space and paid off only in very large houses. Maybe the residents of the House of the New Hunt found living space rather cramped, which would have made it easier to give up the luxury of a classical peristyle. This argument is not totally convincing, given that the enclosure of the porticoes increased the size of public reception halls, not of private rooms. It seems, rather, that domestic space underwent a drastic change, and I am afraid that in many cases excavation may have eliminated ancient walls mistakenly identified as late additions. They were late additions in a sense, yet part of the evolution of domestic space rather than signs of decadence. It remains to be seen what this evolution meant. It may be useful to consider the parceling up of the vast central space of many homes in light of what I said earlier about the proliferation of private baths and latrines. Houses became increasingly independent of communal facilities, while at the same time their interiors were further compartmentalized and specialized. Both developments were probably related to an idea that gained currency in the Late Empire: the idea of the individual. Increasing hierarchy in social relations, divinization of authority, and greater emphasis on personal modesty are various aspects of a single phenomenon, perhaps most succinctly characterized as a regression of rationality and nakedness in the face of "mystery" in all its various forms. This was the climate in which the peristyle, a coherent space with a variety of functions, was divided up and transformed into a suite of adjoining rooms.

## The Message of the Architecture

The design of individual rooms and the overall organization of a building, taken together, emphasized the power of its owner and provided a prestigious background against which he played his assigned social role. Not until the Renaissance do we find in Western cities such a large number of private homes so clearly designed to allow their owners to live luxuriously while meeting the obligations incumbent upon men of high rank.

The significance of the surroundings is emphasized by the decor. Only in rare cases do we know how walls and ceilings were decorated, so our attention must focus primarily on the mosaic floors. These were immovable decorations, usually assembled on the property, and hence inseparable from their architectural setting. Vitruvius emphasizes that a room's decor must be adapted to its purpose; he might well have added that its sumptuousness must be strictly in keeping with the importance of the room.

This brings us to a theoretical issue: What was the owner's role in deciding how the house ought to be decorated? Was there a decorative "program"? The two questions are related, and most contemporary scholars answer both negatively. The owner, we are told, had little to do with the choice of decorative motifs; mosaicists had a repertoire of designs from which the homeowner had to choose. The designs had little symbolic significance, and it is wrong to "overinterpret" themes that at most referred vaguely to a cultural heritage shared by everyone and expressive of no one in particular.

These arguments are welcome correctives to the torrent of speculation set loose by some of the more fascinating mosaics, speculation which, though ingenious, goes far beyond the evidence. But the corrective also goes too far. It accords to the ancient artist-artisan a role he never played. The man who commissioned the work played the decisive role. He decided what themes interested him, perhaps even the way in which they were to be treated. We need only consider how

Fig. 36. Dionysus and Ariadne. (Mosaic of Thuburbo Maius, Tunis, Bardo Museum.)

Fig. 37. Funerary mosaic from Thina. (Museum of Sfax.)

the style and motifs of the mosaics evolved in parallel with other social developments and, more specifically, with the new needs of the late imperial ruling class. The idea that an illustration has meaning and is not chosen without reason cannot be rejected out of hand merely because it is "obvious."

Decor employing scenes from pagan mythology raises the issue in a particularly acute form. It has been fashionable of late to argue that such scenes in no way reflected owners' religious leanings. We are told that mythological subjects are the sterile remains of a "culture," in the most banal sense of the word. But the argument anticipates what would occur several centuries later, when Christianity, by then dominant, would adapt for its own use scattered elements of a disintegrated but still prestigious ancient culture. In late imperial times, however, the political, cultural, and religious situation was different. Although it is denied that pagan mosaics have any religious significance, no one would consider using the same argument about mosaics with Christian motifs; it would make sense to treat pagan themes so differently from Christian ones only if Christianity had been the only religion in the Late Empire. Similarly, it is frequently asserted that the juxtaposition of Christian and pagan mosaics proves that the latter had lost all meaning. How, then, can we explain why some pagan mosaics were deliberately destroyed? In one recently

Fig. 38. Bulla regia, House of the New Hunt, seen from the east. Foreground: exedra; in background, beyond peristyle: triclinium.

Fig. 39. Mosaic of Iulius from Carthage. (Tunis, Bardo Museum.)

excavated building in Mactar in central Tunisia a marine mosaic decorating a basin and a mosaic of Venus decorating a fountain (fig. 46) were both covered over with a layer of cement; all signs suggest that this destructive act was the work of Christians. Given the way in which the Christian religion spread, it is not surprising that we find pagan and Christian motifs side by side. Christianity was not the cause of a radical mutation in society and individuals; its growing popularity is but one sign of a broad evolutionary process. It was this evolutionary process that brought Christianity to the fore, not the other way around. Apart from a minority for whom conversion to Christianity was a spiritual revolution and a dramatic change in practice, the new beliefs did not replace the old as much as they were added to them. The practice of juxtaposing mosaics with incompatible motifs must be viewed against this background, and it is not by chance that private homes are an ideal place for observing the way in which different attitudes coexisted. Owners were freer at home to exhibit their personal convictions than they were elsewhere. Augustine vehemently attacked the view that a man is fully a king in his own home (*Sermons, 224, 3*). All men, regardless of religious belief, believed at this time that the world was in the grip of malevolent demons. While it was up to the city to defend the community at large, it was up to each man to protect his own home. Accordingly, many people set alongside the Penates and other pagan deities the symbols of another religion that claimed to offer protection and cited miracles in support of its claim. It would be far more surprising if the head of a family had deliberately and definitively renounced any guarantee of well-being. People did not change their view of the world because they became Christians; they became Christians because they changed their view of the world. The transitional period was inevitably quite long.

The extreme scarcity of overtly Christian motifs in the late mosaics of wealthy African homes is striking. One has to wonder whether Christianity penetrated the African ruling class very deeply until quite late, the fifth century at the earliest. It is as if African notables, remote from the central government and its political and religious dictates, were able to maintain both a culture that was essentially classical and a religion that was essentially traditional until quite late. The private house, once the ideal place for expressing these religious and cultural attitudes, eventually became the only place where they could be expressed at all.

Although it is risky to ask mosaics more than they are prepared to tell, it is foolish not to ask them anything at all. There may be proof that a mosaic was intended to convey a message explicitly intended by its owner. A house in Smirat in Tunisia has a mosaic commemorating the public benefaction of one Magerius, who paid for games in the amphitheater.[16] The names of the gladiators and leopards that took part in the contest are listed in legends. Dionysus, Diana, and Magerius himself presided over these games, and a central figure in the mosaic is shown carrying cash prizes to the victors. This figure is wreathed with an inscription that proves that the mosaic

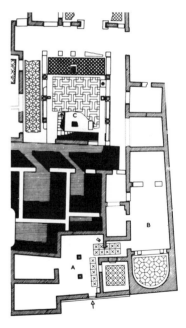

Fig. 40. Bulla Regia, House no. 3 (see fig. 6). Another house with underground rooms, partially excavated. A: secondary entrance; B: private basilica; C: peristyle.

Fig. 41. Bulla Regia, House
of the Hunt: private latrines,
photographed from the south.

commemorated a specific event, not some sort of symbolic
contest. The text tells how Magerius, cheered by the crowd,
rewarded the participants in a manner likely to remain in the
memory of all who witnessed and hailed his magnificent generosity: "That is what it means to be rich! That is what it
means to be powerful!" The famous day was immortalized in
mosaic for the greater glory of the master of the house.

The link between mosaic decoration and events in a family's history can also be seen in the House of Castorius at
Cuicul (fig. 19), where some mosaics carry inscriptions. Two

Fig. 42. Thugga: western portico of House of Dionysus and Ulysses.

Fig. 43. Mosaic from Carthage showing portico with draperies.

are well enough preserved to be intelligible. The first, located in the eastern portico, is wreathed by a crown of laurels and in all probability celebrates the owner of the house, one Castorius, who undertook to repair some of the floors. We do not know when Castorius or his ancestors acquired this house with peristyle, one of the finest in the area, but the quality of the mosaics for which he takes credit suggests a lower level of wealth and culture than such a setting would lead one to expect. Does this indicate the decline of a family or an entire neighborhood or a social class? The second inscription, though damaged, confirms this impression and offers a striking example of the social pretensions of what we might today call the "middle class." The inscription reads: "This house [*haec domus*] is the home of these illustrious young men . . . distinguished, they are clerks in the courts of fortunate *Lybia* . . . happy are the parents so blessed."[17] The office in question was unimportant, even if it does suggest that these sons of a well-to-do family had found employment in the entourage of the provincial governor. This desire to exalt a relatively minor accomplishment recalls a passage in Augustine's *Confessions* (II, 5), in which he describes his father's efforts to enable him

Fig. 44. Bulla Regia, House of the New Hunt: eastern portico photographed from the south.

to continue his studies: "After my return from Madaura (a neighbor city whither I had journeyed to learn grammar and rhetoric), the expenses for a further journey to Carthage were being provided for me; and that, rather by the resolution than the means of my father, who was but a poor freeman of Thagaste . . . Who did not extol my father, for that beyond the ability of his means, he would furnish his son with all necessaries for a far journey for his studies' sake? For many far abler citizens did no such thing for their children."

Fig. 45. Bulla Regia, House of the New Hunt: western portico, photographed from the south.

There were more modest but no less effective ways to exalt the splendor of the domus. Responding to a need for aristocratic propaganda, mosaicists in the Late Empire created new themes, in particular those involving great hunting scenes. All the many variations on this theme depict the *dominus* and his friends on horseback hunting a variety of animals with the help of numerous servants, who handle the dogs, set traps, retrieve game, and dispose of the remains.

Houses were thus decorated with scenes of aristocratic enjoyment. The economic consequences of these amusements were not negligible, and the occasions themselves were a good opportunity for men to get together. (Unlike women in some societies, Roman women were excluded from the hunt.) That

Fig. 46. Mactar, House of Venus. Mosaic of Venus. (Museum of Mactar.)

the owner was intimately involved in the decoration of his house is often attested by legends inscribed beneath these hunting scenes, which indicate the names of the master's dogs and horses; it is hard to believe that these were merely conventional.

Yet these images were not just realistic; they were also, in an essential way, symbolic, a social manifesto: the superiority of the dominus and his companions was indicated by their equipment (only they are on horseback, for instance), their activity (they confront the animal, while their servants only help out or trap living game), and their costume. Despite the strenuousness of hunting, masters wear the gaudy clothing that was one of the primary external manifestations of power in the Late Empire. Physical exercise was not allowed to perturb the vestimentary display, "which reveals each man's rank" (Augustine, *De doctr. christ.*, II, 25). Even when thrown from the saddle a dominus remained a dominus, immediately recognizable as such (fig. 47).

The mythical dimension given the hunt in these mosaics amplified their social message. The allusion was sometimes direct. In a mosaic from the city of Uthina, close to the site of present-day Tunis, the mosaicist has depicted an estate that is the scene of farming as well as hunting. One of the hunters who, armed with a spear, confronts a boar is shown nude, that is, in the manner of a mythical hero. He is being compared to Meleager, vanquisher of the monstrous boar that wreaked havoc on the fields of his city.

Apart from funerary art, metaphors of this kind were not

Fig. 47. Bulla Regia: detail of mosaic in the triclinium of the House of the New Hunt.

popular, probably because they deprived the master of the external tokens that had become an essential ingredient of power. But hunting scenes could be used to glorify the owner of a house by establishing an analogy between him and the emperor. Skill in hunting had long been one of the ways in which the *imperator* manifested his *virtus,* the essential quality that guaranteed prosperity—a gift of the gods. To overcome an animal's strength and savagery by means of stamina, intelligence, and skill became one of the signs of power. This may have been artistic rhetoric, but the ideology had concrete embodiments: Commodius did not hesitate to descend into the arena to fire arrows at lions pitted against him.

The aristocracy, by decorating its houses with scenes of hunting and its risks (accidents were often portrayed), turned this imperial ideology to its own advantage. Lion-hunting was a monopoly of the emperor, so aristocrats had to settle for confronting boars or chasing hares and jackals. Yet on occasion nobles were represented in battles worthy of an emperor, as in the mosaic of the triclinium of the House of the New Hunt at Bulla Regia, in which we see not only boars but such wild animals as a panther (fig. 49) and two lions.

Study of the decor of aristocratic houses in Africa leads to a more general question of political organization. How was power distributed from echelon to echelon? The prince, model of all forms of power, left his mark on the lower echelons as well. But did his inferiors confine themselves to respectful imitation, or were they potential rivals? Clearly the owner of the (relatively modest) House of the New Hunt did not aspire to the throne. The lions in his triclinium were not usurped imperial symbols; more likely they referred to a favor that the emperor often granted to African nobles: permission to hunt the imperial animal (*Theodosian Code,* XV, 11, 1). Perhaps it was because the owner of the House of the Dionysiac Procession at Thysdrus lacked this privilege that he was obliged to decorate his triclinium with a mosaic showing animals attacking other animals (fig. 48) rather than succumbing to his own skill as hunter.

Simply to ask whether such representations were or were not illicit avoids more fundamental issues. On the one hand, imperial power, whose mystical dimension grew steadily over the centuries, was the only possible model for other kinds of power. On the other hand, the very fact that the basis of imperial power became more and more mystical and irrational made it fragile and encouraged competition. In the end was

Detail of mosaic of Smirat (see page 112): the servant delivers four bags of a thousand denarii each, one for each leopard killed.

victory not the only justification of power? The scenes of lion-hunting that decorate so many private homes express this ambivalent attitude toward an eminently public problem, that of power. Bear in mind that on several occasions the African aristocracy either threw its welcome support to the reigning emperor or produced its own candidates for the throne.[18] Notables built homes that allowed them to live everywhere not just in the Roman manner but as veritable local emperors. In the vast majority of cases they intended nothing more than respectful imitation of the model par excellence. Nevertheless, ambiguity was always present; in the long run it was surely important that the aristocracy conceived of its local power as a mirror of the central power, down to matters of imagery and ceremonial.

Fig. 48. Thysdrus, mosaic from triclinium of House of the Dionysiac Procession. (Museum of El Jem.)

# ✒ Conclusion

T HE private home was an essential element of social life, and the word *domus,* which means "house," especially a sumptuous house, also connoted related matters, such as the family. People and their dwellings were indistinguishable: domus referred not only to the walls but also to the people within them. Evidence for this is found in inscriptions and texts, in which the word refers now to one, now to the other, but most often to both at once, to the house and its residents envisioned as an indivisible whole. The architectural setting was not an inert vessel; the *genius* of the domus, honored by a cult, was the protector of both the place and the people who lived in it. The idea of the domus thus draws on religious, social, and economic sources. It is an enduring structure, sustained by a material base and an accompanying ideology. The great families of Africa, like those of Italy, worshiped their ancestors and the past. Past events were commemorated in paintings (Apuleius, *Metamorphoses,* VI, 29); certain mosaics served the same purpose. Moreover, a workshop has been unearthed in Thysdrus in which death masks were made. Obviously the practice of maintaining portrait galleries of ancestors was not unknown in Africa. The domus, then, struck roots into the past. For this reason the term could be stretched to signify "the fatherland."

We must not exaggerate the strength of the bond between house and family. In the upper reaches of the elite, career and business affairs could take a man to the far corners of the Empire, and houses had long been commodities bought, remodeled, and sold according to the professional and family needs and wealth of the owner. Wealthy notables usually owned not one old house filled with memories but a number of different residences.

We have little reliable information about how owners' attitudes toward their homes may have changed over extended periods of time. Only in rare cases do we know the names of a series of owners of a given property, and in no case can we follow the way in which the property was transmitted from generation to generation. This ignorance is but one aspect of an even more glaring deficiency: our lack of knowledge concerning the way in which the social elite reproduced itself. How much new blood was admitted into the elite in each new generation, and how much of a part was played by inherited wealth? On occasion epigraphs enable us to reconstitute a family's genealogy and the network of relations thereby created, especially as that network relates to matrimonial strategy; yet it is difficult to know whether these cases are typical or exceptional. At any rate, it is difficult to tie whatever conclusions one draws from this still fragmentary research to the archaeological remains.

For the time being we must content ourselves with speculating about the relationship between the few families whose histories we know fairly completely and the ruins of sumptuous houses. Architectural programs were very ambitious. Although the size of houses varied considerably, the similarity of architectural and decorative principles shows that the ambition remained the same. Whatever their actual power, members of the elite patterned their private dwellings after a single model.

The organization of space within the home also follows a fixed model. Given the wide range of activities that the Romans classified as "private," it was necessary to provide a number of rooms intended for different purposes and to take great care in establishing the way in which these rooms related to one another. A key role was assigned to the peristyle, not only as an element of architectural composition but also as a device for organizing activity within the home. The multiplicity of its functions reflects the diversity of private activities. The colonnaded courtyard typifies the aristocratic home. Complemented by corridors and anterooms, the peristyle contributed in a major way to the solution of an apparently insoluble problem: how to provide a homogeneous space suitable for heterogeneous activities. These contradictory requirements could have produced at worst an incoherent hodgepodge, at best a mere juxtaposition of "public" and "private" areas. Fortunately builders and their clients were able to transcend the contradictions and create a unified space that faithfully mirrored the African elite.

Fig. 49. Another detail of the mosaic in the triclinium of the House of the New Hunt (see also fig. 47).

Manuscript, 9th century. Emperor Charlemagne and his son Pepin, king of Italy, each holding the scepter of justice and wearing a sword, jointly preside over a tribunal. Below, a cleric seated before an open law book, with a reed pen in one hand and a knife in the other, prepares to record their judgment. (Modena, Capitulary Library.)

# ❧ 4 ❧

# The Early Middle Ages
# in the West

Michel Rouche

Face of Merovingian gold coin worth a third of a solidus and struck at Toulouse in the early 7th century. The coin is copied from a Roman model showing Romulus and Remus suckled by a wolf, illustrating the survival of Roman influence, particularly in Aquitania. The coin was struck by the minter Magnus. (Paris, Bibliothèque Nationale, Cabinet des Médailles.)

# Introduction

*by Paul Veyne*

THREE centuries have passed. Clovis was baptized in 496 and received the insignia of a consul of Rome (that is, of Byzantium, capital of the Roman Empire minus its western provinces, which were occupied by barbarians). In the West, at the dawn of the modern age, the Greco-Roman world was no more. As Machiavelli said, "Men, who had been called Caesar and Pompey, now became Johns and Peters and Matthews." In the Byzantine East the Roman system remained intact until Hellenism emerged as sole master.

The West was barbarized—not so much through the blows dealt by the Germans, great admirers of Roman grandeur, as in reaction to their assumption of political power. Humiliated by loss of power, the old aristocracy of notables, the city fathers and civil servants of old Empire, found that life no longer held meaning for them. They gave up the ghost and thereby lost what had made Roman society "civilized": its unconscious desire for self-stylization. Only the Church, for its own ends, retained something of that desire.

Barbarism or culture? Societies called barbarian have a culture; those called civilized give themselves one with great effort—for better or worse. Puritanical, aesthetic, highly militarized, and capitalist free-enterprise societies are all "civilized." The drama of the great invasions lay not in the collapse of the imperial apparatus or in the realms of economics or demography but in the obliteration of hitherto crucial social distinctions: between those who read and those who do not, for example, or between those trained to work hard and those not obliged to undergo such training. Such transformations of self are not wrought by schools or other institutions, which are really effects rather than causes, but by what is called, quite inappropriately, education. Education occurs when a social group that seeks unwittingly to adopt a distinctive style influences the behavior of its members. But at the first sign that the older generation does not practice what it preaches, the younger generation ceases to heed its elders. The sermons of the elders must be backed by real authority if they are to be believed.

In the West, with the great invasions of the fifth century, that authority vanished, a tradition of self-stylization came to an end, and what we sometimes call the "Dark Ages" began. The existence of a civilized culture, of deliberate self-cultivation, is thus an anthropological fact, a characteristic feature of certain societies; like any tradition, it cannot be taught or imposed by force. Culture has nothing to do with what some censorious people like to think of as hard work and strict upbringing. Culture needs to be saved from its friends: no deliberate effort can substitute for the realities of power or compensate for humiliation. The transformation of self, when effective, is not demanding work. It is rather like an ambition, a game, a luxury, even a form of snobbery. Some people, no matter what they say, detest culture not merely for its class content, but because it works against nature.

# ☙ Historical Introduction

I N 584 King Chilperic had a son, whom he had "brought up in the manor of Vitry, for he was afraid that, if he appeared in public, some harm might befall him and he might even be killed."[1] In a few words, Gregory, bishop of Tours, gives us an accurate indication of the atmosphere in which private life in the early Middle Ages unfolded. Something of importance had just happened to the king: a son had been born to him. Only a male child was worthy of interest. Nothing is said about the child's mother, whose name we do not know. Perhaps she was a concubine. No sooner was the child born than the king sent him from the city (in this case, Cambrai) to the country, where he lived with his nurse. Childhood, years of fragility, had to be spent hidden away lest some harm come to pass. The world was such a threatening place! The birth had scarcely taken place before the father's thoughts had turned to death. And indeed, of Chilperic's five children only this one, the future Clotaire II, would survive. With his help we already have a sense of what private life was like in the early Middle Ages: it was a life of love, violence, anguish, and death, for all its pretense of bucolic happiness.

   Private life assumed much greater importance in the Middle Ages than it had in Roman antiquity. The eclipse of the city by the countryside is the most striking proof of this. The joy of living, once cultivated in urban streets and buildings, now took refuge in rude houses, even huts. The Empire had held up public life as an ideal, promoted by its laws, its troops, and its aediles. But in the age of the Germanic kingdoms the cult of urbanity collapsed, and private life took its place. For the newcomers, the Germans, practically everything fell within the private domain.

Reverse of Merovingian gold coin worth a third of a solidus and struck at Toulouse in the early 7th century. Like the coin shown on page 412, this copies a Roman model, but a Christian rather than a pagan one. The man wears a helmet and laurel wreath and carries a triumphal cross in his hand. (Paris, Bibliothèque Nationale, Cabinet des Médailles.)

It should come as no surprise that I shall have much more to say about northern Gaul, the area north of the Loire, than about southern Gaul. In the latter, which remained relatively Roman in spirit until the ninth century, little documentation of private life has survived. Very few Aquitanian or Provençal writers have left descriptions of the marriages or burials of their contemporaries or of what they ate or what they did in bed. Powerless, they could do nothing but look on in horror as the public institutions of Roman Gaul collapsed and as frightful new customs invaded their lands. The best of them later sought to convert the pagan intruders from the north and east to Christianity.

The invaders, on the other hand, tell us much, through their laws and their conflicts with the Church, about the importance for them of personal property, food, the body, women, and the family. We learn of their fears and their desire for vengeance, their aggressiveness and their hopes, their conceptions of the sacred, and, finally, their understanding of the inner life. The imbalance in the portrait is the history of an invasion of privacy, which proceeded from north to south.

Crucified thief, 8th century. The last known private mausoleum, the hypogeum of Mellebaude, an early-8th–century abbot and mystic, typifies the manner in which bodies were placed under the protection of the crucified Christ. (Poitiers.)

*Life of Saint Radegund*, 10th–11th century. Radegund is seated at the table of her husband, King Clotaire. The king's table differs little from that of a private individual; bread, a fish in a bowl, and a knife suggest that, however formal the dress, food was eaten with the hands. (Poitiers, Municipal Library.)

# ᷇ Private Life Conquers State and Society

T HE new governments established in fifth-century Gaul, be they Visigoth, Burgundian, or Frank, had little success imitating either the political institutions or the social arrangements of the Roman Empire. From the court down to the lowest official, in city and countryside, in religious and professional organizations, private persons took center stage. Wealth itself became a personal matter, and individuals sought to make everything, from their homes to their tables, private.

In the Late Empire the state had been glorified and the law promoted as a means of establishing peace and eliminating war. To Gallo-Romans, the Germanic tribes that established the new monarchies were nothing but barbarians and slaves, whose only duty was to submit to Constantinople, the new Rome. Gregory of Tours, an excellent observer of the monarchy and the new society, explicitly reserves, in his *History of the Franks,* the word "republic" for the Eastern Roman Empire. The *res publica,* or "public thing," a notion requiring a certain capacity for abstraction, was incomprehensible to barbarians. There was no such thing as a "barbarian state," because barbarism (a subjective term that did not necessarily refer to all Germans and may have included the Celts of Britain and various depraved Gallo-Romans) was a quality of soldiers, who bristled at the slightest injury and knew only violent emotions. They were extremely simple country people, who ate themselves sick and drank themselves into a stupor, and wherever they went they pillaged the people and picked the earth clean. Even after a more temperate examination of the "governmental" structures of the Franks and others, we must concede that this judgment was not without foundation.

*The Confusion of Public and Private*

Merovingian signet ring in gold, 7th century. The ring, which bears its owner's name, was used to seal letters and personal notes, property deeds, and other public and private documents. (Paris, Bibliothèque Nationale, Cabinet des Médailles.)

In the Germanic tribes, power, whose origins were at once magical, divine, and military, was exercised jointly by the king, elected to command, and his troops of free warriors. This unstable amalgam, which consisted of a *heer-könig,* who was condemned to conquer in order to maintain his authority, and warriors who remained faithful as long as their leader was the strongest, constituted a new type of "state" (if it can be called that), a sort of community of soldiers without fixed residence or assured survival. What held the group together was not, as in Rome, the idea of public safety and the common good, but private interests, joined together in a provisional partnership perpetuated by victory. The Franks, for example, hesitated in choosing a leader. At first they elected Childeric. Later, they expelled him and chose a Roman general, Aegidius. After he was assassinated, they recalled Childeric from Thuringia. And Childeric, as everyone knows, was the father of Clovis and was buried in Tournai in a Gallo-Roman cemetery in the midst of civilians and soldiers—a private warrior among others, yet remarkable for the sumptuous furnishings of his tomb. From that time forward the fundamental features of the Frankish state were established once and for all, despite the fact that Clovis was able to eliminate all his rival commanders and all his relatives who claimed the right to succeed him.

The king was master of the booty of war and of whatever territory his troops conquered. When he died his property was divided equally among his heirs as though it were private property: the kingdom was a form of patrimony. This reduction of the state to the level of mere private real estate led to bloody civil wars and resulted in the division of Merovingian Gaul into independent regions: Burgundy, Aquitania, Provence, Brittany, and so forth. The Carolingians, another noble family that seized power by force, also divided the kingdom as if it were private property: between Pepin and his brother Carloman I in 741, and between Charlemagne and Carloman II in 768. Charlemagne himself had planned to divide his empire among his three sons in 806; only the fortuitous deaths of the two younger brothers of Louis the Pious allowed the Carolingian Empire to remain unified from 814 to 840. The weight of German custom was such, however, that, despite the advice of ecclesiastics who wanted the state once again to become public property—a *respublica christiana,* they called it— the emperor's entourage of nobles, abetted by the empress Judith, who wanted to do something for her dear little son

Charles the Bald, pressed for and between 817 and 840 received at least four possible plans for dividing the empire.

The Treaty of Verdun (843), which even today makes the map of Europe look like an exercise in baroque marquetry, was a logical consequence of the principle that the kingdom is patrimony. Lotharingia itself fell victim to this practice, when Lothair I, upon his death, divided his kingdom among his three sons, thereby shattering the central axis of Europe, whose fragments today constitute the Netherlands, Belgium, Lorraine, Switzerland, and Italy. There is no escaping the fact that this concrete and carnal concept of the state, which held that it was the personal property of the potentate, was shared by all who wielded power in the early Middle Ages. What is more, the Capetians might well have perpetuated this concept had they not recognized in the end that the return to a notion of the state as public good, a notion foisted on them by clerics imbued with Roman law, actually served their interests much better.

The Merovingians and Carolingians who preceded the Capetians could not understand what seems self-evident to us because Germanic law unwittingly confounded public and private. Consider how the laws of the Germans were elaborated. Visigoths, Burgundians, and Franks, for whom the written word was limited to a few religious runes, during their years of wandering entrusted rules of law to the memory of designated specialists, whom the Franks called *rachimburgs*. These men learned each article by heart and memorized the most recent decisions, which created a body of precedents. Living libraries, they were law incarnate, unpredictable and terrifying. Simply let a judge pronounce in Old High German the words *friofalto uaua buscho* (free man maimed on the grass), for instance, and sentence was automatically passed: "A fine of 100 gold solidi." Because justice was primarily oral, the judicial act was singularly personal and subjective; no one other than the specialists knew the law.

What is more, each man's origin determined the law to which he was subject: that of the Salian Franks, that of the Ripuarian Franks (those from the Rhine region), that of the Burgundians, or that of the Visigoths (better known as the Code of Euric). The personal nature of the law reinforced the compartmentalization of society and deprived justice of any claim to universality. Roman Law had in its favor the fact that it was applicable to all citizens of the Empire. Hence in quick succession the laws of the various German tribes were com-

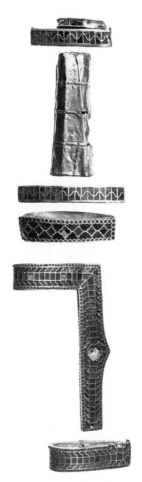

Sword handle and scabbard from tomb of Childeric, 5th century. Of the long sword of Clovis' father, found in Tournai, only the upper guard, the handle, and the lower guard in gilt cloisonné survived. The scabbard shown here is for a scramasax, a dagger sharpened along one edge; its chape and neck are also of gilt cloisonné. The wooden sheath has disappeared. (Paris, Bibliothèque Nationale, Cabinet des Médailles.)

Triumphal arch designed by Eginhard, biographer of Charlemagne. This 17th-century engraving was based on the original. Here again the memory of Rome was glorified and Christianized at the same time. Eginhard dedicated this arch not to the emperor but to God, lending mililtary significance to the victory of the Church over evil, symbolized by the horseman treading on a dragon. (Paris, Bibliothèque Nationale.)

mitted to writing: the Code of Euric in 461, the Law of the Burgundians in 502, and a first version of Salic Law in 511. Despite this, the laws continued to be memorized as they were applied until at least the tenth century, perhaps later. They perpetuated a concept of law radically different from that of Roman Law. Of 105 articles in the Law of the Burgundians, only 6 pertained to "public law." Similarly, in Salic Law, only 8 of 78 articles were concerned with the public sphere. Other articles oddly mingle the rights of the king and his treasury with those of private persons. By contrast, the Theodosian Code, promulgated in 438, included several dozen laws in sixteen books. Only half of Book VIII and all of Book IX are exclusively concerned with private law. The proportion is the reverse of that found in German law. The Roman tradition was perpetuated in Gaul by an abridged edition, the Breviary of Alaric, published in 506 and applied to Gallo-Romans living south of the Loire and to the Christian clergy. (Book XVI pertains to the Catholic Church, although it is still public and not yet canon law.) It is obvious that the expansion of the domain of private law at the expense of that of public law was a German innovation. Frankish judges devoted as much care to a case involving the theft of a dog as Roman judges did to cases involving the fiscal responsibility of *curiales,* or municipal councilors.

Private affairs were paramount in Frankish, Merovingian, and Carolingian justice. Boundary disputes, contested wills, complaints by buyers against sellers, and disputes among heirs all but overwhelmed the judges, including the royal courts. Among the few surviving examples of Merovingian public edicts, it is not surprising to find a judgment such as that of Dagobert (629–639) confirming the division of the legacies of Chrodolenus and Chaimedes between their heirs Ursinus and Beppolenus, or that of Clotaire III (657–673), organizing and disposing of the legacy of a certain Ermelius.

Of course most such cases involved very powerful noble families. Yet the fact that questions of family property assumed such proportions indicates the range of private inter-

Decree of Charlemagne on parchment, 14 September 774, granting ownership of the forest of Kinsheim. The text is written in a careful Merovingian cursive script. Note the signum and monogram Karolus at the bottom. (Paris, National Archives.)

Crypt of Gourdon (Saône-et-Loire), buried ca. 525. This paten and chalice with bird's-beak handles, used for consecrating bread and wine, are among the finest surviving examples of liturgical goldsmithing from this period. (Paris, Bibliothèque Nationale, Cabinet des Médailles.)

ests. An even clearer sign of this is the number of cases involving theft of moveable property. For the Germans, who, except for the Visigoths, had little experience with property in land, ownership took the form of jealous and watchful conservation of precious or vital goods, such as jewels, tools, foodstuffs, or family livestock. Given such attitudes, the theft of a pot of honey by a slave in sixth-century Angoulême could assume dramatic proportions. The man would probably have been hanged had not a hermit named Cybard intervened to save his life. In 798 Theodulf, bishop of Orléans and a man of Roman civilization, complained bitterly when, during a circuit of *missus dominicus* made in the Narbonne region, he witnessed the punishment of theft by death and of murder by the payment of a sum of money. These priorities were an ineluctable consequence of a warrior society's preference for personal possessions over life and limb. Having was more important than being for nations living on the edge of survival. Saint Ambrose called this attitude "avarice," and Gregory of Tours called it "rapacity." But for the errant and triumphant Germans, those high-flying eagles, death was the best way to mark the unbreachable boundary drawn around their private goods.

To the German warriors it made more sense that the gold drained away to the imperial treasury by the complex Roman tax system should remain, along with war booty, in the king's personal treasury. Each warrior was entitled to part of this booty, as the celebrated episode of the vessel or ewer of Soissons reveals.[2] What is more, each warrior expected gifts from his king in exchange for his services. The Merovingians, like the Carolingians after them, were lavish with gifts of gold coins, gold cloisonné, cut glass, and swords whose handles were encrusted with jewels taken from the royal coffers or from the booty wagons—fifteen of which, each drawn by two oxen, were needed to carry away the spoils of the victory over the Avars in 796!

This mutual exchange of gifts between the king and his noble warriors—ostentatious and obligatory generosity—reinforced the bonds between the royal power and its troops. It was a far cry from taxation. The Merovingian kings recognized that the blood tax paid by the Franks who served them created an exemption from payment of the tax levied on the vanquished Gallo-Romans. Nevertheless, with the help of functionaries in the south, they sought to maintain the capitation and land tax on their other subjects.

The monarchy lost this long battle over taxation in the

Carolingian period, and the private appropriation of what had once been direct public taxes was so successful that historians often disagree about whether the dues paid by peasants on various large Carolingian estates were originally public or private. Inevitably the word "franc" (Frank) came to mean "free," hence exempt from taxation. Anyone who paid taxes bore the stigma of servitude, and the tax itself was degraded to a level equal to that of any other private service. Taxation as such disappeared, a fact that was to mark France until the end of the Hundred Years' War. The king was supposed to live off his own property like any other landowner. Private life strangled the state by depriving it of financial resources.

The army held out longer and more successfully. Yet even here the German monarchs very early introduced a major innovation: personal bodyguards. Called *hirdh* by the Scandinavians and *truste* by the Merovingians, the bodyguard consisted of young warriors, equal among themselves, who swore to be faithful to their king even unto death. Among the Celts these were often the king's foster sons, sworn to defend their foster father. They took their meals with their commander, or, as Salic Law puts it, they shared his bread, hence they were the companions (*cum panis,* from which *companio*) of the king, bound to him almost as if by blood ties. Blood shed in battle fortified these ties and unified the king's protectors, his "enforcers." Accordingly, the *antrustions,* or members of the truste, were very valuable property. A person who killed one of them was obliged to pay a fine of 600 gold pieces, the highest fine imposed for any murder. By the fifth century this fine was established throughout the Roman Empire, owing to the continual attempts to murder important men. The Romans and Visigoths called such warriors *bucellaires,* biscuit eaters, for the army's best bread was reserved for them. Their loyalty to their patron was so great that it continued after his death. The emperor Valentinian III, afraid of the ambitions of General Aetius, assassinated him in 454, only to have his throat slit by Accila, one of Aetius' bucellaires, and his brother-in-law Trasila. Here, two non-natural forms of kinship, commensal and adoptive, led to behavior no different from what would have been expected of a blood relative. War became a private affair owing to the usurpation of state power by bonds of flesh and blood.

What Fustel de Coulanges called "absolute monarchy tempered by assassination," with murder the only limitation on the king's omnipotence, brought with it an extraordinary

Merovingian gold coins, 7th century. Above: Dagobert I, king of Austrasia and, later, king of Gaul from 629 to 639. This coin was mounted as a medallion, showing that coins were readily used as jewels. Below: 1/3 solidus, struck at Chalon. The king is shown full-face rather than in profile, a common practice in Byzantium and among the Spanish Visigoths. (Paris, Bibliothèque Nationale, Cabinet des Médailles.)

Phalerae of gilded silver, 7th century. These harness ornaments were found in a horseman's tomb at Ittenheim in Alsace. One shows a boar being hunted in a swamp, the other a soldier wearing a Roman officer's uniform and helmet with plume and holding his shield and lance. (Strasbourg, Rohan Museum.)

confusion between public and private in what passed for central government in the barbarian kingdoms. The famous "mayor of the palace," who brought down the Merovingian dynasty and created the Carolingian, was originally nothing more than the steward of the royal estates inherited from the Roman treasury. The Romans had distinguished between state property, imperial property, and the emperor's private property; the Merovingians confused all three categories. The mayor of the palace became the greatest landowner in the kingdom. Accordingly, the Carolingians did away with the office. But in their attempt to restore the state, they fell into old errors. Was the seneschal—*sinis kalk* in Old High German—the most senior of the king's servants, truly a high official? Not to judge by what he did, namely, wait on the royal table. Similarly, we might mistake the king's butler for little more than a sommelier if we did not know the important "political" role of the "wine of honor," the cup drunk in honor of one's guests and dinner companions. As for the prestigious titles of "constable" and "marshal," recall that the words originally referred to the stable master (*comes stabuli*) and horsetender or blacksmith (*maris kalk*), indispensable for the king's travels. The chamberlain, too, was a servant, responsible for changing the royal bed hangings and linen and for watching over the coffers containing property deeds, sacks of gold, and royal jewels.

Such confusion between public and private, such inability to rise above strictly personal and concrete realities, explains why no Merovingian officials were able to conceive a notion of the common good, with the exception of clerics formed by Roman culture. Great aristocrats sent their young sons to the courts of Neustria and Austrasia to learn tasks that they would later perform in the cities and countryside. They were called *nutriti,* "fed ones," for they were fully taken in charge by the king, who became a sort of adoptive father, gave them room and board (and I should imagine a good scrubbing), and kept them under his own roof. This close relationship had its emotional side, marked by specific gestures that triggered responses of filial obedience. Since everyone at the king's table (and at every other table, for that matter) ate with the fingers, it was a coveted duty to hold the king's napkin whenever he washed his hands. The *mapparius* (napkin holder) was therefore a much more important man than his modest duty suggests. The monarch was able to observe the child from age seven to fourteen, when nothing can be hidden, and could judge his affection and loyalty before naming him count or duke.

What an odd form of leadership training, in which heart counted for more than competence! This community of apprentice functionaries, called a *schola,* was maintained by the Carolingians. But since "the heart has its reasons that reason does not know," these former companions of the king or emperor also confused public duty with private possession. The revolt of Carolingian officials, which began in 840, and their seizure of rights that had been the king's, resulted in that

Psalter of Utrecht (816–835). Official entry into a fortified city. A captain, accompanied by his personal guard, is triumphantly welcomed at the city gate, as the residents prepare to acclaim him. Boats are anchored along the river banks. In the sky the hand of God blesses the scene. (Utrecht, Library of the Royal University.)

Merovingian gold coins, 6th and 7th centuries. Three Merovingian kings are shown in imperial costumes. Left: Theodebert I (534–548) wears the crown of the Byzantine emperor. Center: Childebert I (511–538) is shown in profile, wearing a toga, diadem, and neck ribbon. Right: Dagobert (629–639) wears a gold band around his head, a Roman imperial insignia. The coins were struck in a royal workshop. (Paris, Bibliothèque Nationale, Cabinet des Médailles.)

expansion of local powers which we call feudalism. As one annalist wrote in 888, "every man in those days wanted to make himself king out of his own entrails." There can be no better definition of the triumph of the private over the public. Nor should it be forgotten that the roots of rebellion lay not merely in ambition but in the balance of love and hate in feelings toward the father-king. For Reginon, royal power was literally secreted by the paternal gut, the seat of tenderness. No man can be his own father. To attempt this impossible feat was the absolute affirmation of self.

Appropriation of public goods can be seen in other areas. The mint, a royal monopoly par excellence, is a good example. As early as 560–580, the first private minters did not hesitate to put their own names on coins in place of the king's name. Charlemagne in 790 reclaimed all his rights in this respect and forbade individuals to strike coinage. But with Eudes, the first non-Carolingian king, the plundering returned, and a few years before 918 a former functionary, Guillaume, duke of Aquitaine, had a denier struck at Brioude. He thus opened the way to a proliferation of feudal coinage. Another royal prerogative inherited from the Romans was the right to maintain roads and build fortifications. The Merovingian kings, as well as Queen Brunhilde, kept up the Roman roads; "Brunhilde's roads," as they are called, can still be seen crisscrossing rural France. Charlemagne, too, maintained the roads. But the shock of the Scandinavian invasions was such that no one repaired damaged bridges and flooded roadways. In the tenth century new roads, called "routes," appeared in various places as the result of private initiative. And while Charlemagne built stout citadels of wood and earth to consolidate his conquests, Charles the Bald, in 864, complained that some men were on their own initiative building *haies et fertés,* fortifications made of trees and thorn bushes tightly woven together, as well as houses surrounded by palisades. By 950 feudal promontories were rising throughout the kingdom. As Georges Duby has written, feudalism was nothing less than the "fragmentation of authority into a host of autonomous cells. In each of these, a master held, as his private right, the power to command and to punish. He exploited this power as part of his hereditary patrimony."

---

Among the Roman laws in Alaric's Breviary is one that vainly attempted to prevent landowners from building houses against citadel walls, thereby avoiding the expense of building a fourth wall but impeding the free movement of the garrison. Similarly, we find private spaces being carved out everywhere, along with horizontal private bonds that bypassed hierarchical institutions or resulted in the creation of new institutions. The term *schola*, which once referred to the imperial guard, came to be applied in turn to a train of warrior-servants who waited on the king, to the group of clergymen who waited on the bishop, to the monks of a monastery, and ultimately to a choral society; it did not mean "school" before the ninth century. The antrustions had their counterpart in civil society, namely, the vassals. The etymology of the word is particularly enlightening. It comes from the Celtic *gwas* (from which the French *gars, garce,* young man or woman). It designated a young male slave, as is proved by its Latinized form, *vassus,* in Salic Law. The vassus was ranked with the other household slaves: the blacksmith, the goldsmith, and the swineherd. A great landowner might own several, even as many as a dozen. These young men (*juniores*) submitted to the authority of an older man, or *senior* (from which seigneur), in a curious ceremony, the "commendation," in which the younger man placed his clasped hands between the hands of the master, who enfolded them in his own. The vassus thus entered into a new realm of protection and mutual services. Through the touching of hands the warrior chief caused to pass from his own body into the body of the vassal something like a sacred fluid, the *hail.* Made taboo, as it were, the vassal thereupon fell under the charismatic power, pagan in origin, of the lord: his *mundeburdium,* or *mainbour,* true power, at once possessive and protective. This ceremony went beyond the mere notion of paternal protection and filial service. This new kind of relationship, of inferior to superior, derived its force from pagan

*The Proliferation of Small Groups*

Charlemagne, 9th century. This portrait introduced a collection of capitularies compiled by Ansegisus. The emperor, holding the scepter of justice, is depicted as the supreme judge and legislator. (Paris, Bibliothèque Nationale, Latin 9654.)

notions of interpersonal relations. Behind every individual who wielded power the pagans saw the cosmos itself, which they represented anthropomorphically. Like the power of nature, the power of man was ambivalent, sometimes beneficial, sometimes destructive. Minors, women, slaves, and servants belonged to the father or chief. Similarly, the chief literally breathed life into his vassals, structured their very being, with his mainbour. Under the heat of these emotional and religious relations, social differences literally melted away, and the *freund* became *frei*: the slave friend was liberated. Hence it is not surprising that vassals became free men in the Carolingian era, and that these groups of warrior-servants who took their meals together with the king contributed greatly to the Carolingian seizure of power. These ties of man to man seemed so strong and so solid to Charlemagne that he thought it wise to use them to consolidate his government. He therefore introduced vassalage into the political society of his time, adopting the practice of giving each vassal the income from an estate and multiplying the number of vassals of the king, princes, counts, and so forth, thereby creating a pyramid at whose summit he saw himself. What happened was in fact the opposite. At the time of the civil wars among the sons of Louis the Pious, the vassals obeyed the lord to whom they were closest and not that remote lord, the emperor, for they feared the wrath of the nearby master much more than the anger of the prestigious sovereign. As Robert Folz has pithily observed, "Charlemagne [and his successors] were betrayed by men."

Each vassal faced a difficult personal problem: that of lying, perjury. In a society dominated by youth, young men absorbed in enjoyment of the present moment were scarcely troubled by promises they had given. To dominate duration and time is a weak old man's pretension. False witness and perjury were so common that Salic Law, whose articles generally consist of no more than three or four lines, devoted three paragraphs to these offenses. One, concerning the man who refused to respect an oath given to another, was thirty-eight lines long! The subject must have been an important one, and Theodulf, after observing a trial, is dismayed by the litany of false oaths sworn by accused and accusers alike, to say nothing of their assorted supporters and witnesses. And what about the "Field of Lies," the Lügenfeld, thirty-odd miles from Colmar, where on one tragic night the "loyal" vassals of Louis the Pious crept out of camp to join his sons, abandoning the emperor to his fate? Never was the weakness of direct bonds between man and man so clear as on that night of repudiated friendship, especially when Louis exhorted his few remaining men to abandon him, "lest they lose life or limb on his account." Lying, then, was eminently subversive. The Church was so conscious of this that almost all early medieval penitentials rank perjury first among sins. In the penitential of Saint Columban, the most widely disseminated and copied of all, the man who commits perjury out of self-interest is condemned to remain shut up inside a monastery for life, and the man who commits perjury out of fear is condemned to seven years' penance, the first three on bread and water, unarmed in exile—a horrible punishment for that time; he also had to give alms and free slaves! In short, if vassalage began as a nursery school for future friends, a fellowship of youthful supporters of an aged king, or a shock troop, it was also a snake pit, and the lord could easily find himself bitten by one of his vassals.

The group of vassals was much less cohesive than other groups. Not all the old Roman corporations had disappeared. It seems likely that the stonecutters and glassmakers survived, carefully guarding their trade secrets and know-how. Gregory

Merovingian glass work, late 5th–6th century: a bottle, two drinking glasses without feet, a carafe, and a bowl. (Epernay, Historical Museum; Saint-Germain-en-Laye, Museum of National Antiquities.)

of Tours mentions an architect who suddenly loses all memory of his art and techniques. The Virgin appears to him in a dream and restores his knowledge. The story says a great deal about the importance, even for southerners imbued with Roman civilization, of memorized knowledge and oral transmission of culture.

More is known about the marginal communities denounced as "conjurations" by the clergy and called "guilds" by others. Men of all sorts—peasants, artisans, and, above all, merchants—swore a mutual oath among equals to support one another, come what may. These oaths were sworn on the twenty-sixth of December, feast day of the pagan god Jul, when it was possible to couple with the spirits of the dead and with demons that returned to the surface of the earth. Guild members prepared huge banquets at which they ate themselves sick and drank themselves silly until, in a state of total stupor, they were ready to enter into communion with supernatural forces. Then each man swore a solemn oath, to kill So-and-so, to back So-and-so in a business deal, and so forth. Many clerics denounced these conjurations as being not only a threat to public order but also, more serious in their eyes, satanic and immoral. Hincmar, in 858, sought in vain to Christianize them. In reality, these self-defense organizations proved quite useful in the fight against the Vikings, in 859, in the area between the Seine and the Loire. Merchants' guilds were often quite necessary for dealing with pirates on the high seas or setting prices in foreign ports. The guilds (so called because of the money, or *geld,* deposited in common funds) were probably quite effective. They were able to impose their own economic laws, which explains the persistent hostility of the Church as late as the eleventh century. Here again these curious associations practiced both legitimate self-defense and the law of the jungle, prandial fraternity and leveling egalitarianism.

Jewish communities were even more closed than the guilds. Born of the twofold Roman diaspora of the first and second centuries, they established themselves in the cities of Roman Gaul in Merovingian times and consolidated their position during the Carolingian era in Septimania (lower Languedoc), the Rhineland, and Champagne. Life for them revolved around the Torah, which, along with the rest of the Bible, became their real fatherland. Communities of Jewish households administered themselves through a council of elders, which recognized no higher spiritual authority. Rabbis

Ebbo's gospel book, 9th century. On the lower portion of church facade, a peasant is shown sowing seed. (Epernay, Municipal Library.)

were merely teachers, and each believer had a precise place in the social hierarchy. The community designated one of its members to negotiate with the *goyim,* or pagans—in reality Christians—over problems of coexistence, taxes, and so forth, with the result that Gallo-Romans and Franks knew nothing about the inward, intimate life of the Jewish families living among them. The hermetic solitude of the Jewish communities, coupled with the intellectual superiority of Jews, who digested huge volumes of abstract commentaries on Scripture, aroused fantasies in the minds of Christians confronted by these autonomous, anonymous, but fiercely unified groups, these roving traders who made homes in one place but seemed to have roots elsewhere—in Spain, Egypt, Italy, and the like.

Christians were much more tolerant of monastic communities, which they viewed as islands of repose and springboards to eternity. There the Christian mysteries ceased to seem strange and came to be embodied in an ideal microcosm, an antisociety, ridiculously small and vulnerable compared with the world of *homo homini lupus* outside. To be sure, the first monastic rules followed in Gaul, as early as the fifth century, still bore the imprint of joyous anarchism left by those religious athletes, the illiterate Egyptian peasants, cham-

Marble floor, 11th century. These ancient marble tiles traveled by donkey from Italy. Early medieval churches had splendid interiors, particularly around the altar. (Saint-Benoit-sur-Loire, Loiret.)

pions of fasting and mortification of the flesh. Soon, however, with the help of the Irish monk Saint Columban, who combined the ancient rules with that of Saint Benedict of Norcia (died ca. 560), the cloistered monasteries, guarded by gatekeepers, became throughout Gaul oases that revealed characteristic traits of each region's physical and mental landscape. As Saint Benedict said, "The monastery should, if possible, be constructed in such a way that everything necessary, which is to say, water, a mill, a garden, and various trades, can be found inside, so that the monks are not obliged to seek every which way for their needs, for to do so is not at all good for their souls."

Unlike the Jewish communities, the monks did not cut off all relations with the outside world and form a cyst in the tissue of society. Guests, pilgrims, and novices were received inside the walls, which were closed as much as possible for the monks seeking God, but partially open for lay brothers. The council of brother monks was always received by the father abbot, who was obliged to consult on many decisions. The community was organized horizontally and vertically; its private space was a bridge between two worlds, the terrestrial and the divine. Louis the Pious assigned his adviser, Benedict of Aniane, to apply the Benedictine rule throughout the Empire, after the decision of the Council of Aix in 817. Monasteries then proliferated like social microbes, living, fraternal utopias. Adalhard, abbot of Corbie, said in 822 that no monastery should house more than four hundred persons, including lay servants, for otherwise there was a danger of anonymity and the heart might be cut out of personal relations. Benedict held that the abbot (from *abba,* "papa" in Aramaic) should be an attentive father, that he should watch over and direct his spiritual sons on the road to knowledge of God and teach them the virtues of silence and humility. The monasteries also became model artistic workshops as well as schools of spirituality. Benedict was so insistent on the importance of a stable community living according to the rule that he disapproved of gyrovagues, wandering monks of the sort found in Ireland and Egypt, who roved from cell to cell unsupervised; he stipulated that hermits should not be authorized to live in solitude until they had passed many years in the monastery.

| | |
|---|---|
| *The Weakness of the Lone Individual* | In this respect Benedict was bucking the tide, because hermitism, which came in several waves, was one of the more startling new developments in the Germano-Latin countries. |

Praying figure, 11th century. A man makes the ancient gesture of appeal as he stands alone and prays to God. (Crypt of Cruas, Ardèche.)

The extent of the phenomenon is surprising, since the extraordinarily violent character of medieval life made it imperative that every individual seek the protection of a community. Nevertheless, some individuals did not hesitate to lose themselves in the vast forests of Gaul, which probably covered more than two-thirds of the country, and to live as savages, that is, as woodsmen (*silvaticus,* savage; from *silva,* woods). The quest for solitude had nothing to do with the fierce misanthropy of the superior man contemptuous of moral decay among his contemporaries. It was dangerous, because the hermit was lumped together with the outlaw, the man abandoned by his tribe, whom anyone was at liberty to strike down, like a mad dog. And many anchorites were indeed murdered.

Renunciation of the world was, as Jean Heuclin has shown, a matter of taking one's distance, of seeking a personal relationship with God; God then sent his faithful worshiper, overwhelmed with love, back to conquer the world. The desert gradually became populated around the hermit; monasteries and soon cities flourished. In northern Gaul alone, from the fifth to the eleventh century, more than three hundred and fifty hermits spiritually and materially transformed their social—ecological and, above all, human—environment. There were three great waves of eremitism. The first came in the fifth century, and the second in the sixth and seventh

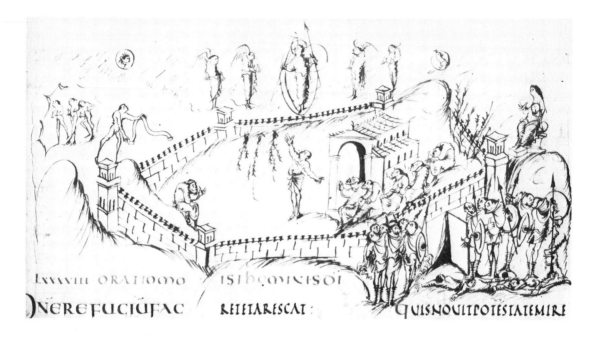

LXXXVIII ORATIOMO    ISIBCOIVISOI

)NEREFUCIÚFAC    RETETARESCAT:    QUISNOUITPOTESTATEMIRE

Psalter of Utrecht (816–835). A fortified city: God is like a fortified city, according to the psalm. Inside the walls men engage in peaceful prayer, while outside the enemy tramples on the bodies of the vanquished. (Utrecht, Library of the Royal University.)

centuries, spearheaded by highly cultivated Irish and Aquitanian monks. Then a crisis developed and the movement came to a halt in the wake of Carolingian legislation aimed at creating an orderly society and embodying the suspicious attitudes of Benedict of Norcia toward gyrovagues. The new standard was applied even to recluses who shut themselves up in small cells or, like Hiltrude at Liessies, in an oratory attached to the church, with which she communicated through a small window. The rule of Grimlaic, from the first half of the ninth century, all but put an end to the practice, which was authorized in only a few cases so as to weed out the madmen.

The third wave of eremitism did not begin to gather force until after 850. Meanwhile an important change had taken place. In the seventh century common folk and women were prominent among God's mendicants, but by the end of the Carolingian era the majority of hermits were male and noble. Prophetic solitude, a marginal and ultimately subversive way of life, was hard to maintain in the face of an increasingly organized church. It took an important personage to hold out. Still, these extraordinary men, symbols of all that society was not, continued to enjoy popular favor. Preachers, land-clearers, farmers, they lived on herbs, roots, bits of dry bread, and foul water. Constantly praying in silence, they healed body and soul and exorcised demons, the old pagan gods. Their rude huts were bare of furniture. The hermit was the opposite of society: a countermodel, who refused the anxious quest for possession, preferring instead the joy of simple existence.

It took uncommon courage and an extraordinary personality to face the difficulties inherent in this kind of spiritual journey with its risks of solitude and renunciation. For weaker men it was easier to seek shelter in one of the places that the Church had established as sanctuaries for the "poor," that is, people without well-placed protectors. Here people came in search of refuge from the consequences of a crime or a false accusation. The impoverished could find shelter in any church, cathedral, or rural parish chapel by placing their names on a list, or register, along with twelve other companions in misfortune (the number was symbolic), to whom the church authorities offered food and shelter. The fugitive slave, the hardened murderer, and the abandoned woman could all seek refuge in the church's "parvis," the triple colonnaded gallery adjoining the western facade. The perimeter of the parvis was sacred, hence inviolable, because it was land belonging to the patron saint.

These asylums sheltered entire families, pitiful human flotsam, hopeless drunks—a veritable pandemonium of vagrants. Longtime residents fell into bouts of drinking and adultery, while their enemies, furious that their prey had escaped, lurked outside awaiting the moment when the marked man inadvertently set foot outside the sanctuary, so that they might slay him on the spot. Gregory of Tours tells how Duke Claudius laid a trap for a man named Eberulf inside and outside the basilica of Saint Martin in Tours. The ambush degenerated into a riot involving slaves of both men, vassals of the duke, and churchwardens—a riot that left the pavement covered with blood. Despite these flaws, or perhaps because of them, the right of asylum was a constant of early medieval society, a ray of hope for the weak and a place of respite for the cynical.

The same concept of protected space in which the unarmed were safe from armed thugs seems to me to have inspired the privilege of immunity. Upon the request of a bishop or abbot the king granted to land owned by a church or monastery dispensation from any visit, inspection, or tax that a royal official might otherwise be legally entitled to make. With church lands thus immunized against the petty tyrant of the village, the bishop or abbot, who could not wield

Trenching of grapevines. Gelasian sacramentary known as the "de Gellone." Flavigny, 755–787. Grapes require a great deal of manual labor, especially in the spring. After the dressing of the vine, the soil is turned with the hoe around the base of the growing stalk. (Paris, Bibliothèque Nationale, Latin 12048.)

"The labors of the months," 809–818. Spring sowing, the plowing of fallow land in June, hay cutting, harvesting, the sowing of winter wheat, and the picking of grapes alternate with tasks in uncultivated areas, hunting with hawk, boar-hunting, and dressing of the hog. (Vienna, Austrian National Library, taken from the *Astronomical Notices* found in Salzburg.)

a sword, was free to use the income from that land as needed for construction and poor relief.

In Merovingian and Carolingian society enclosures were fundamental in establishing the notion of protected private property. When the Saxons settled in the Boulonnais, they established villages of huts surrounded by thorny hedges called *zaun*. The word has left traces in present-day place names such as Landrethun and Baincthun (*zaun* having yielded *thun* and, in English, *town*). The hedge was a dividing line that made the town an islet of private life. Burgundian and Salic Law often mention tree lines, boundary markers, and hedges protecting fields. Vineyards required special protection, and any domestic animal that trampled or ate vine shoots and grapes was subject to immediate slaughter. With much legalistic complication the Frankish rachimburgs punished those who stole baled hay, cut down an apple or pear tree, stole another man's fodder, or, worst of all, broke down an enclosure, with fines ranging from 3 to 45 solidi. A man who pulled up several stretches of hedge or who hauled stolen hedges away for his own use or who hid them was subject to a fine ranging from 15 to 62½ solidi. These were enormous sums, since a slave or a horse was worth only 12 solidi! The Franks must have cared deeply about protecting private property if they attached such value to enclosures. The laws of the Bretons reveal similar predilections and tell us much about the Celtic and Germanic origins of the *bocages,* enclosed fields that are so prominent a feature of the landscape of western France today.

The most prized of all enclosed spaces was the garden. The Franks kept some gardens exclusively for turnips, chickpeas, fava beans, and lentils. More commonly gardens were used to grow a wide variety of vegetables. Fortunatus, bishop of Poitiers, describes a friend's garden in a poem: "Here crimson-colored spring brings forth the green grass and the air is redolent with the heavenly fragrance of roses. And there young vine shoots offer protection from the heat of summer and shelter the vines heavy with grapes. The whole enclosure is covered with a thousand flowers. Some fruits are white, others red. Summer here is sweeter than anywhere else, and a discreet breeze gently shakes the apples in the boughs. Childebert grafted them with love." An intimate, quiet place, a spot where a man could work alone, the garden was a world unto itself where people tasted life's pleasures and sampled fruits and vegetables they grew themselves, far more delicious, as everyone knows, than fruits and vegetables grown by anyone else. The gardener laboriously turns the earth and painstakingly tends his vulnerable young plants, thereby establishing a tangible connection between himself and the earth and its produce. There were gardens in the monasteries and in the huts of peasants, in Saint Gall and in every great Carolingian manor. All required much work with the hoe, seeding, setting of seedlings, weeding, and repair work on walls and fences. Nearby stood the orchard, often with just one of each kind of fruit tree. Monks were advised to devote strips of their gardens to medicinal herbs such as abrotanum, which cured gout; fennel, good for constipation, coughs, and diseases of the eye; chervil, used for stopping hemorrhages; and absinth, for con-

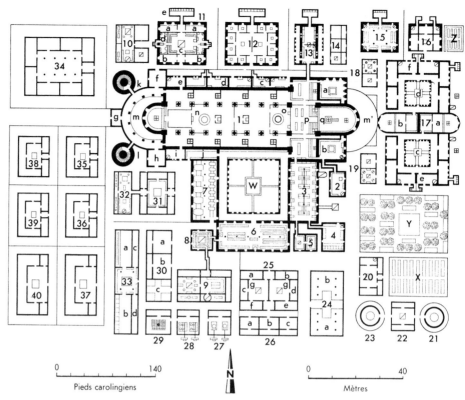

Plan of the monastery of Saint-Gall. Drawn by Heito for the abbot of Saint-Gall, this plan was actually used in construction, as archaeological excavation has shown. Building 11 was a guest house for guests of high rank and building 31 a guest house for paupers and pilgrims, both with adjoining service buildings. (Charlemagne Exposition, Aix-la-Chapelle, 1965, pp. 400–401.)

trolling fevers. Lovingly cultivated, gardens yielded not only delightful desserts but also useful medicaments.

Gardens were good for entertaining visitors. Travel was tiresome and dangerous. The abbot Loup of Ferrières advised a friend to take several stout companions with him on a journey in case he should encounter thieves along the road. Such risks were soon forgotten, however, when the weary traveler was welcomed at the hostelry of a monastery or noble household. Hospitality was obligatory. According to Burgundian Law, "anyone who refuses to offer a visitor shelter and warmth shall pay a fine of 3 solidi." In winter hay or barley had to be provided for the horses. Any free man called to join the army had to be given water and grass for his horse, according to an Aquitanian capitulary of 768. Charlemagne, in 789, stressed the need for hostels "for travelers, places for receiving the poor in monasteries and clerical communities, for on the Day of Judgment the Lord will say, 'I was a guest and you welcomed me.'" The allusion is both to the Gospel and to the Rule of Saint Benedict. Hospitality was a sacred duty, religious in its essence (both pagan and Christian). The plan of the monastery of Saint Gall shows, to the right of the entry, a house for pilgrims and paupers, a square room with benches, two dormitories, and outbuildings containing kneading troughs, an oven, and a brewery; to the left of the entry we find a guest house with two heated rooms, servants' bedrooms, and stables for the horses.

All this was a heavy financial burden, whether for hospitals in the strict sense, called *xenodochia,* or hospices for pilgrim monks, mainly Irish, the *hospicia Scottorum,* who traveled across Gaul toward Rome and the East. It was difficult to plan. At Corbie the monks counted on sheltering twelve paupers every night, and one and a half loaves were set aside for each one for dinner and for the road, with an additional twenty-seven loaves in case of unforeseen arrivals. But Saint-Germain-des-Prés received one hundred and forty guests per day in 829. Every bishop and every abbot actually set up two hostels, one for the poor and another for the rich, the count-bishops and other dignitaries traveling on business. Travelers could not take for granted that they would be sheltered along the way, however. Saint Boniface reports that female pilgrims to Rome, Anglo-Saxons like himself, were forced to prostitute themselves in every town along their route in order to reach their goal. Because of this withholding of alms, which induced these women to engage in an unusual means of mortifying the flesh, the Church was obliged to forbid women to embark on pilgrimages. Salic Law imposed a heavy fine, 300 solidi, on anyone who killed a guest of the king, an intimate who shared the king's bread. If a dinner guest was killed, everyone at the

Model of house built on cellar. Cannon foundry, Douai, 6th–7th century. Built of wood with thatch roof and walls, the floor of this hut was raised above ground atop a cellar used for storage and weaving. The roof extends well beyond the walls to protect the house from runoff. (Douai, Museum of Natural Science and Archaeology.)

Merovingian ceramics from Oise, 6th–7th century. These black pots, decorated with repeating motifs using an embossed roller wheel, were used for cooking and serving meals. (Saint-Germain-en-Laye, Museum of National Antiquities.)

dinner was obliged to pay the price for the man's murder. Since "stranger" was always more or less synonymous with "enemy," this was an important law. And it was important for the future that the Rule of Saint Benedict prescribed that "the abbot and all the monks shall wash the feet of all the guests." Therein lay the seeds of an extraordinary reversal of attitudes.

## The Warmth of the Home

The foregoing discussion of hospitality has brought us to the threshold of the home, the true sanctuary of private life. Beautiful Gallo-Roman *villae* with marble and mosaic floors still existed south of the Loire. Descriptions left by Sidonius Apollinaris in the fifth century and Fortunatus at the end of the sixth century prove that nothing of the Roman art of living had been lost at Aydat in Auvergne or at Bourg, Besson, Beaurech, and Pregnac in the Bordelais, with all the comforts of the city available in the countryside, just as in the time of Pliny the Younger. But archaeological excavation at Séviac in Gascony reveals that the villas were at some point abandoned or altered. New construction was undertaken with more rustic stone, and the plans of seigneurial and royal houses on the great Carolingian estates are much simpler than those of the Gallo-Roman villas. The best known is the manor house at Annapes, from the early ninth century, "a very well built house, made of stone, with three parts: the whole upper portion of the house, surrounded by wooden galleries, included eleven small, heated rooms; below was a cellar; and two porticoes. Inside the court were seventeen other heated houses made of wood, with as many rooms and other dependencies in good condition, a stable, a kitchen, a bakery, two corn cribs, and three barns. The court, stoutly defended by a hedge with a stone gate, had a wooden gallery above for storing provisions. A small courtyard, also surrounded by a hedge, was nicely laid out and planted with trees of various kinds."

The reader will have noticed the importance of walls and enclosures and the use of wood construction alongside buildings of stone. Most houses must have been built of wood, with cob walls and thatched roofs. Fortunatus, though an Italian used to stone construction, admired what he called a "palace of boards" joined in such a way that "one does not see the cracks." This masterpiece of carpentry must have been a luxury dwelling. Excavation by archaeologists has given us a good idea of the huts occupied by peasants, "miserable dwellings . . . covered with leaves," Gregory of Tours described them. Digs at Brebières and Proville in the Nord have shown that these huts ranged from 6 to 13 feet in length by 6 feet in width. The excavations have actually unearthed cellars. Two, four, six, or eight beams carried thatched roofs that reached down to the ground. The smallest huts, with cellars of approximately 25 square feet, would have covered 50 square feet of ground space. No trace of a hearth has been found in any of these dwellings, which must have been temporary houses or buildings used for weaving or perhaps toolsheds. Nearby were a number of garbage pits and grain silos in the shape of bottles. Only a few signs of hearths have been found outside the huts. In Douai, alongside these primitive huts, Pierre Demolon has found two rectangular wooden farmhouses, one Merovingian, the other, built on top of it, Carolingian, 50 feet long and 13 feet wide. This house had corner pillars of stout oak sunk into the soil with mortar bedding at the base, proof that the building was sturdily constructed. Analysis of traces of wood and excrement has shown that paths bordered by wattle fences of hazel led from one building to another and allowed the whole area to be fenced off. Men and animals must have lived together in the largest building. Suddenly we can see how men and women lived at close quarters, hiding their grain and wine in silos and cellars, sharing the warmth of the animals, slogging through dung and mud. Similar farmhouses, but made of stone, existed in the south, for example, at Larina, in Burgundy, in the fifth century, but their roofs were made of flat stones rather than thatch.

What was stored in the cellars and storehouses must have attracted thieves, because Salic Law prescribed a fine of 15 solidi for anyone who burglarized an unlocked *screona,* or weaving cellar, and 45 solidi for robbing a locked one. But the huts themselves were poorly furnished: a few round pots of red, gray, or black ceramic, cauldrons hung over the fire by handles, some bone picks, and a few knives. Decorated ceramic plates were found only in the south, where the early Christians produced embossed ceramics. In the Carolingian period there were also the so-called Pingsdorf or Badorf ceramics, a kind of pitcher. Although the wealthiest families had glass goblets and plates of silver or bronze, there was little variety overall. The only major innovation was in eating utensils: plates supplanted cups and other vessels that could be held in one hand. The goblet and truncated conical vessel became

A key, symbol of woman's power, was used to lock treasure chests and cellars. (Museum of Metz.)

Anthology of medical treatises. Pen and ink on parchment, ca. 850. This ancient work describes medicinal plants, indicating their specific qualities along with formulas for combining herbs to produce a variety of effects. (Paris, Bibliothèque Nationale, Latin 6862.)

increasingly common, as early as the fifth century in the case of early Christian ceramics. This proves that the Gallic habit of taking meals seated around a table had won out, even in the south, over the Roman custom of banqueting while lying supported on one elbow. The Germans had long eaten sitting up. Sitting permitted the use of knife and spoon and, above all, made it possible to eat with both hands, quite often with the fingers. This, in turn, made it necessary to wash one's hands frequently, a practice that was hygienic as well as pagan.

Meals were veritable religious rituals, with the evening meal always more important than the noon meal. It was unthinkable to harm a person with whom one shared a meal. Banquets welded the community together and established communion with the gods, the source of life and regeneration. The voracity of the Gauls was already celebrated in the lifetime of the Aquitanian Sulpicius Severus in the fourth century. The Germans only added to their reputation. The Franks invented soup, a concoction of boiled meat served with bread at the beginning of the meal. Chilperic, hoping to soften Gregory of Tours, who had called him the Nero and Herod of his day, offered him a more sophisticated soup, to which chicken and chickpeas had been added. Gregory was careful

not to taste it, for to do so would have been to approve Chilperic's policies. The Gallo-Romans ate a puree of dried vegetables called *pulmentum* to start the meal. Then came sauced and grilled meats—beef, mutton, pork, and game. The meal was served with cabbage, turnips, and radishes and seasoned with garlic, onion, and abundant spices, including pepper, cumin, cloves, cinnamon, nard, orange pimento, and nutmeg. Spices were thought to aid in digestion. Various dishes were served with *garum,* a salty condiment obtained by marinating the intestines of mackerel and sturgeon in salt, along with oysters, rather like the Vietnamese *nuoc-mam.* Fortunatus describes meals worthy of Pantagruel, which he left with his "stomach swollen like a balloon." Gregory of Tours was still furious when he told the story of the two bishops, Salonius and Sagittarius, who spent the night eating and drinking, got up from the table at sunrise, slept all day, and then at nightfall "sprawled on the table again for another all-night supper." In the circumstances it is easy to see that fasting was not a hygienic necessity but a religious countervalue intended as criticism of the cult of the stomach. The wealthy Briton Winnoch ate nothing but uncooked herbs. One monk in Bordeaux "did not even eat bread and drank nothing but an infusion once every three days." Some people drank even more than they ate. At the end of one banquet in Tournai, "after the table was taken away, everyone remained seated on their benches. They had drunk so much wine and had so gorged themselves that the slaves [and the guests] lay drunk in every corner of the house, wherever they happened to stumble." For minds used to regarding drunkenness as a gift of the gods and a form of true ecstasy, sobriety was no virtue. What is more, wine was then the only tonic available to everyone.

It would be naive to think that gluttony and drunkenness were exclusive privileges of the wealthy. Slaves drank their share, as we saw a moment ago. Overindulgence was a vice shared by nearly everyone in Merovingian and Carolingian society. Saint Columban, who counseled his monks to eat "roots [turnips, radishes, etc.], dried vegetables, and porridge with a little biscuit in order to keep the stomach from growing too large and the mind from asphyxiation," would have been surprised to see how much monks consumed. In the euphoric years of Carolingian prosperity, monastic rations were increased considerably. Each monk consumed, on the average, 3.7 pounds of bread every day (nuns ate only 3 pounds), along

Aesculapius discovering betony. Pen and ink on parchment, ca. 850. This anthology was widely used, as is shown by glosses added in the margin. (Paris, Bibliothèque Nationale, Latin 6862.)

with a quart and a half of wine or beer, 2 or 3 ounces of cheese, and a puree of lentils or chickpeas amounting to 8 ounces (4 ounces for nuns). Laymen, both servants of the monastery and outsiders, had to make do with only 3.1 pounds of bread, but they made up for it with a quart and a half of wine or beer plus 3 ounces of meat and 6 ounces of pureed dried vegetables and, to end the meal, 3 ounces of cheese.

These rations amounted to some 6,000 calories, twice what is now considered necessary for the average active man and a third more than is needed by a man engaged in hard labor. The medieval diet was based on the conviction that only heavy and fatty foods were nourishing—bread, milk, and cheese, especially bread. Everything served in addition to bread was secondary: "herbs," roots, fruits, even meats and purees. When there were not enough dishes to go around, people ate these snacks on slices of bread. There is a word that expresses this veneration of bread: *companaticum,* that which accompanies bread, from which came the Old French *compa-nage*. The other necessity at mealtime, to aid in the digestion of all these dishes, was obviously wine, probably a very light wine. When only beer was available, the ration was doubled. Given the monotony of the menu, condiments, spices, and *garum* were indispensable for whetting the appetite and awakening dormant taste buds.

The diet just described was the normal one, that eaten even by hard-working peasants. On feast days people indulged to excess. Holiday rations for monks, canons, and laymen were one-third greater than normal rations, and the Christian calendar included at least sixty holidays. In addition, the birthdays of certain honored saints were celebrated, and in large monasteries meals were eaten in honor of members of the Carolingian family. At holiday banquets monks consumed the same quantity of bread as on ordinary days, but the ration of wine and dried vegetables was doubled, and each man received six eggs and two chickens. On certain holidays the canons of Le Mans received a kilogram of meat as well as "potions" consisting of about a half-liter of wine flavored with fennel, mint, or sage. During Lent, meat and chicken were replaced by plaice, haddock, eels, and conger. Rations ran as high as 9,000 calories daily.

How and why were such meals ingested? Offering excessive amounts of carbohydrates and proteins and insufficient vitamins, they took a long time to digest. Siestas were essential, and the ubiquitous belches and farts were produced as noisily as possible, as a sign of good health and of gratitude toward one's host. The guest was not happy until his belly bulged. These feasts were not luxurious, sophisticated meals, but gullet-stuffings intended to ward off hunger pangs brought on by the unbalanced diet. The diet made people fat and potbellied; they felt constantly unsatisfied. Charlemagne developed an aversion to his doctors because they forbade him to eat roast meat on account of his overly sanguine complexion. The torture of hunger ended in the martyrdom of obesity.

A pagan religious idea, reinforced by Christianity, was behind these Gargantuan feasts. The German practice of dynastic commemorative meals originated in pagan rituals of sacrifice, mimicked, as we saw earlier, by the guilds. Eating a great deal was supposed to make a man sexually vigorous. By making the Carolingians healthy and mentally sound, these fabulous meals, accompanied of course by prayer, were supposed to bring stability to the monarchy and protect the dynasty. Prayers were also said for the queen or empress, that she might bear children. In a curious but pious gastric alchemy, the monk's paunch was the counterpart of the pregnant queen's belly. The Carolingians did not distinguish between mind and body, faith and intelligence, heart and reason. If a quarter or two-fifths of liturgical time was devoted to these banquets, the choice was deliberate. The point of such gastronomic extravaganzas was to make people feel the unity of spiritual joy and material well-being. Prayers and banquets secured the safety of the empire and the emperor, the health of his wife and offspring, the victory of his army, and the abundance of the harvest. Piety insinuated itself into the gullets of the faithful in a veritable incarnation, a "fleshification" of faith—faith in God and in those to whom he had given power.

This veritable cult of dietary excess, typical of men and women capable of feeling only strong emotions, came to an end in the tenth century, at least for ordinary meals; banquets lasting two or three days continued to be held. The councils of the eleventh century put the Carolingian diet out of bounds for monks and clergymen, although it remained the norm for married men and women. This persistent gluttony, which neither the physicians who took dietary recommendations from Anthimus' *De observatione ciborum* and the dietetic calendars nor the clergymen and religious legislators who condemned the obsession with wine could stamp out, was rivaled only by another form of sin: avarice.

*The Lust for Gold*

The feeling of power associated with the possession of gold and silver was exhilarating to those who managed to accumulate hoards of the two metals. This evil was denounced by Gregory of Tours, who tirelessly repeated the lines of Virgil: "Accursed lust for money, to what do you not drive the hearts of men!" Apart from princely fortunes, the wealth of certain leading laymen was impressive. One Merovingian general, Mummolus, left 250 talents of silver and more than 30 talents of gold in the form of coins, vases, and silver plates, one of which weighed 170 pounds—a total of 13,750 pounds of silver and 1,650 pounds of gold. The silver basin alone weighed almost 125 pounds! A Frankish landowner, who held the son of a southern senator hostage and made him a slave, demanded as ransom 7,200 pounds of gold, an amount equivalent to the price of thirty slaves. A cultivated slave by the name of Andarchius, who took care of his master's business affairs, was able to convince a noble lady whose daughter he wanted to marry that he possessed 16,000 solidi of gold (150 pounds). Greed spared no one. Gregory of Tours tells of a peasant to whom a saint appeared in a vision, asking the peasant to clean his oratory. The peasant did not comply with this request, so the saint returned and beat the peasant with a stick, but to no avail. On a third visit the saint left a gold coin in plain view next to the peasant's bed. Miracle of miracles, this time the peasant understood what was being asked of him!

The end of the Merovingian era was a period of hoarding, and huge personal and ecclesiastical treasures were amassed. In 621, for example, Bishop Desiderius of Auxerre, a native of Aquitania, bequeathed to his church some 300 pounds of liturgical objects in gold. Lust for jewels was such that Fredegund, who detested her daughter Rigunth, set the following trap for her, according to Gregory of Tours: "She led the way into a strong-room and opened a chest which was full of jewels and precious ornaments. For a long time she kept taking out one thing after another and handing them to her daughter, who stood beside her. Then she suddenly said: 'I'm tired of doing this. Put your own hand in and take whatever you find.' Rigunth was stretching her arm into the chest to take out some more things, when her mother suddenly seized the lid and slammed it down on her neck. She leant on it with all her might and the edge of the chest pressed so hard against the girl's throat that her eyes were soon standing out of her head." Rigunth was saved by her slaves. For her marriage to the king

Merovingian metalwork. Top: cross-belt of damascened iron, silver, and brass, 650–700, from the Burgundian cemetery in Burgundy. Center: part of cross-belt for holding sword, made of iron plated with silver and brass. Early 8th century. Bottom: cast bronze clasps for fastening clothing at the neck. All 6th century. (Belfort Museum; Auxerre, Museum of Fine Arts; Saint-Germain-en-Laye, Museum of National Antiquities.)

Silver basin, 4th century. Found in the Rhone Valley near Avignon, this basin, almost 30 inches in diameter, depicts the return of the captured Briseis to Achilles, who listens, head bowed, to a speech of Ulysses. Precious items such as this were found in the private treasuries of leading Merovingian aristocrats. (Paris, Bibliothèque Nationale, Cabinet des Médailles.)

of Spain she had obtained fifty wagons filled with gold, silver, and precious clothing. Carolingian laymen amassed impressive fortunes, as their wills prove. In the year 865, Evrard, founder of Cysoin, owned nine swords with gold-decorated hilts and tips, six gilt cross-belts encrusted with precious gems and ivory inlay, and vessels of horn and marble covered with gold and silver, to mention only a few of his possessions. Here we touch upon yet another Carolingian tradition: opulence as a quality of being, an element of status.

The work of the Merovingian and Carolingian goldsmiths is probably unsurpassed. Aesthetic concerns, however, were not uppermost in the minds of the smelters, engravers, and goldsmiths, of whose work only a few marvels have survived the centuries, such as the sword belts inlaid with silver of the Paris cemeteries or the chalice of Tassilon. They started out making protective amulets, whose function soon turned to show. From the fifth to the eighth century sword buckles, filigreed cross-belts, cloisonné glass beads, garnets in cabochon, round and arched fibulae, purse clasps, earrings, and hairpins grew steadily in size. Signet rings, often made of gold, were proof of personal power. Arnegund, one of the wives of King Clotaire I, wore hers on her right thumb. Such rings were used to emboss a mark in the wax seal at the bottom of a public document and so displayed the wearer's rank and wealth. Other rings bore ancient intaglios, and Merovingian engraving was in no way inferior to that of the fourth century. Excavation of cemeteries has revealed that the wearing of precious stones gradually came to be limited to women, while only arms, worn exclusively by men, continued to be embellished with gold. Does this division of buried wealth suggest that violence was the exclusive province of men and wealth of women?

Bible of Charles the Bald, after 840. Inside an initial letter the illuminator has depicted the family of Moses around his cradle; below the baby is cast adrift on the Nile, where Pharaoh's daughter discovers him. (Paris, Bibliothèque Nationale, Latin I.)

# ~ Body and Heart

URBICUS, bishop of Clermont-Ferrand, separated from his wife when he became bishop, as was customary. But, "the bishop's wife burned so hot with passion . . . that she made her way through the pitch-black night to the church house. When she found that everything was shut up for the night, she started to beat on the doors of the church house and to shout something like the following: 'Bishop! How long do you intend to remain asleep? How long do you propose to refuse to open these closed doors? Why do you scorn your lawful wife? Why do you shut your ears and refuse to listen to the words of Paul, who wrote: "Come together again, that Satan tempt you not"' (I Cor. 7:5). As she went on in this vein for quite some time, the bishop finally weakened. He ordered that she be ushered into his bed and, after having intercourse with her, turned her out." A short while later, as though in counterpoint, the same author, Gregory of Tours, tells the story of a young married couple who swore they would practice continence and did so throughout a long life of sharing the same bed. When they died, their heavy sarcophagi were placed along opposite walls; but the next morning the two were found side by side. People referred to their tombs as those of the "Two Lovers." Celibacy versus marriage, exigent libido versus affectionate continence: these pairs of opposites defined the place of the heart and the body in Christian life. To make sense of the apparent contradictions we must understand more about the demography of the period.

---

*The Body*

Clothes, though generally made of sewn fabric, were quite ample, attached by means of belts and buckles. Gallo-Romans and Franks differed little in this regard. Everyone

wore knee-length linen shirts and tunics with long or short
sleeves (the same costume can be seen in Auvergne today, the
so-called *biaude*), trousers with anklets or puttees, and either
leather half-boots or wooden shoes, depending on social rank.
Over the tunic women wore floor-length gowns, open in front
of lifted up by chains so that they could walk. In cold weather
people added jackets of animal hide or fine fur or cloaks
consisting of a square piece of wool thrown over the back and
held in front by a clasp that attached over the right shoulder.
Social differences were indicated only by the richness of the
fabric and the wearing of arms and jewels. People went nude
only when they swam or bathed or slept.

The Roman baths were kept up for some time, even in
monasteries, but they were reserved increasingly for the ill.
For swimming there were rivers and pools at the hot springs,
such as those at Aix, where Charlemagne liked to swim with
as many as a hundred guests. The Carolingian princes bathed
and changed their clothes on Saturdays. Each sex had its
grooming rituals and carried combs, tweezers, and other such
items on their belts.

The Franks wore their hair as their kings did, quite long.
The Romans cut theirs at the neckline. The Franks kept their
hair off their necks and foreheads and plucked their beards.
Slaves and members of the clergy were tonsured. Priests and
monks kept only a crown of hair or, like the Irish, a band of
hair running from ear to ear. The symbolism is clear: long
hair stood for strength, virility, and liberty. The tonsure was
a sign of slave status, which the clergy used to signify subservience to Christ. Women's hair was left uncut, and judging
by the long hairpins that have survived, it must have been
artfully displayed. To tonsure a free boy or girl was an offense
punishable by a fine of 45 solidi under Salic Law, reduced to
42 solidi in the case of girls under Burgundian Law. Burgundian Law further specified that the offense should not be punished if it occurred outside the girl's house during the course
of a battle in which she took part.

Salic Law was equally severe on what pagans regarded as
offenses against the body. If a free man touched the hand of a
woman, he was obliged to pay 15 solidi; if he touched her
arm up to the elbow, 30 solidi; above the elbow, 35 solidi;
and if he finally reached the breast, 45 solidi. Why was the
female body taboo? Certain penitentials reveal that in some
pagan ceremonies a young girl or woman undressed completely in order to call forth the fertility of the fields, bring on

Among the objects commonly
worn on the belt was the ring
of soft iron, which could be
struck sharply against a rock to
start a fire. From Jandun
(Ardennes.)

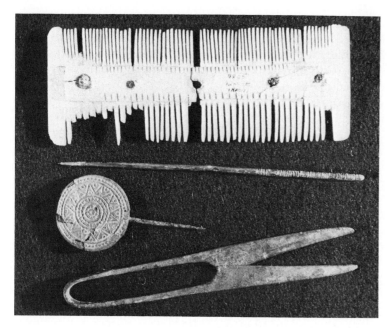

Feminine toilet articles: bone comb, hair pins, and a pair of shears. (Strasbourg, Archaeological Museum.)

rain, and so forth. Touching a woman, therefore, was interfering with the life processes. Men and women could be naked together in only one place: the bed in which they jointly made children. Nudity was sacred.

The significance of nudity in Christianity was quite different. Until the beginning of the eighth century men and women were baptized naked, on the night of Holy Saturday, in an octagonal basin attached to every cathedral. Naked as Adam and Eve at the Creation, they emerged from the water dead to the world of sin and resurrected for all eternity. Their nakedness signified the fact that they were God's creatures, sinless, in a state of prelapsarian grace. The naked Christian stood for a created being, the naked pagan for a procreator. The disappearance of baptism by immersion in the Carolingian era gave nudity a sexual connotation that it had previously lacked for Christians, linking it to the pagan symbolism of the bed. As early as the sixth century the Church had felt a need to suppress crucifixes on which Christ was depicted nude, like any other crucified slave. A priest in Narbonne one day had a vision of a naked Christ who asked to be clothed. It was around this time that it became common in Byzantium to show Christ on the cross wearing a long tunic, the *colobium*. People obviously had begun to react against what had come

Bronze medallion depicting Theodoric the Great (ca. 454–526), king of the Ostrogoths ca. 493. Although the king is shown wearing the uniform of a Roman general, he has the long, carefully curled hair that was a sign of freedom among the Germans. (London, British Museum.)

Fragment of ivory diptych, early 5th century. Christ's baptism by immersion in the River Jordan. A glorification of the human body, created by God but encouraged to grow by the Holy Spirit, which hovers over the waters as at the Creation. Possibly from Amiens. (West Berlin, Prussian State Museum of Culture.)

to be considered an indecent and, what is more, a dangerous spectacle, the danger being that Christ would be worshiped by women as a fertility god, like Priapus or the Viking god Freyr, whose sculpted images with erect phallus leave no doubt about his function. Dressed, bathed, combed, and cosseted, the body came to be revered. To avoid idolatry it had to be clothed. Well aware of this, Saint Benedict advised his monks to sleep fully dressed. "Each one shall have his own bed," says the Rule, and, "if possible, all should sleep in the same room . . . so that . . . when the signal is given, they may wake without delay and race to be first to set about God's work." The monk's night was consecrated to the love of God through prayer.

This pagan adoration of the body as usual elicited its opposite: hatred and fear of the body. Salic Law dealt harshly with rape and castration. (I shall have more to say about rape presently, but it is curious to note that neither Roman Law nor Burgundian Law penalized this act.) Castration must still have been commonplace in the eighth century, for Charlemagne was obliged to increase the fine for castration from 100 to 200 solidi and to add to the law the new crime of "castration of an antrustion," punishable by a fine of 600 solidi. In the collective unconscious of the Franks castration was equivalent to death, although a fee of 9 solidi was allowed for the physician who treated the victim. Slaves who stole could be castrated but were more commonly whipped. In disputed cases they were tortured.

Roman Law provided for torture for all condemned criminals. Gregory of Tours tells tales that reveal the extraordinary sadism of torturers and the crowds that watched them. Healed wounds were reopened, and physicians were brought in to treat torture victims so that "the torture might go on." Gregory manages to save the deacon Riculf from the death penalty but not from torture: "Nothing, not even metal, could bear such blows as this wretched creature had to endure. From the third hour of the day he hung suspended from a tree, with his hands tied behind his back. At the ninth hour he was taken down, racked with the rope and pulley, and then beaten with sticks and staves and double leather thongs, not by one man or by two, but everyone who could come within reach of his wretched limbs." These practices continued in the Carolingian era. The ordeal, of pagan origin, was much more frequently used than in the past. The most common form of ordeal was to force the accused to walk barefoot over nine white-hot plowshares. Providence was supposed to protect the innocent person from any burn, and the accused had only to appear some days later with soles more pink than shriveled purple in order to be acquitted. God moved in pure bodies but refused all contact with bodies tainted by murder. This pagan notion, though opposed by some bishops, survived in Christianity until the twelfth century, thanks chiefly to the support of Archbishop Hincmar of Rheims.

---

The human body was the primary battleground in the war between good and evil, malady and miracle. A miracle was a manifestation of divine power, often obtained by dint of prayer to a saint. Men were not the only source of physical woe. Plague epidemics ravaged Gaul in the sixth and seventh centuries. The appearance of buboes in the armpits heralded a speedy death. The great Gallic sanctuaries chiefly sheltered not healed plague victims but patients with slowly evolving diseases.

*Sickness and Health*

Numerous reports of miraculous cures were prepared in hundreds of copies in Carolingian as well as Merovingian times by physician-monks who knew how to make diagnoses in the manner of Hippocrates. Using these documents, we can gauge the state of health of the population and establish a map of human suffering. At important pilgrimage stations throughout Gaul, we find that 41 percent of these healing reports concern cases of paralysis, listlessness, or spasm; 19 percent, blindness; 17 percent, various diseases; 12.5 percent, madness and possession; and 8.5 percent, deafness, muteness, and deaf-muteness. Most of the paralyses can be accounted for by the dietary deficiencies noted earlier, especially vitamin deficiencies, which can cause polyneuritis, as well as such other diseases as trachoma, glaucoma, and especially rickets in children, large numbers of whom were counted among the wretched occupants of the sanctuaries. Neglect of the aqueducts led to the drinking of stagnant water, and swamps proliferated as cultivated land was abandoned. The result was an upsurge in polio, malaria, and paratyphoid fevers. Many children were handicapped by peri- or postnatal diseases, and the large numbers of such children suggest that both infant mortality and childbirth mortality rates must have been quite high. Many women and couples came to ask for an end to their sterility or for a successful childbirth, which shows that procreation came close to being an obsession.

Talisman of Charlemagne. This crystal, surrounded by gold and precious gems, was supposed to ward off illness—something of a cross between a magical amulet and a religious relic (Rheims, Cathedral Museum.)

Sculpture, 11th century, showing two trees, a stag, and a
hunter, symbolizing the solitude of the Christian caught
between the savagery of nature
and the savagery of man.
(Priory of Notre-Dame-de-
Salagon, Mane, Alpes-de-
Haute-Provence.)

With that we come to the psychosomatic and mental
illnesses. Some paralyses were the result of nervous diseases,
as were many sensory problems. But there were also cases of
hysteria and split personality, and manic disorders accompanied by logorrhea, often of alcoholic origin. The monk-
physicians were often quite perceptive in describing manic and
depressive illnesses associated with epilepsy, which for religious minds raised the problem of demonic possession. Even
though the authors of the reports believed firmly in possession, they regarded the possessed as sick people, mentally and
physically infected by Satan. They emphasized that the ex-
pulsion of the demon was invariably accompanied by elimination of vicious, bloody, or purulent humors and pestilential
exhalations. The bodies of the sick were racked by suffering.
All bore some measure of guilt, owing to the constant wav-
ering between execration and adoration of the flesh.

What we learn from study of the body—of the importance
of clothing and hair styling, the taboo on nudity, the morbid
interest in castration and torture, and organic and mental dis-

eases—reveals that people in the early Middle Ages placed extreme value on strength, procreation, and physical and mental health, probably because these were indispensable in an unstable, threatening, and incomprehensible world.

---

Studies of the population of one village from the fifth to the eighth century reinforce these findings. The work of anthropologist Luc Buchet on the cemetery of Frénouville in Normandy has thrown much light on the demography of the period; his results have been confirmed by smaller-scale studies in the Nord. Broadly speaking, the infant mortality rate was extremely high, around 45 percent. The life expectancy at birth was scarcely thirty years. Average life expectancy was around forty-five years, but only thirty to forty years for women, many of whom died in childbirth or of puerperal fever at from eighteen to twenty-nine years of age. Survival therefore required large numbers of women and children. Old people were rare, but if a person lived to be forty, his or her chance of survival doubled. Jean Heuclin has calculated that female hermits died at age sixty-seven on the average and male hermits at age seventy-six. True, hermits ate a more balanced diet than most other people, but many eighth-century bishops also attained respectable ages.

What we are detecting here is probably the well-known longevity of religious celibates, whose lives were less agitated than those of laymen. Examination of skeletons has shown high rates of endogamy and consanguinity, leading to degenerative diseases that hastened death. Average height was low: 5 ½ feet for men, just over 5 feet for women, no doubt owing to poor nutrition. These peasant populations had scarcely changed since the neolithic age. Remains of foreign occupiers as tall as 5 foot 10 inches have been found in only a few places. Yet despite all the handicaps, the population of some Merovingian villages seems to have doubled or even quintupled. Though closed in upon themselves, villages grew.

Merovingian society, with its paradoxical victory of life over death, was not unlike Third World society today, although infant mortality, without vaccines and antibiotics, was higher than it is now. Study of Carolingian polyptychs confirms this observation. Mme Zerner-Chardavoine has recently analyzed records from the estates of Saint-Victor of Marseilles for 813–814. She finds that the birth rate surged upward at irregular intervals, with a high level of infant mortality and

*Demographics*

Late-5th-century marble plaque showing Abraham about to sacrifice Isaac, who is eventually replaced by the ram at left. This common image was a symbol of hope in the resurrection to come and proof that children could no longer be victims. (Crypt of Saint Maximin, Var.)

high fertility rate. As a result, 22 percent of the populations consisted of children under twelve and 38 percent of unmarried young people. The average number of children per family was 2.9. The mentally retarded were carefully noted, and retarded girls outnumbered retarded boys. Families were not yet of the Christian or nuclear type: father, mother, and children. A society with more than 60 percent of the population under age twenty-five could not avoid being youthful and energetic, no matter how often death struck. Previously I deduced that early medieval society emphasized the youthful values of physical strength, procreation, and physical and mental health; here is positive corroboration.

The Franks openly encouraged procreation. Anyone who killed a free woman of childbearing age was obliged to pay 600 solidi, as much as for the murder of an antrustion; but a woman killed after menopause rated a fine of just 200 solidi. A pregnant woman who was struck and killed brought a fine of 700 solidi, but only 100 if she lived and the child was subsequently aborted. King Guntram added a further stipulation in the late sixth century, probably because crimes of this kind were on the rise. He imposed a fine of 600 solidi for killing a pregnant woman, with an additional 600 solidi if the dead fetus was a male. He could hardly have been more explicit. Since a boy under twelve was "worth" 600 solidi and a girl under twelve was "worth" only 200, a hierarchy of values was established: at the bottom of the scale were young girls and older women incapable of bearing children; in the middle, young boys; at the top, pregnant women. Since, moreover, the age of marriage was still quite close to the age of majority, twelve years (Fortunatus tells of the young maiden Viltutha, who married at thirteen and died in childbirth shortly thereafter), and since King Guntram thought it wise to impose a fine of 62½ solidi on any woman who gave another woman a magic potion of herbs and other plants intended to induce an abortion, which potion resulted in permanent sterility, it seems fair to say that women were respected only as mothers. Pagan religion and the need to survive both converged on the same goal: the child.

---

*Children: Slaves or Princes*

"A woman of Berry gave birth to a crippled, blind, and mute son, more monster than human being. She tearfully confessed that he had been conceived on a Sunday night and that she did not dare kill him, as mothers often do in such

cases. She gave him to some beggars, who put him on a cart and dragged him around for people to see." In this case the wrath of the gods made itself manifest, literally visible, in the shape of a monster. That wrath was particularly severe because the Christian prohibition against intercourse on the Lord's Day had been violated. The pagans had long practiced exposure of newborns, but leaving a baby still bloody from birth at the door of a church no longer resulted in death. The priest would announce the discovery to the congregation and, if no one claimed the child, would give it to the "inventor," who became its owner, raised it, and made it his slave.

Generally speaking, however, children were well cared for; the wealthy gave them to nurses, and common folk breast-fed their children until the age of three. Much evidence could be cited to show that parents were attached to their children despite the frightful infant mortality rates. The most touching testimony is that of Gregory of Tours, who confesses to having suffered horribly at the death of young orphans whom he had personally taken in and spoon-fed but who fell victim to an epidemic. Protectiveness toward children manifested itself during wartime in a paradoxical way. A child was a precious commodity, as precious as a woman, and as such was part of the spoils of war. Whenever a city was captured, the victors slaughtered "everyone who could piss against the wall." In other words, they led away into slavery all the women and nursing children, including boys under the age of three; older boys were killed along with their fathers. This practice gave rise to the custom of referring to the child as a "slave" (*puer* in Latin).

Infants were treated more tenderly than older boys and girls, who were often disciplined harshly. This difference of treatment is clearly evident in monastic rules, which once again ran counter to common practice outside the monasteries. To be sure, monks were quite willing to receive a child offered by its family in hope of good fortune; it was a matter of giving to God what one held dearest. The Rule of Saint Benedict states: "If the child is very young, have its parents prepare the petition mentioned above and wrap it, along with the child's hand, in the altar cloth with the oblation and offer it thus." Every monastery sheltered numerous oblates, so that monastic communities became veritable nurseries, especially among the Celts, where adoptive parenthood, of pagan origin, became a Christian value. At majority the oblate was free to take, or refuse to take, perpetual vows. In the meantime, he or she

Merovingian pendant with asymmetrical knotwork. (Metz Museum.)

received an education radically at odds with the educational practices of the time. Rather than teach young boys to be aggressive and young girls to be submissive, the monks spared the rod and sought to preserve the virtues of childhood, considered weaknesses by their contemporaries. Bede the Venerable, and many others after him, admired the young male: "He does not persist in anger, he bears no rancor, he does not delight in the beauty of women, he says what he thinks." Last but not least, he was a docile pupil. In short, the monks sought not to harden the heart but to open it up. But when puberty came they were out of their depth. Forced to confront the sudden transition from childhood to adulthood, they resorted to old-fashioned strictness. The child's place in the family varied from one extreme to the other. In Merovingian cemeteries the corpses of children have left almost no trace alongside the tombs of their parents, whereas children in the Carolingian era were cherished little dolls, as is suggested by the first recorded use of a cradle. A slave in the household, a prince in the monasteries, the child was two persons, at once absent and present.

The same could be said of the elderly, of whom there were very few, mostly useless except for the *seniores,* old men, lords, heads of clans, tribes, parentelas, or great noble families. That Brunhilde should have lived past eighty years of age was considered a prodigy of the devil that had to be exorcised by capital punishment, but that Charlemagne should have lived to age sixty-seven was considered proof of the divine protection he enjoyed. An old man behaved acceptably only if he gave constant proof of his maturity and self-control. Otherwise he was expected to make a gift to an abbey, in exchange for which he received a prebend and could retire there to finish his days. Contracts specified the number of loaves and the quantity of wine or beer that the old man would receive each day. In the Carolingian era the charity registers were often filled with the names of old women and grandfathers (*nonnones*). The barbarian laws had no provisions that applied specifically to the elderly, but that may mean simply that there were very few "elderly" people in the current sense of the word, especially in Merovingian times. Children were in the majority, and youth, as we have seen, set the tone for all of society. The weak, or *pauperes,* paupers—that is, women and children—therefore outnumbered everyone else and may have accounted for as much as three-quarters of the population! This disproportion of women and children relative to adult males necessitated extensive family structures, with widows and young orphans, nephews, and nieces living together with male and female slaves, all under the power of the male head of the family. The family head descended from a *stirps*, an ancient and well-known clan or dynasty. This broad structure, referred to by some authors as an "extended family" and by others as a "patriarchal family," was called simply *familia* by early medieval writers, who used the word to denote a complex, ramified community whose essential function was one of protection.

*The Parentela*

Salic Law makes it clear that an individual has no right to protection if he is not part of a family. "If a person wishes to quit his family, he must come before the judge or centenar and break over his head four alder branches, and he must throw these into the four corners of the courtroom. Then he must say under oath that he abjures any protection, bequest, or property coming from any member of his family. If later some kinsman of his dies or is killed, he does not inherit from him or receive any fine paid in compensation. If he himself dies or is killed, any fine paid as compensation and any estate go not to his parents but to the treasury." A veritable moral person, the Frankish family was the protective unit par excellence; in return it demanded obedience of its members. To ward off the otherwise inevitable catastrophe, the man who wished to quit his family, who committed the crime of individualism, broke alder branches over his head—alder being the tree of misfortune, which grows beside treacherous waters and burns quickly, giving off little heat. This pagan practice was supposed to prevent sudden or violent death. But the expression of such fears betrays the somber reality. In Roman society greater legal protections made possible smaller "families," limited to no more than grandparents, parents, children, and slaves. By contrast, in Frankish society, or, rather, in the society north of the Loire, shaped by Celtic and Germanic traditions, families had to be large if they were to survive and if property was to be transmitted from generation to generation. Large families were the price that had to be paid for the lack of any notion of the public good; adoption and vassalage provided the numbers needed for strength.

The advantages of numbers were considerable. Armed companions were always at the ready, if needed for protection. A poor man faced with a stiff fine could call upon relatives and neighbors for help. Pecuniary solidarity was obligatory. Strict rules of inheritance governed the transmission of property from one person to another. Every blood line was associated with some piece of property, its seat. This property, called "Salic land," could not be inherited by a woman; otherwise her clan would have ceased to exist, would have been absorbed by her husband's clan. This article of Salic Law was misunderstood by royal jurists, who in 1316, upon the succession of the direct Capetians, interpreted it as prohibiting women from acceding to the throne. In fact, women were allowed to inherit property, except for this one piece of ancestral land, without which the Frankish system of private protection would have collapsed.

Several dozen persons lived at times in great, hangarlike wooden houses, where uncles and aunts, male and female cousins, children, slaves, and servants all slept together, naked, around a common fire. The number of such dwellings diminished in Carolingian times, owing to the Church's championing of the nuclear family; nevertheless, the officials who prepared the polyptychs recorded precise numbers of inhabitants per hearth, and the figures range from one or two to eight, ten, or even twelve, creating the misleading impression that the average was around four. A slave was marked down as a *familiaris,* or family member. Thus the family, in this extended sense, was the basic social unit. Monks used the same word, *familia,* to refer to their community, which included both monks and laymen, some living inside the cloister walls, some outside.

For survival the family also needed women. The man who headed the bloodline, guardian of the purity of the blood, was owner of his children's *mund.* He delegated his protective power to his sons-in-law through the marriage, or rather, the engagement ceremony, which was not so much a survival of the old custom wherein the would-be husband purchased his future wife from her father as it was a guarantee against violence and a certification of the bride's purity. During the engagement ceremony the girl's parents received a sum of money, a token of the purchase of paternal authority over the bride. Among the Franks this amount was 1 solidus plus 1 denarius for a first marriage and 3 solidi plus 1 denarius for a remarriage. The ceremony was public, and the gift obligatory and irrevocable. A man who married a woman other than his fiancée had to pay a fine of 62½ solidi. Among the Burgundians the gift exchanged for the mund, called a *wittimon,* was also

Capital from Saint-Benoît-sur-Loire, 11th century. Two monks digging in the monastery's garden, symbolizing the "family" at work.

Capital from Saint-Benoît-sur-Loire, 11th century. Exterior of narthex. An eclectic work, but perfectly in keeping with ancient norms, this capital depicts, between two volutes, a very rare image, that of a tumbler.

compulsory, and breaking the bond thus established called for payment of quadruple damages. The Theodosian Code and Roman Law in general accorded similar importance to the earnest money paid at the time of engagement. The payment of earnest money was equivalent to marriage, even though a year or two might pass before the union was completed, since the parents made the decision alone, without consulting the prospective bride or even the groom. A glance at any number of hagiographies, such as those of Saints Geneviève and Maxellende, reveals what a scandal could be caused by a girl's refusal to marry. Officially, the Merovingian councils and the decree of Clotaire II in 614 prohibited marrying a woman against her will. In practice, however, but for rare exceptions—a few strong-willed Christian women—young women and young men were presumed to assent to their parents' wishes. "When Leobard reached the appropriate age, his parents, according to the usages of the world [an expression showing that the practice in question was not Christian], obliged him to give earnest money to a girl and later forced him to take her for his wife. The father easily persuaded his son, still quite young, to act contrary to his will." A woman who disobeyed her parents in this regard was considered to have committed adultery, to have placed herself morally beyond the pale. A son who disobeyed had to pay his parents twice the "nuptial price"—that is, the amount of his mund— but he was free to remarry. A Burgundian, of great family or small, who married a girl without her father's consent "must pay three times the mund to his father-in-law for not having asked his permission, 150 solidi to his father, and 36 solidi as a fine to the treasury." But in this case the marriage could not be undone, because the carnal union had occurred at the man's initiative and there was no reason to consider the woman to be impure.

The foregoing remarks apply only to the engagement. The engagement ceremony, which outshone the marriage ceremony, was marked by a great banquet accompanied by much drinking, singing, and deliberately obscene jokes intended to spur the fertility of the newlyweds. The fiancée then received gifts. These gifts, conveyed by written deed under Roman Law or certified before three witnesses among the Germans, always included domestic animals, clothing, jewelry, precious stones, coins, a strongbox, a bed with covers, utensils, and so forth—mainly moveable property. In an old Gallic custom, the fiancé offered a pair of slippers as a token of domestic tranquillity. Roman custom was for the fiancé to give a gold ring, a symbol of the oath he had sworn, in which the unbroken circle of the ring symbolized eternity. The Romans wore the ring either on the right middle finger or the left ring finger, from which, according to ancient Egyptian physicians, a nerve led directly to the heart. Finally, the engaged couple exchanged a kiss on the mouth, a symbol of the union of their two bodies. In short, the marriage was complete before the marriage ceremony proper. This was true of the Gallo-Romans as well, who followed Roman customs in marriage, concluding by escorting the couple home, since, "according to custom, the newlyweds are placed together into the same bed."

Among the Franks and the Germans generally, consummation was the essential feature of marriage, and cohabitation in itself constituted marriage. Yet the gift given by the groom to the bride on the morning of the wedding night, the *mor-*

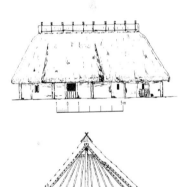

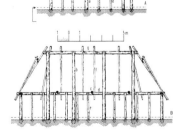

Reconstruction based on archaeological findings of a house, some 40 feet long, made entirely of wood covered with thatch. (Bonn, Landesmuseum.)

*gengabe,* was important too. It was customary among Burgundians as well as Franks. This gift was a token of the groom's gratitude at finding his wife a virgin and a sign that any children she bore would indeed be his. The morgengabe gave evidence of the purity of the bride's blood. It was not given, accordingly, at second and third marriages, which, though quite common, were not highly esteemed. A widowed woman kept a third of the morgengabe and returned the rest to the family of her late husband. Thus, a woman was protected only if she was a virgin, for the offspring and the inheritance were ultimately more important than the marriage itself. The woman's purity was essential for both religious and social reasons. A notion deeply rooted in the collective unconscious was that purity and cleanliness are identical, and that whatever could be done should be done to protect women

Plan of the village of Gladbach, 7th–8th century. Around the great house stood huts, storehouses, and silos. Each great house was enclosed by a hedge. (Bonn, Landesmuseum.)

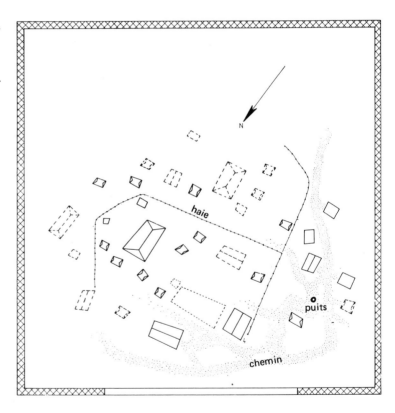

Construction rasée

Grande maison-halle    Autre maison, plus petite

Maison sur cave    Hutte sur cave

from pollution. The equilibrium of all society was at stake. This was a survival of the old Roman pagan idea of stuprum, or violation of chastity, which created an indelible stain that made marriage impossible.

---

In these troubled, violence-ridden times, the virgin represented the future of the bloodline. Steps were taken to punish the breaking of engagements and acts, such as rape, that made marriage impossible. Rape, abduction, incest, and adultery had to be avoided. Many articles of Roman and Germanic law deal with these crimes. Among the Franks and Burgundians, the female body was taboo. Rape of female slaves was punished, but the damage was already done; rape victims were deemed to have been "corrupted." The Gallo-Romans punished the rape of a free woman by death, the rape of a slave by a fine equal to her value. A corrupted woman had no further value. She even lost the right to own property, as the Visigothic Code of Euric stipulates in the case of a widow, "who is convicted of having debased herself by adultery or unlawful union." More than likely such women had no alternative other than prostitution, which was strictly forbidden but common nevertheless. In the sixth century the Franks punished the rape of a free woman by a fine of only 62½ solidi; Charlemagne increased the fine to 200 solidi, evidence perhaps that the crime had become more common.

Abduction, which often ended in rape, was often treated the same way, though the causes of the two offenses were different. Among the Gallo-Romans wealthy heiresses were often the prey of abductors, whereas Germans commonly resorted to abduction in order to extort consent from reluctant parents. Once the girl was abducted, perhaps with her consent, and duly deflowered, the marriage was a fait accompli. The parents had no recourse but to accept from the abductor the price of the mundium plus 62½ solidi. It was better not to prove that the girl had given her consent, for then she became a slave. By accepting the fait accompli, honor was saved and the purity of the blood protected. The importance of virginity is corroborated by detailed examination of Burgundian Law. If a girl returned to her father's home "uncorrupted," her abductor had to pay six times the mund and a fine of 12 solidi. If he did not have the amount required, whether he kept the girl or not he was handed over to her parents, who could castrate him. The wayward or dishonored daughter was

*Love: Instinct or Sentiment*

Merovingian jewels, 5th century. The *baugen,* or gold bracelet, signified royalty among the Franks. The signet ring, also of gold, bears the name of its owner, Hiva. (Metz Museum.)

then left with her absurd eunuch and no heir. This law of vengeance proves that rape and abduction were often the only means available to a man of seizing a woman and thereby acquiring power. The cult of the intact hymen was intended to edify society in quite a literal sense.

Even more serious was the discovery, after consummation of a marriage, of incest or adultery. Here, Salic Law, heavily influenced by pagan religion, agrees with the texts promulgated by the Merovingian councils, which strictly prohibited marriages that were called "incestuous," even though not involving relations between parent and child or brother and sister. Saint Paul (I Cor. 5:1) had already referred to relations between a son and his father's wife as incest. Indeed, any relations between relatives by blood or marriage were denounced as incest. Burgundian Law prohibited relations with "a female relative or the sister of one's wife"; Frankish Law, relations with "the daughter of a sister or brother, or the wife of a brother or an uncle." Such "criminal" marriages bore the "mark of infamy," and the guilty parties were separated. King Childebert II, in an edict at the end of the sixth century, made this condemnation even stronger. He also ordered that anyone guilty of abduction be put to death and stipulated that a man guilty of incest, already excommunicated by the Church, should be declared an outlaw and treated as a foreigner, meaning that sooner or later he was likely to be killed.

It seems reasonable to deduce that abduction and incest were on the rise. That is not surprising, since, as Merovingian cemetery excavations have shown, endogamy was common, extended families were quite broad, and it was a firmly established belief that kinship by marriage was the same as kinship by blood. Endogamy, branded incest, continually strengthened the solidarity of the parentela. In the circumstances, it is hardly surprising that the following passage should have appeared in one penitential: "If, in your wife's absence, and unbeknownst to her or to you, your own wife's sister came into your bed and, thinking that she was your wife, you had intimate relations with her . . ." The occurrence must have been commonplace, given the darkness of the night and the common sleeping quarters. All these "incestuous" practices, which made it seem normal for a widower to marry his first wife's sister or a late uncle's wife or a cousin german, were common in Merovingian times, for the kings refused to prohibit marriages between fourth-degree kin. Not until the Council of Mayence in 814 did such "impure" marriage begin to disappear.

---

If "incest" between relatives was considered normal, adultery was not. The "stench of adultery," to borrow a phrase from Burgundian Law, was so reviled that an adulterous woman was likely to be turned out of her house immediately and later perhaps strangled and thrown to rot in a swamp. As for the Gallo-Romans, a law promulgated by the emperor Majorian authorized a husband who caught his wife and her lover in the act to kill them immediately, "with a single blow." The Franks were even stricter. Not only the husband but his entire family, as well as the family of the adulterous woman, considered the adultery a stain on their escutcheon, and the guilty woman was condemned to die. Gregory of Tours cites numerous cases in which close relatives, that is, members of the parentela, went to the unfaithful woman's father and challenged him "either to justify your daughter under oath, or else she must die." The two families often came to blows and slaughtered one another: "As for the woman, called to judgment a few days later, she was strangled to death." Other women were burned alive or subjected to the ordeal of water to prove their innocence. A heavy stone was tied around the woman's neck and she was thrown into the nearest body of water. If she floated, which was most unlikely, her innocence was proven.

The Burgundians extended the notion of adultery to

*Women: Pure and Impure*

maidens and widows who slept with a man of their own accord. Tainted ever after, they were treated as untouchable. The Franks applied the term "adultery" to the crime of a man who slept with another man's slave. If the union became known, it meant slavery for the guilty man. The same punishment applied to the free woman who committed the analogous crime. The taint of adultery was darkened by the mark of the slave. Sexually and socially, the moral connotations of the two stains were the same. This calls to mind the dream of a priest in Rheims, who saw two doves perched on his hand, one black, the other white. The following morning, two fugitives arrived in Rheims. One, a slave, had helped the other, his master and the son of a senator, to escape. The priest immediately identified the black dove with the slave and the white dove with his master. Here we confront a pervasive, Manichaean religious mentality. More than rape or abduction (which, being deeds of men, could ultimately lead to marriage), adultery resulted in pollution of the woman and her offspring, poisoning the future. Any coupling in contempt of social differences was unthinkable because socially subversive. Similarly, the adulterous woman, by her own act, subverted her children's claim to authenticity and destroyed the charisma

This fourteen-year-old German girl (from Windeby) was blindfolded, garroted, and deliberately drowned in the 1st century, probably in punishment for adultery. (Schleswig, Schleswig-Holstein Museum for Prehistory and Early History.)

in her blood. The rapist or abductor was severely punished, but not the adulterous man. For the former two directly attacked the power of the clan heads, whereas the latter did no harm to his own parentela, and any children born of his illicit union belonged to the woman's husband. Last but not least, his copulation did not pollute him. The woman, on the other hand, committed a genuine crime by blotting out the future. The woman's personal life, unlike that of the man, was in the end wholly public, because of the consequences it could so easily entail.

This difference between men and women—the man master of his mund, the woman hedged about with taboos—is even clearer in the case of divorce. We do not know if the Franks permitted divorce. They did prohibit the breaking of a betrothal, which was tantamount to marriage; the fine for violating this law was 62½ solidi. Burgundian and Roman Law, defying the Church, did authorize divorce, but under conditions almost always unfavorable to the woman. A man could legitimately turn out his wife if she committed "one of the following three crimes: adultery, malefice [the use of potions to induce abortion or impotence], or violation of a grave." Roman Law substituted "poisoning or procuring" for the two last-named offenses. But if a woman ever dared turn out her husband, she could be strangled and thrown into the mud, for only adultery could prompt such an action.

The Gallo-Romans practiced divorce by mutual consent. Women could repudiate husbands who committed murder or violated a grave. Here we touch upon a distinction that is commonly drawn between the two civilizations. The Romans thought in terms of equality between the sexes; the Germans placed the man above the woman. More should be said on this subject, but it is worth noting that, since neither civilization punished male adultery, the distance between them was less great than it might at first appear. Separation of married couples, with remarriage permitted, was common in the Merovingian era. Roman legal formulas used by notaries prove that this was the case throughout southern Gaul, in Tours, Angers, and even as far north as Paris, at least until 732, when the formulary of Marculf was compiled. A late-sixth-century document from Angers is quite revealing: "Mrs. So-and-so states that her husband Mr. So-and-so, far from showing affection toward her, behaved in an arrogant and unbearable manner. It is known to all that, owing to the work of the devil and despite the divine interdiction, they can no longer

Ivory pyxis, second half of 5th century. The ancient motif, which depicts Dionysus conquering the Indians, is treated in a crude, violent manner typical of a military culture. The gods are larger in size than the men. Below right, a satyr prepares to decapitate a prisoner. (From Trier, now in Vienna, Museum of Art History.)

live together. They have therefore agreed, between themselves and in the presence of the council of elders, that they must release each other from their promises. This has been done. Wherever the husband wishes to take a wife, he shall have the power and liberty to do so. By the same token, wherever the woman named above wishes to take a husband, she shall have the power and the liberty to do so. And if, from today, either one attempts to contravene this letter or to challenge its provisions, he or she shall pay the sum of so many solidi to his or her former spouse by way of legal compensation, upon order of a judge. He or she shall obtain none of the claimed damages. This letter shall remain in force for the years to come." The Church must have tolerated divorce by mutual consent, particularly when, as here, it was initiated by the woman, whereas the barbarians found such divorces immoral and scandalous. Other evidence, from as late as the eighth century, shows that separations were encouraged in certain delicate cases. At the root of marital discord might lie abuse of the woman, her desire to take vows, the husband's impotence, pagan ideas, adultery, sterility, leprosy, and so forth.

Once the Church was able to prohibit divorce completely, a victory finally won during the reign of Emperor Louis the Pious (814–840), it encountered yet another obstacle in the behavior of private individuals. Franks settled by Charlemagne in military colonies in southern France had taken wives. Upon their return to Austrasia they took second wives. Many saw nothing wrong with keeping both wives or renouncing one as it served their interests. Among the high nobility especially, where marriage increasingly took on social and political importance, where endogamy, which strengthened the solidarity of the family or parentela, was still advantageous, and where the outbreak of civil war in 830 made it easy to rupture an alliance by repudiating one's wife, leaving her her personal property and morgengabe, monogamy and indissoluble marriages were seen as intolerable shackles. In his epic on the Viking siege of Paris in 855, Abbo of Fleury held that one reason for the invaders' success was the nobles' immoderate love of women and penchant for marrying kin. The relation of cause to effect may not be obvious, but the marriages in question were real. Hincmar, archbishop of Rheims (840–882), had no compunctions about describing how certain great lords rid themselves of troublesome wives: sent to inspect the kitchens, the women had their throats slit by the slave butcher otherwise occupied with the slaughter of pigs. After such a

Retable of Goenels-Elderen, ivory plaque, 8th century, depicting the Coronation of the Virgin and the Visitation. The latter is a delicate portrayal of tender affection between relatives. (Brussels, Royal Museum.)

"Carolingian divorce," the husband, having duly paid the compensation for homicide to the woman's family, was, as a widower, free in the eyes of the Church to enter into a second marriage.

The great obstacles to indissoluble marriage remained the well-established practice of polygamy among the Germans and the Gallo-Roman custom of taking female slaves as concubines. The laws condemned and set fines for rape, abduction, or intercourse with another man's slave, even with her consent, because such acts harmed the slaveowner's property and offended his honor. But there was no law against a master's sleeping with his own slave. Such a union resulted not in marriage but in concubinage. In Roman Law, if a child born to a concubine was not freed by her master, that child remained a slave; in any event the child of such a union was at the bottom of the social scale. Only marriage ensured that children would be born free. Gallo-Roman and German masters of all social ranks were in the habit of fathering children on their female slaves. Polygamy, on the other hand, was practiced by relative newcomers to France, the Franks and, later, the Vikings, who made "Danish marriages" (*more danico*) in Normandy as late as the eleventh century. Many factors conspired to produce endogamy among the Germans. It was in no one's interest to force a girl to leave one parentela and join another, for she took her personal property along with her. Parents chose for their sons officially sanctioned brides from a closely related branch of the family. It was, however, lawful for a man to take a second-class wife, a free woman, to recognize a preexisting sexual bond. These were called *friedlehe,* tokens of peace. Finally, it was always possible for a man to have one or more slave concubines. There was only one marriage, but several wives. Officially, monogamy reigned; in practice, there was polygamy. The official wife enjoyed the fullest rights; the second-class concubine, or friedlehe, lesser rights; and the third-class concubine, or slave, the least rights of all. Only the children of the official wife could inherit property. If a friedlehe was repudiated, she left without her dowry. Her children were regarded as free but bastards, with no claims on the estate unless the official wife was sterile, an important consideration in the eyes of contemporaries. Slave wives had no power but that which they derived from the master's passion. If this complex system of polygamy provided for posterity, it suffered from one major drawback: it pitted woman against woman in fierce battles for their man's heart, and hence for power.

Royal families and the nobility were particularly affected by these harem battles. On occasion they had disastrous political consequences, owing to the heritability of the crown; other times they were merely sordid. From Clovis on, nearly all the Merovingian kings had several wives. Clotaire I (511–561), whose wife asked him to find a good husband for her sister Aregund, could think of no one better than himself, so he made her his concubine. Here polygamy was complicated by incest (in the broad sense discussed earlier). Theudebert (543–548) had chosen a Roman matron from Béziers, Deuteria, as his free concubine. Her daughter by a previous marriage grew up to be a beautiful woman, and Deuteria feared that she would steal the king's heart. She therefore placed the girl in an ox-cart and sent it hurtling into the Meuse at Verdun. Everyone knows about the famous quarrel between Brunhilde and Fredegund, but no one bothers to point out that the civil war that they unleashed, which lasted from 573 until 613, was due to the murder of Chilperic's official wife, Galswinth, Brunhilde's sister. Chilperic was so inflamed with passion for his slave Fredegund that he did not shrink from having his wife strangled so that he might put his favorite in her place. Remember, too, that the Carolingian dynasty was founded by a bastard, Charles Martel, son of a concubine, who first had to prevent his widowed mother-in-law from ruling through her grandsons. It was the son of a concubine of Charlemagne, Pepin the Hunchback, who fomented a parricide-regicide in 792, the last regicide in France until the murder of Henri III in 1589. Finally, recall that Charlemagne, a womanizer, had four successive official wives and at least six concubines. Concubines quite often brought sisters, cousins, or nieces into their master's harem. When the master died his concubines moved on to the bed of his heir. This was double or triple incest in the eyes of the Church, which for a long time could do nothing about it. In attempting to eradicate endogamous polygamy, the Church adopted all the futile interdictions of the Merovingian councils concerning indissoluble marriage and monogamy. These were broadened by the Council of Mayence in 813. Marriage was henceforth forbidden on grounds of consanguinity to relatives as distant as second cousins. This legislation aroused innumerable protests. The most serious was that of Lothaire II, king of Lotharingia (later Lorraine), who, having had no child by his wife Theuberge, wanted to repudiate her and marry his concubine Waldrade, who had given him a son. He clashed with the intransigent Hincmar, archbishop of Rheims, and Pope Nicholas I. Theuberge, as a good wife concerned about her husband's succession, swore falsely that she had been raped and sodomized by her brother, the abbot of Saint-Maurice d'Agaune; she hoped that her marriage would be annulled on grounds of incestuous and impure sexual relations, in accordance with pagan beliefs. But nothing came of her charges. Lorraine, for want of an heir, was divided among the king's brothers. For the first time, a rule of private life—the prohibition against divorce—prevailed over reasons of state.

Monogamy and indissoluble marriage did not become general practices until the tenth century, first among the common people and later among the nobility, with Gallo-Romans preceding Franks. The behavior of people in the south seems to have changed radically between Merovingian and Carolingian times. In the sixth century, for example, Gregory of Tours told an anecdote that must have been inspired by a recent occurrence: "Count Eulalius had married Tetradia . . . But this man made concubines of his slaves and began to neglect his wife. When he returned from one of his prostitutes, he used to beat his wife . . . Finally, in an appalling situation and stripped of the honor she had enjoyed, this woman conceived a desire for her husband's nephew, named Virus . . . He promised to marry her, but, fearing what his uncle might do, he sent her to Duke Desiderius with the intention of marrying her later. She took with her all of her husband's fortune, gold, silver, clothing, in fact whatever she could carry . . . Eulalius, nursing his resentment, waited a while before attacking and killing his nephew. Desiderius then married Tetradia. Whereupon Eulalius abbducted a girl from a convent in Lyons and made her his wife, but his concubines became jealous, or so it is said, and cast a spell over him by witchcraft."[3] Every conceivable marital trouble is contained in this story: adultery with the nephew, theft of the husband's property, murder of the lover, abduction of a nun, madness brought on by concubines' black magic. But in the ninth and tenth centuries such practices seem to have ceased in southern Gaul, for no source mentions them. To be sure, concubinage with servants, found in every rural society, continued, but divorce and polygamy came to an end.

We are now ready to consider the sentiment of love in the early Middle Ages. No source, secular or clerical, uses the    *An Unruly Passion* word *amor* in a positive sense. Love is always a sensual, un-reasonable, and destructive passion. It is applied to relations between parents and children as well as between lovers. Never, so far as I know, is the term "love" used in connection with an official marriage. In referring to the sentiment of conjugal love, Pope Innocent I (411–417), in a letter to Bishop Victrice of Rouen, used the term *charitas conjugalis,* which is difficult to translate but obviously involves both conjugal grace and a mixture of tenderness and friendship. Others used the word *dilectio,* signifying preference and respect. Jonas of Orléans, in the eleventh century, frequently used the word *caritas* in refer-ring to conjugal love, love that embraced both *honesta copulatio* (honorable, temperate sexual relations) and fidelity coupled with sensible and disinterested devotion. These characteriza-tions of love were not merely expressions of pious wishes by moralists or utopian Christians but maneuvers in a battle being waged against the common equation of love with violent desire. The new conception of love was put into practice by certain cultivated lay persons. The *Manual* of Dhuoda, wife of Marquis Bernard, which was intended for her son William, is a good example of the contrast between a woman's respect-ful and tender feelings toward her husband and her ardent feelings toward her son: "Thy mother's heart burns ardently for thee, my first-born." Conjugal love and maternal love are here clearly opposite sides of the same coin. As for Eginhard, a contemporary of Dhuoda who lost his wife in 836, just after completing his biography of Charlemagne, Stéphane Lebecq has pointed out how his loss reveals the depths of a love that possessed him body and soul. In a letter to his friend Loup, abbot of Ferrières, Eginhard indicates his tender feelings to-ward a woman who was at once wife, sister, and companion. Despite his faith in resurrection, grief, sorrow, and melancholy have brought him to the brink of a nervous breakdown. Given Eginhard's shrewd psychoanalysis of his grief over the loss of the woman he loved, it is hard to deny that Christians did indeed experience conjugal love. This is something quite dif-ferent from the Platonic relationship praised by Gregory of Tours. It is no longer the dream of a monk who reviles the flesh, or of a couple like Melanie and Pinien who in the fifth century, after discharging the obligation to produce offspring, joyously separated so that each might at last enjoy mystical marriage with God through cloistered prayer. It is, rather, a love between a man and a woman who together experience the difficulties and pleasures of a love that is both physical and

Bronze medallion depicting Theodoric the Great (ca. 454–526), king of the Ostrogoths ca. 493. Although the king is shown wearing the uniform of a Roman general, he has the long, carefully curled hair that was a sign of freedom among the Germans. (London, British Museum.)

spiritual. Make no mistake, however: such couples were quite rare.

By now it should be clear why the word "love" was not used in connection with marriage in the early Middle Ages. The influence of Ovid's *Amores* was insignificant, since the work was scarcely known at the time. Instead, people were convinced that love was the result of an irresistible sensual impulse, of desire inspired according to the pagans by the gods and according to the Christians by Satan, but in any case a subversive, destructive passion. This conviction was as firmly established in the schools as it was in people's minds. A scholastic exercise discovered in an eleventh-century manuscript in a Belgian abbey by Jean-Pierre Devroey describes the theological virtues and their exaggerations and opposites: "Love, desire seeking universal possession. Charity, tender unity. Hatred, contempt for the vanities of this world." Love is the opposite of charity, its negative. The Germans had another word for this unreasonable and possessive spirit: *libido*. This always stemmed from the woman. Gregory of Tours used the word in describing the poor woman abandoned by her husband Urbicus when he became bishop, and also in connection with Tetradia. A special edict was promulgated in 517 by the Burgundian king Sigismund concerning a widow, Aunegilde, who was engaged to remarry a man named Fredegiscle with the approval of both their parents. But, "burning with hot desire (*libido*), she broke her pledge to the court and ran to Baltamod, taking with her not her vows but her shame." She would have been put to death had she not received a royal pardon at Eastertime. Similarly, any widow who, "overcome by desire (*libido*), freely and spontaneously has sexual relations with a man, and that fact becomes known," immediately loses her rights and cannot marry the man in question. Such desire was seen as base and unworthy of marriage, a serious flaw. Love is destructive.

This deeply rooted belief was reinforced by another belief encountered in the story of Count Eulalius: the idea that concubines used spells, potions, amulets, and magic of all sorts to inflame passion and hold onto their lovers. Women were thought to be property of the cosmos, of the infernal and nocturnal powers, since their menstrual cycle, like the moon's, was twenty-eight days. Imagine the terror that gripped entire populations when there was an eclipse of the moon! People believed that the world was about to come to a standstill and that women would bear no more children. The shadows had to be driven from the moon with the help of "noisy ceremonies" called *vince luna,* or "victorious Moon," which were condemned by the Council of Leptines in 744. Although Isidore of Seville's brief work *De natura rerum* made available to the clergy a scientific explanation of the moon's eclipses, the Church had a hard time persuading people that women were human rather than cosmic beings. The Council of Leptines remarked that some people believe that "women surrender to the moon like pagans so as to capture the hearts of men." For many men, woman remained a mystery, sometimes good, sometimes evil, a source now of happiness, now of sorrow, at once terrifyingly pure and destructively impure. To calm anxieties and appease the gods, newlyweds were given a cup of hydromel, alcohol obtained from fermented honey (also known as mead). Tranquilizer, euphoric, and love-potion antidote, this drug, at once strong and sweet, was supposed to give the couple courage to penetrate the mysteries of the flesh. This is the origin of "honeymoon," that time of coming together and feeling at one with the world known to all newly married couples. The honeymoon exorcised the demons of love and enabled the couple to survive many more moons, thereby preserving the order of things.

On this long, and still pagan, journey from the body to the heart, we have discovered that the naked body was sacred and that the marital bed was the temple of procreation and affection. But the body, however venerated, was also detested. Rape, castration, and torture were constant threats, as were innumerable mental and physical diseases. Adored or reviled, racked by microbes and anxieties, obsessed with survival, medieval bodies were mostly young; there was little room in society for the elderly, and women of childbearing age enjoyed every protection. Children were a precious, though fragile, commodity. The purpose of the parentela, headed by the family chief, was to protect the weak: unmarried men, married women, children, slaves, and so on. Marriages were arranged by parents; children had no say. The bride had to be a virgin in order for her offspring to be considered authentic and of pure blood. Hence everything possible was done to prevent abduction, incest, adultery, and, to a lesser extent, divorce. Endogamy and polygamy tended in the opposite direction, however, giving rise to pollution, corruption, indecency, and filth of all sorts, which had either to be purified by iron and fire or drowned in water and mud. Impurity attached mainly to women, even though most sexual offenses were committed by men. Woman, blamed as the source of the destructive folly of love, had to be wrested from the cosmos, or at any rate from the world of wickedness, and made safe for the dignity of marriage and tender motherhood, the basis of society. The sacredness of the body and the need to exorcise passion account for the status of women and of the family in general.

Stele, 7th century, depicting a Frankish warrior combing himself. In his hand he holds a sheathed sword, while a two-headed monster threatens him in the background. Alongside him stands a ceramic pitcher. From the cemetery of Niederdollendorf. (Bonn, Rhine State Museum.)

# ᪥ Violence and Death

M ANY crimes are committed nowadays," wrote Gregory of Tours in 585, to which the biographer of Saint Leger added, in 675, "every man sees justice in his own will." There is no better way of saying that violence had become a strictly private affair; if childbearing was the symbol of womanhood, murder was the symbol of manhood. What mechanism led from aggressiveness, an indispensable quality, to destructive violence and death, from innocent games to hunting to rioting to the quiet of the graveyard and phantasms of the afterlife?

---

The intellectual education of young boys, except where placed in charge of a preceptor, ceased to be a private act and moved into the monastery or cathedral schools, but physical education, through sports and hunting, continued to be a family responsibility. This part of a boy's training usually began after the *barbatoria,* the ceremony that followed the boy's first shave. The presence of facial hair was proof that the boy's aggressiveness, a fundamental attribute of the male, was ripe for encouragement. The Franks had been able to defeat Rome only by dint of constant cultivation of the military virtues. Indeed, the word "frank" comes from the Old High German *frekkr,* which means bold, strong, courageous.

From the age of fourteen or even earlier, swimming, running, walking, and horseback-riding were sports that boys quickly learned and practiced constantly, because the skills involved were indispensable. Because the stirrup did not come into use until the ninth century, the young boy had to leap onto the horse like a modern bareback rider. To dismount, the rider brought one leg over the horse's back and then

*Education for War*

Codex Legum Longobardorum, 11th century. Kings Pepin of Italy and Lothaire I. The two Carolingian kings are shown in formal dress and carrying the scepter of justice. Lothaire is followed by a warrior, who carries a lance and wears a hunting horn affixed to his neck. (Cava dei Tirreni, Italy, abbey archives.)

jumped, feet together, to the ground. A bond quickly grew up between boy and horse, a bond so strong that in 793, when a Moslem army attacked Conques, a young Aquitanian aristocrat named Datus chose to keep his horse rather than exchange it for his mother, who had been taken prisoner. The enemy soldiers tore off the woman's breasts and beheaded her before the eyes of her son, who later felt horrified.

Men were similarly attached to the swords they received from their fathers or lords after the dubbing ceremony. Dubbing seems to have been a very ancient practice. The word comes from the Frankish *duban,* meaning "to strike." Military training included lessons in the use of sword, bow, and battle-axe, or francisc, a weapon which, well thrown, could smash an enemy's shield and lay him open to the final charge. When training was complete, the boy's biological or foster father had him kneel and struck him a hard blow on the shoulder to test his resistance. Dubbing was a rite of passage, proof that the young man could hold his own in battle and kill to protect his clan. Now real battles could begin. Games were apparently of little importance, except for dice, which were thrown by Gallo-Roman aristocrats in the time of Sidonius Apollinaris (late fifth century), and chess, which was played by all Celtic and Germanic nobles for it was still regarded as training in military tactics.

The most important lessons were in hunting, where the

boy learned to kill big game and catch small animals. He drew closer to the domestic animals that helped the hunters and developed hostility and aggression toward the wild and uncultivated. The mysterious wild, devoid of men, was called *for-estis* as early as the seventh century, from which comes our "forest." Originally the word referred to wild nature outside (*for*) the reach of man. In the minds of the Franks wild nature could be subdued only by violence, at the moment when it was most vulnerable, in autumn, when plants began to die and young animals no longer needed their mothers. Then began that contest between man and animal to see which was stronger, nature or culture, instinct or intelligence.

The purpose of hunting was not only to supply the kitchen with venison but to train young men in the arts of war and killing. Frequently men were the victims. During a hunt in the forest of Bondy, east of Paris, in 675, the Merovingian King Childeric II ceased to be hunter and became the hunted; rebellious nobles led by Bodilon slit his throat as if he were a stag, along with the pregnant Queen Bilichilde. Charles the Bald's son, Charles the Child (the epithet suggests how precocious this episode was), died in 864 after a hunting accident, as did a nephew, Carloman II, wounded by a boar in 884. And Carloman's brother, King Louis II, who had triumphed over the Vikings only two years earlier, had nothing better to do than hunt more tender game, a young girl, who fled into her cottage. Forgetting that he was on horseback, the king galloped toward the door and fractured his skull on the lintel. The pleasures of the hunt had their darker side.

The war between man and beast yielded not only the pleasure of slaughter but also that of a close relationship with hunting animals, whose instincts had to be trained by man. The Gallo-Romans used two types of hunting dog, Umbrians and mastiffs, possibly equivalent to latter-day running dogs and bulldogs that caught the prey by the neck. The Burgundians used the boarhound, a fast runner, the segusiave, which led the pursuit, and the petruncule, possibly another kind of bulldog. Anyone who stole a dog was obliged to kiss its behind in public, or, if he refused this dishonor, to pay 5 solidi to the owner plus a fine of 2 solidi. The Franks assessed a much higher fine: 15 solidi. A tame stag, branded by its owner, was "worth" 45 solidi if stolen. The old Celtic practice today known as *chasse au brame,* troat-hunting, involved placing a rutting stag in a U-shaped trap of trees and nets; when the

Man shooting a bow. Ebbo's evangelary, 9th century. The bow was used by both soldiers and hunters. Here it is wielded by a simple peasant. (Epernay, Municipal Library.)

Buckle and component of harness, made of bronze and silver-inlaid iron, from the late 6th or early 7th century and the first half of the 7th century, respectively. (Metz Museum.)

stag began to troat, does and other stags would approach and be caught. Equally precious were birds of prey, which were quite difficult to train. For stealing a falcon on its perch, hence ready for use, the Franks imposed a fine of 15 solidi, and for stealing a falcon locked in its cage, a fine of 45 solidi—as much as for a trained stag and three times as much as for a slave. To discourage such thefts the Burgundians hit on an even better solution: the stolen falcon would be allowed to devour five ounces of red meat from the thief's chest, a thrust of the beak away from pecking out an eye.

This passion for hunting, for hunting animals, and for birds of prey was universally shared in Merovingian and Carolingian Gaul. Louis the Pious, in a capitulary, states that if a man wished to pay a *wergeld,* or compensation for murder, in kind rather than cash, his sword and his sparrow-hawk should be an obligatory part of the payment, for a man attached such emotional value to those two indispensable companions through thick and thin that he invariably overestimated their actual worth. Two hunting weapons apparently considered less valuable, although just as essential, were the bow and the boar-spear. The bow and arrow were used for hunting birds. Sidonius Apollinaris depicts Theodoric II, king of the Visigoths (451–462), bird-hunting on horseback; he shoots deliberately, using a bow already armed by a squire in his train. The boar-spear was used, in 456, by Avitus, a senator from Auvergne who became emperor of Rome; he had to dismount and approach the boar on foot, then sink the spear into the body of this most dangerous of all game. The bow and the spear must have been cheaper and easier to obtain than the sword or the hawk, and men were not so attached to them as they were to the latter, for everyone cherished childhood memories of blows well struck with the Frankish sword, that marvel of supple keenness, or of years spent training a faithful dog or hawk that never missed its prey.

A complex relationship developed between hunter and prey, one of imitation mingled with fear. Wolves were then common, and in very cold winters they came, starving, to fortified towns; in Bordeaux, in 585, they devoured many dogs. Early in the ninth century, Charlemagne, in his capitulary *De villis,* ordered his masters of the wolf hunt to cross the moat and trap wolves, especially cubs in the month of May. Frothaire, bishop of Metz, praised the emperor's forests in a letter to Charlemagne: "I killed more than a hundred wolves in your forests." To kill wolves, traps consisting of a lure and a stretched bow were set in the "desert," that is, in uncultivated areas. Merely touching the trip was enough to fire the arrow and kill the curious animal, or man. In order to prevent this kind of accident, Burgundian Law specified that a trap must be marked by one sign on the ground and two in the air. Wolves terrorized human populations and were considered as dangerous as the boar, which, when attacked, became an aggressive animal capable of killing with a thrust of its tusks. Hunting it was so difficult that a fine of 15 solidi was assessed against any hunter who stole or killed a boar that other hunters had started. Sows were never hunted, for, unlike the male, which attacks at once, the sow runs away. The Franks could hardly avoid drawing a parallel between the aggressive boar and man, on the one hand, and between the fleeing sow, protective of her offspring, and woman, on the other. Animal nature literally dictated to humans the roles of male and female: respectively, aggression and tenderness, superiority and inferiority.

Not only feared, animals were also imitated. In the second half of the fifth century it became less and less usual for Gallo-Roman aristocrats and even commoners to call people by three names; single names were in vogue. The Franks followed suit, choosing names composed of two roots. Often, in the hope of securing for a child the qualities of an envied wild animal, they chose names that referred to the beast: Bern-hard, strong bear; Bert-chramm, shining crow; and Wolf-gang, walks like a wolf (implying for a long time).

Since the name makes the man, the Gallo-Romans were slowly won over to the same way of thinking. Duke Lupus (wolf) had a brother, Magnulfus (great wolf), and two sons,

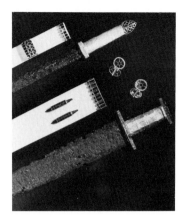

Germanic weapons, late 5th century, from a princely tomb at Pouan in Aube. From top to bottom: scabbard for scramasax, scramasax, two belt buckles, scabbard for sword, and sword. These sumptuous arms, embellished with gold cloisonné, probably belonged to a general. (Troyes, Museum of Fine Arts.)

Johannes and Romulfus (Roman wolf, a clever, Latino-Germanic allusion to the origins of Rome). Impressed by northerners' name choices, southerners, even clergymen, gradually adopted Germanic names with martial or animal connotations. South of the Nantes-Besançon line, only 17 percent of bishops had Germanic names in the sixth century; by the seventh century the figure has risen to 67 percent. This change suggests that Merovingian society in general had become more aggressive, and hunting was now more widely practiced than in the past. Not all German-sounding names were totems of anthropomorphic cults, however, and apart from areas in which the Franks had settled it seems likely that almost no one understood exactly what these names meant.

Nevertheless, as we learn from reading the condemnations repeatedly issued by Merovingian and Carolingian councils against members of the clergy who bore arms and hunted with dogs and falcons, the art of killing became for many a devouring passion that attacked even those who should have been peaceful pastors. At the time of independence in the eighth century, the bishops of Aquitania were renowned for their skill with the lance. Although things had begun to change by the ninth century, Jonas of Orléans complained of men who loved hunting and dogs so much that they neglected themselves and the poor. "In order to kill beasts fed by no one, the powerful dispossess the poor." These criticisms had little effect, for hunting was both a stimulant of, and a release for, aggressive instincts. During the siege of Paris by the Vikings in 885, some defenders kept their hawks with them, as today's soldier might keep a handkerchief. And the most ardent fighter of all, helmeted, armor-clad, sword in hand, dispatching pagan after pagan, was the city's bishop, Gozlin.

Article 36 of Salic Law provides that if a domestic quadruped kills a man, its owner shall pay half the compensation set down for homicide, and the offending animal shall be turned over to the plaintiff. This practice, out of which grew the later custom of trying animals in court, reveals the profound belief in the destructive capacity of beasts, in the dark violence of a nature that had to be subdued. The point was not merely to prove that an animal was guilty in order to avoid suspicion falling on man—such commonsensical reasoning is quite anachronistic. People sensed, rather, a complicity between man and beast, a shared death instinct.

The same feelings gave rise to the German custom of dressing in fur. Roman disgust for the barbarians stemmed not only from such habits, widespread among Burgundians, as greasing the hair with rancid butter and eating garlic and onion, but also from the custom of going "clad in fur," to the Romans a sure sign of savagery. Now, along with Germanic names, the wearing of fur jackets spread throughout the population. Charlemagne wore one, as did peasants in winter, but with the hair turned inward, a significant detail noted by Robert Delort. People wished to acquire the animal's qualities, but to show hair on the outside was to look so much like an animal as to run the risk of being possessed by one. It was to be reduced to the level of the beast, to take on its essential qualities and its way of killing.

If hunting established ties with death, fishing seems to have been oddly attached to life. Not that people did not enjoy eating fish; fishing just did not mobilize their energies. Salic Law specified that stealing fish was as serious an offense as stealing hunting animals or prey, but it gives no further details. Fishing was too peaceful an activity to provoke theft. Imperial

Portion of consular diptych showing combat with animals in an amphitheater, 400–450. Hunting games were very popular in Roman cities until the middle of the Merovingian period. (Museum of Bourges.)

Sarcophagi, 6th–7th century. These sarcophagi, of limestone from the Poitou, are decorated with multibranched crosses and are typical of Gallo-Roman cemeteries south of the Loire. (Poitiers, Baptistry of Saint John.)

game wardens were supposed to keep as close a watch on rivers and hatcheries as on nets and warrens, but we know nothing about what conflicts might have resulted from thefts of fish or diversion of streams. Fish were in fact closely associated with monks. The Rule of Saint Benedict specifies that "concerning the flesh of quadrupeds, all must totally abstain from eating any, except for patients in very weak condition." During Lent and on Fridays lay people imitated the monks by eating only fish. The consumption of salt-water fish increased slowly until, some time in the tenth century, it exceeded that of fresh-water fish. In social and dietary symbolism, however, eating fish continued to be associated with the monks who had initiated it. It was the food of peace, of unarmed men, and, owing to its aquatic origins, a source of life associated with woman. In extreme cases fishing was despised as the antithesis of hunting, an ignoble, demeaning occupation unfit for a nobleman.

*Arson and Theft: Capital Crimes*

Theft and arson were private acts of great importance in the mechanism of escalating violence. The elders who drafted the Salic Law were obsessed with theft. Of 70 articles, at least 22—nearly a third—are concerned with theft in one way or another. By contrast, Burgundian Law devotes only 13 out of 105 articles to the subject. Such details suggest that the Burgundians, and the Goths generally, had known real property longer than the Franks, for whom moveable property was the essence of wealth and ostentatious display.

The enumeration of offenses in Salic Law is almost maniacal. After the theft of hogs we find theft of cattle, sheep, and goats, hunting dogs, birds of prey, roosters, chickens, tame peacocks, geese, turtledoves, and other birds caught in traps. Next come thefts of hives and swarms of bees, the only source of sugar at that time, followed by slaves of all sorts: swineherds, vine tenders, stablemen, blacksmiths, carpenters, goldsmiths, and so on.

The lawmakers clearly listed the most common offenses first, followed by the rarest. They also indicated the value of each type of property. Some of these estimates are surprising: 45 solidi for a stolen jar of honey, but only 35 for a slave or a mare (increased to 62½ if the slave was a skilled artisan). Men had no intrinsic value, only use value. The highly prized cart horse or stallion was worth 45 solidi—more than an ordinary slave. Objects of all sorts were stolen: sow's and sheep's bells, flour from the mill, sewing thread, barrels of wine, hay, and so on. The portrait that emerges is one of a fussy, possessive society, where no detail was too small to be noticed, every loss became a personal insult, and the thief caught in the act might pay for his crime with capital punishment. Theft by a slave, on the other hand, was punished by 120–150 lashes, torture, or castration, because slaveowners did not wish to lose their capital.

It would be easy to emulate the Christian clergy of the time and pronounce moral judgment at this point. But these harsh laws were in reality a means of regularizing relations among the Franks. They were shaped by the Frankish concept of wealth and the elders' knowledge of the envy that lies at the root of larceny. This in the face of increasing social differentiation, which heightened the distinctions between once equal warriors and made some clans more powerful than others. These draconian measures were intended to establish a distinction between the spoils of war, or legal theft at the expense of an enemy, and theft pure and simple, theft from other Franks, which provoked intestine conflict. Torn between war and their land, these soldier-peasants made no distinction between outward and inward aggression, between theft and plunder. And they were ready to risk life and limb over a trifle. Proof of this assertion can be had from a glance at Burgundian Law, where the crimes already enumerated,

which seemed so important to the Franks, are characterized as minor and punished by a fine of 3 solidi. Only the theft of a plowshare or a pair of oxen with their yoke was considered serious. For such a crime the thief was condemned to slavery. Clearly, landed property was of much greater importance to the Burgundians. (And, a fortiori, to the Gallo-Romans, whose laws are filled with questions of displaced boundary markers, fraudulent sales, burned deeds, invaded estates, and so on.)

But to consider these matters would take us too far afield, since we are concerned here with private business, not business transacted through notaries. What is more, brigands, thieves, *latrones,* also known in Gallic as *bagaudes* (people who band together), preyed upon rural Gaul from the fifth through the tenth century. When caught by the king's troops, these bandits were condemned to slavery, imprisonment, or death. Such "criminals," unafraid of torture or punishment, made people anxious and worried, and they frequently barricaded themselves in their homes for protection.

If theft was an attack on the person, arson was an attack on the community and clan, and people found it even more terrifying. Nothing could have been simpler than to set fire to a thatched cottage, a salt sieve, a granary, barn, pigsty, or stable. Salic Law imposed heavy fines on anyone who committed such crimes while people were sleeping. An indemnity had to be paid for each person killed and for each who escaped alive. Yet the arsonist was not personally punished. By contrast, Roman Law provided for banishment of noble artisans and sentenced free commoners to hard labor in the mines. If the arson caused major damage, the perpetrator could be condemned to death. In both cases I am speaking of arson committed with malice against one's neighbors; Roman Law, for its part, distinguished carefully between criminal arson and accidental destruction of a neighbor's property caused by a fire started for the purpose of clearing land and which subsequently spread uncontrollably.

Rather than explain the difference between Roman and Salic Law as a difference between two civilizations, something needs to be said about the depths of the collective psychology of Romans and Franks. Fire was perceived as an instrument of purification. A person threatened or injured in his own home, in whose hearth burned the beneficial fire par excellence, considered himself accursed and impure, no matter whether the fire that did the damage was accidental or deliberately set. In the minds of Gallo-Romans and Christians, cities that burned—such as Tours on several occasions, Bourges in 584, Orléans in 580, and Paris in 585—were being punished for their sins or destroyed by the demon. A defense had to be found, some form of protection. Homes were protected by crucifixes or tau crosses. An image of Saint Martin

Gallo-Roman mosaic from Lillebonne, 250–300, depicting troat-hunting. The central panel shows Apollo pursuing Daphne, while the four side panels depict hunting for stags, using a doe tied up and concealed behind bushes. Her troating attracts the male deer. This technique was still in use in Merovingian times. (Rouen, Departmental Museum.)

might be placed inside, or relics on a private altar. "When the city of Bordeaux was ravaged by a fierce fire, the home of the Syrian Euphron, though surrounded by flames, was not damaged in the slightest," because he had a bone from Saint Sergius' finger atop one wall. Rumor had it that Paris had been racked by fires ever since one day somebody, cleaning the drains, "had removed a snake and dormouse made of bronze, which had somehow previously consecrated them." This story, from Gregory of Tours, shows that even heaven's fire could be demonic and even chthonian, subterranean, one with the darker forces of the cosmos. The only way to stop it was with apotropaic symbols of animals themselves drawn up out of the earth, like the snake and the dormouse, which spend a part of the year underground.

The Franks shared this view, but they disagreed with the Gallo-Romans when it came to the guilt of the arsonist. They held that if the fire proved lethal, the crime was one of murder, which as we shall see was not a reprehensible act but a form of masculine aggressiveness, a human invention. Do not forget that men were buried in the Merovingian cemeteries with oval rings of iron, used for lighting fires, attached to their belts. Held firmly in one hand, these rings were struck against flint with a series of sharp blows to start the fire. Cut flints have been found clutched in the hands of some cadavers. This method of starting fires recalls another, even older method called *nodfyr,* "fire of necessity." A stick of hard, dry wood was turned rapidly with the aid of a short cord in a piece of soft, dry wood; eventually the tip of the stick would become hot, turn red, and produce a flame. This technique was believed to be magical, and the fire thus obtained was thought

Cover of evangelary in ivory, 840–870. It shows the pilgrims of Emmaus meeting Christ at the gates of Jerusalem. Like the illustration on page 498, it emphasizes the protective role of the city, the only secure place in an exposed and violent world. (Paris, Bibliothèque Nationale.)

to be a gift of the gods. The practice was condemned by the Council of Leptines in 744, but to no avail. Men who committed arson armed with such sacred fire inspired holy terror. It was best not to touch them.

The Church, however, found a way to deal with these untouchable arsonists, without admitting it in so many words. The penitentials provided a penitence for masturbation. It was insignificant for children but increased to a year for an adult male and three years for a female. Now, as C. G. Jung has pointed out, nearly all arsonists are masturbators. The cases he cites show that there is a profound connection between arson and masturbation, two ways of producing a "heat" that is at once destructive and creative. The arsonist committed both acts simultaneously; fire literally spurted out of his body. The penitentials explained that the prohibition against masturbation was necessary to punish an excess of desire (*libido*), greater in women than in men, a point corroborated by Jung. No explicit connection was made with arson. It is possible, nevertheless, that masturbation was seen as a dangerous practice. Thus theft, regarded as a masculine act, and arson, regarded as more feminine than masculine, reveal the sexual origins of aggressive behavior.

---

The conjunction of sex and death brings us to the widow. Widowers are never mentioned in early medieval society, probably because they did not exist: the male death rate was extremely high owing to public and private violence. The laws of the Germanic peoples did what they could to prevent widows from remarrying, because their *libido* was considered dangerous. Because widows required economic independence, they retained their dowry and morgengabe. Burgundian Law stipulated that if the children of a widow married they should inherit at most two-thirds of their father's property lest their mother fall into misery. Hence some widows became powerful, even domineering figures, especially since control of the family passed to them on the husband's death. On the other hand, if a woman remarried she came once again under the mundium of her new husband. The Franks in fact required the second husband to pay 3 gold solidi to the woman's kin, a sum known as the *reipus,* or gold of maturity. It is proof that, although women, or at any rate widows, could be powerful and respected figures, they could never be totally free because they required men to perform acts of violence on their

*Murder, Torture, and Vengeance*

Bible of Charles the Bald, ca. 846. Saint Paul is shown being healed in Damascus by Ananias. (Paris, Bibliotèque Nationale, Latin 1.)

behalf. The widow's ripe sexuality and established fortune made her at once vulnerable, attractive, and powerful.

Violence was much more common in the early Middle Ages than it is today; wounds and blows sometimes claimed lives. The weary indifference found in the writings of Gregory of Tours and the cries of horror that can be heard in the poetry and sermons of Theodulf, bishop of Orléans, and Hincmar, archbishop of Rheims, suggest that violence was an everyday affair. No one will be surprised to learn that laymen slaughtered one another, but what about clerks who rebelled against their bishop? And what are we to think of the nuns of Sainte-Croix in Poitiers, who abused their abbess and bishop, disrupted a council and caused it to disperse, gathered "an army of murderers, sorcerers, and adulterers," and attacked their own convent? Pierre Riché mentions a ninth-century case involving the bishop of Le Mans, who, unhappy with his priests, had them castrated. Charlemagne had to intervene to have the madman evicted from his see.

It would be wrong to think that all such acts were the result of mental aberration. Aggression was routine, as the assassination of Archbishop Fulk of Rheims at the instigation of the count of Flanders early in the tenth century points out. The wise elders who framed the Salic Law rehearsed a whole litany of violent acts culminating in murder, punishable by the so-called *wergeld,* "man gold," money paid in compensation for murder. Only gold could stem the flow of blood. Cases envisioned by the law ranged from murder by poisoned arrow to bludgeoning that caused blood to drip upon the ground. Three punches rated a fine of 9 gold solidi. A hand or foot cut off, an eye plucked out, a sliced ear or nose rated 100 solidi. If, however, the hand or the thumb remained attached, the fine was reduced. The reckoning was complex, because an index finger, which was used in shooting the bow and arrow, was worth 35 solidi, whereas a little finger was worth only 15. Worse still, some brutes went so far as to pluck out their enemy's tongue, "so that he cannot speak"; the penalty for this atrocity was 100 solidi.

It is not hard to guess the reason for such ferocity: vengeance. Why else take the trouble to perform difficult "surgery" on a screaming patient held down by accomplices unless there was a profound urge to annihilate that part of the body which had wronged the attacker? It is easier just to kill a man; one can do it alone, and it cost no more in fines unless the victim was an antrustion or guest of the king. Every murder was categorized by the social status of the victim. The fine paid to the victim's family was the same whether he was a Frank or a Roman. Only the place in the social hierarchy made a difference—king's man or mere free man. For the third time we come upon the curious Frankish custom of putting thieves to death but fining murderers. It is particularly astonishing in light of the fact that both the Romans and the Burgundians provided the death penalty for murder. Among the Burgundians murder committed in legitimate self-defense led to the payment of half the applicable compensation to the family, depending on the victim's status: noble, free man, or man of inferior rank.

Something more needs to be said about the notion of vengeance, "that vengeance against a kinsman that we call *faide,*" in the words of Reginon of Prüm. As soon as a murder was committed, the victim's family incurred a religious duty to avenge the death against either the murderer or his family. That victim's family then incurred a similar obligation, and so on, ad infinitum. The training in violence culminated in an endless series of private vendettas, sometimes lasting centuries, and reported to us from the time of Gregory of Tours in the sixth century down to Raoul Glaber in the eleventh. It was considered shameful not to avenge one's family. After learning from the murderer himself that his parents' throats have

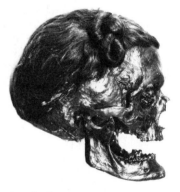

Head of man preserved in a peat bog, 1st century. A man about fifty years old was decapitated, as a surviving cervical vertebra proves. His blond hair was knotted on the right side, as was common among the Suevians. After decapitation the head was thrown into a swamp at Osterby. (Schleswig, Schleswig-Holstein Museum.)

Gospels, 800–850, possibly from Chartres. The beheading of Saint John, as Salomé dances before King Herod. (Paris, Bibliothèque Nationale, Latin 9386.)

been cut, young Sichar, though a Roman, says to himself that if he does not avenge his parents he is not worthy to be called a man, that he is nothing but a "feeble woman." Whereupon he saws off the head of the sleeping murderer. After the murder of Chilperic, King Guntram cries out: "If I do not succeed in avenging Chilperic's death before this year is up, I ought no longer to be held a man." Again, the equation of murder with virility.

The act of killing was not reproved; indeed, it became a habit. "If a man finds at a crossroads a man whose enemies have left him without feet or hands . . . and if he finishes that man off, he shall be subject to a fine of 100 solidi." Or again: "If a man beheads a man whose enemies have set him upon a stake without prior approval . . . he shall be subject to a fine of 15 solidi." Incomprehensible as these acts are to us, they were serious matters. In both cases the victims had been exposed in sacred places—at a crossroads or on the stake of an enclosure—to signify that a religious duty had been discharged, that vengeance had been exacted for some wrong. If a third party intervened in these *faides,* another round of vengeance might be triggered, a third clan might become involved. Such affairs could become quite complicated. Queen Brunhilde escaped from one tangled situation by getting the members of two warring clans drunk and then having them slaughtered by her henchmen.

As Sylvie Desmet points out, however, there was a simple way of breaking the chain of violence: payment of the wergeld. Since every wound and every person literally carried a "price tag," private vengeance could be halted if one family accepted payment of the wergeld by the other. In a society where human life counted for nothing and all that mattered was the damage sustained, this was obviously a tempting solution. The sums involved were large and could result in instantaneous enrichment. But greed was often outweighed by hatred, or by the fear of being called a coward or a woman. If men did not behave as men, the equilibrium of the society was threatened. Often the wergeld was not paid and vengeance followed its own course.

Vengeance was obligatory. Earlier I mentioned banquets at which the guests swore to kill someone or to defend their companions come what may. The men who drafted a new chapter added to Salic Law in the late eighth century were well aware of such obligations. They felt the need to state that, "when the law was set down in writing, the Franks were

Gold coin worth ⅓ solidus, from Le Mans, 7th century. The cross, symbol of protection and triumph, appears on the front and the back. Such coins were used to pay fines for theft and other offenses. (Paris, Bibliothèque Nationale, Cabinet des Médailles.)

not Christians. Hence they swore oaths with their right hands and upon their arms." Subsequently they accepted the Christian manner of swearing oaths. But the old manner of swearing, sealed with symbols of death, did not suddenly die out. Men were still quick to draw their swords. The Burgundians punished anyone who did with a fine, but they seem to have been less violent than the Franks, for their laws were concerned mainly with questions of teeth being knocked out by fists. The hand and the weapon were one and the same thing, and there was nothing to tame the instinct to shed blood at the slightest provocation. Impulse was not distinguished from premeditation, nor were words distinguished from actions, particularly among the Franks, though other peoples followed suit. Why? Because insults made violence obligatory.

Laughable or pitiful as it may seem that lawmakers were reduced to evaluating the severity of different kinds of insults, the fact remains that honor was at stake: the honor of the insulter as well as that of the insulted. Not to respond was to accept that the insulting characterization of oneself was true. For a weak man, vulgar insults were the only means of attacking a powerful enemy. People believed implicitly in the power of words. The Romans settled for punishing only insults made in public. The Germans, however, believed that all insults were destructive, because they attacked the private virtues by which the pagans set such great store. The most dishonoring of all insults was to call someone a prostitute; for this the fine was 45 solidi. This is but another instance of the obsession with female purity. Less serious were various insults applied to men. Punishable by a fine of 15 solidi was the accusation of pederasty. Below that, at a fine of 3 solidi, was the charge of *concagatus* (*conchié* in Old French, soiled with excrement). The proximity of these two insults in the law shows that in the martial, rural world of the Franks the male homosexual was no longer the lustful lover of ancient renown but a mere "buttsucker," base and ignoble. All sexuality was supposed to be pure, even in private.

Righteousness was esteemed, and it was considered insulting to call a man a fox, a traitor, or a slanderer. Physical courage was also esteemed, so that it was an insult to declare that a man had thrown down his shield in the midst of battle or had run like a scared rabbit. Here, again, we see the identification with animals and their vices. The whole panorama of insults suggests an individualistic, prelogical mentality, as well as certain collective obsessions with dishonoring acts.

No one would deny that words can do injury, but in the early Middle Ages the psychosomatic damage was palpable. No insult could be allowed to pass, and violence became obligatory.

---

I have said nothing thus far about the most damaging insult of all, for it involves the powers of the underworld and brings us face to face with the question of the afterlife. "If a person calls another person a witches' servant or accuses him of carrying the bronze cauldron that the ghouls use for cooking . . . he shall be subject to a fine of 62½ solidi." "If a ghoul eats a man . . . she shall be subject to a fine of 200 solidi." Witches who required the entrails of men for their brew were particularly feared. Associated, like the priestess of Vix's crater, with the infernal powers, they foretold the future with the help of human blood spread over the insides of their cauldrons. Witches were called bloodsuckers and cannibals. Woman, the creator of life, was also a cause of death. The ambivalent attitude toward death of the Franks, and of pagans in general, is clearly visible here. On the one hand, death is not something to be afraid of, but on the other hand, those familiar with its mysteries sow fear. Like sex, death fell within the province of the *sacer*. Because no one knew what harm the dead could do to the living, death caused fear and trembling. But it was necessary to kill in order to live, as is shown by the human sacrifices still practiced by the Franks as late as the sixth century, but even more because war was essential to the survival of the tribe.

People therefore took their distance from death, stood apart fearful and full of respect. The living created a separate place for the dead, the cemetery, which in Merovingian times was always located far from the village and its dwellings. This was not unlike the Roman practice of burying the dead along roads outside the city walls. But the Germans developed their own unique brand of rural burial grounds, which they set, if possible, on the south slope of a hill, near a well, or in the bed of a dry stream or the ruins of a Gallo-Roman villa. The fashion quickly spread from north to south. In Frankish territory the body was often buried naked in the ground, sometimes surrounded by a caisson of vertical stones. South of the Loire sarcophagi of stone or marble were common. Wooden coffins with ironwork fittings were also used frequently. Children's graves were sometimes grouped around the tombs of

## Fear of the Dead

Buckle of engraved bronze, ca. 400, from the Cemetery of Landifoy (Aisne). The engraving depicts two women, one dressed as a warrior, the other wearing a hairpiece, along with two seated lions. The buckle probably belonged to a Roman centurion. (Laon, Municipal Museum.)

Crater of Vix and Cauldron of Gundestrup, 5th century. The crater depicts a female chimera with a petrifying stare; her protruding tongue signifies death, an allusion to the bloody sacrifices she demanded. On the Celtic cauldron below, a priestess performs such a sacrifice. For the Franks such practices were still current or else remained fresh and vivid memories. (Châtillon-sur-Seine, Archaeological Museum; Copenhagen, National Museum.)

their parents. Originally cremation was universal, and in the fifth and sixth centuries it was still practiced in the north in some Saxon and Frankish cemeteries. Its purpose was chiefly to prevent the dead from returning to haunt the living. Thorny shrubs were frequently planted on the grave to confine the dead to their own world. The Franks used a stake or bridgelike stele for the same purpose.

The increasing recourse to burial, even prior to Christianization, tended to foster belief in the notion that the dead inhabit a world of their own. The rural cemetery recreated the endogamy of the village. The dead were always clothed before burial. Only a few buckles have survived in the graves of the poorest people; from the late seventh century we have hooked fasteners that were used to secure the burial shroud. Some men, especially blacksmiths, were buried with their tools. At Hérouvillette a complete set of blacksmith's tools was found in one grave. The *fèvre,* as the smith was called in the Middle Ages, knew the mysterious arts of taming fire and bending metal. He cut a distinctive figure in the village—part sorcerer, part sawbones. A piece of the sacred was his; hence he had a place apart in the cemetery. Other men were buried in small groups with their weapons (sword, scramasax, lance, shield) and domestic implements (comb, hair tweezers, flint and iron). Women were consigned to the earth with jewels, necklaces, bracelets, earrings, round and bowed pins, hairpins, purses filled with gold, and silver-tipped anklet laces. The graves of princes such as Hordain in the north or Aregund at Saint-Denis were often extraordinarily sumptuous. A kinswoman of Duke Guntram Boso was buried with "much-prized jewels and a great deal of gold." Accompanied by familiar objects, the dead passed from private life to private death, but they remained separated from the living by an invisible frontier.

The various funerary fashions of the Merovingian era give some idea of the ambiguous relation of the living to the dead, at once intimate and estranged. The first duty was to make sure that the corpse was well buried, set up on its own in the afterlife. A half-dozen tombs from north of the Seine indicate that horses were sacrificed and buried along with the body. This custom was an allusion to Wotan's horse Sleipnir, a solar symbol and servant of the war god who carried the dead back to earth once a year, on December 26, the feast day of the pagan god Jul. Less commonly, a stag, symbol of royalty, was buried with the body. To keep the dead confined in the other world, magic talismans and phylacteries were also buried:

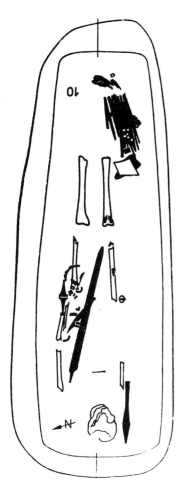

Grave of the blacksmith of Hérouvillette (Calvados), 6th century. This grave, located in the center of the Hérouvillette cemetery, held the weapons of a man who was a soldier as well as a blacksmith. It also held his blacksmith's tools, including a hammer and tongs, along with a number of coins; these would prove useful in the man's journey through the other world. (Caen, CRAM.)

necklaces of amber pearls, crystal pendants, boar's tusks, bear's teeth. Rare stones were credited with the power to ward off demons. The teeth of wild animals were supposed to preserve a man's strength. Pouches of hair and fingernail trimmings were supposed to impart vitality because hair and nails continue to grow after death.

Sometimes Christian influence led to the burial of relics. The coin placed in the mouth of a cadaver to pay the boatman for taking the body across the River Styx (Charon's obolus) was replaced by a host, despite a Church ban on the practice. Ceramic pitchers and glass goblets or flagons were sometimes placed at the feet of the body, offering terrestrial nourishment for the long journey into eternity. On occasion archaeologists have recovered the remains of food offerings that were placed in these vessels, compounded of meats, porridges, and nuts. Symbols of masculinity were included, such as hazel branches and cut flints (we have already seen why), as well as symbols of femininity, such as seashells, whose white mouths were thought to resemble the vulva. In short, the corpse ate, fought, and loved like a living person.

Materially, the life of the dead offered an exact parallel to the life of the living. Everything possible was done to keep the dead happy—in their own world. Some bodies, thought to be particularly dangerous, had their demons exorcised in cruel ways. Stillborn children were impaled, for it was believed that innocents could not remain underground. They tended to wander upward toward the surface of the earth,

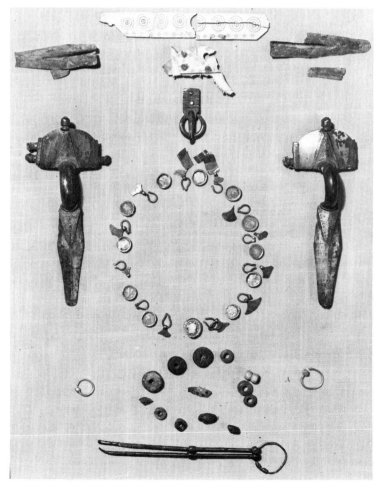

Young girl's jewelery from a cemetery near Strigny, 6th–7th century, including two curved silver fibulae, a necklace, a bracelet, gold earrings, a pair of stylets, pieces of a comb, and a buckle, typical of the jewels buried with the bodies of well-born women. (Chalon-sur-Saône, Danon Museum.)

Model of Hordain cemetery, 6th–7th century. Amid ordinary earthen graves stands a stone building intended to receive a personage of some importance. (Douai, Museum of Natural Sciences and Archaeology.)

where they reproached the living for not having been allowed to live, or beyond, to heaven. Others, possibly sorcerers or criminals, were nailed into their coffins, mutilated, decapitated, or surrounded by a circle of purifying charcoal.

Fear of death made it imperative that the needs of the dead be provided for. Hagiography and archaeology show that bodies were embalmed with myrrh and aloe. The body of Queen Bilichilde was discovered in Saint-Germain-des-Prés with a cushion of aromatic herbs under the head. Obviously such practices were employed only by wealthy families. Others cared for their dead in more prosaic ways, essentially in order to comfort themselves, to make life triumph over death by means other than lending to the cadaver the appearance of life. The body was placed on a stretcher and taken from the village to the cemetery in a procession, with a cloth or handkerchief over the face to avoid the evil eye. The body was carried at knee-height so that it would not escape the attraction of the underworld. Relatives came at regular intervals for commemorative banquets at the graveside, and archaeologists have even discovered the diners' refuse. Church councils, such as the Council of Tours in 567, protested: "Some people, perpetuating ancient errors, bring food to the dead for the Feast of Saint Peter [February 22] . . . and eat vegetables offered to the demons." These memorial banquets reaffirmed family ties and, it was thought, calmed the dead. We find traces of the practice as late as the eleventh century. There were also night vigils and nocturnal dancing and singing intended to drive away ghosts. Through such practices people brought peace to the cemeteries and calmed their own anxieties.

One final precaution had to be taken: the living had to be prevented from opening graves. The practice was common enough. How many archaeologists have been disappointed to

Gallo-Roman cemetery at La Gayole (Var), 5th–6th century. In contrast to the cemetery shown in the preceding illustration, we find heavy stone sarcophagi laid out in rows, illustrating the difference between egalitarian and hierarchical attitudes toward death.

find tombs in which they were interested already broken into, and how many sarcophagi can be seen today in our museums, smashed or with holes through which deft hands were passed to rob the cadaver of his weapons and jewels! Grave-robbing often occurred right around the time of the burial. Gregory of Tours mentions several instances, the best-known being that of a female relative of Guntram Boso, who was buried in a basilica in Metz; shortly thereafter the duke's "servants made their way into the church . . . shut the doors behind them, opened the tomb and stole as many of the precious objects from the dead body as they could lay their hands on." For contemporaries this kind of crime had two disastrous results. The individual whose grave was robbed lost his or her rank and returned at night to haunt the living. Such beliefs were at the root of legends of nocturnal phantoms, who followed either Diana and her dogs (as the Gallo-Romans believed) or Hilda (as the Germans believed) in a screaming train.

In order to quell such nightmares, steps had to be taken against the impious, whom greed made fearless of death. Some went so far as to rob a slain man's body before he had been laid in his grave; others waited until after the burial. "If a person breaks open a man's grave and robs it, he shall remain an outlaw until he has paid compensation to the relatives of the deceased. Until then no person shall give him bread or afford him hospitality. He shall pay the relatives or the wife or a close friend . . . 15 solidi. The author of such a crime shall be liable to a fine of 200 solidi." As we can see, the smaller amount went to the parentela, the larger amount to the representative of the king. The crime injured not only the deceased but also his kin. Solidarity continued beyond the grave, and it is not hard to understand why relatives were upset whenever a grave was robbed. It is more accurate, perhaps, to speak of graves being "violated" rather than "robbed." The crime, whether committed by a man or a woman, was grounds for divorce among Romans and Burgundians. The sexual connotations of "violation," with implications of necrophilia, would certainly suggest that the guilty party made him- or herself impure. Grave violation was seen as nothing less than adultery with the dead. Sex and death, both hedged about with taboos, were not supposed to come in contact, lest the world be turned upside down.

The final resting place was supposed to be strictly private. Contact between cadavers might disrupt the order of things and trouble the living. "If any person places one dead man on

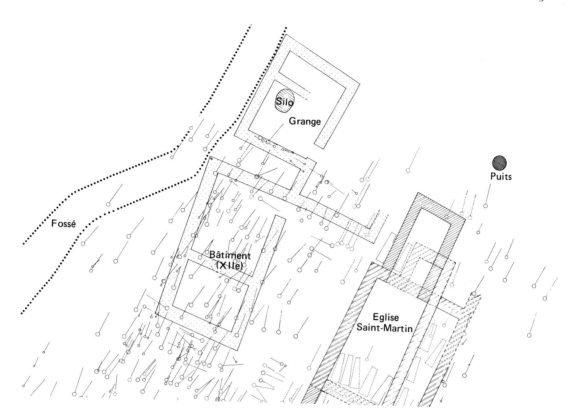

Silo

Grange

Puits

Fossé

Bâtiment
(XIIe)

Eglise
Saint-Martin

top of another in a coffin or a tomb . . . he shall be liable to a fine of 45 solidi." King Guntram extended this prohibition to include those who buried bodies in either an ordinary funeral basilica or a basilica containing the relics of a saint. There must have been sharp battles over the enforcement of such regulations, for archaeological excavation has shown that double and even triple burials were quite common. It was difficult to protect the intimacy of the tomb. This body of taboos was more restrictive than the set of marriage regulations, because it dealt with subjects that were at once public and private: burial and death, social status and tombs. When it came to sexuality, it was easier just to impose a strict set of rules on women to keep them from going astray. But try to keep an eye on a dead man! Doubts persisted all the more because they pertained to something invisible.

The Church took action, seeking to make death a public event so as to quell anxieties about the unknown and to make the moment of death and the state of being dead part of a journey toward another life, a reason for hope. The turning

Plan of Mondeville cemetery (Calvados). This is the oldest known example of a cemetery built next to a parish church (Saint-Martin of Mondeville, which dates from the second half of the 7th century). (Caen, CRAM.)

point seems to have come in the second half of the seventh century. The last private hypogea and mausolea date from around 750; in the meantime cemeteries were moved from the village outskirts into the parish churchyard. The oldest example, and the most surely dated (sometime between 650 and 700), is a cemetery at Saint-Martin-de-Mondeville in Normandy, discovered by Claude Lorren. It was patterned after suburban funerary basilicas dating back to the sixth century. Burial near the principal altar and the bodies of saints yielded a promise of salvation that pagan burial practices were unable to match. At the same time, the tombs of the privileged, of princes and military leaders, were distinguished from those of ordinary mortals and gathered together under the floors of churches or even in private chapels.

Thus death became a public phenomenon. The faithful stood on the bodies of their loved ones as they prayed. The world of the living and the world of the dead were united, separated only by a symbolic divide, the church floor, and sharing the same sacred space. The anxiety of private death gave way to the calm of public death, although women continued to wail, flay their cheeks with their fingernails, and tear out their hair to appease the deceased. Still, a definitive page in the history of death had been turned. Twentieth-century archaeologists, hoping for a major find in a Carolingian cemetery, have been frustrated by the new practice of mingling the dead with the living inside the village sanctuary. The thousands of skeletons that had slowly accumulated in Merovingian necropolises were now piled up in the shade of the parish orchard. Death was integrated into humankind.

*Fantasies of the Afterlife*      The struggle against death's terrors stirred the prophetic and eschatological imagination. The afterlife became increasingly important as a category of thought, and the clergy attempted to reshape the religious imagination, transmuting sublunary terrors into fears for eternal life. As the dead were moved from unconsecrated to hallowed ground, pastors sought to shift worries and fears about the end of the world from the present to the more or less distant future. This would allow human energies to be devoted to the transformation of humankind in preparation for eternal life rather than to warding off the forces of nature. The eschatological visions of private authors, made public by books and preaching, had a major impact on private psychology. They altered the human

Soissons, crypt of Saint-Médard, 7th–9th century. Sculptures of the Merovingian princes were placed in these sacred surroundings, bringing temporal power under the mysterious protection of the saint.

imagination forever. As early as the sixth century a few inspired leaders had sought in vain to herald the coming of a
new world. By the end of the seventh or the beginning of the
eighth century, however, a number of visionaries had come
forward in response to anxieties stemming from the crisis of
the Merovingian monarchy and the advance of Islam in the
Mediterranean region. Crises of civilization always produce
mystics capable of crystallizing the secret hopes and fears of
many people. This crisis was no exception, yielding its share
of pessimistic as well as optimistic visions.

The monk Baronte was a converted Frankish noble who,
in the course of a journey through the other world, was
reproached by demons for "having had three wives, which is
not allowed, and for other adulteries." In other words, this
former functionary had practiced polygamy and concubinage,
and the sins weighed upon his conscience. In his monastic
retreat in Méobecq (Berry), he imagined, some time before
678–679, a journey through heaven and hell, which gave him
a foretaste of the afterlife. Hell, according to Baronte, was
not, as the pagans had said, underground. It is somewhere in
space, outside our world. Hence it is impossible for the dead
to return to earth to torment the living. The damned can never
escape: "Thousands of men emitting melancholy moans,
bound and garroted by demons, who hover like bees around
the hive . . . Overwhelmed by their torture, they scream end-
lessly." The devils are black. They first tear their victims with
their nails and fangs, then devour them. Clearly the focus of
anxiety has been shifted away from the present. In painting a
terrifying image of the fate in store for sinners, Baronte hoped
to shock his readers and bring about an inward conversion
such as he himself had experienced. Finally, accompanied by
the archangel Raphael, he passes through three gates and
comes to a fourth, the gate of heaven, guarded by Saint Peter.
But Peter bars the entry. The time has not yet come. Baronte's
journey through the other world ends just short of ineffable
happiness, which the soul must merit. Thus hell provokes
anxieties, the purpose of which is to transform the present and
thereby force open the gates barring the way to the mysterious
future. The imagination being absorbed in the afterlife, realism
prevails in everyday life; Christian man was free to acknowledge history, as pagan man had never done. The pagan cosmos
had neither beginning nor end and was ruled by eternally
recurring forces. But the Christian visionary evoked fears of
damnation, not today but tomorrow. He broke the endless

Jouarre, tomb of Bishop
Agilbert, late 7th–early 8th
century. One of the finest Merovingian sculptures, it is an image of the resurrected Christ in
triumph.

cycle of spring, summer, autumn, and winter, of birth, maturation, harvest (or razzia), and death, and thus swept aside the pagan myth of eternal recurrence, substituting instead a new vision, that of irreversible, linear time.

A man's work, this pessimistic vision was addressed to the overgrown children, the eternal youths, who composed Merovingian society. Violent men, the only lesson they understood was that of corporal punishment. A more optimistic vision, this one the work of a woman, was addressed to a different audience and fostered a different kind of imagination. Aldegund, a young noblewoman, had refused several offers of marriage. Her parents finally accepted her decision, and she founded a convent at Maubeuge, where she died in 684. There she had twelve visions, which she recounted to her nuns for

Jouarre, tomb of Bishop Agilbert, late 7th–early 8th century. The resurrection of the dead, whose joy at being released from their graves is evident. This vision of hope was located in a convent.

Plaque used to separate choir from nave, which is to say, clergy from faithful, in the 8th century. Two birds peck at a vine, symbol of eternity. (Metz, Church of Saint-Pierre-de-la-Citadelle.)

their spiritual edification. Whereas Baronte had drawn upon pagan anxieties about the cosmos, Aldegund concentrated her attention on the pagan sexual dilemma: destruction or procreation. She sought to overcome the contradiction by drawing a parallel between male-female relations and the relations between humans and the God who created them. In a highly personal style, reminiscent in some ways of the *Song of Songs,* she describes her quest for God in concrete images. Then, in her sixth vision, she tells of the intoxicating encounter with her Beloved, a moment of ineffable happiness followed by sudden loss. There follows a scene of darkest night, reminiscent of Theresa of Avila. Aldegund writes of the impossibility of love, of its inevitable failure before the strangeness of the Other. The luminous globes that had lighted the convent give way to thirst, pallor, affliction, caustic fire, ardent heat, and the temptation to renounce the quest. Suddenly, the heavenly spouse is rediscovered and the ultimate union takes place, freely accepted after so much suffering. The original instinct has been transformed into acceptance of a beloved quite different from the nun's first image of Him. Here, the earth has been projected into heaven, and the optimistic nun has placed amorous passion, the bane of terrestrial marriage, at the center of her vision of heavenly marriage. What was to be feared on earth becomes constructive in heaven, provided that one first dies to the world and to one's own instincts. The imagery of heavenly marriage is thus diametrically opposed to the imagery of earthly marriage. Baronte was content to use fear of damnation to obtain good behavior and hence salvation. Aldegund transformed passion into love of liberty, a response to the love that saves. This was something of which only a small minority were capable, perhaps only a few individuals. But the fact that they were able to broaden their imaginations to such a degree proves that Christian culture had become firmly established. Private life took on a new dimension: the relation of the self to the afterlife, whether in salvation, damnation, or self-realization.

In visionary literature, which abounded in Carolingian times, the supernatural is omnipresent. Premonitory dreams, descriptions of infernal tortures and glorious arrivals in paradise, proliferated and spread outside the monastery. Most if not nearly all followed the pessimistic line traced by Baronte. The punishment of the great of this world was a nearly universal theme. At least three such essays were produced after the death of Charlemagne, all foreseeing his damnation unless prayers were said asking forgiveness for his sexual sins, presumably with his many concubines (relations with whom, as we have seen, were considered a form of incest). The Carolingians were as realistic as their predecessors: wild animals devour the parts of the damned responsible for their sins; dragons breathe fire; pitch, sulfur, lead, and wax are melted in ovens. The visionaries could draw upon a large arsenal of purifying instruments, and the way in which each did draw upon that arsenal reveals his or her obsessions. As in earlier periods, those obsessions grew mainly out of troubled consciences, especially in the wake of a rising tide of civil war and defeat at the hands of the Vikings after about 830. People worried that their failure resulted not from neglect of the laws of this world but from the indirect influence of the other world. Heaven and earth were in communication. Sex and death therefore appeared in a new light: Would they stand in the way of man's future happiness?

Monk reading. Ivory, 9th century. (Montpellier, Fabre Museum.)

# ❧ Sacred and Secret

THE burden of violence and fear of sex and death gave rise to obscure feelings of guilt. With the victory of Christianity over paganism the relations between each individual and God assumed paramount importance. The meaning of intimacy and inwardness changed. The Church made writing sacred, and the clerk and the scribe—mediators between man and God who knew, or perhaps revealed, everyone's inner secrets—played a key role in promoting new kinds of behavior. Everything was questioned, and much ambiguity lay in the answers.

In 391 Christianity replaced paganism as the state religion in Gaul and throughout the West. Denounced by miracle-working saints and condemned by church councils, pagan religious practice became steadily more private and, increasingly, hidden. Paganism took refuge in nocturnal cults, divination, magic, and folklore, or, better still, donned Christian garb. For paganism the "sacred" meant an amalgam of cosmic powers subsuming men and things, powers that anyone could use for good or ill, for himself or others, by performing the appropriate rituals, based on the idea of a strict exchange of gifts. As the official cults disappeared, particularly after the Council of Leptines in 744, which probably shut the last rural temples, or *fana,* pagan faith, henceforth restricted to the countryside, was increasingly subject to Christian influence through the penitentials, guidebooks of the confessors. Although these guides were eventually molded rather effectively to their purpose, they showed little grasp of the fear and anguish that underlay pagan religious attitudes.

---

*Pagan Survivals*

Bishops and clergy complained, more or less constantly until at least the tenth century, about the continuation of pagan

Hooked lance, second half of 5th century. Sarcophagus in the Capuchin cemetery at Bourges. This iron lance, with two side hooks terminating in animal heads attached to the central shaft, bears the inscription *patricius regis,* king's patrician. It must have belonged to a high official of the Visigoth king. (Bourges, Museum of Berry.)

practices, particularly in northern Gaul, Friesland, and Saxony, all recently conquered regions. Many private observances continued unchanged for more than five centuries, as did such pagan public holidays as New Year's Day (which has continued to do rather well). Traditional methods of divination, both Roman and German, helped people cope with anxiety about the future. A squawking crow that circled to the left foretold a happy journey. Barley that leapt into the air when thrown on hot coals was an omen of danger. Careful study of the snorting and excrement of horses and oxen could reveal whether the day would be good or bad. Soothsayers sometimes called upon the dead. At a sacred spot such as a crossroads they would sit, for instance, on the hide of a bull, bloody side up so as to force the demons to come up out of the earth. In the dead of night they held mysterious communication with spirits, thanks to which they were able to predict the outcome of a battle or the reason for a disaster.

Such arts, long practiced by the Gauls and Celts, are mentioned by Burchard of Worms as late as 1008–1012. Burchard also says that women were still being used as mediums. The Celtic *filida* were supposed to be able to foretell the outcome of future battles. Among the Germans, women were the keepers of the sacred runes, used by the Vikings in the ninth and tenth centuries. The word "rune" means "secret," but also "tender friend." The mystery of the runes was just one of the untold riches believed to be possessed by the female sex. Every letter contained secrets of the gods. The rune *y* signified wealth and favor; *n,* misery, misfortune; *t,* victory; *j,* a good harvest and a prosperous year. The letters were carved on sticks, which a woman drew at random, like lots. Even after Christianization the runes were still thought to tell the future. Indeed, the practice was Christianized to such a degree that it was at times tolerated by the Church, which referred to the runes as the *sortes sanctorum,* or saints' lots.

Of forty-six known penitentials, twenty-six mention, without particular disapproval, the practice of having a child or priest open the Bible at random and read the first line on which his eyes happened to fall; this was believed to reveal a true prophecy. Gregory of Tours mentions the practice several times. The career of Gundovald the Pretender, which ended tragically at Saint-Bertrand-de-Comminges in 585, was predicted in another way—by interpretation of a natural disaster. Lifted up on the *pavois,* or shield that soldiers wore on their shoulders, the new king stumbled and nearly fell to the ground. Later there was an earthquake, and a column of fire hung in the sky with a star perched on top of it. In Gregory's mind these portents foretold Gundovald's violent death.

Christian or pagan, these methods of fortune-telling were based on a fear that God or the gods had willed a certain fate, nullifying free will. When this happened, a person could only try to gain some control over the sacred powers that held the future in their hands. In this civilization of oral tradition, books, indeed anything couched in written form, became mysterious and sacred objects. This was unprecedented. The latest example of this state of mind is the *Domesday Book*—the very name is revealing—promulgated by William the Conqueror in 1086. In reality of course the book had nothing to do with "doomsday" at all; it was merely a compendium of what was due the king and his lords, so detailed that a glance at the page pertaining to this or that estate was enough to put an end to any dispute and make definitive judgment possible. To the illiterate, writing therefore appeared magical and prophetic.

The Council of Paris (829) renewed earlier condemnations

Manuscript from Aratos, 9th century. Diana, the moon goddess, holding a large reed pen, rides in a chariot drawn by two oxen. This work on astronomy and astrology mingled a little scientific knowledge with a lot of belief in the influence of the stars. (Boulogne-sur-Mer, Municipal Library.)

of these beliefs, which influenced even the clergy. Pierre Riché has discovered Carolingian manuscripts bearing magic squares, which state that an illness can be ended "by combining the letters of one's name with the numbers of the days on which one became ill." Incantations in macaronic Latin were used as remedies for hemorrhage, dropsy, eye ailments, and so forth. Secret magic could be used to do good or harm to others.

Magic, though strictly prohibited, was the ideal expression of ambivalent pagan notions of the sacred. It was used, in particular, as a means of altering one's relations with other people. Earlier I mentioned the use of amulets and phylacteries to protect the dead. The living also wore these magic charms, the most famous example being the crystal talisman that Charlemagne wore around his neck. Belt buckles were decorated with designs supposedly capable of fending off evil. Bundles of herbs were tied to arms or legs as good-luck charms. Oaths were sworn by a man's hair or beard, so that in case of perjury one became subject to the vital force that supposedly issued from the head. Rabanus Maurus reports that the skulls of dead men were sometimes reduced to ashes, from which a therapeutic potion was prepared. A magical medicine sought to capture whatever effluvia of the divine the cosmos contained. No effort was spared to save a sick child. The mother might place the child at a crossroads in a tunnel of earth closed by thorns at either end. Contact with mother earth was supposed to simulate a return to the maternal breast. The underworld somehow trapped the evil, and if the child ceased to cry, it was cured. Children with whooping cough were placed inside a hollow tree. For each disease, a way had to be found to tap the forces of the occult, to work an exchange, draw off some flux, or barricade the route.

I shall say nothing about the gathering of herbs and medicinal plants, carried out, to the accompaniment of incantations, on the first of every month. These practices were quickly Christianized through the recital of a Pater and a Credo. More interesting were the potions, which embodied common ideas about sex and death and reveal the extent to which private life was racked by dark combats and constant obsessions. Everyone believed in evil spells, as the laws attest, and most spells were associated with magic potions, which could do good or ill. The penitentials corroborate these assertions. Twenty-six of them state that poisons obtained by mixing, among other things, belladonna and honeysuckle could

Handle, bronze, 7th century. This late Merovingian piece depicts a man brandishing two crosses designed to ward off evil spirits. (Metz Museum.)

Baptistry of Saint John, Poitiers, 6th century. One of the few Merovingian monuments to have survived, despite the elimination of baptism by immersion.

cause death or abortion. There are forty-eight references to love potions, twenty-six of which were prepared by women. To make a man impotent it seems that sewing ribbons to the clothes of the man and his wife was not enough. A woman who wished to cause impotence undressed, covered herself with honey, and rolled around on a pile of wheat. The grains were then carefully removed, placed in a hand mill, and ground by turning the handle clockwise rather than the normal counterclockwise. With the flour thus produced, the woman baked a bread which she gave to the man she wished to "castrate." Since the flour had been milled in the wrong direction, the stimulating effects of nudity and honey were nullified and the man was unsexed. If, however, the flour was milled normally and the dough kneaded between the woman's thighs (that is, on her genitals), the result was the opposite; bread baked with this dough could be used to arouse desire in a woman's husband or a man she wished to seduce. Another magical technique involved placing a fish in a woman's vagina until the fish died. Thereby imbued with generative and aphrodisiac powers, the fish was cooked, seasoned, and given to the woman's husband. This not only worked as an aphrodisiac but also prevented the husband from taking a mistress. No wonder men of the early Middle Ages were convinced that women possessed not only the secrets of that folly, love, but also the keys to that precious treasure, life. The Celtic myth of the love potion that brought Tristan and Isolde together despite themselves, a myth spread by word of mouth long before it was written down in the twelfth century, must have had its counterpart in real life. To believe in the folly of love was to experience it.

I shall not dwell further on other types of love potions, concocted of such ingredients as menstrual blood, sperm, and urine. The principle in all cases was the same: to capture the vital forces contained in various emanations of living bodies. The great secret of the soothsayers, sorcerers, and women who frequented the sacred woods (*nimidas, nemeton*) by night, who joined in ritual dances to secure fertility and prosperity, to keep the dead in their graves, and to ward off ghosts, was knowledge of how to tame the sacred, how to approach stealthily its dangerous power.

## The Dawn of Conscience

How was the transition from the pagan sacred to the Christian sacrament effected? How could beliefs impregnable because domestic and intimate be Christianized? How was one to find God in one's heart, when previously divine power had been experienced as something external? The creation of new sacred spaces, basilicas and sanctuaries, the development of the cult of the saints, and liturgical processions and celebrations helped to make faith public. We have already seen why the cult of the dead became public. In order to "privatize" Christian belief, two courses of action were available: evil magic could be attributed to Satan, or beneficial magic could be transformed by Christianization. I have mentioned the way in which the Christian imagination incorporated the devil into its vision of the afterlife. The devil was also incorporated into life here below. Idol worship was branded a manifestation of Satan: the idol was itself a demon. Similarly, potions, incantations, *sortes sanctorum,* and magic of all kinds were condemned as demonic. The Councils of Agde (506) and Orléans

(511) condemned soothsayers and pythonesses as "possessed by demons." Demons, described as incorporeal but real beings and symbolized by lions and serpents, were useful as personalizations of the obscure cosmic forces feared by the ancient pagans. Naming the enemy shifted the balance of power. Demons could change their shape at will; we saw how they were driven from the bodies of the possessed in the sanctuaries. Gregory of Tours tells us that the devil "soiled the bishop's throne, on which he sat in mockery, dressed as woman." He attacked the weak: "Women, cringing creatures, must always fear him." He could also become an enemy within, insinuating himself into evil thoughts, deceptive actions, and jealous feelings. Fear of the devil became the new name for the feelings of anxiety people felt toward the world's evil forces. Fortunately the saints were nearby to nullify the devil's work with their powerful patronage. Threateningly vast, untamed nature left plenty of room for a duel with the

Crypt of Saint-Germain of Auxerre. Tomb of Saint Germain.

devil, a combat rather than, as with the pagan gods, a legalistic arrangement occasionally violated by ruse.

Evidence as to the inner reality of this changing perception of the devil is lacking, however, for autobiography, a new genre inaugurated by Augustine's *Confessions,* was abandoned in the seventh century. It does not reappear until the twelfth century, with Raoul Glaber and especially Guibert of Nogent. If we turn to hagiography for information about the internalization of religious feelings, we encounter the same obstacles and obtain at best indirect evidence, notably in connection with cases of possession. By contrast, there are numerous examples of the Christianization of pagan behavior. In the compendia of miracles a fair proportion (as high as 26 percent) are concerned with accidents and maladies, particularly paralysis, that befall men and women, often of high rank, when they refuse to obey a saint's orders or indicate their skepticism or hide their sins. These "miracles" of punishment suggest that the punished themselves felt latent guilt, particularly in the Carolingian sanctuaries of northern France. Such phenomena are rarer in Merovingian times, and when a sinner is punished, the saint heals but does not cause the punishment; in other words, the saint's role is external. Therein lies a crucial difference between these two important phases of Christianization, as though the nature of conscience had shifted from external awareness of wrongdoing to internal awareness of responsibility.

In order to gain a better grasp of this important phenomenon, the development of an inner conscience, we should examine changes in the sacraments. Baptism in the Carolingian era was limited to children (except in missionary territories). Aspersion replaced immersion. Water stood now for regeneration rather than a source of life; it symbolized the passage from death to resurrection. Baptism was perceived as a sacrament that washed away sin and brought the individual into the Church, into society, and into Christendom, while holding out the promise of salvation. In a sense, baptism was believed to work automatically, almost magically, and this notion was responsible for Charlemagne's forced baptism of the Saxons, over the protests of Alcuin.

Baptism established a spiritual kinship between the infant, the godmother, and the godfather, which became a canonical impediment to marriage between godparent and child. The Council of Rome (721) imposed on couples who violated this prohibition seven to fifteen years' penitence and forced them to separate. The Carolingian clergy believed that such marriages were a form of incest. In effect, godmother and godfather became members of the child's kinship group. Stress was placed on the "new birth" represented by baptism. But the death rate in those days was high, and many children must have found themselves orphans with godparents as their guardians. There must have been pressure on the godparents to become parents in the flesh, that is, to marry, since adopting a child created a strong emotional bond. Marriages between godparents must have become common as the baptism of children became increasingly popular. Baptism, like relationships created by marriage, vassalage, and so on, was a way of fostering solidarity. The councils dealt severely with endogamous marriages, common among pagans, owing to the Augustinian principle that marriage is a *seminarium caritatis,* a seed of love, meaning love as distinct from kinship. Because parental, filial, and spiritual love already exists in a family, it is pointless and dangerous to reinforce it, but indispensable and creative to draw that love out of the family and "sow" it elsewhere. Thus, the view that baptism somehow implies adoption of the child by the community worked against the endogamous family and served to counter the forces of attraction that the baptism ceremony, like similar pagan ceremonies, tended to unleash.

Another revealing change concerns the eucharist. In Merovingian times the consecrated bread was placed in the hands of the communicant at mass. But the Council of Auxerre (561–605) stipulated that when a woman received the body of Christ, she must wrap her hand in her dress, as though some trace of impurity, having to do with menstruation, attached to her flesh. The Carolingian church did not go so far as the Byzantine church in this regard, but when the Roman liturgical reform was adopted, Alcuin took advantage of the occasion to win approval of the principle that, in order to avoid sacrilege, the communion wafer (now of unleavened bread) should be placed directly into the mouth of the communicant.

The use of unleavened bread was a point of constant dispute with the Byzantine church. There can be no doubt that it gave concrete representation to what was at bottom a pagan, magical notion, that the eucharist was nonperishable and untouchable. The idea of the bread of the eucharist as a natural nourishment was thereby obscured, supplanted by a supernatural idea, and the relationship with God lost something of its human aspect. Christianity asked each believer to

Pair of pagan idols: a male on the left, a female on the right. Wood, 5th century, from the Braak Marshes. These crudely sculpted branches exemplify pagan beliefs in fertility gods. (Schleswig, Schleswig-Holstein Museum.)

Life of Saint Radegund, 11th century. Radegund is shown seated beside her husband Clotaire I. Disgusted by his polygamy, she sought and obtained permission to separate and entered a convent at Poitiers, which she dedicated to the Holy Cross. (Poitiers, Municipal Library.)

make a considerable leap, from belief in distant and terrifying gods to belief in one God, good and immediately present. With the acceptance of large numbers of Germans into the Church, compromise became necessary, and fear of a transcendent God may have been the least objectionable pedagogical alternative for approaching Him with respect.

If the eucharist became less familiar than it had been in late antiquity, penitence evolved in the opposite direction. Until the time of Caesarius of Arles (503–542) absolution was freely offered to sinners who wished to be shriven of sins. The sinner who desired healing joined a special group, the order of penitents. This joining was a public event, and absolution was granted only once in a person's lifetime. Such public dishonor was inconceivable for German warriors. People were afraid of being damned if they died after repeating a sin for which absolution had already been granted. Hence late-sixth-century Celtic monks proposed a new manner of reconciliation with God: private penance with auricular confession, a secret avowal of sins coupled with a whole schedule of punishments, rather like the schedule of punishments in the Germanic laws. This proposal met with immediate success and enjoyed continued popularity for many years to come, since the last penitential, that of Alan of Lille, dates fom 1180.

Just as death was made public in order to eradicate fear of the dead, penitence became private in order to help people cope with the fear of dying.

At first glance, it seems unlikely that penitential literature should have changed the way people thought, given the close kinship between the Germanic laws and the penitentials, particularly those composed prior to the ninth century. For each sin the penitentials specified a punishment consisting of a certain number of years on bread and water. If a person could not or would not fast, he or she was allowed to pay so many solidi per year of fasting in lieu thereof. Such a practice could hardly foster the development of conscience, since no account was taken of the sinner's intention, recidivism was always possible, and the commutation of sentence by payment of cash perpetuated the notion that salvation could be bought. In short, the old pagan contract *do ut des*—I give you so that you will give me—was maintained. The free grant of God's mercy was totally neglected. Accordingly, the Council of Paris (829) condemned the penitentials and ordered all of them burned. Again, however, the high Carolingian clergy was totally out of touch with its flock, for in practice, of the two or three books that a country priest would have owned in the ninth and later centuries, one was always a penitential. The prescriptions contained therein obviously responded to deeply felt needs of the faithful and must have alleviated their anxieties.

Whatever concessions the penitentials may have made to pagan religious attitudes, they nevertheless resulted in a complete reversal of the values embodied in the Germanic laws. Whereas the latter considered theft a more serious crime than murder, and rape and abduction more serious than polygamy and concubinage, the penitentials placed three major sins at the top of the list: fornication (a term applied to sexual sins of all sorts), acts of violence, and perjury. Perjury was the only common concern of lay and clerical lawmakers. To give in to the temptations of the flesh, to kill a man, or to swear falsely were the sins most often committed and most reprehensible in the eyes of all. Another innovation was that the penalty for each sin took no account of the sinner's social status (although it is true that only the wealthy could afford to pay to have their penance commuted). It made no difference whether a man was a slave, a free man, a noble, a royal antrustion, or what have you. Equality before God was genuinely affirmed, and the arbitrary power of masters over slaves was denounced. Penance for a given sin did vary, however, depending on whether the sinner was a layman or an ecclesiastic. From psalmist to bishop, penances were graduated; and in any case they were always greater than for laymen. But among the latter no account was taken of sex, occupation, or ethnic origin. Penalties for sins helped to establish equality among laymen and "sacrality" among clerics, which is why the penalties on the clergy were so harsh. The penitentials gave currency to the notion that priests and monks ought to be absolutely impeccable, thereby setting them apart from other Christians.

That said, it should come as no surprise that a lay murderer was liable to a penance of three to five years, whereas a bishop who committed murder lost his episcopal status and was obliged to fast on bread and water for twelve years. In punishing violence, the penitentials reflect a heightened sense of personal responsibility, a shift toward primacy of being over having. Theft, with the exception of church- and grave-robbing, which represented an attack on sacred values, was not severely punished in comparison to murder. The Code of Euric had stipulated that a slave who committed a crime on orders of his master should not be punished. The penitentials went even further: they stated that the slave's master bore responsibility for the crime and should be required to pay damages. Such a statement would have been impossible in the fifth century, as would the notion that a master who beat his slave to death should be obliged to do four or five years' penance, just as if he had killed a free man.

The real innovations lay elsewhere, however. Certain penances seem to have been aimed at violence within the clan. A master who raped his slave was obliged to make amends (in certain cases) by manumitting the woman. Many masters must have gnashed their teeth over this affront to what they considered their right. Even harder to accept was the punishment of *faide,* murder for vengeance. The Church was tolerant of this crime at first, but from the ninth century on, murder committed with malice aforethought was punished much more severely than other kinds of murder. Judges took note of the criminal's subjective intentions, even if this was never stated in so many words. After A.D. 800 penances for murder of a bishop, spouse, or lay person for reasons of vengeance were increased in an effort to put an end to these crimes, not new to be sure but increasingly considered intolerable in this age of Carolingian renaissance. This is particularly clear, I think, in the case of the murder of a woman by her husband.

Soldier trampling his en-
emy. Ivory, 9th–10th cen-
tury. (Florence, Bargello.)

Penitentials prior to the ninth century do not mention this crime, though far be it from me to suggest that the Merovingians did not murder their wives; remember that Chilperic had Galswinth strangled. In those days, however, the need to get rid of one's wife, especially in the nobility, was not as great, given the practice of polygamy. But the new emphasis on monogamy and indissoluble marriage resulted in an increase in what I called "Carolingian divorce." Something had to be done to stem the rising tide of murders. Wife-murder was therefore declared the most serious kind of murder. Three penitentials condemned the murder of a lord or a father or "of one's wife, who is a part of oneself." The wife who poisoned her husband was included in the same group. Men and women were here treated equally, even if married women enjoyed special protection. The penance for adultery, which prior to the Carolingian reform had been three years, was increased to seven years. Murder of a spouse, which had been punished by fourteen years' penance in the ninth century, demanded lifetime penance in the eleventh. With such severity the frequency of the practice decreased, to judge by the chronicles. Nobles who wished to get rid of sterile, ill-tempered, or useless wives, or simply of wives who stood in the way of their political ambitions, had to concoct falsehoods about being more closely related than canon law allowed, in the hope of being granted an annulment and permission to remarry.

The authors of the penitentials were much less severe toward rape and abduction. The penance for these crimes, around three years, did not increase, unless clerics were involved. Why? For the same reasons responsible for severity regarding wife-murder: the Church sought to allow women equality with men and freedom in marriage. The ecclesiastical authorities began to take an interest in cases concerning abductions and rapes committed by youths seeking to circumvent parental opposition to marriage, in order to determine whether the parties had consented, on the grounds that "mutual consent makes marriage." In northern Gaul a curious custom known as the *stefgang,* or walk between stakes, appeared. If a family complained that a daughter had been abducted and raped, the girl was obliged to stand between two stakes; behind one stake stood her own family, behind the other the family of her abductor. She had to decide which to choose. If she chose her own family, the compensation for abduction and rape had to be paid. If she chose her abductor's family, her marriage was officially celebrated. Thus, in order

Abbot wearing liturgical robes and holding a crook. Gelasian sacramentary known as "de Gellone," Flavigny, 755–787. (Paris, Bibliothèque Nationale, Latin 12048.)

to validate the mutual consent of the two parties, given in private, that consent had to be made public. A woman's private life thus became fully autonomous, a first step toward a certain equality.

The penitentials really did change private life insofar as outward behavior was concerned. A more delicate question, however, is whether auricular confession actually altered private marital behavior, for here the clash between the Christian ideal and pagan beliefs and practices was clear. What did people confess to priests that paganism had not disapproved? Many real sins were acknowledged to the confessor, sins that paganism did not punish. In order of seriousness it seems that bestiality, often linked to sodomy, ranked first, followed by oral sex, incest in the broad sense, divorce and indeed all forms of marital separation, especially after the ninth century and in particular on grounds of sterility of the woman.

The latter prohibition was totally incomprehensible to the new Christians, as was the condemnation of female homosexuality, which pagans did not consider a grave matter. These two attitudes were patently contradictory, in that the sterile woman was held to be damned by the gods, while the lesbian, unlike the pederast, remained pure. Less serious sins incurred milder punishments, generally a few fortnights rather than the three to seven years incurred for the graver sins; included were masturbation and the use of sexual positions other than face to face. In addition, it was recommended that couples abstain from sex for three days prior to Sunday, Easter, Christmas, and other holidays. (From penitentials such as Finnian's in the sixth century it has been calculated that no more than two hundred days remained during which couples could have legitimate intercourse.)

By now we have a fairly clear picture of what the confessors rejected out of hand and what they strongly recommended. In keeping with the Bible, they opposed any union that did not mirror the union of Christ with the Church, that is, monogamous and indissoluble. They sought a natural order, at once divine and human, both in society and in psychology. It followed from this that women needed some measure of protection from men, that blood vengeance had to be quelled, and that desire had to be channeled toward useful ends. Pleasure in sexual intercourse was never condemned for itself, only when it became an end in itself. Pleasure does not seem to have been an overwhelming preoccupation of the male at this time. Fellatio, for example, is condemned not because

Bible of Charles the Bald, ca. 846, showing Saint Jerome translating the Bible. (Paris, Bibliothèque Nationale, Latin 1.)

the male seeks pleasure but because the woman performs it on her husband, "so that he will love you by dint of your diabolical exertions." Many sexual practices must have been considered pagan, magical, or demonic. That is why the pejorative term *amor,* unruly passion, and its opposite, *caritas,* chaste conjugal love, do not appear in these purely disciplinary texts. Only once does Halitgaire of Cambrai employ the word *amor* in his penitential: "If by casting a spell someone seeks to obtain the amor of someone else." The word here clearly refers to unruly passion. By contrast, *libido, desiderium, concupiscentia,* and *delectatio*—lust, desire, selfish desire, and pleasure—occur frequently. In sharp contrast to the Germanic laws, however, both sexes are treated alike. Whereas pagans held that woman alone produced passionate desire, Christians blamed both men and women. This helps explain the clash between pagan and Christian outlooks and the serious conflict that occurred in the ninth century between Church and nobility over the question of marriage.

The change in mental outlook did not occur overnight. Violence perpetuated male superiority, as did a linguistic phenomenon about which little is known: the shift from vulgar Latin to proto-French. Although Carolingian councils such as the Council of Compiègne (757) proclaimed "a single law for men and women," people were slow to accept the idea. Evidence for this assertion can be found in the words of one bishop to the synod of Mâcon in 585, words that are all too well known: "He rose to say that a woman cannot be called man (*homo*), but he calmed down when the bishops explained to him that the Old Testament says: 'Male and female created

He them,' and called them Adam, which means man (*homo*) made of earth; at the same time He named the woman Eve [the living]. In other words, he said that both were men." This text, responsible for the legend that a council denied that women have souls, actually reveals a linguistic mutation from which modern French still suffers. When the bishop raised the question, he was thinking of *homo* in the sense of *vir,* the male, rather than "humankind in general." His question was perfectly logical, but his Latin was already French, and French, which had dropped the term *vir,* still lacks a specific word for man in the sense of male (whereas German distinguishes between *der Mann* and *der Mensch*). The dual meaning of "man" (human being and male) perpetuated the conviction that one sex was superior to the other, whereas the biblical text implied strict equality. Here the gap between the pagan and Christian mentality is patent, and because of the power of the signifier to obscure the signified, the distinction remains irremediable even today.

If the Church's intransigence on questions of sexuality and marriage divided pagans and Christians, there were nevertheless points of agreement. The penitentials reveal how Merovingians and Carolingians sought to make private life fruitful and pure. Sodomy and adultery had been considered grave sins by the pagans. But the penance for adultery by a woman had been greater than that for adultery by a man up to the ninth century, when the two became equal. In other words, Christianity rejected the pagan notion that adultery pollutes the woman but not the man. Pagans and Christians were in accord when it came to the condemnation of abortion; contraception (including the use of pessaries and philters); mutilation, especially castration; the prohibition of nudity (for which reasons were never given); and banning sexual relations during menstruation or after childbirth (for reasons of impurity). The penitentials adopted two important religious intuitions of the pagans: that the purpose of marriage is procreation; and that this purpose cannot be realized unless both husband and wife are completely pure. (Here the misogyny of paganism reemerges: abortion, infanticide, and contraception are considered acts for which the woman bears sole responsibility, and the remarriage of widows was still considered inadvisable.) Woman is impure by dint of her blood and all that flows out of her. One cannot help being struck by the total contradiction between these prescriptions and the words of Matthew 15:18: "What comes out of the mouth proceeds from the heart, and

Psalter of Utrecht (816–835). Soldiers pray, their lances stuck into the ground, while the besieged citizens beg the Lord to send his angels to close the city gates. The mystery of trust in God. (Utrecht, Library of the Royal University.)

this defiles a man." Here again we encounter the confusion of purity with cleanness. Pagan ideas clearly influenced Christian behavior. But in a rural civilization, where men and women lived in mud and dung, how could such confusion have been avoided? Daily life was unclean, hence private life was also contaminated, and in these conditions moralism flourished.

---

*Inwardness through Prayer*

Such were the secrets whispered into the ear of the confessor in an atmosphere of ambiguous sacredness, now in agreement, now in disagreement with the pronouncements of the Church. Confession was a positive counterpart to pagan proscriptions and Christian anathemata; it created a conscience in laymen and even more in monks and priests, whose sins were punished much more harshly than those of the laity. Much literature was addressed to laymen in order to form their moral judgment. The *Mirrors* of the princes sought to foster a Christian political judgment based on justice and obedience. *De institutione laicali* by Jonas of Orléans disseminated an ideal of Christian marriage based on restraint and chastity. Dhuoda, in the manual she addressed to her son, sought to teach the future warrior about loyalty, charity, and prayer. Halitgaire of Cambrai produced a penitential enumerating the qualities that one should seek to develop in a Christian, be he active or contemplative: faith, hope, and charity, the latter still defined as love ("He who does not love does not believe and hopes in vain"), prudence, justice, strength, and temperance. Prayer was the ultimate education.

The initiator of this education of the heart in Gaul was John Cassian, who founded a monastery and convent in Marseilles in 417. His *Institutes of the Cenobites, Conferences of the Elders,* and, above all, *Collations* were read constantly, at supper (from which comes the modern sense of "collation," meaning "light meal"). They helped develop a method for gaining knowledge of God based on study of the Bible, or *lectio divina,* divine reading.

Based on the psalms and on the internal experiences of the first monks, divine reading was a rumination "of mouth [out loud] and heart," called divine because it was the word of God proffered in the presence of God. ("Wherever two or three people pray to me, there I shall be found," said Jesus.) Knowledge of God came from listening to the words, much as in the course of a long conversation each participant lets others know who he is by what he says. Reading and rumi-

Saint Luke. Ivory, 9th–10th century. The evangelist is shown here writing in the classical pose of the scribe, seated on a cushion. (Lyons, Museum of Fine Arts.)

nation eventually impressed the word of God upon the minds of those who prayed. Then, even in the midst of manual labor, meditation could arise from the depths of one's being, meditation being a combination of dialogue and emotion welling up from the words engraved upon the heart. Cassian also provided a stratagem against vice and a form of therapy: each monk should confess his every wicked thought to the elder who served as his spiritual guide. Such deep psychological introspection was radically new. Conscience ceased to be

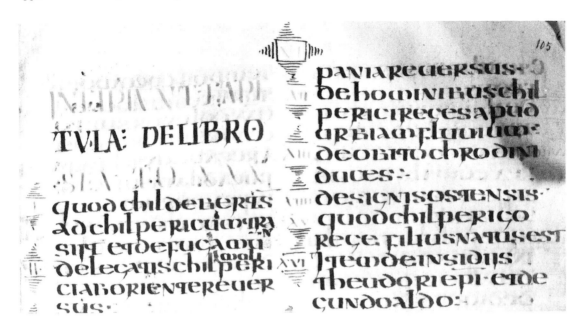

Manuscript of Gregory of Tours, 7th century. His *History of the Franks* was written between 567 and 593. Shown is the table of contents to Book 6. (Cambrai, Municipal Library.)

merely a vague sense of guilt imposed from outside and became a method of observing and analyzing inner spiritual conflict.

Saint Benedict of Norcia, whose rule was adopted in 817 by all monasteries throughout the Carolingian Empire, further developed Cassian's innovations in the direction of a personal relationship with God. "We must prepare our hearts and bodies [note that minds are not mentioned] for combat under holy obedience to the divine commandments . . . We are therefore going to establish a school in which one may learn the service of the Lord." Once the young monk learned to read and write by committing all 150 psalms to memory, "rumination" allowed him to embark upon meditation. The rule required each monk to chant or recite all the psalms every week. Fifty-two times each year, the monastic community sang all 150 psalms. The rule even specifies, in a seemingly tedious chapter, the order in which the psalms are to be intoned. But the point is really to suggest the course that each monk ought to follow in his personal relationship with God, from praise of His greatness to the suffering of the forsaken sinner to thanksgiving for the Lord's gifts. The poetic language of the psalms makes impalpable eternity seem real, lifting the monk above this fallen world. Spiritual culture becomes second nature, and renunciation of the world slowly effects a change of attitude, as the monk comes to trust in his Protector. At a time when violence was the way of the Franks and even the Gallo-Romans in the world outside, the monks in the monasteries shunned that world and turned elsewhere for strength and assistance.

Yet conquest of the inner dimension meant not abandonment of the world but transformation. The break with the world and the struggle with vows of poverty, chastity, and obedience enabled the monk to return to the natural world once his personality was defined. The whole Benedictine ideal has been summed up in the phrase "Pray and work" (*ora et labora*). This represents quite a departure from the Roman ideal of cultivated leisure, *otium*. Although (or perhaps because) Benedict was originally a well-born Roman, he condemned *otium* and praised its opposite, *negotium,* work viewed as suffering. Why? Because "idleness [*otiositas*] is the enemy of the soul. Hence the brothers must be occupied during specified hours with manual labor, and at other times with divine reading." A radical revolution! Hard physical labor became an ideal, and intellectual work, whether solitary or communal, ceased to be recreation and became work like any other. It is not surprising that the monasteries, while encouraging inner life (and so long as they did not lose their equilibrium), succeeded in building a new world.

These innovations were considerable, for they emphasized the importance of inner conviction, as opposed to instinctive, subjective reaction to danger, as a cause of action. The changes required intense intellectual activity, including common reading at meals and after complin and sometimes even during work in the kitchens and elsewhere. Guests of the monastery also listened to the readings. Saint Benedict carefully delineated the time set aside for personal reading: two hours every morning from Easter until the first of November, and three hours in winter. During the siesta, "if someone wishes to read, he may do so, provided he does not disturb anyone." Reading was almost always out loud, since in those days the texts had no punctuation and words were not separated. Silent reading was a difficult feat in a society where solitude was rare, the result, as the pagans said, of "a hatred of humankind." But Benedict did not hesitate to encourage it and even to make it compulsory. During Lent, Sundays were also set aside for private reading. At the beginning of Lent the brothers took "a book from the library that all would read in turn." There were more than twenty hours of private reading each week. This discipline was so difficult to maintain that two senior monks were assigned to keep watch during reading hours, looking for chatterers, idlers, and others who succumbed to *otium* or *acedia* (spiritual torpor). Those who wished to read at night were given light. The aim was to press each monk toward the oratory. "If he wishes to pray alone, in private, he may enter and pray silently, not out loud, but with tears and twinges of the heart." Silent prayer was thus the result of intense asceticism and of intellectual labors that seemed extraordinarily difficult to contemporaries. And it was done without words, spoken or unspoken—another intolerable form of suffering.

*The Discovery of Silence*

Solitary reading was intended to enforce silence, silence without which it was impossible to gather one's thoughts. "The ninth degree of humility," the Rule says, "is that the monk forbids his tongue to speak and, maintaining silence, he waits until spoken to before uttering a word . . . At all times monks should cultivate silence, but especially during the hours of night . . . Upon leaving complin no monk shall be allowed to say anything to anyone." The goal of silence was, in Augustine's phrase, to cultivate the inner man. This, too, was a new value. Benedict insisted upon it, at times with severity and irritation, for in his eyes it was essential if monks were to arrive at the goal of desiring eternal life with "all their spiritual desire" (*concupiscentia spiritualis*). The word "concupiscence" is here deliberately chosen to make it clear that the relationship with God is a kind of love, not selfish and limited by the flesh but all-encompassing and transcendent. In the privacy of cloister and oratory Benedict and his followers fashioned a ramifying subjectivity in which the analysis of emotions, feelings, and spiritual progress paved the way for the discovery of all the riches of the human personality, free at last of bondage to this world. No longer a slave, man could dream of becoming a master. The example of the great monks, like Boniface, Benedict of Aniane, and Odo of Cluny, shows that a new type of man had been created, outwardly isolated and weak but in fact strong for having confronted the rigors of silence.

Another solitary figure reveals similar progress of the inner life: the scribe. Scribes were monks who, less fortunate than their brothers, were obliged to spend long hours away from the warmth of the stove and who often complained, in inscriptions left on the colophons of manuscripts, that they

GLATULSDSFORTITUDO
MEA·QUAREMEREPPULIS
TISIQUARETRISTISINCEDO·
DUMADFLICITMEINIMICUS

C IINTROIBOADALTAREDI
ADDMQUILAETIFICAT
IUUENTUTEMMEAM

S PERAINDŌQNMADHU
CONFITEBORILLI·SALU
IAREUULTUSMEIETDSM

were cold or that the dinner hour was still a long way off or that the ink was freezing in the inkwell. Of all the actors on the historical stage, there are few about whom we know less. The scribe's task was facilitated by the abandonment in late antiquity of the rolled papyrus scroll, and the adoption of the *codex,* whose pages (made of parchment) we still turn today. This invention had important psychological repercussions. For one thing, it was no longer necessary to have a slave-reader if one wished to take notes. The text could be held with one hand and notes taken with the other. This practice of simultaneous reading and writing, which encouraged the shift to silent reading, seems to have been common in Carolingian times. It made possible an inner dialogue between reader and text. Besides affording an opportunity to meditate upon what one read, the codex made it easier to copy texts or to compare several versions of a manuscript.

A scribe's work was nevertheless quite demanding. Even when several scribes worked together in the same room, they had to keep silent in order to concentrate. The book or scroll to be copied was placed on a stand. The scribe wrote with a split reed or, in the Carolingian era, more commonly with a quill, either on his knees or on a board or table. Before beginning his copying he had to trace horizontal and vertical

Psalter of Utrecht (816–835). God punishes the city, whose residents pray in vain at the altar as the enemy storms the gates. (Utrecht, Library of the Royal University.)

lines with a drypoint, indicating the margins and rows. Besides the copyist there were other solitary workers: correctors, rubricators, painters, illuminators, and binders. The "Carolingian minuscule" was invented at Corbie in the late eighth century and later gained in popularity. This highly legible character (our Roman font) had to be drawn calligraphically rather than written at one stroke, like the quick Merovingian cursive. The change was a progressive one, but it increased the toil of the scribe. It was hard work, according to one: "It clouds the sight, makes one hunchbacked, pulls in the chest and stomach, and causes back pain. It is hard on the whole body. So, reader, turn the pages gently and do not put your fingers on the letters." Copying, like praying and fasting, was a truly ascetic endeavor, an antidote to the passions and a rein on the imagination because of the attention that the work demanded and the strain on the fingers. It took a man one year to copy a Bible. We are indebted to these Carolingian scribes for more than eight thousand manuscripts, among which are contained most of the known works of the ancient authors.

What went through the minds of the scribes as they copied pagan texts that often may have seemed false, insignificant, or indecent? They never made selections from or censored what they copied. The scribes were faithful to their text. Few have left any record of their impressions. Hrostvita, a nun at Gandersheim in the tenth century, who copied comedies modeled on those of Terence, admits that certain expressions of the author, even transcribed outside their obscene context, made her blush. But other copyists held their peace. As Dom Leclercq points out, "an element of mystery remains that we had better respect." It is clear that the texts were honored and respected, and no effort was spared to embellish them. Books were very expensive. To copy Cicero or Seneca required enough parchment to consume an entire flock of sheep, at four folios per head. The bindings and cover plates were often done in cloisonné gold with insets of precious gems, books being like reliquaries in this regard. The taste for beautiful books made of the written work something of a sacred object, worthy of sharing the private life of the medieval man of letters. In monks, for whom other pleasures, sophisticated or vulgar, were out of bounds, the taste for beautiful verse is easy to understand. Abbot Loup of Ferrières, who rejoiced at sending a friend a gift of juicy peaches, never tired of the most sonorous verses of Virgil, while in the previous generation Paul the Deacon amused himself by writing "gently satirical" poems. The solitude of the scribe and of all authors encouraged the search for beauty of expression, and a nicely turned phrase gave almost ineffable pleasure.

Could the pleasures of such an intense life of the mind be conveyed to others? There was of course the time-honored literary correspondence, the masters of which remained Pliny the Younger and, above all, Sidonius Apollinaris, who died bishop of Clermont-Ferrand in 484 after defending the culture and the faith against the Visigoths. Only the ninth-century Loup of Ferrières rose to their heights of eloquence, but he remained the exception, and his literary apostolate had no heirs, except perhaps for Eginhard, a layman as cultivated as the learned bishop. Correspondence was more commonly a matter of business, as in the insults exchanged between Bishop Importun of Paris and Bishop Frodebert of Tours (ca. 665) or the innumerable letters written by Hincmar, archbishop of Rheims, who worked indefatigably to retrieve lands stolen from his church. Others, like Alcuin, begged in letters that prayers be said to win pardon for their sins and repose for their souls. The increasing emphasis placed on prayer led to the formation of communities of priests and laymen who pledged themselves to pray for any brother who fell ill, to attend his funeral, and to celebrate masses in his honor after his death. Churches and monasteries sent round scrolls on which were inscribed the names of their dead, so that prayers might be said for their souls. Pierre Riché notes the formation of an association whose members were Saint-Germain-des Prés, Saint-Denis, and Saint-Rémi-de-Reims in 842. When a monk died, other monks recited the psalter for a month. The priests celebrated masses on the first, seventh, and thirteenth day after death. This was the precursor of the prayers for the dead, the great specialty of the monks of Cluny in the tenth century. But such prayers threatened to degenerate into mere mechanical recitation, and were a far cry from the fervent inner prayer of the great monks of old.

Monks and priests were believed to be privileged intermediaries between ordinary people and God. Having a personal relationship with things divine, they could be useful for life in this world as well as the next. These men, who created holy spaces for themselves in monasteries, churches, and asylums, who stood watch over the relics of the saints and the sacred books, and who abstained from sex, cut themselves off from the rest of the population. They more or less consciously

Manuscript of Alaric's breviary, 700–750, showing Lodhari, king of the Alemanni, conveying the law of his people to a bishop, a duke, and a count. (Paris, Bibliothèque Nationale, Latin 4404.)

maintained the confusion between *sacer* and *sanctus,* taboo and holy. At the end of the Carolingian period, moreover, the clergy's deliberate reversion to a religion of fear and trembling, the only effective means of combatting the unbridled violence of the times, heightened the sense that the Church was in possession of the sacred.

To be saved, an individual had to take possession of the Church: a simplistic notion responsible for the development of the so-called private church, or *Eigenkirche.* From the beginnings of the mission in Gaul, Germanic aristocrats helped the missionaries by granting them land and other essentials for building the first churches. In their minds they believed that they owned the new church, both the buildings and the men who staffed them. Nothing was easier for an aristocrat than to choose some peasant slave, emancipate him to satisfy the laws of the Church, and pay for his training as a priest. The lord thus acquired his own private priest whose job was to secure his salvation through prayers and masses. The same more or less conscious calculation was made by princes who

Bible of Charles the Bald, ca. 846. Moses bringing the law tablets to the Hebrews. A Carolingian version of the only law that mattered, the law of God, here entrusted to the king and his officials. (Paris, Bibliothèque Nationale, Latin 1.)

founded monasteries and bishoprics. The private church system turned priests into servants, particularly in the north, in Francia. As Jonas of Orléans put it quite bitterly: "There are priests so poor and so deprived of human dignity, and so scorned by some laymen, that they are used not only as stewards and accountants [only the priests knew how to read and write] but as domestic servants, and are not allowed to eat at their lord's table." Powerful laymen held the clergy in such a tight grip that by the tenth century the situation had deteriorated to the point where it was intolerable. The result was the Gregorian reform, nothing less than a liberation of the clergy. Only a few pious laymen such as Girard of Vienne and Gerald of Aurillac had seen the danger in the late ninth century and founded monasteries exempt from all secular authority. But Gerald was one of the few nobles of his day who led a pious life while remaining in the world. Not only did he recite psalms from the moment he awoke, even as he dressed, but he had biblical texts read to him at table and personally commented on and explained them to his guests.

Wherever the inner life was held to be important, relations between laymen and clerics had a pious foundation. But where inner life was unimportant, the clergy was viewed as a sacerdotal caste and the church as a private possession. Incomplete Christianization of private life helped revive pagan notions of the sacred. By the year 1000 we find powerful lay lords eager to gain possession of the clergy's secrets and magical formulas in the hope of alleviating anxieties that the exercise of political power, by this time totally private, could no longer quell.

Thus, Christianization, although more thorough in Carolingian than in Merovingian times, was unable to eradicate pagan beliefs. Prelogical knowledge, female intuition, magical formulas, potions, philters, and the like were all related to obsessions with love, death, and the afterlife. The Church attempted to dispel fears of malevolent forces by ascribing them to a concrete agent, the devil, in order to liberate the individual conscience. But the slow transition from an external to an internal—and more personal—conscience remained incomplete. Sacraments such as baptism and the eucharist were not exempt from a touch of magical thinking. Penitence and marriage were probably the most effective means of Christianizing private life. To be sure, a look at penitentials from the sixth to the eleventh century shows that there was undeniable progress in creating a moral conscience. The Church was genuinely uncompromising with regard to murder, polygamy, and divorce; it insisted that all laymen were equal with regard to sin, and to some extent that women were equal to men. Being took precedence over having. In all these ways the penitentials were totally in contradiction with the laws of the Germans and contributed to profound changes in personal and social behavior. As for marriage, the sudden emphasis on indissolubility and on a natural order of sexual relations met with vehement opposition, of which the Lothaire–Theutberge affair was a relatively minor manifestation.

The bishops were well aware, however, that the penitentials tolerated a considerable degree of compromise with pagan beliefs, as is evident from the fact the synods attempted to prohibit their use. All too often, acknowledgment of sin was akin to acknowledgment of a crime or physical defect rather than to acknowledgment of refusal of divine love. The automatic penance made the religious bond equivalent to a kind of contract. Acceptance of pagan reasons for refusing certain practices led to contradictions with the Gospel. Finally, since intentions were not taken into account (except in cases of vengeance), there was no consciousness of the motives behind sinful actions. There was progress, since now the results were judged rather than the damages sustained, but this only called for further progress that had to await the work of Abelard.

Individual conscience emerged slowly from the Church's contradictory efforts. Intransigent on some points, compromising on others, over the course of ten centuries the Church saw love and death move from the realm of the pagan sacred to that of the Christian secret. Yet the primitive mentality survived. Any process of acculturation exhibits a combination of rigor and laxity. Jacques Maritain speaks of "kneeling before the world" to describe the way in which the Church respected and even capitulated to non-Christian values. The early medieval Church, in taking possession of the pagan sacred, was playing with fire, but it rescued individuals from that fire so that they might become themselves.

Shaping the inner life through prayer, solitude, and silence was the only way to prepare for the eventual "desacralization" of the subjective relationship with God. Here no ambiguity was tolerated. Asceticism of body and heart took its place, through manual and intellectual labor, fasting, and prayer. Benedict of Norcia launched an intellectual revolution by introducing *lectio divina* and reading in general. Like the scribe in his lonely labor over his parchment, the man of prayer did violence to himself in order to open his mind and heart to the needs of others. The prestige of the praying monk, coupled with the sacralization of the clergy (through the severity of punishment for its sins, as prescribed by the penitentials) and of books and writing, turned the tables on powerful lay lords, who then seized those vestibules of the afterlife, the monasteries and churches. The praying monk and the priest became magical instruments for gaining access to paradise. The inner life, a private discovery that could not be conveyed to others, was transformed into a vulgar formula.

Emperor Louis the Pious, included at the beginning of his own capitularies. The emperor, holding the scepter of justice, dictates the law to a scribe. (Cava dei Tirreni, Italy.)

# ✒ Conclusion

FROM the state as private property to the private church we have come full circle. In politics and religion the early Middle Ages were marked by powerful individual personalities; it was a time of rejection of abstraction and long views, a time for small groups and warmly emotional communities. Instinct was the primary value; voraciousness and rapacity were the leading qualities of a world avid for life and pleasure. The body and the heart were at odds. Nature set out to conquer culture. Animals fascinated men. The body was venerated, mutilated, tortured. Violence was the only means of survival. Death was at everyone's back.

This is no Romantic image, no Hugo-esque panorama of the origins of France painted in hues of blood, gold, and royal purple. Think, rather, of the early Middle Ages as our collective unconscious, as the time when our spontaneous passions were buried for good, when the repudiation of all public institutions laid bare the nature of our instincts and thus paved the way for the building of a new man. Think of it as a time of combat between two religions, pagan and Christian, over the family, sex, and death.

The obsession of Gaul's invaders, which they communicated to the Gallo-Romans, was survival. Born of harsh experience on the poor land and in the brutal forests of Europe, this obsession forced them to reduce their concept of man to the art of killing and of women to childbearing. Sexuality was a tool for building society, which had to be used in accordance with nature's teachings. The lesson of nature was that only the fittest survive and that wives and mothers must be pure. Love, a destructive madness, was banished. The beneficent powers of the mysterious cosmos had to be harnessed, and the malevolent powers repulsed. Death, the possession of the invisible underworld, was as dangerous as sex. Violence was inescapable. It was in this climate that endogamous villages grew, burying their dead in outlying fields.

Countering the religion of fear was a religion of hope, both sympathetic and hostile to the pagan legacy. The new religion accepted pagan beliefs about the child and the purity of marriage but sought to destroy the parentela by imposing monogamous marriage. In a compromise with paganism, the Gallic church Christianized pagan practices. It made important progress in two areas, public and private. To combat anxiety over death, it moved the dead to the churchyards, where the living could see them. To combat the fear of punishment, it moved penitence from the marketplace into the confessional. Last but not least, to men who knew only the hard life of marital camaraderie, the Church offered the lonely hermit and the prayerful monk as alternative models. However ambiguous the Church's influence on private life may have been, this slow process of acculturation, impeded by many failures and most notably by the failure of the Carolingian Empire, helped make individual human beings increasingly independent of their environment. Once fearful of the world, man had to learn contempt for the world before he could set forth to conquer it.

Constantinople, the Golden Horn at the beginning of the century.

# ❧ 5 ❧

# Byzantium in the Tenth and Eleventh Centuries

## Evelyne Patlagean

Quadriga of heavy silk, 8th century. (Paris, Cluny Museum.)

# ᔑ The Byzantine Empire

"**B**YZANTIUM" refers to a millennium of history; to a capital, Constantinople; to an immense empire; and to a society shaped and reshaped by the centuries. My focus here is on the period 900–1060, which covers Byzantium's apogee in the tenth century and its first steps toward modernity in the eleventh. Like any healthy society, the Byzantine expressed itself in voluminous documents, many of which shed revealing light on the cultural and mental categories with which this book is concerned: the contours of private space and private time, the activities conducted within that space, and the things that were said there. First let me set the stage and introduce the cast of characters so that the reader, before being forced to confront the complexities of the documentation, can appreciate the social variety subsumed under the term "Byzantine Empire."

As this period opens the Byzantine Empire was bounded on the east by the Armenian foothills of the Caucasus and the upper Euphrates and on the southeast by the Taurus Mountains. In the Balkans it stretched along the left bank of the Danube, separated by the lower stretches of that river from the Bulgar kingdom, born in 681 and converted to Christianity in 864 by a Byzantine mission. After a ninth century marked by the political emancipation of Venice and a running struggle with the Arabs, in which the prizes were Sicily, Crete, and the islands of the Aegean, the tenth century was one of triumphant reconquest. Byzantium recaptured Crete; it reestablished its colonial presence in southern Italy with a new province whose centers were Bari and Tarentum (Taranto); and it

*Geography and History from the Ninth to the Eleventh Century*

again invaded Mesopotamia, capturing Edessa. On the lower Danube it formed an alliance against the Pecheneg Turks with the Russian government of Kiev, which had entered into trade relations with Byzantium earlier in the century and joined the Byzantine church in 988. Then, in 1014, Byzantium defeated the Bulgar Empire. In the eleventh century an influx of Italian merchants and western mercenaries, coupled with the rise of the Seljuk Turks, gradually changed the picture.

This history is of little importance to my subject. Suffice to say that the Byzantine Empire subsumed a variety of societies and cultures, on which the sources shed varying amounts of light. We do know something of the life of Constantinople, which was not only the greatest city of the Empire and of all Christendom but the "reigning city," the capital, within which stood a veritable city within a city: the imperial palace. The sources also cast light on the eastern frontier from the Taurus to Armenia and, further north, on Thessalonica, "the great city," the only city at all comparable with the capital, but different. In the background we catch glimpses of the peninsula of Mount Athos, where monks settled in the ninth century and organized in the tenth. Farther to the west lay southern Italy, present-day Apulia and Calabria, with its coastal cities Bari and Tarentum and its wooded mountains to which monks retreated, turning their back on Arab incursions farther to the north, toward Rome. It is hard to believe that such diverse populations, living in such disparate surroundings, shared a common civilization.

Yet there was a Byzantine civilization, shaped by a political history that involved not only the palace in Constantinople but the entire Empire. In 867 Emperor Michael III was assassinated by his favorite and co-emperor, Basil, about whose provincial origins little is known. Basil founded a dynasty that endured until 1056, when Theodora, his last descendant, died. With the accession of Basil's son Leo VI, however, political tensions developed between the palace, seat of the dynasty and center of power, and the empire's great generals, indispensable in time of war. Basil's assumption of power marks the beginning of a policy of reconquest, not to say aggression, that continued until the death of Basil II, aided by fruitful missionary efforts aimed at the young Slavic states to the south and east.

It was this policy that gave such an important role to play to the generals, whose families dated back no earlier than the eighth century and whose success was commemorated by the

Bronze charioteer, Constantinople, 10th century(?). (Paris, Mallon Collection.)

King Solomon holding the
Book of Wisdom. Enamel,
Constantinople, 10th century.
(Venice, Crypt of the Cathedral
of Saint Mark.)

adoption of a family name derived from an adjective or familiar word. The most celebrated of the generals were natives of eastern and southeastern Anatolia and the Armenian border region. A residence in the capital, a short distance from the palace, was the mark of a general's eminence, but the source of power remained property and loyal supporters in the provinces. Even the throne was not out of reach, although in principle it passed from father to son, because the emperor could form an alliance with a particular general who thereby became co-emperor. Romanus I Lecapenus (920–944) obtained his position in this way, and his daughter married the adolescent Constantine VII.

In 963 Nicephorus II Phocas, from the fourth generation of a family that had risen to the first rank, married Theophano, widow of Romanus II, the son of Constantine VII. He was murdered and replaced in 969 by his sister's son John I Tzimisces, the empress' lover as well as a brilliant general related to the important Sclerus clan. On John I's death in 976, Basil II, son of Romanus II, was old enough to rule personally and was forced to defend his throne against a formidable uprising in eastern Asia Minor during which he played one powerful relative, Bardas Phocas, off against another, Bardas Sclerus. Officially associated with his brother Constantine VIII, he reigned without partner or spouse until his death in 1025, followed by the death of Constantine in 1028.

In the absence of any sons, the dynasty was carried on by Constantine's daughter, Zoë, who had two marriages, one with Romanus Argyrus (Romanus III), whom she had executed in 1034, the second with Michael IV, brother of a court eunuch (1034–1041). She then adopted the latter's nephew, Michael V, who was deposed in 1042, after which Zoë shared the throne with her sister, the nun Theodora, while marrying the aristocrat Constantine Monomachus (Constantine IX). Zoë died in 1050, Constantine IX in 1055, and the dynasty ended with Theodora in 1056. In 1057, her hand-picked successor, Michael VI, was eliminated by Isaacius Comnenus (Isaac I), first of the Comnenus dynasty. The Comneni regained the throne in 1081 after the reigns of two Ducae, Constantine X (1059–1067) and Michael VII (1060–1067 and 1071–1078), as well as Romanus IV (1068–1071) and Nicephorus III (1078–1081). The accession of Isaac's brother Alexis I began the century of the Comneni, another era.

I have chosen the dates of rulers as chronological milestones, not out of idiosyncratic preference but because the

sources make such a choice unavoidable. Our knowledge of the social history of the period is not limited to anecdotes about Basil I, his descendants, and the great dynasties, however. The eastern frontier of the empire had a life of its own, remote from the cultural and political forces of the capital and in contact with the periphery of the Islamic world. To be sure, this border region was administered by Constantinople, divided up into districts each under the command of a local general ensconced with his troops in a fortress. These generals were in some cases local leaders who had been integrated into the Byzantine defenses. But the official organization of this defensive system tells us nothing about the liberty of the soldiers themselves. Nor does it help define the unique aspects of a civilization that would gradually disappear in the eleventh century, when the empire came increasingly to rely on mercenaries, and the Turks emerged as a new force. In the capital, civil and religious leaders mingled: palace personnel, officials of the imperial bureaucracy and the courts, and officials of the patriarchal bureaucracy and courts. All defined and distinguished themselves by their learning and skill with language, that is, by their knowledge of the genres and rules of rhetoric and their familiarity with the cultural heritage of pagan and Christian antiquity. This high culture, which ultimately in-

Gregory Nazianzen, *Collected Sermons,* showing the tax-collector Julian performing his duties. (Paris, Bibliothèque Nationale, Greek 550, a 12th-century copy made at Constantinople.)

Fragment of winding-sheet of St. Lazarus. Byzantium, 11th–12th century. (Paris, Cluny Museum.)

cluded knowledge of the law, was imparted by schools that prepared students for careers in government and the church. Throughout this period the emperors took a great interest in the running of these schools. The central authorities ramified in the provinces, to which the emperor sent his functionaries and the patriarch his bishops.

The real center of society and productive activity was the countryside, which was inhabited by peasants, some of them smallholders, others sharecroppers, and still others slaves. Most lived in villages, but in border regions particularly one finds them also on large estates established on virgin lands. Landowners formed a diverse class, varied in wealth, social influence, and political power. Central and eastern Anatolia, a region which traditionally boasted many large estates, was not typical. The monasteries also owned land, a considerable amount overall but, again, unevenly distributed. During the period in question, moreover, urban revival is evident in the Byzantine Empire as in other parts of the world, a revival sustained by the work of artisans and by trade. The tenth century witnessed the development of trade on a large scale, involving such goods as silk fabrics, spices, furs, and slaves. If the traders were often Jews, Muslims, or Italian merchants from Amalfi and Venice, the great marketplaces were Constantinople, Thessalonica, and Trebizond. Foreign merchants were granted concessions in the capital: the Russians were the first to obtain a concession, in the early tenth century, followed by the Venetians at the very end of that century. The trend continued in the eleventh century, establishing Constantinople as a major international marketplace. In the eleventh century the capital took on more and more of the features of a big city, with a complex, diversified, and bustling urban society.

Alongside civil society stood the church. Church and society were related by family, local, and cultural ties. The Byzantine church survived a major crisis in the ninth century, when icon worship was definitively reinstated. Justified by the cult of the saints and, in the last analysis, by the dogma of the Incarnation, this practice left a unique stamp on collective and individual piety. Once this crisis had been resolved, the organization of the church changed little. The patriarch, backed by his bureaucracy and his courts, ruled the church, meaning bishops, parishes, laymen, and even monks (so long as their monasteries were not autonomous and under the direct jurisdiction of the emperor).

In reality the monks were paramount in the Byzantine

church, and in Byzantine Christendom, throughout this period. The manner of shunning the world had changed since the first flowering of monasticism between the end of the third and the end of the fifth century. The religious as well as the political authorities had worked to eradicate the freer, more individualistic forms of monastic life, and social forces probably worked toward the same end. Domestic asceticism, for example, had all but disappeared. The principle that monks should live in a community of some sort had prevailed over hermitism, and monasteries played an increasingly important role in urban life. The status of monasteries varied: some were imperial, some patriarchal, some subject to the local bishop, some autonomous or even private, that is, the property of an individual, a family, or even another monastery. The leading centers of monasticism were Brusa and especially Mount Athos, the "holy mountain," a monastic republic (a smaller replica of which was established in southern Italy). In Constantinople, the Studion monastery, a center of religious radicalism, enjoyed an official priority of sorts. The emperors had their favorites, however, particularly those not belonging to the dynasty of Basil I. Nicephorus II Phocas and his brother Leo founded the Lavra monastery of Athos; Alexis I and his mother lavished their attentions on Saint John of Patmos. Private persons great and small gave gifts and made bequests to the monasteries. But there was religious dissidence in the Byzantine Empire, especially in the eleventh century.

*Sources*

This brief geographical and social sketch should help explain the kinds of sources that Byzantine society produced, as well as why some survived and others did not. Archaeology of the medieval Byzantine Empire has yet to produce results comparable with those found in the West. Earthquakes have caused extensive damage, as did classical archaeologists of the nineteenth century, who razed the Byzantine strata of Athens in their fervor to get at more ancient remains. Sites are now excavated more carefully than in the past, so as to preserve traces of the long transition from antiquity to the Ottoman Empire. The Byzantine levels are not always accessible, however, as in the case of the Istanbul site. The archaeology of villages and fortresses is only just beginning, though the exploration of the well-known cave churches of Cappadocia has yielded interesting data. In short, excavation sites and monuments have little to say about the period in which we are

Ivory-covered wooden chest, 10th–11th century. Right: Adam at the forge. Left: Eve works the bellows. (Darmstadt, State Museum of Hesse.)

interested. There is no dearth of objects, however, some common, others rare, including precious gems, ivory pieces, silk fabrics, jewels, and especially the instruments of personal communion with the realm of the invisible, such as icons and amulets.

Many painted images—manuscript miniatures—have survived, and it is tempting to use them to fill the gaps in the archaeological record. But such evidence is not easy to handle. A great deal of illustration was done in the tenth and eleventh centuries both in Constantinople and in the provinces. Books were quite often produced on commission, in which case their decoration depended on the desires and wealth of the client, possibly the emperor himself. Among the extant items are a psalter and menology (a calendar of the saints' festivals) allegedly made for Basil II. Certain texts called for illustration: the Gospels, psalters, collections of the *Homilies* of Gregory Nazianzen, one of the Fathers of the Greek church. But one copy of a treatise on snake bites contains painted illustrations.

A manuscript I shall cite often is the *Chronicle* of John Scylitzes, written in the late eleventh century and concerned with recent history. Though recopied in the thirteenth century, it apparently contains partial reproductions of miniatures contemporary with the original draft. One wonders about the topicality of the images. The meal at the marriage of Cana, the demon standing beside the simoniac priest, and the peasant tending to his labors—were these drawn from a book of models or inspired by the times? Or is it idle to raise such a question with regard to a civilization where progress was slow, unless there are explicit references to ancient sources of the sort tenth-century authors were fond of making?

Archival documents have suffered more than other sources from the ravages of history. What has survived from this period comes from the monastic cartularies, primarily those of Mount Athos. Others may not yet have delivered up all their secrets. I shall cite a number of foundation charters, monastery rules (*typikon*), anticipated donations, and wills that in one way or another came to be stored in the cartularies. Wills were made on the eve of entering a monastery, since monks were not allowed to own property. Other wills tell us how widows acquired the capacity to manage family property. By contrast, the only marriage contract with information about what wedding gifts were given is a Jewish document drafted in 1022 at Mastaura, on the banks of the Meander, and discovered outside the Empire, in the celebrated archives of a synagogue of Old Cairo. The dearth of private documents is partly compensated by a remarkable collection of decisions of the judge Eustathius the Roman, who heard cases in the capital during the first thirty years of the eleventh century. The briefs are excellent, and we have several conjugal and familial lawsuits from which to choose. Lastly, there is evidence in books themselves. Copyists sometimes did more than just sign their work. Book owners signed their names, annotated their books, and sometimes transcribed documents onto blank pages. Modern Hellenism also began to take shape in this period. The spoken language, the invaluable evidence of family names, and various beliefs, proverbs, and songs traces of which have survived come under this head.

The lives of Byzantine men and women were supposedly governed by edicts of the sovereign and the church, through which we can sometimes discover what practices the authorities approved or tried in vain to stamp out. The Novels (laws) of Leo VI from the late ninth century suggest a systematic plan to revise the legal code; this is less true of tenth- and eleventh-century Novels, whose number is much smaller. The church, for its part, waged a steady campaign, continued over several centuries. The Council of 692 took important steps to eradicate customs and festivals that it deemed polytheistic. The Second Council of Nicaea, which temporarily reinstated icon worship in 787, did important work concerning the discipline of clerics, monks, and laymen and helped to establish how these different orders of Christian society should relate to one another. The Council of Constantinople (861) dealt with similar issues. The patriarchate of Constantinople relied on a permanent synod, whose decisions we know at least indirectly. Much of the penitential literature is still unpublished; in any case it is not as rich a source as penitentials in the West for this period. In the twelfth century the councils of 692, 787, and 861, among others, were commented on by three students of canon law: Theodore Balsamon, the patriarchate's greatest jurist and functionary and, later, Patriarch of Antioch; John Zonaras; and Alexios Aristenos. Finally, two pamphlets—one, from the early eleventh century, signed by a monk named Euthymius, the other, from the reign of Alexis I Comnenus, signed by yet another Euthymius—attacked heresy in terms that signal a change in the nature of piety.

I shall also be citing many other documents, some signed, others anonymous, but all examples of a particular genre: letters. The information these letters contain is in part determined by the rules of the epistolary genre. Byzantine culture always sought to wrap itself in tradition, whether authentic or apocryphal. It is all too often believed that it was therefore lifeless and static. Emphasis on tradition only defined the rules

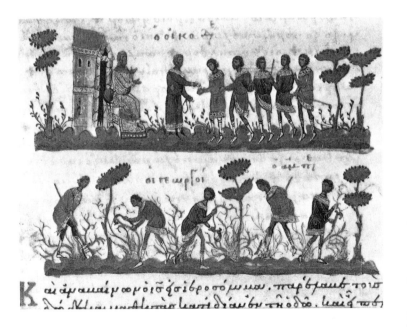

Gospels, Constantinople, mid-10th century. Above: payment of ground rents. Below: labor in a vineyard. (Paris, Bibliothèque Nationale, Greek 74).

of the game. Nevertheless, these rules make it difficult to ferret out evidence for the history of ideas and attitudes.

Monastery of Daphni (Greece), 11th century.

Hundreds of tenth- and eleventh-century letters have survived, not by simple accumulation in the archives but by the deliberate choice of Byzantine librarians, who compiled epistolary anthologies and preserved the letters of certain distinguished writers, such as Michael Psellus, an important political and cultural figure of the eleventh century. These letters express the view of a homogeneous social group, all of whose members were men: high functionaries, bishops, assistants to the sovereign, and on occasion the emperor. In addition to these letters we have a document unique in its form and personal tone, the *Counsels and Stories* composed between 1075 and 1081 by Cecaumenus, an aristocrat who had retired from imperial service and returned to his native province. Although I have made little use of the learned poetry written by men of letters, I do use the epic of Digenis Acritas, because beneath the Romanesque trappings one can discern the epic subjects of which early tenth-century itinerant musicians used to sing

John Damascene, Florilegium (*Sacra Parallela*), 9th century, Italy or southern Palestine. Above: preparation of medication. Below: a painter. (Paris, Bibliothèque Nationale, Greek 923.)

as they made their way from castle to castle along the eastern frontier. An oral form of the epic itself was probably current in the eleventh century, disseminating, far from the capital, models of heroism, seduction, and love.

Monastic and private libraries contained books for use in prayers for all occasions, household medicine, and the interpretation of dreams. They are particularly hard to date; the liturgy of Constantinople was already established by the eighth century, as one manuscript reveals. The Hippocratic tradition left its mark on such works as a pamphlet on gynecology and a dietary calendar indicating what foods should be eaten throughout the year to maintain health. The science of dream interpretation, old as antiquity, in Byzantium took at least two forms. I will examine Achmet's *Oneirokritikon;* the author is mysterious, but the work, composed between 813 and the end of the eleventh century, adds new observations to ancient material.

In answer to the question of whether biographies from this period have survived, I should point out that the lives of the saints were biographies of real individuals as well as exempla for the faithful. The biographical aspect is especially prominent in tenth- and eleventh-century hagiography, although the exemplary aspect is not lacking. Hagiographies were composed for the glory of a monastery or sanctuary associated with a particular saint or to aid in the celebration of the saint's festival. Although all the authors are monks, they exhibit a good deal of cultural diversity. The saints themselves are a diverse group. I shall discuss some twenty in all from the tenth and eleventh centuries, a few women but mostly men. None were from the lower classes, for that would have been inconceivable, but before entering the monastery or convent these saints had led a variety of lives in the world. The biographic (as opposed to exemplary) parts of the hagiographies feature different geographical and social settings, from Constantinople to a province in Asia Minor or southern Italy to the trails of Mount Athos. The historical literature of the period is no less rich, but it is more difficult to use. Histories focused on the palace when they were not directly inspired by the emperor. Hence information about the emperors must be treated with caution and cannot be compared directly with information about other individuals because of the symbolic importance attached to the person of the emperor. Still, the histories do contain information unavailable elsewhere about the aristocracy that gravitated toward the seat of ultimate power.

The foregoing, though not an exhaustive survey of sources concerning the Byzantine Empire in the tenth and eleventh centuries, does list materials useful for research into private life in this period. The Greek language will show us the way. Greek has a word for private in the sense intended here. Old words persisted: affairs (*pragmata*) in the broad sense, as opposed to rest (*hesychia*), whether profane, political, or spiritual, and "leisure" (*schole*). We have private in the patrimonial and social sense (*idios,* from which *idiazein,* to live in private) and private (*oikeios*) in the sense of a person or good belonging to the household (*oikos*). But history had profoundly altered the traditional meanings of some other words. The city (*polis*) was now usually fortified (*kastron*), in the provinces at any rate, and populated not by citizens (*politai*) but by mere inhabitants (*oiketores*). *Politikos* meant civil, particularly in the tax classifications, where it was opposed to *stratiotikos,* military. Socially there were the powerful (*dynatoi*) and the poor (*penetes*). The government (*demosion*) meant the sovereign together with his fiscal and judicial bureaucracies; the people (*demos*) had long since been reduced to little more than a figure in the imperial liturgy, a group that acclaimed the emperor in ceremonies. The *demotes,* man of the people, was just the man in the street or, worse, a good-for-nothing; this changed somewhat in the eleventh century. The revival of urban life meant that *democratia* ceased to be mob rule and became, at least for a while, a matter of political pressure exerted by a population of artisans and merchants.

These changes in public terminology show the effects of the long decline of the ancient city as the center of social and political life and the rise of imperial government, with its principle of centralized uniformity. The change was too dramatic not to have left its mark on the realm of the "private," even if the vocabulary appears to have remained static. As for the religious realm, the *laikos* was one of the Christian people (*laos*). Here the "private" was perhaps that which escaped from the supervision of clerics and monks, such as ceremonies that the church did not recognize. I should point out that by "public" I do not mean merely the state, but collective life, external life, in general, in all its manifestations. By "private" I mean intimate life, life among those to whom we are closest, as well as the inner life, the life of the "self" that each of us becomes when we are free to be as we wish.

*Words*

Monogrammed ring, not earlier than the 6th century. (Paris, Bibliothèque Nationale, Cabinet des Médailles.)

Set of keys with mono-
grammed key-ring. (Menil
Foundation, Baltimore,
The Walters Art Gallery.)

# ᴥ Private Space

THE household defined the limits of private space. In Greek a distinction is made between *oikos,* household, meaning the people who worked and resided in the house, and *oikia,* the house per se. Right away, then, we see that the oikos was defined in terms of a space and a group of people, and by the relations between the two. That the household was a closed, intimate space, set apart from the world outside, is suggested by Achmet's *Dream Key,* in which oneiric significance is attached to the various parts of the body: "The mouth is man's household (*oikos*), which contains all that is personally his . . . the teeth are to be understood as the man's relations." In fact, molars stand for children: uppers for boys, lowers for girls.

---

*The Secular Household*

The oikos, however, was not entirely private; it stood at the junction between two realms. In some respects the home was a public place. In the villages, assemblies of "heads of household" shouldered judicial and, more importantly, fiscal responsibilities, with all households included in the tax census represented. Certain families, designated "military households," were required to send to the army a family member fully equipped for combat. We read in the histories, moreover, of this or that aristocratic oikos settled in the capital. The core of the oikos consisted of the family members, but they were joined by *oikeoi,* or familiars, servants, some of whom were slaves (*oiketai*). The terms *anthropoi,* men, and *philoi,* friends, were also used. The aristocratic oikos played a political role at the palace, to which it gained access through the military exploits of the family head or by way of hereditary connections or marriage. In case of disgrace brought about by the discovery of a conspiracy or a change in the political climate, the family retreated to its residence. *Hesychia* (repose) was at times "retirement" enforced by dismissal from the imperial entourage. The aristocratic oikos was an ambivalent place. At the antipodes from the palace, the political heart of the Empire, it could be either a hotbed of political intrigue or a retirement retreat. The same is true of the country seats of the great families, which could at any time become the center of some political scheme. When Basil II stopped at the country seat of one of the great magnates of his day, Eustathius Maleinus, the emperor took his sumptuous welcome, with his host's private army massed nearby, as a sign of subversive intentions.

Each oikos formed part of a larger kinship group, or parentela. Starting in the ninth century, perhaps even as early as the late eighth century, kinship groups began to identify themselves by adopting family names, which were then transmitted from generation to generation. Historians often mentioned a man's family and place of residence in Constantinople in order to identify him. The few surviving tax documents from this period indicate the names of peasant families. These did not live together under one roof, since more than one head of household is listed. According to the *Life of Philaretos* (ca. 821), the house of that wealthy but saintly landowner was home to three generations. The *Life of Mary the Younger* (died 902; biography written after 1025) and the *Life of Cyrillus of Philea* (died 1110) show families with young children. The records of Judge Eustathius prove that men sometimes moved in with their wives' families. Peasant wills and household inventories attest that some households were headed by widows. One letter-writer lived with his mother, who died after forty years of widowhood; many others were celibate clerics who never mention any relatives.

Servants were not distinguished from what we would now call the family. Despite the ambiguity of the terminology, it is clear that many servants were slaves. Theodorus, metropolitan of Nicaea, says in one letter that he left his house in Constantinople in the middle of the night, heading for the Church of the Holy Apostles where he intended to honor Saint John Chrysostom. A nephew mounted on an ass preceded him, and two servants followed, worthies who proved incapable of defending him from attackers. Exiled, the same bishop left his house in the keeping of a lone caretaker, who daily made sure that all the doors and windows were barred. Manumission of slaves was so common that the prayer books

Gospels, Constantinople, mid-11th century: swineherd with swine. (Paris, Bibliothèque Nationale, Greek 74.)

contained an appropriate ritual. It was often accomplished posthumously, by will: in 1049, Gemma, widow of a functionary in southern Italy, freed her slave Maria. The slave was to receive the bed in which her late owner had slept and four measures of wheat from the coming harvest.

Families received guests and visitors of all sorts. The lives of saints who came as children or adolescents to Constantinople (such as Evaristus, a monk of Studion, or Nicephorus, bishop of Miletus) show that these youngsters were taken in by well-placed relatives or patrons. Concubines (*pallakai*) may have lived in the homes of their lovers. Each great house had a chaplain to celebrate religious services. And when Digenis leaves his provincial home for his first hunt, he is accompanied not only by his father and maternal uncle but also by a group of boys (*agouroi*) who live in the same house. City houses were sometimes arranged in such a way as to unite related families without forcing all to share the same roof; several houses might open onto a common *aule,* or courtyard, each with its own entrance.

Multistoried buildings in cities housed several families. An artisan lived, worked, and sold his wares in his *ergasterion,* or shop. The sources sometimes refer to an *oikiskon,* small cottage. People of modest station often rented lodging. Aristocratic houses, by contrast, were presumably freestanding buildings. Interior courts with galleries, terraces, corbeled windows, large halls, smaller rooms, and baths were the theater of urban life, grand or modest, according to the family's fortune. In rural areas the freestanding house served both ends of the social spectrum: slaves and tenant farmers lived in huts on the large estates, and great magnates occupied splendid country seats. Some of these villas date from antiquity; excavation has revealed fine specimens in Syria and Palestine from the early years of Islam. From there the model was reintro-

Tile depicting Virgin with Child. Ceramic polychrome (white earth), Constantinople region, 10th century (30 cm x 29.8 cm x 1 cm). (Sèvres, National Museum of Ceramics.)

duced into the Byzantine Empire, especially in the east, and the palace voluptuously described in the Digenis epic is a fanciful remembrance of one such villa. What the house in which Eustathius Maleinus received Basil II with such impudent opulence looked like, however, we do not know. At Cavusin, near Urkup, a castle embedded into rock with a fortified tower has been discovered, along with a church whose donors, painted in the apse, are identified as Emperor Nicephorus II Phocas and his wife Theophano; his father, Bardas Phocas; and his brother, Leo Phocas. Peasant dwellings were grouped together in villages; proximity, kinship, and joint ownership fostered solidarity as well as conflict. And a few homes usually stood apart from the rest of the village.

The typical home was an intimate, probably comfortable, haven. Alexandros, metropolitan of Nicaea, loudly demanding to be released from prison where he had been sent in connection with an obscure libel case, complained that he missed his house and was forced to make do without bath or privy. Theodorus, another metropolitan of Nicaea, wrote to someone in a position to help end his exile: "Can you give me back my house (*oikia*), from which I have been expelled, as from the capital itself, as if I were filth, so that now I sleep out under the stars, living like a wild animal, I who must contend every day with my maladies and my liver pain, who need medicine and treatment. And may the Lord give you in recompense a home in heaven." The house—closed as tightly as the mouth—was protected by an elaborate system of locks, examples of which have survived. Interiors were divided by curtains (which are raised by the characters in Scylitzes' *Chronicle*). These not only served as partitions but also helped to prevent drafts, about which Bishop Liutprand of Cremona complained bitterly when, during his embassy to Nicephorus II, he was lodged in a rather breezy palace. It was customary to cover walls with ceramic tiles depicting animals or bouquets of acanthus.

The variety of personal and household objects is evident from the list of trades in Constantinople compiled by the prefect under Leo VI. Boxes of sculpted ivory and fragments of dinnerware have survived. It is not clear, however, whether certain rooms were permanently set aside for specific purposes such as receiving guests. Household furnishings do not enlighten us, and there is nothing in the surviving sources comparable to the estate inventories that we have for medieval and later periods. This dearth of evidence is not accidental. The Jewish bride who married in Mastaura in 1022 brought with her not only a personal trousseau but linen and utensils for the house; unfortunately, her marriage contract is an isolated piece of evidence in two senses. The few surviving eleventh-century wills do not list furniture and common household items, partly by omission. When the wealthy provincial Eus-

Ivory-covered wooden chest (15.7 cm x 23 cm x 16 cm), Constantinople, second half of 10th century or first half of 11th century, depicting ancient warriors, Dionysiac figures, and animals. (Washington, Dumbarton Oaks, Byzantine Collection.)

Tile decorated with peacock. Ceramic polychrome (white earth), Constantinople region, 10th century (29.3 cm x 30 cm). (Sèvres, National Museum of Ceramics.)

Frieze of animals. Ceramic polychrome (white earth), Constantinople region, 10th century (7.8 cm x 32 cm). (Sèvres, National Museum of Ceramics.)

tathius Boilas disposed of his property in 1059, the only inventory worthy of the name pertained to his donation to the domanial church, which included icons, books sacred and profane, and precious metal utensils. No detailed information is given concerning the division of his real and moveable property among his married children. The will of the widow Gemma (1049) is similar. She left "the entire house, as is, to Kostas and Petros, sons of [her] nephew Leo." There was apparently no need to inventory the contents of the house. In the same will, however, Gemma does bequeath a number of items of furniture.

It would be wrong to conclude that material life was impoverished; the sources belie any such claim. But living arrangements do not seem to have been highly elaborate and may have been rather fluid. This would explain why no fixed distribution was set in wills. A major exception to this rule, however, was the imperial palace in the tenth century, whose routine and formal uses are known from the histories and, above all, from the *Book of Ceremonies* compiled under Constantine VII. But what are we to make of this? In the palace we find not only rooms for audiences, offices, libraries, and copying but also dining rooms, an oratory, and the imperial bedchamber. Was all this nothing more than an elaboration of an aristocratic way of life? What about the bath where the emperor's wife bathed on the eve of the marriage and the "purple residence" that marked an imperial birth as legitimate?

The palace also contained an area that was exclusively private by definition: the section reserved for women. Not that Byzantine women were recluses. Thomaïs was able to travel freely to the temple of the Virgin of Blachernae in a suburb of the capital and even spent the night there in prayer. The mother of Nicephorus, bishop of Miletus, came to Constantinople to see her son, who had been sent there as a child; she went to school with him to protect his purity, behavior held up as exemplary by the hagiographer. But an illustration in Scylitzes' *Chronicle* shows that women, or at any rate one wealthy widow, traveled with a whole entourage—she is carried on a litter and surrounded by servants—suggesting that wealthy women who left home took the entire gynaeceum with them.

Women and girls were kept strictly segregated from the outside world. The *Life of Philaretos* (ca. 821) describes his indignation when imperial envoys, seeking a wife for the young sovereign, asked to see his granddaughters. He apparently gave in, however, because one of the girls was chosen. A similar question regarding the role of women tormented old Cecaumenus at the end of the eleventh century. He was vehemently opposed to allowing guests to sit at the same table with the women of the family; as proof that women should be served apart, he tells of a wife seduced and a husband deceived. Honor is of paramount concern: "An unchaste daughter is guilty of harming not only herself but also her parents and relatives. That is why you should keep your daughters under lock and key, as if proven guilty or imprudent, in order to avoid any venomous bites." To be sure, Anna Dalassena, mother of Alexis I, summoned Cyrillus of Philea to her bedroom when she wished to make his acquaintance. But she was an old woman and he a saint. The segregation of women was the first principle of interior design. Michael Psellus' *Chronography* confirms that in the eleventh century both the palace and private homes contained a *gynaikonitis,* or woman's apartment. Of what social classes this was true, however, we do not know. In principle, outsiders were not allowed to frequent the women of the house, but as Cecaumenus' story shows, the principle was not always respected.

Dining served a complex social function. At the very least, holidays were observed at family dinners. When, during the reign of Basil I, Mary the Younger was falsely accused of illicit relations with a servant, her husband was so angry that he refused to allow her to come to table even for the first Sunday of Lent, and "he remained alone with his brothers [or brother and sister, according to the story] and intimates, eating and drinking." Imperial dinners were charged with political

Silver ewer. (Paris, Hayford Pierce Collection.)

significance, but it is worth mentioning that Eudocia Ingerina,
the mistress of Michael III whom he gave to Basil to marry,
was present at the supper where Basil murdered the emperor.
Some information can be gleaned from manuscript illustrations. The Madrid manuscript of Scylitzes shows the widow
Danielis seated, as mistress of the house, between her son and
the future emperor Basil, who is still unknown but whose
future greatness Danielis divines. The two men eat from the
same plate; the woman, with the guest seated on her right,
does not share the meal. Another scene shows an official meal
after Basil has assumed the throne: he is alone at a separate
table set at right angles to a long table full of men, over which
he presides. Women are allowed at dinners, say the canonists,
provided they are not "drinking bouts" (*symposiai*), that is,
banquets punctuated by dubious entertainments. The presence
of a woman at such an occasion was grounds for her husband
to sue for divorce; male guests, however, were not criticized
for being there.

The imperial couple, according to the *Book of Ceremonies,*
normally shared the same room and bed. Scylitzes, in his
account of the murder of Nicephorus II Phocas in 969,
describes the emperor as an ascetic who was repressing a
monastic vocation. In observance of periods of abstinence
prescribed by the church, he slept outside the imperial bedchamber. His murder took place during Advent, and the murderers were forced to wander through the palace looking for
him, finally locating him asleep on a bearskin, gift of his
maternal uncle the monk Michael Maleinus, wearing a purple
cap. The instigator of the crime, John Tzimisces, sat on the
imperial bed waiting for the blow to be struck. The empress

Fabric with griffins in medallions, 10th–11th century. (Florence, National Museum.)

Zoë shared the bed of her husband Romanus III as well as that of her young lover, the future Michael IV. But Constantine IX met his lover Scleraina outside the palace, while Leo VI slept with his mistress, Zoë Azoutzina, in a country residence when the empress was absent. An empress gave birth not in the bedroom where the imperial couple conceived its children but in the "purple residence" reserved for the purpose, probably because of the impurity inherent in childbirth, which would have been incompatible with the sacred dignity of the Empire.

We know less about the habits of ordinary married couples, apart from the customs of the wedding night. Luke the Stylite, who lived in the tenth century, restored life to a baby whose parents had accidentally suffocated it in their bed. By contrast, Mary the Younger's husband did not sleep in her room but entered in the morning, where he found her asleep with an infant in her arms. The Church prescribed periods of abstinence, in particular during Lent and on Saturdays and Sundays. Although observance of this rule was a condition for receiving communion, we have no way of knowing whether it was actually respected. Nor do we know if sexual relations, or at least sharing of the marital bed, were in fact halted during menstruation or during the period between childbirth and the subsequent "churching." Miniatures show sick patients, the dying, women in childbirth, and corpses in very narrow beds, but with frames mounted on legs and headboards. The paralytic of the Gospel, however, is carried on his back on a light cot.

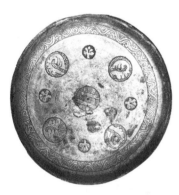

Ceramic plate with engraved decoration, 12th century. (London, British Museum.)

Private worship services were held in the oratories of great houses and in domanial churches that landowners had been building on their estates since the fourth century. In his will of 1059 Eustathius Boilas bequeathed a collection of books and precious objects to furnish his private church. Some Cappadocian churches may have belonged to specific families, to judge by the named statues of donors found in them. Private ownership of churches was something upon which the Church had long cast a suspicious eye, because it opened the way to heresy. But the demand continued, and priests were authorized to hold private services with approval of the local bishop, although not outside their own parishes. (The rule was widely flouted, particularly since the private churches allowed abuse of the rules concerning offerings.) Evidence of private worship has survived, as is seen in small, portable icons, painted on wood and decorated with silver; hard stone icons; ivory cas-

καὶ ἡ τῆς εὐχαριστίας ἁφαι
μ ζαιδοχολογία· ἦλθε γὰρ ἦ άγα
λλίασις· ἐπὶ τῇ χαρᾷ.
καὶ γάρ τῷ μὲν μέ χίρω προτέ
θειται· ὡς ἄ μιμφευτος προκέκρι
ται μι φη· τὸ τε παλαιόν μξ
ψορὲ κ του καὶ ἡ υτρέπω ση μερ

χάρι τος ἀπο μι ὣ εἰ φρο σύνης·
ὡ φαιδρό τητος τῆς ἐπι ρου
σκηνι ἐθραι· ὡς δ ἐωπιᾳ τις

James of Kokkinobaphos, *Homilies on the Virgin* (12th century), illustrated by the author or under his supervision: Joachim and Ann give thanks after the birth of the Virgin. (Paris, Bibliothèque Nationale, Greek 1208.)

kets and reliquaries; and probably also some of the surviving liturgical items in bronze and silver. The corner reserved for icons in Orthodox homes then and now is prefigured in an illustration in the Madrid manuscript of Scylitzes, which shows Theodora, wife of Theophilus, the last iconoclastic emperor, secretly worshiping holy images arrayed in a secret closet in her apartment.

In wealthy homes there was a place for reading and, if need be, writing, although we cannot say exactly where it was. Numerous representations of the evangelists have made us familiar with the image of a man writing, with the necessary implements arranged on a small desk illuminated by a hanging lamp and standing next to an open cabinet filled with books. This image may be misleading because it is elliptical, but the library is undoubtedly that of the copyist in his studio and the reader in his home. Did people read themselves (as opposed to being read to)? The answer is that they did, judging by the reading notes of the ninth-century patriarch Photius. Each page begins with the words: "Read such-and-such a work." But if we believe the evidence of a manuscript preserved in

Gregory Nazianzen, *Selected Speeches:* St. Gregory officiating. Constantinople, 12th century. (Paris, Bibliothèque Nationale, Greek 543.)

the Athonite monastery at Vatopedi and copied in 1021 by Basilius, "reader and chronographer, man of Lord Nicolaus," the answer is negative. True, this characterization may be nothing more than a clerical rank. Basil I, a man of obscure origins, had books read to him and also practiced calligraphy. Many aristocrats and members of the urban middle classes knew how to read. Women also learned to read, to judge by contemporary hagiographies, even if they did not read the same things as men. Reading was a leisure activity. Cecaumenus insists on this point, and one letter-writer suggests this as an excuse for his correspondent's tardiness. Books were purchased from booksellers, especially in Constantinople, or ordered directly from copyists and monasteries. Different styles were practiced in Constantinople, on the eastern frontier, and in southern Italy. In addition, the palace, noble houses, and monasteries had copying done on the premises.

Writing is another matter. Not that writing was considered, as in some societies, a subaltern occupation: in the tenth century even emperors practiced calligraphy. But written communication was complex, as surviving letters attest. Some are complete in themselves; others are mere eloquent, well-turned "cover letters," accompanying a messenger who conveyed the real news orally. Not all letters were physically transcribed by their authors; many were dictated to secretaries. Sometimes a writing assistant (*grammateus, grammatikos*) was put in charge of the master's correspondence and library or even made an assistant in creative endeavor; this is suggested by a scene of dictation in a manuscript of the *Acts of the Apostles* copied in 1045 (Paris Greek 223).

---

*Monastic Households*

The monastery was also referred to at times as an oikos as well as a place of repose (*hesychia*). It was home to a symbolic family, the brotherhood (*adelphotes*) of monks, or brothers (*adelphoi*), under the authority of a hegumen, or spiritual father (*pater pneumatikos*), not only of the monks but also of lay children (*tekna*), who might or might not remain in the world. At least three monks were required to constitute a monastery, and one large Mount Athos monastery was home to as many as seven hundred. Donations, foundations, and the taking of vows were common in this period, as if the cloister were the ultimate goal of all life, the final retreat, to which men were sometimes driven against their will.

Like the military household, the monastic household per-

Saint George killing the dragon, 11th-century fresco. (Church of the Serpent, Göreme [Cappadocia].)

formed a recognized public service; it therefore enjoyed various tax privileges and received income from a variety of sources. In the tenth century, and even the eleventh, the wealth of the monasteries and their exemption from taxation was not justified by their charitable role but by the universally acknowledged power of the monks to intercede with God and to offer spiritual guidance to ordinary men. It was desirable and profitable for real estate to be granted monastic status, and this no doubt played a role in the upsurge of private foundations and, in the eleventh century, in the practice of lay management of the temporal property of monasteries. With regard to discipline, Greek monks still adhered to the principles elaborated in the fourth century by Basil of Caesarea. But Theodorus developed a rule for the Studion in Constantinople, whose period of glory began with him in the ninth century. This rule inspired the monks of Mount Athos and elsewhere, including monasteries founded by monarchs in the new Slavic states. The councils of 787 and 861 elaborated the rule still further. Yet every monastery founder, monk or layman, continued to establish his own rule, covering such matters as operational details, prayers to be said, and charitable endeavors.

Monks were not supposed to own property. Once a monk chose a monastery he was expected to remain there forever; he made his will, if need be, before donning the habit. Some monks paid to be admitted into monasteries, but once admitted they lived, in theory, by working in the community, though in fact (in this period) largely from the income generated by the monastic estates. Twelfth-century satirical poems written in Constantinople depict the superiors of the monasteries as gluttons and satyrs who bathe weekly and have doctors in attendance at their bedsides, while the poor monks live in discomfort and destitution. The agreement signed by the Athonite monastery at Lavra and the monk Athanasius reveals a sorry state of affairs. Nephew of the previous superior, Athanasius gave his private monastery at Bouleuteria, with its cells, church, and vineyards, to the Lavra monastery, which improved the establishment. For himself Athanasius asked to be made a member of the community in which he had taken vows. The contract guaranteed him his choice of lodging, upkeep for his three servants, and a boat, a horse, and annual rations; it was further stipulated that his family would inherit the contents of his cell when he died.

On occasion the emperor granted use of a monastery to

Annotated gospels,
Constantinople, early 11th cen-
tury: Saint Luke writing.
(Paris, Bibliothèque Nationale,
Greek 64.)

Top: Scylitzes' *Chronicle:* the monk Lazarus resumes painting icons in the convent of St.-John-the-Precursor after he is martyred. Bottom: Empress Theodora, wife of Theophilus, secretly venerates an icon in her apartment. (Madrid, National Library.)

a layman who took vows for this very purpose. This was in accordance with a general tendency in the late eleventh century for the central government to assign incomes to private individuals. In 1083, for example, Alexis I Comnenus ordered that, in reward for his services, one Stephanos. also known as the monk Simeon, be given the Athonite convent at Xenophon, together with all its possessions. Stephanos, a eunuch and admiral who had served the preceding emperor Nicephorus III, had expressed a desire to quit the world. Stephanos, his three "boys," and his familiars became monks, as is shown by the fact that they changed their names and were tonsured. A document intended to put an end to subsequent spoliation of the property mentions this fact and presents an inventory of properties belonging to the monastery, icons, and additions made to its library of 130 volumes.

The private monastery was a prominent feature of Byzantine society in this period. It was not unusual for private houses to be transformed into monasteries. In Constantinople, for example, there was the house of the strategos Manuel (ca. 830); the home of one Mossele, whose family, of Armenian origin, had been closely involved with palace affairs since the late eighth century; and the home of Romanus I himself, which after Romanus became co-emperor was transformed into the convent of the Myrelaion. A document from Lavra, dated 1016, indicates that a woman named Glyceria and her late husband had given their "poor home" to the convent so the woman might take vows as a nun. Many other monasteries were built specifically as private establishments, both in Constantinople and in the provinces, where great landowners had monasteries built on their property. The Argyroi owned a patrimonial monastery consecrated to Saint Elizabeth; it was located in the Charsianon district, where so many aristocrats had country estates, and was founded by the *tourmarchos* (troop commander) Leo, grandfather of one Eustathius Argyros, a contemporary of Leo VI. Euthymius the Younger (died 898), scion of a relatively modest military household, built a monastery and a convent for his descendants. Some private monasteries were quite modest. A law of 996 notes that the inhabitants of certain rural villages had built private churches and small neighboring convents for themselves and possibly two or three others. Private monasteries could of course be sold or given as gifts, and records of such transactions are preserved in the archives at Mount Athos.

Not all monasteries founded by private individuals were

Communion plate. Onyx and gold cloisonné, 10th century. (Brussels, Stoclet Collection.)

destined to remain private monasteries. The monastery of Backovo, today in Bulgaria, was founded and endowed in 1083 by two Georgians who had made careers in Byzantium: the great *domestikos* Gregorios Pakourianos (Bakouriani) and his brother. The monastery was said to be independent, but relatives, servants, and compatriots of the two brothers were given preference for admission. By contrast, in 1077 the judge Michael Attaleiates chose wording that kept his foundation in the private realm: in his will he bequeathed the monastery, which housed seven monks in the capital, to the Creator, whom he names as "heir . . . administrator and master." But the actual administration was reserved, using the same language, to the judge's direct descendants, including female descendants if no male were available to take up the responsibility.

Private monasteries served as family burial places and ensured that deceased members of the family would be remembered. The body of Eustathius Argyros was buried in his family monastery. Michael Attaleiates stipulated that prayers should be said for himself, his relatives, his two successive wives, several persons named but not identified and, finally, the emperors. Burial in a monastery was no doubt a spiritual privilege that the wealthy procured for themselves and granted to their protégés. Basil the New, a strange seer who frequented the great houses of Constantinople in the mid-tenth century, was buried in a monastery owned by one of his followers. Now we can understand why Simeon the New Theologian found so many lay tombs when he took over as director of Constantinople's monastery of Saint Mamas, and why, as part of his campaign of reform, he had bodies that did not belong removed from the premises. Some private monasteries were apparently dependencies of laymen's homes. The eunuch Samonas, Leo VI's evil genius, once received the emperor in a monastery that he owned. Some men took vows in their own monasteries or even in their own homes transformed into monasteries.

The council of 861 denounced these common and well-known practices. The transformation of a private home or construction of a private convent was sometimes nothing more than a profitable sham; taking the tonsure in one's own house did not necessarily infringe on a man's customary pleasures. The council therefore required that no home be turned into a monastery without approval of the local bishop, with whom an inventory of property had to be filed. Men who

Lavra monastery, Mount Athos.

took vows in monasteries they owned had to be received by a hegumen. Hagiographers were careful to give their stories the proper moral. An extreme case is that of Cyrillus the Phileote, a contemporary of Alexis I. Having received the call after a stint in the navy, he at first acceded to his wife's pleas that he not abandon her and make orphans of his still young children and that he not give his wicked neighbors cause to rejoice. "Retire from the world in our own home," she said. He lived in a cell near his house for a while but finally entered a monastery. The central thread of the story is the saint's quest for hesychia, or repose, which introduces him to the spiritual life. Most hagiographies associate this repose with the cloister, however, and do not fail to recount how ardently the hero waits for his chosen spiritual father to grant him the hooded black habit and tonsure along with a new name.

Under what conditions did monks live in the monasteries?

Windows of the Church of Hosios Lukas (Greece), 11th century.

The hagiographies and monastic rules tell us a great deal about the nature of monastic repose in the tenth and eleventh centuries. Traditionally monks lived alone (even if they had servants) in a *kellion,* or cell. In cities all the kellia of the monastery were generally grouped together in a building, separated from the street by an enclosed space. As for Mount Athos, the documents sometimes mention isolated cells or small groups of cells, but these were satellites of a monastery, which imposed discipline and took care of the liturgy. The common areas included the refectory, the chapel or church (which in the cities received lay worshipers from outside the monastery), the library, the treasury, the archives (entrusted to a conservator), a bath, and an infirmary. Convents for women were similarly organized. We also know something about how people lived inside the cloister. The *typikon,* or rule, specified what should be eaten on ordinary days and holidays, as well as what should be given to the sick and the poor and what clothes should be worn the year round. As we saw earlier, however, the rule was sometimes evaded. The principle that monks should work was also unevenly respected. The rule of the Studion in the early ninth century was intended to make the monastery self-sufficient. But in this period monks increasingly lived off the income from their lands. Lavra, in the mid-eleventh century, distinguished itself by engaging in commercial shipping and fishing.

Comparison of the monastery with the lay oikos reveals two points of difference. The principle that women inhabit a place apart was transposed, or, rather, extended in the monasteries to exclude women entirely (and in the convents to exclude men). Not only were women excluded, so was anything that might serve as a similar temptation, such as female animals (the penitentials are explicit on this point) and beardless youths (pupils were housed separately). Under the patriarchate of Nicholas III (1084–1111), a scandal was provoked at Athos by the Vlaques, a nomadic shepherd people, when it was discovered that their wives and daughters, disguised as men, grazed the monks' flocks and served in the monasteries. Eunuchs had their own convents. Michael Attaleiates set his aside for them and stipulatated that the only exceptions to this rule should be his own relatives, or men of stainless reputation above the age of fifty who owned land. The principle had to be modified for women's convents (many of which were founded by men), because a male priest was required to exercise sacerdotal authority.

Mount Athos.

The penitentials imply what one might have suspected, that not all monks and nuns scrupulously observed the rule of segregation; but that does not make the rule any less significant. The inhabitants of the cloister were cut off from the outside world. Monks were not allowed to leave without

authorization from their superior. Council after council repeated the prohibition against peripatetic monks. When the
patriarch Michael Cerularius, who entertained a suspect interest in magic and fortune-telling, was accused of wrongdoing
in a document drafted after 1058 by Michael Psellus, he was
charged with having met three people who constitute a perfect
triumvirate of evil: a pythoness disguised as a male and two
monks with whom she traveled about the country.

The ultimate monastic repose was found in the individual
cell. Rules prescribed that monks must do their work in their
cells but forbade any conversation or activity requiring more
than one person. According to the typikon of Pakourianos,
monks were supposed to pass their time "in private" (*idios*).

Frontispiece of an anthology of laws. Above: three imperial lawgivers; left to right: Justinian, Leo III, and Constantine V. Below: table for computing degrees of kinship. Probably from Calabria, A.D. 1175. (Venice, Marciana Library, Ancient Holdings, Greek 172.)

# &#8766; Self and Others

THE relations between self and other and self and others still define the axes, or, rather, the circles of private life. In Byzantine society during this period these relations were of course different from what they are today. The boundary line between public and private life was also different, according to our model. Nowadays the family is, in theory, entirely a private affair in regard to both property and emotional attitudes. Various aspects of social practice frequently contradict this theory, but the principle remains, rightly or wrongly, the basis of our consideration of societies remote from us in time and space.

In tenth- and eleventh-century Byzantium relations between individuals were differently organized. To begin with, relations between equals were distinguished from relations between superiors and inferiors—meaning servants, slaves, and followers. A person's equals were divided into two groups regardless of sex: relatives and friends. The terms may be familiar to us, but their meanings were quite different. Kinship was determined by recognized criteria such as birth, adoption, marriage, and ritual. And friendship applied to a whole range of relations not covered by these various kinds of kinship, which one might be tempted to call free relations were it not for the fact that they were often sealed by sworn pacts. This system of classification interacted with the household classification described earlier, but the two were not identical. For example, the servant, or oiketes, was part of a man's household, but the familiar, or oikeios, had a more ambiguous position, somewhere between an equal and an inferior. The division between public and private, as well as that between lay and religious, further complicated the picture.

*Families and Their Strategic Choices*

The kinship group, or *parentela*, was conscious of its extent both horizontally and vertically and could be expanded in either direction in a variety of ways. Its importance can be traced in fact to remote Greco-Roman antecedents. But the prominence of such groups in Byzantine social history varied with time. In one sense the social history of Byzantium can even be viewed as a dialectic between the kinship group and the state, where the latter term refers to the legislative, fiscal, and judicial authority subsumed by the Greek term *demosion*. The tenth and eleventh centuries were part of a longer period, which began during the eighth century at the latest, in which kinship groups openly figure in the investment strategies of the state and its church. Hence it is misleading to look at the kinship group as a setting for private life until we have defined the limits of its more public role.

To clarify what I mean, let me discuss two examples from different levels of the social hierarchy. The first has to do with the high politics of the tenth century. Multiple marriages linked the three leading families of the time—the Phocas, Sclerus, and Maleinus clans. Nicephorus II Phocas, who became emperor in 963 through his marriage with Theophano, widow of Romanus II, was the great-grandson of one Phocas, whose given name became the family name in the next generation. This Phocas was a man who, according to one chronicler, enjoyed military success because of his "extraordinary strength." His son, Nicephorus the Elder, had an illustrious military career in the early ninth century; his grandsons, Bardas and Leo, soon found high positions in government service. Bardas, father of the future emperor, married a Maleinus woman. The Maleinoi were then in their third generation, illustrious on both sides. Manuel Maleinus, brother of Bardas' wife, became a spiritual master of Athos under the monastic name Michael, indeed the superior of the founder of Lavra, the monastery that would be favored by his nephews Leo and Nicephorus even before the latter acceded to the throne. The Maleinoi are also known to have been important landowners in Cappadocia. To Bardas Phocas and the Maleinus woman he married (women are almost never identified by first name, except for the wives, sisters, and daughters of emperors) were born, so far as we know, Nicephorus and his brother, Leo, as well as two girls. One of the latter married an illustrious general by the name of John Curcuas and became the mother of John Tzimisces, who murdered and succeeded his uncle in

969. When he in turn married the empress, Tzimisces was a widower; his first wife was a woman from the Sclerus family, which, like a number of prominent families, was of Armenian origin but present in the upper reaches of the military hierarchy since at least the beginning of the ninth century. The end of the tenth century was marked by an uprising in Asia Minor, which essentially pitted the provincial clients of the Phocas and Sclerus families against Basil II, who became emperor in 976. Basil II fostered conflict between Bardas Phocas, son of Leo, the brother of the assassinated emperor, and Bardas Sclerus, brother of Tzimisces' first wife and of the wife of Bardas Phocas. With this complicated background in mind, it is easy to understand the furious, or perhaps merely objective, note found in the margin of the Novel (or law) of 996 whereby Basil II sought to eliminate various abuses committed by "powerful clans" to the detriment of the central government and its taxpayers. The note identifies these clans as the "Phocades, Scleroi, and Maleinoi."

My second example, less resounding though in other respects quite similar, comes from the *Life of Theodora of Thessalonica,* a nun who died in 892. Born in 812, she was the third child of a priest from the island of Aegina. Her mother having died in childbirth, Theodora's father turned the child over to her godmother to raise; she was affianced to a local notable at

Scylitzes' *Chronicle:* baptism of the son of Leon VI, the future Constantine VII, by the patriarch Nicolas Mystikos; at right, the godfather, brother of the emperor. (Madrid, National Library.)

the first legal opportunity, when she turned six. Theodora married and was the mother of three children when in 826 an Arab invasion forced the family to flee to Thessalonica. Her elder sister, who was dead by this time, had been a nun. Her brother, massacred during the invasion, was a deacon, which is to say that he had embarked upon a clerical career. In Thessalonica, Theodora's father ended his days as a monk. After her two youngest children died, the future saint offered the eldest, her "first fruit," to the Church. The little girl was taken to Sister Catherine, sister of the archbishop of Thessalonica, and a "relative" of the family. After the death of her husband, the heroine of the story also enters a convent, to which she gives a portion of her estate and whose superior is another "relative." Later she meets her daughter, who has become her sister in religion and the superior of her convent.

The hagiographer, a Thessalonican priest and contemporary of the saint, has no purpose in writing other than to edify the faithful and to glorify his city and Theodora's convent. But his account can be read as an illustration of the way in which a typical provincial clan invested its all in the church, placing its sons in the clergy and some of its daughters in convents. Taken together, these two examples show how private families controlled public goods. This fact has a bearing on the manner in which the question of the family's relation to private life ought to be posed. I shall not delve deeper into

Scylitzes' *Chronicle:* marriage (Greek rite) of Constantine VII to Helen, daughter of Roman I Lecapenus. (Madrid, National Library.)

these strategies, which also cast doubt on the meaning of the public category. Let me simply say that the kinship group straddled the divide between public and private and that I am considering only the private aspects of kinship group behavior.

The forms of kinship proliferated because family connections were socially useful. Kinship served as a metaphor for many other kinds of relationships. Marriage rules were stated in terms of degree of kinship, and marriage was an important part of every family's strategy for social advancement. In the fourth century, the church, whose decisions were backed by imperial edict, established the principle of "not confounding names," that is, not assimilating the relations of the bride and the groom into a single family. Sisinnius issued explicit rules in 997: second cousins and second cousins once removed were forbidden to marry; two brothers (or sisters) could not marry two women (men) who were second cousins of each other; a man and his nephew could not marry sisters; a woman and her niece could not marry brothers; marriages between uncle and niece (or aunt and nephew) had long been prohibited; and, finally, a man could not marry two sisters in succession, nor could he marry a woman and then marry her mother.

Bracelet in cloisonné enamel, 11th century. (Budapest, National Museum.)

Adoptive kinship and kinship through baptism incurred the same prohibitions as biological kinship. Marriage between a man and his goddaughter had been prohibited since the sixth century, but the council of 692 took a decisive step by prohibiting marriage between a child's carnal and spiritual parents, that is, between mother and godfather. The reason given for this was that "kinship according to the spirit" is superior to "kinship according to the flesh." Church doctrine was perfectly in harmony with the objective, common to all kinship groups, of extending the network of solidarity as broadly as possible. In practice people shunned some marriages not prohibited by canon law, as between a man and the daughters of a family that adopted him. In the tenth century the aristocracy also sought to forge alliances between established clans or between an established clan and an impressive new arrival on the scene. It did so because it had still not consolidated its position and was open to new members. The example of the Phocas, Maleinus, and Sclerus families suggests that access to the aristocracy had already become more difficult by the end of the tenth century.

Questions addressed to the patriarchate call attention to otherwise obscure families that chose marriage strategies intended to fortify existing solidarities rather than create new ones; in other words, they chose marriage partners from a relatively limited circle of prospects. Consider this case, which was presented to the patriarch Alexis the Studite (1025–1043). Georgios had received blessings for his marriage with Theodota, then five and a half years old, but the child died a short while afterward. The patriarch invalidated the benediction on the grounds that the girl was too young, but this was in order to authorize a marriage that the little girl's widowed mother wished to make with a man who was Georgios' second cousin. The closeness of kinship groups is seen not only in patriarchal decisions but also in the obsessive fear of "mixing of the blood," which is to say, of incest, whether in marriage or not, as is shown by the minute detail in which the penitential rehearses the list of marriages prohibited by canon law. History and hagiography mention only the usual connections; in politics partnerships are formed mainly between brothers, fathers-in-law and sons-in-law, and between a man and his sister's husband. At times the entire kinship group (*syggeneia*) or at least the household becomes involved. Maternal uncles often set examples for nephews who chose a monastic or religious life. Other relations are simply referred to as "kin." But the patriarch's answers show that degrees of relation could be specified in detail when necessary. In some surviving wills nephews inherit for want of direct heirs: Gemma, for example, left most of her estate to her nephew in 1049, after making provisions for her servants. And one letter-writer assigned his nephew the place of the son he never had.

Adoptive kinship was less prominent in practice than in legislation. Leo VI granted authority to adopt to women and eunuchs as well as to men, based on the principle that the spiritual takes precedence over the carnal in founding the bond of kinship. In the shadows we also glimpse the ancient custom of adopting a man as a brother, which was repudiated by the church, perhaps owing to suspicion of homosexuality. Although almost never mentioned in the histories and hagiographies, this practice was sufficiently common, despite church opposition, that prayer books included a special ritual, probably intended to substitute for the age-old gesture of exchanging blood, a blessing given in church by a priest. (Interestingly, the adoption of brothers has survived in an extensive portion of what used to be Byzantine territory, notably the Balkans.) The histories mention godfathers, especially when the godfather is the emperor, which could be an important factor in a man's career. Grandfathers and uncles could serve as god-

Pair of gold earrings.
Constantinople, 10th century.
(Washington, Dumbarton
Oaks, Byzantine Collection.)

fathers. The honor was reciprocal, and the bond between godfather and godson was, and still is, socially recognized in the Christian societies of the Mediterranean. The validity of this bond between men contrasted with the prohibition against marriage, or indeed any form of carnal relationship, between a child's godfather and its mother. This point is stressed not only in the penitential but also in tales of the afterlife and the punishment of sinners, as well as in the "Letter fallen from heaven," an apocryphal and variable text that first appeared in the fifth century and subsequently incorporated, in its various Greek versions, most of the common clerical injunctions. The godfather at baptism was designated to serve as godfather at his goddaughter's wedding, holding the marriage crown of the Greek rite over her head. He may have played a role in that key element of family strategy—arranging the marriage—but this we do not know for certain.

Arranging the marriage was the key but not the only element of family strategy. Choice of career was also important, at least for those families whose lawsuits are recorded in the register of Judge Eustathius and whose questions are recorded in the archives of the patriarchate, as well as a few families mentioned in the hagiographies. These were aristocratic families attracted to the capital, as well as middle-class and clerical families, often well placed in public service, and for the most part urban, possibly residents of Constantinople. Marriage could further a man's career and did not prevent boys from entering the clergy. The monastery was another avenue of advancement. Castration of young boys was still practiced, although the law limited it in theory to cases where medically indicated; it could open the way to a lay or clerical career. The history of the Byzantine eunuch has yet to be written, and the period in which we are interested was the period of the eunuch's greatest importance. The eunuch was not at all the figure of fun that he became for Enlightenment writers fond of tales of the romantic Orient. He was seen, rather, as a third sex, in which nature was entirely abolished and only culture remained. A variety of consequences flowed from this abolition of nature.

The family, and in fact the entire kinship group, chose futures for its offspring. The sources vary as to the age at which the choice was made. Most of the hagiographies depict adolescents or young adults who choose the ascetic life when a marriage is proposed and rejected. Euthymius the Younger, who died in 898, agreed to marry at age eighteen to ensure the continuation of his house, a provincial family of "military" landowners; he fled to the monastery only after his wife had become pregnant and his sister had married. Thomaïs of Lesbos, who in the mid-tenth century, in obedience to her parents' wishes, renounced her desire to remain a virgin, did not marry until age twenty-four. Other young people were in more of a hurry, either because the need was urgent or there was some opportunity to seize. Prepubescent youths, could, if not marry, at least become engaged, although consent to either marriage or a monastic career could not be given, in theory, until one had reached the age of reason. But the ancient theory of the ages of life served families that were in a hurry, and the age of consent was fixed at the beginning of the seventh year of life, when the child's elementary education, based on reading and the psalter, was complete. Such early consent was obviously unreliable; nevertheless, children, especially little girls, continued to be sent to the cloister. The council of 692 and legislation of Leo VI established a limit of age ten, but this was probably not always observed in practice. I noted that the daughter of Theodora of Thessalonica was placed in a convent at age six, and this fact is mentioned in a hagiography, which held itself up as a model. Problems raised by early marriage were even more complex.

Culminating a lengthy evolution, a late-eighth-century law made obtaining the nuptial benediction the necessary and sufficient condition for celebration of a marriage. But from at least the sixth century on, the betrothal had assumed increasing importance, to the point where the consequences of betrothal were almost the same as those of marriage. Betrothal therefore became a solution for families in too much of a hurry to await the legal age of marriage, which had long been set at twelve for girls and fourteen for boys, because engagement could be celebrated as of the age of consent. The records of Judge Eustathius contain lawsuits stemming from broken engagements. These give some idea of actual practice, at least among the aristocracy. The betrothal was recorded in a notarized document, which specified a date for the marriage, the amount of the dowry, and possibly a forfeit for breaking the engagement.

Consent of the parents was required for unemancipated children, regardless of their age: one unemancipated young man married a young woman in her home, after which the couple went together to the church, but the marriage could not be validated owing to the refusal of the groom's father to

Dancer, from crown said to be of Constantine Monomachos, probably given by him to King Andrew I (1046–1060) of Hungary. Enamel and gold cloisonné. (Budapest, National Museum.)

give his consent. Widows of the family, such as a mother or grandmother, were normally authorized to conclude marriage contracts. The residence of the betrothed couple was often a matter for negotiation. The father of one prepubescent girl took his future son-in-law into his home without a formal betrothal but after obtaining benediction for the marriage; the situation was deemed irregular and the contract was annulled without difficulty. The court pointed out that even if a girl was betrothed, received the nuptial benediction, and went to live in her husband's home, she could not become a legitimate wife until her twelfth birthday. We do not know whether such marriages were prematurely consummated, nor do we know the median age of female puberty in Byzantine society.

Golden bird with stud pattern, 10th–11th century. (Lausanne, Dr. Reber's collection.)

The court's insistence on the legal norms suggests that they were commonly violated. Consider the following curious case, in which the groom, a young member of the Comnenus family, went to live with his bride's family. He had made a written promise of marriage but later repudiated it, claiming that he was underage (he was eighteen at the time). The judge found against him, criticizing the youth for having entered an aristocratic household, "seen the girl, spent time with her, and remained in the house after promising to marry her." Again we cannot say to what lengths cohabitation was carried, but the same judicial archives include the case of a bride who, at the moment of consummation, was found to be "spoiled." Yet her husband turned her out illegally, since in such cases the man was expected to leave the bedchamber at once and call "friends and relatives of the woman" in as witnesses. A contemporary pamphlet on gynecology gives hints on how to recover the appearance of a lost virginity.

Marriages were generally arranged by parents or relatives. On this point the hagiographies corroborate the information contained in Judge Eustathius' records. The widowed mother of Euthymius the Younger searched for a young woman of good family for her son; the husband of Mary the Younger's sister offered Mary's hand to his friend. The law required parents to find spouses for their children, and a young woman who remained unmarried at twenty-five had the right to insist that her parents find her a husband. Some of the cases heard by Judge Eustathius show that the wishes of the children were not always disregarded. The *protospatharios* Himerius, for example, "fell in love with a girl from a senator's family . . . took her to bed, and deflowered her without her father's knowledge. Later, she became pregnant and her father learned what had happened, and Himerius and the girl hastened to the church." The marriage took place, but Himerius was then still under the legal authority of his own father, after whose death he attempted to have it annulled, thereby precipitating the lawsuit. Cecaumenus, we recall, was well aware that his daughters were not inaccessible. Girls were not only seduced in their homes but sometimes abducted; in such cases there was always a presumption of a secret agreement. In the twelfth century Theodorus Balsamon was particularly severe in one canonical commentary concerning the case of a girl who had read the marriage contract drawn up by her father for her betrothal to a man whom she did not wish to marry. She alerted her beloved, who spirited her away, but Balsamon declared that the marriage was impossible, even with the consent of the girl's father. The marriage of the parents of the hero Digenis involved kin on both sides: a young emir fell in love with a Christian girl of noble family and abducted her, after which the girl's brothers became involved, followed by the parents of both bride and groom.

In seeking a marriage partner, families considered wealth and connections. Once the choice was made, the couple was expected to produce children. As Achmet's *Dream Key* shows, having children was a concern of both men and women in their dreams.

---

*Marriage, Family, and Feelings*

The church followed the ancient teachings of Paul in recommending marriage as the only solution for men and women who could not attain the higher good of virginity or continence. Religious preaching about marriage in fact changed while appearing not to; the changes came, no doubt, in response to social evolution and the increased emphasis on kin-group solidarities. The church remained reticent about sexuality, legitimate or not, as can be seen from its prohibition of third marriages and its stress on the positive value of widowhood. Hagiography continued to promote the virtues of the cloistered life. But some saints actually married prior to taking vows, and this was new, if not in reality then at least in hagiographic literature, in which female saints now began to appear with some frequency. In some examples of the genre, such as the *Life of Thomaïs of Lesbos,* written sometime between the birth of Romanus II and his accession to the throne, marriage itself became a scene of merit and happiness. Kale (Beauty), mother of Saint Thomaïs, "took upon herself

Adulterous woman: detail of a fresco of Sant'Angelo in Formis (Italy), school of Cassino, 11th century.

the golden yoke, which she wore in concord thrice happy, blessed, and evangelical, observing the divine commandments." She and her husband rivaled each other in spiritual merit, living together in perfect harmony. Their marriage was motivated "not by physical pleasure but by the desire for a virtuous child," a theme that the author of this hagiography develops at length. After the traditional period of waiting, found in so many saints' lives, a child was finally born to them: Thomaïs.

The poor child was less fortunate than her mother but even more virtuous. She preferred virginity but accepted marriage, "two things universally praised and respected," and her husband's blows made her a saint. Mary the Younger was also mistreated after a false accusation that she had sinned with a servant. Her husband locked her up and questioned her favorite maid, "with cross looks and a gruff voice." Despite the maid's denials, Mary was beaten, drawn by horses, and kicked until she nearly died. This account may reflect monastic hyperbole in treating the vexations of marriage, but similar horrors can be found in the archives of Judge Eustathius. In a case involving the property of a woman who fled her husband and went to a convent, the husband was allowed six months to persuade his wife to return; her relatives were forbidden to prevent him from seeing her. It was up to the husband to "flatter her with words, to lay a full table before her, and to do everything in his power to rekindle old feelings, but without violence or assault." A third person, apparently a nun from the convent, was to stand by during these interviews and intervene if the last-named condition were violated.

The use of *pallakai,* concubines, though disapproved by the church, was common. Men dreamed of having one, and the penitential drew a parallel between a man's concubine and his wife (*metruia*) when it came to the violation of sexual taboos. Many concubines must have been women of the lower orders, and their children would have faced many difficulties. Judge Eustathius heard one case involving a man whose mother had died and the daughter of a servant whom the man's father had impregnated and later married after his first wife's death. A will, dated 1076 and drawn up by Genesios, son of Falkon, just before entering a monastery, confirms his grant of freedom to one Loukia (Lucia), "my slave, purchased for cash," along with a bequest to the woman's daughter, Anna, to which he adds two vines, "because of the care and attention she showed them," even though she had no idea that

they would one day be hers. Given that all the other legatees are nephews and nieces, it is tempting to conclude that Anna was Genesios' daughter. Romanus I, father-in-law of Constantine VII and co-emperor, had a son by a concubine (whose name we do not know) along with numerous legitimate offspring. The boy was castrated, which prevented him from founding a rival dynasty but not from making a career in politics—a brilliant career thanks to the fact that his nephews were still minors. Another interesting case is the imperial ménage à trois described by Psellus. Zoë, who became the legitimate ruler after the death of her uncle Basil II and her father, Constantine VIII, was old—in her fifties—when she married Constantine Monomachus. Now, Constantine lived openly with a woman of the Sclerus clan, the niece of his second wife. He visited his mistress in her own home and, while waiting for Zoë to die so that he might be free to marry, formed with her an unprecedented *philia,* or friendship, which scandalized the Senate. But the mistress died before Zoë. Apart from the political aspects, such situations may have been common, for Psellus shows no compunctions about saying that Zoë's age justified the arrangement.

There were well-defined standards of female conduct, infringement of which a man could cite as grounds for repu-

Scylitzes' *Chronicle:* acrobatic interlude at the hippodrome. (Madrid, National Museum.)

diating his wife. Judge Eustathius mentions baths and lavish dinners with men from outside the family and trips to the races at the hippodrome. The law specified grounds for divorce, which over time became increasingly narrow: adultery by the woman, impotence on the part of the man, attempts on the life of a spouse, and leprosy. In theory, adulterous couples had their noses cut off, and the woman was sent to a convent. The husband was allowed two years to take her back. But theory and practice did not coincide. Couples separated by common agreement and entered the cloister, and some wives chose on their own to enter convents. The first wife of Basil I was turned out summarily, without legal proceedings of any kind, so Basil might marry Eudocia Ingerina; so was the wife of Romanus III Argyrus, so that he might marry Zoë. Such practices were tolerated by the church, which had so strongly condemned the fourth marriage of Leo VI and raised objections to the marriage of Nicephorus II and the imperial widow on grounds of spiritual kinship. Does this mean these practices were not unusual?

Finally, some of the lawsuits already cited show that families occasionally adopted matrimonial strategies that required earlier marriages to be annulled. The loss of a spouse offered new opportunities, but it is difficult to say how those opportunities were used in practice. The church, backed by the law, prohibited third marriages, and even second marriages were not fully approved. That widows served as heads of household for tax purposes and had charge of community property for the purpose of making wills is attested in the sources; they could also serve as guardians responsible for finding marriage partners for their children and grandchildren. Eustathius Boilas, from whose autobiographical testament I shall cite frequently, never remarried after losing his wife early in the eleventh century, while he was still young; he considers the fact worthy of note. Marital decisions, especially the choice of a mate, were influenced by considerations of property. "The engagement was broken off for reasons of inadequate wealth," states one affidavit in the archives of Judge Eustathius. The widow's legal capacity made matters easier; broken promises of all sorts made them more difficult.

It is almost impossible to delve into the realm of intimate feelings. Two convergent historical factors make it difficult to know what they were. In the first place, the family was defined by a set of publicly accepted values and by behavioral choices dictated by those values. The *History* of Leo Deacon, a late-tenth-century historiographer, can be read as political history, as a chronicle of the reigns of John Tzimisces and the young Basil II and of the great aristocratic uprising in Asia Minor. It can also be read as dynastic history, illustrating the effects of family solidarity and vengeance. The theme raised by Cecaumenus, of family honor endangered by wives and daughters, is not really a matter of intimate feelings. Families are discussed in documents whose purpose and genre left no room for individual expression, apart from rare exceptions and writers willing to bend the rules. We must examine each genre separately and make no mistake about the intentions of our texts. The eleventh-century sources discuss feelings with a freedom more modern than was possible in the austerely classical climate of the tenth century, and the behavior they describe was perhaps also more liberated.

Much attention has been devoted to hagiography in this period, and a good deal of information has been gathered about the saints as children and adolescents, about their education and family plans. But the purpose of hagiography is neither documentary nor anecdotal nor entirely biographical, because biography is constrained by the mold of sanctity; its only purpose is to demonstrate the holiness of the future saint, and every detail is nothing but a prefiguration of a sainthood that will be proved, ultimately, by miracles. The precocious greatness of the hero or heroine rubs off on the parents, particularly the mother. The mother's desire to have a child is in effect a desire for edification, as is clear from the words of the Virgin announcing the birth of Thomaïs to her mother.

Hagiography tells us that mothers played a role in early education, even of boys; this, in any case, was an ancient tradition. The mother of Nicephorus of Medicion (died 813) is held up as an example in the life of that saint, written between 824 and 827, because she gave her three sons a good education. She found teachers to "teach them holy letters" and kept them away from amusements tainted by association with the old cults, such as carnivalesque dances, races at the hippodrome, and plays in the theaters—all the sorts of things, says the hagiographer, that delight young children. In the tenth century, when the mother of Nicephorus of Miletus, who was a child during the reign of Romanus I, protects his purity by changing his little shirt for a longer garment and accompanying him to school, she is laying the groundwork for his future merit; the child's early castration for the sake of his career occasions no comment, however.

It was common to say that such and such a child behaves like an old man and shows no interest in childhood diversions,

Gregory Nazianzen, *Selected Sermons:* Cover page of "Discourse on
the love of the poor." The star-shaped composition depicts various
scenes of relief for the poor. In the margin, children play with swing.
Constantinople, 12th century. (Paris, Bibliothèque Nationale, Greek 550.)

as though this were some sort of miracle. The adult saint had to exhibit the ultimate in virtue; eulogistic rhetoric demanded it, and hagiographers, trying to outdo one another, could make do with no less. So Euthymius the Younger leaves his pregnant wife without a sigh, and Theodora of Tessalonica overcomes her worry about her little daughter's harsh life in the convent, and Mary the Younger overcomes her sorrow at losing two children. In death Mary will appear to a reclusive painter and inspire him to paint her own icon, which shows her flanked by her two dead children and her faithful servant. To be sure, a personal accent can sometimes be heard even in hagiography. When, around 821, the monk Nicetas wrote the life of his grandfather and godfather Saint Philaretos, emulator of Job, he was in fact compiling a family chronicle that Philaretos himself had asked him to write. The writing, however, bears the undeniably intimate stamp of a happy childhood.

Texts intended for private use probably have more to offer. Nothing could be less revealing, however, than the many bravura pieces composed in docile obedience to the laws of ancient rhetoric or the rules of such genres as letters of condolence and marriage congratulations. Though full of information about social and cultural models, they are without exception extremely disappointing to anyone in search of the intimate secrets of Byzantine life. In letters addressed to freely chosen correspondents, by contrast, writers were free to talk about themselves and their correspondents, at least in those letters collected for posterity, written exclusively by men under the sign of *philia,* or friendship. In particular, letter-writers often excuse themselves by explaining the reasons for a long silence or delay in answering. Constantine VII, for example, tells one of his correspondents, the *logothetos* and *magistros* Simeon, of his concerns about his children, especially his youngest child, who has been ill. Private wills and monastic foundations left room for the expression of some family feelings, for such documents could be drafted in a rather free style—rhetoric had no part in their composition. Eustathius Boilas begins his will, drafted in 1059, with an autobiographical sketch. He recalls how, shortly after his family moved into its present home, "my son, who had just finished his third year, left this life in the sixth indiction; and in the ninth [that is, three years later], his mother, my wife, her head shaved and clad in a nun's habit, followed her child, by divine Providence leaving behind our two daughters and, for my lifetime, myself." That is all—and it is enough. When Genesios, son of Falkon, was seized by the desire to enter a monastery, he divided his property, near Taranto, by drawing up a will in the year 1076. He leaves something to Falkon and Gemma, the children of one of his brothers, and adds a further bequest "for Gemma alone, whom I loved for her fine manners and for the respect that she was pleased to show me." Therein lies a clue, to be sure, but to what, we will never know.

Couples, married or not, come to life in eleventh-century texts. This does not mean that the couple came into being at that time but, what is more significant, that people began to see it and hear it. Amorous ways were recognized, albeit for purposes of mockery and criticism. Psellus describes with cruel precision the seductive maneuvers that young and handsome Michael used to win the overripe and overpassionate Zoë, who held legitimate title to the throne: "He behaved as lovers do. Taking her in his arms, he gave her quick kisses, he touched her neck and hand, following the instructions of his brother [the eunuch John] . . . Then their kisses led to intercourse, and they arranged to be found sleeping together in the same bed by many eyes." Cecaumenus also knew how a woman's favors were won and why no woman of his family could be trusted alone with a visitor: "If he thinks he can get away with it, he will give your wife an affectionate nod, he will stare at her without reserve, and he will even sully her if given the chance." This severe provincial goes on to tell the true story of a man from Constantinople who is sent away on a mission only to find a seducer in his house when he returns three years later, a man who had introduced himself as a relative of his wife's. The woman's sin caused the unfortunate husband and his relatives great distress. "As for the young man, he boasted of his exploit as though it were one of the Labors of Hercules."

Psellus also described the passion that joined Constantine IX and Scleraina: "They were both so involved in love (*eros*) that neither could stand to be without the other, even in circumstances where they seemed to be courting woe." The epic of Digenis, as it has come down to us, depicts the hero as a man fully involved in a flourishing marriage but also irresistibly, if remorsefully, drawn to the pleasures of adultery. The text cannot be adduced here as evidence, however, because we are unsure of the dates of the surviving written versions. The subject itself, though bearing traces of ninth-century events, dates from the eleventh or twelfth century.

The poor of the cities were often forced to turn to charitable institutions when they became sick or grew old. These were modeled on institutions that developed between the fourth and sixth centuries in the cities, especially the larger cities, of the late Roman Empire. Founded by the emperor or by private individuals and managed by monks, hospitals enjoyed, after a long period of decline, a revival in the eleventh and especially the twelfth century, a development related to the revival of the cities that began as early as the ninth century. The Hospital of Christ the Omnipotent, established and provided with a detailed set of regulations by John II Comnenus in 1126, is the best known and most fully developed example. On a more modest scale, Michael Attaleiates, in a will (1077) cited previously, established a hospice along with his monastery. In the urban houses of the well-to-do and probably also in the huts of peasants, one came into the world, suffered, and died at home. That physicians came to their patients' bedsides is attested by letter-writers. Midwives did the same, and if some miniatures depict the rooms in which the Virgin or Christ were born, others show the birth itself: Rachel and Rebecca bring their sons into the world either seated or standing up. The *Life of Mary the Younger* recounts her death in the bosom of her family, of injuries sustained when she was beaten by her husband. The onlookers burst into tears when the time comes to prepare the funeral bath, a scene represented in innumerable illustrations.

*Spiritual Kinship*

The monastic oikos was a metaphor suggesting an analogy between the brotherhood of monks and the household of an ordinary family. The reality of this metaphoric kinship is attested by its legal consequences and its effect on the transmission of property. It was an unusual form of kinship in that marriage did not exist. The brotherhood (*adelphotes*) lived in an oikos and possibly other secondary residences (*metoikia*) under the authority of a father (*pater*). This father was chosen in various ways set down in the rule of the monastery, usually involving the monks and the descendants of the monastery's founder. The brotherhood (sisterhood, in the case of convents) grew and perpetuated itself by accepting new members, individuals who in theory decided voluntarily to take vows but in fact were often obliged to do so for one reason or another, as in the case of children, women turned out by their husbands, and defeated politicians. After a period of probation,

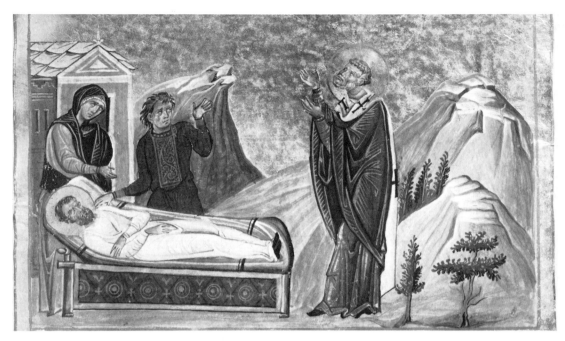

So-called menology of Basil II, Constantinople, late 10th century: death of Saint Martin of Tours. (Rome, Vatican Library, Greek 1613.)

the postulant was accepted and tonsured (in a symbolic negation of sexuality) by the father, who gave the new monk a habit and a new name, symbolizing the beginning of a new life. Similarly, in convents, the sisterhood lived under the authority of a mother, whose lack of sacerdotal authority meant that convents could not function as perfectly closed communities, a difficulty that was met in a number of ways.

The brotherhood of monks was an idealized, which is to say fleshless, reflection of ordinary kinship. It had nothing to do with godparenthood or fraternal adoption, these being strictly worldly customs. Nor did monks own slaves. These, at any rate, were the interdictions set forth in the founding rule of the monastery of Lavra in 963, and similar rules existed in other monasteries. In reality, things were not quite as specified: monks kept free servants, and ordinary kinship relations did not disappear when private homes were turned into monasteries; for example, brothers, uncles, and nephews entered the Studion monastery. The *Life of Theodora of Thessalonica* tells of a mother and daughter meeting in a convent and insists that profane feelings of filial affection gave way to the love that one nun feels for another; even more praiseworthy, the mother is obedient to her daughter, who has become abbess of their convent. Lay persons were at times taken into the monastic family by spiritual adoption. In 1014 Constantine and Mary Lagudes, who had no children or other heirs, bequeathed their belongings to the monastery of Lavra, with which they enjoyed a spiritual relationship. Above all, the "spiritual father" played an extraordinarily important role as the director of individual conscience from the ninth century on; he established a link of the utmost importance between the world and the cloister.

The spiritual father was always a *hieromonachos*—a priest as well as a monk—even though there was more to his role than merely hearing confessions. His spiritual kin included both monks and lay persons, and the latter sometimes left property to the monastery. In 1012 the monk Eustratius, later hegumen of Lavra, received a gift from a childless couple, the *koubouklesios* (patriarchal chamberlain) John and his wife, Glyceria. When the local bishop attempted to get hold of the property, Glyceria, who had in the meantime been widowed and taken vows as a nun, signed a confirmation of the gift. This document shows explicitly that the paternal metaphor carried real force. Our knowledge of the relation between spiritual father and his children comes from the models and exempla that monastic authors of the ninth, tenth, and eleventh centuries set for themselves. The importance of the spiritual father figure matched the monks' growing and increasingly open insistence that their way of life was the best and that they as a group should enjoy social supremacy in Byzantine Christendom.

By 837, when the *Life of Peter of Atroa* was written shortly after his death, confession had become a central theme. Peter identifies hidden sins. He briefly resurrects a monk who died while he was away from his monastery, unable to confess to Peter as he had wished, whereupon the monk declares: "Peter, I never allowed myself to look upon you or listen to you as a mere human being. I looked upon and listened to you as though you were an angel from on high, and all my life I have taken your words to me as commandments of divine origin." Peter also hears the confessions of lay persons and assigns them penances. Here we witness a development that went far beyond the scale of spiritual penalties attested as early as the fourth century. The *Life of the Patriarch Euthymius,* written a few years after Euthymius' death in 917 by a monk in his monastery, can be read in one sense as a chronicle of the reign of Leo VI. Its real purpose, however, was to exhibit the sovereign authority of the "father" over the emperor himself and the emperor's entourage. This authority is seen at work in times of political difficulty and crisis and outside any sacramental context.

Another tenth-century text also makes a point of exhibiting spiritual authority over the emperor, for to exercise such authority was to rule beyond all argument. The text to which I refer is the rule of Athanasius, who founded the monastery of Lavra on Mount Athos in 963. Athanasius mentions that Nicephorus II Phocas participated in this project before assuming the throne and alludes to Nicephorus' monastic vocation at that time. Then Athanasius himself enters the story. He points out that Phocas became emperor, left the construction site, and went to the capital, and he reproaches him vehemently: "I called the most pious emperor to account, for I knew that he would quietly suffer me to say what I had to say." Indeed, Phocas does apologize for his behavior. The letter-writers of the tenth century give us a more down-to-earth, if more ornately expressed, view of the affection bestowed upon the "spiritual father" (although certain letters suggest that the person referred to is actually a godfather).

As a final example of spiritual fatherhood, consider the relation between the monk Simeon of Studion and his disciple, Simeon the New Theologian, who was born in 949 or 950 and died in 1022, hegumen of the monastery of Saint Mamas in Constantinople. The latter Simeon is a key figure of the eleventh century and of Byzantine mysticism. We know him through his work, portions of which are now attributed, in fact, to his master, and through his *Life,* written by his own spiritual son, Nicetas Stethatus, some time after 1054. At the heart of his story Nicetas placed two themes: the illumination of Simeon the New Theologian, who received his doctrine and liturgical hymns directly from the Holy Spirit, and his close relationship with his spiritual father, Simeon. This relationship was so close that when Simeon died his disciple had his icon painted and also established in his honor a public holiday that enjoyed great success. These two themes probably also figured in the charges brought against him by the patriarchal tribunal, where he explained at great length, in terms recounted in the *Life,* the nature of the holiday and the cult of holy men. Both the claim of personal revelation and the unprecedented exaltation of the spiritual father, emphasizing that the relationship with him must be one of total obedience and complete frankness, represent a sharp break with monastic tradition, at once a disintegration of monastic brotherhood and emancipation from its bonds. What is more, Nicetas saw himself in a similar relationship to the New Theologian. The latter, a young eunuch from a good provincial family, renounced a political career while still an adolescent and came to receive the tonsure from the monk who also gave him his name and who was already his spiritual father in the world. Their intimacy was such that the postulant slept in his master's cell, "for want of space." At the end of the story, Nicetas has a vision of the New Theologian, now dead, lying on a bed in an imperial residence. Simeon "took [Nicetas] in his arms and kissed [him] on the mouth" and then handed him a written document that he wished published. These physical contacts are supposed to demonstrate to readers of the *Life* that holy men have been granted the reward and grace of "insensibility" (*apatheia*). The theme is related to the question whether the body dies a real or symbolic death, which, as his biographer points out, is an important part of the New Theologian's ascetic meditation.

Although the examples mentioned thus far involve only men, the penitentials also provided for confessions by women, both nuns and laywomen. Spiritual kinship with women developed in similar ways, as is shown by the relation between the patriarch Nicholas I and Empress Zoë, mother of Constantine VII. But the fundamental asymmetry due to the sacerdotal power of men and the segregation of women caused problems, which neither the sacrament of penance nor the duty to confess to the mother superior could entirely overcome.

*Friends*

As fundamental and as broad as the kinship metaphor was, it did not cover all types of private relations, for the society was too complex. A person could be another's "man," for example; Boilas in his will refers to someone as his "lord" (*authentes*). I shall say nothing here about this kind of relationship, which is not the aspect of private life under scrutiny in this book. Kinship was also linked to friendship (*philia*), whose meaning was complementary and in a sense residual: friendship described those relationships not compelled by biological kinship, kinship through marriage, or metaphorical kinship stemming from a ritual of some sort.

Most of the sources concern friendship between men, where friendship, at least at first glance, means much the same thing as it does today. It was about this sort of friendship that

Scylitzes' *Chronicle:* conversation among men. (Madrid, National Library.)

men expressed their personal feelings in letters. Of course people of the class that wrote letters straddled the divide between public and private, and their friendships were implicated in both realms. The histories show that friendship, often sealed by a solemn oath, was frequently the prelude to political conspiracy, in which case even relatives could become "friends." The fathers of a married man and woman, for instance, might form a friendship as an additional bond between their two families, a bond freely chosen, hence all the more effective. "Friendship" also described the illicit pact between the eunuch Samonas, Leo VI's trusted secretary, and two Greek merchants, whom he helped to obtain a profitable monopoly in trade with Bulgaria.

On a more mundane level, friendship was often the grounds for recommending a friend's protégé or relative for special favor. Correspondents kept each other informed about their careers and exchanged news of mutual friends. This was perfectly traditional behavior, as can be seen from a glance at fourth-century correspondence. Less traditional is the lack of reserve with which letter-writers described their moods and detailed their illnesses. Today's reader finds rather disconcerting the ardent if stereotyped phrases in which letter-writers expressed their feelings about a friend's absence; it is for such feelings that the letters were preserved. The fragments of private correspondence judged worthy of inclusion in an anthology or in someone's *Works* can hardly pass for intimately personal texts. They must have been composed in keeping with rules of rhetoric of which they were deemed worthy exemplars, owing in part to the identity of their authors but in part, too, I should imagine, to their fine style. Byzantine society emphasized friendship between men; no epistolary evidence of friendship between women or of a love affair has survived. What is more, masculine friendship is expressed in terms that nowadays would raise questions about the nature of the relationship. For example, Simeon Magister, a high fiscal official in the latter part of the tenth century, wrote to a correspondent who was either a monk or the "son" of a common spiritual father in these terms: "You are with me constantly in my soul, my desired brother, and thoughts of your tender company are ever on my mind." Elsewhere in the same letter we read: "I have received your very dear letter, and the more deeply I delved into its characters, the more love (*eros*) I felt." It would be easy to multiply examples in which letter-writers use the vocabulary of the heart. Desire (*pothos*) is felt for the absent individual; it is a matter of nostalgia rather than sexuality. Tenderness (*agape*) is intense but nonspecific. Love often seems questionable, but suspicions are invariably dispelled by further reading. On the whole, it seems fair to say that among members of the social elite, educated in good schools, the rules governing talk about feelings were different from what they are today and different from what they were for monks at the time.

Hunter with hare; use of sword, pike, and bow. Sides of a wooden chest, 10th–11th century. (Museum of Rheims.)

# ✒ The Inner Life

Let me move on to the self, to the inner life of the individual. Again the evidence comes exclusively from men, adults, notables; what information we glean about others must be read between the lines. We can only hope that what these writers have left is a fairly comprehensive portrait of the human condition in Byzantium.

At first glance Byzantine writers seem wholly without reserve when talking about their bodies. We have seen how Theodorus of Nicaea detailed his ailments in a letter asking to be allowed to return home. John, a monk of Latros, adopts a similar tone in excusing his failure to write: "Rest assured, most dear and desired friend, that I have not seen the pure light for one single day, nor have I had any appetite for food or drink, nor have I slept, even though I have plenty of leisure, afflicted as I am and tormented by a disease that I can only call invisible. To those who see me I seem to be in good health. In fact I am not entirely well." Theodorus of Nicaea paints what seems to be a caricature of himself but is in fact quite a literary portrait: he is, he says, a man "with a thick beard, fat neck, and protuberant and swollen stomach," as well as a bald head and a scowling look, yet innocent of the crimes of which he stands accused, despite this unprepossessing appearance. In the dreams interpreted by Achmet all the parts of the body and all its secretions and evacuations play a part. Yet one must not place too much trust in these.

A more attentive reading shows the tension that existed in the high culture of the elite between ancient heritage and contemporary practice. One place where this tension was strongest had to do with the visible presence of the sexualized

*Awareness of the Body*

617

body. On ivory caskets one sees the nudity of Adam and Eve in precise anatomical detail, as well as mythological figures depicted according to the ancient taste. Manuscript paintings were quite different. In the Scylitzes manuscript in Madrid, for example, we see only a silhouette of the widow Danielis on her travels, closely wrapped. On a psalter painted in Constantinople in the late eleventh century, the dancers are sumptuously but fully clothed; even their hands are hidden in long sleeves, and they wear tall hats upon their heads. Men worked and fought with bare legs, but in the cities it was rare to see a gentleman's ankles.

Attention should be paid to the ways in which sexual desire was made explicit. Lay writing displays a crudity that had less to do with individual candor than with fidelity to an ancient literary tradition. Consider the letter that Theodorus Daphopates, secretary of Romanus I, wrote in the name of the *protospatharios* Basilius to a friend of the latter who had married the night before—a letter shocking to the unprepared modern reader. Theodorus tells how he imagined the sequence of events on the wedding night, using the customary martial metaphor; he goes on to explain how his imagination affected him physically, describing in precise detail what took place. What the reader must understand is that this text belongs to a traditional genre, the *epithalamios,* or nuptial compliment, and that Theodorus is merely making use of the well-known ancient theme of a man witnessing his friend during a night of love. Still, the writer made free use of this classical remembrance in a letter so far from being intimate and confidential that it was copied and included in an epistolary anthology.

The medical rather than the literary tradition undoubtedly did most to shape the attitudes of both laymen and monks in regard to sex and the body. Private libraries contained books of domestic medicine, especially dietary calendars which described, in accordance with the Hippocratic doctrine of the four humors, what foods should be eaten at different times of the year. The same venerable authority assured men that women, too, experienced desire and pleasure and, moreover, that these were essential for conception. The resulting ideas and customs were explored in an essay on the "female pathology of the womb," written at some point between the sixth and the twelfth century and signed by one Metrodora, whose name seems too eloquent to be real. The basis of this essay is the presumed fundamental importance of the womb in determining the health of women. The author (possibly a

Button, gold and enamel cloisonné (3.2 cm x 1.5 cm). Constantinople, 11th century. (Washington, Dumbarton Oaks, Byzantine Collection.)

John Damascene, Florilegium (*Sacra Parallela*), 9th century. Ezechias, ill, with the prophet Isaiah. (Paris, Bibliothèque Nationale, Greek 923.)

woman) details an astonishing variety of ailments developed by women "who became widows in their flower, or virgins who allowed the crucial moment of marriage to pass them by." These maladies are explained as resulting from the fact that "natural desire has remained unemployed." Although this is a secular work, the proposed cure is not sexual activity but the use of various remedies, whose composition is given. There are preparations for treating diseases of the womb and problems of conception and childbirth as well as for determining virginity without local examination, concealing the loss of virginity, extracting confessions of adultery, preventing sexual relations with a third party, and heightening the pleasure of the woman or the couple. The treatise also contains formulas for making the breasts beautiful and the face "white and brilliant." In general, the detailed observations and the doubtless largely traditional pharmacopoeia respected the prevailing distinction between the married and the unmarried woman.

Male sexual desire also received attention from the doctors because of the need to suppress it for ascetic purposes. This obstacle in the way of any man seeking the holy life had always been a theme of hagiography. The hagiographer Nicephorus of Miletus, monk and later bishop, developed the theme in order to justify the presence in one particular hagiography of a person who had been castrated in his youth. The man's purity was such that he never allowed himself to be touched or even looked at by members of his own family. That, the author tells us, will not seem especially remarkable to those unscathed by the struggle with desire, "but those who, in conformity with the human condition and the laws of generation laid down by the Creator, know the violence of combat with this bit of flesh, who are assailed by impure thoughts, and who are inured to the painful struggle with carnal ideas and desires—they will deem remarkable and worthy of recounting"—a fact that proves that the saint avoided occasions that might provoke even the thought of pleasure. The hagiographer goes on to hope that his readers will not protest that "removal of the testicles" was responsible for this remarkable fortitude, "for, as physiologists are well aware, the drive for carnal union is stronger and fiercer in [eunuchs] than in those whose bodies are unmaimed and intact." He cites ancient sources in support of this assertion. What is more, in the original Greek the *Life of Nicephorus of Miletus* develops a terminology for the psychic sources of sexual desire whose subtleties cannot be adequately rendered in translation.

The link between medicine and asceticism is also evident in another classic issue of monastic discipline: nocturnal emissions. An *Essay on the Government of Souls,* addressed by Leo VI to the superior of his imperial monastery, Euthymius (possibly the future patriarch), discusses this question in terms of Hippocratic concepts. Shortly after becoming a monk John Zonaras wrote a brief treatise on the subject, entitled *To those who regard the natural flow of semen as unclean.* He thinks that the position stated in his title is not only extreme but also marked by a rather Jewish adherence to Old Testament scripture, and he refutes it with arguments drawn from physiology. Victims of nocturnal emission, he argues, should not be indiscriminately barred from the sacraments and contact with icons. Each man should examine his conscience. When the flow of semen is merely a natural consequence of a superfluity, there is nothing to reproach; a sin is committed only where desire for a woman has been nursed to the point where it satisfies itself in a dream.

The tradition just discussed dominates the surviving texts, but there is evidence that some Byzantines adopted different attitudes toward the body. Achmet's *Dream Key* takes readers' sexual aims into account as a matter of course. No one will be surprised to learn that hair signified both political and sexual

Nicander, *Theriaca* (a treatise on snake bites and their remedies), 10th century. A garden is cleared of serpents, after which a man walks peacefully through the area. (Paris, Bibliothèque Nationale, annex to Greek 247.)

Ivory-covered wooden chest, 10th–11th century: Adam and Eve nude. (Darmstadt, State Museum of Hesse.)

potency, and Achmet devotes several paragraphs to the growth and loss of hair on various parts of the body. The set of a man's shoulders can reveal whether he has concubines and prefers them to his legitimate wife. A nod to a woman is a sign of future relations; this was the gesture that the suspicious Cecaumenus feared. Anyone who puts on new sandals but does not walk in them will find a wife, or, if married, a new concubine. If a man dreams of kisses or even bestiality, the interpreter of dreams is not surprised. On the other hand, ninth- and tenth-century hagiographies of both men and women still exhibit the ancient theme of flight from marriage and desire in order to protect one's virginity, and it would be wrong to view this as a mere commonplace of monastic authors. There is all too clearly a connection between the choice of virginity and the ideal of hesychia, or repose. In the case of women we must also take account of the situation or situations in which they lived.

The eleventh century was a more loquacious time, and its attitudes were perhaps somewhat different from those encountered thus far. Laughter at the body was an ancient tradition, though one disapproved of by Christianity. But Christian censorship seems to have been lifted when Michael Psellus drew the portrait of Constantine IX Monomachus, that is, the portrait of a Constantinople aristocrat who, in the mid-eleventh century, came to the throne by means of a late marriage. "The soul of the monarch smiled at amusements of every sort, and he wanted constant distraction." Nothing amused him more than speech defects, and he made a great favorite of one man who humorously accentuated his impediment and who, through his off-color remarks about the empress Zoë, wife of Constantine IX, and her sister Theodora, became the darling of the court. "He claimed to be the child of the elder sister, and he swore by his great gods that the younger sister [a nun] had given birth and gave details of the circumstances. And as he remembered his own delivery, he recounted the sequence of his sufferings and shamelessly described a woman's womb." The same sovereign is depicted, after the death of his mistress Scleraina, "turning over the subject of love (*eros*) in his intimate conversations. He wandered off into all sorts of digressions, imagining the most extravagant scenes. For he was by nature curious about the things of love (*erotika*), and he was incapable of putting an end to his troubles through facile intercourse. He preferred to let himself be racked by wave after wave of desire before attempting a first embrace." Psellus assures us that he blushes to tell of it; yet his whole portrait stands in sharp contrast to the grandiose austerity of the preceding century.

Ascetic discourse in this period is new in its accents, although traditional references can still be found. We saw how Simeon the New Theologian claimed to have achieved a personal relationship with the Holy Spirit in the solitude of his cell. He made no claim, however, that his brand of asceticism was new, and he traced its origins to a phrase in the treatise of John Climacus on the contemplative life. While visiting his family Simeon found this book, which had been widely read in the seventh century, in the family library and read that "not to feel is to cause the soul to die; it is the death of the spirit before the death of the body." Struck by this idea, Simeon spent nights in prayerful vigil over the tombs of the dead, "painting their image in his heart." He repeated this practice whenever he fell victim to the ascetic's peculiar form of "discouragement": "He sat down and imagined in his mind the dead beneath the earth. Sometimes he remained in mourning, sometimes he spoke out, his voice in tears . . . Like an image painted on a wall, the vision of those dead bodies was impressed upon his mind." Soon all his perceptions changed to the point where everything seemed "truly dead." To achieve

"There was Abraham buried, and Sarah his wife." Genesis 35:10. (Rome, Vatican Library, Greek 747.)

the death of the senses through concrete imagination of actual individual death represents a sharp departure from the practices usually described in hagiography, however venerable the reference adduced in justification.

Also new on the scene were the heretic Bogomiles, whose puritanism was heir to a long tradition of radical denial of the flesh and repudiation of the ecclesiastical institution; and for just as long the radicals had been suspected of transgressions and all sorts of iniquities. The name Bogomile is attested in Bulgaria as early as the tenth century, but the sect did not become prominent in Byzantium until the eleventh. Like Simeon, the Bogomiles were not so much perpetuators of tradition as they were harbingers of things to come or symptoms of changes already under way. This important movement will be discussed more fully later. For now let me simply cite the description of the Bogomiles given by Anna Comnena during the reign of her father, Alexis I: "The Bogomile kind are frightening for their simulation of virtue. You will not see a hair on a lay Bogomile. The evil is dissimulated under cassock and hood. The Bogomile looks somber, he is covered down to his nose, he walks with his head down, and he murmurs in a low tone." A lay asceticism? The princess concludes: "Inwardly, however, he is an uncontrollable wolf."

---

*Dreams and Visions*

Traditionally the Byzantine paid attention to dreams, which were believed to be premonitory messages received during sleep. Romanus I wrote anxiously to Theodorus Daphnopates, saying that he had seen himself the previous night in a dream inside a temple that at first seemed splendid, well lighted, and full of treasures but then turned dark, tottered on its foundations, and became filled with dead animals and black Ethiopians wielding bloody swords. In response the secretary offered an edifying interpretation, based on the idea that man is a divine temple. The histories tell of the dreams of emperors and other political figures; iconography represents them. The dreams of private individuals were interpreted in terms of social position and sex. The influence of tradition is clear and not surprising: the section of Achmet's manual devoted to animals can be compared with ancient bestiaries like the *Physiologos*. Along with asses, pigs, sparrows, and wolves, we find, in imperial dreams, the eagle and lion as well as the dragon; the camel and elephant lent an exotic touch. Achmet's dreamers also have visions of such religious figures

Lion devouring a gazelle,
10th–11th century. (Athens,
Byzantine Museum.)

as the prophet Elijah, the Virgin Mary, and Christ. Today we
regard dreams as commonplace but visions as extraordinary;
in Byzantium, however, visions were considered a normal and
rather common experience. For the Byzantine a vision was
not a feat of the imagination but a religious experience. For
Achmet's readers there was no difference between dreaming
about a living person and dreaming about Christ; in both
dream and vision the individual confronted the other just as
he would have done in real waking life. The dividing line
between real and imaginary was not the same as it is today;
whether the imagined experience was frightening or magical
in content made no difference.

Fictional stories, whether told or read, unquestionably
belonged to the realm of the imagination, however. Once
again we must consider the question of private as opposed to
public reading. What court officials were by and large obliged
to read I call public reading, which was closely connected with

John Damascene, Florilegium
(*Sacra Parallela*), 9th century.
David and Bathsheba. (Paris,
Bibliothèque Nationale, Greek
923.)

the vogue for classical culture. Here, however, I am interested in something else: private reading, which was a leisure activity. What did people read in private? The private reading of a public man is decribed in the *Life of Basil I,* which was inspired or written by his grandson, Constantine VII. Basil's reading included historical narratives, political counsels, moral exhortation, patristic and spiritual literature, and accounts of the lives and exploits of great generals, emperors, and saints.

Similar reading matter can be found in the library—probably representative of the private libraries of the aristocacy—of Eustathius Boilas, whose will (sealed in 1059) was cited previously. Apart from the Bible, he mentions a number of volumes of history and hagiography. But he also owned a *Dream Key* and a *Romance of Alexander.* The fact that Cecaumenus' reading was fairly similar shows that private reading was not strictly for amusement; some was for instruction, whether spiritual or profane. The line between the two is not always easy to draw, as I shall try to show by discussing two works.

*Barlaam and Josaphat* takes place in India, that continent of delights to which the Byzantine imagination so often turned for escape. The story concerns a Christian mission that succeeds in inspiring a monastic vocation in young Josaphat, son of the king of India and later king himself. The missionary is the monk Barlaam, who comes disguised as a merchant from the desert of Senaar. The story's central theme, that of a king who is also a monk, had topical resonances in tenth-century Byzantium. The work, traditionally attributed to John Damascene, a doctor of the eighth-century Greek church, may in fact date from that era in both its Greek and Georgian versions. Although the question does not concern us here, I want to emphasize that Byzantine works always announce the genre to which they belong, and the subtitle of this work is "history (*historia*) useful to the soul," which suggests that it was one of the many edifying and marvelous tales told about the desert anchorites, a genre that was popular in late antiquity and still read, to judge from the manuscripts, in later centuries. This example of a work that is both an edifying tract and an adventure story shows how difficult it is today to distinguish between what was diverting and what was utilitarian in Byzantine literature. I should add that the work was often accompanied by illustrations.

Even more complex and interesting is the *Romance of Alexander,* whose hero's incomparable renown had made him, ever since the third or fourth century, the central figure in stories set not only in India, from which he wrote letters to his mentor Aristotle, but also in heaven and in a subsea otherworld. The exceptionally rich Alexandrian tradition was further developed in Byzantium and elsewhere during the Middle Ages, though we have no idea which version of the legend was contained in Boilas' library. Like *Barlaam and Josaphat,* and despite its different subject matter, *Alexander* combines the charm of heroic characters with adventures in far-off places and pious Christian wisdom.

It is difficult to know just how much literary pleasure women were allowed. Edifying works were probably available to them, and the comparative importance of hagiographies of female saints in this period is a point in favor of this hypothesis. Yet, as we have just seen, the term "edifying" covered a far broader range of literature than one might expect. On the other hand, young girls and women were deprived of access to classical culture, at least in theory. This was still true in the mid-twelfth century, when George Tornikes composed the funeral eulogy of Anna Comnena, daughter of Alexis I. Tornikes points out that the princess began the study of classical literature (*grammatike*) without the knowl-

Scylitzes' *Chronicle:* philosophers and their pupils. (Madrid, National Library.)

Gospels, Constantinople, 12th century: Saint Luke. (Paris, Bibliothèque Nationale, Greek 189.)

edge of her parents, who were quite properly afraid that she, a girl of pure virtue, would become acquainted with myths "containing many gods and hence no God" and possibly suffer moral harm. Anna managed to overcome all the obstacles in her way, but she never escaped from the domestic confinement to which women of good society were subjected. If she learned medicine, she practiced it only in her home. At best she gave a scholarly turn to homely skills that, to judge by the compendia of medical wisdom discussed earlier, were widely shared. How did women of this social class spend their time? Some decades earlier the empress Zoë had taken a passionate interest in the manufacture of cosmetics. (Recall that the work of Metrodora contained both beauty secrets and medical remedies.) But Psellus tells us that Zoë never practiced "woman's work"— meaning sewing and knitting, as well as embroidering—although the surviving samples of embroidery all postdate the eleventh century.

*Beyond the Household*

Thus far our portrait of private life has scarcely moved outside of private homes and monasteries—homes that were open in one degree or another to visitors. The sources tell us little about sociability in the tenth and eleventh centuries. About street life we know nothing. Certain humble trades are mentioned in a compendium compiled by the prefect of Constantinople in the tenth century. The wretched poor who lived under the porticoes and the lowlife who frequented the taverns furnish the background to various episodes in the *Life of Andrew the Mad,* but this work, generally said to date from the tenth century, may be based on an earlier period of urban ascetic life. To learn more about these aspects of private life we must await the twelfth century, by which time the importance of urban life had increased even further and taste in literature turned more to realism, still tinged, however, with preciosity.

Too many of our sources are urban for us to expect them to devote much attention to nature. They are urban not only as a matter of fact but also as a matter of cultural heritage, through an unbroken tradition stretching back to classical antiquity. The discomfort of the countryside and the savage state of its inhabitants are a common refrain in letters written by exiles or by men of letters sent to serve in remote bishoprics, such as Theophylactus, bishop of Ohrid from 1090 until his death in 1108. In this same period Cecaumenus, in retirement, took an interest not in nature as such but in the operation of his estates, also a part of antique tradition.

Only the hunter and the ascetic saw solitude and wilderness as positive values. Hunting had both public and private significance, or perhaps one should say that, no matter whether the hunt was public or private, its meaning was the same: to make the hunter a hero through his victory over game. This was the purpose of the elaborate protocol of the imperial hunts, and it also explains why accidents that occurred during these affairs were taken as warnings; it enables us, too, to interpret young Digenis' first hunt as a rite of passage. Nothing surprising here—yet the texts are remarkably alive. One shows the aging Basil I in hot pursuit of a giant stag, which leads him far from his escort, turns to face the hunter, lifts him by the belt, and drags him helplessly away. Another portrays Digenis as an adolescent begging his father to allow him at last to undergo the trial until finally, one morning, the two leave their castle in the company of the boy's maternal uncle and a band of *agouroi,* or young companions.

Similar remarks can be made about asceticism. Since the fourth century, when Christianity developed its model of saintliness, the desert (*eremos*) had been the place where the

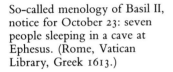

So-called menology of Basil II, notice for October 23: seven people sleeping in a cave at Ephesus. (Rome, Vatican Library, Greek 1613.)

saint proved his mettle through mortification of the flesh, renunciation of civilization, and struggles with demons. Saints turned their backs on the city, but for a few insignificant if not frankly heretical exceptions. Fifth- and sixth-century saints were for the most part founders of monasteries, and hagiographies from this period generally divide neatly into two parts: one recounting the hero's initial spiritual experience, which takes place in solitude; the other a chronicle of the monastery of which the saint is the pride and glory.

By the ninth century the picture has changed somewhat. The venerable model of spiritual combat in the wilderness has given way to a new model emphasizing conventual values, obedience foremost among them. Yet the original model survived both in narrative and in practice. Consider the case of Paul, son of a squadron commander and founder of the important monastery of Latros near Miletus. He takes to the mountains with a single companion, a friend who eventually leaves him; Paul then lives on acorns, endures the assaults of demons, and survives his time in "solitude" (*monosis*), even though he is in fact not far from a semi-conventual monastic establishment (*lavra*). Until his death in 955 his life is a series of retreats and returns, covering an ever wider expanse of territory. In reality, however, the monastic church of the ninth and tenth centuries took an increasingly dim view of the completely solitary life, for it allowed a man too much freedom. Athanasius, who in 963 founded the Athonite convent of Lavra, brought back into the fold the hermit Nicephorus the Naked (as he was called). Was it significant that Nicephorus was a native of Calabria?

The most eloquent tales of the beauty and attractions of nature produced in this period did in fact come from this Byzantine equivalent of the Far West. The masterpiece of the genre is the *Life* of Nil of Rossano, who died in 1004. The text, which bears some resemblance to the *Life* of Paul of Latros, recounts Nil's slow journey from the Gulf of Taranto to Rome, near which he founded the monastery of Grottaferrata. His travels take him through a wooded, mountainous region, far from the coasts that were so vulnerable to attack by Arabs. The model, as one might expect, was exclusively masculine, although the ninth century did produce a new version of Mary the Egyptian in the story of Theoctiste of Paros, which emphasized, in its edifying way, the return of the female body itself to a state of nature.

The forty martyrs of Sebaste and Christ in majesty. Ivory plaque, Constantinople, 10th–11th century (17.6 cm x 12.8 cm). (Berlin, Prussian State Museum of Culture.)

# ⚜ Private Belief

BYZANTINES believed that their world was part of a
much vaster universe, whose structure had been worked
out in an earlier time. There was a place for the saved and a
place for the damned. The distinction between public and
private carried over into this universe without destroying its
fundamental unity. Public religion, led by the emperor and
the patriarch, sought the protection of heaven for the community and its armies. That is why Leo VI preached in person
at Saint Sophia and led the people of Constantinople to the
port of that city to receive the relics of Saint Lazarus, accompanied by a hymn that he himself had composed. The sovereign's liturgical role was part of religion's public side, as were
the government's requests to monks to intercede with heaven
on behalf of the state.

Certain forms of religious devotion were also part of
public religion: the entire Empire honored Christ in majesty;
Mary, the protector of its armies; and Saint Michael, a warrior
who led the souls of the dead to the other world. Saint De-
metrius watched over Thessalonica, the second most important city in the Empire. The house of Basil I prayed to the
prophet Elijah, whose solar imagery accorded well with the
traditional symbolism of imperial power. Also public in a
rather different sense were the cults of the saints, which honored their tombs and icons. And finally there were public
religious traditions that dated back for centuries, such as the
custom of casting a horoscope whenever a child was born to
the imperial couple; or the Dionysiac carnivals that were always banned by the Church and always celebrated by the
crowd: masked men and women engaged in lascivious dancing
in the streets and laughed—a serious matter, for Dionysus had

been demoted to the rank of demon, and demons delighted in laughter.

Private religion was built from the same constituents. The few estate and donation inventories that we possess attest the private ownership of liturgical objects such as sacred books and icons. Certain surviving religious books and objects may well have served private devotions. This was certainly true of various icons and reliquaries, and of crosses and medallions bearing images of the saints that were worn around the neck. Icons played as important a role in personal piety as they did in public religion. These strictly regulated and widely reproduced images drew upon the dogma of the Incarnation and the charisma of the saints. Christian transcendence, vision, icon, and physical presence of the saint—all entered into a coherent system in the hagiographies. From the seventh century on, pious tales were told of icons intervening in human affairs, helping, for instance, to bring about the signing of a contract. Believers worshiped familiar icons in their own homes. Psellus tells us that the empress Zoë spoke to her icon of Christ.

The most popular private cults were the same as the public ones, especially the cult of Mary. In the lives of the saints it is Mary who announces long-awaited births, and the women of Constantinople prayed to her at night in her temple in the Blachernae. Even in private, however, Mary was not yet the wholly feminine and maternal figure with which we are familiar. Lay and monastic cults honored a variety of saints, but the Church eventually sought to impose limits on this freedom. In the tenth century an official compilation was made of the traditional hagiographies and an iconographical canon was imposed on icon painters, most of whom were monks.

Enamel medallion of Christ (3.3 cm diameter), set in a frame of silver on wood. Constantinople, mid-11th century. (Washington, Dumbarton Oaks, Byzantine Collection.)

A new cult could come into existence at any time. Miracles performed by living persons earned them veneration, but there was no cult in the strict sense until veneration was organized around the tomb. Hagiographies by definition dealt with cults that had become public, that is, communal and official. The control exerted by the authorities over the proliferation of new cults is evident in the charges brought against Simeon the New Theologian as reported by his biographer, Nicetas Stethatus. Simeon established a cult in honor of his spiritual father, the Studite monk Simeon: he established a holiday and had an icon made, and followers gathered at his invitation. In doing these things, however, he was obeying an inspiration vouchsafed to him alone, and for this he was

Christ on the cross between the Virgin and Saint John. Portable icon of steatite, 10th–12th century. (Paris, Bibliothèque Nationale, Cabinet des Médailles.)

brought before the patriarchal tribunal. The case shows what tension existed between ecclesiastical authority and personal spirituality.

*Demons and Primitive Beliefs*    Private religion involved coexistence with demons (*daimones*)—demons more complex and domestic than the carnival Dionysus. Demons lurked everywhere but especially in the home, as well as in deserted places, ruins, and bodies of water. In ninth- and tenth-century hagiography they are neither as primordial nor as undifferentiated as they are in stories about the ascetics and miracle workers of late antiquity. These latter-day demons, no longer faceless, prefigure the demons of modern Greek belief. Many have names, are associated with specific places, and are endowed with particular skills; like angels they have bodies. No Byzantine at any level of society disbelieved in demons, as is shown by the gold-mounted amulets that women of the tenth-century wore as pendants or, still more telling, the importance of demons in the work of Michael Psellus and his eleventh-century contemporaries, after the great renaissance of classical learning in the preceding two centuries.

Humanist learning, far from introducing a rationalist corrective to popular beliefs, nourished and enriched those beliefs with new questions, references, and allusions. Probably before this renaissance, moreover, Slavic influence affected the belief in demons, perhaps accounting for the importance of water demons and certain methods of fortune-telling. Belief in some demons, such as the horrible Gyllu, who attacks women in labor, has survived down to our own time. The old deities, long since demoted to the rank of demons, continued to play a part in private rites of magic; in the eleventh century they attracted the worried interest of learned theologians.

In this respect the high culture of the time was quite primitive; knowledge was supposed to achieve practical effects. Astrology, magic, and alchemy were part of the intellectual landscape for a Psellus or his contemporary, the patriarch Michael Cerularius. After the latter was deposed in 1058, Psellus prepared for the synod an astonishingly ambiguous indictment against him. Tenth- and eleventh-century prayer books show signs of a similar concern with efficacy. Cecaumenus reproaches "uneducated people," who turn to fortune-tellers to know the future. But this preoccupation was not the exclusive province of the uneducated.

Medallion-amulet of lead, with ring, showing figure on horseback. (Paris, Bibliothèque Nationale, Cabinet des Médailles.)

Around the turn of the eleventh century, Simeon the New Theologian and the Bogomile sect attempted to alter the relation between the church and the faithful in novel but not unprecedented ways. Although the approaches of Simeon and the Bogomiles were different, there is a striking historical similarity between them. Simeon's position was discussed earlier, albeit too briefly; here I want to focus mainly on the significance of Bogomile practices. The *Treatise* of the Bulgarian priest Cosmas, which appeared in 972 or shortly thereafter, attacked the Bogomiles of Bulgaria, a country profoundly influenced by all forms of Byzantine culture. In Byzantium itself the Bogomiles were the subject of two orthodox tracts written by two monks of the Peribleptos monastery in Constantinople. Both monks were named Euthymius; one wrote his tract around 1050, the other during the reign of Alexis I Comnenus (1081–1118).

The Bogomiles eliminated the distinctions on which the Christian social structure was based. Churches, they said, are mere "common houses." Baptism is nothing but water and oil; the eucharist, bread and wine. They recognized neither priesthood nor sainthood, did not venerate the cross, uttered no prayer but the Pater Noster, rejected marriage, and urged married couples to separate. They held that Christ was bap-

*Other Religious Experiences*

Barberini Psalter, ca. 1092. Folio 16v: "Hades receiving sinners driven by an angel." (Rome, Vatican Library, Greek 372.)

tized by the spirit, and they sought to reproduce that baptism in their neophytes. After examination, neophytes received the imposition of the Gospels and of the hands of those in assistance, men and women alike. The Bogomiles practiced mixed mutual confession. Finally, all Bogomiles inhabited by the Holy Spirit were worthy to be called *theotokos,* progenitor of God (a term normally reserved for the Virgin Mary), because the Word was also in them. All these details stem from a dissident position with respect to the Incarnation, the fundamental principle of the Christian social order. As a result, the sect lived what can be considered a private form of religious life within Byzantine society.

The Bogomiles participated fully in the common religious life, but each individual Bogomile interpreted the meaning of ordinary religious practices as he or she saw fit. Their masters exhibited a knowledge of Scripture and the Church Fathers that the official church considered to be inspired by the devil. Orthodox baptism did not trouble them, for they held that it had no effect; nor did Bogomiles disdain to wear monastic habit. They attended church services, the better to conceal themselves. Inwardly they believed that the term "sinner" designated the orthodox; that Bethlehem, birthplace of the divine Word, signified their own church; and that Jerusalem, still under Jewish rule, meant the official religion. Their dis-

Barberini Psalter, ca. 1092, illustration in margin: simoniac ordination. The black silhouette of a demon stands beside the corrupt priest. (Rome, Vatican Library, Greek 372.)

sidence was not new, in that it continued ancient tendencies in eastern Christianity associated with the Paulicians in the ninth century before being taken up by the Bogomiles in the tenth. The Bogomile movement, however, attained an unprecedented level of theoretical vigor and social importance in the eleventh century, and it is tempting to link this fact to the progress of urban society. Indeed, the first Euthymius mentions the cities of Thrace and the region of Smyrna as the target of successful proselytizing by John Tzourillas, who is said to be well known "for having left his wife after having made her a false nun, he himself having become a false monk."

Repressive measures instituted by Alexis I Comnenus suggest how important the sect had become in Constantinople. In the wake of this repression the Bogomiles seem to have adopted still more elaborate forms of dissimulation and mental reservation. The sources are more explicit, to be sure. But it was a new age, in which the Bogomiles' experiments with a private, inward form of religion, not unrelated to that practiced by Simeon the New Theologian, exerted a tremendous fascination.

Convent of Göreme (Cappadocia), 11th century.

# ❧ Conclusion

I SHALL end with the dawn of the twelfth century. What I hoped to show was not that private life existed in tenth- and eleventh-century Byzantium; that was obvious from the start. All societies of any complexity distinguish between public and private. But the definition and structure of the private vary from one society to another, depending on such variables as power, religion, housing, and the family. It is primarily cultural discourse that determines what is private and what is not. Using the written records of the government and the social elite, the only evidence we have, we have examined the private life of Christian society in the eastern Mediterranean region around the year 1000: Byzantium in the period we call medieval. We have discovered that the eleventh century was distinguished from the tenth by a change of tone. Private experience, corseted by classicism in the tenth century, seems to have emancipated itself in the eleventh, in a society undergoing broad structural change. Was this merely a change in what people said or was it a change of conscience? That is hard to say. What we can say is that the twelfth century continued the trend and carried it yet another step forward.

# Notes

# Bibliography

# Notes

## 1. The Roman Empire

1. The importance of gymnastics and music in Greek-inspired education during the imperial period (see Marcus Aurelius, I, 6) was confirmed by Louis Robert, in the proceedings of the international congress on epigraphy held in Athens in 1982 (I, 45). The basic reference on Hellenistic and Roman education is Ilsetraut Hadot, *Arts libéraux et Philosophie dans la pensée antique* (Paris: Etudes agustiniennes, 1984).

2. Bacchic imagery is more than decorative and less than religious (in the full sense). The key to this problem is an idea attributable to Jean-Claude Passeron, which seems to me of great theoretical importance. The language of images, Passeron says, is not "assertoric." An image can neither affirm nor deny what it depicts, nor can it add modifiers such as "a little," "perhaps," "tomorrow," and so on. Bacchic imagery is an attractive proposition that requires no response and leaves the question of its reality in suspense. The point is not, as is often said, that all symbolism is fluid and admits of a thousand different interpretations. It is rather that symbolism does not require us to respond yes or no. Spectators need not know what they think about Bacchus. The image, being less than an assertion, takes no position and does not require its viewer to take a position. But to say that an image is not assertoric in no way implies that it is merely decorative.

## 2. Late Antiquity

1. Musonius Rufus, fragment 14, ed. and trans. Cora E. Lutz, *Yale Classical Studies*, 10 (1947): 93. The words quoted in the next paragraph are from fragment 12, p. 87.

2. II *Baruch* 85.3; lines in the next paragraph are from II *Baruch* 85.4.

3. Cited in E. Urbach, *The Sages: Their Concepts and Beliefs* (Jerusalem: Magnus, 1979), p. 358.

4. Galen, cited in an Arabic author; see R. Walzer, *Galen on Jews and Christians* (Oxford: Oxford University Press, 1949), p. 15.

5. F. Nietzsche, *Die fröhliche Wissenschaft* 358 (Stuttgart: Kroner Taschenbuch, 1956): 251.

6. *Sentences of Sextus* no. 236.

7. J. Doresse and E. Lanne, *Un témoin archaïque de la liturgie copte de S. Gasile* (Louvain: Bibliothèque de Muséon, 1960), p. 28.

8. John Chrysostom, *Homily 11 in 2 Thessalonians* and *Homily 1 in Titus,* trans. Library of the Nicene Fathers (Grand Rapids, Mich.: Eerdmans, 1979), 13:373, 479.

9. E. Diehl, *Inscriptiones latinae christianae veteres,* no. 2157 (Berlin: Wiedman, 1925), 1:423. The following paragraph closes with *Inscriptiones* no. 967, p. 179.

10. *Historia Monachorum* 10.

11. John Chrysostom, *On Virginity* 73.1.

12. John Cassian, *Collationes* 12.8.

13. Cited in M. Mueller, *Die Lehre von dem heilige Augustinus von der Paradiesehe* (Regensburg: F. Pustet, 1954), p. 152, n. 79.

## 3. Private Life and Domestic Architecture in Roman Africa

1. R. Etienne, *Le Quartier nord-est de Volubilis* (Paris, 1960), pp. 121–122.

2. R. Rebuffat, "Enceintes urbaines et insécurité en Maurétanie Tingitane," *Mélanges de l'Ecole française de Rome-Antiquité,* 86 (1974): 510–512.

3. G. Picard, "Deux sénateurs romains inconnus," *Karthago,* 4 (1953): 123–125.

4. N. Duval, "Couronnes agonistiques sur des mosaiques africaines," *Bulletin archéologique du comité des travaux historiques,* n.s., 12–14 (1976–1978): 195–216.

5. For an overview of the current state of this question, see N. Duval, "Les origines de la basilique chrétienne," *Information d'histoire de l'art,* 7 (1962): 1–19.

6. G. de Angelis d'Ossat, "L'aula regia del distrutto palazzo imperiale di Ravenna," *Corsi di cultura,* 23 (1976): 345–356.

7. J. Lassus, "Une opération immobilière à Timgad," *Mélanges Piganiol,* pp. 1120–1129.

8. Y. Thébert, "Les maisons à étage souterrain de Bulla Regia," *Cahiers de Tunisie,* 20 (1972): 17–44.

9. Y. Janvier, *La législation du Bas-Empire romain sur les édifices publics* (Aix-en-Provence, 1969).

10. C. Boube-Picot, "Les bronzes antiques du Maroc. II: Le mobilier," *Etudes et travaux d'archéologie marocaine* 5 (Rabat, 1975).

11. Y. Thébert, "L'utilisation de l'eau dans la maison de la pêche à Bulla Regia," *Cahiers de Tunisie,* 19 (1971): 11–17.

12. G. Picard, "La maison de Vénus," *Recherches archéologiques franco-tunisiennes à Mactar,* 1 (Rome, 1977): 23.

13. This and other quotations from Augustine are from *The Confessions of Saint Augustine,* trans. E. B. Pusey (New York: Dutton, 1951).

14. P. Veyne, "Les cadeaux des colons à leur propriétaire," *Revue archéologique* (1981): 245–252.

15. A. Corbin, *Le miasme et la jonquille. L'odorat et l'imaginaire social* (Paris, 1982), p. 269.

16. A. Beschaouch, "La mosaïque de chasse découverte à Smirat en Tunisie," *Comptes rendus de l'Académie des inscriptions et belles-lettres* (1966): 134–157.

17. M. Blanchard-Lemée, *Maisons à mosaïques du quartier central de Djémila (Cuicul),* n.d., pp. 166ff.

18. The debate that has raged for decades about the opulent villa at Piazza Armerina in Sicily typifies the confusion inherent in the emerging society of the Late Empire. The magnificence of its architecture and the use of porphyry (which, like lion-hunting, was supposedly an imperial privilege) have involved scholars in a lengthy debate on the identity of the owner: great lord or imperial personage? The fact that such a building could have been built at all reveals the ambitions of the elite.

## 4. The Early Middle Ages in the West

1. Unless otherwise noted, this and subsequent quotations are from Gregory of Tours, *History of the Franks,* trans. Lewis Thorpe (London: Penguin, 1974).

2. For those who may not be familiar with this episode, here is a brief résumé. Clovis' troops had plundered many churches, and from one they had taken a large, carefully wrought ewer. The bishop of this church asked Clovis to return the ewer. The king told the bishop's messengers to follow him to Soissons where the booty would be divided, promising that if the ewer fell to his share, he would return it to the church. In Soissons he put it to his men that they grant him the ewer over and above his regular share. One man demurred, saying that the king should have only his share and no more, then took an axe to the ewer, smashing it. Later, when Clovis inspected his troops, he found fault with this man's equipment, and when the man bent forward to pick up his weapons, split his head open with a battle-axe. A full account may be found in Gregory of Tours' *History of the Franks.* (Translator's note.)

3. This passage was retranslated from the author's French rendering, which varies somewhat from the standard English version of Gregory's account used previously.

# Bibliography

## 1. The Roman Empire

Alföldy, G. *Die Rolle des Einzelnen in der Gesellschaft des römischen Kaiserreiches: Erwartungen und Wertmassstäbe.* Sitzungsberichte der Heidelberger Akademie, 1980, VIII.

Ameling, W. *Herodes Atticus.* 2 vols. Hildesheim, 1982.

André, J. *L'Alimentation et la Cuisine à Rome.* Paris: Les Belles Lettres, 1981.

André, J.-M. *Les Loisirs en Grèce et à Rome.* Paris: Presses Universitaires de France, 1984.

Andreau, J. *Les Affaires de Monsieur Jucundus.* Rome: Ecole française de Rome, 1974.

*Aufstieg und Niedergang der römischen Welt. Geschichte und Kultur Roms im Spiegel der neuren Forschung,* ed. H. Temprini and W. Haase. Several volumes have been published in Berlin and New York by W. De Gruyter.

Balland, A. *Fouilles de Xanthos, VII, Inscriptions d'époque impériale du Létôon.* Paris: Boccard, 1981.

Blanck, H. *Einführung in das Privatleben der Griechen und Römer.* Darmstadt: Wissenschaftliche Buchgesellschaft, 1976.

Bleicken, J. *Stattliche Ordnung und Freiheit in der römischen Republik.* Frankfurter Althistorische Studien 6. Kallmünz: Lassleben, 1972.

Blümner, H. *Die römischen Privataltertümer.* Handbuch der klassischen Altertumswisswnschaft, IV, 2, 2. Munich, 1911.

Boulvert, G., and M. Morabito. "Le droit de l'esclavage sous le Haut-Empire." *Aufstieg und Niedergang,* II, vol. XIV, p. 98.

Brödner, E. *Die römischen Thermen und das antike Badewesen.* Darmstadt: Wissenschaftliche Buchgesellschaft, 1983.

Brunt, P. A. "Aspects of the Social Thought of Dio Chrysostom and the Stoics." *Proceedings of the Cambridge Philological Society,* 1973, p. 9.

——— "Charges of Provincial Maladministration under the Early Principate." *Historia,* 10 (1961): 189.

——— *Social Conflicts in the Roman Republic.* London: Chatto and Windus, 1971.

——— "Stoicism and the Principate." *Papers of the British School at Rome,* 43 (1975): 7.

Buti, I. *Studi sulla capacità patrimoniale dei "servi."* Pubblicazioni della Facoltà di giurisprudenza dell'università di Camerino. Naples: Jovene, 1976.

Cagnat, R., and V. Chapot. *Manuel d'archéologie romaine.* 2 vols. Paris, 1916.

Canas, B. A. "La femme devant la justice provinciale de l'Egypte romaine." *Revue historique de droit* (1984): 358.

Christes, J. *Bildung und Gesellschaft: die Einschätzung der Bildung und ihrer Vermittler in der grichisch-römischen Antike.* Darmstadt: Wissenschaftliche Buchgesellschaft, 1975.

Cockle, H. "Pottery Manufacture in Roman Egypt." *Journal of Roman Studies,* 71 (1981): 87.

Corbier, M. "Les familles clarissimes d'Afrique proconsulaire." *Epigrafia e Ordine senatorio,* 5 (1982).

——— "Ideologie et pratique de l'héritage (ler siècle avant Jésus Christ – IIe siècle après Jésus Christ)." *Index,* 1984. Proceedings of the GIREA colloquium, 1983.

Cotton, H. "Documentary Letters of Recommendation in Latin from the Roman Empire," *Beiträge zur klassischen Philologie.* Hain: Königstein, 1981.

Crook, J. *Law and Life of Rome.* Ithaca, N.Y.: Cornell University Press, 1967.

Daremberg, Saglio and Pottier. *Dictionnaire des Antiquités grecque et romaine.* Paris, 1877–1918.

D'Arms, J. H. *Commerce and Social Standing in Ancient Rome.* Cambridge, Mass.: Harvard University Press, 1981.

David, J.-M. "Les orateurs des municipes à Rome: intégration, réticences, et snobismes," *Les Bourgeoises municipales italiennes.* Paris and Naples: Centre Jean Bérard, 1983.

De Marchi, A. *Il Culto privato di Roma antica.* 2 vols. Milan, 1896–1903.

De Robertis, F. *Lavoro e Lavoratori nel mondo romano.* Bari: Laterza, 1963.

Dill, S. *Roman Society from Nero to Marcus Aurelius.*

647

New York, 1904. Reprint. New York: Meridian, 1957.

Dunbabin, K. *The Mosaics of Roman North Africa. Studies in Iconography and Patronage.* Oxford: Oxford University Press, 1978.

Etienne, R. *La Vie quotidienne à Pompeii.* Paris: Hachette, 1966.

Eyben, E. "Family Planning in Graeco-Roman Antiquity." *Ancient Society,* 11–12 (1980–1981): 5.

Fabre, G. *Libertus, recherches sur les rapports patron-affranchi à la fin de la République romaine.* Rome: Ecole française de Rome, 1981.

Finley, M. I. *The Ancient Economy.* Berkeley: University of California Press, 1973.

——— ed. *Slavery in Classical Antiquity.* Cambridge, England: Cambridge University Press, 1960.

Flory, Marleen B. "Family and Familia: A Study of Social Relations in Slavery." Ph.D. dissertation, Yale University, 1975.

Foucault, M. *Histoire de la sexualité,* vol. 2, *L'Usage des plaisirs;* vol. 3, *Le Souci de soi.* Paris: Gallimard, 1984.

Friedländer, L. *Darstellungen aus der Sittengeschichte Roms in der Zeit von August bis zum Ausgang der Antonine.* 9th ed. Edited by G. Wissowa. 4 vols. Leipzig, 1920.

Frier, B. W. *Landlords and Tenants in Imperial Rome.* Princeton: Princeton University Press, 1980.

Gabba, E. "Ricchezza e classe dirigente roman." *Rivista storica italiana,* 93 (1981): 541.

Galbraith, J. K. *The Nature of Mass Poverty.* Cambridge, Mass.: Harvard University Press, 1979.

Gagé, J. *Les Classes sociales dans L'Empire romain.* 2d ed. Paris: Payot, 1971.

Garnsey, P. "Independent Freedmen and the Economy of Roman Italy under the Principate." *Klio,* 63 (1981): 359.

——— ed. "Non-slave Labour in the Graeco-Roman World." *Cambridge Philological Society,* supplement VI, 1980.

Goldschmidt, V. *La Doctrine d'Epicure et le Droit.* Paris: Vrin, 1977.

——— *Le Système stoicien et l'Idée de temps.* Paris: Vrin, 1953.

Gombrich, E. *The Image and the Eye.* Oxford: Phaidon, 1982.

Gourevitch, D. *Le Triangle hippocratique dans le monde gréco-romain: le malade, sa maladie et son médecin.* Rome: Ecole française de Rome, 1984.

Hadot, I. *Seneca und die grichisch-römische Tradition der Seelenleitung.* Berlin: W. De Gruyter, 1969.

——— "Tradition stoïcienne et idées politiques au temps des Grecques." *Revue des études latines,* 48 (1970): 133.

Hadot, P. *Exercices spirituels et Philosophie antique.* Paris: Etudes augustiniennes, 1981.

Hands, A. R. *Charities and Social Aid in Greece and Rome.* London: Thames and Hudson, 1968.

Harris, H. A. *Sport in Greece and Rome.* London: Thames and Hudson, 1972.

Helen, T. *Organization of Roman Brick Production in the First and Second Centuries A.D.* Helsinki, 1975.

Hengstl, J. *Private Arbeitsverhältnisse freier Personen in den hellenistischen Papyri bis Diokletian.* Bonn: Habelt, 1972.

Jerphagnon, L. *Vivre et Philosopher sous les Césars.* Toulouse: Privat, 1980.

Kampen, N. *Image and Status. Roman Working Women in Ostia.* Berlin: Mann, 1981.

Kaser, M. *Das römische Privatrecht,* vol. 1, *Das altrömische, das vorklassische und klassische Recht.* Handbuch der Altertumswissenschaft, III, 3, 1. 2nd ed. Munich: Beck, 1971.

——— *Das römische Zivilprocessrecht.* Handbuch der Altertumswissenschaft, III, 4. Munich: Beck, 1966.

Kelly, J. M. *Roman Litigation,* Oxford: Oxford University Press, 1966.

Kleiner, D. *Roman Group Portraiture: The Funerary Reliefs of the Late Republic and Early Empire.* London and New York: Garland, 1977.

Koch, G., and H. Sichtermann. "Römische Sarkophage," *Handbuch der Archäologie.* Munich, 1982.

Krenkel, W. *Der Abortus in der Antike.* Wissenschaftliche Zeitschrift der Universität Rostock, 20, 1971, p. 443.

La Rocca, E., M. de Vos, and F. Coarelli. *Guida archeologica di Pompei.* Milan: Mondadori, 1976.

Laubscher, H. P. *Fischer und Landleute. Studien zur hellenistischen Genreplastik.* Mainz: von Zabern, 1982.

Leveau, P. *Caesarea de Maurétanie, une ville romaine et ses campagnes.* Rome: Ecole française de Rome, 1984.

Lewis, N. *Life in Egypt under Roman Rule.* Oxford: Oxford University Press, 1983.

Lilja, S. "Homosexuality in Republican and Augustan Rome." *Societas scientiarium Fennica, Commentationes humanarum litterarum,* 74, 192.

Linnott, A. W. *Violence in Republican Rome.* Oxford: Oxford University Press, 1968.

MacMullen, R. "The Epigraphic Habit in the Roman Empire." *American Journal of Philology,* 103 (1982): 233.

——— *Paganism in the Roman Empire.* New Haven: Yale University Press, 1981.

——— *Roman Social Relations, 50 B.C. to A.D. 284.* New Haven: Yale University Press, 1974.

Mallwitz, A. *Olympia und seine Bauten.* Munich: Prestel, 1972.

Marquardt, J. *Das Privatleben der Römer.* Handbuch der römischen Altertümer, VII. 2d ed. 2 vols. Leipzig, 1886.

Marrou, H.-I. *Histoire de l'éducation dans l'Antiquité.* Paris: Seuil, 1965, expanded 6th ed. For a non-functional methodological approach to the history of education, see M. Nilsson, *Die hellenistische Schule.* Munich, 1955, which reaches different conclusions.

———— "Mousikos Aner," *Etude sur les scènes de la vie intellectuelle figurant sur les monuments funéraires romains.* Rome: Erma, 1965.

Martin, R. "La vie sexuelle des esclaves d'après les 'Dialogues rustiques' de Varron," in J. Collart, ed., *Varron, grammaire antique et stylistique latine.* Paris: Les Belles Lettres, 1978, p. 113.

———— "Pline le Jeune et les problèmes économiques de son temps." *Revue des études anciennes,* 69 (1967): 62.

Mocsy, A. "Die Unkenntnis des Lebensalter im römischen Reich." *Acta antiqua Academiae scientiarum Hungaricae,* 14 (1966): 387.

Moreau, P. "Structures de parenté et d'alliance d'après le *Pro Cluentio,*" *Les Bourgeoises municipales italiennes.* Paris and Naples: Centre Jean Bérard, 1983.

Nardi, E. *Procurato abortonel mondo greco-romano.* Milan: Giuffrè, 1971.

Neraudau, J.-P. *Etre enfant à Rome.* Paris: Les Belles Lettres, 1984.

Nilsson, M. *Geschichte der griechischen Religion,* vol. 2, *Die hellenistische und römische Zeit.* Handbuch der Altertumswissenschaft, V, 2. 2nd ed. Munich, Beck, 1961.

Nock, A. D. *Essays on Religion and the Ancient World.* 2 vols. Oxford: Clarendon, 1972.

Nörr, D. "Zur sozialen und rechtlichen Bewertung der freien Arbeit in Rom." *Zeitschrift der Savigny-Stiftung, Roman. Abt.,* 82 (1965): 67.

Paoli, U. E. *Vita romana. La vie quotidienne dans la Rome antique,* trans. J. Rebertat. Paris: Desclée de Brouwer, 1955.

Pauly-Wissowa. *Realencylopädie der klassischen Altertumswissenschaft.* Stuttgart, 1893–1981.

Picard, G.-C. *La Civilisation de l'Afrique romaine.* Paris, Plon, 1959.

Pleket, H. W. "Collegium juvenum Nemesiorum: A Note on Ancient Youth Organization." *Mnemosyne,* 22 (1969): 281.

———— "Games, Prizes, Athletes, and Ideology: Some Aspects of the History of Sport in the Greco-Roman World," *Arena,* 1 (1976) 49.

———— "Urban Elites and Business in the Greek Part of the Roman Empire," in Garnsey et al. *Trade in the Ancient Economy.* London, 1983, p. 131

———— "Zur Soziologie des antiken Sports," *Mededelingen van het Nederlands Instituut te Rome,* 36, (1974): 57.

Pohlenz, M. *Die Stoa, Geschichte einer geistigen Bewegung.* 5th ed. Göttingen: Vandenhoeck und Ruprecht, 1978.

Pomeroy, Sarah B. *Goddesses, Whores, Wives, and Slaves: Women in Classical Antiquity.* New York: Schocken, 1975.

Prachner, M. *Die Sklaven und die Freigelassenen im arretinischen Sigillatagewerbe.* Wiesbaden: Steiner, 1980.

Quet, M.-H. "Remarques sur la place de la fête dans le discours des moralistes grecs." *La Fête, pratique et discours. Annales littéraires de l'université de Besançon. Centre de recherches d'histoire ancienne,* 42 (1981): 41.

Rabbow, P. *Seelenführung Methodik der Exerzitien in der Antike.* Munich: Kösel, 1954.

Raepset-Charlier, M.-T. "Ordre sénatorial et divorce sous le Haut-Empire." *Acta classica universitatis scientiarum Debrecenensis,* 17–18 (1981–1982): 161.

Ramin, J., and P. Veyne, "Les hommes libres qui passent pour esclaves et l'esclavage volontaire." *Historia,* 30 (1981): 472.

Rawson, B. "Family Life among the Lower Classes at Rome," *Classical Philology,* 61 (1966): 71.

———— "Roman Concubinage and Other De Facto Marriages." *Transactions of the American Philosophical Association,* 104 (1974): 279.

Reekmans, Tony. "Juvenal's Views on Social Change." *Ancient Society,* 2 (1971): 117–161.

Robert, J., and L. Robert. *Bulletin épigraphique,* in *Revue des études grecques* since 1938 (collected in indexed volumes since 1971). Contains a wealth of facts and ideas, the majority of which pertain to Greek areas of the Roman Empire or under Roman domination.

Robert, L. *Opera minora selecta.* 4 vols. Amsterdam: Hakkert, 1974.

Saller, R. P. *Personal Patronage under the Early Empire.* Cambridge, England: The Cambridge University Press, 1982.

San Nicolo, M. *Aegyptisches Vereinswesen zur Zeit der Ptolemäer und Römer.* Munich: Beck, 1972.

Schmitt-Pantel, P. "Le festin dans la fête de la cité hellénistique," *La fête, pratique et discours.* Annales littéraires de l'université de Besançon. Centre de recherches d'histoire ancienne, 1981, vol. 62, p. 85.

Schuller, W., ed. *Korruption im Altertum*. Munich: Oldenburg, 1982.

Syme, R. *Roman Papers*. Oxford: Oxford University Press, 1979.

———— "Greeks Invading the Roman Government." *Brademas Lectures*. Brookline, Mass.: Hellenic College Press, 1982.

Thomas, Y. *Paura dei padri e Violenza dei figli: immagini retoriche e norme di diritto*. In Pellizer and Zoerzetti, *La Paura dei padri nella società antica e medievale*. Bari: Laterza, 1983.

———— "Remarques sur le pécule et les *honores* des fils de famille." *Mélanges d'archéologie et d'histoire de l'Ecole française de Rome. Antiquité*, 93 (1981): 529.

Toynbee, J. M. C. *Death and Burial in the Roman World*. London: Thames and Hudson, 1971.

Turcan, R. A. *Mithra et le Mithriacisme*. Paris: Presses Universitaires de France, 1981.

Vallat, J.-P. "Architecture rurale en Campanie septentrionale," *Architecture et Société*. Rome: Ecole française de Rome, 1983, p. 247.

Versnel, H. S., ed. *Faith, Hope and Worship. Aspects of Religious Mentality in the Ancient World*. Leyden: Brill, 1981.

Veyne, P. *L'Elégie érotique romaine*. Paris: Seuil, 1983.

———— "Le folklore à Rome et les droits de la conscience publique sur la conduite individuelle." *Latomus*, 42 (1983): 3.

———— "Suicide, Fisc, esclavage, capital et droit romain." *Latomus*, 40 (1981): 217.

———— "Les saluts aux dieux et le voyage de cette vie." *Revue archéologique*, 1985.

———— "Mythe et réalité de l'autarcie à Rome." *Revue des études anciennes*, 81 (1979): 261.

Ville, G. *La Gladiature en Occident, des origines à la mort de Domitien*. Ecole française de Rome, 1981.

Wissowa, G. *Religion und Kultur der Römer*. Handbuch der Altertumswissenschaft, IV, 5. 2nd ed. Munich: Beck, 1971.

## 2. Late Antiquity

Although recent historiography of the later Empire has produced many reliable surveys of the political, social, and religious history of the late antique period, it offers no single treatment of the age from the viewpoint of this series. The short work of a master is closest to such a survey: H.-I. Marrou, *Décadence romaine ou antiquité tardive?* (Paris, 1977). In the English-speaking world, William Lecky, *History of European Morals from Augustus to Charlemagne* (London, 1869), summarizes a traditional attitude. A. H. M. Jones, *The Later Roman Empire*, vol. II (Oxford, 1964), esp. pp. 873–1024, contains much evidence but little comment. Without the work of Paul Veyne, I would have lacked not only the information necessary to venture along this new path but also the courage, which I owe largely to his vigor and deep erudition in handling subjects rarely approached in the same manner by other scholars.

The world of the city: P. Veyne, *Le Pain et le Cirque* (Paris: Seuil, 1976), and R. MacMullen, *Paganism in the Roman Empire* (New Haven: Yale University Press, 1981). Education and socialization in the city: H.-I. Marrou, *Histoire de l'éducation dans l'Antiquité* (Paris, 1948; reprint, Paris: Seuil, 1981, 2 vols.), remains unsurpassed; this is true also of A. J. Festugière, *Antioche païenne et chrétienne* (Paris, 1959), esp. pp. 211–240. A. C. Dionisotti, "From Ausonius' Schooldays? A Schoolbook and Its Relatives," *Journal of Roman Studies*, 82 (1982): 83, makes available a charming new document.

Sexuality, deportment, and medical images of the body: P. Veyne, "La famille et l'amour sous le Haut Empire romain," *Annales*, 33 (1978): 35, and "L'homosexualité à Rome," *Communications*, 35 (1982): 26, represent a new starting point for discussion; Aline Rousselle, *Porneia: de la maîtrise du corps à la privation sensorielle* (Paris, 1983), is exceptionally illuminating. The stability of normative values on inscriptions: L. Robert, *Hellenica*, 13 (1965): 226–227, to begin with, as any other of the many passages dedicated to such issues from the pen of an unrivaled connoisseur of the Greek world under the Empire.

Social distance: R. MacMullen, *Roman Social Relations* (New Haven: Yale University Press, 1974), is convincing. *Popularitas* and the moral quality of the shows: L. Robert, *Les gladiateurs dans l'Orient grec* (Paris, 1940), sees an ugly matter with unfailing precision; see also G. Ville and P. Veyne, "Religion et politique: comment ont pris fin les combats de gladiateurs," *Annales*, 34 (1979): 651. The democratization of philosophical ideals in Christian circles: H. E. Chadwick, *The Sentences of Sixtus* (Cambridge, Eng., 1959), and the humane and learned introduction and notes of H.-I. Marrou (with M. Harl) to *Clément d'Alexandrie: Le Pédagogue*, Sources chrétiennes 70 (Paris, 1960).

On the "heart" and the "evil inclination" in late Judaism, J. Hadot, *Penchant mauvais et volonté libre dans la Sagesse de Ben Sira* (Brussels, 1972), is a good introduction; G. F. Moore, *Judaism* (Cambridge, Mass.: Harvard University Press, 1950), pp. 474–

496, assembles the rabbinic evidence. The sociology of the early Christian community in Corinth has been studied by G. Theissen, especially in articles in *Zeitschrift für neutestamentliche Wissenschaft*, 65 (1974): 232, *Novum Testamentum*, 16 (1974): 179, and *Evangelische Theologie*, 35 (1975): 155: these are translated in *The Social Setting of Pauline Christianity* (Philadelphia, 1982). Wayne Meeks, *The First Urban Christians: The Social World of the Apostle Paul* (New Haven: Yale University Press, 1983), represents a quantum-jump in sociological sophistication. For the remaining centuries, we are left with the work of an *Altmeister*, A. Harnack, *Mission und Ausbreitung des Christentums* (Leipzig, 1902). H. Gülzow, Kallist von Rom, *Zeitschrift für neutestamentliche Wissenschaft*, 58 (1968): 102, and L. W. Countryman, *The Rich Christian in the Church of the Early Empire* (New York, 1980), are revealing.

On almsgiving and shifts in popular morality, P. Veyne, *Le pain et le cirque*, pp. 44–50, and remarks in "Suicide, Fisc, esclavage capital et droit romain," *Latomus*, 40 (1981): 217, are the best starting point. Celibacy and marital rigorism in the Early Church: C. Munier, *L'Église dans l'empire romain* (Paris, 1979), pp. 7–16, is a clear summary. *Etica sessuale e matrimonio nel cristianesimo delle origini*, ed. R. Cantalamessa (Milan, 1976), contains some excellent essays, esp. P. F. Beatrice, "Continenza e matrimonio nel cristianesimo primitivo," p. 3; *Les Actes Apocryphes des Apôtres: Christianisme et monde païen*, ed. F. Bovon (Geneva, 1981), touches on related issues. On the issue of sexual renunciation in late antiquity, I am in disagreement with the luminous little book of E. R. Dodds, *Pagan, and Christian in an Age of Anxiety* (Cambridge, Eng., 1965).

Social structure and city life in the later Empire: Peter Brown, *The Making of Late Antiquity* (Cambridge, Mass.: Harvard University Press, 1978), pp. 27–53, advances an interpretation and assembles much secondary literature; C. Lepelley, *Les cités de l'Afrique romaine au Bas-Empire*, 2 vols. (Paris, 1979–1981), is a definitive addition; see also R. Krautheimer, *Three Christian Capitals: Topography and Politics* (Berkeley, 1983). On costume: R. MacMullen, "Some Pictures in Ammianus Marcellinus," *Art Bulletin* (1964): 49, and G. Fabre, "Recherches sur l'origine des ornements vestimentaires du Bas-Empire," *Karthago*, 16 (1973): 107; acute and concrete, Marrou, *Décadence romaine*, pp. 15–20, sees the importance of such changes.

Urban ceremonial and the mystique of power: H. Stern, *Le Calendrier de 354* (Paris, 1953), remains essential; M. Meslin, *La fête des kalendes de janvier* (Brussels, 1970), describes a significant mutation in pagan folklore; J. W. Salomonson, *Voluptatem spectandi non perdat sed mutet* (Amsterdam, 1979), illustrates the continuity of a mystique of the games in Christian circles. The relation between the palaces of the *potentes* and the ideology of their power registered in mosaics has been recently studied by K. M. D. Dunbabin, *The Mosaics of Roman North Africa* (Oxford, 1978). The mosaics of the villa at Piazza Armerina in Sicily have provoked much discussion; see S. Settis, "Per l'interpretazione di Piazza Armerina," *Mélanges d'archéologie et d'histoire: Antiquité*, 87 (1975): 873; for the discovery of similar mosaics at Tellaro and Patti, see Lellia Cracco Ruggini, *La Sicilia tra Roma e Bisanzio: Storia di Sicilia* (Naples, 1982), III, 66.

City and basilica: R. Krautheimer, *Rome: Profile of a City* (Princeton, 1980), is a masterly supplement to the monumental study of C. Pietri, *Roma cristiana*, 2 vols. (Paris, 1977). For changes in ecclesiastical ceremonial and almsgiving, see Peter Brown, "Dalla plebs romana alla plebs Dei. Aspetti della cristianizzazione di Roma," *Passatopresente*, 2 (1982): 123, and *The Cult of the Saints: Its Rise and Function in Latin Christianity* (Chicago, 1981), pp. 39–49. On poverty and almsgiving, E. Patlagean, *Pauvreté économique et pauvreté sociale à Byzance* (Paris, 1977), marks a new departure in the study of late Roman society and the influence of Christianity on the urban community.

The idiosyncracy of pagan epitaphs is well presented by R. Lattimore, *Themes in Greek and Latin Epitaphs* (Urbana, Ill., 1962). The care of the dead in Christian communities receives outstanding treatment by P. A. Février, "Le Culte des morts dans les communautés chrétiennes durant le iiième siecle," *Atti del ix° congresso di archeologia cristiana* (Rome, 1977), I, 212, and "À propos du culte funéraire: culte et sociabilité," *Cahiers archéologiques*, 26 (1977): 29, and by R. Krautheimer, "Mensa, coemeterium, martyrium," *Cahiers archéologiques*, 11 (1960): 15. These and others contributed to the interpretation in Brown, *Cult of the Saints*, pp. 23–38. B. Young, "Paganisme, christianisme et rites funéraires mérovingiens," *Archéologie médiévale*, 7 (1977): 5, is an important contribution for one region; Y. Duval, *Loca sanctorum Africae* (Rome: École française de Rome, 1982), is a magnificent collection for another. V. Saxer, *Morts, martyrs, reliques en Afrique chrétienne* (Paris, 1980), documents clerical attitudes.

For the antecedents of monastic spirituality, see A. Guillaumont, "Monachisme et éthique judéo-chrétienne," *Judéo-Christianisme: volume offert au car-*

*dinal J. Daniélou: Recherches de science religieuse*, 60 (1972): 199. The impact of monasticism is best approached through the work of its major exponents in an urban environment: *Jean Chrysostome: La Virginité*, ed. B. Grillet, Sources chrétiennes 125 (Paris, 1966), and *Grégoire de Nysse: Traité sur la Virginité*, ed. M. Aubineau, Sources chrétiennes 119 (Paris, 1966)—the latter particularly useful. The theoretical radicalism of the monastic paradigm can lend itself to serious exaggeration of the rigor of the ascetic practices of the monks; not even the best accounts are immune, notably Festugière, *Antioche*, pp. 291–310, and A. Vööbus, *A History of Asceticism in the Syrian Orient*, vols. 1 and 2 (Louvain, 1958 and 1960). D. Chitty, *The Desert a City* (Oxford, 1966), an exceptionally learned and humane book, and E. A. Judge, "The Earliest Use of 'Monachos,'" *Jahrbuch für Antike und Christentum*, 20 (1977): 72, provide correctives. Monastic poverty and its relation to the self-image of a Christian society, shown to be crucial by Patlagean, *Pauvreté*, has been studied in the Pachomian communities by B. Büchler, *Die Armut der Armen* (Munich, 1980). Oxyrhynchus is discussed in J. M. Carrié, "Les distributions alimentaires dans les cités de l'empire romain tardif," *Mélanges d'archéologie et d'histoire: Antiquité*, 87 (1975): 995, and by R. Remondon, "L'église dans la société égyptienne à l'époque byzantine," *Chronique d'Égypte*, 47 (1972): 254. Monastic education and the city: Festugière, *Antioche*, pp. 181–240, and Marrou, *Histoire de l'éducation*, pp. 149–161, see issues clearly; *Jean Chrysostome: Sur la vaine gloire*, ed. A. M. Malingrey, Sources chrétiennes 188 (Paris, 1972), is the most revealing source. On monastic introspection and sexuality: F. Refoulé, "Rêves et vie spirituelle d'apres Évagre le Pontique," *La vie spirituelle: Supplément*, 14 (1961): 470; M. Foucault, "Le combat de la chasteté," *Communications*, 35 (1982): 15, and A. Rousselle, *Porneia*, pp. 167–250, are new approaches to a topic usually covered with platitudes in scholarly treatments; *Évagre le Pontique: Traité pratique ou le moine*, 2 vols., ed. A. and C. Guillaumont, Sources chrétiennes 170 and 171 (Paris, 1971), is invaluable.

Byzantine marital morality and urban conditions: C. Scaglioni, "Ideale coniugale e familiare in san Giovanni Crisostomo," *Etica sessuale*, ed. Cantalamessa, p. 273, and the contributions in *Jean Chrysostome et Augustin*, ed. C. Kannengiesser (Paris, 1975), mark a beginning. *Barsanuphe et Jean de Gaza: Correspondence*, trans. L. Regnault (Solesmes, 1971), gives a delightful picture of the moral problems on which laymen and monks sought the advice of a local holy man. Sexuality as a remedy for mortality

in Greek Christian thought: Ton H. C. van Eijk, "Marriage and Virginity, Death and Immortality," *Epektasis: Mélanges J. Daniélou* (Paris, 1972), p. 209, is the most important study.

A. Kazhdan and A. Cutler, "Continuity and Discontinuity in Byzantine History," *Byzantion*, 52 (1982): 429, discusses medieval Byzantine society problems that could be applied to the fifth and sixth centuries. Peter Brown, "Eastern and Western Christendom in Late Antiquity: A Parting of the Ways," *Society and the Holy in Late Antiquity* (Berkeley, 1982), p. 166, suggests the outlines of possible divergences between East and West.

The attitude of Augustine has been studied at length, but not always about the issues discussed here. Augustine's *de nuptiis et concupiscentia*, written to Count Valerius (418), is a central text, as is Book Fourteen of the *City of God* (420). The *de nuptiis* is edited with an excellent commentary by A. C. de Veer, *Premières polémiques contre Julien: Bibliothèque augustinienne* 23 (Paris, 1974). The letter (421?) of Augustine to the patriarch Atticus of Constantinople is a clear statement of his later views on the sexuality of Adam and Eve and on the nature of present-day concupiscence: J. Divjak, ed., *Corpus Scriptorum Ecclesiasticorum Latinorum* 88 (Vienna, 1981). I find M. Müller, *Die Lehre des heiligen Augustins von der Paradieseche und ihre Auswirkung in der Sexualethik des 12. und 13. Jahrhunderts* (Regensburg, 1954), the most reliable for the later reception of Augustinian doctrine by medieval canonists and authors of confessional manuals.

## 3. Private Life and Domestic Architecture in Roman Africa

Becatti, G. "Case ostiensi del tardo impero." *Bollettino d'Arte*, 33 (1948): 102–128, 197–224.

Boëthius, A., and J. B. Ward-Perkins. *Etruscan and Roman Architecture*. London: Penguin, 1970.

Bruneau, P., et al. *L'Ilot de la maison des comédiens. Délos, XXVII*. Paris, 1970. A detailed list of Greek houses from the second century B.C. in which the interior courtyard was transformed into a peristyle ringed by porticoes.

Clavel, M., and P. Lévêque. *Villes et structures urbaines dans l'Occident romain*. Paris, 1971.

De Vos, A., and M. de Vos. *Pompei, Ercolano, Stabia*. Rome, 1982.

Duby, G., ed. *Histoire de la France urbaine*, vol. 1, *La Ville antique des origines au IXe siècle*. Paris: Seuil, 1980.

Lancel, S., ed. *Byrsa I et II*. Rome: Ecole française de Rome, 1979, 1982.

La Rocca, E., M. de Vos, and A. de Vos. *Guida archeologica di Pompei*. Verona, 1976.

Lassus, J. "Adaptation à l'Afrique de l'urbanisme romain," *8e Congrès international d'archéologie classique, Paris, 1963*. Paris, 1965, pp. 245–249.

Martin, R. *L'Urbanisme dans la Grèce antique*. 2nd ed. Paris, 1974.

Martin, R., and G. Vallet, "L'architettura domestica," in E. Gabba and G. Vallet, eds., *La Sicilia antiqua*, vol. 1, part 2, pp. 321–354.

Pasini, F. *Ostia antica. Insule e classi sociali*. Rome, 1978.

Pavolini, C. *Ostia*. Rome, 1983.

Picard, G. *La Civilisation de l'Afrique romaine*. Paris, 1959.

Picard, G. C., and C. Picard. *Vie et mort de Carthage*. Paris, 1970, esp. pp. 220 ff.

Rebuffat, R. *Thamusida II*. Rome: Ecole française de Rome, 1970. A thoroughgoing reconsideration of African private architecture through the study of individual buildings.

——— "Maisons à péristyle d'Afrique du Nord, répertoire de plans publiés." *Mélanges de l'Ecole française de Rome*, 81 (1969): 659–724; 86 (1974): 445–499.

Romanelli, P. "Topografia e archeologia dell'Africa romana," *Enciclopedia classica*. Turin, 1970.

Van Aken, A. R. A. "Late Roman Domus Architecture." *Mnemosyne* (1949): 242–251.

## 4. The Early Middle Ages in the West

Alvaro d'Ors, E., ed. *Codigo de Eurico*. Madrid, 1960.

*Archéologie médiévale*. Paris: Centre de recherches archéologiques médiévales de Caen, 1971–
This journal publishes a compendium of medieval excavations in France along with important articles.

Baehrens, E. *Liber medicinalis de Q. S. Sammonicus*. Leipzig, 1881.

Bellanger, G., and C. Sellier. *Répertoire des cimetières mérovingiens du Pas-de-Calais*. Arras, 1982.

Beyerle, F., and R. Buchner, eds. *Lex Ribuaria*. Monumenta Germaniae Historica. Hannover, 1954.

Buchet, Luc. "La nécropole gallo-romaine et mérovingienne de Frénouville (Calvados), étude anthropologique." *Archéologie médiévale* (1978): 5–53.

Center for the Study of the Early Middle Ages. Proceedings of the Twenty-Fourth Congress. 2 vols. Spoleto, 1977. On marriage.

Chapelot, J., and R. Fossier. *Le Village et la Maison au Moyen Age*. Paris, 1980.

Coleman, E. R. "L'infanticide durant la haut Moyen Age." *Annales* (1974): 315–335.

Delage, M.-J. *Sermons au peuple de Césaire d'Arles*. 2 vols. Paris: Cerf, 1972–1978.

Demolon, P. *Le Village mérovingien de Brebières*. Arras, 1972.

Devisse, Jean. *Hincmar, archevêque de Reims (845–882)*. 3 vols. Geneva, 1976, pp. 367–468. A discussion of Christian marriage.

Dill, S. *Roman Society in Gaul in the Time of the Merovingian Age*. New York, 1926; reprinted 1966.

Dittrich, Otto. *Sainte Aldegonde, une sainte des Francs*. Kevelaer, 1976. A bilingual French-German edition.

Drew, K. F. "The Germanic Family of the Lex Burgondionum." *Medievalia et Humanistica* (1963): 5–14.

Dubois, Dom J., and L. Beaumont-Maillet. *Sainte Genevieve de Paris*. Paris, 1982.

Eckhardt, K. A., ed. *Pactus Legis Salicae*. 2 vols. Monumenta Germaniae Historica. Hannover, 1862–1969.

Einhard. *The Life of Charlemagne*, with a foreword by Sidney Painter. Ann Arbor: University of Michigan Press, 1960.

Faral, E. *Poème sur Louis le Pieux et Epitre au roi Pépin par Ermold le Noir*. Paris: Champion, 1932.

Ganshof, F. L. "Le statut de la femme dans la monarchie franque," *Recueil de la Société Jean Bodin*, 1962, pp. 5–58.

Gransen, G. "La lettre de Hincmar de Reims au sujet du mariage d'Etienne," *Pascua mediaevalia*. Louvain, 1983, pp. 133–146.

Halphen, L. *Vie de Charlemagne par Eginhard*. Paris: Champion, 1923.

Hartel, C., ed. *Prosper d'Aquitaine*. Vienna, 1894.

James, E. *The Merovingian Archeology of South-West Gaul*. 2 vols. London, 1977.

Joffroy, R. *Le Cimetière de Lavoye*. Paris, 1974.

Kalifa, S. "Singularités matrimoniales chez les anciens Germains, le rapt et le droit de la femme à disposer d'elle-même." *Revue historique du droit français et étranger* (1970): 199–225.

Köttje, R. *Die Bussbücher Halitgars von Cambrai und des Hrabanus Maurus*. Berlin and New York, 1980.

Krusch, B., and W. Levison, eds. *Passiones vitaeque sanctorum aevi Merowingici*. 7 vols. Monumenta Germaniae Historica. Hannover, 1920. An introduction to the private life of the major patrons of Gallic churches.

Latouche, R. *Histoire de France par Richer*. Paris: Champion, 1923.

Lauer, P., ed. *Flodoard, Annales*. Picard, 1905.

——— *Histoire des fils de Louis le Pieux, par Nithard*. Paris: Champion, 1926.

Lelong, Charles. *La vie quotidienne en Gaule à l'époque merovingienne*. Paris: Hachette, 1963.

Léo, F., ed. *Fortunatus*. Monumenta Germaniae Historica. Hannover, 1881.

Levillain, L. *Correspondance (829–862) de Loup de Ferrières*. Paris: Champion, 1927.

Loyen, A. *Poèmes et lettres de Sidoine Apollinaire*. 3 vols. Paris: Les Belles Lettres, 1960–1970.

Manselli, R. "Vie familiale et éthique sexuelle dans les pénitentiels." Rome: Ecole française de Rome. A colloquium on Family and Kinship in the Medieval West. Rome, 1977, pp. 363–378.

Meyer, P., and T. Mommsen, eds. *Codex theodosianus*. 2nd ed. 2 vols. Berlin, 1905.

Moussy, C. *Poème d'action de grâces et Prière de Paulin de Pella*. Paris: Cerf, 1974.

Munier, C., and C. de Clercq, eds. *Concilia Galliae*. 2nd ed. 2 vols. Turnhout, 1963.

Pharr, Clyde. *The Theodosian Code and Novels and the Sirmondian Constitutions*. Princeton: Princeton University Press, 1952.

Riché, P. *Manuel pour mon fils, par Dhuoda*. Paris: Cerf, 1975.

——— *La Vie quotidienne dans l'Empire carolingien*. Paris: Hachette, 1973.

Rouche, Michel. "La faim à l'époque carolingienne: essai sur quelques types de rations alimentaires." *Revue historique* (1973): 295–320.

——— "Les repas de fête à l'époque carolingienne," Congrès de Nice, *Boire et manger au Moyen Age*. Nice, 1982; Paris: Les Belles Lettres, 1984, I, 265–296.

Salin, E. *La civilisation mérovingienne*. 4 vols. Paris, 1950–1959, 4 vols.

Salis, L. R. de, ed. *Leges Burgonionum*. Monumenta Germaniae Historica. Hannover, 1892.

Schmitt, F., ed. *Corpus Consuetudiunum Monasticarum*. Siegburg, 1963.

Simonnot, H. *Le Mundium dans le droit de famille germanique*. Paris, 1893.

Stuard, S. M., ed. *Women in Medieval Society*. Philadelphia: University of Pennsylvania Press, 1976.

Temple, S. F. *Women in Frankish Society. Marriage and the Cloister, 500 to 900*. Philadelphia, 1981.

Theiss, L. "Saints sans famille? Quelques remarques sur la famille dans le monde franc à travers les sources hagiographiques." *Revue historique* (1976): 3–20.

Thevenin, A. *Les Cimetières mérovingiens de la Haute-Saône*. Paris, 1968.

Uddholm, A., ed. *Marculf's "Formulae."* Uppsala, 1962.

Vogüé, A. de. *La Règle de saint Benoît*. 7 vols. Paris: Cerf, 1972–1978.

Wallace-Hadrill, J., ed. *Fredegaire*. London, 1960.

Wasserchleben, F. W. H. *Die Bussordnungen der Abendländischen Kirche*. Halle and Graz, 1958. A collection of penitentials.

Werminghoff, A., ed. *Concilia aevi Karolini*. 2 vols. Monumenta Germaniae Historica. Hannover, 1904–1908.

Zerner-Chardavoine, Mme. "Enfants et jeunes au IXe siècle, la démographie du polyptyque de Marseille, 813–814." *Provence historique* (1981): 355–384.

Zeumer, K., ed. *Formulae Merowingici et Karolini aevi*. Monumenta Germaniae Historica. Hannover, 1886.

## 5. Byzantium in the Tenth and Eleventh Centuries

*L'Art byzantin, art européen. Athens*, 1964.

Beaucamp, J. "La situation juridique de la femme à Byzance." *Cahiers de civilisation médiévale*, 20 (1977): 145–176.

Beck, H. G. *Das byzantinische Jahrtausend*. Munich: Beck, 1978.

——— "Byzantinisches Gefolgschaftswesen," *Sitzungsber. Bayer. Akad. d. Wissensch. Philos. -Histor. Kl.*, vol. 5, 1965.

——— *Geschichte der byzantinischen Volksliteratur*. Munich: Beck, 1971.

——— *Kirche und theologische Literatur im byzantinischen Reich*. Munich: Beck, 1959.

Bréhier, L. *Le Monde byzantin*. 3 vols. Paris: Albin Michel, 1946–1950; reprinted with a bibliographical supplement by J. Gouillard, 1969–1970.

Buckler, G. "Women in Byzantine Law about 1100 A.D." *Byzantion*, XI (1936): 391–416.

*Byzantine Books and Bookmen*. Washington, D.C.: Dumbarton Oaks, 1975.

Centre de recherche d'histoire et civilisation byzantine, *Travaux et Mémoires*, vol. 6, *Recherches sur le XIe siècle*. Paris: Boccard, 1976.

Dauvillier, J., and C. de Clercq. *Le Mariage en droit canonique oriental*. Paris: Sirey, 1936.

Grabar, A. *L'Iconoclasme byzantin*. 2nd ed. Paris: Flammarion, 1984.

———— *La Peinture byzantine.* Geneva: Skira, 1953.

Guillou, A. *La Civilisation byzantine.* Paris: Arthuad, 1975.

Hackel, S., ed. *The Byzantine Saint.* London: Fellowship of St. Alban and St. Sergius, 1981. See esp., R. Morris, "The Political Saint of the Eleventh Century," pp. 3–50, and E. Patlagean, "Sainteté et pouvoir," pp. 88–105.

Hendy, M. F. "Byzantium, 1081–1204: An Economic Reappraisal." *Transactions of the Royal Historical Society* (1970): 31–52.

Hunger, H. *Die hochsprachliche profane Literatur der Byzantiner.* 2 vols. Munich: Beck, 1978.

———— *Reich der neuen Mitte. Der christliche Geist der byzantinischen Kultur.* Graz, Vienna, and Cologne: Styria, 1965.

Hussey, J. M., ed. *The Byzantine Empire.* 2nd ed. vol. 4 of *Cambridge Medieval History.* Cambridge, Eng.: Cambridge University Press, 1967–1968.

Kazhdan, A., with S. Franklin. *Studies on Byzantine Literature of the Eleventh and Twelfth Centuries.* Cambridge, Eng., and Paris: Cambridge University Press, Maison des Sciences de l'Homme, 1984.

Kazhdan, A., and G. Constable. *People and Power in Byzantium: An Introduction to Modern Byzantine Studies.* Washington, D.C.: Dumbarton Oaks, 1982.

Kirsten, E. "Die byzantinische Stadt," *Berichte zum XI internationalen Byzantinisten-Kongress.* 3 vols. Munich, 1958.

Lemerle, P. *Cinq Etudes sur le XIe siècle byzantin.* Paris: Centre Nationale pour la Recherche Scientifique, 1977. Compare A. Kazhdan, "Remarques sur le XIe siècle byzantin. A propos d'un livre récent de Paul Lemerle." *Byzantion,* 49 (1979): 491–503.

Lopez, R. S. *Byzantium and the World around It: Economic and Institutional Relations.* London: Variorum Reprints, 1978.

Mango, C. *The Art of the Byzantine Empire.* Sources and Documents in the History of Art. Englewood Cliffs, N.J.: Prentice-Hall, 1972.

Morris, R. "The Powerful and the Poor in Tenth Century Byzantium: Law and Reality." *Past and Present,* 73 (1976): 3–27.

Obolensky, D. *The Bogomils. A Study in Balkan Neo-Manichaeism.* Cambridge, Eng., 1948.

Ostrogorsky, G. *Histoire de l'Etat byzantin.* Paris: Payot, 1976.

———— "Observations on the Aristocracy in Byzantium." *Dumbarton Oaks Papers,* 25 (1971): 3–32.

*Proceedings of the 13th International Congress of Byzantine Studies.* Oxford: Oxford University Press, 1967.

Svoboda, K. *La Démonologie de Michel Psellos.* Brno, 1927. Compare P. Gautier, "Le *De daemonibus* du Pseudo-Psellos." *Revue des études byzantines,* 38 (1980): 105–194.

Vasiliev, A. A. *History of the Byzantine Empire. 324-1453.* 2nd ed. Madison: University of Wisconsin Press, 1952.

Vryonis, S. "Byzantine *Demokratia* and the Guilds." *Dumbarton Oaks Papers,* 17 (1963): 287–314.

# Acknowledgments

# Index

# Acknowledgments

The authors wish to thank Simone Lescuyer, Agnès Mathieu, and Claude Simion, who supervised the illustration of this book with taste, skill, and originality. We are indebited to Mme Judith Petit, conservator of the Dutuit Collection at the Petit Palais, for illustrations from that collection's catalogue of bronze coins. We also wish to thank Professor Christian Goudineau of the Collège de France and J.-P. Darmon, a research associate at the Centre National de Recherche Scientifique.

The sites and objects illustrated in this book (on the pages noted) are found in various locations, as follows: Aquitaine Museum, Bordeaux, 81; Archaeological Museum, Aquileia, 73, 109, 126, 133, 157; Archaeological Museum, Châtillon-sur-Seine, 504; Archaeological Museum, Milan, 97; Archaeological Museum, Naples, 6, 32, 36, 38, 60, 71, 72, 87, 89, 203, 208, 213, 216, 221; Archaeological Museum, Ostia, 10, 18, 122, 167, 190, 211; Archaeological Museum, Strasbourg, 455; Archaeological Museum, Venice, 204; Arezzo Museum, 161; Austrian National Library, Vienna, 438; Baptistry of Saint John, Poitiers, 492; Bardo Museum, Tunis, 88, 193, 277, 281, 393, 396; Bargello, Florence, 531; Belfort Museum, 449; Berlin Museum, 125; Bibliothèque Nationale, Paris, 293, 422, 430, 437, 444, 445, 452, 496, 498, 501, 532, 534, 543, 544, 557, 562, 564, 569, 577, 578, 581, 606, 619, 621, 626, 628; Bibliothèque Nationale, Cabinet des Médailles, Paris, 46, 209, 281, 283, 298, 301, 307, 412, 415, 420, 421, 424, 425, 428, 450, 502, 565, 635, 637; British Museum, London, 74, 127, 198, 295, 455, 480, 570; Byzantine Museum, Athens, 625; Caen (CRAM), 506, 511; Calvet Museum, Avignon, 180; Capitulary Library, Modena, 410; Catacombs of Saint January, 279; Cathedral, Aquileia, 289; Cathedral Museum, Rheims, 457; Cava dei Tirreni (Abbey archives), 486, 547; Charlemagne Exposition, Aix-la-Chapelle, 440; Christian Museum of Brescia, 294; Christian Museum of the Lateran, Rome, 280, 282; Christian Museum of Manastero, Aquileia, 311; Church of Saint Ambrose, Milan, 284; Church of Saint-Pierre-de-la-Citadelle, Metz, 516; Church of San Vittore, Ravenna, 127; Church of Santa Sabina, Rome, 303; Church of the Serpent, Goreme [Cappadocia], 580; Cluny Museum, Paris, 552, 558; Communal Museum, Velletri, 305; Crypt of the Cathedral of Saint Mark, Venice, 555; Crypt of Cruas, Ardèche, 435; Crypt of Santa Maria, Verona, 267; Crypt of Saint Maximin, Var, 460; Curia, Rome, 261; Danon Museum, Chalon-sur-Saône, 507; Departmental Museum, Rouen, 495; Doria Palace, Genoa, 231; Dresden Museum, 121; Ducal Palace, Mantua, 165; Dumbarton Oaks, Byzantine Collection, Washington, D.C., 571, 596, 618, 634; Episcopal Museum, Trier, 284; Estonian Museum, 124; Fabre Museum, Montpeillier, 518; Hayford Pierce Collection, Paris, 573; Historical Museum, Epernay, 431; Landesmuseum Bonn, 467, 468; Landesmuseum, Trier, 138, 143, 144, 238, 271, 275; Lapidary Museum, Arles, 76; Lateran Museum, Rome, 24 (now at Vatican), 118; Library of the Royal University, Utrecht, 427, 436, 535, 541; Louvre, Paris, 8, 14, 16, 19, 22, 42, 44, 46, 77, 114, 170, 187, 197, 234, 249, 250, 256, 299; Mallon Collection, Paris, 554; Marburg Museum, 13; Marciana Library, Ancient Holdings, Venice, 590; Metropolitan Museum, New York, 224; Municipal Library, Boulogne-sur-Mer, 521; Municipal Library, Cambrai, 538; Municipal Libary, Epernay, 432, 487; Municipal Library, Poitiers, 418, 528; Municipal Museum, Laon, 503; Museum of Ancona, 86, 130; Museum of Antiquities, Leyden, 220; Museum of Antiquities, Rouen (P. Perrin photograph), 454; Museum of the Aquila, 104; Museum of Art History, Vienna, 474; Museum of the Baths, Rome, 15, 39, 54, 58, 78, 80, 84, 120, 195, 206, 222, 251, 258, 265; Museum of Beirut, 187; Museum of Benevento, 50; Museum of Berry, Bourges, 520; Museum of Bourges, 491; Museum of the Conservators, Rome, 26, 43, 47, 94, 96, 106, 135, 143, 225, 236, 246; Museum of Fine Arts, Auxterre, 449; Museum of Fine Arts, Dijon, 255; Museum of Fine Arts, Lyons, 537; Museum of Fine Arts, Troyes, 490; Museum of El Jem, 406; Museum of Gallo-Roman Civilization, Lyons, 11; Museum of Istanbul, 260; Museum of Mactar, 402; Museum of Metz, 443, 462, 488, 522; Museum of National Antiquities, Saint-Germain-en-Laye, 140, 431, 441, 449; Museum of National Science and Archaeology, Douai, 441, 508;

659

Museum of Parma, 182; Museum of Plovdiv, 188; Museum of Portogruaro, 102; Museum of Rheims, 616; Museum of Saint Paul's Outside-the-Walls, Rome, 66, 268; Museum of Sfax, 394; Museum of Syracuse, 99; National Archaeological Museum, Athens, 28; National Archives, Paris, 423; National Library, Madrid, 574, 582, 593, 594, 614, 627; National Museum, Budapest, 595, 598; National Museum, Copenhagen, 504; National Museum, Florence, 575; National Museum, Madrid, 603; National Museum, Rome, 314; National Museum of Ceramics, Sèvres, 572; Ny Carlsberg Glypotek, Copenhagen, 200; Palace of the Sforza, Milan, 147; Palazzo Colonna, Rome, 30; Palazzo Mattei, 247; Palazzo Salviati, 145; Petit Palais, Dutuit Collection, Paris, 4, 48, 49, 59, 62, 90, 93, 142, 143, 175, 212, 213, 214; Prado, Madrid, 196; Priory of Notre-Dame-de-Salagon, Mane, Alpes-de-Haute-Provence, 458; Prussian State Museum of Culture, West Berlin, 456, 632; Dr. Reber's Collection, Lausanne, 599; Rhine State Museum, 484; Rohan Museum, Strasbourg, 426; Royal Museum, Brussels, 476; Saint-Benoit-sur-Loire, Loiret, 433; Schleswig-Holstein Museum for Prehistory and Early History, 472, 499, 527; Staatsbibliothek, Berlin, 272; State Museum of Hesse, Darmstadt, 560; Stoclet Collection, Brussels, 583; Torlonia Collection, Rome, 116, 148, 201; Uffizi, Florence, 83; Vatican Grottoes, Rome, 296; Vatican Library, Rome, 239, 288, 610, 630, 638; Vatican Museums, Rome, 16, 34, 53, 56, 135, 160, 162, 168, 184, 199, 227, 232, 243, 248; Vault of the Catacomb of Saint Priscilla, 252; Villa Albani, Rome, 41, 111; Villa Borghese, Rome, 245; The Walters Art Gallery, Menil Foundation, Baltimore, 566.

Photographs were supplied by the following agencies and individuals: Arabesques (J.-C. et E. Chambrier), 275b, 302; Archives Ph. Toutain, 550; Armand Colin, 440; Bulloz, 4, 48, 49, 58, 59, 62, 70, 90, 93, 140, 142, 175, 212, 213, 214, 241, 281, 423, 457; G. Dagli Orti, 13, 15, 18, 30, 36, 38, 39, 41, 50, 54b, 56, 58, 66, 72, 78, 81, 87, 99, 104, 111, 116, 120, 121, 122, 125, 126, 127b, 143c, 147, 150, 152, 154, 183, 187b, 190, 192, 200, 201, 203, 208, 210, 213a, 243, 251, 258, 260, 267, 268, 279, 289, 295, 418, 431d,e, 441, 455a, 486a, 490, 511, 525, 528, 547, 580, 586, 640; Edimédia, 74, 277; Collection Snark, 396; Giraudon, 8, 16a, 18, 19, 22, 42, 46b, 209, 256, 298, 301, 449b,c, 450, 470, 491, 494, 498, 504, 507, 518, 521, 537, 554, 558, 560, 573, 575, 583, 595, 598, 599, 616, 622, 625, Alinari-Giraudon, 14, 26, 32, 53, 54a,c, 60, 82, 83, 102, 106, 108, 124, 127, 145, 148, 280, 294, Anderson-Giraudon, 6, 70, 94, 118, 154, 160, 184, 196, 206, 236, 264, 278, 286, Lauros-Giraudon, 255, 544, 555; M. Langrognet, 216, 563; Jacques Laurent, Tarbes, 455; Magnum/E. Lessing, 252, 296, 305; ARXIU MAS, Barcelona, 574, 582, 593, 594, 603, 614, 627; C. Michaelides, 288; Roger-Viollet, 76, 98, 100, 164b, 166, 188, 211, 242, 249b, 291, 292, 449a, 585, 588; Hurault-Viollet, 431a,c, Alinari-Viollet, 28, 89, 168, 197, 248, 265, Anderson-Viollet, 35, 195, 199, 282, 314, 601; J. Roubier, 425a, 435, 458, 461, 477, 480, 492, 509, 513, 514, 515, 523; M. Rouche, 465; Scala, Florence, 128, 284b; Y. Thébert, 324, 333, 334, 338, 340, 342, 348, 350, 382, 386, 388, 391, 393, 394, 398, 399, 400, 401, 402, 403, 404, 406, 409; R. Tournus, 77, 249a, 299; private collections, 47, 86, 97, 109, 161, 169, 185, 193, 245, 261, 303, 433.

Credits for color plates, in order of appearance are: Naples, Archaeological Museum, Edimédia © Archives Snark; Naples, Archaeological Museum, G. Dagli Orti; Naples, Archaeological Museum, G. Dagli Orti; Tivoli, Hadrian's Villa, M. Langrognet; Aquileia, Cathedral, G. Dagli Orti; Naples, Catacombs of Saint January, G. Dagli Orti; Bulla Regia, Y. Thébert; Museum of El Jem, Y. Thébert; Bulla Regia, Y. Thébert; Utica, Y. Thébert; Strasbourg, Archaeological Museum, G. Dagli Orti; Château-Landon, G. Dagli Orti; Rome, Vatican Library; Museum of Istanbul, G. Dagli Orti; Madrid, National Library, ARXIU MAS, Barcelona; Rome Vatican Library.

I wish to thank Arthur Goldhammer for undertaking the arduous task of making this book available to an English-speaking audience. Much additional material that was not present in the original French is included in this version; a few minor cuts and corrections have been made.

P.V.

# Index

DATE DUE